Dr. Kevin B. Burr, PhD, Assistant Professor of Bible and Ministry
Harding University, Searcy, AR

Bernardo provides an important foray into the economic world of the New Testament that is thorough, detailed, and impressive in scope. His first move is the right move: he lays out clear definitions of economic terms like "socialism" and "capitalism," which are all too often employed by biblical scholars as euphemisms (respectively) for "good" and "bad" economic policies and practices. With these terms defined, he equips Bible students and scholars alike to take the first steps toward a more nuanced and accurate understanding of the Greco-Roman world's economic realities and how those realities affect modern-day biblical exegesis and application. As Bernardo works through the texts of the New Testament, he rightly highlights both the consistent proclamation that Jesus is King and the clear implication that the Church ought to refuse violence and temporal dominion. Simply put, I find Bernardo's thesis compelling: the New Testament cannot be forced to endorse authoritarian socialism.

Dr. Allan R. Bevere, Professional Fellow in Theology, Ashland Theological
Seminary, Ashland, Ohio

Everyone reads the Bible through interpretive lenses. Alex Bernardo offers us a refreshing and thoughtful way of understanding the New Testament through the lenses of cooperation and nonviolence. Rightfully arguing that modern expressions of conservatism and liberalism are two sides of the same modernist and authoritarian paradigms, Bernardo offers an alternative interpretation of the New Testament that seeks to put Jesus and the writers of the New Testament in their first century context, demonstrating that current paradigms are woefully insufficient in understanding the Christian Scriptures. This book is a must-read.

Dr. Jeffery Degner, Senior Fellow of Economics and Free Enterprise,
Cornerstone University

Alex Bernardo has produced a richly-referenced, thoughtful, and methodical analysis of New Testament theology and its defense of property rights, particularly against the claims made by political elites and authoritarians of all stripes. His clarity, accompanied by his refusal to whitewash modern movements and ideologies set him apart from other authors. Disciplined and historically-grounded, Bernardo assists readers in avoiding categorical confusion that so many have fallen prey to. Readers will gain deeper insight into what Biblical submission really means, along with the boldness to proclaim, "We must obey God rather than men."

particular, trying to understand the relationship of the New Testament to market behavior, political principles, and contemporary practice. Bernardo methodically walks through the relevant passages in the New Testament and discusses the historical context—to arrive at principles for economics, politics, government, money, good citizenship, and the role of policy advocacy within a biblical worldview. As a result, his project will be helpful for anyone looking to merge faith with political practice.

Cody Cook, Author of *The Anarchist Anabaptist*

Alex Bernardo has done a service to both the church and to those who want to make a freer, less violent world. Politics, Economics, and New Testament Interpretation introduces the world of the New Testament and the principles of liberty to new audiences and then corrects the unfortunate tendency of much New Testament scholarship to read pop economics and badly formed political theory into Scripture. Future readings of the New Testament's political and economic framework will need to consider Bernardo's arguments if they want to be historically accurate and make the New Testament relevant to our current time and place.

Politics,
Economics,
and
New Testament
Interpretation

Alex Bernardo

CHRISTIANS FOR LIBERTY PRESS
St. Louis, MO

DEDICATION

This book is dedicated to Bethany and Emily, without whom it would have never been written. Thank you both for your unending support. I truly love our tiny family and am eternally grateful for you both, and I count the two of you as the greatest blessings God has ever granted me. Our best days are still ahead.

TABLE OF CONTENTS

CHAPTER 3 | Liberty and Authority 45

PART II: BACKGROUND AND METHODOLOGY TO NEW TESTAMENT INTERPRETATION

CHAPTER 4 | Method and Modernization. 73

CHAPTER 5 | The Greco-Roman World 97

PART III: NEW TESTAMENT INTERPRETATION

PREFACE

A NOTE ON STYLE

The book you are currently holding in your hands is the result of over twenty years of reading, studying, and reflecting upon the Bible and its relationship to the modern world. I had always dreamed of writing a book distilling my thoughts, and after amassing a large library of works on the Bible, political philosophy, and economic theory, I had the ability to convert my thoughts to words on paper. The research presented in the following pages reflect my own academic interests and reading habits. I did not have access to a university library during the composition of this book, and in many ways I think that fact only strengthens my proposed thesis. By accessing only the best and brightest minds in the relevant fields, I have avoided losing myself in the endless maze of obscure journal articles, out-of-print books, and fringe scholarship. While an assessment and analysis of these sources is intellectually valuable, I wanted to demonstrate that my thesis is compatible with the main currents of scholarly discourse. Anyone interested in pursuing the ideas I put forward in more detail need only consult the works included in the bibliography. There is an endless horizon of ideas waiting for intrepid explorers to traverse, and we must never stop searching for the truth.

A few methodological notes are in order before proceeding. I have chosen to capitalize the word 'Messiah' when referring specifically to Jesus but leave it uncapitalized when denoting general messianic expectations. As a Christian, I have chosen to capitalize both 'God' and 'Holy Spirit' based on my theological conviction that they are personal beings and deserve to be respected as such. I have also elected to capitalize the word 'Gentile'; as I will demonstrate in the following pages, many first-century Jews divided the world into two discrete categories: Jews and Gentiles. Since the term 'Gentile' functions as a proper noun, it seemed historically appropriate for me to capitalize it. When directly quoting scholarship, however, I have left the capitalization of terms like 'God', 'Messiah', and 'Gentile' unchanged to accurately reflect the perspective presented in their own works. Other writers deserve to have their voices fully heard without censorship or modification.

I also made the decision, with which my editor reluctantly conceded, to place punctuation marks and footnote references outside of all direct source quotations included in the book. Language, including the rules of grammar and syntax, are a product of social convention, and it has never made sense to me that American authors add punctuation inside of quotation marks which didn't exist in the original source. This tendency will likely annoy some readers, but I want to clarify that it was intentional and is far from an idiosyncratic novelty or the failure of my editor or proofreaders! Much of the Biblical scholarship I engage with in this book and which influenced my intellectual development was produced by British scholars, where the style of punctuation I employ is actually very common. I count this as one advantage the British have over Americans. While there are many people who have given me input and assisted in the editorial process, I alone determined the finished product. Any mistakes or errors included in the following pages are my responsibility and must not be blamed on anyone who edited or endorsed the book.

ACKNOWLEDGEMENTS AND DEDICATION

This project would not have come to fruition without the support of many incredible people I am blessed to have the privilege of knowing, some of whom might never read a word of this book but nevertheless provided me with the encouragement and motivation I needed to see this work through to the end. I want to thank the Libertarian Christian Institute, particularly Doug Stuart and Norman Horn, for taking on this project, providing an ample amount of helpful feedback, and ensuring my personal dream became a reality. The unique nature of this book would likely never survive the editorial board of any other publisher, but Doug and Norm believed it was valuable enough to pursue. While I am grateful for all of my LCI colleagues, Cody Cook sacrificed a considerable amount of time reading through the rough draft and offering me his thoughts. His own published works are partially responsible for influencing me to write this book, and I am thankful to call Cody a friend. I also want to thank those who looked through the draft and were willing to either comment on the book or endorse it, including Dr. Jeffery Degner, Dr. Allan Bevere, Dr. Gerard Casey, and Dr. Eric Schansberg. A special thanks goes out to Dr. Kevin Burr. I am very grateful for our friendship, your willingness to support this book, and for proving to me that not everyone in the discipline of Biblical studies falls neatly into the progressive-conservative political spectrum.

Friendship is an undervalued asset in modern society, and I want to give full credit to the phenomenal friends who have shaped my life in powerful and tangible ways. I have the privilege of being involved in two amazing small-groups. I would like to thank my Friday night group, particularly Jon, Matt, and Kyle, for always entertaining my crazy thoughts about theology and politics and providing a consistent example of mature Christian faithfulness. Even though I am an old man by comparison, my Sunday afternoon group always asks deep and purposeful questions, and I have been both refreshed and challenged by your desire to seek after God. Because of you I am much more optimistic about the future of the church. I want to thank my Generations family for providing a healthy, missionally-oriented community of believers, and I couldn't think of a better place to worship and serve. I especially want to acknowledge the leaders (both past and present) of our church, Dave, Vince, Patrick, Christina, and Dawn, for building into my family. Our church culture is exceedingly rare and wouldn't exist without your leadership. I am extremely appreciative of my TMS family, particularly the incredible educators whom I have the privilege of working with daily in the 7th grade hallway. I couldn't imagine teaching with a better team of people, and you all keep me sane in a job which can oftentimes be frustrating, irrational, and downright depressing. You make a positive difference in this world, and it is an honor to serve with you.

For the many friends who have stuck with me through the decades, despite being separated by geography and circumstances, I couldn't imagine life without you. To Kyle, Colin, Laura, Gary, Wes, and everyone else, you all are amazing. I am especially grateful for Anthony and Ryan. Your life-long commitment to following Jesus is an inspiration, and I am thankful for the many conversations we have had about God, politics, raising families, great music, and everything else. After twenty years, it feels like our friendship is just getting started. Here is to many more decades of whiskey and great conversations! To my hilarious cousins (and their great parents; I love all my aunts and uncles!) in western Kentucky and Texas, one of the best developments in my personal life over the last two years has been our weekly text exchanges. I wish we would have started this years ago. If you read this, it's 99 time! Tradition has been called, and I expect to see you shortly. Not only do I have an excellent mother- and father-in-law, my wife's entire family is awesome. You all were a package deal with Bethany, and you have all made my life so much better! Thank you all for the unending support you have shown my family, and thank you for openly welcoming me into yours!

To Ross, Rachel, and the kids, I couldn't ask for a better brother and sister-in-law. As the years go on, I really appreciate the positive impact you all have had on our lives and count you both as among a small group of people we can always count on during difficult times. You guys are the best, and I look forward to seeing you raise your family in the years ahead. To my parents, Anita and Rob, you both enabled me to become the man I am today. Mom, you always pushed me to take my education seriously and realize the value of constantly learning, and you taught me to ask difficult questions and stand up for what is right. Dad, your example of hard work and responsibility have shaped my life in powerful ways, and I would never have been able to pursue a project like this without those values which you instilled in me from a young age. To my grandparents, all of whom have passed, thank you for everything. I know we will meet again in the world to come, and I can't wait to see you all again.

Finally, I must express my sincere gratitude to my family, Bethany, Emily, and Bun-Bun. Even though I was completely baited into purchasing a rabbit, our pet Bun-Bun is an incredible addition to our family. Rabbits might not be smart, but they make great pets! Emily, I mean it with all my heart when I say that you are the best kid ever. Your compassion and kindness, desire to question everything, faith in God, and wonderful personality are incredible assets which will serve you well! You bring so much joy to my life and it has been an honor to watch you grow and develop into the young woman you are today. I am very grateful that you were so understanding during the writing of this book, and I promise I will make up for all the lost time we could have spent together! To Bess, I am blessed beyond belief to have married a woman like you. I know that I am sometimes a difficult person to live with (especially when writing a very long book!) but you always offer me support, encouragement, and accountability. Without you none of this would have been possible, and there is no one else I would rather spend my life with than you. You are an incredible mother and I am so thankful for the family we have built together. Your faithfulness, lack of pretension, and realism keeps all of us grounded, and I still believe that the best years of our marriage are ahead of us. It is to you and Emily that I dedicate this book. Thank you both for helping me see this project through to the end, and I am genuinely excited about returning to nights of playing basketball at the park and walking to the cows. You guys are the best!

Alex Bernardo
February 2026

CHAPTER 1 | An Introduction to Categorical Confusion

We Don't Know What We Don't Know

JESUS AND SOCIALISM

I used to believe Jesus was a socialist.

This isn't exactly the perspective a kid who grew up in conservative Kentucky would be expected to hold naturally. I had a tendency, however, of describing him (and other characters in the New Testament) as 'kind of' a socialist. As a bi-vocational minister I habitually attempted to steer conversations with my friends and family members in the direction of faith. On a dark and snowy evening in 2014 I was at a holiday party with several of my friends when the topic turned to the then-controversial issue of gay marriage. As a Christian who believed strongly that the ideal biblical view of marriage was a monogamous, life-long union between a man and a woman in which sexual activity was reserved exclusively for wedlock, I nevertheless took the position that in a free, democratic society like the United States same-sex attracted couples should be able to obtain a legally-recognized civil union. They could, if they chose to do so, even call it 'marriage'. Let churches retain their traditional views about biblical matrimony, and let those who don't attend traditionalist churches do whatever they want. After all, Christians shouldn't be imposing their beliefs on others using the force of the law, right? Isn't faith a personal choice that everyone must make for themselves? And shouldn't Christians be in the business of trying to respectfully convince people of the gospel's veracity? My argument went over well, and, as one of my friends (not quite accurately) observed, my position was similar to those held by 'the liberals'. I (not quite accurately) concurred, noting how I also believed Jesus was 'kind of' a socialist despite my generally conservative and traditionalist theological worldview. While I still believe the former position (same-sex civil unions should be respected, and churches who hold to traditional views of marriage should also be respected), I no longer subscribe to the latter. What changed?

In 2014 I believed that 'socialism' was the moderate approach for Christians who cared deeply about applying biblical principles to the problems of modern society. I was raised in a politically center-right home and my mom made sure our family was actively involved in a local Lutheran church. I began reading Scripture at the age of 14 and was immediately hooked. I found it to be simultaneously provocative and terrifying, and my time in the Lutheran church had taught me one very important lesson: the Bible is authoritative and Christians must conform to its teachings. I still believe that lesson is entirely correct. As I read and reread the New Testament throughout high school, I realized many Christians never actually took it seriously. Very few attempted to read it, much less allow it to shape their lives, and I had burning questions that only a small number of people were equipped to answer. I became somewhat radical through my reading of the text and went to college in pursuit of a degree in Biblical studies. I fell in love with the program and learned how to read the Bible in its historical context. My research helped reframe many of the questions and categories which I had used to interpret the Bible during my formative years in high school. I left college with more questions about the Bible than I had when I was younger but had come to appreciate the complexities of biblical interpretation and developed an acute sense of humility about my ability to read and interpret the Bible accurately. These burning questions drove me to continue studying long after graduation and led organically to subjects outside the field of Biblical studies, hoping to develop areas of knowledge which would enable me to better understand the biblical texts.

The natural progression of life instructed my worldview as well. I had worked a day job through college and during my junior year began serving as the high school student director at my home church. Upon graduation, my day job became a full-time gig while I continued to work bi-vocationally in ministry. I learned several valuable lessons from holding both of these positions simultaneously. As a minister, I realized that human life is incalculably complex. People had real needs and were oftentimes at the mercy of forces which were well beyond their control. My reading of the Bible showed me how the church was a broken world's only hope and that Christians should be committed to radical, sacrificial service by providing charity for those in need. I also noticed that American politics often compromised the witness of the church and started to wonder if American Christians should hold the political process at arm's length. Politics was a necessary evil, I assumed, but our hope should be in Jesus and the kingdom he inaugurated at his resurrection. Those eternal truths should frame the identity of the church.

My full-time job, monotonously working in production at a dry-cleaning facility, also shaped my intellectual outlook in a powerful way. I quickly concluded that limits should be placed on public and private charity. Some people simply don't want to work or take personal responsibility, and those people need to experience real consequences for their actions. I also saw how business regulations and taxation hurt working-class people. I asked my company's owner one day why we couldn't hire people at a higher hourly rate to attract more competent workers. He appreciated the question and showed me the company's spreadsheet, explaining how payroll comprised well over 50% of company expenses, and because our industry was heavily regulated, compliance with state and federal regulations was extremely costly. After utilities, rents and mortgages, supplies, and taxes, industry profit margins were incredibly slim. His explanation made perfect mathematical sense. I also had the common but radicalizing experience of looking at my paystub every week and seeing firsthand how much the government took from me in taxes. I believed we needed some taxes (how else would we pay for the roads, the schools, the military, and entitlement programs?) but that the rates were too high. My low-income coworkers, not to mention myself, could have lived a more materially secure life if the government would just let them keep a larger share of the money they had worked hard to earn.

By 2014 I was well aware of all of these problems. Yet when the topic of Jesus and 'economics' or 'politics' would come up in conversation, I still maintained that Jesus was 'kind of' a socialist. Why? I had been taught to believe, not least by my reading of biblical scholarship, that 'capitalism' is all about greed and consumerism, and all capitalists were evil and immoral people who valued money above everything else. Socialism, by contrast, was about sharing and charity. Nice, kind people believed in socialism, a sentiment appearing to conform with the New Testament, which unambiguously demands charity as an obligation for Christians. My experiences at work and in ministry were revelatory; we absolutely had to impose some limits on charity. Perhaps the government should only take a little bit of money to help people who are truly in need, and maybe Christians should give more of their personal money to charitable organizations? Since I assumed this position was, more or less, the definition of 'socialism', it made perfect sense to identify Jesus as a marginal socialist. As it turns out, I was wrong. I had never stopped and considered what I actually meant when I employed basic political and economic terminology.

DEFINITIONS MATTER

For reasons which will be elaborated in the next chapter I eventually abandoned the position that Jesus was, even 'kind of', a socialist. The problem with terms like 'socialism' and 'capitalism' in contemporary discourse is in their universal lack of precise definitions. In fact, these terms have almost no definitional anchors whatsoever. They are essentially used as synonyms for 'good' and 'evil' political policies depending on which side of the left-right political spectrum the person who employs them happens to fall. This is, in my view, symptomatic of a wider problem in American society. Conversations about politics and economics are hopelessly imprecise. Many Americans simply don't develop the critical thinking skills necessary to assess complex political and economic issues[1], and I will argue in the next chapter that even professional academics fail to think about politics and economics in definitionally or philosophically consistent terms. Politics has become something of a team sport where many Americans support one of the two major parties regardless of the constantly shifting policy platforms each party endorses. Democrat Barack Obama ran his 2008 campaign on a platform of traditional marriage[2], an unthinkable position for a Democratic presidential candidate today, while Republican Donald Trump became the first president to openly support same-sex marriage from his first day in office after he was inaugurated in 2017[3], a position which would have been equally unthinkable for any Republican presidential candidate in 2008. Regardless of these massive policy shifts, voters line up behind their political teams and offer them unconditional support, illustrating how the American voting public either never cultivated political principles or are willing to abandon them as long as their preferred party obtains power.

The problems of division run even deeper. Economist Cass Sunstein argues in his book *Going to Extremes: How Like Minds Unite and Divide*[4] that people tend to become more extreme in their views when they associate only with others who share their views, while dialogue between people who hold opposing

---

1. The shift in public education policy which prioritizes math and language arts standards has no doubt contributed to this phenomenon; for a scholarly analysis of this shift, see McGuinn, Patrick J. 2006. *No Child Left Behind and the Transformation of Federal Education Policy, 1965-2005*. University Press of Kansas.

2. Miller, Zeke. "Axelrod: Obama Misled Nation When He Opposed Gay Marriage In 2008." *Time*, February 10, 2016. https://time.com/3702584/gay-marriage-axelrod-obama/.

3. Gutierrez-Morfin, Noel. "Trump Says He's 'Fine' With Gay Marriage in '60 Minutes' Interview." *NBC News*, November 14, 2016. https://www.nbcnews.com/feature/nbc-out/trump-says-h e-s-fine-gay-marriage-60-minutes-interview-n683606.

4. Sunstein, Cass. 2011. *Going to Extremes: How Like Minds Unite and Divide*. Oxford University Press.

positions tends to moderate the perspectives of both groups. He accurately foresaw in 2011 how social media, with its algorithmically curated echo chambers, was uniquely primed to create deep social and political divisions in the United States[5], a premonition which has undoubtedly come true. This has resulted in American citizens becoming increasingly entrenched and less willing to understand how the other side thinks. Within this polarized battleground, terms like 'capitalism' and 'socialism', as well as theories of political power, become weaponized to attack the other team. These terms and concepts, which desperately need tethering to stable definitions or descriptions, become amorphous and lose much of their rhetorical value. The academic class, which should seek to add nuance and precision into these complex conversations, is often guilty of falling prey to the cultural reductionism of juvenile political pressures. American Christians, who should be shrewdly critical of secular society, have also succumbed to the social forces which promote unclear political and economic thinking. I stand guilty as charged; my own thinking on Jesus and socialism that I held over a decade ago is an excellent example of this prevalent cultural phenomenon. Without ever reading an economics textbook I boldly proclaimed that Jesus must have held socialist beliefs because my perception of his ministry corresponded to my perception of socialism. Even after earning a degree in Biblical studies I was guilty of committing one of the fundamental sins of biblical interpretation: importing my own values, preferences, and ideas back into the biblical texts.

The Bible is a product of particular cultures that existed at particular points in history. The Bible was not written to modern, twenty-first century westerners, and the authors of the Bible, even accepting they wrote under the inspiration of God, were products of the social and historical contexts in which they lived. While Christians generally believe in the authority and reliability of the Bible[6], we also must acknowledge that it was written by people who thought and lived differently than us, to people who thought and lived differently than us, and within cultures that thought and lived differently than us. The task of biblical interpretation is to understand the Bible in its historical context, and then, for the Christian interpreter, assess how we might apply the principles we find there to our situation in the modern world. We acknowledge the two-thousand-year gap between ourselves and the writers of the New Testament, and we appreciate their very real historical differences. That is why we must carefully read and interpret the Bible in its historical context. The problem stems from our inability to think clearly about basic modern political and economic concepts; by attempting to find examples of

---

5. Sunstein, p. 79-83

6. Two categories I will define in Chapter 4.

our flawed definitions in places they were never hiding, we wind up chasing after nothing but our own shadows. Christians of all political persuasions are guilty of going to the text in search of a justification for ideas that simply didn't exist in the ancient world. This is no less true in academia. Nearly every professional biblical scholar has also fallen into one of these modern echo chambers, resulting in scholarly reconstructions of figures like Jesus and Paul which bear a suspiciously striking resemblance to modern social and political paradigms. Since western universities often trend to the left, many scholars uncritically adopt the language of capitalism as a supposed foil to the radical message of Jesus and the apostles. There are no stable definitions of political and economic concepts in the modern world. We find ourselves in a predicament in which we wind up projecting our own biases and prejudices back onto the canvas of history, effectively silencing the voices of those from a distant time who are trying to communicate something we are incapable of hearing. We presuppose the Bible is designed to answer modern social and political questions when it is entirely contingent upon ancient assumptions about the nature of reality.

I understand the desire to want the Bible to speak directly to the political and economic structures of our times. Progressives and conservatives alike, even those who have rejected the ultimate authority of Scripture, search the texts for passages which appear to justify their preferred policy positions. After all, who wouldn't want Jesus on their side in a contentious political debate? The heated yet uninformed nature of American politics causes people to think irrationally about the Bible, and even those who have a rich knowledge of the Bible and understand the importance of historical context in other areas fail to do so when they believe it to be relevant for public policy debates. It seems that the American church is at an impasse; our unclear thinking about modern political problems leads to unclear thinking about the Bible, which is misinterpreted and incorrectly applied to modern questions, thereby creating more unclear thinking. It is, to borrow an old phrase, a vicious cycle.

THE GOALS OF THE BOOK

It doesn't have to be this way. For several years I have labored to reframe the conversation. I believe that anchoring our modern understanding of politics and economics to consistent, irreducible, and universally applicable categories, exploring the differences (and occasional similarities) between ancient and modern political and economic concepts, and analysing the biblical texts in light this data will inject a level of nuance and refinement into a debate which has far too often been hindered by unclear thinking. Even though I am not an expert in any of the areas

I will explore in this book (a lacuna for which I will soon offer an explanation) my research and reflection on the relationship between modern political and economic thought and biblical interpretation has led me to the conclusion that there might just be a way to clarify the parameters of this discussion after all. The basic premise of this book is as follows: biblical scholarship has generally failed to adequately define political and economic concepts, and this failure has resulted in drawing contemporary conclusions from the biblical texts which are diametrically opposed to the original intention of the biblical authors themselves. In particular, biblical scholarship almost always implicitly or explicitly assumes (and sometimes endorses) the political and economic paradigm of modern authoritarian socialism, even when it contradicts certain conclusions scholars derive from their interpretations. By properly defining and delineating the political and economic categories, New Testament interpretation (and the conclusion which believers in the modern world draw from their interpretation) undermines authoritarian socialism and provides us with a more historically satisfying and accurate reading of New Testament texts. This argument of this book can be reduced to a single thesis statement: the New Testament does not endorse authoritarian socialism.

To this end, there are three goals I hope to accomplish by writing this book:

1. Define modern economic and political concepts and compare them with the ancient world in which the New Testament was written.
2. Demonstrate the complexities of applying biblical texts to modern social and political questions and explore the use of modern social and political categories in biblical interpretation.
3. Analyze several prominent New Testament texts which are often assumed to address 'political' and 'economic' issues.

A quick word regarding all three.

The first goal is to do what nearly every professional New Testament scholar or theologian who writes about these issues has failed to accomplish: actually define what we mean by 'capitalism' and 'socialism'. I have spent the last several years studying the Austrian school of economics and it has become increasingly apparent that proponents of the Austrian school have constructed the only categorically consistent and irreducible definition of these terms. Political philosophers who understand the consequences of Austrian economics have provided a more accurate method of understanding modern political dynamics. Instead of the conventional 'left-right' spectrum (associated with the terms 'progressive' and 'conservative', respectively) which is constantly shifting and generally interpreted through the subjective preferences of political commentators, Austrian-informed political theorists have correctly relabeled the political spectrum using the categories of 'libertarian' and 'authoritarian'. I will show that this tradition of economic and political thought is intellectually stable, generally applicable, and less susceptible to subjective misappropriation. Related to this, I want to provide a general overview of the ancient political and economic institutions which impacted the early followers of Jesus and contextualized the works that were eventually included in the New Testament. To that end, there will be chapter-length reviews of both the Greco-Roman and Jewish contexts within which the earliest followers of Jesus were located. By understanding this essential background information we will be in a much better position to interpret biblical texts and demonstrate the ways in which our contemporary categories create more hermeneutical dilemmas than they solve.

This leads me to my second point, which is about the difficulty of applying biblical texts to modern economic and political questions and, vice versa, utilizing modern economic and political categories in biblical interpretation. There are, as a matter of pure historical fact, profound differences between the modern and ancient mind. Our categories for interpreting reality are a product of, to put it broadly, the Renaissance, the Reformation, the Scientific Revolution, and the Enlightenment. These long periods of cultural transformation forever altered the western intellectual landscape and have created such a profound epistemological revolution that we often fail to appreciate just how different the ancient world was from our own. This dynamic stems from the Renaissance itself; the great architect of fourteenth century Italian renaissance thought was Petrarch, who very much understood the times in which he was living as a return to the grandeur of classical Greece and Rome. He is in large part responsible for creating the (mis)perception that the time between Augustine and the rise to prominence of the Italian city-states was a 'dark age' characterized by a European rejection of its glorious ancient past[7], resulting in a popular misconception that the Greek and Romans weren't really too much different from us after all. Even though the Enlightenment problematized over-simplistic Renaissance readings of history[8], in popular reception many western thinkers have internalized Petrarch and assumed we are of one mind with our classical forebears, a myth which has had a profound impact on biblical interpretation.

These differences aren't just restricted to the world of ideas, however. The social, political, economic, and material fabric of antiquity is entirely different from our own. The urban economies of the Roman cities in which Paul evangelized, as

---

7. Cahill, Thomas. 2013. *Heretics and Heroes*. Anchor Books. pp. 67-70

8. Pagden, Anthony. 2013. *The Enlightenment*. Random House. pp. 13-14

well as the agrarian economies of regions like Galilee, were in many respects entirely dissimilar from modern economic systems. Understanding these differences are essential for contextualizing the ministry of Jesus and the works of other New Testament writers. While the underlying market principles of scarcity, choice, supply, and demand are still essential tools for understanding economic dynamics, we must take it for granted that modern industrial economies sharply diverge from those in antiquity, and our imprecise definition of modern economic concepts often obscures this fact. Similarly, the complexities of Roman imperial rule, which was sometimes administered with a light touch and sometimes enforced through a clenched fist, differs in many important respects from our so-called 'modern liberal democracies'. Understanding the nature of Roman imperialism and the very real political power held by local rulers[9] will provide precision and nuance to our understanding of biblical works forged in these contexts of Antiquity. Many New Testament scholars have in recent years attempted to provide a more nuanced analysis of the social and political realities in which the Bible was produced. Several of them explicitly utilize Marxists class analysis, reading biblical texts through the framework of class conflict. An excellent recent example is a book written by James Crossley and Robert Myles entitled *"Jesus: A Life in Class Conflict"*[10]. I will be in dialogue with this and other related works throughout the following pages, and even though I am proposing an alternative framework for thinking about these questions, scholars like Crossley and Myles understand the complexities of reading ancient texts about politics and economics in contemporary contexts. We need more research in this area and I hope to contribute another perspective which draws on much of the excellent research already conducted within New Testament scholarship.

My third goal, which will comprise the majority of this book, requires the shortest amount of explanation. Once I have established definitions, methods, and contexts I will examine passages from the New Testament which are often debated in contemporary political and economic discourse. The scope of this work is much wider than many related monographs, however, as I plan on reviewing texts which are often marginalized or overlooked. I will include material from all twenty-seven works in the New Testament, exhaustively demonstrating the utility of employing precise political and economic concepts in biblical interpretation. The scope is massive, to be sure, but I hope my humble exegetical proposals presented in

---

9. Local authorities like the Sanhedren, which have often been characterized as 'religious leaders' in biblical interpretation, possessed real political power and would have been seen by their contemporaries as 'political' bodies. This is, as we will see, a projection of the post-Enlightenment dichotomy between 'religion' and 'politics' back into antiquity.

10. Crossley, James, and Robert Myles. 2023. *Jesus: A Life in Class Conflict.* Zer0 Books.

this book will help refine a categorically confused conversation. I strongly believe the prevailing modern political category of authoritarian socialism, which I will define below, is entirely incompatible with the principles embedded in the New Testament. A bold proposition demands substantial evidence, but the scales of probability tip in favor of my thesis.

The Outline of the Book

The path ahead is fairly straightforward. The book is divided into three sections. Part One, entitled Background and Methodology to Politics and Economics, comprises Chapters 2-3. In these chapters I will define 'capitalism' and 'socialism', argue that the real political spectrum is not conservative-versus-progressive but rather liberty-versus-authority, and explain how authoritarian socialism became the dominant political and economic ideology of modernity. The second section of the book, Background and Methodology to New Testament Interpretation, provides a philosophical and historical framework for interpreting the New Testament. In Chapter 4 I outline my hermeneutical method for interpreting Scripture and caution against the dangers of modernization, which is the imposition of modern ideas upon ancient biblical texts, while Chapters 5-6 explores the Greco-Roman and Jewish contexts which shaped the New Testament.

In the third and longest section, titled simply *New Testament Interpretation*, I employ the methodology delineated in the first two sections to do exactly what the section title suggests: interpret the New Testament. I turn to the gospels in Chapters 7-10, discussing interpretive methods and themes before providing a detailed analysis of the texts themselves. Chapter 11 is something of an interlude, covering Acts in anticipation of Paul, which will be the subject of Chapters 12-15. As with the gospels, I present a detailed hermeneutical framework for interpreting Paul's letters before analysing them in (mostly) canonical order, saving Romans and the notorious 13:1-7 for the final Pauline chapter, enabling readers to understand this difficult passage within the larger framework of Paul's thought. Chapter 16 covers Hebrews and the Catholic Epistles while Chapter 17 details Revelation. Chapter 19 will draw the book to a close, showing how New Testament scholarship can be improved through clear political and economic reasoning and drawing my long study to a close.

While the book was written to be read as a continuous whole, it was also deliberately structured to be used as a reference work for curious readers who are interested only in particular aspects of this study. For a Christian unfamiliar with political and economic theory, a reader who is intrigued by methodological or historical questions in biblical interpretation, or someone who simply wants to see how specific biblical passages might work within my proposed interpretive framework, much of the book can be profitably read on a chapter-by-chapter or even section-by-section basis. Although I do, as this book's author, encourage you to see how the entire argument fits together, I appreciate your willingness to engage with the ideas presented in the following pages.

My Personal Limitations

We all have personal limitations, and I will not attempt to conceal mine. While I am not a biblical scholar, I have a degree in Biblical Studies and host a podcast where I have spent hundreds of hours talking to some of the world's most prolific biblical scholars, engaging with their work.[11] I routinely read new biblical scholarship and have nearly a decade of experience in ministry, placing me in the category of 'very informed lay person'. For years I have been waiting for some professional scholar to write a book about the Bible, politics, and economics which was definitionally and methodologically rigorous while also incorporating themes and texts often left out of the conversation. I guess I got tired of waiting. While I dream of the day when a 'real' biblical scholar decides to give it a shot, the glaring lacuna in the discipline necessitated a response, and I am confident my attempt stands toe-to-toe with every other attempt to analyze the political and economic context of the New Testament. Love it or hate it, biblical interpretation cannot be confined to the ivory towers of higher education, and I have more than paid my dues. Institutional outsiders such as myself must sometimes be afforded a seat at the table, and I come equipped with an informed perspective regarding political and economic theory which many Biblical scholars lack. In fact, one of my central contentions is that the entire discipline needs to seriously rethink its political and economic priors, and to that extent I am wholly qualified to mount an extended protest against the insular conceptions of modern ideas which plague the field. Even if one is inclined to reject my work outright or, upon reading it, forcefully disagree with my conclusions, I maintain that any book which seeks to analyze the New Testament's political and economic themes must do precisely what I will undertake in the following pages: carefully define terms, explicitly detail hermeneutical method, and, above all, interpret as many texts as possible. I hope my contribution will serve as an example for others to emulate.

I should also place the rest of my cards on the table. I will not pretend to be politically or economically neutral. I am a committed libertarian of the anarcho-capitalist tradition championed by intellectual giants such as the great Murray

---

11. *The Protestant Libertarian Podcast*, available on all podcast streaming platforms.

Rothbard. I am unapologetic and uncompromising in my commitment to this tradition, which I believe to be morally and philosophically consistent. More to the point, I think it is the *only* modern political and economic theory which is compatible with Christian values and the most consistent expression of Christian political thought. I had been reading the Bible for well over a decade and came to many of the theological conclusions which I will articulate and defend below long before discovering libertarianism. I was surprised to find a tradition which seemed to be in harmony with the values of my faith, and further reading and research has only confirmed my initial impressions. That being said, I am not making an argument for Christian libertarianism in this book, and I don't believe for a second that the Bible clearly teaches libertarianism or any other modern political or economic theory, for reasons that will become clear in the following chapters. I am to show the incompatibility of authoritarian socialism with the New Testament. If this results in an abandonment of conservatism or progressivism, then so be it. The stage has been set, and we are now ready to begin our study of politics, economics, and New Testament interpretation. Let's get started.

PART I | Background and Methodology
to Politics & Economics

There are many problems plaguing modern Biblical interpretation, both in academic and ecclesial settings. One glaring issue is a distinct lack of categorical or definitional precision. Nowhere is this more apparent than when interpreters both professional and popular attempt to analyze the political and economic contours of the New Testament, and it is particularly evident when interpreters attempt to draw modern conclusions based on imprecise conceptual premises. The only satisfactory way to break the impasse and think more rationally and historically about politics, economics, and the New Testament is to posit a redefinition of political and economic categories with a view to making sense of how these categories aid in New Testament interpretation and application.

While words are infinitely malleable, I will propose definitions for the terms 'capitalism' and 'socialism' which are consistent, irreducible, and universally applicable. Regardless of whether or not one agrees with my employment of these terms, the referents to which they point will provide us with more conceptual clarity when interpreting the New Testament. Starting from the tradition of Austrian economics, I will demonstrate that 'capitalism' is a decentralized economic arrangement in which the means of production are controlled by those who own them, while socialism is a centralised economic system in which the factors of production are publicly controlled and regulated. The fundamental differences between these two different approaches to economics lies in their use of force; capitalism is based on peaceful, voluntary transactions between cooperative individuals or groups while socialism is predicated upon coercive, involuntary aggression by a ruling class. There are no 'mixed economies'; so long as political authorities are able to arbitrarily intervene in consensual transactions there can be no capitalism. Modern, state-centered economic policy is always socialistic to varying degrees and therefore relies upon the threat of violence to enforce.

Austrian economics generated a political theory based upon the non-aggression principle, the radical but morally consistent idea that no one has the right to initiate aggression against another. While contemporary political discourse divides the world up neatly into a conservative right-wing and a progressive left-wing, both conservatism and progressivism violate the non-aggression principle and are therefore structurally identical. The real political spectrum is not left vs. right but liberty vs. authority, which is reducible to political arrangements based on peaceful consent as opposed to those based on arbitrary authority. To that end the prevailing modern political and economic paradigm is authoritarian socialism, which, as I will argue throughout the book, is incompatible with the New Testament.

CHAPTER 2 | Capitalism and Socialism

Defining Economic Terms

The state is not irrelevant but instrumental to global capitalism's expansion.

Richard Horsley[1]

Under the conditions of global capitalism, capital gravitates towards the hyper-rich.

Douglas Oakman[2]

What began as the parochial ideologies of the disaffected peasantry in Galilee and Judea . . . continues to be embedded in subtle ways within the now capitalist mode of production of our age.

James Crossley and Robert Myles[3]

The economy (that is, the market and capitalism) and the nation state combine to rob ordinary people of resources and livelihood.
Halvor Moxnes[4]

[There are] connections between aspects of the Roman empire and forms of empire today: the global capitalist economy and the powerful . . . United States of America.

Michael Gorman[5]

---

1. Horsley, Richard. 2021. *You Shall Not Bow Down and Serve Them: The Political Economic Projects of Jesus and Paul.* Cascade Books. p. 212

2. Oakman, Douglas. 2012. *The Political Aims of Jesus.* Fortress Press. p. 137

3. Crossley and Myles, *Class Conflict*, p. 263

4. Moxnes, Halvor. 2018. *Jesus and the Rise of Nationalism: A New Quest for the Nineteenth-Century Historical Jesus.* I.B. Tauris. p. 193

5. Gorman, Michael. 2011. *Reading Revelation Responsibly.* Cascade Books. p. 44

WHAT DO WE MEAN?

Most of the contemporary debates about politics, leaving so-called 'culture war' issues to the side[6], are about the size and scope of government power, especially as it relates to the American market in particular and economic activity in general. American progressives on the political left believe the government should have a more active role in regulating the economy and providing social services funded by taxpayer dollars. American conservatives, at least nominally, claim to represent the opposite: they want the government to have a smaller role in regulating the economy and provide fewer social services. To be fair, the massive amount of debt incurred by the federal government under the leadership of both parties[7] suggests that Republican politicians prefer the rhetoric of 'limited government' to its actual implementation, but many GOP voters sincerely believe the role of government in American markets should have defined boundaries.

In popular parlance the political divisions between the American progressive left and conservative right are often characterized in economic terms as a divergence between 'socialism' and 'capitalism'. Progressives, under the oftentimes subconscious influence of Marxist or Keynesian assumptions, claim we need more 'socialism' because socialism is about helping poor people and being generous. Progressive Christians, correctly observing the Bible teaches charity and compassion as virtues Christians must cultivate, have concluded believers are obligated to support 'socialist' policies. Conservatives, on the other hand, have appropriated the term 'capitalism' as a way of referring to their preference for a government that handles the economy with a lighter touch. Few conservatives (especially among elected representatives) would want the government to have no involvement in economic affairs, and, as a matter of fact, many conservatives think the government must retain a substantial involvement in American markets, but there is still a general assumption that the term 'capitalism' denotes at least some limit to government power over the economy.

Christians on both the left and the right have decided, by the way they use these terms, that 'socialism' means more economic regulation and 'capitalism' means less. They then assume that when the writers of the Bible address issues

---

6. This book is primarily about defining economic terms and delimiting general principles of Chrsitian political engagement from a biblical perspective, so I will mostly avoid the controversial 'culture war' debates that generate heated conflict. The more fundamental issues that I address in this book will, I hope, help Christians reflect upon how they ought to navigate complex cultural issues.

7. Fichera, Angelo. "FACT FOCUS: Who's to Blame for the National Debt? It's More Complicated than One Culprit." *Associated Press*, May 18, 2023. https://apnews.com/article/fact-check-national-debt-donald-trump-barack-obama-ee3e613646fe500edf803e57959c776e.

which seem to be related to what we would categorize as 'politics' and 'economics' in the modern world, these terms are an appropriate way of describing how the biblical authors themselves would have thought about political and economic issues in antiquity, and, by extension, how we ought to appropriate and apply these passages in our modern context. The implicit thought process resembles something like this: we have developed the correct language and categories for understanding politics and economics in the modern world, the ancient authors probably thought about them in the same way we do, and our interpretation of passages in the Bible which seem to be addressing politics and economics will result in their support of either 'capitalism' or 'socialism' because this must have been what they were describing all along.

I am going to argue that these definitions of 'capitalism' and 'socialism' are fundamentally unsound. The way in which the terms are often invoked in popular culture and political discourse lack any solid foundation. The catena of quotations I provided at the beginning of the chapter from published works by professional biblical scholars is indicative of this problem. Few ever attempt to define the term 'capitalism', which is, for them, the source of all our modern ills and a system which any accurate interpretation of the Bible must oppose. This, however, leaves the door wide open to a necessary follow-up question: what, if anything, do we mean by 'capitalism'? Few people have walked through the door. Economist F.A. Hayek correctly notes that the modern connotations associated with the word 'capitalism' are largely a product of ideologically-charged interpretations of economic history[8] (a phenomenon which has, without a shred of doubt, influenced academic biblical scholarship), and before we can explore biblical texts which are often thought to relate to 'economic' issues it will do us well to set some parameters for the terms 'capitalism' and 'socialism..

My goal for this chapter is simple: provide consistent, irreducible, and universally applicable definitions of 'capitalism' and 'socialism' which enable us to examine economic categories both ancient and modern. Before we discuss these definitions and categories, it will be helpful to briefly reflect upon the mechanics of language and the necessity of accurately defining terms. We will turn to this important question first.

A WORD ABOUT WORDS: THE PROBLEM WITH LANGUAGE

Human language is entirely subjective. There is not a single word, uttered by a single individual, in any language, in any culture, which possesses a metaphysically

---

8. Hayek, F. A.. 1954. *Capitalism and the Historians*. University of Chicago Press. p. 15

'objective' meaning. Language is, in the purest sense of the phrase, a 'social construct'. Many people would immediately balk at this seemingly bold assertion. "*Well*", they might say, "*we have this book called 'the dictionary' which proves words do have real meanings*". This retort is correct on its face yet false in its substance. What do I mean by this?

Words absolutely do have meanings. When, as an English speaker, I am going for a walk and see another neighbor with an animal on a leash, I can correctly identify the animal using the English word 'dog'. Everyone who speaks American English knows what the word 'dog' means. The word 'dog' refers to the animal which my neighbor is taking for a walk. There are, however, certain instances in which the word 'dog' might be used in reference to something other than a four-legged pet. When a politician acts in a particularly corrupt manner, or when a friend engages in behavior society deems immoral, it is a common convention among English speakers to refer to that person as a 'dog'. In this context, the word 'dog' denotes morally questionable behavior, not a four-legged animal. When someone is making fun of another person one colloquial way of referring to it is 'dogging' the individual. Not a single English speaker would assume, when they heard the phrase "*you are dogging on him*", that the person performing the 'dogging' is literally hitting another person with a dog. A quick Google search will reveal that there are even more perverse uses of the term 'dog' which we need not mention in a book about the Bible. While the word 'dog' does have a definition in English dictionaries, its meaning can change depending on the context in which it is used. Therefore, the word 'dog' does indeed have a meaning, but not a universally objective one.

This is because language is little more than a semiotic system. 'Semiotic' is a technical term which means 'the study of signs or symbols'. Language is, at its heart, a series of signs and those things to which the sign refers (known as a 'referent'). Anyone who has ever driven down a state road or highway has a basic grasp of how semiotics function. If you are on a trip to a major city and you see a sign which has the name of that city and the number of miles it will take you to reach it, it is understood you have not yet arrived at your destination but that the sign is pointing you towards it. The function of language is similar. 'Things' exist in the real world. These 'things' can be tangible (dogs, snow, buildings, grass, etc.) or intangible (love, beauty, peace, frustration, etc.), but they exist. These are the 'referents', things about which humans need to communicate. The words we use to describe these referents are 'signs'. The signs are not the referents, they can only point us to the referents. It doesn't really matter what signs we use so long as in human communication both parties agree that particular signs point to particular referents.

The diversity of human language further clarifies the semiotic nature of language. Imagine two men, one who only speaks English and another who only speaks Spanish, are standing on a street corner. They hear a woman yelling that she has lost her dog. Seconds later, a dog runs by the men on the other side of the street. Both men point at the dog. The English speaker yells "*dog!*" and the Spanish speaker yells "*perro!*", a Spanish word for 'dog'. Both men are correct. Yet the signs they use in reference to the animal are different. How the woman searching for the dog will receive the sign depends on what language she speaks. If she speaks either Spanish or English, she will understand the sign which points to the referent. If she speaks another language, such as Russian, for instance, then the sign will mean nothing to her. This doesn't at all change the referent, the dog, which is still on the loose. It only means that the woman won't understand the sign.

Philosopher Ludwig Wittgenstein explored linguistic phenomena like these in his 1953 book *Philosophical Investigations*[9]. Wittgenstein argues that learning a language is much like learning the rules of a game. He even refers to this process as a "language game", where a speaker must learn the particular rules, conventions, and meanings of words in a given language in order to comprehend how that language works[10]. Language, because it is infinitely malleable, has no concrete or definite meaning. Societies develop the meaning of particular words over time, and in order for a person to play a particular "language game" (i.e. speak the language of a given society), they must understand the rules which govern the use of that language. As Wittgenstein says, "*the meaning of a word is its use in the language*"[11]. Even grammar is entirely arbitrary. Its sole purpose is to control the rules of how particular words are used in particular languages, with the objective of constructing intelligible signs that point to intelligible referents[12].

What, you might be asking, does any of this have to do with capitalism, politics, or the New Testament? The problem with loaded and controversial terms like 'capitalism' and 'socialism' is that they are often used to play different language games. Even among English speaking audiences these terms are employed in diverse and contradicting contexts. As signs they refer to radically different referents but because the referents themselves are abstract the users of these signs often assume they are pointed to a shared referent. The rules for the language game of 'capitalism' and 'socialism' have not been clearly defined, meaning that none of the players can possibly understand the game. Imagine playing a game of pickup

---

9. Wittgenstein, Ludwig. 1953. *Philosophical Investigations*. 3rd ed. (2001) Blackwell Publishing.

10. Wittgenstein, *Philosophical Investigations*, pp. 4-5

11. Wittgenstein, *Philosophical Investigations*, p. 18

12. Wittgenstein, *Philosophical Investigations*, pp. 117-118

basketball when someone who has only ever played soccer joins your team. If they start trying to kick the ball with their foot you would immediately understand that they have confused the rules of basketball with the rules of soccer. They didn't understand the game. This is why, in my opinion, there are many Americans on the left and right (including the professional biblical scholars quoted at the beginning of this chapter) who employ imprecise and contradictory uses of basic economic terms.

My hope is to delineate a clear set of rules governing the game of 'capitalism' and 'socialism', and I believe that the Austrian school of economics has done precisely this. The Austrian conception of these terms are consistent, irreducible, and have analytic applicability to all human economic activity. To be fair, it is entirely possible that you will disagree with the way in which I define these terms. Since language has no objective meaning, you are free to do so. I, however, want to explain very clearly how I will be using these terms in this book, and perhaps introduce unfamiliar readers with a venerable and rich intellectual tradition. With the conclusion of this brief philosophical investigation, we must now define the rules in order to play the game.

CAPITALISM AND SOCIALISM

"In the vocabularies of all languages the words "capitalist" and "bourgeois" signify today all that is shameful, degrading, and infamous. Contrariwise, people call all that they deem good and praiseworthy "socialist." The regular scheme of arguing is this: A man arbitrarily calls anything he dislikes "capitalistic," and then deduces from this appellation that the thing is bad."[13] The great Austrian economist Ludwig von Mises has a point. In the previous chapter I shared my own formerly-held assumptions about the term 'capitalism' and how, as I grew older, I came to realize I hadn't quite understood what it meant. Mises accurately observes that, not only in popular discourse but in academic circles as well, the word 'capitalist' has become a term which primarily denotes a particular judgment about the morality of certain economic arrangements. As a sign, the referent of 'capitalism' is whatever the user of the term deems unsavory or immoral. To this end it has been almost entirely devoid of any specific economic content aside from the fact that detractors of capitalism are generally insistent upon more government intervention in the market. I don't believe this understanding of the term is either accurate or useful, and the scholars I quoted at the beginning of the chapter who use this term (or adjacent

---

13. Mises, Ludwig von. 1949. *Human Action.* Yale University Press; (Martino Publishing, 2012). p. 268

terms like 'laissez-faire'[14]) are certainly employing it in a negative context. The sign has no concrete reference. I believe that needs to change. Before I can explore my own reevaluation of the term and provide a substantive definition, it might be helpful to review how the word came to be evaluated as a synonym for 'evil'.

Who Owns the Capital?: Karl Marx

The word 'capital', from which the world 'capitalism' is derived, simply means "*human-made goods that are used to produce goods and services*"[15]. To put it another way, 'capital' is what humans use to make goods or provide services. Capital is one of the essential means or factors of production. That which contributes to a finished product offered for purchase by a consumer is a form of capital. Tools, factories, trucks, software and the like are all examples of capital. Companies invest in capital not because it makes money in and of itself but because the accumulation of capital is the only way a business can produce goods and services. Capital is worthless unless it is employed to produce something consumers wish to purchase. The greatest factory in the world is little more than a financial liability without production. 'Capitalism', then, is a particular interpretation of the nature and ownership of capital.

Karl Marx and Friedrich Engels, the infamous architects of Communist theory, were, to put it mildly, skeptical about the private ownership of capital, the means of production. They argue in their seminal work *The Communist Manifesto*[16] that history can be understood as a never-ending struggle between different classes, and that, rather neatly, all human relationships can be reduced to a power dynamic between oppressors and oppressed[17]. As the feudalism of the middle ages gave way to modern industrialization, the two classes which had emerged in this new era of history were the bourgeoisie and the proletariat. Whereas in the previous period of feudal production serfs were oppressed by the land-owning lords, the bourgeoisie in the industrial age had gained control over the factors of production (including the all-important capital used to produce goods and services) and were, by

---

14. This is a common error made often by N.T. Wright in particular. Wright is notorious for making deliberately ambiguous claims about the practical application of his theology so that conservative and progressive readers can interpret his statements in a manner which is congenial to their personal preferences. While I can appreciate this as a brilliant marketing tactic it serves to conceal his own political commitments. I will comment on this in more detail below.

15. Irvin, Tucker B. 2013. *Survey of Economics*. 8th ed. South-Western, Cengage Learning. p. 550

16. Marx, Karl, and Frederick Engels. 1848. *The Communist Manifesto*. International Publishers (1948).

17. Marx and Engels, *Communist Manifesto*, p. 9

virtue of the ownership of these factors of production, oppressing the proletariat masses[18]. The goal of Marx and Engels's communist program was to push history forward by abolishing the bourgeoisie and empowering the proletariat. This meant that the private ownership of capital, the method which the bourgeoisie used to oppress the proletariat, had to be eliminated. In the words of Marx and Engels, *"the theory of the Communists may be summed up in the single sentence: Abolition of private property"*[19]. They elucidate this further, stating *"all that we want to do away with is the miserable character of this appropriation, under which the laborer* [the proletariat] *lives merely to increase capital, and is allowed to live only insofar as the interest of the ruling class requires it"*[20]. This includes the abolition of *"free trade, free selling and buying"*[21]. Since history is inevitably driven forward by class conflict, there must one day be a showdown between the owners of capital and those whom they exploit. In the end, the proletariat would prevail and usher in a classless society.

Or so the theory goes. I unironically agree with the great postmodernist philosopher Michel Foucault, whose theories about epistemology and historical knowledge I find compelling, that *"every sentiment, particularly the noblest and most disinterested, has a history"*[22]. All ideas, including Communism and capitalism, are the product of particular historical contexts. Marx and Engels failed to transcend historical subjectivity. Their foundational philosophy, 'historical materialism', asserts that human civilization is shaped and transformed by economic activity and, in particular, specific methods of production. When the methods of production break down, conflict necessarily ensues and humans must adapt to a new method of production[23]. It is this process of materialist conflict that would inevitably led to the abolition of private capital (and property in general) and bring about a golden age of human civilization. The philosophical substructure of Communism, and thus the earliest critiques of capitalism, are framed by several prominent nineteenth-century intellectuals. The most eminent is philosopher G.F. Hegel, whose theory of historical dialectics influenced Marx's understanding of human relations. The dramatically oversimplified explanation of Hegel's most influential insight, which is itself a product of wider nineteenth-century thought, is that history progresses naturally and human beings can, with the correct methodology, step

---

18. Marx and Engels, *Communist Manifesto*, pp. 10-21

19. Marx and Engels, *Communist Manifesto*, p. 23

20. Marx and Engels, *Communist Manifesto*, p. 24

21. Marx and Engels, *Communist Manifesto*, p. 25

22. Foucault, Michel. 1982. *The Foucault Reader*. Edited by Paul Rabinow. Pantheon Books. p. 87

23. Volle, Adam. "Historical Materialism." Britannica. December 2, 2021. https://www.britannica.com/topic/historical-materialism.

outside of the historical process and analyze it objectively. The massive intellectual breakthroughs in the natural sciences which occurred during the Scientific Revolution and the Enlightenment convinced a number of European thinkers that by applying scientific reasoning to social and political phenomena they could 'discover' truths about the workings of humanity. After all, if the universe was a giant machine which operated under a set of natural laws, why shouldn't human society work the same way?

This thinking, according to F.A. Hayek, became deeply ingrained in European philosophical thought, and the notion that natural laws of society could be discovered and subsequently imposed upon humanity had a profound impact on the development of socialism which influenced thinkers like Hegel and therefore Marx[24]. Hayek rejects the notion that human beings can be studied in the same way as the natural world and demonstrates how attempting to discern laws of society and inflicting them by government force through central planning led to the deaths of millions of people in the nineteenth and twentieth centuries. I concur. For our purposes this means Marx, who was heavily influenced by Hegel, has made a grave historical error: perhaps the notion that the private ownership of capital is the mechanism of oppression in this current economic age is flawed. Marx's historical materialism is a chimera. Philosopher Bertrand Russell, certainly no free-market activist, would agree: *"all the elements in Marx's philosophy which are derived from Hegel are unscientific, in the sense that there is no reason whatsoever to suppose them true."*[25] This doesn't mean, however, that Marx has been any less influential[26]. While Marxism has been interpreted and reapplied by many prominent schools of thought, including critical theory and postmodernism[27] (both of which are roundly rejected as 'Marxist' by those who hold to the orthodox teachings of Marx[28]), the main point I wish to make in what appears to be an irrelevant digression is that Marx is primarily responsible for the notion that 'capitalism' is a dirty word which must connote economic systems in need of dismantling. He created both the sign and the referent, and the notion of 'capital' has been tainted

---

24. Hayek, F.A. 1954. *The Counter-Revolution of Science*. The Free Press; (Liberty Press, 1979). pp. 185-193. I will offer a more detailed analysis in the next chapter.

25. Russell, Bertrand. 1940. *The History of Western Philosophy*. Simon & Schuster, Inc.; (Touchstone, 1972). p. 789

26. Nor does it mean that all of Marx's insights are fundamentally flawed. As we will see, there are some surprising similarities between certain elements of Marxists thought and the libertarian tradition for which I am advocating.

27. Bronner, Stephen. 2017. *Critical Theory*. Oxford University Press. pp. 9, 13

28. So, Paul. "Why Critical Race Theory Is Not Marxism." Midwestern Marx Institute. December 2, 2021. https://www.midwesternmarx.com/articles/why-critical-race-theory-is-not-marxism-by-paul-so.

with the stain of oppression ever since. It is this negative association of 'capitalism' with oppression and evil which has influenced biblical scholarship (and thus biblical interpretation), economic theory, and political discourse to this day. It is why I once believed Jesus was a socialist. Why did I change my perspective, and how did I come to disassociate 'capitalism' with moral degeneracy? I read an economics textbook.

Defining Capitalism and Socialism

It was a beautiful Saturday morning in the early fall of 2016. Cool air, orange leaves, and a crystal-clear blue sky; a quintessential autumn day. For several years I had worked two jobs. I was committed to student ministry, and had made it my life's mission, but (unsurprisingly) it didn't pay the bills. To support myself and my young family I worked a full-time day job to make ends meet. I had been grinding it out like that for years before realizing that ministry wasn't going to be my professional career. I decided to return to school and become a teacher and was accepted into the education program at Northern Kentucky University to work on my master's degree. My bachelors in Biblical studies had left a few holes in my academic resume which needed to be filled before starting the program, so I had to complete a handful of prerequisite courses. In the midst of two jobs and a family I decided to work through the small number of undergraduate courses I needed to be eligible for graduate school. I had committed to my church through December, when I would officially step down and focus on my day job and school. I just had to make it through the fall. I took three classes that semester, and one of them was an economics course. I remember being extremely excited about it. Many of the biblical scholars who had most influenced my thinking about the Bible and theology often commented on economic issues, but I knew almost nothing about the subject, except that Jesus was kind of a socialist. I was excited to better understand the field and before the class began started listening to economics podcasts to help me begin thinking about the subject. I had also recently heard Gary Johnson, the 2016 Libertarian Party presidential candidate, on Anderson Cooper and realized my political beliefs were very similar. I was hoping that my economics course would help me think about these issues more clearly. I had no idea what I was in for.

I had a scheduled meeting with a few people from my church at a local coffee shop on that fall Saturday morning. My wife suggested I arrive early and take some time by myself to complete school work, and I took her advice. The weather was so nice I rolled down the windows to my truck and decided to sit in the parking lot before the meeting. I simply needed to read through a chapter in my economics textbook and jot down a few notes for a short reflection. My professor had opted to teach us from only a few chapters in the textbook which we were reading out of order. The book was called *Survey of Economics* by Irvin Tucker (from which I supplied the definition of 'capital' earlier in the chapter), a standard Economics 101 textbook. We had already worked on supply and demand charts and studied scarcity and choice. My professor, wanting us to develop our economics vocabulary, had assigned the final chapter in the book, entitled '*Economies in Transition*[29], which, as fate would have it, included a definition of the terms 'capitalism' and 'socialism'. I was twenty-seven years old, and it was the first time in my life I encountered an actual definition of these two contentious terms. I was about to experience a paradigm shift.

As sunlight poured through the open window of my truck, I read the following:

"Capitalism is an economic system characterized by private ownership of re-sources and markets. Capitalism *is also called the* free enterprise system. *Regardless of its political system, a capitalist economic system must possess two characteristics: (1) private ownership of resources and (2) decentralized decision making using markets."*[30]

It took me by surprise. There was nothing about greed or exploitation and no suggestion that holding these views made somebody a bad person. In fact, based on my (extremely rudimentary) understanding of economics and my (much more developed) theology of the church and charity, I immediately realized I was mostly in favor of the type of economic system outlined by this definition. Just a few pages later, Tucker offered a definition of 'socialism' which was a direct inversion of capitalism:

"Regardless of a society's political system, a socialist economy has two basic characteristics: (1) public ownership and (2) centralized decision making".[31]

There was again no moralizing in this definition. No suggestion that those who believe in socialism are of a superior character or that it is inherently 'good'. Even though, for reasons I will describe shortly, I think these definitions need further refinement, I knew I had never used either term correctly. It made so much sense to me: capitalism is a system where private actors own resources and make

---

29. Tucker, *Survey of Economics*, pp. 491-509

30. Tucker, *Survey of Economics*, p. 498

31. Tucker, *Survey of Economics*, p. 501

individual decisions about how to utilize them, while in socialism the public ('government') controls resources and decisions about their use are centralized. Simple, clean, and comprehensible.

I immediately drew a few conclusions from my newfound understanding of economics: 'capitalism' and 'socialism' are two mutually exclusive methods of economic thinking and Christians could in essence have good-faith debates about which one corresponds more closely to our faith, charity and generosity are not intrinsic to socialism nor antithetical to capitalism, and I needed to seriously reconsider the vocabulary I used to describe my interpretation of biblical texts which address so-called 'economic' issues. It turns out I had been playing the wrong language game all along. So had everyone else. Not long after that perfect fall day I began to describe myself as a capitalist. While Christians were called to radical charity and generous self-sacrifice, neither were incompatible with an economy which was oriented around private ownership and private decision making. It also struck me how many of my favorite biblical scholars who usually conduct careful and thorough research on complex subjects had seemingly failed to use basic economic language in any systematic or coherent manner. Biblical scholarship had genuinely attempted to address economic and political issues, as the proliferation of books offering 'anti-imperial' readings of the New Testament reveals, but much of the literature which had influenced me was obviously using economic terminology in ways that contradicted the simple definitions I had discovered in my Economics 101 textbook. I became disappointed by the lack of clarity.

While I was working through the master's program, my extremely limited amount of free reading time was spent reviewing medieval history, the subject I teach professionally. Much of my economic 'research', if I can even call it that, was through listening to conservative podcasts and reading progressive news outlets. The same problem I saw in biblical scholarship plagued both sides of the political aisle: each persisted in using these two terms without ever defining what they mean. For the progressives, 'capitalism' meant bad and 'socialism' meant good. Conservatives, riding high on the Trump train, inverted the moral assessment. This contradiction made sense: the subjective policy preferences of political commentators were endowed with whichever term they associated with the good, upright and moral. It was as if the words themselves had no objective or concrete meaning. I knew there had to be a better way to conceptualize these terms, and as I began to read more literature on economics I accidentally stumbled upon a school of economic thought offering a definition of 'capitalism' which was even more precise and irreducible than Tucker's. Dubbed 'the Austrian school', economists like F.A. Hayek, Ludwig von Mises, and Murray Rothbard would further refine my conception of 'capitalism' and 'socialism'.

Austrian Economics

The Subjective Theory of Value

There is one tradition of economic thought which offers clear, consistent, and irreducible definitions of these basic economic concepts: the Austrian school. Named after the nationality of its early leading theorists, Austrian economics has its roots in the 'marginal revolution', a transformation of economic thought which took place in the 1870s. Until that point the majority of economists believed that the value of a good or service could be explained by the costs expended to produce it, particularly the labor utilized during production[32]. By the beginning of the 1870s, however, a small number of economists, most notably Austrian Carl Menger, began to argue that value couldn't be quantified by a product's inputs. Steven Horwitz explains the marginal revolution: *"the value of a good or service was the result of subjective perceptions of the usefulness to the consumer of the specific amount required for the use at hand* [thus the *marginal* amount] *. . . goods had value because people thought they were useful, and the specific amount of value they had depended on the particular quantity that was needed to satisfy the user's specific want"*[33]. Regardless of how much it cost to produce a good or service, its real worth was entirely contingent upon how much people wanted the product. Value is subjective. Carl Menger published his book *Principles of Economics* in 1871, becoming a foundational text for the Austrian school. His theoretical approach to economics emphasized both the limited knowledge and subjectivity of human beings. Value can't be reduced to the price of inputs, because people value individual goods and certain quantities of goods differently. In Menger's words, *"value is thus the importance that individual goods . . . attain for us because we are conscious of being dependent on . . . them for the satisfaction of our needs"*[34]. The brilliance of this new approach to economics was in reframing the conversation around how people acted in the real world. It is very much a human-centered approach to the question of economics and emphasises human subjectivity, our inability to know the future, the limits of human knowledge, and the powerful realization that 'markets' are simply euphemisms for the collective total of individual human actions[35]. In other words, the study of economics is really the study of human action. The Austrian

---

32. Horwitz, Steven. 2020. *Austrian Economics: An Introduction.* Cato Institute. p. 4

33. Horwitz, *Austrian Economics*, p. 5

34. Menger, Carl. 2007. *Principles of Economics*. Mises Institute. (1871) p. 115

35. Horwitz, *Austrian Economics*, pp. 6-8

economist who would develop these insights further than anyone else was a man named Ludwig von Mises.

Mises and Human Action

Ludwig von Mises (1881-1973) was an Austrian-born economist who immigrated to the United States in 1940. His prolific output of published works developed the insights of his predecessors and crystalized Austrian economic theory. The crowning jewel of his productive career is the 1949 book *Human Action: A Treatise on Economics* from which I quoted earlier in the chapter. The title betrays his fundamental premise: economics is simply the analysis of humans acting. Mises defines human action as such: *"Human action is purposeful behavior . . . Action is will put into operation and transformed into agency, is aiming at ends and goals, is the ego's meaningful response to stimuli and to the conditions of its environment, is a person's conscious adjustment to the state of the universe that determines his life"*[36]. Mises argues that all human action is purposeful; simply by virtue of doing *anything* the acting being is attempting to reach a certain end[37]. It is these conscious decisions to act which determine the course of world history. The entire human experience can be understood as human action and the consequences that (often unintentionally) result from it. Even 'inaction' is a form of human action, because the acting agent is purposefully choosing to do nothing at all[38].

Mises also argues that praxeology, by which he means the study of human action, must be the starting point for all economic analysis, and indeed *any* analysis of human behavior: *"the category of action is logically antecedent to any concrete act"*[39]. Human action is *a priori* knowledge and also logically irrefutable because even in the act of articulating an argument against human action one would be, in fact, purposefully acting. It is simply inescapable: human beings purposefully act based on subjective value judgments, and these actions produce consequences which shape world history. Mises is also careful to distinguish praxeological analysis from other methods of analyzing human and economic behavior. While many intellectuals such as Marx argue that their philosophies provide true, objective, and absolute observations about the meaning of life and history, often with the view of uncovering 'truths' about the workings of history which enables us to plan for a glorious utopian future, Mises categorically rejects this as an analytic

---

36. Mises, *Human Action*, p. 11

37. Mises, *Human Action*, p. 12

38. Mises, *Human Action*, p. 13

39. Mises, *Human Action*, p. 35

possibility. What praxeology can tell us about ends and meanings are simply the ends which acting humans hope to attain and the subjective meaning to which humans attach their purposeful actions[40].

The logical philosophical corollary of praxeology is *methodological individualism*, which is often radically misunderstood by both critics and proponents of free-market economics in popular discourse[41]. The depressingly vacuous criticism of markets in general and libertarian approaches to economics in particular is that 'individualism' is a western construct which undermines community formation. Kaitlyn Schiess makes this exact mistake in her book on Christian politics entitled *The Ballot and the Bible*: "*the Bible describes a vision of the human that is counter to a libertarian vision of humans*"[42]. This assertion, made in the middle of a discussion regarding economics and a critique of economic systems which are divorced from social realities, betrays a deep misunderstanding of the libertarian conception of individualism and economics. Schiess, only a few words before, ironically and unwittingly concedes one major tenet of the subjective theory of value: "*the economy does not operate outside of broader society*"[43], a nod to the social consequence of human action. In her defense there are indeed many conservatives and a few libertarians who (at least rhetorically) play into the stereotype Schiess attempts to counter, and the mythology of 'rugged individualism' (which may turn out to be but a figment of the progressive imagination) has been used by those on the political left to disparage any emphasis on individual autonomy.

Mises will have none of it: "*Methodological individualism, far from contesting the significance of such collective wholes, considers it as one of its main tasks to describe and analyze their becoming and their disappearing, their changing structures, and their operation . . . we must realize that all actions are performed by individuals . . . a social collective has no existence and reality outside of the individual members' actions . . . In this sense one may say that a social collective comes into being through the actions of individuals. That does not mean that the individual is temporally antecedent. It merely means that definite actions of individuals constitute the collective*"[44]. For Mises and the Austrian school methodological individualism is much more precise and philosophically consistent than the strawmen of individualism erected

---

40. Mises, *Human Action*, p. 28

41. Because, of course, they are attempting to play a language game for which the rules have not been defined. This demonstrates the importance of carefully delineating the meaning of ambiguous but often-used terms.

42. Schiess, Kaitlyn. 2023. *The Ballot and the Bible*. Brazos Press. p. 102

43. Schiess, *The Ballot and the Bible*, p. 102

44. Mises, *Human Action*, pp. 42-43

by intellectuals like Schiess. Communities are essential for human flourishing and make economic change possible; without the purposeful actions of individuals, however, there can be no community. Groups are the spontaneous and organic outgrowth of individual human action, and each human must be respected as an individual being with subjective values and preferences in order to understand how they both shape and are shaped by society. Far from the romantic imagery of the solitary 'rugged' individual who removes themselves from society to live a life of self-sufficiency in the wilderness, praxeology simply treats each individual as an autonomous agent who purposefully acts. The actions of every individual produces the entity we call 'society', without which none of us could survive. But the foundation of all economic analysis, and, as we will see shortly, the concept of 'capitalism' itself, must begin with the individual.

Capitalism and Socialism in the Austrian School

"*The market economy is the social system of the division of labor under private ownership of the means of production*".[45] Mises provides a concise explanation of markets which he elaborates further. In order to define how Austrians use the term 'capitalism', it is important to carefully follow his logic from start to finish. All people act purposefully in order to satisfy perceived wants. In a market economy, the only path to wealth is by providing goods or services which other subjective individuals value. The beauty of this method of production is that in order to satisfy one's own wants, one must produce something which satisfies the wants of others. The market mechanisms of prices (including profits) and capital accumulation are the driving force behind expanded production, which in turn increases the ability of producers to provide more of what consumers demand. Prices are little more than signals which, based on the interplay of supply and demand, show the exchange ratios between those who wish to buy and those who wish to sell[46]. Prices help producers make decisions about what and how much to produce while also informing capital investment. If a producer believes purchasing new capital, costing money in the short run, will increase profits in the long run, then he or she purchases new capital and expands production. This allows more goods and services to be produced that satisfy the subjective wants of acting consumers. Profits and losses in this system are a signal to producers of consumer satisfaction. If a producer is turning a profit, which is the sum total of income minus all expenses (including capital expenses), then his customers are satisfied. If a producer is running at a loss,

---

45. Mises, *Human Action*, p. 258

46. Mises, *Human Action*, p. 259

then his customers are not satisfied. They are entrusting another producer to fulfill their wants. The market economy is driven by consumers; consumers essentially vote with their dollars for which producer they think best satisfies their wants. Once a producer stops satisfying consumer wants, they must shift production or go out of business. This entire system, which relies on the private ownership of capital and economic calculations based on the price system, profits, and losses, is known as 'the market economy'.

This is also precisely what Mises calls 'capitalism'. In order for economic calculation to function as intended there cannot be any coercion or compulsion in the market. Once any arbitrary intervention into the market from either powerful individuals or groups occurs, the entire price system and therefore the rational utilization of capital for production is distorted. The only role of government in a market economy driven by the subjective valuations of individuals is to preserve an environment in which the market can operate. Any interference in the market process by government necessarily compromises this arrangement. This is where Mises clearly articulates the fundamental difference between 'capitalism' and 'socialism' that will serve as our understanding of each term for the remainder of the book. Capitalism, as a shorthand definition of the market economy based on praxeology, economic calculation, and capital, is completely incompatible with its opposite mode of production, socialism. As Mises explains, *"the market economy or capitalism, as it is usually called, and the socialist economy preclude one another. There is no mixture of the two systems possible or thinkable; there is no such thing as a mixed economy, a system that would be in part capitalistic and in part socialistic"*[47]. Capitalism and socialism are mutually exclusive.

For the Austrian, *capitalism* is simply a market arrangement determined by the subjective values of individuals. Capital is privately owned, resources are privately utilized, and buying and selling decisions are based on individual preferences. Any arbitrary intervention in this economic arrangement is, by definition, not capitalism. This is the point at which my Economics 101 textbook needs further refinement. Tucker offered a helpful starting point for thinking about the differences between these terms but unlike Mises doesn't take them to their logical conclusions. Before defining 'capitalism' and 'socialism' Tucker explains the phenomena of 'mixed economies' wherein free markets are combined with government interventions[48], noting that there are no countries in this world where 'pure' expressions of either free markets or governmental control determine all economic activity. On this point, he is absolutely correct. Ultimately, however, this

---

47. Mises, *Human Action*, p. 259

48. Tucker, *Survey of Economics*, pp. 497-498

means that 'capitalism' in the Austrian sense is incompatible with Tucker's 'mixed' economies, which in practice denotes only fewer or greater socialist policies being implemented through government dictate. Tucker also mistakenly assumes that capitalism and socialism can operate "*regardless of* [a country's] *political system*"[49], which is in Misesean terms a logical contradiction. Either a government interferes in the economic activity of private citizens, in which case the economic system is socialism, or it doesn't, in which case the economic system is capitalism. Mises defends an essentially Lockean understanding of the relationship between state and market: if a state is going to exist, its sole purpose should be to protect the life, health, and property of its citizens against those (including politicians and bureaucrats) who seek to destroy it. It creates the conditions for a free market specifically by refusing to involve itself in economic affairs[50]. *Any* state intervention in the market is not capitalism, but, since the resources and capital are being controlled or regulated by those who don't own it, must be labeled 'socialism'.

Hans-Hermann Hoppe, another Austrian economist and political theorist, addresses these definitional problems in his 1989 book *A Theory of Socialism and Capitalism*[51]. Without reference to Wittgenstein he poignantly states the problem of unclear conceptual thinking. In discussing the concept of private property rights, fundamental to the Austrian definition of capitalism, Hoppe comments that "*starting from imprecisely stated or assumed definitions and building a complex network of thought upon them can lead only to intellectual disaster. For the original imprecisions and loopholes will then pervade and distort everything derived from them*"[52]. I am following Hoppe's insight in this book about New Testament scholarship: starting from an imprecise understanding of political and economic concepts, interpreters read the Bible as if it affirms their incorrect understanding of these terms. They then ironically wind up advocating for policies which create the very conditions they strive to critique. The cycle must be broken.

I have until this point sidestepped the concept of 'private property', against which Marx and Engels waged a vicious rhetorical war. Private property, in contradistinction to Marx and Engels, is essential for the Austrian conception of capitalism. Hoppe correctly argues that property rights are fundamental to the human condition. Even in a Garden of Eden-esque state of superabundance every human would still be the owner of their own body, the utilization of their time, and

---

49. Tucker, *Survey of Economics*, pp. 498, 501

50. Mises, *Human Action*, p. 258

51. Hoppe, Hans-Hermann. 1989. *A Theory of Capitalism and Socialism.* 2nd ed. (2013). Mises Institute.

52. Hoppe, *Theory*, p. 19

their labor.[53] Hoppe concludes from this that when an individual uses their body, time, and labor to either originally appropriate property (finding a piece of land and being the first to farm it, for instance) or acquire it through peaceful, contractual exchange with the original owner, they have the natural right to decide how that property is utilized.[54] The attempt to control property by those that did not originally appropriate it or receive it through voluntary, contractual exchange is a moral act of aggression against the rightful owner and incompatible with free-market capitalism. Socialism is the economic and political institutionalization of aggression against private property and individual rights. According to Hoppe, the difference between capitalism and socialism is *"definable in terms of property: aggression being aggression against property, contract, being a nonaggressive relationship between property owners, socialism being an institutionalized policy of aggression against property, and capitalism being an institutionalized policy of the recognition of property and contractualism"*[55].

Mises agrees with Hoppe: *"if historical experience could teach us anything, it would be that private property is inextricably linked with civilization"*[56]. Therefore any property acquired through original appropriation or contractual exchange must be respected as private property. This is the essence of capitalism. We are now in a position to provide a foundational definition of 'capitalism' and 'socialism' which will be used throughout the rest of this book, hopefully providing much needed clarity in debates about the Bible and economics that are often obscure or opaque. Based on the clear, consistent, and irreducible definitions of these terms by the Austrian school, I propose the following definitions for these terms: *capitalism* is an economic arrangement based on voluntary production and exchange free of violent coercion or intervention, and *socialism* is an economic arrangement where non-property owners use aggression to make decisions about the utilization of property. To further simplify these simplified definitions, capitalism is incompatible with government intervention in the market or the violation of property rights, and socialism *is* government intervention in the market and the violation of property rights. This poses a unique moral dilemma for believers: Socialism is synonymous with violence. Few modern Christians would concede the point but it is nevertheless entirely true. I will return to this idea often in the following pages. Can people who claim to follow a crucified Messiah support economic systems which are fundamentally based upon violent coercion? Probably not.

---

53. Hoppe, *Theory*, p. 21

54. Hoppe, *Theory*, pp. 21-27

55. Hoppe, *Theory*, p. 20

56. Mises, *Human Action*, p. 264

An anticipated rejoinder: New Testament scholars and Christian commentators might object to my proposed definitions. I'll concede; language is subjective, they are free to do so. Detractors will then need to manufacture a new set of linguistic rules which makes this game intelligible. My basic contention is that capitalism must be free from intervention while socialism is by default intervention. Most people, including conservatives who would claim to be 'capitalists', believe the state has a right to intervene in economic activity. Socialists who claim to criticize capitalism often directly point to the market problems caused by direct state intervention. Neither of these positions is linguistically or logically consistent. The Austrians have created a vocabulary which allows us to break this impasse and more skillfully play the language game of economics. The definitions of capitalism and socialism offered above will be my framework for understanding both how the writers of the New Testament address economic issues and why New Testament scholars are often either unclear or completely incoherent when they invoke these terms. Before turning to political categories, I wish to briefly explore how one prominent biblical scholar has fallen prey to unclear thinking about economics as an example of the phenomenon I've outlined above. He will serve as a starting point for my critique of New Testament scholarship and unclear economic thinking. I believe the world-famous biblical scholar N.T. Wright is wrong about economics.

N.T. WRIGHT IS WRONG ABOUT FREE MARKETS

I use N.T. Wright as an example of unclear economic reasoning for several reasons. First, he is undeniably the western world's most famous biblical scholar and theologian. His work has been widely read in ecumenical contexts and is appreciated by scholars, pastors, and lay members of churches around the world, and his numerous video, internet, radio, and podcast appearances have helped disseminate his ideas to a wide-ranging audience. When I was working on my degree in Biblical studies in the late 2000s, Wright was the gold standard of Christian scholarship. I have read much of his work and appreciate many of his contributions and insights, even if I have come to disagree with him on a number of important interpretive and theological issues.

Another reason I am singling him out towards the opening of this book is the negative reception of his work among particular groups of scholars. Certain strands of Lutheran, Reformed, and fundamentalist thinkers have rejected his work for, in their view, undermining certain doctrinal tenets of classical protestantism[57].

---

57. For an excellent example of a Lutheran critique of Wright's work on Paul in particular, see Zetterholm, Magnus. 2009. *Approaches to Paul.* Fortress Press. pp. 184-193

On the other side of the academic aisle sit many progressive and secular scholars, including those influenced by Marxist thought, who are critical of Wright for being too conservative and not pushing the boundaries of critical scholarship far enough[58]. One scholar, under the radicalizing influence of critical theory, even suggests that Wright and his contributions to scholarship ought to be *"cancelled"*[59], an assertion as uncharitably condescending as it is superficial. While most scholars in this latter camp would never go to such irrational extremes they nevertheless offer strong (and sometimes deserving) critiques of Wright's approach to the New Testament.

The irony, at least for readers of this book, is that I will be drawing on the work of Wright *and* his critics, all of whom have made important contributions to the subject matter at hand which must to be taken into consideration, even if I want to nuance and reshape some of their scholarly claims. Laying another layer of irony, both Wright and his critics on the theological left and right are guilty of making the same mistakes regarding the economic and political concepts they employ in New Testament interpretation, equally distorting any conclusions about the modern world which are deduced from their exegesis. When it comes to misunderstanding capitalism and socialism, Wright has more in common with his critics than his critics might care to admit. One of the brilliant and frustrating aspects of Wright's work is how the modern applications of his scholarly work are usually just vague enough to avoid engendering controversy. He is obviously aware that his writing is tailored to a diverse audience and tends to use language that won't deliberately offend the centrists who read his work. It is an incredible marketing strategy, and one can hardly fault him for trying to appeal to a wide audience. It does, however, often have the effect of veiling his beliefs.

A perfect example of this dynamic is found in Wright's 2019 book *History and Eschatology*[60]. Included in a section where Wright explains the impact of Enlightenment thought, he describes the reception of Adam Smith's *The Wealth of Nations* and explains how it led to the acceptance by many in the western world of a *"full-on laissez-faire view of economics"*, generating the widely held perspective that the economy would simply *"work by itself"*. He continues: *"this has become highly influential in subsequent economics, being used to justify unfettered industrial expansion within the spreading imperial worlds and ending up with the greed-is-good*

---

58. Galbraith, Deane. 2024. *"Religion, Visions, and Alternative Histories"*. In *The Next Quest for the Historical Jesus* edited by Crossley, James and Keith, Chris. Eerdmans. p. 157

59. Park, Wongi. 2024. *"Race, Ethnicity, and Whiteness"*. In *The Next Quest for the Historical Jesus* edited by Crossley, James and Keith, Chris. Eerdmans. p. 157

60. Wright, N.T. 2019. *History and Eschatology*. Baylor University Press.

philosophy of Ronald Reagan and Margaret Thatcher. No care for the poor, let alone the remission of large debts"[61]. While Wright doesn't explicitly use the term 'capitalism', it is obviously the conceptual referent of his critique. One of his progressive conversation partners, Richard Horsley, has no problem drawing the connection between Ronald Reagan and capitalism[62], thus the justification for reading this passage as a critique of capitalism popularly conceived. Wright has provided us with a classic example of how biblical scholars use economic concepts in an unsystematic manner.

Wright's claim that laissez-faire means the economy somehow 'works on its own' is patently false. As the Misesian articulation of praxeology makes abundantly clear, the 'economy' is simply a description of the totality of individual human actions; there are no metahistorical forces driving economic activity, only the actions of individuals and the consequences which result from them. Subscribing to capitalism simply means recognizing that people should be free to produce, consume, and exchange property without the arbitrary intervention of outside forces. The notion that the economy 'works on its own' is simply the recognition, as we will see when we outline political categories below, that there doesn't need to be a central planning committee in order to produce economic growth. The idea that the economy must at least in some manner be centrally directed, as Wright implicitly suggests, is a product of nineteenth-century thought which relies on a theory that history itself 'works on its own', one which has held a powerful influence over western epistemology ever since[63]. Wright has simply confused categories.

He also attributes to laissez-faire '*greed*' and a disregard for the poor. To revisit the quotation from Mises at the chapter's opening, Wright is clearly using the language of free markets to decry any activity he finds morally deficient. 'Greed' and a disregard for the poor are not intrinsic to the private ownership of capital, private property, or free exchange. Decentralized networks of charity, particularly in communities of faith, have always provided for those in need. Before the Great Depression mutual-aid societies and churches were primarily responsible for taking care of those in poverty without any government intervention[64], and private charity, often distributed at the local level to those who are truly in need, fosters

---

61. Wright, *Eschatology*, p. 19

62. Horsley, Richard. 2003. *Jesus and Empire*. Fortress Press. p. 3. Even though Horsley's scholarship could generally be considered more politically progressive than Wright's, they both share similar views about Jesus, Paul, and empire that will be addressed later in the book. While I disagree with many aspects of their work, both have produced excellent historical scholarship that I will both utilize and critique later in the book.

63. Hayek, *Science*, p. 379

64. Richman, Sheldon. 2001. *Tethered Citizens*. The Future of Freedom Foundation. p. 106

reciprocity and independence, unlike the centralized big-government entitlement programs developed in the wake of the New Deal and Great Society programs which allow politicians to buy votes from particular interest groups and creates a sense of dependency on faraway government bureaucrats instead of local communities[65]. Thomas Sowell has empirically demonstrated these policies almost always lead to more crime, violence, and permanent poverty[66]. Without government confiscation of private property and intervention in the market, the very definition of socialism, private charity was and would be an effective method of helping those who find themselves in need. Wright's inability to comprehend a social order free from state economic intervention does not constitute a failure of the free market but rather an oversight of his own imagination. On a more fundamental level, the idea that it is greedy for people to keep their property but not greedy for politicians to confiscate it from them against their will, popular as it may be, doesn't in any way make it moral. Perhaps Wright should attribute more 'greed' to the politicians who rig the economy than the citizens who are simply trying to earn a living.

Wright claims that '*imperialism*' is a result of laissez-faire free markets. He has obviously never read Mises. Capitalism as defined by the Austrian school precludes the idea of imperialism and any politically-driven 'public policy'. Capitalism respects the private property rights of all human beings and outright rejects any intervention in the free exchange of goods and services between individuals and groups. Imperialism by definition is a project of the state; this point is so glaringly obvious it amazes me how so many professional intellectuals miss it entirely. The idea that governments waging war (often involving conscripted soldiers, fiat currencies, and heavy taxes) in far-away places to control resources which weren't acquired contractually is somehow a manifestation of the respect for private property and free exchange would be comical if it wasn't a generally accepted view among academics. Marx was wrong: the private ownership of capital is not a tool of oppression and imperialism. The arbitrary intervention of the state into economic activity, the very definition of socialism, is what actually drives state-sponsored imperialism. Capitalism is antithetical to imperialism because imperialism is an abandonment of the fundamental presuppositions of capitalism. Wright reveals why defining these terms in a clear, consistent manner is so important; it helps us analyze and assess events as they occur in the real world without unnecessary intellectual baggage.

This leads us to Wright's commentary on the policies of Ronald Reagan and Margaret Thatcher. Observant readers will already anticipate my response: any

---

65. Richman, *Tethered Citizens*, p. 107
66. Sowell, Thomas. 2011. *Economic Facts and Fallacies*. Basic Books. pp. 185-187

so-called 'public policy' where the political class makes decisions about property, resources, or economic activity is by definition not a form of capitalism. The very notion of 'public policy' is antithetical to private property; either those who rightfully own property decide how it is used or someone else does, and if someone else does it isn't capitalism. With that important caveat in mind we slaughter the conservative sacred cow: Ronald Reagan. I won't comment on Thatcher (the last several pages have criticized an English scholar; no need to further offend my readers from the British Isles), but we must seriously reevaluate the capitalistic credentials of Reagan's supposed free-market revolution. In shallow historical evaluations of 1980s American politics Reagan is either the hero of free-market capitalism (for conservatives) or the villain of deregulated imperialism (for progressives)[67]. Both narratives are false because they assume the Reagan administration actually pursued a policy of economic freedom. N.T. Wright uncritically accepts this popular understanding of Ronald Reagan, making his Reaganite critique of free markets historically false.

David Stockman, director of the Office of Management and Budget in the Reagan administration from 1981-1985, resigned from his position after elected Republicans failed to decrease government spending. In his book *The Great Deformation: The Corruption of Capitalism in America*[68] Stockman explains how Reagan and congressional Republicans weren't at all the defenders of free-market capitalism political commentators chalked them up to be. After slashing taxes in 1981, mostly benefiting politically-connected corporations and their sleazy D.C. lobbyists, the Reagan administration failed to cut government spending, predictably resulting in massive budget deficits. The economic logic is elementary. In order to reduce income, the government must reduce consumption. In the following years Reagan signed several tax increase measures into laws, thereby reigning in the deficit[69]. While observers like Wright and Horsley, analysing history with an imprecise definition of basic economic concepts, frame this as a breakdown of the free markets, it was unmistakably the consequence of government policy . A group of politicians make economic decisions which benefit one group of people at the expense of another, it backfires, and so they raise taxes without cutting spending. Had Wright consulted the Austrians, he wouldn't have been so off-base. In the purest sense of the term the Reagan administration was implementing socialist policies.

---

67. Both popular conceptions of Reagan's legacy collapse under even a cursory understanding of Austrian economics.

68. Stockman, David. 2013. *The Great Deformation*. Public Affairs.

69. Stockman, *The Great Deformation*, pp. 96-99

Another nasty and inconvenient fact is often left out of the conversation about concrete economic policies, one with relevance to Wright's assertion regarding the relationship between markets and imperialism. Reagan dramatically expanded the military-industrial complex. Stockman explains how *"a riotous expansion of the warfare state was foremost among the policy errors of the Reagan Revolution . . . the White House made a historically devastating mistake by signing over to the Pentagon a blank check known as the '7 percent real growth top line'. This . . . nearly tripled the annual defense budget from $140 billion to $370 billion . . . it fueled expansionist impulses through the military-industrial complex at exactly the wrong time in history"*[70]. Increasing government expenditures for the warfare state, often to the benefit of politically-connected corporations and further expanding the imperialist ambitions of America's federal government, is the opposite of free-market, laissez-faire capitalism. Resources are being taken by force from private citizens and decisions about the utilization of those resources are made by politicians and bureaucrats. What Stockman is describing can only be described as socialism. The expansion of military power is in violation of economic freedom, private property, and voluntary exchange. That ain't capitalism, friends. Wright has correctly identified an important problem but because of his lack of linguistic and categorical precision he provides an incorrect analysis and proposed solution. Every single scholar quoted in the opening to this chapter has fallen into the same rhetorical trap; unable to provide a clear, irreducible, and universally applicable definition of basic economic categories has distorted economic discourse in biblical scholarship.

It isn't inevitable we succumb to the trap. We need only exercise linguistic and conceptual clarity. The referents of economic language can be clearly differentiated within an Austrian analysis of human action and capricious, violent intrusion. Capitalism stands for voluntary, peaceful, and noncoercive transactions between consenting parties while socialism denotes arbitrary external intervention, prohibiting the free exchange of goods and services. Socialists justify the violence of state intervention with nebulous appeals to justice, fairness, equality, or morality, but the flowery rhetoric should not conceal the only mechanism for implementing socialist policies: the power of violence. The road to hell, they say, is paved with good intentions. I'm not convinced the intentions of socialists are always benevolent. Now that we have delineated the fundamental differences between capitalism and socialism, it's time to reassess our political categories.

---

70. Stockman, *The Great Deformation*, p. 70

CHAPTER 3 | Liberty and Authority

Rethinking Political Categories

So here's what we have: a right-wing cheering gallery and excuse factory for the state's behavior abroad, and a left-wing cheering gallery for its aggression and looting at home. The political "center" cheers both the foreign and the domestic aggression, of course, as evidence of its wise moderation.

Tom Woods[1]

THE BEST OF ENEMIES

Anyone who is curious enough to think critically about our current two-party system of American governance, where "right-wing" Republicans are engaged in an existential conflict with 'left-wing" Democrats, might arrive at the controversial conclusion that the two factions bear an uncanny resemblance to each other. I would argue, in fact, that the similarities are greater than the differences. To the causal observer this suggestion appears patently false. "Why", they might rightfully ask, "do the press, the universities, the politicians, friends and family members, and my social media feed portray this grand battle between two mutually exclusive ideologies if they aren't really that different". To be fair, political discourse is rarely that incisive and articulate; a more realistic response might be "screw you, you're an idiot". At least that has been my experience posting content which reveals uncomfortable similarities between the left and right on social media. The American public isn't much more polite offline either.

The idea that western politics can be divided neatly into two competing categories, one which must be 'good' and the other which must be 'evil', is deeply

1. Woods, Thomas. 2014. *Real Dissent: A Libertarian Sets Fire to the Index Card of Allowable Opinion*. Self-published. p. 134

ingrained in the modern psyche. It is thoroughly embedded in the cultural fabric of contemporary society and functions as an often unacknowledged presupposition in political discourse. No citations are needed to prove the point. Everything from sports to movies to elections to sermons to relationships have been politicized with an increasingly restless unease about conforming our decisions to a particular party line. Regardless of your political perspective, it is obvious that our politics are growing more and more divisive with each successive news cycle. It feels impossible to escape the political black hole. We are all pulled into the dark and distorting vortex of left-right political thinking.

New Testament scholarship does not escape the immense gravitational force of the left-right divide in politics. As we will see in later chapters, biblical scholars have been hopelessly and sometimes unwittingly shaped by these sweeping political trends and are sometimes themselves responsible for deepening this binary political entrenchment. An excellent example of this on the left can be found in the work of Richard Horsley, who, as we saw in the previous chapter, is openly hostile towards what he mistakenly calls 'capitalism'. Towards the end of his 2003 book *Jesus and Empire*, Horsley explains the rise of American imperialism during the 20th century. He lists a series of military actions conducted under various presidential administrations, starting with Theodore Roosevelt and including Eisenhower, Nixon, H. W. Bush, and W. Bush, all of whom expanded American military influence around the globe and helped bring about what he correctly terms the "*sole superpower*" status of the United States[2]. The presidents included in his analysis absolutely do deserve blame for the rise of American imperialism, and he is, in that regard, technically correct. The United States has imperial aspirations and each of these presidential administrations contributed to the export of American dominance.

The problem, however, is what his list (deliberately?) omits. An informed observer has cause for suspicion: Horsley fails to name a single politician affiliated with the Democratic party in his analysis of escalating American militarism. Based on the overall argument of his book, motivated by a concern to present Jesus as an erstwhile opponent of all imperialisms modern and ancient, Horsley is operating within a framework of political assumptions which cast the Republicans as the bad guys and the Democrats as their benevolent opponents. For scholars like Horsley, this means the Republicans and not the Democrats are solely responsible for the rise of imperial institutions which Jesus would have opposed. This results in the unstated but obviously intended conclusion that Jesus agrees with people who have the same political worldview as Horsley. Everyone else (read: Republicans)

---

2. Horsley, *Empire*, pp. 140-141

are simply rejecting the teachings of Jesus. This is a clear projection of the left-right political binary onto the canvas of both American history and the historical Jesus. What if, however, we attempted to step outside of this political dichotomy and explore the contributions made to American imperialism by Democratic presidents? As it turns out, both sides are equally guilty.

Democrat and progressive hero Woodrow Wilson probably deserves more blame than anyone on Horsley's list. Regardless of how one interprets the geopolitical morality of World War I, Wilson believed he was destined to remake the world in America's image. Involving the United States in a far-away European war was a critical step towards achieving this lofty goal.[3] After the war ended Wilson supported the Treaty of Versailles, assigning guilt to Germany and imposing heavy reparations on the country, paving the way for the rise of Nazism and World War II.[4] It was under the leadership of four-term president and Democrat Franklin D. Roosevelt that the United States entered World War II, after which our country became the only western superpower. Roosevelt's successor, Democrat Harry Truman, made the fateful decision to drop two newly-created nuclear weapons on civilian targets, despite the opposition of nearly every general and politician in his orbit.[5] The bombings of Hiroshima and Nagasaki are, in my view, two of the greatest atrocities in human history and mark the beginning of the Cold War and the atomic age. Horsley acknowledges the role nuclear weapons played in the expansion of American imperialism but conveniently forgets to mention that the decision to use them was made by a Democrat. Jesus is on their side, after all, and an admission of guilt might complicate an otherwise pristine historical narrative. Horsley also correctly states that the disastrous Vietnam War was imperial in nature but yet again refuses to mention it was declared and waged by another Democrat, Lyndon B. Johnson![6]

President Jimmy Carter, also a Democrat, manufactured the 'Carter Doctrine', a policy devised in the midst of Middle Eastern turmoil during the late 1970s which declared the Persian Gulf to be of vital strategic importance to the United

---

3. Herman, Arthur. 2017. *1917: Lenin, Wilson, and the Birth of the New World Disorder*. HarperCollins. pp. 14-15. This book demonstrates that Vladimir Lenin and Woodrow Wilson had similar grand ambitions of reshaping the direction of world history and are largely responsible for our current global dysfunction in ways that many contemporary political commentators would be uncomfortable admitting.

4. Powell, Jim. 2005. *Wilson's War: How Woodrow Wilson's Great Blunder Led to Hitler, Lenin, Stalin, & World War II*. Crown Forum. pp. 226-253

5. Horton, Scott. 2022. *Hotter Than the Sun: Time to Abolish Nuclear Weapons*. The Libertarian Institute. pp. 418-422.

6. Horsley, *Empire*, 141

States and committed the American military to defending it.[7] It became the political justification for both the Gulf War and the Bush administration's response to 9.11, resulting in the War on Terrorism. Horsley blames both Bush administrations for the American intervention in the Middle East but, once again, is silent about the Democrat who forged the policy regime which made those interventions possible. Since Horsley's book was written in 2003, it is impossible to know for sure what Horsley would have made of Democrat Barack Obama's expansion of the War on Terror[8] or the Biden administration's unequivocal support of Israel's brutal war against the Palestinians[9], but it is a safe bet he would have placed the blame of American foreign policy solely on the shoulders of W. Bush and Trump while eliding the responsibility of Obama and Biden. We will explore later in the book some of Horsley's more recent works and discover that he never can quite bring himself to place any blame on politicians who happen to identify with his side. It would reveal a truth Horsley apparently wishes to keep hidden: the Republicans *and* Democrats are responsible for American imperialism, which, coming full circle, brings us back to my initial claim that the American left and right aren't as far apart as many imagine.

This dynamic exemplifies a set of issues I wish to address in this chapter which will be essential for our interpretation of passages in the Bible as well as our critique of the ways in which biblical scholars utilize political concepts in their writing and research. Horsley's left-right binary perfectly encapsulates the problem with contemporary political discourse. His work implicitly assumes a political framework which looks something like this: there are two sides to every political conflict, these sides are mutually exclusive, and one is good while the other is evil. His biblical interpretation and the conclusions he draws from it are forced into this matrix, and those who disagree with Horsley's political analysis are, by association, disagreeing with Jesus himself. I believe that Christians who identify with both the political left and right are guilty of playing this same game by reading their personal political commitments back into the Bible. All of this is a result of unclear political thinking.

---

7. Horton, Scott. 2021. *Enough Already: Time to End the War on Terrorism.* The Libertarian Institute. pp. 16-18

8. Schuler, Eric. "Obama's Most Important Legacy: Endless, Limitless War." Antiwar.com. May 6, 2016. https://www.antiwar.com/blog/2016/05/06/obamas-most-important-legacy-endless-limitless-war/.

9. DeCamp, Dave. "Support for Israel Has Cost US Taxpayers At Least $22.76 Billion in One Year." Antiwar.com. October 7, 2024. https://news.antiwar.com/2024/10/07/support-for-israel-has-cost-the-us-taxpayer-at-least-22-8-billion-in-one-year/.

In this chapter I will reframe our understanding of basic political concepts. In ideological terms the American political left and right are defined as 'progressivism' and 'conservatism', associated with the Democrat and Republican parties respectively. I intend to explain these terms and expose their shared structural assumptions. I will then explain how political philosophers working within the tradition of Austrian economics have produced a more consistent analysis of political power which is universally applicable and based upon fundamental principles, particularly the concept of non-aggression. Progressivism and conservatism both rely on varying degrees of authoritarian violence to seek their preferred social ends, the shared political presupposition of both ideologies. This insight obligates us to reconceptualize popular political categories, deemphasising superficial dissimilarities and interrogating first principles. A better conception of the political spectrum, stripping away the aesthetic divide supposedly separating left and right, would examine political action as choice between liberty and authority, with progressives and conservatives falling squarely on the side of 'authority'. In order to substantiate my thesis we must analyze the essential relationship between left and right.

PROGRESSIVISM AND CONSERVATISM: TWO SIDES OF THE SAME AUTHORITARIAN COIN

Progressives and conservatives *hate* each other. That probably accounts for Richard Horsley's attempt to blame American imperialism solely on conservative Republicans; not only are they wrong about politics, their ideology is fundamentally immoral. Any political philosophy which leads to war and imperialism must be evil, right? How could someone with Jesus on their side possibly be implicated in crimes against humanity? The moralising which lurks behind the employment of popular economic terminology also characterizes debates about politics and political power. Even when the political process is conceptualized in utilitarian terms, where voters support policies which they might concede are morally questionable in the short run but will (supposedly) accomplish righteous goals in the distant future, there is an underlying assumption that taking the 'correct' side of a political debate makes one morally superior to those who hold opposing views. This generates an impression that each side must be different because they proceed from divergent starting points and result in conflicting policy proposals. I don't believe a word of this is true.

Let me be clear: I am not arguing that American progressives and conservatives support the same political policies. They most certainly do not. The so-called 'culture war' issues are so controversial for this very reason; debates about who can use which bathrooms, gun ownership, prayer in schools, and the sexuality of

Disney princesses cause massive controversy, and it is usually possible to determine which side of an issue someone supports by their personal political identification. My argument rests on the claim that these differences are a facade. The real political assumptions of American progressives and conservatives are, at the most fundamental level, completely identical. It is a bold but demonstrably plausible thesis which can be supported by appealing to the ways in which these terms are generally defined and identifying their unstated but genuine similarities.

In *The American Vision*, a popular older American history textbook designed for high school students, the authors provide a definition of 'conservative' and 'progressivism' which closely approximates the popular usage of each term. A conservative, according to *The American Vision*, is "*a person who believes government power, particularly in the economy, should be limited in order to maximize individual freedom*"[10]. Notice the definition doesn't perfectly correspond to the Austrian definition of 'capitalism', which argues that there should be *no* government interference in economic activity. Instead, a conservative wants '*limited*' government power, the end of which is to increase personal freedom. While *The American Vision* provides an excellent definition of conservatism as an ideology it is easy to see how this could be subjectively applied. Exactly which government powers ought to be limited, how much control government should have over the economy, and how to increase individual freedom are all open to interpretation. There is no stable, consistent, or irreducible articulation of conservative principles because conservatives might differ over particular political policies based on how they delineate the limits of government power. It is also impossible to equate conservatism with capitalism in the irreducible Austrian sense of the term. Hoppe correctly notes that "*conservatism must, and indeed does, advocate the legitimacy of noncontractual means in the acquisition and retention of property and income derived from it*"[11]. While no American conservative in good standing would self-identify as a socialist they must nevertheless support at least some socialist policies under the guise of 'limited government power'. To be charitable and honest, personal experience has taught me that most self-described conservatives generally do want, at least nominally, less government. What exactly this means in practice, however, is difficult to determine.

Progressivism as an ideology suffers from the same lack of specificity. *The American Vision* defines progressivism as "*a political movement that crossed party lines which believed that industrialism and urbanization had created many social problems and that the government should take a more active role in dealing with these problems*"[12].

---

10. *The American Vision*. 2011. 1st ed. McGraw-Hill Glencoe. p. 1086

11. Hoppe, *Theory*, p. 89

12. *American Vision*, p. 1091

The historical roots of progressive thought are deeply anchored in the soil of nineteenth-century thought, and we will analyze its development below. A critical examination of the definition, however, reveals it is also open to interpretation. What, exactly, were the *'problems'* created by industrialism and urbanization and what, exactly, is the role that government should play in solving them? In theory this definition could include both full-blown Marxists (or at least those who think they represent Marxism[13]) and those on the center-left who simply want to retain certain entitlement programs or other social services. There is a massive ideological gulf between the two but the term is equally applicable to both. Progressives strongly believe in government intervention but for many American progressives there is an outer limit to government power. The fundamental assumption underlying progressivism is that state power should be employed to make society progressively better and in many (or most, depending upon just *how much* one is progressively inclined) cases progressives openly support socialist policies.

I don't want to overstate my case; there are very real differences between the progressive and conservative philosophies of government. That cannot be denied. It is equally untenable to view them as antithetical. They are not separated by a wide, deep ideological valley as popular political discourse would lead us to believe, they are rather opposite sides of the same coin. Or, to shift the metaphor slightly, if there is a modern political spectrum, progressivism and conservatism represent different points *on only one side* of that spectrum. Their stark similarities are obscured by the heated political debates between proponents of each ideology, but by stepping back examining them philosophically it becomes readily apparent that the conflict between progressivism and conservatism is more like a sibling rivalry or a civil war. They are battling for control of common ground, both willingly embracing state power to achieve their desired ends.

The quote from Tom Woods included at the beginning of the chapter, reflecting on the American left and right at the height of the 'War on Terrorism' in 2007, summarizes this dynamic succinctly: *"So here's what we have: a right-wing cheering gallery and excuse factory for the state's behavior abroad, and a left-wing cheering gallery for its aggression and looting at home. The political "center" cheers both the foreign and the domestic aggression, of course, as evidence of its wise moderation"*[14]. In the age of Trump and Biden political commitments have changed. The conservative right has become more skeptical of war (save for Israel) while the progressive left,

---

13. As I hinted in chapter one, my anecdotal experience with self-described 'orthodox' Marxists revealed that many of them reject progressivism and specifically the appropriation of Marxist rhetoric to perpetuate progressive political agendas.

14. Woods, *Real Dissent*, p. 134

comically appropriating Cold War-era talking points, support any American military intervention which they believe damages the credibility of Donald Trump.[15] It also turns out conservatives aren't a bastion of domestic economic freedom as the corporate press likes to portray them. Many conservatives are willing to affirm the economic viability of tariffs despite the conspicuous increase in economic control tariffs delegated to government officials.[16] In David Stockman's book *Trump's War on Capitalism* he breaks Trump's first term down by the numbers and proves mathematically that Donald's *"Greatest Economy Ever"* was little more than a chimera; in Stockman's judgment, Trump was *"a big spender, easy money-man, hard-core protectionist, immigrant-basher, militarist, and all around Big Government statist"*[17], charges offensive to MAGA acolytes but by every objective metric entirely true. Do Trump conservatives want less government than their progressive Democrat opponents? Yes. Does this mean they want a government inconsequential in size and scope? No.

Herein lies the paradox: despite the ever-shifting policy platforms of conservative Republicans and progressive Democrats neither side is willing to offer a wholesale alternative to the current governmental structures which dominate global politics. Both seek to seize the reigns of power and use them to achieve their own subjectively defined ends. It is incontestable that the goals of American conservatives and progressives are radically different, but they both arrive at their preferred destinations by driving the same vehicle: authoritarian state power. In truth the difference between conservatives and progressives is simply a matter of perspective and time: once we have accepted that both sides presuppose the existence of a government which has the authority to influence social interactions, particularly with respect to economic exchange, then it becomes little more than a matter of tracking the policies each side supports at given points in history. The objective policies of each group are like rapidly shifting sands in a desert windstorm; when the dust settles not a single grain remains in place, but the desert itself is still a never-ending horizon of sand. The policies have moved, but the motives and presuppositions are the same: we need a strong government which enables us to implement our goals for society. Human history has a destination which can only be reached by ensuring that the right people control the levers of power and exercise authority over those who might dissent.

---

15. Zlotow, Walt. "Why So Many Progressives Promoting Endless Ukraine Bloodbath?" Antiwar.Com. June 7, 2023. https://www.antiwar.com/blog/2023/06/07/why-so-many-progressives-promoting-endless-ukraine-bloodbath/.

16. O'Keeffe, Conner. "Tariffs Will Not Make America Great Again." Mises.Org. January 29, 2025. https://mises.org/mises-wire/tariffs-will-not-make-america-great-again.

17. Stockman, David. 2024. *Trump's War on Capitalism*. Hot Books. p. 2

Most residents of the contemporary west, not least Americans, couldn't imagine a world where the political institutions and philosophies which undergird them are fundamentally challenged. The hubris of modernity rests upon a notion that we arrived at this point in history for a reason coupled with a concurrent failure to imagine any future political arrangement which is structurally independent from the present. The uncomfortable point stands: progressivism and conservatism are opposite sides of the same coin, weakening to the core any supposed differences between the two groups and making it nearly impossible for those who don't acknowledge the underlying similarities to think critically about political realities. This is precisely what Horsley's analysis of American imperialism neglected. Those 'conservatives' who helped construct the greatest empire in world history aren't really that much different from their progressive counterparts. Democrats deserve just as much of the blame. Both progressivism and conservatism rely to greater and lesser degrees on state authoritarianism, meaning adherents to both traditions are political authoritarians. Both parties reject the Austrian conception of capitalism and maintain that the government has a responsibility to *in some way* manage the personal and economic lives of its citizens.

This brings me to the next step in my argument: if both progressivism and conservatism are in practice only contrasting examples of authoritarianism, is there any political alternative? Along with precisely defining in economic language, we need to develop political categories that are consistent, irreducible, and universally applicable. Since the political left and right are both equally manifestations of authoritarianism, I would like to propose an actual alternative: libertarianism. In the same way that 'socialism' denotes any arbitrary third-party interference in economic affairs and 'capitalism' is a rejection of *all* arbitrary economic interventions, 'authoritarianism' denotes any political philosophy which affirms the arbitrary authority of one person or group over another, and 'libertarianism' is an outright rejection of all arbitrary authoritarian power. Despite the ridiculous caricature of libertarians as either "Republicans who like to smoke pot" or "Democrats who like to shoot guns", libertarianism is a rejection of all authoritarianism along with the violence which necessarily accompanies it. The theory rests upon a set of philosophical assumptions that will help us conceptualize political power more clearly.

THE LIBERTARIAN ALTERNATIVE: NON-AGGRESSION AND THE STATE

The Non-Aggression Principle

Murray Rothbard was a true polymath. A brilliant historian, Austrian economist, and political philosopher, Rothbard took the economic and political insights of

Mises and Hayek to their logical conclusions and developed an articulation of libertarian political philosophy which is, commensurate with the goals of this book, consistent, irreducible, and universally applicable. He understood the underlying authoritarian nature of left-right political posturing and proposed an audacious alternative. Rothbard condenses the core insight of libertarian philosophy: "*The libertarian creed rests upon one central axiom: that no man or group of men may aggress against the person or property of anyone else. This may be called the "nonaggression axiom"*".[18] There is an easily discernible difference between the authoritarianism of conservatism and progressivism, which both rely on at least some utilization of arbitrary state power to interfere in the affairs of private individuals, and the libertarian principle[19] of non-aggression which rejects it as immoral. Rothbard, on the same page, further refines his definition: "*"Aggression" is defined as the initiation of the use or threat of physical violence against the person or property of anyone else. Aggression is therefore synonymous with invasion*"[20].

The non-aggression principle is the fundamental tenet of libertarian political philosophy, and the starting point from which we derive a general theory of political power. While progressives and conservatives believe in state regulation of personal behavior and economic activity to achieve subjective, predetermined social ends, the libertarian contends that every human deserves the right to be free from arbitrary aggression. This is why, as Rothbard notes, libertarians support the freedom to speak, publish, assemble and engage in activities which others deem immoral so long as all activity is consensual, voluntary, and non-aggressive. Libertarianism opposes legislating against the subjective preferences of private citizens; controversial cultural issues like pornography, drug use, gun ownership, and same-sex marriage, regardless of how libertarians morally assess these behaviors, cannot be categorized as 'criminal activity' because, as Rothbard explains, "*the libertarian does not regard* [behaviors and institutions like these] *as "crimes" at all, since he defines a "crime" as violent invasion of someone else's person or property*"[21]. Progressives and conservatives alike want to criminalize, restrict, or regulate certain voluntary behaviors which they believe are harmful to society, with the often unspoken corollary that the threat of violence is *necessary* for the enforcement of authoritarian dictates. Violators of legally criminalized activity will either have their

---

18. Rothbard, Murray. 2010. *For a New Liberty: The Libertarian Manifesto*. 2nd ed. Mises Institute. p. 27

19. Most libertarians refer to Rothbard's *"non-aggression axiom"* as the non-aggression *principle*, often reduced to the acronym "NAP". Unless directly quoting an author, I will retain the more common 'principle' when referring to this fundamental libertarian insight.

20. Rothbard, *Liberty*, p. 27

21. Rothbard, *Liberty*, p. 27

property stripped from them or be thrown in a cage should they fail to comply with the authoritarian mandate. The libertarian alternative defines 'crime' in the strictest sense of the word as a violation of natural rights. Nothing else is properly 'criminal' and should not be suppressed with violence.

Libertarianism is the only morally consistent political philosophy. While most progressives and conservatives sincerely presume their preferred political and economic policy agendas are for the good of society, they can only be properly enforced by employing violence against peaceful people. That authoritarians fail to realize their political and economic assumptions are predicated on violence against innocent people is not an ethical excuse. Rothbard discusses the consistency of libertarianism as opposed to the inconsistency of authoritarianism on the left and right: "[The libertarian] *sees his own position as virtually the only consistent one, consistent on behalf of the liberty of every individual. For how can the leftist be opposed to the violence of war and conscription while at the same time supporting the violence of taxation and government control? And how can the rightist trumpet his devotion to private property and free enterprise while at the same time favoring war, conscription, and the outlawing of noninvasive activities and practices that he deems immoral?*"[22]. Rothbard's *For a New Liberty* was originally published in 1973, and the political policies supported by the left and right have since shifted, but his critique remains prescient. For authoritarians, political power must always be used to achieve specific (yet subjective) social ends. Libertarians, on the other hand, refuse to accept authoritarianism as morally or philosophically consistent.

This same observation applies to property rights, which is why libertarians embrace the Austrian definition of 'capitalism' and renounce every manifestation of socialism. Marx and Engels, as I explained in the previous chapter, argued that "*the theory of the Communists may be summed up in a single sentence: Abolition of private property*"[23]. While most progressives and conservatives wouldn't argue for the abolition of *all* private property they do affirm that in some (or many, or most) instances it must be regulated by state authorities. Hans-Hermann Hoppe, friend and colleague of Rothbard, explained that the fundamental unit of private property was the human body, and that the time and labor expended in production belongs to the individual alone.[24] Although we discussed his argument vis-a-vis economics in the previous chapter, it is helpful to revisit it in the context of politics here. He argues that concepts such as "*aggression, contract, capitalism, and socialism . . . are definable in terms of property:* aggression *being aggression against*

---

22. Rothbard, *Liberty*, p. 28

23. Marx and Engels, *Communist Manifesto*, p. 23

24. Hoppe, *Theory*, pp. 21-27

property, contract *being a nonaggressive relationship between property owners*, social-ism *being an institutionalized policy of aggression against property, and* capitalism *being an institutionalized policy of the recognition of property and contractualism*"[25]. He further elaborates on the relationship between socialism and political authori-tarianism, observing that socialism is "*more precisely . . . a transfer of property titles from people who have acquired them contractually from persons who have done so previously onto persons who have neither done anything with the things in question nor acquired them contractually*"[26]. Authoritarians on the left and right, whether implicitly or explicitly, accept these violations of property rights as a necessary condition for achieving political ends.

Marx, Engles, and all political authoritarians fail to appreciate a horrifying truth: the willingness to violate property rights amounts to slavery. Far from the abolition of private property, communism and all forms of socialism transfer the ability to make decisions about property which has been peacefully acquired over to those who were not involved in the process of acquisition or production. One class or group of people 'own' the property because they have the final say in how it is utilized and thereby, at least in part, 'own' the bodies and labor of those involved in original appropriation or contractual exchange. The English word for this kind of economic arrangement is '*slavery*'. There is no way around it. One group is forced to work against their will for another group under the threat of violence. Rothbard elaborates: "*Consider, too, the consequences of* denying *each man the right to own his own person* [and thus the fruits of his labor] . . . *a certain class of people, A, have the right to own another class, B . . . while Class A deserves the rights of be-ing human, Class B is in reality subhuman . . .* [this arrangement] *contradicts itself in denying natural human rights to one set of humans*"[27]. This moral and political evil is not only an attribute of full-blown communism but is in fact the political arrangement supported by conservatives and progressives, even if they fail to rec-ognize it as such. Libertarianism consistently condemns arbitrary violence and coercion in favor of what has become the definitional gold-standard of this book: a consistent, irreducible, and universally applicable definition of political categories. Authoritarians on the left and right believe in varying degrees of socialism and the necessity of violence against peaceful people, and libertarians believe in the non-aggression principle which regards violence against peaceful people and their property as always and everywhere immoral. This is why, according to Rothbard, "*the libertarian, in short, insists on applying the general moral law to everyone, and*

---

25. Hoppe, *Theory*, p. 20

26. Hoppe, *Theory*, p. 33

27. Rothbard, *Liberty*, p. 34

makes no special exemptions for any person or group"[28]. Because of this, we must naturally reassess the nature of state power.

The State

Murray Rothbard, in his classic essay *Anatomy of the State*[29], describes in cold, calculating detail the true nature of arbitrary human government. The state is always and forever opposed to libertarian values. Rothbard defines the state as follows: "*the State is that organization in society which attempts to maintain a monopoly of the use of force and violence in a given territorial area; in particular, it is the only organization in society that obtains its revenue not by voluntary contribution of payment for services rendered but by coercion*"[30]. There are two characteristics which define a state: it is the institution that possesses a monopoly on violence and generates its revenue through coercion. Regardless of the categorical form it takes (monarchy, democracy, oligarchy, etc.), the behavior of every state throughout human history can be reduced to these two aspects. For the libertarian who upholds non-aggression, the state is the direct antithesis of consistently applied moral principles.

Rothbard expands his definition of the state: "*while other individuals or institutions obtain their income by production of goods and services and by the peaceful and voluntary sale of these goods and services to others, the State obtains its revenue by the use of compulsion; that is, by the use and the threat of the jailhouse and bayonet. Having used force and violence to obtain its revenue, the State generally goes on to regulate and dictate the other actions of its individual subjects. One would think that the simple observation of all States through history and over the globe would be proof enough of this assertion; but the miasma of myth has lain so long over State activity that elaboration is necessary*"[31]. This is a remarkably consistent and generally applicable articulation of state action. It doesn't matter if a state takes the form of an ancient empire (a category relevant to our interpretation of New Testament texts), a medieval kingdom, or a modern democracy. The state possesses the power to tax and regulate, a privilege which state actors refuse to share with any other organization in society. This is why the state is both inherently monopolistic and inherently violent.

---

28. Rothbard, *Liberty*, p. 28

29. Rothbard, Murray. 2000. *Egalitarianism as a Revolt Against Nature and Other Essays*. 2nd ed. Mises Institute. pp. 55-88. Originally released in this collection of essays originally published in 1974, *Anatomy of the State* has been reproduced as a booklet and in digital form at the Mises Institute. I highly recommend reading the essay in full.

30. Rothbard, *Essays*, p. 57

31. Rothbard, *Essays*, p. 57

For authoritarians of both the progressive and conservative variety, the state is an essential component of society. Most people, including morally upright Christians, take it as a given that the group of individuals who we happen to call 'the government' can and should exercise arbitrary power over others. For those of us who view every person as a morally autonomous individual, accountable to the same moral standards as everyone else, the idea that state actors should receive a special dispensation to act in an immoral manner is philosophically untenable. If it is wrong for someone to steal what belongs to their neighbor, how does being born into a royal family or winning an election suddenly confer an ethical permission to take without consent what isn't rightfully theirs? If my neighbor is engaging in behavior I find immoral and I kidnap them, locking them away in my basement, I would be rightfully regarded as a deranged criminal. If some politicians, however, pass a law about that same immoral behavior, can those political authorities actually be granted, *ex nihilo*, a moral license to jail people with whom they disagree? Of course not.

Nearly everyone in the western world accepts that government operates with a set of special moral exemptions which are not granted to the rest of us, and they use this quasi-magical (dare we say 'theological'?) conception of 'the state' to justify the gross immorality of state action. Most people believe that the so-called modern democratic process legitimizes the use of force against peaceful people, but if those peaceful people didn't vote for the person who happens to win an election, why should they under threat of violence be forced to submit to their rule? Sure, the progressives generally want to grant the state a greater degree of arbitrary power and the conservatives want to grant the state a lesser degree of arbitrary power, but both parties assume the state has a right to exercise violence and confiscate that it didn't produce, even if there are constitutional limits to government pillaging. This is why authoritarianism and libertarianism can be the only two categories for understanding political action: authoritarians can debate about the scope and extent of political authority, but they all tacitly accept state violence as morally permissible and socially desirable. Libertarians believe, on the other hand, that moral principles must be universally applicable and reject as unethical any and every violation of the non-aggression principle. Liberty and authority are our only two options. Either one accepts the legitimacy of the state, or they deny it.

Tying the argument in this chapter together with the economic analysis of the previous one, it is impossible to reconcile the authoritarian state with capitalism as understood in the Austrian tradition. Rothbard recognizes what N.T. Wright and Richard Horsley fail to appreciate: *"since the State necessarily lives by the compulsory confiscation of private capital, and since its expansion necessarily involves ever-greater incursions on private individuals and private enterprise, we must assert that the State is profoundly and inherently anticapitalistic. In a sense, our position is the reverse of the Marxist dictum that the State is the "executive committee" of the ruling class in the present day, supposedly the capitalists. Instead, the State—the organization of the political means—constitutes, and is the source of, the "ruling class" . . . and is in permanent opposition to genuinely private capital"*[32]. Once we have a firm understanding of the inherent antithesis between capitalism and socialism it is evident that authoritarian forms of government must *necessarily* rely on socialist economic policies and why libertarianism and capitalism are a rejection of arbitrary control by state actors over peaceful people. Socialism and authoritarianism, by their very definitions, violate the non-aggression principle.

One of the points which will emerge in my engagement with New Testament scholarship is how the field is universally dominated by the presuppositions of authoritarian statism as described by Rothbard. Although I have had the privilege of meeting (and even befriending) a small number of biblical scholars and theologians who understand the political dynamic I have articulated above[33], most simply assume the necessity of state intervention, particularly in the economy, and read that assumption back into the New Testament. This inevitably, ala Horsley and Wright, results in interpretive conclusions and modern applications of those conclusions which further legitimize their preferred approach to authoritarian government, justifying personal policy preferences by claiming they were found prototypically in the teachings of Jesus, Paul, and other early Christian leaders. One problem: the Bible itself doesn't justify this approach. To further corroborate the claims about fundamental political categories I have made thus far, I will offer a truncated analysis of how the western mind came to believe in the necessary power of centralized statism and the very real consequences which result from that belief. There is one particular Austrian economist who analyzed the nineteenth-century roots of modern authoritarianism and explained why *'the road to serfdom'* always ends in disaster. We will now turn to the work of F.A. Hayek.

THE MYTHOLOGY OF CENTRALIZED STATE ACTION

Nobel Prize-winning[34] Austrian economist F.A. Hayek, a student of Mises and an associate of Rothbard, is best known for his 1944 book *The Road to Serfdom*, a

---

32. Rothbard, *Essays*, p. 79

33. I won't mention any names; holding the state in contempt is a hazard to continued employment in many academic institutions. Believe me when I say, however, that libertarian-oriented biblical scholars and theologians do exist.

34. He was awarded this honor in 1974. We mustn't allow subsequent winners to sour our opinion of Hayek's excellent work.

devastating critique of centralized economic planning and the authoritarianism which inevitably results. We will return to that classic work in time. Less well known is his 1954 publication *The Counter-Revolution of Science* in which Hayek examines how the concept of state planning became *the* mainstream political ideal in the nineteenth century. Since both progressivism and conservatism assume the necessity of authoritarian state power, a brief review of Hayek's thesis in *The Counter-Revolution of Science* will enable us to see how these ideas became ubiquitous in western culture and, by extension, subtly but thoroughly shaped the discipline of New Testament scholarship.

Before the year 1800 all academic disciplines utilized methods which were suited to address the questions posed by their particular fields of research. It was assumed, for example, that the discipline of linguistics required a set of methodological tools which were applicable to the study of language, while disciplines such as theology needed alternative methods since they were, quite obviously, addressing a different set of questions. As the field of natural sciences yielded revolutionary results in the human understanding of nature, bringing about massive advances in technology, medicine, and production, other disciplines began to imitate the method and language of the natural sciences, hoping that the same incredible breakthroughs happening in the natural sciences could be replicated in their own respective fields of research. This resulted in a philosophy called 'scientism', which is the application of the methods of natural sciences to fields that study fundamentally different subjects.[35]

Hayek contends that scientism is nothing more than a category mistake. The study of rocks, plants, stars, and oceans is materially different from the study of other subjects, particularly the study of human beings and society in general. Nature is objective, predictable, and repeatable while human beings are deeply subjective. Consistent with the Austrian school's praxeological emphasis on subjective human action, Hayek explains how academics in the social sciences, particularly in the fields of politics and economics, are charged with the task of analyzing the beliefs and behaviors of people, regardless of whether their beliefs are true or their behaviors are reasonable. The data researchers in the social sciences examine are actions, ideas, and concepts, which are all different in kind from studying predictable and repeatable events in nature such as the reactions of various chemical compounds.[36] The conclusions drawn from these observations make perfect sense: natural science as a discipline is invaluable to human flourishing and has achieved incredible results, but its precise methods are not universally applicable to other

---

35. Hayek, *Science*, pp. 19-25
36. Hayek, *Science*, pp. 41-60

fields of research, especially the very subjective field of social sciences. While this should have been a common sense observation, by the middle of the nineteenth century scientism had come to dominate the social sciences despite a glaring methodological incongruity between the two disciplines. How did this intellectual coup d'etat happen?

As early as 1783 French intellectual Nicolas de Condorcet publicly suggested that the study of society was in desperate need of methodological innovation. A brilliant mathematician, Condorcet was also a keen observer of the advances in scientific research occurring across Europe and came to conclude that perhaps the problems of society could be solved by filtering social research through the matrix of scientific methodology and mathematics.[37] This provocative assertion would eventually catch on in France, aided by the massive social dislocations caused during the French Revolution. At the epicenter of the European Enlightenment, French intellectuals served as the vanguard of this advancement in human knowledge, with the French university system producing classically trained scholars who, like Condorcet, were competent in multiple fields. During the Revolution, however, the university system was disrupted and education in France became more narrowly focused on the development of technical skills, particularly those which, building on developments from the natural sciences, produced engineering and technological advancements. The humanities, once deemed essential knowledge for an educated individual, would be supplanted by purely technical knowledge. This would ultimately lead to the hegemonic rise of scientisim in France; on the one hand, the intellectual class would receive little to no training in the social sciences while on the other hand inculcated with a belief that the methods of the natural sciences should be replicated in other fields of research, even if scientific methodology was ill-suited for the analytical subjects of those fields.[38] It wouldn't take long for someone to follow in Condorcet's footsteps and suggest that human society posed a "scientific" problem which could only be solved using the methods of the natural sciences.

The person responsible for walking Cordorcet's fateful path was Henri de Saint-Simon. Saint-Simon was a wealthy, intellectually self-confident aristocrat who believed society was in desperate need of systematic reorganization and that using the analytical tools of science could expose certain 'natural laws' of society which could then be imposed upon the human race through blunt authoritarian force. The logic, for Saint-Simon, appeared flawless. Once the underlying scientific 'truths' of society were discovered, every individual could therefore be assigned

---

37. Hayek, *Science*, pp. 191-192

38. Hayek, *Science*, pp. 185-211

an occupation which would contribute to the good of the entire human race. But who is responsible for discovering, teaching, and implementing these laws? A 'Council of Newton', named after the father of modern science, would possess the intellectual foresight to understand these laws of society and, by virtue of their superior intelligence, granted a right to impose these laws upon an ignorant and epistemologically inferior population. No need for abstract philosophy, economic reasoning, or theology; 'science' will solve all of humanity's problems, if only a brave council of leaders had the tenacity to follow through with Saint-Simon's bold proposals.[39]

While Saint-Simon's personality alienated many would-be allies and tarnished his personal legacy, several of his associates developed his scientistic ideas and enabled them to reach a wider audience. The most significant of these figures was Auguste Comte, who in 1817 became Saint-Simon's secretary. Comte would collaborate on a number of projects with Saint-Simon, further refining and popularizing the belief that a scientific reorganization of society was not only possible but necessary for human flourishing.[40] The first of these publications was released in 1819. Entitled *Organisateur*, this series of essays and articles laid the intellectual foundation for the organization of society around a political system which would provide much-needed direction for all social activity. Based on the extremely fashionable "law of progress", the notion, popularized by the Enlightenment, that the application of 'science' and 'reason' to all areas of life would necessarily result in the world becoming 'progressively' (hence "*progress*") better[41], Saint-Simon and Comte argue that previous methods of social, economic, and political thinking must be replaced by scientism, reorganizing the political and economic systems of the day and directing humanity to its grand, inevitable destiny.[42]

Within this framework of thinking about society scientifically, concepts like 'liberty' and 'individual freedom' were deeply incompatible with new conceptions of scientific social organization. Hayek notes, "*Saint-Simon sees more clearly than most socialists after him that the organization of society for a common purpose, which is fundamental to all socialists systems, is incompatible with individual freedoms*"[43]. If individuals were free, then they might act in 'non-scientific' ways and impede the omniscient Council of Newton's grand plans for humanity. Individual liberty,

---

39. Hayek, *Science*, pp. 213-234

40. Hayek, *Science*, pp. 235-239

41. 'Better' being a subjective and therefore morally problematic goal, especially when the 'better' must be imposed by force upon those who have a different conception of the 'better'.

42. Hayek, *Science*, pp. 240-248

43. Hayek, *Science*, p. *249*

therefore, had no place in this new scientistically organized world. In later writings, Comte and Saint-Simon would further develop ideas which would become central to socialism, progressivism, and conservatism. All social and economic activity needed to be centrally planned by scientistically-minded 'experts'. The greatest threat to human progress was the freedom of ignorant individuals to think and act for themselves.[44]

These ideas caught on like wildfire and spread rapidly throughout the European intellectual class. Even though Saint-Simon's name would become historically marginalized due to his pugnacious and off-putting personality, his ideas, carried on by associates and successors like Comte, would become so deeply embedded in the structure of European thought they forever redrew the boundaries of social, political, and economic discourse. His ideology would soon move into Germany where a number of Hegelian disciples would absorb and adapt them to their own philosophical system. Marx and Engels were both heavily influenced by Saint-Simonianism, and prominent scholars in all fields of research adopted and promoted Saint-Simonian scientism, further popularising the belief in the scientistic reorganization of society. Napoleon III and Otto von Bismark, two of the most influential nineteenth-century European statesmen, were not only intellectually impacted by Saint-Simonianism but incorporated his ideas into their policy platforms: central banking, the cartelization of industry, and state-run school systems were all designed to impose uniformity and control over an unruly population based on the implicit notion that a good society must be centrally planned.[45] Two prominent theologians, D.F. Strauss[46] and Ernst Renan[47], both of whom contributed to the construction of modern biblical scholarship, were awash in the tides of Saint-Simonianism sweeping across Europe[48]. The intellectual transformation was all encompassing: by the end of the nineteenth century, the ideological juggernaut of centralized authoritarian statism had conquered the mind of nearly

---

44. Hayek, *Science*, pp. 248-262

45. Hayek, *Science*, pp. 291-320

46. Hayek, *Science*, p. 303

47. Hayek, *Science*, pp. 362, 374

48. The implications of these insights for modern biblical scholarship, formed within the context of nineteenth-century Europe and reflecting the cultural biases of the period, are massive. My working theory is that the social, political, and economic assumptions of figures like Strauss and Renan permeated their scholarship in ways which set the parameters for biblical interpretation, influencing modern scholars such as Wright and Horsley. It is beyond the reach of my ability or the goals of this book to trace these influences in detail, but my hope is that perhaps a competent scholar will one day produce a study examining this historical dynamic. It is a story obscured by the shadows of history which must be brought into the light.

every politician, intellectual, and informed citizen throughout Europe and North America. It persists to this day.

Hayek accurately perceived the dangerous consequences of Saint-Simonian authoritarianism. It became the unspoken justification for nearly every political program from the mid-nineteenth century down to this day. In his 1944 classic *The Road to Serfdom*[49], Hayek provides a devastating philosophical critique of authoritarian centralized planning, revealing how nearly all western nations had incorporated the assumptions of authoritarianism into their public policy programs. Saint-Simon and his disciples manufactured the mythology of scientistic technocracy; intellectual elites must manage society and bring 'rational' order to an otherwise chaotic world. There was only one mechanism capable of forging a glorious scientistic utopia: state authoritarianism.

Reflecting on the rise of Nazism in Germany, communism in Russia, and fascism in Italy, Hayek perceptively noticed that politicians of all stripes in Allied countries supported policies which were remarkably similar in kind to their totalitarian counterparts. As in Germany, Russia, and Italy, central planning must inevitably result in unimaginable tyranny. As a matter of brute fact, Saint-Simonianism was little more than a scientific rationalization of absolute power: *"the desire to organize social life according to a unitary plan itself springs largely from a desire for power . . . in order to achieve their end, [planners] must create power—power over men wielded by other men—of a magnitude never before known, and that their success will depend on the extent to which they achieve such power"*[50]. Authoritarianism is the product of the political will to power and leads to ever-increasing appropriations of arbitrary forcer: *"by concentrating power so that it can be used in the service of a single plan, it is not merely transformed by infinitely heightened"*[51]. The fatal flaw with Saint-Simonianism and any pretentious 'Council of Newton' is epistemological. Human beings are fallible and infinitely subjective. The idea of a grand central planning committee capable of stepping outside the boundaries of limited human knowledge is a pipedream. When given power, it is *"inevitable that they [the authoritarian planners] should impose their scale of preferences on the community for which they plan"*[52]. Instead of bringing human history to its eschatological, predetermined destination, authoritarianism is always nothing more than the imposition of one person or group's subjective preferences onto a society which may

49. Hayek, F.A. 2007. *The Road to Serfdom: The Definitive Edition*. Edited by Bruce Caldwell. The University of Chicago Press.

50. Hayek, *Serfdom*, p. 165

51. Hayek, *Serfdom*, p. 165

52. Hayek, *Serfdom*, p. 106

or may not agree with them. And, if the twentieth century taught us anything, authoritarianism has saddled the human race with nothing but pain and suffering.

Yet progressives and conservatives, still deeply indebted to nineteenth-century conceptions of authoritarian power as the only means of achieving glorious political ends, persist in promoting policies which are predicated upon, even if unconsciously, the idea that, at least in certain situations, authoritarian power should be violently wielded against a peaceful population. This type of political thinking, in the same manner as imprecisely defined economic terminology, has permeated the field of biblical scholarship and constricted both the methodological possibilities and interpretive conclusions of New Testament texts thought to reflect economic and political issues. We need a new paradigm for thinking about these questions. I return to the thesis of this chapter: the real political spectrum is not progressivism-versus-conservatism but libertarianism-verses-authoritarianism. Properly reframing the political spectrum allows us to accurately evaluate the political challenges posed by biblical texts.

LIBERTY AND AUTHORITY

Believing the world can be neatly divided up into 'good guys' and 'bad guys' based on the conservative-progressive duality of modern political discourse is a false starting point, one which has entrapped otherwise talented and accomplished scholars who have failed to think critically about fundamental political concepts. The problem with Richard Horsley's characterization of the rise of American imperialism is not in his conclusion, which is factually correct, but rather the means by which he arrives at it. Blaming one political party, the so-called 'right-wing' or 'conservative' faction, while completely refusing to acknowledge the wicked imperial contributions of politicians who happen to be on his preferred side perfectly exemplifies the dangers of unclear political categorization. Progressive and conservatives alike are both responsible for the dysfunctional American imperial order. Both sides share a common set of assumptions about the nature of planning and power, and the real conflict between the two is about how power ought to be managed, not if it should be arbitrarily granted at all. They fight each other because they think their side would do a better job at wielding political power than their opponents. Authoritarianism, in the progressive and conservative worldview, is necessary for a properly organized society.

In the strictest sense of the terms both sides are committed to at least a marginal degree of socialism, the institutionalization of aggression towards people and property. This is a categorical rejection of the non-aggression principle. Even if a reader were to disagree with my classification of political categories, without an adherence to the non-aggression principle their preferred political solutions require initiatory violence and the control or regulation of property by those who did not consensually produce or acquire it. Libertarian capitalism is the absolute rejection of violence against the person or property of others, while all other political arrangements are variations of authoritarian socialism predicated upon violence. Scholars such as Horsley, shrouding their authoritarianism in the moralizing rhetoric of 'justice' and 'love', are blind to the fundamentally violent nature of their political and economic worldview. Authoritarians need to either admit they believe in the necessity of violence or embrace non-aggression.

It's a tragedy that so many New Testament scholars and theologians see the clear biblical injunctions against violence and exploitation but fail to appreciate how their interpretive conclusions only perpetuate systems of violence and exploitation. It is not unique to the field. Most of Western political thought is plagued by the same conceptual and linguistic imprecision which denigrates biblical scholarship. Many of the intellectuals responsible for shaping my worldview and whose work we will rely on in this book for historical reconstructions of ancient economic and political systems have fallen prey to these rhetorical ambiguities. I hope that my small contribution will inject the conversation with some much-needed precision. Redefining economic language and reconceptualizing political categories will allow us to think more clearly about the Bible and its application in the modern world. The choice is between violence and peace. There is no other option. Before I begin interpreting the New Testament in light of these conclusions I will outline my interpretive methodology and provide an overview of the social and economic contexts of the Greco-Roman and Jewish worlds. This will be the burden of my next three chapters.

AN AUSTRIAN EXCURSUS: HOPPE, MARXISM, AND CLASS CONFLICT

Much of the scholarship included in this book is either explicitly embedded in the Marxist tradition or has been subtly influenced by aspects of Marxist ideology. Marxists, because of their concern with economics, have produced some of the best research on ancient economic and political systems. While I have been critical of Horsley in this chapter, Marxists of his ilk share a few common assumptions with the Austrian school. Far from disrespecting the excellent scholarship of Horsley and others in his tradition, my goal is to challenge the lack of political and economic conceptual clarity which limits the efficacy of their work. Before proceeding we will unpack the surprising similarities between the Marxist and Austrian schools as well as highlighting where the two traditions diverge.

Hans-Hermann Hoppe penned a perfect study exploring the relationships between Marxist and Austrian interpretations of political and economic structures. In his 1990 article *Marxists and Austrian Class Analysis*[53], Hoppe elucidates the conception of class conflict shared by Austrians and Marxists. History has indeed been characterized by class struggle, the ruling class is inherently exploitative, competition within the ruling class leads to the further centralization of power, and class rule will ultimately become incompatible with the development of productive forces.[54] Marxists are also generally correct about the nature of state power. The state is interested in suppressing class consciousness in order to consolidate its rule and uses redistributive policies to entice popular support. The state also relies on ideological propaganda and mystification to justify its existence; 'exploitation' means 'freedom', taxation is 'voluntary', we all rule each other, and other contradictory statements are lies told by the state to legitimize and maintain its power. States exist by forming tight bonds between political and corporate power; cartelization or outright control of certain industries, particularly money and banking, guarantee government control over the means of production.[55] Hoppe agrees with this entire set of Marxist claims.

The flaw in Marxist analysis of class conflict is a deficient conception of economic exchange. After presenting the similarities between Marxism and the Austrian school, Hoppe concludes: "*All of these theses are perfectly justifiable, as I will show. Unfortunately, however, it is Marxism, which subscribes to all of them, that has done more than any other ideological system to discredit their validity by deriving them from a patently absurd theory of exploitation*"[56]. It is with respect to the concept of 'exploitation' that the Marxists are in error. Marx failed to notice the underlying moral distinction between working as a free laborer under a system of property rights and the real exploitation which occurred under feudalism, where self-ownership and contractually acquired property rights didn't exist. Building from the Austrian tenets of subjective value and human action, Hoppe argues that because people have different preferences, especially regarding employment and expected compensation, wage-earning cannot be regarded as 'exploitative' in any meaningful sense. Business owners assume risk by investing in capital and thus have a lower time preference, meaning they are willing to take on the increased hazards of saving and investing in the present for a potentially high profit in the

---

53. Hoppe, Hans-Hermann. "Marxist and Austrian Class Analysis." *Journal of Libertarian Studies* 9 *No. 2*, (1990): 79-93.

54. Hoppe, *Class Analysis*, pp. 79-80

55. Hoppe, *Class Analysis*, pp. 86-87

56. Hoppe, Class Analysis, p. 80

future. If the business venture fails, owners incur the greatest loss. Many free laborers have a higher time preference and prefer immediate income, working for a wage, without assuming the risks associated with capital accumulation and investment. Far from being in conflict with one another, business owners and laborers are free to enter into mutually-beneficial contractual arrangements which satisfy the subjective preferences of both parties.[57] As Hoppe puts it, *"their interests are not antagonistic but harmonious"*[58]. He elaborates on this point further, and it's worth quoting in full:

> *"The starting point for the Austrian exploitation theory is plain and simple, as it should be. Actually, it has already been established through the analysis of the Marxist theory: Exploitation characterized the relationship between slave and slave master and serf and feudal lord. But no exploitation was found possible under a clean capitalism. What is the principle difference between these two cases? The answer is: the recognition or non-recognition of the homesteading principle* [original appropriation or contractual exchange of property]. *The peasant under feudalism is exploited because he does not have exclusive control over land that he homesteaded, and the slave because he has no exclusive control over his own homesteaded body. If, on the other hand, everyone has exclusive control over his own body (is a free laborer, that is) and acts in accordance with the homesteading principle, there can be no exploitation. It is logically absurd to claim that a person who homesteads goods not previously homesteaded by anybody else, or who employs such goods in the production of future goods, or who saves presently homesteaded or produced goods in order to increase the future supply of goods, could thereby exploit anybody. Nothing has been taken away from anybody in this process, and additional goods have actually been created. And it would be equally absurd to claim that an agreement between different homesteaders, savers, and producers regarding their non-exploitatively appropriated goods or services could possibly contain any foul play. Instead, exploitation takes place whenever any deviation from the homesteading principle occurs. Exploitation occurs whenever a person successfully claims partial or full control over scarce resources he has not homesteaded, saved, or produced, and which he has not acquired contractually from a previous producer-owner."*[59]

---

57. Hoppe, *Class Analysis*, pp. 80-82

58. Hoppe, *Class Analysis*, p. 82

59. Hoppe, *Class Analysis*, p. 83

The relevance of this lengthy quote is self-evident. Exploitation is only possible when an individual or a group violates the rights of another individual or group. As the Marxists contend, the state is inherently exploitative. What Marxists fail to see, and what Marxist New Testament scholarship has perpetuated, is a fundamental misunderstanding of exploitation. The state, having a monopoly on violence and generating revenue through coercion, is the institutionalization of exploitation. When corporations, industries, or banks participate in state exploitation, *which is the way all modern Western economies are structured*, there can be no human liberty. The entire system survives through violence and coercion. My point has been made: any interference in the free exchange of goods and services between peaceful individuals is not capitalism. It's socialism. Both progressives and conservatives believe in varying degrees of socialism and are therefore political authoritarians.

Industrial cartelization, war, and central banking all contribute to the growth of state power and are therefore inherently 'exploitative'.[60] Richard Horsley devotes an entire chapter in one of his books to railing against the failings of so-called 'global capitalism'.[61] Quite literally every problem he identifies in the modern world is a result of political authoritarianism and socialism. The policy proposals he endorses are *exactly* the same ones which brought us to this exploitative destination in the first place. He argues, more insidiously, that the New Testament *condones* his proposed policies, all of which must be enforced by the authoritarian coercion of state violence. He correctly diagnoses many diseases which plague the modern world and then offers the very same 'treatments' which brought about the illness. This is a textbook example of the problems identified and explained by Hoppe: Horsley understands the dynamics of class conflict and the exploitative power of the ruling class, but, because of unclear economic and political thinking, he entirely misunderstands 'exploitation' and in fact argues the world needs more of it. The Bible says it, so it must be true. The rest of this book will challenge these prevailing economic and political assumptions to their core.

---

60. Hoppe, *Class Analysis*, pp. 87-90

61. Horsley, *Bow Down*, pp. 190-219

PART II | Background and Methodology to
New Testament Interpretation

The Bible, written by many authors over the span of hundreds of years in a cultural context which is entirely different from our own, offers few simple answers to complex historical questions. While as a believer I affirm that, in accordance with 2 Timothy 2:16-17, "*All Scripture is inspired by God and profitable for teaching, for reproof, for correction, for training in righteousness; so that the man of God may be adequate, equipped for every good work*", and that the Scripture can deeply enrich the untrained through the power of God's Spirit, we must carefully discern how to interpret and apply the Bible if we want to do so faithfully and with precision.

In this section I lay out my methodology for interpreting Scripture. I warn against the dangers of attempting to remake Jesus and the New Testament which represents him in our own image, careful to avoid the modernizing trap which peers into documents which were written thousands of years ago to see little more than our own contemporary preferences. I discuss the hermeneutical and exegetical methods which will be employed in this book, including the constant need to be sensitive towards the historical and narrative contexts of the works which are included in the New Testament. I then argue for the reliability and authority of the Bible for those who follow Jesus, demonstrating that both of those categories allow us to be sensitive to the historical dynamics of the New Testament writings. I also detail my admirable goal of avoiding unnecessary theological controversies and appealing to a wide ecumenical audience, an objective which I (mostly) successfully accomplished.

I will then paint a picture of the historical contexts in which the New Testament was produced. Rome had just become the de facto master of the Mediterranean world only decades before the birth of Jesus, and Roman imperialism shaped both the life of Jesus and the character of his earliest followers. It is impossible to fully appreciate the New Testament, Acts, and Paul's letters in particular, without understanding the Greco-Roman world which they inhabited. I provide a historical analysis of the ancient Mediterranean and the political, economic, and social institutions which shaped it, all with an eye to better interpreting complex New Testament texts. Just as important, if not more so, than the Greco-Roman background of the early Jesus movement is its foundation in Second Temple Judaism. I briefly review the narrative of the Old Testament, examine the impact of the exile and restoration under Persian rule, the development of Judaism in the Second Temple period, the way in which Judaism interfaced with pagan imperialism, and the major beliefs and hopes which emerged with the Judaism of that period. Our analysis of political and economic themes in the New Testament will be deeply rooted in the soil of methodology and its first-century historical context.

CHAPTER 4 | Method and Modernization

How To Read (and Not to Read) the Bible

There is no historical task which so reveals a man's true self as the writing of a Life of Jesus.

Albert Schwitzer[1]

The gospels do not give us all the information we need, especially for the inner life of Jesus . . . these lacunae are naturally filled by modern persons with modern content.

Henry Cadbury[2]

THE PERIL OF MODERNIZATION

Jesus was not a modern man. Neither were Paul, Peter, James, or any other leader in the apostolic church. We must take it for granted, as a matter of pure historical reality, that they therefore did not think in the same way as those of us who happen to live in the twenty-first century. Post-Enlightenment political, economic, and social categories would have been incomprehensible to the earliest followers of Jesus; assuming we can read the texts they produced, which would ultimately become the New Testament, and find comprehensive articulations of contemporary ideas is entirely anachronistic. Our assessment of biblical texts must begin with a self-reflexive exercise in intellectual humility: they are a product of very particular historical and cultural contexts which are dramatically different from our own. The Bible is difficult to understand because the documents which form the canon were written by and to people who bear very little resemblance to ourselves. If we fail to appreciate this consideration we will inevitably read the Bible not as a window

---

1. Schweitzer, Albert. 1968. *The Quest of the Historical Jesus*. Macmillan. p. 4.
2. Cadbury, Henry. 2006. *The Peril of Modernizing Jesus*. Wipf and Stock. pp. 28-29

into the past but as a mirror which reflects our modern prejudices. As subjective knowers we sometimes analyze the world around us as if everyone throughout history has experienced it in the same way. This is simply not the case. The only way we can limit our subjectivity is by acknowledging it exists and honestly assessing our biases.

Idiosyncratic readings of biblical texts are the rule. Even professional biblical scholars who have carefully constructed complex interpretive methodologies are guilty of projecting their subjective preferences onto the texts and presenting historical reconstructions which are congenial to their own social, political, and economic biases. It is often the case that sophisticated interpretations are even more indebted to the interpreter's mind; the biases become more obscured due to the complex exegetical results, but still they lurk, just below the surface, influencing the conclusions an interpreter draws from the text. This is the inevitable result of our own limited intellectual capacities, and to that extent all of humanity stands guilty for the crime of interpretive bias. That doesn't mean we should ignore it or pretend academic biblical scholarship hasn't suffered the same fate. It's a specter which has haunted the discipline since its modern inception in the late eighteenth century.

Albert Schweitzer became the first scholar to fully articulate this insight. Originally published in German in 1906, Schweitzer's *The Quest for the Historical Jesus* was a review and critique of nineteenth-century biblical scholarship, culminating in his own proposal that Jesus should be understood as a Jewish apocalyptic prophet. En route to drawing this conclusion, Schweitzer explores the works of several prominent intellectuals and, importantly for our conversation, demonstrates how they were all influenced by their social and cultural contexts, producing reconstructions of Jesus which bore a striking resemblance to their own subjective preferences. Schweitzer puts it well: "*The historical investigation of the life of Jesus did not take its rise from a purely historical interest; it turned to the Jesus of history as an ally in the struggle against the tyranny of dogma . . . it sought to present the historic Jesus in a form intelligible to its own time . . . thus each successive epoch of theology found its own thoughts in Jesus; that was, indeed, the only way in which it could make him live*"[3]. Within the rapidly-changing social, political, and economic landscape of nineteenth-century thought, which, as we noted earlier, produced the hegemonic belief in scientist authoritarian socialism, scholars looked to Jesus as a source of inspiration in those dark and troubled times; having Jesus on one's side goes a long way towards legitimizing favored subjective cultural preferences, and it is little surprise that the presentations of Jesus produced during the formative era

---

3. Schweitzer, *Quest*, p. 4

of biblical scholarship were congenial to the ideals of European intellectuals. Just as Richard Horsley would never allow Jesus to openly critique his own political team, biblical scholarship often functions, like I previously noted, less as a window into the past than as a mirror reflecting the biases of individual scholars.

This is especially true when the issues at stake are contentious. Political and economic debates, which are almost always arguments about which group of people ought to be given arbitrary power over everyone else (and almost never about whether arbitrary power should exist at all), provide particularly fertile soil for planting the seeds of one's own viewpoints in the garden of New Testament interpretation. Quaker biblical scholar Henry Cadbury, building on the work of Schwitzer, dedicated an entire book to analyzing this exact dilemma. Entitled *The Peril of Modernizing Jesus*, originally published in 1937, this important book explains the dangers of expecting Jesus to answer all of our pressing modern questions and the ubiquity with which interpreters believe he can. Cadbury clearly states the problem: *"Anachronism in thinking about Jesus has been largely due to excusable ignorance. The gospels do not give us all the information we need, especially for the inner life of Jesus . . . great gaps are left to be filled by inference and conjecture if we would know the mind of Christ. These lacunae are naturally filled by modern persons with modern content. They infer what Jesus would have thought and felt from what we should think and feel . . . they do not notice that, to use the gospel metaphor, they are stitching a new patch on an old garment"*[4]. We have already observed biblical scholars such as N.T. Wright and Richard Horsley openly (if inaccurately) expressing their own political and economic preferences; is it really a stretch to imagine that, at least in some cases, they read the Bible through the lens of their contemporary worldviews instead of allowing the Bible to challenge those worldviews? Hardly.

Perfectly delineating this phenomenon, Cadbury writes *"The unconscious process behind our claiming Jesus as one of ourselves is easily understood. There is usually even in the most emancipated minds a feeling that Jesus was probably right. In few circles would a proposal be damaged if shown to be in accordance with the mind of Christ. Everyone likes to find his own sentiment independently and unexpectedly sponsored by others. The agreement guarantees . . . the correctness of one's own opinion."*[5] Regarding modern economic and political concepts, there could be no higher authority than that which comes from Jesus himself. If a biblical text, especially a saying or teaching in the gospels, can be plausibly argued to support a modern policy proposal, how could anyone, let alone a practicing Christian, possibly disagree? And if Jesus endorses the policy, why not use state power to impose it upon

---

4. Cadbury, *Peril*, pp. 28-29
5. Cadbury, *Peril*, p. 37

society? This conviction, shared by the conservative right and the progressive left, is based on an implicit assumption that at least some force is necessary to achieve preferred social ends.

Cadbury realizes the powerful personal incentives of modernizing Jesus's teachings: "*Nearly every word of enthusiastic praise for truths we think we find in him is really only a claim of his support for our own viewpoint . . .* [if] *we can argue that he does agree with our standards then we can claim—ostensibly to his honor, but really to our own—that Jesus saw ahead of his time and has been gloriously vindicated by modern experience and knowledge*"[6]. Further driving the point home, Cadbury states "*the most effective reason why the modern student . . . transports* [Jesus] *to our own mentality . . . is the tacit assumption that our own outlook is correct and that Jesus inevitably shared it*"[7]. Biblical scholarship, with all its pretensions to academic objectivity, particularly as it relates to modern political and economic applications of biblical interpretation, is a product of these forces. While every effective commentator understands the limits of their own intellectual horizons and takes great caution when using ancient texts to legitimate modern ideas, we have already seen in the work of Wright and Horsley how easy it is to assume Jesus validates popular modern conceptions and then read those conceptions back into the text.

Cadbury devotes a long chapter in his book to critiquing 'modernized' social gospel readings which were prevalent in the 1930s and based upon the use of Jesus and the New Testament to justify progressive policy platforms endorsed by liberal theologians.[8] This was, and continues to be, an extremely influential method of applying the Bible to our modern context. Liberal theology, based on a flawed definition of 'socialism' and contemporary assumptions about the nature of authoritarian state power, was assumed to be the worldview Jesus *must* have held because Jesus was a nice guy and liberal theologians believe in being nice. My sarcasm isn't far from the truth. According to liberal theology progressive policies help people, so Christians must support them because they reflect the values of Jesus. Cadbury was more skeptical: "*We must be particularly careful not to quote* [Jesus] *as the ally and prophet of our modern social programs and reforms. There may be reasons for a modern Christian to espouse prohibition, pacifism, socialism or communism as so many liberal Christians do. But to claim Jesus as holding in any explicit, literal, or conscious way such modern philosophies is the grossest anachronism. Of course by the same token the capitalists and militarists have no more right to claim him. His teaching*

---

6. Cadbury, *Peril*, p. 38

7. Cadbury, *Peril*, p. 72

8. Cadbury, *Peril*, pp. 86-199. The chapter, entitled *Limitations of Jesus' Social Teachings*, is essential reading for anyone interested in the arguments I am making in this book.

only in the remotest way lies parallel to these modern "isms' and none of them, not even the best of them, can be wisely or safely promoted by a partisan dishonesty to the facts of history"[9]. Ancient figures like Jesus, Paul, and the writers of the New Testament were not modern liberal theologians and their categories of thought differ radically from our own. Acting as if we can draw a straight line through two-thousand years of history from a small collection of written documents to our complex modern society is bound to result in failure. At best we are incorrect. At worst we misrepresent Jesus. Modern interpreters must carefully avoid both pitfalls.

Halvor Moxnes and Post-Nationalism

The methods of contemporary biblical scholarship are much more refined and complex than those developed by liberal theologians in the 1930s, but the modernization of biblical texts to support complex social agendas remains equally pervasive. A particularly egregious example can be found in the otherwise brilliant book *Jesus and the Rise of Nationalism*, written by scholar Halvor Moxnes. It is an exceptional work of reception history. Moxnes, self-consciously following in the footsteps of Albert Schwitzer, analyzes the concurrent rise of European nationalism and historical Jesus research which occurred in the nineteenth century. He explains quite persuasively how reconstructions of Jesus produced during this period were heavily influenced by nationalistic ideals and often used in support of nationalist movements. Intellectuals such as D.F. Strauss and Ernst Renan[10], two towering figures in early biblical scholarship, were themselves deeply steeped in the ideology of nationalism. Their context distorted both their perception of Jesus and, more importantly, the categories which subsequent scholarship have utilized in historical Jesus research. Moxnes correctly argues that scholarship needs to be aware of this historical dynamic and rid itself of the categorial vestiges associated with nineteenth century nationalism. The bulk of his book is entirely compatible with the work of Cadbury and serves as a profound example of the historical deformations caused by reading New Testament texts through the matrix of modern ideas.

Moxnes doesn't always take his own advice. In the concluding chapter, *"Jesus Beyond Nationalism"*, subtitled *"Imagining a Post-National World"*, Moxnes argues against nineteenth-century nationalistic ideology but advocates for a replacement which is no less a product of his twenty-first century political ideology. He argues

---

9. Cadbury, *Peril*, p. 112

10. Each scholar was, as I noted in the previous chapter, heavily influenced by Saint-Simonianism. This is an interesting connection that, lamentably, Moxnes does not explore in his work. As we will see, it might complicate his modern political conclusions.

that *"writing about Jesus can be a resource for thinking about the political future and not just personal inspiration"*[11] and questions whether the *"terms for describing society that originated with nationalism in the nineteenth century are appropriate or sufficient today"*[12]. I believe he is correct on both counts and will make similar arguments throughout this book. Had Moxnes ended his analysis there I would have no objections. His proposed solution to the problem of nationalism, and his employment of Jesus and the gospels to justify it, is equally unsatisfactory.

Moxnes argues at the outset of his final chapter that the *"most pressing question today goes beyond the nation; it is the need to think of a future for all of humanity"*[13] and asks how Jesus research might be relevant for a *"new world order"*[14]. He argues that the ways in which Jesus related to people should be interpreted through the (modern) approach of intersectionality, which is capable of identifying and addressing true discrimination. Intersectional theory has been utilized by the United Nations and therefore the issues facing humanity today *"require global solutions"*[15]. The culprit, of course, is *"the economy (that is, the market and capitalism) and the nation state* [which] *combine to rob ordinary people of resources and livelihoods"*, which he describes as an *"empire"* shortly before labelling the globalized market as *"the most serious problem in the world today"*[16]. The antidote to our current global 'capitalist' dysfunction[17] can be found in the words of Jesus.

He claims that the economic teachings of Jesus aren't simply designed to regulate private behavior but should *"pose challenges on a structural level . . . his sayings were directed at the ways society generally works"*. He also argues that the Kingdom of God was in complete opposition to the rule of the day, which was *"characterized by exploitation and oppression"*, and that the *"economy of the Kingdom"* challenges Christians to rethink social structures.[18] I agree. So how does Moxnes propose we go about doing this? Building on the work of philosopher Jurgen Habermas, Moxnes contends that the *"present concern is how this democracy can be preserved and developed in a postnational situation"*. This can be achieved by European Union states developing a *"self-understanding of egalitarian universalism"*, a restructuring of the United Nations, and creating a *"global community"* that could *"make*

---

11. Moxnes, *Nationalism*, p. 181

12. Moxnes, *Nationalism*, p. 182

13. Moxnes, *Nationalism*, p. 179

14. Moxnes, *Nationalism*, p. 183

15. Moxnes, *Nationalism*, p. 189

16. Moxnes, *Nationalism*, p. 193

17. Moxnes predictably provides no concrete definition of 'capitalism'.

18. Moxnes, *Nationalism*, p. 195-195

a change of course towards a world domestic policy". Nations must no longer act in their own self-interest but "*as part of global governance in the key of domestic policy*", which will give "*democratic legitimacy to the global negotiation process towards a global domestic policy*".[19] In other words, Moxnes wants to replace a subjective nineteenth-century nationalism with his own preferred 'objective' twenty-first century globalism. It sounds like the logical progression of Saint-Simonian centralized authoritarian socialism because that is precisely what it is.

The goal of politics, for Moxnes, is "*to work towards a good life for all and to engage in democratic discussions of the responsibility of society*"[20]. What exactly constitutes a 'good life' will be determined by intellectuals like Moxnes, and in the future "democratically" legitimated globalists will benevolently impose this goodness upon all of humanity, even if the peoples of individual nations have a conception of the 'good' which differs from his. He approvingly cites the work of John Caputo, who writes about the imperative for those living in "*a small town in America*" to deconstruct their understanding of Christianity and instead embrace his; if Jesus was to go to that small town he would certainly implement the ideals of 'social justice' held by Moxnes and Caputo.[21] No concern is given whatsoever for the supposed "democratic" rights of "*small town*" Americans; since Jesus is on the side of Moxnes, the great post-nationalist global government possesses a rightfully, morally unimpeachable mandate to impose his preferred policies by force on the entire human race. It is, after all, for our own good. Right? As a Christian living in an American small town, I sincerely doubt that some European academic teaching at an urban university in Norway truly has my best interest in mind. He should have absolutely no say over how I live my life. Yet Moxnes believes Jesus is on his side, granting him a magical ethical obligation to make decisions on my behalf. The Bible says it, Moxnes believes it, and that settles it.

The economic and political deficiencies with his proposals have been adequately addressed in the previous two chapters. These contemporary categories within which he interprets the Bible are no less 'modern' or 'subjective' than those employed in nineteenth-century Jesus research. Even though Moxnes is an erudite and sophisticated academic his work is a product of his subjective social and political biases and serves the purpose of legitimizing his preferred conception of global authoritarianism, all under the false assertion that Jesus would endorse his every policy proposal. In two hundred years some scholar could write a book entitled *Jesus and the Rise of Globalism*, and Moxnes would be an excellent case

---

19. Moxnes, *Nationalism*, pp. 196-197

20. Moxnes, *Nationalism*, p. 197

21. Moxnes, *Nationalism*, p. 182

study of the same phenomena he rightly decries in his own work. In evaluating the shortcomings of one modernization of Jesus, he simply substitutes it with another. The substructure of modern Western political and economic thought, that at least some degree of authoritarian socialism is necessary for a functioning society, is the unstated presupposition of Moxnes's worldview.

We find ourselves in another quandary: how exactly do we adjudicate what constitutes a 'biblical' view of economic and political principles? Let's take, for example, the following passage from the gospel of Matthew: *"Jesus called them to Himself and said, "You know that the rulers of the Gentiles lord it over them, and their great men exercise authority over them. It is not this way among you, but whoever wishes to become great among you shall be your servant, and whoever wishes to be first among you shall be your slave; just as the Son of Man did not come to be served, but to serve, and to give His life a ransom for many."*"[22]. On my reading of the text, Jesus is the example of humble servanthood, standing in stark contrast to Gentile rulers, with the implication that true power is found not in political domination but through self-sacrificial service. This text could, for modern Christians, inculcate a suspicion towards *all* forms of political authoritarianism, calling us to personally imitate the suffering Son of Man in our relationships with other people. Moxnes, on the other hand, would use this passage to justify political authoritarianism, and on a global scale to boot. How do we make rational interpretive decisions about complex biblical texts without becoming entangled in the trap of modernization?

Let's be honest: humans are unable to completely transcend cultural contexts. Our precritical worldviews are predominantly determined by the social, political, economic, and theological influences which we take for granted. How we are raised, the company we keep, the media we consume, the education we complete, our hobbies and interests, and every other aspect of our lives both shape and are shaped by our accidental social location. The reason people who grow up in the Middle East think differently than those of us who were raised in the West demonstrates this point perfectly. We find it difficult to communicate because we have been enculturated into entirely different social orders, and these contexts in large part determine our values, beliefs, and interests. It also inevitably informs the way we read the Bible, which is how a European academic and an American public school teacher come to different interpretive conclusions despite reading the same New Testament texts.

Not only is the 'culture gap' an interpersonal problem which determines how different groups of people read the Bible in the twenty-first century, there is an even greater difference between the modern era and the world of Greco-Roman

---

22. Matthew 20:24-28

antiquity. It must be taken as an a priori fact that the writers of the Bible do not share our modern assumptions, therefore we must be careful not to read our own culture back into texts which were produced in and for a different one. I again concur with Cadbury that *our age differs more from Jesus' age in ways of thinking than in ways of living*[23], an observation we would do well to remember. While we may not be able to entirely avoid the problem of modernization when reading the Bible, we can take steps to limit it.

The rest of this chapter is devoted to setting parameters for biblical interpretation. If I am going to analyze the New Testament in its historical context and make the case that biblical scholarship has imposed flawed modern social and political concepts on the text, producing distorted modern applications of those interpretations, then I need to outline my own interpretive methodology. None of what I say in the following pages is controversial in professional biblical scholarship; in fact, my own approach to Scripture is a result of the work produced by the scholars I am challenging, including Halvor Moxnes. By utilizing their work, reframing social and political categories, and reevaluating texts in light of these categories I hope to expand the boundaries within which modern Christians construct political and economic theologies . With these goals in mind, it is time to talk about method. How, exactly, was the Bible intended to be read?

THE HISTORICAL PROBLEM

The Bible is complicated. Even to modern Western Christians who grow up in churches which hold the Bible in high regard, a close reading of any given passage leaves the reader with an impression that the biblical world is located in exotic territory. Superficial observations such as differences in names, technology, and customs are just the start. Paul seems to be obsessed with circumcision[24], Jesus is in constant conflict with the Jewish leadership in Jerusalem, and Revelation is full of incomprehensible imagery. The Roman imperial order lurks in the backdrop of several New Testament texts, and Paul, apostle of the crucified Jewish Messiah and hero of the church, seems to find himself in perennial controversy among both Jews and Gentiles. All of these prominent features in the New Testament are, quite literally, foreign to the modern reader. Such is the study of history. The works which are included in the Bible were written to, by, and for people who lived in either the ancient Near East (the Old Testament) or the Greco-Roman Mediterranean basin (the New Testament). Not only were ancient lifestyles materially dissimilar,

---

23. Cadbury, *Peril*, p. 4
24. See Romans 2-4, Galatians 2-3, and Phillipians 3.

the ancients also thought in different categories, held conflicting values, and interpreted reality through the matrix of ancient assumptions. They occupied a place in history which is not like our own, and in order to understand them we must account for *their* history.

I was fortunate enough to take a Latin class in high school. The teacher was a very educated woman who divided our coursework into a study of both the Latin language and Greco-Roman culture. As a new Christian I had spent the year prior reading and rereading the New Testament and I was interested in learning more about the Roman world. While my immature and admittedly lazy teenage mind struggled to grasp the language, I was immediately struck by how studying Roman society transformed my reading of the Bible. From that moment forward I was convinced that history was the key to a deeper engagement with Scripture. biblical interpretation, then, can only proceed fruitfully by situating the texts in their historical context. We cannot escape the gravity of history; the New Testament authors are not modern, twenty-first century Western thinkers and should not be treated as such. From fundamentalists who believe in theories of divine dictation to agnostics who argue the Bible is little more than the product of fallible men, we must all accept that the Scriptures were produced at a particular point in history and were indelibly influenced by that context.

In an introductory book on New Testament interpretation, scholars John Hayes and Carl Holladay make four important points about the relationship between history and interpretation which are relevant to this study.[25] First, the Bible was not originally addressed to modern readers. Every work in the Bible had an original intended audience, and it wasn't us. This is clearly demonstrated in the opening passages of the first canonical letter, Romans. Written by the apostle Paul[26], it is addressed *"to all who are beloved of God in Rome"*[27], which, obviously, means that it was written to people who lived in the ancient city, and, once again, not modern Americans. Secondly, the Bible was not written in a modern language. The New Testament is composed entirely in Koine Greek, and even though our grasp of this ancient language is comprehensive, there are words and concepts in Greek which have no perfect parallels in English. There are many excellent modern translations, but differences between these various translations reveal that those who translate from Greek into modern English disagree about how to best represent the ancient language in modern form. The third observation made by Hayes

---

25. Hayes, John, and Carl Holladay. 1987. *biblical Exegesis: A Beginner's Handbook.* John Knox Press. pp. 14-15

26. Romans 1:1

27. Romans 1:7

and Holladay is the *"enormous cultural gap"*[28] between antiquity and modernity, which we have already addressed. Those who haven't thought about historiography often reduce these cultural differences to superficial external differences such as preferences in dress, food, architecture, and technology, but the "cultural gap" is much wider. Their underlying assumptions about the world, nature, divinity, and, importantly for this study, categories such as 'economics' and 'politics' are nothing like our own, and we will always misinterpret Scripture when we ignore cultural differences. Fourth and finally they explain the cultural gap between us and them: there are two thousand years of history between the first century and the twenty-first century, and, plainly stated, a lot of stuff happened between then and now. Human civilization has changed during the previous twenty centuries and historically viable interpretations of Scripture must account for those differences.

Where does this leave a committed Christian such as myself? I am a Protestant who holds to the authority of scripture[29] and believes it should be the foundation upon which my practice and theology rests. What are we supposed to do with a collection of ancient texts which are supposed to inform our modern worldview? Old Testament scholar John Walton says it best: the Bible *"was written for us . . . but it was not written to us"*[30]. As a confessional Christian, I believe God intended for us to have the works which are included in the biblical canon, but we must also humbly accept that we are not the original intended audience of Scripture. The Bible begs to be interpreted in their terms. The process of reading the Bible in its original context is called *exegesis*.

EXEGESIS, HERMENEUTICS, AND THE NEW TESTAMENT

Scholars Gordon Fee and Douglas Stuart offer a simple and helpful definition of 'exegesis': *"Exegesis is the careful, systematic study of the Scripture to discover the original, intended meaning. This is basically a historical task"*[31]. The primary meaning of any text, indeed any transmission at all, is the intention of its author. Consistent with a praxeological understanding of economic activity, all human communication has an intended purpose. An author wants to communicate a specific idea (or set of ideas) and employs linguistic tools to accomplish their goal. Even if the recipient, the author's intended audience, misunderstands the transmission, it doesn't

---

28. Hayes and Holladay, *Exegesis*, p. 15

29. I will provide an explanation for the phrase "authority of scripture" below.

30. Walton, John. 2009. *The Lost World of Genesis One*. IVP Academic. p. 7

31. Fee, Gordon, and Douglas Stuart. 2003. *How to Read the Bible for All Its Worth*. 3rd ed. Zondervan. p. 23

in any way change the basic insight that the real 'meaning' of the communication was what the author *hoped* to convey by writing. Exegesis, when applied to the Bible, is "*the attempt to hear the Word as the original recipients were to have heard it, to find out what was the original intent of the words of the Bible*"[32]. Returning to the opening lines of Romans, Paul, the author, intends to communicate a particular message to his recipients, the church in Rome, and if we want to make any sense of Paul's complicated letter (Romans 13, anyone?) we must account for what Paul was trying to say and how he expected his audience to receive the letter. This is the task of biblical exegesis. Careful historical analysis of biblical texts minimizes the dangers of modernization.

For our purposes there are two broad contexts we must take into consideration when interpreting any text in the Bible: the historical context and the literary context. We have already partially addressed the *historical* context, which is basically the realization I had in my high school Latin class. Fee and Stuart provide an excellent short summary: "*The historical context, which will differ from book to book, has to do with several things: the time and culture of the author and his readers, that is, the geographical, topographical, and political factors that are relevant to the author's setting; and the occasion of the book* [why the author wrote it in the first place], *letter, psalm, prophetic oracle, or other genre. All such matters are especially important for understanding*"[33]. A historical analysis of Romans would include asking who Paul was, how many Christians lived in Rome, what was the socio-economic status of Paul's audience, when was the letter written, and how were letters structured in the Greco-Roman world. These types of questions help us better understand the context of Romans. Good exegesis must be rooted in history.

The second important exegetical consideration is the *literary context*, which includes asking what the author is attempting to communicate within an individual work. It is important to remember that 'the Bible' is not a single book, but a collection of unique, often independent texts, each conveying a particular message to a particular audience. Any individual passage in a biblical text will only make sense within the larger context of the entire work in which it is included. Fee and Stuart explain: "*this is the crucial task in exegesis . . . literary context means first that words only have meaning in sentences, and second that biblical sentences for the most part only have clear meaning in relation to preceding and succeeding sentences. The most important contextual question you will ever ask—and it must be asked over and over of every sentence and every paragraph—is, "What's the point?". We must try to trace the*

---

32. Fee and Stuart, *Bible*, p. 23

33. Fee and Stuart, *Bible*, p. 26

author's train of thought[34]. Indeed. No one would open up a modern novel, read a random line from the middle of the book, and adequately comprehend what the isolated line meant. The only way to understand a sentence, a paragraph, or a chapter of a modern novel is by reading it as one part of a larger literary whole. The Bible is no different. While we have been conditioned in the Western world to read the Bible in short verses or passages drawn from several different books, we can't make sense of a single line in Romans without asking what Paul is doing within the epistle as a whole and how the individual verse or passage relates to the entirety of his letter. Paul didn't write the Roman church an incoherent string of isolated sayings, he wrote them a unified letter containing a unified message.

When interpreting contentious passages like Romans 13 only a small number of historical factors are usually taken into account and the passage in question is commonly divorced from the text as a whole. When the narrative context is evoked, interpreters generally situate the passage within the narrow context of Romans 12 and the rest of Romans 13. In order to understand Romans 13 properly, we must explain how it works within the larger function of Romans, opening at 1:1 and concluding with 16:27, the end of Paul's letter. Failure to account for these factors will result in sloppy exegesis, and, more ruinously, modern applications which actually contradict the intended meaning of Paul's rhetoric. Michael Gorman correctly states that good exegesis provides *"a means of disciplined investigation"*[35] without which we will inevitably misrepresent what the writers of the Bible were trying to say, hindering our ability to apply biblical teaching in the modern world.

The term which denotes critical biblical interpretation in search of contemporary application is *hermeneutics*. Fee and Stuart explain that *"although the word "hermeneutics" ordinarily covers the whole field of interpretation, including exegesis, it is also used in the narrower sense of seeking the contemporary relevance of ancient texts"*[36]. The hermeneutical task, then, is to interpret (i.e. 'exegete') the Bible in its historical and literary context, thoughtfully discerning its relevance for today. That is the goal of this book. Historical exegesis controlled by hermeneutical considerations must refine the way we think about politics, economics, and the New Testament by diminishing unwarranted modernization. The Bible cannot and should not be employed in ways it was never intended to be used, and I believe that New Testament scholarship, operating with unstable conceptions of political and economic concepts, have blatantly committed this error. Fee and Stuart

---

34. Fee and Stuart, *Bible*, p. 27

35. Gorman, Michael. 2001. *Elements of biblical Exegesis.* Hendrickson Publishers. p. 141

36. Fee and Stuart, *Bible*, p. 29

expound this dynamic perfectly: "*the only proper control for hermeneutics is to be found in the original intent of the biblical text . . . we want to know what the Bible means for us—legitimately so. But we cannot make it mean anything that pleases us and then give the Holy Spirit "credit" for it . . . A text cannot mean what it never meant . . . the true meaning of the biblical text for us is what God originally intended it to mean when it was first spoken*"[37].

This approach to Scripture has traditionally been called the "historical-critical method". Drew Holland has recently argued that "historical-critical method" is much too nebulous a category and has suggested interpreters employ the phrase "historical criticism" instead.[38] I agree. In this book I will use historical criticism to analyze New Testament texts. I will often need to explain historical and literary details which are only tangentially related to political and economic themes in order to properly frame what the biblical authors were intending to communicate. We must not assume that every passage in the Bible which seems to address a 'political' or 'economic' question has a precise modern parallel. Too many excellent scholars have unwittingly made that exact mistake. Famous passages like Romans 13 or the so-called parable of the rich young ruler[39] are forced to answer modern political and economic questions which are filtered through the lens of nineteenth-century authoritarian socialism, resulting in a distortion or outright subversion of the author's intention. We must take hermeneutics seriously. We can't escape the powerful pull of history; the only way out of the shadows and into the light is through the long corridors of contextual exegesis conditioned by historical criticism. Another question presents itself. How do we apply ancient biblical texts in the modern world?

RELIABILITY, AUTHORITY, AND BIBLICAL PRINCIPLES

The Greco-Roman and Jewish worlds of antiquity are different from ours both culturally and intellectually. It is impossible to draw a straight line from *any* biblical text and assume it possesses a direct corollary in the modern world. The historical chasm is simply too wide to bridge without assistance. This means, of course, that the Bible can't explicitly endorse *any* modern concept, because the contemporary world neither thinks nor lives like the ancients who wrote and received the texts which became canonized. It is a category mistake to assume the Bible perfectly endorses socialism, technocratic authoritarianism, capitalism, libertarianism,

---

37. Fee and Stuart, *Bible*, pp. 29-30

38. Holland, Drew. 2025. *The Place of the Past*. Cascade Books. p. 4

39. Mark 10:17-31, Matthew 19:16-30, and Luke 18:18-30

progressivism, globalism, conservatism, or any other modern "-ism". Adherents to each belief are guilty of claiming the Bible 'clearly' teaches their preferred political or economic policy theory. Because of our historical location, there is actually very little in the Bible which is entirely clear to a modern audience, and assertions to the contrary are usually made by those who obscure the text with uncritically articulated modern ideas. Far from leaving us hopeless, however, hermeneutically informed exegesis can help us think about how the texts work historically and enable us to draw provisional conclusions about how we might apply them today.

Christians have been arguing for the last two millennia about biblical interpretation and its relevance for belief and practice. Divergent theological traditions have employed various hermeneutical frameworks, many of which are mutually incompatible. Such is the nature of epistemological subjectivity; millions of readers can examine the same biblical text and yet produce diametrically opposed interpretations. Practicing Christians aren't the only ones at fault. Even secularists who believe the entire Bible is a product of primitive man and has no relevance for today are engaging in the process of interpretation and application; the interpretation is that the Bible does not bear any marks of divine inspiration and therefore should not be applied at all. For skeptics, Christian Scripture is almost entirely irrelevant for modern man. Far from the confident philosophical assertions of post-Enlightenment rationalists, reducing the biblical texts to inconsequential historical artifacts is no less 'biased' than affirming its enduring contemporary relevance. Billions of people believe the Bible still matters, including its critics. biblical interpretation will produce no fruits unless directed by a coherent hermeneutical theory.

In my American context, two terms have been influential in shaping the way Christians think about Scripture: *inerrancy* and *infallibility*. Both of these terms were popularized in the *Chicago Statement on biblical Inerrancy*, originally published in 1978[40]. Article XI explains how these two terms function: "*WE AFFIRM that Scripture, having been given by divine inspiration, is infallible, so that, far from misleading us, it is true and reliable in all the matters it addresses. WE DENY that it is possible for the Bible to be at the same time infallible and errant in its assertions. Infallibility and inerrancy may be distinguished, but not separated.*" The Bible must be true and without error. The Chicago Statement was signed by an impressive array of Evangelical scholars and pastors but has itself been subject to various interpretations, including among its original signatories. Since this book is designed to be ecumenical in nature, I have no desire to wade into the fraught debates

---

40. "The Chicago Statement on Biblical Inerrancy." Defendinginerrancy.com. https://defending inerrancy.com/chicago-statements/.

regarding the precise meaning of the Chicago Statement's conceptualization of 'inerrancy' and 'infallibility'. Wittgenstein's insights about the malleability of words and the need for linguistic rules make me wary about openly endorsing one side of this contentious question.

Might there be a better way to conceptualize the significance of Scripture? Given that 'inerrancy' and 'infallibility' are definitionally contested even by those who affirm the Chicago Statement, a hermeneutical reorientation is in order. It must be ecumenical in scope, broad enough to encompass interpretive methods from various orthodox traditions, and sensitive to the objectives of historical criticism. I propose two categories: *reliability* and *authority*. The biblical witness *reliably* conveys divine guidance for the church, mediated through the historical context and intent of its original authors, and it functions as the final *authority* for Christian faith and practice. Few believers would object to these proposed categories, and since reliability and authority anchor the hermeneutical presuppositions of my exegetical methods a more detailed explanation of each term is in order.

'Reliability', a broad concept largely compatible with a number of interpretive approaches to Scripture, is general enough to incorporate historical-critical analysis of the original intentions of biblical texts within their own historical and literary contexts. Wooden interpretations of 'inerrancy' and 'infallibility' (which, I hasten to add, are *not* necessarily held by the majority of Christians who employ them) might reject, for instance, an interpretation of the gospels which asserts the evangelists recount the life of Jesus in a nonchronological order. If the Bible is 'without error', how could the evangelists mix up the order of major events in Jesus's life? If we accept Scripture as reliable, however, supposed lapses in chronology might not pose a problem for us at all. There is, as we will see in later chapters, good reasons to suppose that the evangelists were not as concerned as modern historians about chronological order and preferred to arrange material topically. It is quite possible the gospel writers even embellished stories to make certain points about Jesus which helped contribute to a more reliable portrayal of him. There are a growing number of scholars who believe that the gospels are a form of ancient Greek biography and share the characteristics of that genre. Helen Bond explains how *"all Greek biographies have two things in common: (1) the desire to commemorate a great life (or to occasionally record a dissolute one); and (2) a hope that their audience would learn from it . . . a person's life was laid out for others to imitate"*[41]. Bond continues: *"while biography was closely related in many ways to history, and often took "historical" subjects as its focus, we need to be careful about assuming that*

---

41. Bond, Helen. 2024. *"Biography"*. In *The Next Quest for the Historical Jesus* edited by Crossley, James and Keith, Chris. Eerdmans. p. 65

biographers were interested in history for its own sake. Their purpose was not to provide an accurate list of all that their subject did and said, but to lay bare the essence of the man, to re-create a living character"[42]. On this theory, which I find convincing, the gospel writers wanted to reliably depict Jesus through the genre of ancient biography which would have allowed them space to chronologically rearrange, embellish, or edit the Jesus tradition. So long as the final product, the gospels themselves, accurately reflect the essence of Jesus, the details are of minor consequence. If the evangelists were attempting to convey Jesus within this popular ancient genre, and their audiences would have understood the rules of ancient biography, we should allow our own modern standards of historiographical accuracy to inhibit our engagement with the gospels. If Matthew and Luke share a similar story with different details, we should ask how these details contribute to the biographical goals of commemorating Jesus' life and encouraging others to emulate him, the two purposes of ancient biography. The evangelists aren't just making stuff up for fun; minor variations in detail do not constitute 'error' within the rules of Greek biographical writing.

Reliability allows us to accept these historical contingencies, especially when it appears the Bible doesn't quite measure up to modern historical or scientific standards. Since the New Testament was written in a cultural context where modern criteria were either understood differently or intellectually irrelevant, the Bible is neither 'in error' or 'failed' if the intention of the author was to communicate something which was comprehensible and legitimate for his intended audience, even if it is at odds with our contemporary cultural values. Remembering Walton's dictum that the Bible was written 'for us, not to us', 'reliability' as a hermeneutical starting point for Christian biblical interpretation intersects perfectly with the method of historical criticism. We are interested in what the writers were originally aiming to communicate and have assurance they provide generally reliable information without imposing modernizing categories on ancient biblical texts.

'Authority', on the other hand, means Scripture is the basis for Christian doctrine and practice. If a doctrine or teaching demonstrably contradicts the Bible then it must be rejected. The same is true for Christian morality; our behavior should conform to the ethical exhortations contained within the canonical texts. Both of these claims are uncontroversial for believers. The Protestant Reformation, for all of the bitter disagreements between Protestant leaders, revolved around one central tenet: Scripture is the ultimate source of authority. That, at least, was accepted by all the reformers, and thus *sola scriptura* became the theoretical foundation of

---

42. Bond, *Biography*, 69-70

Protestantism[43]. The Catholic church, in spite of unfair caricatures leveled against it by certain Protestant sects, also binds Catholic doctrine and biblical authority, seeking to demonstrate how its doctrines correspond with Scripture.[44] Not to be forgotten are Orthodox Christians who also appeal to biblical authority and have made it central to Orthodox faith and practice.[45] Christians from every denomination and tradition can all agree on one claim: the Bible is authoritative. This doesn't mean we are in agreement about what Scripture says, but the concept of biblical authority and its impact on doctrine and practice is common to all believers.

Yet we immediately face another historical challenge. Every text in the Christian canon is culturally embedded, inextricably bound to their historical contexts. How can we possibly apply teachings from first-century literature to Christian practice in the twenty-first? An excellent example occurs in 1 Corinthians 8-10[46], where Paul addresses the thorny cultural practice of eating meat sacrificed to idols in a pagan temples. Some in the Corithian community do not object to the consumption of idol-meat while others opposed or were tempted into idolatry by this practice.[47] Bruce Winter explains the conflict: "*Paul noted that some Christians had reclined in the idol temple at a feast and did so on the grounds of what he emphatically described as 'this right of yours'* . . . *they also encouraged 'weak' Christians who had reservations about reclining at dinner in the temple to do the same as they did*"[48]. Paul explains that those who eat meat sacrificed to idols hold the correct theological perspective, stating there "*is no such thing as an idol in the world, and that there is no God but one*"[49], but other believers view the act as idol worship[50]. His conclusion is straightforward: if eating meat sacrificed to idols causes a brother to stumble, the community should abstain from eating meat. 1 Corinthians 9-10 develops this point in greater detail.

---

43. "Theoretical" being the operative term here; unfortunately too many Protestants read the Bible through the lens of their particular theological traditions, resulting in biblical interpretation that is subordinated to dogmatic concerns, which in turn subverts biblical authority and replaces it with that of the tradition. A consistent expression of biblical authority must make one skeptical about *all* theological claims and instill a willingness to change positions if a cherished doctrine is found to be in tension with Scripture.

44. *Catechism of the Catholic Church*, 2nd ed. (Vatican City: Libreria Editrice Vaticana, 1997), § 74-131.

45. "Bible." Orthodox Church in America. https://www.oca.org/questions/scripture/bible.

46. We will return this passage in Chapter 13.

47. 1 Corinthians 8:4-13

48. Winter, Bruce. 2001. *After Paul Left Corinth: The Influence of Secular Ethics and Social Change.* Eerdmans. p. 280

49. 1 Corinthians 8:4

50. 1 Corinthians 8:7-11

How might a long discussion about eating meat sacrificed to idols possibly be of any relevance in our modern context? The likelihood of a supermarket in the United States offering meat processed in honor of a pagan deity is exceedingly low. Is 1 Corinthians 8-10 in any way relevant to modern Christians? Alan Johnson indicates there is more to this passage than meets the eye: *"Chapters 8-10 form a unit about Christians and food sacrificed to pagan temple deities. It is at once an exciting and a challenging section . . . despite the first appearance, we are approaching material that is highly relevant to our times, but also quite often misunderstood"*[51] Ancient Corinthians were not modern Westerners, but Paul has in this passage generated a universally-applicable principle: Christians, including those on the 'correct' side of a theological debate, must cultivate a sacrificial disposition towards other believers. As Johnson states, *"Paul makes it an absolute principle for himself that he will eat no food that causes another Christian to stumble . . . Christian identity is first of all a sense of being known by God . . . then to walk in love both toward God and toward others"*[52]. Even though we do not share a historical and cultural context with the Corinthian church, this principle of self-sacrifice on behalf of others is binding for Christians seeking to follow biblical teaching, regardless of when or where they happen to live. While 1 Corinthians 8-10 was shaped by its historical context, the principle of self-sacrifice articulated in this passage is *supra*historical; it isn't simply confined to the context of idol meat but must be applied by Christians living in different cultures and at later stages in history. The historical context helps us recognize an underlying principle which we must thoughtfully implement in a cultural context that differs from the Corinthian church.

The main point I wish to make regarding the nexus between biblical authority and Christian practice today, by extension impacting our political and economic commitments, is related to the culturally-embedded principles contained in Scripture. The principle of self-sacrifice is foundational for New Testament ethics, and reappears across the literature in different contexts and genres. While modern Christians probably don't have to worry about consuming or abstaining from idol meat, 1 Corinthians 8-10 nevertheless expresses a universal ethical principle. Believers are obligated to foster a sacrificial, others-oriented disposition towards all people without exceptions. By doing so Christians are submitting to the authority of Scripture. Because the Bible is an historical artifact it can give us no direct guidance with respect to the novel challenges of modern life. Missing are instructions regarding the proper use of the internet or social media, electric instruments in church, the ethics of IVF, R-rated movies, work-life balance, foods produced

---

51. Johnson, Alan. 2004. *1 Corinthians*. InterVarsity Press. p. 132

52. Johnson, *1 Corinthians*, p. 142

with industrial chemicals, or many other relevant questions generated by modern intellectual or technological developments. This includes political and economic categories constructed during the Enlightenment and Industrial Revolution. Christians should have good-faith conversations about all these important issues, but we must be careful not to assume the Bible offers specific answers to questions which were impossible for the ancients to even ask.

What we have instead are biblical principles, fixed as they are in antiquity, which must be interpreted and then reapplied to our unprecedented contemporary context. If we believe in the authority of Scripture it is incumbent upon us to work out these principles in the modern world and allow them to shape our beliefs and practices. We live in a world formed by ideas that are only a few hundred years old, and the intellectual framework of Western thought is in the twenty-first century still under construction. We can't escape our modern patterns of thought. Pretending we are somehow 'objective' and capable of stepping outside history is a fever dream induced by nineteenth-century thought. While there is little direct correspondence between the cultures of antiquity and modernity, biblical principles can and should be used to judge modern ideas and practices; if we find a modern value in conflict with biblical principles, we denounce modernity.

This means in practice that all of our beliefs, including those cherished deeply or which seem perfectly 'normal', must be subjected to the rigorous standard of biblical principles. Once we account for the ancient context and discover these underlying principles, we are then in a position to begin the equally difficult task of working out how they ought to be applied today. This is especially true for modern political and economic categories. We have already seen how Wright, Horsley, and Moxnes all accept as morally legitimate the modern conception of centralized authoritarian state socialism, which is, to varying degrees, the presupposition for conservatism and progressivism. Nearly everyone accepts the hegemonic legitimacy of centralized state power. If, however, we find that biblical principles contradict this pervasive modern ideal, then perhaps it is time to reevaluate our commitment to the modern ideal. If we believe in both the reliability and authority of Scripture, we must allow it to inform our engagement with modernity. Before we tie the threads of this chapter together, a quick note on theology and my ecumenical aspirations are in order.

THEOLOGY AND ECUMENISM

In academia there is a distinction between the disciplines of Biblical studies and systematic theology. While the two are often conflated they nevertheless approach the Bible differently and employ their own unique methodologies. While the best biblical scholarship is informed by a knowledge of systematics and the best theology is informed by historical insights from biblical scholarship, they remain two separate disciplines. My own experience attending a Christian university also revealed there is often professional animosity and contention between scholars who work within either field, a dynamic I never anticipated when beginning my college career. Biblical studies is, broadly conceived, a subdiscipline of history, and therefore concerned primarily with understanding the Bible in its historical context. Systematic theology seeks to construct a philosophically coherent analysis of the nature of God (and other related concepts) and is, predictably, much closer to the field of philosophy. The two are not mutually exclusive; biblical scholars and theologians need to be competent in a number of related fields, and biblical scholars operate with theological assumptions just as theologians operate with historical assumptions. It is important, however, to treat each field as its own unique entity.

That being said, this book falls firmly within the goals and objectives of biblical scholarship, and, although relying on the work of several excellent theologians, I am not attempting to construct a systematic theology. While I find the field fascinating, my own training was primarily within the scope of biblical scholarship, and my interests lie predominantly within the boundaries of that discipline. This is a matter of genre above all else; I will in fact be making several theological claims in the following chapters, but they are all directly derived from an *historical* analysis of New Testament texts. I situate the New Testament within its historical context, discover principles which are contained therein, and challenge modern political and economic assumptions that are often uncritically justified by appeal to Scripture. I am a Christian, after all, and I believe the Bible is binding for believers. I can't help but reflect upon the theological consequences of biblical scholarship. It's the entire reason I study the Bible. Nevertheless my interpretive method is aligned with the discipline of biblical scholarship. Because of this objective I will mostly avoid reference to the many systematic political theologies which have been developed throughout the centuries. While this might disappoint some readers, I hope that my historical analysis will be of some value to the ongoing debates about political theology. I hope you will be persuaded both by my historical research and theological conclusions.

I will also avoid, as much as possible, passionately advocating for contentious theological positions. While I do have a perspective on many hot-button, controversial theological debates, I will do my best to shy away from them here. The purpose is twofold. First, I want this book to have a wide, ecumenical appeal. I believe my interpretive work is broadly compatible with Catholic, Orthodox, and most Protestant traditions. While I must discuss, at least tangentially, issues such as justification, the Gospel, salvation, and other topics which Christians vehemently disagree upon, few of my conclusions will hinge on a particular interpretation of these doctrines. I do not want to alienate any of my readers by taking a stand on doctrinal questions which have nothing to do with critiquing modern economic and political concepts in light of biblical principles. Second, I become more convinced with each passing year that these vexing theological questions are infinitely complex. I am also increasingly less confident that my intellectually limited mind could perfectly solve them. I am more interested in learning *why* people come to certain theological conclusions and creating an environment where we can have open, honest, and respectful debates about different beliefs. This is, in my view, the only possible way for us to ever expand the repository of human knowledge, and as we discuss the nature of an infinite, transcendent God a little bit of humility keeps us in check. To that aim, I will not deviate from the primary goal of this book and extend an open invitation to Christians from every tradition to participate in the conversation with me.

Conclusion: Ancient Principles, Modern Problems

Drawing all of these ideas together, I will offer an introductory exegesis of nearly every New Testament text which could influence modern political and economic debates. My hermeneutical method will include analyzing these texts in their historical and literary contexts, paying close attention to authorial intention and how the original recipients would have understood them. While the New Testament, as a product of the first century, does not directly address complex modern problems, there are principles which can be discerned from these texts which must be applied by believers in the modern world. If we accept the reliability and authority of scripture then our faith and practice must be measured by the degree to which it is in alignment with biblical principles. This method enables us to avoid the modernizing tendencies inherent in conversations about the Bible and reframe how we think about Scriptural implications for contemporary life.

The Bible cannot explicitly teach any of our modern economic or political concepts. Socialism, capitalism, conservatism, progressivism, and libertarianism as developed ideological theories are foreign to the ancient mind. It is both anachronistic and disingenuous to assume Jesus, Paul, or any other historical figure would have subscribed to these ideologies and articulated them coherently in antiquity. Despite scholars like Wright, Horsley, and Moxnes paying lip-service to the historical gulf between antiquity and modernity, the conclusions they derive from their reading of the New Testament either tacitly or explicitly endorse the dominant economic and political ideology of our day, centralized authoritarian socialism. New Testament scholarship has fallen into the modernizing trap of employing ancient texts to justify specific modern policy proposals, all of which necessitate a rejection of the non-aggression principle. Even when scholars like Moxnes construct compelling criticisms of the illegitimate modernization imposed upon the Bible by scholars of previous eras, they simply replace older modernized concepts with newer ones which are more congenial to their agenda of global political technocratic authoritarianism.

This isn't to say from the outset their ideas are necessarily incorrect. When the Bible is read from a principlist perspective, which acknowledges that the texts are historically embedded and must be analyzed contextually to derive principles that can then be applied in different historical contexts, the question we must ask is not whether the Bible explicitly teaches modern ideas (which we would all agree it cannot) but rather *which modern ideas best correspond to biblical principles*. This is at the heart of the argument I am making in this book; given the methodological considerations I have addressed above, a historically and narratively-grounded interpretation of the New Testament will produce principles which can be used to determine if particular modern ideas are either broadly congruent or in blatant contraction with them. If a biblical principle is determined to be compatible with a modern idea, then those who accept the notion of biblical authority are justified in holding it. Conversely, if a biblical principle seems to contradict a modern idea, no matter how popular that idea may be, then Christians have a responsibility to question and ultimately abandon it.

I will be arguing in this book that the dominant political and economic paradigm of the modern world, authoritarian socialism, is entirely incompatible with New Testament principles and that Christians should ultimately reject this pervasive contemporary worldview. This is not a popular position to take since it results in a condemnation of both "right-wing" conservatism and "left-wing" progressivism, but attempting to faithfully embody biblical principles should often put one at odds with dominant cultural ideologies. While the New Testament scholars we reviewed thus far have picked a side in contemporary political debates, I believe that the Bible forces us to reject the conception of 'sides' entirely. Modern Christians believe there is an optimal arrangement of authoritarianism which can be legitimized by Scripture, savagely arguing about which authoritarians should be in power or which authoritarian policies should or should not be implemented. If we can liberate ourselves from the ideology of authoritarianism and our modernized reading of the New Testament, we just might be empowered to rethink our commitment to political and economic systems.

There is one final, and very important, point I need to make in closing this chapter. I am not arguing *for* libertarianism or capitalism as precise expressions of New Testament teachings. The Bible, as I have argued, cannot completely articulate concepts which were not developed until later periods in history. While I believe that the best modern expressions of New Testament political and economic instruction are essentially libertarian and capitalistic, this is a very different proposition than claiming the writers of Scripture explicitly endorsed them, a genuine historical impossibility. I am instead arguing *against* authoritarian socialism as a model for New Testament exegesis (the implicit paradigm guiding much New Testament scholarship) and Christian practice. Political authoritarianism and economic socialism are neither taught by the writers of the New Testament nor compatible with biblical principles. In fact, these prevailing categories of our time are in direct contradiction to the witness of Scripture. Before, at long last, we begin our examination of the New Testament and drawing exegetical conclusions about the principles contained within, I must provide a broad overview of the political and economic contexts of the Greco-Roman and Jewish worlds within which the writers of the New Testament composed their texts. This task will occupy the next two chapters.

CHAPTER 5 | The Greco-Roman World

Contextualizing the New Testament

If the New Testament texts were written to make sense to people in the first century, then we must try to put ourselves into their places in order to determine what the writers of the New Testament intended their readers to understand by what they wrote.

James Jeffers[1]

Indeed, if Christianity did not have these linguistic and cultural contacts with the first-century Mediterranean world the presumption would be that it was a fiction originating in another time and place.

Everett Ferguson[2]

INTRODUCTION: POLITICS AND ECONOMICS IN ANTIQUITY

The discipline of economics has, in its relatively short history, revealed insights about the nature of human behavior which are critical for conceptualizing society. Scarcity, the idea that all material resources necessarily exist in limited quantities, and the concurrent response by humans who must make choices regarding the appropriation, utilization, and allocation of finite resources, are universally true and valid irrespective of culture. No one, no matter how much they wish it wasn't so, can escape the reality of scarcity and choice. Nothing material is infinite, and every human action is a response to scarcity. Scarcity and choice are intrinsically related to supply and demand, which determine the allocation of scarce resources. In a market economy supply and demand both coordinate and are coordinated

1. Jeffers, James. 1997. *The Greco-Roman Worlds of the New Testament Era*. InterVarsity Press. p. 11

2. Ferguson, Everett. 2003. *Backgrounds of Early Christianity*. 3rd ed. Eerdmans. p. 2

by the price system, with government intervention necessarily distorting the price system[3]. These economic laws are universally valid, irrespective of historical and cultural contexts. Political systems likewise change and develop over time, but, as both orthodox Marxists and Austrian libertarians have observed, these systems inevitably result in the production of a ruling class which governs at the expense of its population.

It's just a fact: certain axioms of economic theory are always true. From this perspective, there is no difference between first-century Judea and Galilee under Roman occupation and twenty-first century North America. Within the parameters of economic and political generalities, the world continues on as it always has. Theory, however, is where historical similarities end. Antiquity bears only a hazy and distant resemblance to modernity, and in few places is this more true than with respect to concrete political and economic systems. Fundamental assumptions about political power, divine intervention, economic exchange, and a host of related issues are not transferable from one culture to another, and, like language, must be carefully interpreted in order to understand what those who lived in other contexts actually experienced. We have already addressed the challenge of historical distance and the dangers of modernization in previous chapters, and Bruce Malina and Richard Rohrbaugh summarize the problem succinctly: "*We must also recognize . . . that the distance between ourselves and the Bible is social as well as temporal and conceptual. Such social distance includes radical differences in social structures, social roles, values, and general cultural features.*"[4] In order to avoid imposing our contemporary assumptions about political and economic thought anachronistically upon New Testament texts we must necessarily account for the sociological factors which shaped the first century.

Issues that are relevant to our interpretation of New Testament passages must be understood within their own historical context. Outlining the broad contours of Roman imperial administration, taxation, economic exchange, and social relationships are essential for comprehending the Bible. We must also grasp the Jewish context which shaped Jesus, Paul, and other early Jesus-followers. That Jesus was a Jew is historically uncontestable and must be the starting point for any serious reconstruction of him as a historical figure[5]. His ministry in Galilee and

---

3. This is often the stated purpose of various economic regulations, including subsidies and tariffs; by modifying a price through intervention, governments are attempting to divert consumer purchasing decisions from one commodity to another.

4. Malina, Bruce, and Richard Rohrbaugh. 1992. *Social-Science Commentary on the Synoptic Gospels*. Fortress Press.

5. See the excellent discussion in Reinhartz, Adele. 2024. "*Beyond the Jewish Jesus Debate*". In *The Next Quest for the Historical Jesus* edited by Crossley, James and Keith, Chris. Eerdmans. pp. 49-61

Judea, Jewish territories under Roman occupation, is incomprehensible without analyzing the political and economic structures of that region. Paul, despite the unfortunately popular caricature which presents him as the founder of a new 'religion'[6], was born and raised a Jew[7]. Being brought up in the city of Tarsus in the eastern Mediterranean[8] made him the ideal "apostle to the gentiles"[9]. Paul spent most of his adult life in urban environments throughout the Roman empire, and the letters he wrote during the course of his ministry are a product of both his own Jewish identity as well as Greek culture and the Roman imperial and economic order. Any informed reading of the New Testament must account for the wider cultural, social, and historical contexts in which the works included therein were produced.

This approach to biblical interpretation is generally labeled 'social-scientific criticism'. As a method of interpretation it is foundational to modern biblical scholarship and has positively informed the discipline of systematic theology. Explained shortly, *"the critical focus of social-scientific criticism is not limited to the textual evidence, but also includes reconstructions of the social contexts of the authors and/or recipients. This allows social scientific critics to chart how particular texts may reflect, challenge or subvert aspects of the environments of which they are a part"*[10]. In other words, social-scientific criticism seeks to explain how people in the first century thought and lived by reconstructing their social background. While the dangers of modernization are everpresent, mooring our readings of biblical texts to the docks of plausible historical backgrounds diminishes the likelihood we will drift into the turbulent seas of anachronism. Ensuring that our readings of the New Testament are rooted in first-century soil is an interpretive priority.

This is no easy task. Having spent much of the last two decades reading biblical scholarship informed by social-scientific criticism, I present two observations that are relevant for this study. First, reconstructing either the Greco-Roman or Jewish context of the first century is notoriously difficult. While scholars work with a large (and growing) number of primary source materials, there are still massive gaps in our knowledge of antiquity which must necessarily be filled with creative interpretation. In a learned and detailed book on precisely this issue, Everett

---

6. Which is itself, as we will see shortly, a problematic category in antiquity.

7. According to his own autobiographical statements; see Romans 9:3-5, Galatians 2:15, and Philippians 3:4-6.

8. Acts 22:3; the significance of Paul's social location will be discussed in a subsequent chapter.

9. See, for example, Acts 13:44-47, Romans 11:13, and Galatians 2:7-9

10. Lawrence, Louise. 2013. *"Social-Scientific Criticisms"*. In *Dictionary of Jesus and the Gospels*, 2nd ed. edited by Green, Joel. InterVarsity Press. p. 874

Feguson laments about the difficulties of reconstructing the Roman economy alone: "*the subject of economic conditions in the Roman world is too large and complex for an adequate sketch . . . even the standard synthesis given in the bibliography are in need of correction and supplementation, so that only specialists have a command of the subject*"[11]. It's complicated. Second, professional scholars of the highest caliber disagree on a number of important contextual issues. Not only do they draw different conclusions about the function of individual biblical texts, they also disagree on what the primary sources say about the Greco-Roman and Jewish context of the first century. While there may be some general consensus regarding a handful of broad topics, the specifics are hotly debated. Such is the nature of historiography; many of the most pressing historical debates will never reach a conclusive settlement. Context is essential to interpretation, but the context itself must be interpreted. Nothing comes easy.

I am under no illusion I can put to rest these perennial historical questions in one chapter. I fully acknowledge my intellectual limitations. But I cannot avoid the pressing need to contextualize the New Testament within the boundaries of first century Mediterranean life. While the issues are complicated and the debates intense, I strongly believe that a general (if imperfect) orientation to the world of antiquity is possible and will help us illuminate biblical texts that are shrouded in the darkness of modernized political and economic exegesis. My goal in this chapter will be to sketch (in the purest sense of the term) a basic outline of the Greco-Roman context in which the New Testament was written, focusing particularly on political and economic realities that directly impinge upon the texts we will be interpreting in later chapters. This chapter cannot be exhaustive, and there are several extremely important historical circumstances that will, due to the limited goals of this book, remain overlooked. My hope is that readers will have the basic tools they need to think historically about controversial New Testament passages and how they could have been received in antiquity. I would also encourage those who are interested in examining the historical background of the New Testament in greater depth to read the secondary source material with which I am engaging in this chapter. The footnotes below and the bibliography at the end of the book provide curious readers an opportunity to further refine their knowledge of the first century, which will elucidate much more than the selection of texts we explore in this book. We will in this chapter examine how the ancients understood politics and economics, and why we can't, as modern thinkers often unfortunately do, separate these concepts from what we might call 'religion' and 'society'. What we have divided into distinct categorical concepts in the modern world were all

---

11. Ferguson, *Backgrounds*, p. 82

happily interrelated in antiquity. We will then examine the Greco-Roman context of the first century, including Roman imperialism and administration, the Roman economy, the patron-client system, and the socioeconomic makeup of the urban house to whom Paul wrote his letters. We now turn to the ancient conceptualization of politics and economics.

HOW THE ANCIENTS UNDERSTOOD 'POLITICS' AND 'ECONOMICS'

The Bible Isn't About 'Religion'

Reflecting on the nature of biblical literature, Richard Horsley accurately states "*the texts were about all aspects of life, more specifically, about the concrete political-economic-religious realities of ancient societies*"[12]. "*They are not*", he argues, "*about religion separate from political-economic life, but about political-economic-religious life more completely. The texts and the characters in the texts, God and people, are* concerned with all aspects of life"[13]. Despite making these claims to promote an explicitly Marxist reading of Scripture, Horsley is entirely correct. In the modern world, 'religion' as a concept has been separated from 'politics', 'economics', and 'society', with both casual observers and professional interpreters assuming that the Bible is essentially 'religious' and can (or perhaps *should*) be marginalized or distanced from the political process or economic exchange. The constructed category we call 'religion' overlaps little with other, more important areas of life, and many Christians are content to keep 'religion' within these culturally circumscribed boundaries.

The problem, however, is that the ancients did not neatly divide the world into separate spheres in which 'religion' could be isolated from the rest of human experience. Brent Nongbri, in his masterful study of the history of 'religion' as a concept, argues that "*religion is a modern and not an ancient concept . . . the existence of the religious/secular division is part of what constitutes the modern world*"[14]. While modern thinkers posit a sharp divide between religion and other aspects of the human experience, ancient thinkers did not. Nongbri demonstrates that the Latin word *religio*, from which is derived the English word 'religion', had a variety of meanings in antiquity, none of which were a reflection of the modern religious/

---

12. Horsley, *Bow Down*, p. 3

13. Horsley, *Bow Down*, p. 171

14. Nongbri, Brent. 2013. *Before Religion: A History of the Modern Concept.* Yale University Press. p. 12

secular divide.[15] While the development of this concept over the last two thousand years has a long and tortuous history, the idea that religion as a category could be separated from the rest of life emerges from the Renaissance, the Reformation, the Age of Exploration and the Enlightenment, particularly in the work of John Locke.[16] Separating 'religion' from other areas of life "*is not as natural or universal as it is often assumed to be*"[17] and "*prevents one from seeing how ancient people might have organized their worlds*"[18]. The division of the world into separate spheres of religion, politics, and economics reaches its climax, according to Horsley, in the aftermath of the French Revolution, and, from this point on, "*Biblical studies and reading of the Bible in general then projected this assumption that religion and politics and economics are separate spheres of life and institutions back onto the biblical texts and the contexts they address*"[19].

It is inappropriate, therefore, to assume the ancients, including New Testament authors, were operating within a religious/secular framework and addressing specifically 'religious' issues. This was simply not an option in the first century, therefore the Bible isn't a 'religious' text in a narrow modernist sense of the term. It is about the whole of life, and neither the texts, those who wrote them, or their ancient audience would have conceptualized 'religion' as we do in modernity. This also means, directly relevant to the case I am making in this book, that politics and economics were neither divorced from 'religion' nor somehow separated from the whole of society; all of these ideas which have been clinically dissected and separated in the modern world were happily integrated in antiquity. In my opinion, one of the major flaws in contemporary Western Christianity is an overspiritualization of biblical texts which were never intended to be read within the framework of 'religion', thus failing to comprehend what the biblical authors intended to communicate. At the center of Paul's gospel, for example, is the proclamation that Jesus is the Christ, which denotes his status as king.[20] For Paul, as we will see, the Messianic status of Jesus is no metaphor; he believes Jesus rules over all of creation, and not just in a subjective, private 'religious' sense. The notion of Jesus as 'king in our hearts' may be popular in a modern context where 'religion' is easily divisible from 'politics', but, consequential as it may be, Paul is making a much larger claim

---

15. Nongbri, *Before Religion*, pp. 26-34

16. Nongbri, *Before Religion*, pp. 106-131

17. Nongbri, *Before Religion*, p. 154

18. Nongbri, *Before Religion*, p. 156

19. Horsley, *Bow Down*, p. 1

20. The classic texts are Romans 1:1-5, 1 Corinthians 15:3-5, and 2 Timothy 2:8.

which cannot be separated from political and economic considerations. There was, in antiquity, no separation of church and state.

If we are ever going to take the message of Scripture seriously, we must push beyond the artificial distinction between what is religious and secular which characterizes the modern mind and understand reality as a complex, interwoven intellectual tapestry. No one in antiquity would have recognized these facile distinctions, and fully appreciating the New Testament means learning to think without them. It is important to remember that even when we are addressing passages which are often labeled as 'religious', 'political', or 'economic', the original authors never intended these ideas to be separated from one another. We are now in a position to examine how the ancients broadly conceptualized 'politics' and 'economics'.

Politics Encompasses the Whole of Public Life

The English word 'politics' connotes in popular parlance various aspects of the political process: elections, governments, laws, politicians, bureaucrats, news media, and the like. Similar to the term religion, 'politics' has been neatly classified and domesticated. Even if a precise definition remains elusive, English speakers understand the term's referent. Politics is often seen as antithetical to religion and is regarded as a topic to be avoided in polite conversation. Most employers prohibit discussing politics at work, and many families have strict rules about abstaining from political debates at holiday dinners. People become quickly uncomfortable when political topics are broached, even among close friends, and overtly political sermons are usually seen as cringy and in bad taste, a sentiment with which I agree. Most of us have been in a situation where someone initiates (usually without invitation) a political conversation in bad faith, an uncomfortable breach of polite social etiquette. Unfortunately the very narrow conception of 'politics' as 'that which is related to the political process' is often imposed upon the New Testament, resulting in popular (and sometimes scholarly) interpretations of biblical texts that reflect our modern political sensibilities.

The ancients did not conceptualise politics in this way. The Greek word *politeia*, from which our English word 'politics' is derived, encompasses more than the political process. Bruce Winter explains how *politeia* "*is immediately divested of much of its first-century meaning if it is assumed that* politeia = 'politics*", and argues importantly that "[politeia] *has a much wider application than the term 'politics' does today. The term referred to the whole of life in the public domain of a city, in contrast to private existence in a household*"[21]. Politics in the ancient world wasn't simply

---

21. Winter, Bruce. 1994. *Seek the Welfare of the City*. Eerdmans. p. 2

confined to the political process, but instead incorporated the entirety of one's social life outside of the household. The phrase 'public life' is a better conception of politics in antiquity because it implies that everything one does in public is "political'. While the term does include what we would understand as political arrangements and the operation of government, it is much broader: how a person interacted with society in general, including the worship of Greek and Roman deities, involvement in civic associations, work and labor, social relationships, and other activities which took place outside of the home all fall under the label of *politeia*.

Early Christians, who by default participated in wider Greco-Roman society, were certainly aware that their faith had 'political' implications which would necessarily impact their relationship with the outside world. While I believe that the New Testament envisions, at least eschatologically, a dramatic transformation (or perhaps destruction) of the structures of human government, it is also concerned with the Christian witness and relationship to those outside the church. Given this wider definition of *politeia*, Christianity is inherently political. Winter correctly explains how a misunderstanding of *politeia* as 'politics' in the narrow modern sense has constricted our ability to think critically about the nexus between faith and politics: "*the discussion of Christians in 'public life' has proceeded along the Western world's concerns of the narrow, well-worn track of 'church and state'. . . because of this limited focus on what* politeia *is perceived to have meant, much material which is relevant for the Christian's participation in* politeia *has been overlooked*"[22]. By widening our understanding of 'politics' in antiquity to include the whole of public life, we are in a better position to understand how this concept is integrated with other important theological claims in the New Testament. Certain beliefs about Jesus necessitate a change in how Christians engage with the non-Christian world and would be interpreted by ancient observers as political (i.e. 'public life') action.

The comprehensive scope of *politeia* doesn't exclude our narrower, contemporary conception of politics, and Scripture must shape the ways in which believers reflect upon the political process. History is still our guide. In antiquity, the general theory of government was that it existed to reward good conduct, promote public morality, and punish wrongdoing. As Najeeb Haddad points out, both the Greek philosopher Aristotle and the Jewish philosopher Philo are in agreement: government is responsible for upholding the good and punishing the bad, and this conception of the role of government and its relation to public life (remembering they are inseparable to the ancient mind) is standard throughout the Greco-Roman

---

22. Winter, *Welfare*, p. 2

world.[23] Both Paul and Peter, in their vexing passages about governing authorities, reflect this general Greco-Roman explanation of government[24]. Far from legitimizing the modern separation of church and state, the two apostles appeal to prevailing political norms which are concerned with promoting the public good and administering justice.[25] Seen in this light, both Romans 13 and 1 Peter 2 are not as straightforward as often assumed. I will address both of these passages in due course. It is important to remember these broad considerations about *politeia*. In antiquity, the concept includes the whole of public life, not simply the political process. As an extension of public life, government in antiquity was believed to uphold the good and administer justice to the bad. Both of these concepts must frame our understanding of 'politics' in the first century, which can't be separated from other areas of life. We will turn now to the ancient conception of economics.

Economics and Society

In an excellent chapter from New Testament scholar Peter Oakes's book *Empire, Economics, and the New Testament,* entitled '*Methodological Issues in Using Economic Evidence in Interpretation of Early Christian Texts*'[26], Oakes claims that all ancient economies are "*embedded*" economies. In embedded economies "*financial decisions . . . [are] rarely taken for financial reasons alone*"[27]. He contrasts this with mainstream economic theory which is based upon abstract concepts like choice, scarcity, and incentives. He writes "*the focus on choice is problematic in a society where most economic activities are governed more by custom or compulsion*", but adds the following qualifier: "*I suppose it works fairly reasonably as long as one remembers that the choices lie with the powerful elite. The stress on incentives might be useful, but only if it is realized that, for most people, they were generally of an "offer you can't refuse" type. There was not the kind of varying levels of inducement that a modern market system might include*"[28]. While he is correct that many mainstream economic models cannot account for the 'embedded economies' of antiquity where many economic decisions are not made for purely financial reasons, the Austrian school

---

23. Haddad, Najeeb. 2021. *Paul, Politics, and New Creation.* Lexington Books/Fortress Academic. pp. 66-67

24. Romans 13:1-7 and 1 Peter 2:13-17

25. Winter, *Welfare*, pp. 4-5

26. Oakes, Peter. 2020. *Empire, Economics, and the New Testament.* Eerdmans. pp. 65-90; this is required reading for anyone interested in the relationship between economic analysis and the New Testament.

27. Oakes, *Empire*, p. 67

28. Oakes, *Empire*, p. 67

of economics, with its praxeological emphasis on human action and the subjective theory of value, easily accounts for market transactions which aren't aimed purely at profit.[29]

Oakes, however, is entirely correct: the ancients were unshackled by post-Enlightenment economic theory, and many economic decisions were made for reasons other than monetary profit[30]. In the Greek and Roman cities where Paul founded and sustained churches, the patron-client system of benefaction, elite land control, and local cultural customs dominated economic life, while the socio-economic status of early Christians had a major impact on the challenges faced by Jesus-followers in the first century. Roman economic conditions differ considerably from those experienced by Christians today. Grasping first-century economic realities, which will be described in detail below, empowers us to reexamine common interpretations of passages such as 1 Thessalonians 4:9-12 and 2 Thessalonians 3:6-12 which are usually cut straight out of their historical context and stitched into the fabric of modern economic debates. Jesus's warning about sewing new patches on old garments[31] is, when decontextualized, an excellent analogy for uncritically employing biblical texts in contemporary economic discourse. Oakes does recognize that economics as a study of the allocation of scarce resources is perfectly acceptable for analyzing the Roman economy so long as we acknowledge that the motives and mechanics of economic exchange differ in many important ways from the modern world.[32] Making this point even clearer, the Greek etymological ancestor of the English word 'economy' is *oikonomia*, which is, in agreement with Oakes, a much wider and less precise concept than its modern counterpart. The ancient mind would not have distinguished trade, agriculture, and taxation from other forms of social interaction, which is why *oikonomia* is 'embedded' in social relationships more generally.[33] We must also emphasise just how unsystematized the Romans were when thinking about their own economies. As historian Greg Woolf helpfully summarizes, "[The Romans'] *very practical understanding of economic activity did not include the use of predictive or descriptive modelling, they gathered little data from which they could have analyzed trends, and*

---

29. For a review of the Austrian school and its relevance in this study see Chapter 2.

30. I am not sure Oakes is correct when he implies the modern economy is based entirely around rational financial calculation, but I remain convinced that the concept of an 'embedded economy' accurately describes Roman economic thinking.

31. Matthew 2:16/Mark 2.21/Luke 5:36

32. Oakes, *Empire*, p. 68

33. Downs, David. 2013. *"Economics"*. In *Dictionary of Jesus and the Gospels*, 2nd ed. by Joel B. Green, InterVarsity Press. p. 219

the ancient science had no concept of the economy as a separate entity"[34]. It is important to keep these first century economic realities in mind when thinking about how the writers of the Bible deal with what we now consider 'economic' issues.

I will make one final point before proceeding. Since the ancient economy was not based entirely upon financial calculation and the Roman world had no mechanism for thinking systematically about economic activity, it would have been impossible for the writers of the New Testament to provide us with anything approaching a macroeconomic theory. Because the culturally embedded texts of Scripture are always conditioned by the historical circumstances in which they were produced, we must carefully attempt to reconstruct the context which lies behind the text, deduce a principle which the writer employs to instruct his audience, and think critically about how that principle is applicable to Christians today. I wish it wasn't this complicated, but I don't dictate the terms of reality. Any political or economic interpretation of a biblical text which fails to grapple with these realities will be forever doomed to failure. With these broad considerations about the nature of ancient political and economic thought in mind, let's begin our exploration of the Roman and Jewish context which informed the New Testament.

ROME: THE ETERNAL EMPIRE

The Roman Imperial Order

Luke, author of both the gospel which bears his name and Acts, appreciates the sheer power of Roman imperialism. Luke and Acts, which form one long story about the ministry of Jesus and the early church, begins and ends with an acknowledgement of Roman rule. In Luke 2:1 he explains exactly why Jesus's parents had to make the long and arduous journey to Bethlehem from Nazareth in Galilee: "*Now in those days a decree went out from Caesar Augustus, that a census be taken of all the inhabited earth*". The ruler of the Mediterranean, whose quarters were nearly fifteen hundred miles away from Judea, declared a census, and Jews in the far-flung corners of his empire had no choice but to respond. In the closing passages of Acts we find the apostle Paul living in the imperial capital of Rome, "*preaching the kingdom of God and teaching concerning the Lord Jesus Christ with all openness, unhindered*"[35]. The New Testament story about Jesus and his church begins and ends under the shadow of Rome. Or perhaps it begins in the shadow of Rome and

---

34. Woolf, Greg. 2012. *Rome: An Empire's Story*. Oxford University Press. p. 193

35. Acts 28:30-31

ends with Rome in the shadow of God's kingdom. Either way, it is impossible to avoid the stark reality of Roman rule and its indelible impact on the early Jesus movement.

At the birth of Jesus the Roman empire as such was still in its infancy. The story of Rome's dramatic transition from Republic to empire begins with a failed land reform measure proposed to the Senate by the Gracchi brothers in 133 BCE. Perceiving reform as a threat to its power, both brothers were eventually murdered by opposing factions in the Senate. The lesson learned from this event by the Roman elite was that violence was an effective method for solving political problems; this lesson would be applied time and time again over the following century.[36] As political violence intensified in the capitol, Roman generals in the field became less accountable to the Senate and more politically ambitious. Towards the end of the second century BCE a man named Marius was given military leadership by the people in clear defiance of the Senate's prerogative to determine military affairs. The Roman army was open to voluntary enlistment, and payment for services and retirement benefits were now doled out to soldiers directly by the military commander Marius instead of the Senate. Marius was buying their loyalty; his soldiers now answered to him, not the state. A bloody civil war ensued between him and another general, Sulla, which ended with Marius's defeat in 80 BCE. From this point forward, military leaders understood that the pathway to power was through controlling the loyalty of their troops, Roman Republican values be damned. This created a situation in which "[Roman generals] *thought in the short term. They took spectacular risks, attacked Rome's neighbors without the permission of Senate or people, handed over conquered territories to be exploited by their political allies, and gave little thought to the long-term security of Rome*"[37]. Chaos at home and abroad would characterize the final century of Roman Republicanism.

The political and military turmoil spawned by Marius and Sulla created a ripple effect which rocked the Roman world, leading to another infamous civil war between Pompey and Julius Caesar. Caesar defeated Pompey in 48 BCE, declared himself dictator for life, and was, like the Gracchi brothers, murdered by the Senate in 44 BCE. Caesar's death did not result in the Republican restoration many Roman elites had envisioned and would soon engulf the Mediterranean in yet another civil war, this time between the nephew and adopted son of Caesar Octavian and rival Marc Antony. Octavian ultimately defeated Antony at the battle of Actium in 31 BCE, and Antony would commit suicide the follwing year. Actium marked the end of civil war but also the Roman Republic. Octavian, who

---

36. Ferguson, *Backgrounds*, p. 24

37. Woolf, *Rome*, p. 5

would later take the name Augustus, emerged as the Mediterranean's most power-ful man, and he sought to reestablish order over what had been nearly unmitigated disruption.[38] Through political genius and pure power, Octavian would oversee the transition of Rome from a fragile Republic to the greatest empire in human history. Woolf summarizes the life and legacy of Augustus perfectly: "*The long reign of the first emperor, Augustus—he died in AD 14—is the fulcrum of Roman history. Before him there was the Republic: after him only emperors*"[39].

Cleaning up the wreckage strewn by nearly one hundred years of war and political subterfuge would not be easy, but the deft and cunning statesman was more than up to the task. While it was clear to everyone that Octavian was the master of the world, conservative factions in the Senate needed to be reassured that, at least nominally, Roman political president wouldn't be breached. It was imperative Octavian had support from the governing class, and by appealing to Republican sentiments he won the hearts and minds of reluctant politicians. The borders of Roman land, some of which had become porous due to neglect during the civil wars, needed shoring up. Most importantly, Octavian needed to restore order and stability, an important objective for both citizen and provincial alike.[40] The Senate granted Octavian the title 'Augustus' in 27 BCE, a nebulous term which was categorically imprecise but insinuated he possessed more-than-human qualities. The imperial cult, a significant force in Roman political propaganda during the first century CE but also sometimes severely overexaggerated in New Testament scholarship, can trace its history back to Augustus. As an act of brilliant political posturing, Augustus accepted another title, *princeps*. Meaning 'chief citizen', Augustuus wisely balanced his unique position of authority with his Roman citizenship, a gesture of nominal equality with his senatorial colleagues.. This posturing allowed him to assuage conservative fears while steadily accumulating more political power.[41]

With both public and political support behind him, Augustus went about the task of securing the borders and promoting peace and order. He engaged in military campaigns of conquest which quelled unrest. Roman provinces through-out the Mediterranean became more effectively managed and were governed in a systematic manner, greatly improving many of the haphazard political arrange-ments which had become common during the civil wars. Many Roman politi-cians and aristocrats were appointed as provincial governors or had a large hand in

---

38. Ferguson, *Backgrounds*, pp. 24-26

39. Woolf, *Rome*, p. 5

40. Ferguson, *Backgrounds*, p. 26

41. Ferguson, *Backgrounds*, pp. 27-29

administering Roman provinces. Opportunities for political advancement created bonds of loyalty between the Roman elite and their august *princeps*. Augustus granted control of the Roman army back to the government, paying Roman soldiers directly from the treasury and sealing fidelity to the Roman state instead of individual generals. He secured the Mediterranean, improved infrastructure, and, most importantly, created a perception of peace and stability for millions of people living under Roman rule. The *Pax Romana* wasn't just a theory, it was reality. The accomplishments of Augustus were so profound that for the next several hundred years his imperial system would endure. Although his immediate successors, Tiberius (14-37 CE), Caligula (37-41 CE), Claudius (41-54 CE), and Nero (54-68 CE) were never able to fully emulate his accomplishments, the structures of government put in place by Augustus remained uncontested. After Augustus, few envisioned a return to Republicanism. As Woolf puts it, *"from this point on, the question was always simply Who should be emperor?"*[42].

With the proliferation of empire criticism in New Testament scholarship during the last thirty years, one might conclude that all Jews and Christians were vehemently opposed to Roman imperial rule. Certainly scholars like Horley, Moxnes, and Wright, with more than one eye open to the modern political consequences of their scholarship and operating within the prevailing nineteenth-century framework of authoritarian socialism, have tended to oversimplify the complex nature of Jewish and Christian attitudes towards Rome. Augustus, it was widely perceived, had ushered in an age of unprecedented peace for which many in the empire were thankful: *"The early Roman empire was a world at peace. Warfare was minor in scale, and emperors rarely had difficulty in restricting it to the frontiers. The economy and population grew. The number of Romans increased as provincial aristocrats, former soldiers, and freed slaves were granted citizenship . . . new technologies of architecture and manufacturing spread in the provinces . . . Shared cultures of bathing, of education, of eating emerged in the cities of the empire. Even the poorest spectated at gladiatorial combats, beast hunts, athletic festivals, and other ceremonies."*[43] Compared to the tumultuous first century BCE, post-Augustan Rome was peaceful, stable, and prosperous.

Ferguson comments on the significance of these developments for early Christianity: *"The contributions of Augustus of significance for early Christianity include peace, economic prosperity, improved communications, stable government and a sense of renewal . . . There was a strong sense of a new beginning, an old era of upheaval and warfare ended and a new era of peace and prosperity beginning. Christian authors*

---

42. Woolf, *Rome*, pp. 6-7

43. Woolf, *Rome*, pp. 7-8

later concurred with this sentiment, but saw in it an even deeper meaning, for Jesus had been born under Augusts's reign"[44]. This complicates the oftentimes one-dimensional picture which has been painted by many New Testament scholars eager to use Rome as a negative cipher in support of their preferred brand of contemporary authoritarianism, but as a historical reality many within the new Roman imperial order appreciated at least some of the benefits it provided. While early Christian writers clearly portrayed the Roman empire as a new Babylon[45], believed Jesus is the one true king[46], and taught that the kingdom of God had come[47], it is entirely within the realm of historical possibility that the new imperial order was preferable to the old Republican one. Instead of starting with the assumption that the earliest believers were all angrily antagonistic to every facet of Roman rule, the evidence is more complicated. Perhaps the earliest Christians had mixed feelings about Roman imperialism. Oakes highlights this dynamic perfectly: "*The list of Christian attitudes to Rome that I have arrived at is the following . . . awe, appreciation, resentment, contempt, denial of ultimate authority, and expectation of overthrow*"[48]. As we will see in due course, this accurately encapsulates the image of Rome presented in the New Testament. Immediately after becoming the most powerful man on the planet, Caesar Augustus set about the task of organizing a vast empire. It is to this imperial political restructuring we will now turn.

Roman Political Administration

In 27 BCE Augustus passed the Acts of Settlement, aimed at streamlining provincial administration. The Roman empire was divided into two types of provinces, senatorial and imperial, and regions not under direct provincial control were administered by client-kings loyal to the Roman state. The Roman *provincia* was not simply a geographical entity but denoted a particular set of responsibilities designated to the Roman officials or allies who oversaw them.[49] Senatorial provinces were administered by either proconsuls or proprietors who had risen to the heights of political power in Rome. These provinces had fully accepted Roman authority and would not threaten Roman rule, therefore the Romans felt no need to station large amounts of troops in these areas. Propraetors or proconsuls, which

---

44. Ferguson, *Backgrounds*, p. 30

45. 1 Peter 5:13; Revelation 17:5, 18:1-3

46. Acts 2:36, Philippians 2:9-11, Revelation 1:5

47. Mark 1:14-15, Acts 28:31, 1 Thessalonians 2:12, Revelation 11:15

48. Oakes, *Empire*, pp. 157-158

49. Beard, Mary. 2015. *SPQR: A History of Ancient Rome*. Liveright. p. 196

are mentioned three times in Acts[50], possessed the *imperium*, meaning they were able to make political decisions without the consent of the Senate or emperor. So long as they didn't brutally subject or defraud provincials and maintained peace in their provinces, the administrators were granted broad political autonomy.[51]

Imperial provinces, on the other hand, were mostly located near the borders of the Roman empire. Most of the Roman legions, which Augustus had placed under direct imperial control, were stationed in these provinces, mainly to provide security and prevent political unrest. The boundaries of Rome needed protection, as the people who lived on the margins of the empire were more likely to ask hard questions about the legitimacy of Roman rule. The imperial provinces were administered by either legates (in provinces where troops were stationed) or procurators/prefects. Both held *imperium* and were given the right to intervene in local affairs when they believed it was necessary. Procurators, such as the notorious Pontius Pilate, were generally in command of locally-assembled auxiliary troops and were sent to govern smaller areas which presented political obstacles to Roman imperial rule. Judea was one such region for much of the first century.[52]

Many territories in the eastern Mediterranean were governed by client-kings. These were local rulers who had demonstrated fidelity to the Roman government and were entrusted with maintaining order. Since the Greek east was culturally diverse, keeping local leaders in place allowed the Romans to rule without upsetting the native population; they were less suspicious in general of client-kings than of direct Roman governors. Judea oscillated between rule under client-kings (the dynasty of Herod, for instance, ruled Judea from 40 BCE-6 CE and again between 41-44 CE) and Roman procurators (the critical period between 7-40 CE and after 44 CE). The dynamics of imperial Rule in Judea and Galilee are of great importance for understanding the first-century Jewish context in which Jesus proclaimed the kingdom of God.[53]

While provincial governors were granted the *imperium* and invested with the full authority of Roman imperial power, much actual political decision making was delegated to local officials in cities throughout the empire. "*The Roman empire, as far as power and government were concerned, was a collection of cities*"[54]. Jeffers concurs, noting "*the Romans governed thought the cities of the Empire . . . In some respects it is best to think of the Empire as a collection of cities of varying sizes that controlled*

---

50. Acts 13:7-12, 18:12, and 19:38

51. Jeffers, *Greco-Roman World*, p. 112

52. Jeffers, *Greco-Roman World*, p. 113

53. Jeffers, *Greco-Roman World*, pp. 113-114

54. Ferguson, *Backgrounds*, p. 40

the farmland around them"⁵⁵. Cities throughout the Roman empire were divided into four main types: colonies, municipalities, temple cities, and Hellenistic cities. Colonies and municipalities (which were also known as 'free' cities) had the closest ties to Rome. Colonies such as Corinth or Philippi were founded and managed by Roman citizens, exempt from most forms of taxation, and possessed a Roman constitution. Municipalities (free cities) had allied with Rome at some point in the past, and the local government was usually left in place to manage the city's affairs. While residents of these cities were not necessarily granted Roman citizenship they received an exemption from tribute taxes and did not have to defer to the provincial governor. As long as Rome trusted the city's leaders to keep the peace and remain loyal, municipal free cities retained their political autonomy. Athens, which Paul visits in Acts 17, is the quintessential example of a free city.⁵⁶

Temple cities like Jerusalem were generally granted certain privileges based on local customs, and the priesthood and other local officials were left in charge of local affairs. When Jesus is brought before Caiaphas the high priest and, in the words of Mark, "*all the teachers, the chief priests, and the elders and the teachers of the law*"⁵⁷, the watching crowds would have properly viewed them as 'political' authorities even though Pilate, the Roman procurator, retained his *imperium*. The false modern assumption that the Jewish leadership acted as purely 'religious' figures while the Roman governor was the real 'political' authority is not historically viable. We will discuss the complexities of political rule in Judea below. Hellenistic cities, the final of the four broad types of Roman cities, were culturally Greek but had been absorbed into the Roman orbit, and many of them were allowed to follow traditional customs as long as taxes were paid and the residents were at peace.⁵⁸ Paul would visit several of these cities on his missionary journeys.

While the provincial system enabled the Romans to effectively control a large and diverse empire, its primary function was to facilitate peace and the payment of taxes. Provincial governors were given the power of *imperium* and accountable to the emperor and Senate, but much of the daily management was delegated to local authorities centered in major cities throughout the empire. Roman public law was not automatically applied to every resident living in the provinces, and many legal matters were adjudicated through regional precedent and customs. Local courts handled much of the jurisdiction, and, as with the trials of Jesus and Paul, determined whether a legal case was significant enough to bring before the governor.

---

55. Jeffers, *Greco-Roman World*, p. 115

56. Jeffers, *Greco-Roman World*, pp. 116-117

57. Mark 14:53; see also Matthew 26:57 and Luke 22:66

58. Jeffers, *Greco-Roman World*, p. 117-118

The purpose of these trials was to decide which charges, if any, would have necessitated Roman intervention. Cases which local courts wanted settled with capital punishment were ultimately decided by the governor, while lesser punishments could in many circumstances be issued without his consent. [59] The irony in this political arrangement, significant for many New Testament texts, is that while the Roman authorities held absolute power, most of the political decisions were highly decentralized, made by local leaders following local customs.

Jeffers succinctly describes the reality of provincial government during the early imperial period: "*The small staff of a provincial governor could not hope to and never intended to directly govern the provinces. Rome did not care how local cities and regions in the provinces were governed, so long as the taxes were collected and allegiance to Rome remained firm. In this sense the Empire was an association of over a thousand cities ruled indirectly by Rome. Direct government normally was left to provincials who Rome had co-opted into its system*"[60] The Romans were less concerned with justice and interested mostly in maintaining the imperial order. The story of Gallio, proconsul of Achaia, ignoring the complaints of local Jewish leaders regarding Paul because Gallio believed it should be settled according to Jewish law[61] is a perfect example of this dynamic.[62] The Romans ruled the Mediterranean by a heavy hand with a light touch. So long as peace was kept and taxes paid, the Romans mostly remained distant, disinterested rulers. Any threat to peace or revenue, however, would be swiftly neutralized by the Roman sword. This is a lesson the people of Judea would painfully learn some forty years after the death of Jesus.

Taxation

The vast Roman empire was expensive to maintain. Like all imperial powers, balancing an extensive budget became the primary concern of Roman politicians. Subjected people were naturally expected to foot the bill, and because of the millions of inhabitants spread throughout the Mediterranean, the Roman tax system was complex and in a constant state of flux.[63] Historians estimate that the average annual revenue generated by Roman taxation was between one hundred and two hundred million denarii[64], and, as Rome began slowing its military expansion,

---

59. Ferguson, *Backgrounds*, pp. 64-65

60. Jeffers, *Greco-Roman*, p. 115

61. Acts 18:12-17

62. Jeffers, *Greco-Roman*, p. 115

63. Woolf, *Rome*, p. 185

64. The denarius was a standard Roman silver coin.

taxation became the primary source of state income. The expenses of the more precarious imperial provinces, where Rome stationed many of its legions, were paid for directly out of the Emperor's personal treasury, keeping soldiers unwaveringly loyal to Rome instead of some charismatic field commander. Augustus had learned a valuable lesson during the final days of the Republic: loyalty could usually be bought for the right price.[65]

The *Pax Romana* was expensive. Augustus knew this and sought to streamline the process of taxation throughout the Roman empire. Roman citizens were exempt from many forms of taxation, so tax burdens rested primarily on the shoulders of non-citizen provincials. There were two types of direct taxes (known as *triubuta*) levied on imperial subjects. The first, called the *tributum soli*, was a property tax placed foremost on land as well as slaves, houses, and ships. The second, called the *tributum capitis*, was a head tax placed on all adult provincial residents. Periodic censuses undertaken by the Roman government[66] accounted for the *tributum capitis*.[67] Besides these direct taxes, Rome levied several indirect taxes on its provinces. Indirect taxes included customs or tolls on roads, imports and exports, the transportation of goods, and harbor dues. Cities throughout the empire could impose local taxes, and as long as Rome received its cut cities were entitled to keep any excess revenues generated by these taxes. Jews, both in Judea and in the diaspora, were required to pay taxes for the construction of Herod's Temple and to support the priestly class in Jerusalem.[68]

The Jesus tradition as recorded in the synoptic gospels consistently portrays Jesus consorting with tax collectors.[69] The calling of Levi/Matthew[70] results in Matthew becoming a member of Jesus's inner circle, one of the twelve disciples.[71] Luke has a unique parable in which Jesus contrasts the righteousness of a Pharisees with that of a tax collector where the tax collector repents and receives God's mercy.[72] Besides Jesus's willingness to associate himself with tax collectors, the tradition also reveals this was perceived by many who witnessed it, particularly his opponents from the Judean upper class, as a suspicious and controversial decision. Why was this the case?

---

65. Jeffers, *Greco-Roman*, p. 143

66. Of which Luke 2:1-5 is the most famous biblical example.

67. Ferguson, *Backgrounds*, p. 95; Jeffers, *Greco-Roman*, pp. 142-143

68. Jeffers, *Greco-Roman*, p. 144

69. Mark 2:15, Matthew 11:19, and Luke 5:30, for example.

70. Mark 2:13-14, Matthew 9:9, Luke 5:27-28

71. Matthew 10:3, see also Luke 6:15

72. Luke 18:9-14

While direct taxes were collected by imperial officers, most indirect taxes were collected by *telonai*, relatively wealthy men who would contract with local rulers and gather taxes paid to Rome. Both tax collectors mentioned by name in the gospels, Levi/Matthew and Zacchaeus[73], were most likely employed by Herod Antipas, the Roman client-king who ruled Galilee from 4 BCE—39 CE. They were not employed directly by Rome but rather assessed what needed to be paid and enforced the collection. Collectors of indirect taxes were stationed along the many trade routes which spanned the region. They were often compensated on a percentage basis, meaning that efficiency in assessing and collecting taxes could lead to financial gain.[74] Tax collectors were widely perceived as turncoats who betrayed their fellow Jews by aligning themselves with the occupying Roman forces. The average Palestinian Jew would have viewed tax collectors as traitors, precisely why Jesus was met with suspicion for associating with them.[75] Although he is working within an implicitly Marxist framework and overstates his case, Douglas Oakman correctly observes how the Roman tax system was *"always biased towards the elites"* and had the tendency to keep those in poverty perpetually poor[76]. If a prophet from Galilee were to proclaim *"The time is fulfilled, and the kingdom of God is at hand; repent and believe in the gospel"*[77], his audience just might have expected the abolition of Roman taxation and swift judgment for colluding tax collectors. Taxes were essential to the maintenance of Roman imperial power and an inevitable part of life for those living within the first-century Mediterranean world. Any hope for the abolition of taxation was, for most, little more than a fleeting fantasy. Payment of taxes reassured the Romans a region was not seditious. Those who wanted to keep peace with Rome, even if for purely pragmatic reasons, paid their taxes. The alternative was far too dangerous.

Agriculture, Commerce, Trade, and Banking

The Neolithic Revolution, which began around 10,000 BCE, was the most consequential turning point in human history. Until then, humans had been unable to settle in one place and spent much of their short lives hunting for food or gathering what grew naturally from the earth. Settling in one place for too long was suicide, guarenteeing an eventually depletion of the food supply. With the invention

---

73. Luke 19:1-10

74. Ferguson, *Backgrounds*, pp. 95-96

75. Jeffers, *Greco-Roman*, p. 146

76. Oakman, *Political Aims*, pp. 62-64

77. Mark 1:15

of farming, humans learned to cultivate a plot of land and produce crops year after year. This allowed for the construction of permanent settlements and eventually led to the formation of antiquity's greatest empires. Although agricultural techniques would continue to develop over the millenia, labor-intensive farm work required a majority of the human population to produce enough food. Without large numbers of agricultural workers, the human race would have starved.

Paul's letters were written to churches which had been formed in some of Rome's largest cities. Acts records his missionary journeys to those cities, and Revelation was addressed to seven churches in Asia minor located in significant urban centers. Absent modern farming technology, however, most of the Roman population, like nearly every civilization between the Neolithic and Industrial Revolutions, worked in agriculture. Around ninety percent of the Mediterranean labor force was devoted to farming and herding.[78] A flourishing agricultural base made life in Roman cities possible. Farming was essential to the growth of Roman imperial power: "*The olive, the vine, grain, and sheep were the basis of the agricultural economy of the Mediterranean world*"[79]. Many of the parables found in the Gospels accurately reflect the mechanisms of the first century agrarian economy.[80] Many small farms were privately owned and operated with supplemental labor provided by either hired day laborers or slaves. Many Mediterranean farms operated above subsistence and sold the surplus in local markets. Larger farms would employ higher numbers of day laborers, but it became increasingly common among the Roman elite to rely on slave labor since slaves worked longer and were not subject to the military draft. The Romans valued and respected wealth derived from agriculture, and large farming estates could be a source of tremendous economic income. Herding was also an important part of the agrarian economy, with sheep, goats, pigs, and cattle as the most prominent livestock. In general the Roman elite were suspicious of herders and viewed their profession with contempt. The fishing industry could also be profitable but geographically confined to regions near major bodies of water as in Galilee.[81] Much of the Roman food supply, particularly grain, came from Egypt and Africa.[82]

Given that the Roman empire was a constellation of cities which were supported by their surrounding farmland, Douglass Oakman explains how Roman elites were able to accumulate land by increasing taxes and issuing unpayable loans

---

78. Jeffers, *Greco-Roman*, p. 20

79. Ferguson, *Backgrounds*, p. 82

80. Mark 12:1-9, Matthew 20:1-6, and Luke 15:11-31 are excellent examples.

81. Jeffers, *Greco-Roman*, pp. 19-22

82. Ferguson, *Backgrounds*, p. 82

which would force small landowners into debt, causing them to sell their land and become day laborers. In Roman Palestine and Herodian Galilee this policy created a situation in which Jews grew increasingly resentful towards the upper classes. The message of Jesus, who preached in rural villages directly afflicted by predatory land acquisitions, was, according to Oakman, mostly directed against the ruling elite and the social dislocations caused by their economic policies.[83] Based on our historical analysis of the early Roman imperial period this thesis, although exaggerated, is entirely plausible. While there were several historical and theological reasons for Jewish discontent towards Roman rule, the Herodians and Jerusalem political class enforced political and economic policies which caused real, tangible harm. When Jesus, as a part of his prophetic proclamation of the kingdom of God, announced that *"many who are first will be last, and the last, first"*[84], it is likely Jesus had these predatory policies in mind and that his audience would have perceived him to be addressing them. Oakman employs his theory as a biblical critique of *"global capitalism"*[85], but as the Austrian school elucidates these economic arrangements, which are imposed upon society by the political class, can hardly be classified as *'capitalism'*. This is a clear example of good historical research being muddled by unclear economic thinking. His point, however, stands: the Roman economy is based on agricultural production, and the Roman elites constructed policies which placed them in charge of Roman land.

While agriculture dominated Mediterranean economic activity, cities were the cultural, social, and political heart of the Roman empire. Most Mediterranean cities were built around a central marketplace, often a large, rectangular open area surrounded by shops and offices. Not only would city residents meet in the marketplace to shop and conduct business, they would also converse with friends, share news, and come in contact with philosophers spreading new ideas.[86] Although Roman elites were suspicious of the trades, most city-dwellers were involved in manufacturing. Anyone traveling through a Roman city would see rows of shops specializing in the production of pottery, clothing, tools, and other manufactured goods, while restaurants, barber shops, and similar services were readily accessible. By far the most important industry in the Roman world was weaving; several businesses producing cloth could be found in nearly every Mediterranean city. While it was difficult to become rich in manufacturing and the lack of modern mechanization mostly limited production to local markets, many urban residents

---

83. Oakman, *Political Aims*, pp. 35-43

84. Mark 10:31

85. Oakman, *Political Aims*, p. 137

86. Ferguson, *Backgrounds*, p. 83

in the Roman empire made a living producing and selling goods. Workshops were usually on the ground floor of a large apartment complex or the front room in an artisan's home. Workshops might be converted to living quarters at the end of a day's work, and families usually lived and worked in the spaces they owned or rented.[87] Many of the churches to whom Paul wrote would have met in the houses and workshop spaces of successful merchants.[88]

The era of peace ushered in by Augustus made it safer, easier, and cheaper to trade and travel than ever before. Even though merchants and artisans generally produced goods and services which were sold in local markets, the relative safety of Roman roads and travel routes caused an explosion of trade throughout the Empire, much of which was based around exotic imports from places as far away as India and China. The Romans built thousands of miles of quality roads and cleared the Mediterranean of pirates; these accomplishments facilitated trade at a rate which was unprecedented in antiquity. Travellers would follow these routes, and Paul's missionary journeys recorded in Acts, far from being haphazardly planned, correspond directly to land and sea passages commonly used for travel and trade in the early imperial period.[89] Unsurprisingly, elite Romans viewed trading with scorn despite the fact that some savvy investors quietly might make a large profit on commercial trade, and adventurous traders were one of the few groups of people in antiquity with the potential for upward social mobility. The dirty business of trade was also extremely lucrative.[90]

Banking was an important industry in the Mediterranean world, although, much like today, the issuance of loans often led to crippling debt and the confiscation of property as collateral by city elites.[91] Many Romans who lived above subsistence would keep some money either in temples (where they sought protection from the gods), bury it in remote locations, or keep it in a home safe, most would deposit much of their money in banks with the intent of earning interest. Regional institutions such as the temple in Jerusalem offered banking services[92]. Many wealthy Roman families acted as independent banks, lending and investing with interest for commercial or personal profit. Many wealthy lenders would forgo

---

87. Jeffers, *Greco-Roman*, pp. 24-27

88. As, for example, when the Phillipian Christians meet in the house of a merchant named Lydia (Acts 16:14, 40).

89. Ferguson, *Backgrounds*, pp. 86-90

90. Jeffers, *Greco-Roman*, p. 22-23

91. Oakman, *Political Aims*, pp. 39-40

92. The temple 'money changers' found in Mark 11:15 and Matthew 21:12 were functional bankers.

charging interest but could call in their debt at any time; creditors, backed by local courts, could confiscate property from and even enslave those who failed to pay back their debt.[93] The banking system was rigged in favor of the elites by a legal system which privileged wealth. Some things never change.

Despite increasing prosperity throughout the Mediterranean in the first century, most farmers, artisans, and merchants lived at or just above subsistence. An injury, increase in rent, or bad harvest could lead to financial ruin. Free laborers were paid low wages by their wealthy employers who spent massive amounts of money on public benefactions such as games, festivals, and buildings.[94] This secured respect and loyalty from the population to the wealthy patron and was often craftily dispensed to garner social or political capital. Not only were gifts lavished on cities as a whole, the wealthy gave money to specific individuals in exchange for personal fidelity. Benefaction was a critical part of Roman social life, and as a system in which patrons would bestow material benefits (including money) upon grateful clients without expecting direct financial reciprocation it is a perfect example of the 'embedded economics' of the Roman world as well as, being public-facing, a 'political' act. Known as the patron-client system, I will briefly explain how it functions.

Benefaction and the Patron-Client System

The "*definition of patronage is complex but its core characteristics are that it is a non-market relationship between socially unequal people in which dissimilar benefits are exchanged*"[95]. Patronage was essential to Roman society. Building on Oakes's definition, Ferguson offers a thorough explanation of the patron client relationship, where benefactions were exchanged for loyalty: "*Patronage was a reciprocal relationship, in which both patron and client had duties to each other, was a personal and not a business or commercial relationship, existed between parties of different status, and was a voluntary (not a legal) relationship that could be initiation by either party, but the social conventions were stronger than any regulations of law.*"[96] At its core, the patron-client system was about giving and receiving. Often these arrangements were political in the wider sense of the term *politea*. A wealthy patron would give gifts of money, food, or clothing to a less wealthy patron, and in return the patron

---

93. Jeffers, *Greco-Roman*, pp. 23-24

94. Ferguson, *Backgrounds*, p. 85

95. Oakes, *Empire*, p. 109

96. Ferguson, *Backgrounds*, p. 76

would provide the client with loyalty, honor, and social prestige.[97] 'Benefaction' is the term used to describe the daily handout received by clients from their patrons.

This system was especially pronounced in urban environments, where wealthy, powerful Romans sought to expand their influence and prestige. Clients appeared at the homes of their patrons every morning, offering them honor, and requesting gifts. Clients were expected to show unquestioning loyalty to their patrons in matters personal and political, and a major status symbol for the Roman upper class was the number of clients one held in their retinue. Freed slaves regularly became clients of their former masters, and the daily gifts of money or food granted by the patron would ensure reciprocal loyalty. Wealthy patrons might also extend dinner invitations to clients on certain holidays or provide them with legal assistance. Although formal patronage was usually limited to benefactions given by those of a much higher social status to those far below, the ethos of patronage and benefaction influenced all social relationships: *"Everyone from slave to aristocrat felt bound to display respect to someone more powerful than himself, up to the emperor."*[98]

Archaeological evidence suggests that the patron-client system even determined the layout of large cities. Marketplaces at the center of cities often included statues and inscriptions dedicated to Romans who had provided benefactions for that city, and the presence of imperial busts reminded those visiting the market that the Roman emperor was the Mediterranean's chief patron. Large houses, in which the most prominent patrons would live, were often scattered throughout Roman cities, making it easier for their clients to visit them each morning.[99] The houses themselves were architecturally designed to accommodate the meeting of clients, with large doors and reception rooms facilitating a daily flow of guests. It is quite possible that some of Paul's wealthy companions, such as Aristarchus[100], might have been patrons themselves.[101] Given the cultural ubiquity of the practice it is quite possible that Paul's desire to offer the gospel without expecting direct financial compensation[102] was in part a deliberate maneuver to avoid the social obligations accompanying benefaction, and, as I will argue in a later chapter, lies behind Paul's instructions to the Thessalonian church that they *"work with* [their]

---

97. Winter, *Welfare*, p. 46

98. Ferguson, *Backgrounds*, p. 67

99. Oakes, *Empire*, pp. 110-113

100. Acts 19:29, 20:4

101. Winter, *Welfare*, p. 46

102. 1 Corinthians 9:15-18

hands"[103] and "[those] *not willing to work . . .* [are] *. . . not to eat, either*"[104]. It is important to be aware of these deeply embedded cultural expectations. Despite their unfamiliarity to modern thinkers, patronage and benefaction were crucial social assumptions in antiquity and are implicit in several New Testament texts.

Slavery

Another universal social and economic assumption in antiquity was the legitimacy of slavery. It is well-documented that slavery in the Greco-Roman world was structurally dissimilar to the racial slavery of antebellum America, but it was far from glamorous or desirable. The Romans didn't necessarily believe that slaves were inferior by nature and did not consider skin color to be of any particular significance. Slavery was not deemed respectable and there were certain jobs slaves were *not* allowed to perform because upper class Romans believed they should be reserved for citizens of higher status. Like every civilization in antiquity, slavery was an accepted fact of life. There was no organized opposition to the institution of slavery. Even among early Christians, who believed all social status was relativized before God, no one seriously considered the possibility of abolition.[105]

A person became a slave by being captured in war, left for exposure[106], to pay off a debt, as punishment for a crime, or born of a slave. Slaves had no legal rights and were subject to the whims of their masters. Slaves performed a wide variety of jobs from teaching, craftworking, mining, farming, and administrative work. Those who were fortunately assigned to bureaucratic roles or worked for the Roman elite might find themselves living comfortably and exercising power on behalf of their masters. Slaves doing menial work in the fields or the mines, however, had a much shorter life expectancy and lived in conditions which were nothing short of atrocious. Most slaves fell somewhere between these two extreme ends of the spectrum.[107] Slaves were considered part of the Roman household but were not on equal footing with family. The male head of the household, called the *paterfamilias*, held nearly absolute power over his slaves. While many masters had

---

103. 1 Thessalonians 4:11

104. 2 Thessalonians 3:10

105. Jeffers, *Greco-Roman*, pp. 226-227

106. 'Exposure' is the practice of abandoning unwanted babies or children in a publicly accessible area. Romans who took in exposed babies raised them as slaves.

107. Ferguson, *Backgrounds*, pp. 59-60

respectful or even affectionate relationships with their slaves, the social imbalance between slave and free was always assumed by both parties.[108]

Roman citizens routinely freed their slaves. While freed slaves would gain the title of 'freedman' or 'freedwoman', many of them were also granted citizenship. The possibility of emancipation was an incentive for slaves to work hard and cultivate positive relationships with their masters, and they were even permitted to work on the side, earn money, and purchase freedom on their own. When freed slaves regularly become either employees or clients of their former masters, offering them social and political support in exchange for a salary or benefactions. Once freed, former slaves could rise through the ranks of Roman society and attain positions of prominence.[109] Slavery was still awful, of course, but as a system it was much more diverse than its institutional manifestation in early American history.

Statements found in passages like Galatians 3:28, where Paul claims that *"in Christ there are . . . no slave and free"*, were radical in his time and, as we will see, have massive yet often unexplored consequences for the way we interpret passages about political power in the New Testament. Paul's letter to Philemon was written to a slave owner regarding his slave, Onesimus, who befriended Paul and became a believer. Paul writes to Philemon that he should take Onesimus back *"no longer as a slave, but more than a slave, a beloved brother"*[110]. While Paul is under no illusion that his instructions to Philemon will lead to the abolition of slavery (or even the manumission of Onesimus), it challenges the social value of slavery to its core. After Peter instructs his audience to *"submit to every human institution, for the Lord's sake"*[111], he issues advice about political authorities in 2:13-17, slaves and masters in 2:18-25, and wives and husbands in 3:1-7. Nowhere does he challenge the existence of these relational arrangements, but he certainly redefines them in a way which poses a deep structural defiance of their social value. In Christ, slaves and wives have the same status as masters and husbands, even if the culturally-enforced hierarchies remain intact. Modern readers are quick to congratulate themselves for living in societies which have rejected slavery and enforced patriarchal marriages. Rightly so. Why can't we extend this insight to Peter's statements on the relationship between the government and the governed. As I will argue at several junctures in later chapters, I think it's time we should.

---

108. Jeffers, *Greco-Roman*, pp. 228-229

109. Jeffers, *Greco-Roman*, pp. 232-233

110. Philemon 1:16

111. 1 Peter 2:13

The Composition of Early House Churches

To round out this chapter we will examine the socio-economic composition of house churches in Greco-Roman cities. Paul issues two statements in his letters which provide us with information about church demographics. In 1 Corinthians 1:26, Paul says to the church *"consider your calling, brethren, that there were not many wise according to the flesh, not many mighty, not many noble"*, implying that most of his audience was not from the educated upper class. We should take him at his word. Conversely, in Philippians 4:22, Paul relates a greeting to the Philippians from *"those of Caesar's household"*, which could theoretically be referring to slaves but may also mean there were those in Paul's churches who came from the upper crust of Roman society. Paul in 1 Corinthians 1:26 says *"not many"* were wise, might or noble, but not 'all'.

Peter Oakes has attempted to address this question in detail. Based on archeological research conducted in Pompeii and other sites around Italy, he estimates based on the size of craftworker homes, the likely place where urban believers gathered to worship in Greek or Roman cities, the average size of a congregation would be around thirty people. This would include the craftworker, his family, and their slaves, other householders, family members of householders who were not a part of the church, some slaves, freedmen, and tenants, as well as some which were homeless.[112] Oakes infers that the craftworker with the biggest home would also be the wealthiest person in the congregation unless a member of a weather family whose *paterfamilias* did not participate in the church attended. Envisioning these churches as a group of around thirty people not from the upper classes of Roman society does not preclude social stratification: *"The key impression is of social diversity and social hierarchy, even when the wealthiest member is only a craftworker with a modest household . . . [this is] a way of raising possibilities for what he [Paul] intended in terms of the practical application of what he was writing"*[113].

Oakes spends the rest of his chapter exploring how people from different social or economic stratums would have heard Romans 12; slaves and craftworkers, for instance, likely walked away with differing impressions about what Paul's instruction meant for them. Oakes rightly underscores the difficulty of making interpretive decisions based on this evidence, but it is important enough to note that Paul understood his audience and would tailor his message to address their concerns. Reminding ourselves that the early Jesus movement was mostly (but not

---

112. Oakes, Peter. 2009. *Reading Romans in Pompeii*. Fortress Press. p. 96
113. Oakes, *Pompeii*, p. 98

entirely) relegated to the urban lower and working classes can inform our perspective on political and economic contexts in the New Testament.

With a firmer grasp on the historical, cultural, political, economic, and social contexts of the early Roman imperial period influencing the New Testament, we must now explore its other foundational context: Judaism. In fact, if we were to rank the cultural influences of Judaism or Greco-Roman culture on the New Testament, Judaism has a more pervasive impact. The Christian cannon is undeniably embedded in the thought-world of ancient Judaism and our sources simply cannot be comprehended without reference to their Jewish context. We now turn our attention to ancient Judaism.

CHAPTER 6 | Judaism and Empire

The Hope of Israel

Thus says the Lord of hosts, the God of Israel, to all the exiles who I have sent into exile from Jerusalem to Babylon . . . Seek the welfare of the city where I have sent you into exile, and pray to the Lord on its behalf; for in its welfare you will have welfare.

Jeremiah 29:4-7

Though Babylon should ascend to the heavens, And though she should fortify her lofty stronghold, From Me destroyers will come to her, declares the Lord.

Jeremiah 51:53

INTRODUCTION: SECOND TEMPLE JUDAISM

In 538 BCE, one year after Persian king Cyrus the Great overthrew the mighty Babylonian Empire, a small group of people who had been displaced from Judea by the Babylonians, which had conquered the region between 587-586 BCE, were granted the right of return to their ancestral homeland. Now known as 'Jews', this homecoming under the benevolence of Persian imperial rule was bittersweet. While they were, geographically, back in the land which God had promised their forefathers, Jerusalem, the political and theological capital of the region, was in ruins. The first six chapters of Ezra describe the years following Cyrus's edict and the opposition Jews faced from those living near their land. Against vicious opposition, the Jews began rebuilding the temple in Jerusalem and, under Darius, successor of Cyrus, the project was fully sanctioned by the Persian imperial order.[1]

The period from 516 BCE, when the temple in Jerusalem was reconstructed, to 70 CE, when it was destroyed by Roman armies, is known as "Second Temple

---

1. Ezra 6:1-15

Judaism". It is the historical, social, political, and theological developments which took place during this period that produced the cultural background of Jesus, Paul, and the entire early Christian movement. In order to think clearly about how texts in the New Testament which relate to political and economic issues would have been read in context, it is essential we understand the basic contours of this period. In this chapter we will review the historical events and ideas which defined Second Temple Judaism.

CREATION, COVENANT, EXILE, AND RESTORATION

The Jews remained under Persian rule from 539 BCE until the conquests of Macedonian Alexander the Great in 333 BCE. Cyrus allowed the Jews to return home from their exile in Babylon during 538, facilitating the rebuilding of the second Temple. For his generosity Cyrus becomes the only pagan in the entire Hebrew Bible to be granted the title 'anointed'.[2] The two most important figures in Judaism during the Persian period are Ezra and Nehemiah, each of whom receive eponymous works in the Old Testament. In 458 BCE[3] Ezra leads a wave of exiles back to Jerusalem, teaches and encourages keeping of the Law, and attempts to set firm social boundaries between his Jewish compatriots and their non-Jewish neighbors.[4] Nehemiah, the respected cup-bearer for emperor Artaxerxes I[5], is granted permission to guide two more waves of exiles back to Jerusalem in 445 BCE and 432 BCE.[6] His vocation is similar to that of Ezra's; Nehemiah believes that Israel was unfaithful to their covenant with God by refusing to keep the Law and, as a punishment for disobedience, was sent into exile. In order for God to restore his people they must repent and keep the Law, drawing sharp boundaries between Jews and their pagan neighbors.[7]

Since Israel had been thrust into exile by failing to keep the Law, Ezra and Nehemiah encouraged the Jews to repent and turn back to God, specifically by keeping the Law which He gave to His people through Moses. Ezra, who was "*a*

---

2. Isaiah 45:1; the Greek term for 'anointed', *christos*, is a title universally applied to Jesus in the New Testament. The relevance of this designation will play a major role in advancing the thesis proposed in this book.

3. The dating is contested.

4. Ezra 7-10

5. Nehemiah 1:11-2:8

6. Cohen, Shaye. 2006. *From the Maccabees to the Mishnah*. 2nd ed. Westminster John Knox Press. p. 2

7. Nehemiah 1:4-11

scribe skilled in the Law of Moses, which the Lord God of Israel had given"[8], and had "*set his heart to study the Law of the Lord and to practice it, and to teach His statues and ordinances in Israel*"[9], took upon himself the responsibility of compiling the Pentateuch and teaching it to the people in the land, advocating faithful adherence to the Law and a universal separation from foreigners.[10] This was no innovation or newly created Law code but a restoration of the Law God had given to Israel which they had failed to keep.[11] Ezra would become the priest and scribe of the rebuilt Jerusalem temple while Nehemiah would govern on behalf of the Persians.[12] Together they gathered the people and set out to teach them the Law of Moses.[13] Upon hearing the Law, the Jews "*separated themselves from all foreigners, and stood and confessed their sins and the iniquities of their fathers*"[14]. Nehemiah 9:5-38 contains a stylistic confession which also serves as a succinct overview of several major Old Testament themes which became central to the development of Jewish worldviews during the Second Temple period. As an abbreviated summary of the Old Testament narrative, Nehemiah 9 provides readers with a thematic framework for interpreting how Jews of this period were reading their own scriptures and, most importantly, how they believed God would restore Israel in the future. Any discussion regarding the political or economic consequences of New Testament texts must account for these important pillars of Jewish thought.

Creation and Kingship

The corporate confession of Nehemiah 9 begins with an acknowledgement of God's lordship resulting from His creation of the heavens and the earth.[15] A quote from 9:6 reveals the tight relationship between God's identity as creator and king: "*You alone are the Lord. You have made the heavens . . . The earth and all that is on it*". This confession recalls the twin creation narratives of Genesis 1-2 in which God, after ordering the universe, creates humans in His image and likeness while granting them dominion over all creation.[16] In the context of the ancient Near

---

8. Ezra 7:6

9. Ezra 7:10

10. Bruce, F.F. 1997. *Israel and the Nations.* InterVarsity Press. pp. 101-104

11. Kidner, Derek. 1979. *Ezra and Nehemiah.* InterVarsity Press. pp. 113-114

12. Nehemiah 8:9

13. Nehemiah 8:1-8

14. Nehemiah 9:2

15. Nehemiah 9:5-6

16. Genesis 1:26-28

East, God is depicted as a king or lord who entrusts land within His kingdom to vassals which will rule over it on His behalf.[17] As Stephen Dempster puts it, *"the entire* [creation] *account reflects the sovereign power of the Creator . . . From other ancient Near Eastern creation accounts we learn that creation means enthronement"*[18]. Nehemiah's appeal to God as creator and lord is foundational to the entire biblical narrative and the Second Temple Jewish worldview inherited by New Testament authors. Since God alone created the world, He rightly rules over it as king.

Several passages from the Psalms make this connection explicit. Psalm 10:16 states *"The Lord is King forever and ever, Nations have perished from his land."* Psalm 47:7 concurs: *"For God is the King of all the earth"*. Psalm 93, though short, makes it clear that the God who *"firmly established"* the world also sits upon an everlasting throne.[19] In prescientific societies like the ancient Near East the gods functioned as an explanation for what are now known to be natural phenomenon: the rain, sunshine, crop harvests, war, marriage, and every other aspect of life was explained by appeal to transcendent beings working behind the scene to control and manipulate world events, and offering the proper sacrifices to those gods brought insured security and success. The Israelite tradition outright rejects this conception based on God's unique status as creator and king. The futility of idol worship is mockingly dismissed by Isaiah, who frames his critique of pagan idolatry by asserting that Israel's God created the world and rules over the nations.[20]

While the God of Israel rules over all creation, He is also the rightful king of Israel. The Decalogue, popularly known as the Ten Commandments, is, in the context of the ancient Near East, a classic example of a suzerain-vassal treaty. This is a conventional political tool in antiquity which defines the relationship between an emperor (suzerain) and his subject kings (vassals). Suzerain-vassal treaties include a description of the benefits provided by the suzerain on behalf of the vassal and an outline of the services which would be reciprocally provided by the vassal. Exodus 20:2, in which God reminds Israel that He delivered them from captivity and exhorts them to have *"no other gods"*, would have been recognized by its original audience as a reciprocal suzerain-vassal treaty.[21] This underscores a major theme in the Old Testament: God is the only absolute king and His people are expected to regard Him as such. The question of kingship in the Old Testament and how it shaped the hope of Second Temple Judaism will be discussed in more

---

17. Richter, Sandra. 2008. *The Epic of Eden.* InterVarsity Press. pp. 92-93

18. Dempster, Stephen. 2024. *The Return of the Kingdom.* InterVarsity Press. p. 13

19. Psalm 93:1-2

20. Isaiah 40:12-26

21. Novick, Tzvi. 2018. *An Introduction to The Scriptures of Israel.* Eerdmans. pp. 70-71

detail below, but it is important to note the centrality of divine kingship. While often neglected by casual modern readers, it cannot be divorced from other aspects of Old Testament theology. For Ezra, Nehemiah, and the Second Temple Jewish tradition they helped shape, Israel's only hope was in returning to the God they once rejected. This God had brought everything into being and was the only true king; by appealing to the Lordship of Israel's God at the beginning of Nehemiah's corporate confession, His fundamental identities as creator and king permeate the sad narrative which follows it.

Covenant and Exodus

Nehemiah 9:7-15 recounts three of the most crucial events in Israel's long and storied history: the calling of Abraham, the exodus from Egypt, and the giving of the Law. Abraham was, of course, chosen by God because of his faithfulness. As a result, God makes a covenant with Abraham, promising that his family would grow, become a great nation, and ultimately bless all the families of the earth.[22] God also promises Abraham a large family which will be delivered from oppression[23], and seals the covenant by requiring Abraham and all of his male heirs to undergo circumcision, which becomes the physical mark of God's promise to Abraham.[24] Abraham is the father of all Israel, and the Jews assembled before Ezra and Nehemiah in Jerusalem would have traced their lineage back to him. The author of Nehemiah asserts that God has righteously fulfilled his promises to Abraham.[25]

As foretold by God in Genesis 15, Abraham's family, Israel, finds themselves enslaved in Egypt, but through the prophet Moses God faithfully delivers his people from bondage.[26] God speaks to Moses on Mount Sinai and explains the covenantal relationship He made with Israel: *"Now then, if you will indeed obey My voice and keep My covenant, then you shall be My own possession among all the peoples, for all the earth is Mine; and you shall be to me a kingdom of priests and a holy nation"*[27]. The concept of 'holiness' is a central theme in both the Old and New Testaments. The Hebrew term *'qdš'*, from which the English word 'holy' is translated, refers not to an exceedingly moral person but rather a *status* of being 'set apart'. God is holy,

---

22. Genesis 12:1-3

23. Genesis 15:1-16

24. Genesis 17:1-14

25. Nehemiah 9:8

26. Nehemiah 9:9-12; see Exodus 1-18

27. Exodus 19:5-6

differentiated from the rest of creation, and confers the status of holiness upon his people Israel as a part of the covenant He establishes with them.[28] Abraham's family as a community is set apart for a particular purpose: revealing God's holiness to the world. John and Harvey Walton explain the relationship between covenant and holiness: "*When Yahweh makes the covenant with the Israelites and declares them to be his holy people—that is, declares himself to be their God and thereby declares that his identity will be reflected by and through them—their status changes*"[29].

How, then, does Israel keep covenant with God and live out the status of 'holy' which He conferred upon them? By following His Law. In Exodus 20, as we saw above, God gives the Ten Commandments which serves as a foundation for the rest of the Laws outlined to Israel in Exodus, Leviticus, Numbers, and Deuteronomy. Not only does the Law reveal God's kingship over Israel, it is the foundation of the covenantal obligations owed to Him by Israel. Since God made a covenant with Abraham to give him a family, rescued that family out of Egypt, and conferred upon them the status of 'holy', Israel was to respond by following the Law and, in doing so, revealing God's holiness as creator and king to the pagan world. This is precisely what Israel was called by God to do, and Nehemiah correctly frames God's Law as the climax of the Exodus: "*You gave them just ordinances and true Laws, Good statues and commandments*"[30]. God rescued Israel for a reason, and in response Israel must remain faithful to the covenant by following God's Law.

But, as Nehemiah will show, Israel repeatedly disobeys God. After God delivered Israel out of Egypt and sustained them through the desert, they violated the Law and breached covenant with God. Exodus 32, recounted in Nehemiah 9:18, narrates Israel's construction of an idol as a repudiation of God's rule. Israel is forced to repent and God graciously continues to work with them. This act of defiance serves as a foreshadowing of Israel's future disobedience to God and the covenant. Nevertheless God guides His people through the wilderness and eventually allows them to enter the land which He promised to Abraham.[31]

The Law which Ezra and Nehemiah were attempting to restore in Jerusalem is the covenantal crux of God's relationship with Israel. God called Abraham and his family to be holy, or set apart, and one of the great refrains in Leviticus, which

---

28. Walton, John, and Harvey Walton. 2019. *The Lost World of the Torah*. InterVarsity Press. pp. 54-62

29. Walton and Walton, *Torah*, p. 57

30. Nehemiah 9:13

31. Nehemiah 9:18-25

outlines the Law, is that Israel must "be holy"[32]. There are several places in Leviticus where the author explains the logic behind holiness and the covenant. In Leviticus 20:22-26, Israel is commanded to keep the Law which God has given them. They are not to embrace the customs of the nations which surround them, whom God is going to remove from the promised land, because that would compromise their unique identity and relationship with Him. The Law is what separates Israel from the nations so that they may reveal the creator God to a world which has rejected him. Obedience to the covenant results in God bringing his plans for Israel to fruition[33] while disobedience brings about punishment[34].

Deuteronomy intensifies the language of covenantal obedience. In Deuteronomy 4, Israel is urged to keep the commandments in the Law, with the same pattern of blessing for obedience and punishment for disobedience found in Leviticus. God's wisdom is revealed to the world when Israel keeps covenant: "*So keep and do* [the Law], *for that is your wisdom and your understanding in the sight of the people who will hear all these statues and say, 'Surely this great nation is a wise and understanding people. For what great nation is there that has a god so near to it as the Lord*"[35]. The famous *Shema* is found in Deuteronomy 6:4, "*Hear, O Israel! The Lord is Our God, the Lord is one!*", and is followed by the corollary "*You shall love the Lord your God with all your heart and with all your soul and with all your might*" in 6:5. 'Loving God' means following his Law, a direct extension of creation and kingship. Commenting on the *Shema*, scholar Albert Baylis explains, "*The commitment of Israel to Yahweh also may be summarized by that one word, love. Because Yahweh, the God of Israel, is the one true God, God's people are to pursue total commitment . . . The type of love we are talking about is not a gushy, surface emotion—but a total involvement that demands complete commitment*"[36]. Tzvi Novick agrees, stating "*The love prescribed here and elsewhere in the book of Deuteronomy undoubtedly has an affective or emotional aspect to it, but it involves, first and foremost, exclusive loyalty*"[37]. Put simply: God has made a covenant with Israel, and Israel has an obligation to keep it. Failure to do so will bring punishment.

Deuteronomy 27-30[38] is a climactic statement about the expectations of Israel's covenant with God. As Israel approaches the promised land, Moses reminds

---

32. Leviticus 11:44, 19:2, 20:7, 20:26, 21:8

33. Leviticus 26:1-13,

34. Leviticus 26:14-33

35. Deuteronomy 4:6

36. Baylis, Albert. 1996. *From Creation to the Cross*. Zondervan. p. 148

37. Novick, *Scriptures*, p. 71

38. Deuteronomy 31-32 builds upon the blessings and curses outlined in Deuteronomy 27-30.

them of their obligation to follow God's Law. In Deuteronomy 27, Moses condemns all those who would defy God's Law. If Israel remains faithful to the covenant, God will bless them: *"Now it shall be, if you diligently obey the Lord your God, being careful to do all His commandments which I command you today, the Lord your God will set you high above all the nations of the earth. All these blessings will come upon you . . ."*[39] and then proceeds to explain in 28:3-14 how Israel will live comfortably in the land and be respected by the nations who will see the wisdom of Israel's Lord. If Israel fails to follow the Law, God will curse them by cursing their land[40] and allowing foreign nations to dominate them[41]. The rest of Deuteronomy 28 profiles the brutal punishments which will befall Israel, ultimately ending in exile from the promised land.[42] Nehemiah knew Israel's history: the sorry state of Jerusalem under Persian rule in the fifth century BCE was a direct result of Israel's failure to keep God's covenant and the subsequent punishment of exile.

Nehemiah 9:26-31 deftly summaries Israel's history as a cycle of disobedience and punishment followed by God's deliverance (an excellent summary of Joshua-2 Kings) until ultimately, after years of warning, God *"gave them into the hand of the peoples of the lands"*[43]. From Nehemiah through the first century CE, Jews reflected on their own history as leading to the punishment of exile with the hope that one day God would rescue His people from the curse of the Law. The writer of Deuteronomy seems to presuppose that Israel will fail and explains in 30:1-10 how, after suffering the consequences of disobedience, God would restore His people. Ezra and Nehemiah hope that teaching the Law and encouraging returning Jewish exiles to follow it, remaining separate from the peoples of the land, would bring about the promised restoration. Before moving on to the final section of Nehemiah's corporate confession, it will be helpful to understand the basic contours of the long, complex story which begins with God giving Israel the Law and ends with the return to Judea under Persian rule. How exactly did Israel find itself in exile, and what did it mean for those who had been allowed by Cyrus to return to their land?

---

39. Deuteronomy 28:1-2

40. Deuteronomy 28:16-25

41. Deuteronomy 28:25-37

42. Deuteronomy 28:58-66

43. Nehemiah 9:30

Exile: All Roads Lead to Babylon

The corporate confession in Nehemiah views Israel's covenantal history with God as one of abject failure, and the works contained in the Old Testament fully support Nehemiah's thesis. Israel had yet to see the promised land before crafting a golden idol and complaining about God's provisions. After Moses starkly presents the consequences of covenantal obedience and disobedience in Deuteronomy 27-30 Israel finally enters the promised land. Israel, under the leadership of Joshua, is tremendously successful in expelling the inhabitants of the land, but an Israelite soldier named Achen defies God's parameters for war and brings calamity upon Israel.[44] The people repent, God relents, and *"Israel served the Lord all the days of Joshua and all the days of the leaders who survived Joshua"*[45]. It would be one of the few bright spots in Israel's otherwise bleak history.

Israel's descent into disobedience accelerates in Judges. Since God was Israel's king, Abraham's family wasn't supposed to appoint a king to rule over them like all the other nations. In Judges Israel sins against God, receives a punishment, and causes God to raise up temporary leaders called 'judges' to deliver Israel from the consequences of their disobedience. This cycle is repeated throughout the work and shows Israel progressively becoming like the Canaanites they were supposed to expel; Judges 2:11-23 is a thematic introduction to the main contours of Judges. In fact, the entire narrative logic of Judges is centered around Israel's covenant disobedience. David Beldman explains: *"The author has brilliantly arranged and crafted these events and set them within the cyclical framework so as to reinforce one of his main purposes for writing: to demonstrate the deterioration of Israel"*[46]. A common refrain in Judges is that there was *"no king in Israel"*[47], and while many interpreters have assumed the statement refers to a human king like the Cannanites, Beldman rightly contests *"the "No king in Israel" refrain* [refers] *not to human kingship but divine kingship. In other words, the author uses the refrain to highlight the fundamental problem in Israel during the time of the judges: They had rejected their redeemer king, Yahweh. The results of their treason are devastating"*[48]. God was king over creation in general and Israel in particular, but Israel was rejecting His kingship. At one point in the narrative the wicked Israelites ask a judge named Gideon to rule over them like a king, to which Gideon responds *"I will not rule over you, nor shall my son rule*

---

44. Joshua 7

45. Joshua 24:31

46. Beldman, David. 2017. *Deserting the King.* Lexham Press. p. 34

47. Judges 17:6, 18:1, 19:1, and 21:25

48. Beldman, *Deserting the King,* p. 50

over you; the Lord shall rule over you"[49]. As the narrative progresses, Israel doubles down on its disobedience.

Israel will finally reject the kingship of God. Israel's tribal leaders gather before the prophet Samuel and demand a king: "*all the elders of Israel gathered together and came to Samuel . . . and they said to him, "behold . . . appoint a king for us to judge us like all the nations.""*[50]. Israel, supposedly separate from the nations through following God's Law, were openly spurning His covenant. A crestfallen Samuel complains to God, who reminds him "*they have not rejected you, but they have rejected Me from being king over them*"[51]. Through Samuel, God explains to Israel how being under a king will result in war, conscription, crippling taxation, and slavery.[52] The warnings fell on deaf ears: "*Nevertheless, the people refused to listen to the voice of Samuel, and they said, "No, but there shall be a king over us, that we also may be like all the nations*"[53]. History will vindicate Samuel.

The first king of Israel, Saul, is declared ruler over Israel in 1 Samuel 10, but only a few chapters later disobeys God and is rejected by Him through the prophet Samuel[54]. God's Spirit then falls upon David, youngest son of Jesse the Bethlehemite, to replace Saul in 1 Samuel 16. Saul is understandably upset about this unfortunate turn of events and spends the rest of his life attempting to kill David. After Saul meets his untimely end in 1 Samuel 31, David becomes king. This results in a short but bloody civil war between David, rightful king of Israel, and Ish-bosheth, one of Saul's sons who declared himself king. David prevails and an uneasy peace is restored[55]. It would be a portent of events to come. David, despite his glaring personal flaws, is described as a "*man after [God's] own heart*"[56] whose rule stands at the pinnacle of Israel's monarchy. In 2 Samuel 7, a passage which will be discussed in greater detail below (and which should have a major impact on how modern Christians think about political power), David requests through the prophet Nathan that he build a temple for God in Jerusalem.[57] God reminds David that He never needed a temple and He had plans to rescue Israel from its wickedness. This would happen by raising up one of David's sons, who

---

49. Judges 8:12-13

50. 1 Samuel 8:4-5

51. 1 Samuel 8:6-7

52. 1 Samuel 8:10-18

53. 1 Samuel 8:19-20

54. 1 Samuel 15:17-23

55. 2 Samuel 2-5

56. 1 Samuel 13:14

57. 2 Samuel 7:1-3

would build a house for God's name and, significantly, inherit an everlasting king-dom. David's line will rule on behalf of God.[58] David responds by praising God, acknowledging He is the one true king over Israel forever.[59]

The latter half of David's life, recounted in 2 Samuel, is plagued by personal scandal and political unrest. Even the greatest king in Israel's history could not avoid the prophetic condemnation of monarchy articulated by Samuel in 1 Samuel 8: a kingship modeled on Israel's foreign enemies was a curse. David dies and is replaced by his son Solomon, who must also quell sedition from those within Israel eager to acquire power.[60] The first years of Solomon's rule are a monumental suc-cess. Solomon asks God for wisdom, which God generously granted, and Solomin increases in power, builds God a temple, and earns the respect of other rulers in the region.[61] Despite his great wisdom, Solomon's many foreign wives became a snare, influencing him to worship other gods. In response God promises Solomon's great kingdom would be divided.[62] Jeroboam, son of Solomon's servant, becomes king in the north while Rehoboam, Solomon's own son, becomes king in the south. From this point forward, Israel was divided into two separate political entities. The Northern Kingdom and the Southern Kingdom would fight for power and influence, corrupting God's Law. In the long run God's patience runs out and both kingdoms suffer the covenantal curses proscribed in Deuteronomy.

While works like Deuteronomy, Joshua, Judges, 1-2 Samuel and 1-2 Kings are based on traditions which, in my view, originated at the time the events recounted in these narratives took place, the final forms of these texts incorporated into the Old Testament canon were edited to include thematic connections between what may have originally been disparate texts. The effect of this editing has been to cre-ate what scholars call 'Deuteronomistic History', which is a way of casting Israel's story as a rejection of the covenant outlined in Deuteronomy and the hope for a future covenantal restoration.[63] After the death of Solomon and the division of Israel in 1 Kings 12, the rest of 1-2 Kings evaluates the subsequent rulers of the Northern and Southern Kingdoms by their fidelity to the Law of God. Every sin-gle Northern king is portrayed as wicked, and only a small number of Southern kings uphold the Law.

---

58. 2 Samuel 7:4-17

59. 2 Samuel 7:18-29

60. 1 Kings 1-3

61. 1 Kings 4-10

62. 1 Kings 11:1-13

63. Novick, *Scriptures*, p. 78

Despite God sending a number of prophets to turn His people from their sinful ways, they refuse repentance. God, always faithful to the covenant, brings upon his people the curses of Deuteronomy. In 2 Kings 17:1-6 the Assyrian empire besieged the Northern Kingdom, defeated them in battle, and took the survivors into exile. By 722 BCE, the Northern Kingdom was no more. The author of 2 Kings issues a postmortem: *"Now this came about because the sons of Israel had sinned against the Lord their God, who had brought them up from the land of Egypt . . . and they had feared other gods and walked in the customs of the nations whom the Lord had driven out before the Sons of Israel, and in the customs of the kings of Israel which they had introduced"*[64] Despite sending his prophets, the people of Israel rejected God's Laws and His covenant, following after the nations around them and worshiping their gods.[65] As a result, *"the Lord removed Israel from His sight, as He spoke through all His servants the prophets. So Israel was carried away into exile from their own land to Assyria until this day"*[66]. In 586 BCE, the Southern Kingdom would suffer the same fate at the hands of the Babylonians. Because of their sinfulness, Jerusalem was sacked and the people of the Southern Kingdom were taken into exile in Babylon.

The corporate confession in Nehemiah concisely recounts Israel's history: *"You bore with them for many years, And admonished them by Your Spirit through Your prophets, Yet they would not give ear. Therefore You gave them into the hand of the peoples of the lands. Nevertheless, in Your great compassion, you did not make an end of them or forsake them, For You are a gracious and compassionate God"*[67]. Nehemiah offers no excuses for Israel's reckless behavior. Despite the hardships which had befallen His people, God remained committed to the covenant and was exceedingly faithful to Israel.[68] God's judgment was, however, righteous: *"You are just in all that has come upon us; For You have dealt faithfully, but we have acted wickedly. For our kings, our leaders, our priests and our fathers have not kept Your Law Or paid attention to your commandments . . . But they, in their own kingdom . . . Did not serve You or turn from their evil deeds"*[69].

While the Jews of Israel's Southern Kingdom had been allowed under Persian rule to return to Jerusalem, Nehemiah articulates what would become a central feature of the Second Temple Jewish worldview: despite returning from geographical

---

64. 2 Kings 17:7-8

65. 2 Kings 17:9-18

66. 2 Kings 17:23

67. Nehemiah 9:30-31

68. Nehemiah 9:32

69. Nehemiah 9:33-35

exile, Israel was still suffering the consequences of their rebellion against God. Nehemiah 9:36-37 perfectly describes the historical tension within which Jews of this period would live: *"Behold, we are slaves today, And as to the land which You gave to our fathers to eat of its fruit and its bounty, behold we are slaves in it. Its abundant produce is for the kings Whom You have set over us become of our sins; They also rule over our bodies And over our cattle as they please, So we are in great distress"*. The punishment for rejecting God as king, breaking His covenant, and rejecting His Law still hung over the Jews, despite rebuilding the temple and reoccupying the land. N.T. Wright summarizes the situation beautifully: *"When the great moment had come, and Babylon had been destroyed, Israel did not become free, mistress in her own land: the Persians, who had crushed Babylon, were generous overlords to the Jews, but overlords none the less"*[70]. The covenantal curses of Deuteronomy 28 were still in effect, and the promised restoration of Deuteronomy 30 remained relegated to an unknown future.

The themes of creation, kingship, exodus, covenant, exile, and restoration would have a powerful impact on Jewish practice and hope during the Second Temple period. For Ezra, Nehemiah, and their successor, the problem was evident: Israel had been punished because they rejected God as their king and refused to follow the Law enshrined in His covenant. The entire story of Israel was one long decline into failure. Since Israel had compromised its status of holiness, becoming exactly like the nations which surrounded them, boundaries had to again be erected. Ezra and Nehemiah would both advocate for a separation from the pagan nations and a return to God's Law. Israel's Scriptures would regulate the life of Jews who had returned to the land. Israel found itself in this mess because they broke the Law, and the only way out was through returning to the Law, following the covenant, and defending themselves from the encroaching cultural influences of paganism. It is these twin goals of Law-keeping and separation which would dominate Jewish culture in antiquity.[71]

Tzvi Novick, discussing the intellectual changes which took place in Judaism during and after the Babylonian exile, highlights the increasing prominence of monotheism, the temple cult, and Israel's Law as enshrined in Scripture. Monotheism, temple, and Torah[72] became central to the identity of Judaism, and the various Jewish sects which would arise during the Second Temple period were

---

70. Wright, N.T. 1992. *The New Testament and the People of God*. Fortress Press. p. 157

71. Bruce, *Nations*, pp. 99-106

72. The first five books of the Old Testament, also known as the Pentateuch, became the foundation of Judaism; this is so prevalent that the term 'Torah' was often used as a shorthand for the entire Jewish Scriptures. I will use many of these terms interchangeably.

all, in their own ways, attempting to work out what adherence to all three entailed.[73] Monotheism was predicated upon God's identity as creator and king but had been rejected by Israel when they capitulated to other gods. The temple was the locus of God's activity and constructed in Judaism's holiest city, Jerusalem. Maintenance of the temple cult and centralizing the worship of God in Jerusalem prevented Israel from breaching covenant and worshiping false gods. We must remember, as I will argue below, that the temple was as much a *political* institution as a theological one, and debates over the legitimacy of the temple leadership would characterize the ministries of John the Baptist and Jesus. The Law, of course, was the foundation of the covenant and, like monotheism and the temple, was not consigned to the isolated category of 'religion' in antiquity. Failing to follow the Law had led to exile and punishment, and adherence to the Law would, following Ezra and Nehemiah, bring restoration. The geographical return from Babylonian exile generated as many social and political questions as it did theological ones, all of which were inseparable. Jews would fiercely debate about who controlled the temple in Jerusalem and the correct interpretation of the Law. Early Christianity, which should be seen historically as one among many sects of Second Temple Judaism, has a particular stake in these Jewish conversations.

Returning to the Law, separating from the nations, upholding the unique status of Israel's God, and maintaining the temple were seen by Jews following Ezra and Nehemia as the means by which God would bring about the promised restoration and finally rescue Israel from their covenantal sins. But what, exactly, does this restoration entail? Before exploring how Jews negotiated the post-exilic world of antiquity, we must explore how they conceptualized the coming restoration. It is to this important question we will now turn.

The Restoration of Israel

The biblical prophets, channeling Deuteronomy 30, anticipate a day when God will finally rescue His disobedient people and reestablish the covenant. These prophecies are complex and interpreted differently by various Jewish groups in the Second Temple period, but there are a few important themes which directly relate to the arguments I am advancing in this book. First, a general word on prophecy.

Old Testament scholar John Walton explains, contrary to popular modern conceptions of prophecy, how prophets in the ancient Near East were primarily spokespersons for their particular deity. Prophets were not often concerned about predicting the future but rather tasked with revealing God's (or the gods') plans

---

73. Novick, *Scriptures,* pp. 139-149

and purposes for his people.[74] Samuel and Nathan are both responsible for holding the kings of Israel accountable to God, and the primary role of figures like Elija, Elisha, Isaiah, Jeremiah, Amos, and other famous prophets was to hold Israel accountable for the covenant they made with God by drawing the people back to His Law. Instead of making precise predictions regarding the distant future, prophets reminded Israel about the Deutoronomic choice between blessing and curse: repentance leads to blessing while continued disobedience leads to curse. Ezekiel 33:11 exemplifies the role of the prophet as it relates to Israel's lack of faithfulness: "*I* [God] *take no pleasure in the death of the wicked, but rather that the wicked turn from his way and live. Turn back . . . O house of Israel*". Just as God relented when the Ninevites repented in Jonah 3, if Israel turned back to God He would faithfully deliver them from calamity. Failure to repent results in covenantal curses.

When prophets do make statements about the future they are always within the framework of covenant. If Israel is faithful, the blessings outlined in Deuteronomy 28:1-14 will enable them to thrive in the land. If they are faithless, then the curses of Deuteronomy 28:15-68 will befall them. Israel chose the latter option. The prophets witnessed Israel failing and looked to the restoration promised in Deuteronomy 30 for guidance. There is no one singular prediction which perfectly encapsulates the coming restoration of Israel, but rather a constellation of various themes characterizes prophetic hope. Walton explains how prophetic fulfillment follows oblique trajectories and can be fulfilled in many ways, including those not fully intended by the prophets. Since prophecy is not a clear prediction of future events but rather a message from God to His people regarding the covenant, we shouldn't expect surgical precision.[75] It is this inherent ambiguity in Jewish prophecy which will lead to the diversity of eschatological hope in Second Temple Judaism. There are several important themes that are relevant for this study which emerge from the prophetic literature.

In Isaiah 9-11, the prophet announces Israel will be rescued from bondage by foreign powers and that the throne of David (remember 2 Samuel 7) will be reestablished as an eternal kingdom.[76] In Isaiah 10:1-19, Assyria is God's instrument for judging the Northern Kingdom but will themselves be judged by God in the end. God's faithful remnant will return to the land and will truly rely on the Lord.[77] Isaiah 11 famously describes the restoration of David's house ("*Then a shoot will spring from the stem of Jesse*", referring to the father of David in verse

---

74. Walton, John. 2024. *The Lost World of the Prophets*. InterVarsity Press. pp. 35-39

75. Walton, *Prophets*, pp. 102-107

76. Isaiah 9:2-7

77. Isaiah 10:20-23

1) and, as a result of his rule, the world will finally be at peace because *"the earth will be full of the knowledge of the Lord, As the waters cover the sea"*[78]. Isaiah 11:10 proclaims the nations will finally turn to God's righteous king, and Israel, who had been punished and cast into exile, will be restored and return to their land.[79] These themes are ubiquitous in Old Testament prophecies of restoration. Israel's rescue from bondage, a return to covenant faithfulness, punishing and revealing God to the wicked nations, and the reestablishment of David's line are the cornerstones of prophetic hope. The literature is overwhelmingly saturated with these themes, either implicitly or explicitly, and a short foray through a few significant prophetic passages will demonstrate just how deeply these themes run throughout the Jewish scriptures.

Jeremiah issues a series of climactic prophecies in which God declares that *"days are coming . . . when I will restore the fortunes of My people Israel and Judah . . .* [and] *bring them back to the land that I gave to their forefathers"*[80]. The family of Abraham, which had been divided after the death of Solomon, would be reunited and return to the promised land. Their slavery to foreign powers will end because *"they shall serve the Lord their God and David their king, whom I will raise up for them"*[81], and, as a result, Israel *"shall be my people, And I will be your God"*[82], clearly echoing the refrain of faithfulness in Leviticus. God will make a *"new covenant"* with the house of Israel, writing His Law on their hearts so that He might be their God and they might be His people, and He will forgive their sins against the covenant, forgetting them forever.[83] When Israel is forgiven for their sins the nations will see God's mercy and offer praise[84] before the son of David who executes judgment and rules on God's behalf. The temple will be rebuilt and priests will offer God righteous sacrifices[85]. While the prophecies in Isaiah and Jeremiah are structurally different, the themes are identical.

Ezekiel follows the pattern set by Isaiah and Jeremiah. In Ezekiel 34 the prophet condemns Israel's wicked leaders because they have led the people astray. Israel is presented as a flock of sheep without a shepherd to guide them. God promises that after the exile he *"will search for* [his] *sheep and seek them out. As a*

---

78. Isaiah 11:9; read 11:1-8 for context.

79. Isaiah 11:11-16

80. Jeremiah 30:3

81. Jeremiah 30:9

82. Jeremiah 30:22

83. Jeremiah 31:31-34

84. Jeremiah 33:8-9

85. Jeremiah 33:14-22

shepherd cares for his herd in the day when he is among his scattered sheep, so I will care for my sheep and will deliver them from all the places to which they were scattered on a cloudy and gloomy day"[86]. God will perform a second exodus, delivering His people from captivity in a foreign land. He will accomplish this by "*set*[ting] *over them one shepherd, My servant David . . . And I, the Lord, will be their God, and My servant David will be prince among them*"[87]. These themes are found yet again in Ezekiel 36:22-38: God will rescue his people from exile, forgive them of their sins, place His spirit upon them, and reveal Himself to the nations. Israel will finally serve God, and, echoing Leviticus, "*you will be My people, and I will be your God*"[88]. In Ezekiel 37 Israel is compared to a valley full of dry bones, which are reanimated when God pours out His spirit upon them. The themes of return from exile, forgiveness of sins, enthronement of a Davidic king, and the revelation of God to the nations are woven into the chapter. Ezekiel 40-48 envisions a restoration of the temple in Jerusalem where God communes with His people. While Ezekiel is stylistically distinct from Isaiah and Jeremiah, the message is the same: God will rescue his people (including restoring faithfulness, land, and temple), install the David king, and reveal himself to the nations.

This comprises the hard core of Israel's prophetic hope, and Jews of the Second Temple period, in glorious diversity and variation, attempted to discern exactly how God planned on bringing these prophecies to fruition. What it looks like in practice was anyone's guess, and the thematically clear but specifically imprecise nature of prophecy made concrete predictions futile. God would, at some point in history, and probably as a result of Jews faithfully following the Law (ala Ezra and Nehemiah), restore his people, return them to the land and their temple (free of Persian or other foreign rule, of course), reestablish the line of David, and reveal Himself to the nations. Jewish eschatology, variegated as it was, revolved around these major themes. There is one, however, which requires a closer look because of how significant it is for our reading of the New Testament. That theme is the reestablishment of the Davidic monarchy.

The Eternal Kingdom of David

From the beginning of creation, God ruled as king over everything. When He made a covenant with Israel, God was their exclusive Lord; Israel was to give their loyalty to no one else, and the divine kingship of Israel's God was one of the many

---

86. Ezekiel 34:11-12

87. Ezekiel 34:23-24

88. Ezekiel 36:28

factors separating them from the foreign nations whom, according to the calling of Abraham in Genesis 12:3, Israel was supposed to bless. We have already seen how the book of Judges was crafted to portray Israel rejecting God as their king, with Gideon explicitly turning down the offer to rule as a human monarch in Judges 8:22-23. When Israel fatefully begs for a king in emulation of the nations in 1 Samuel 8, it is depicted as a rejection of God. The grand narrative which runs from 1 Samuel-2 Kings exhibits king after king betraying God, ignoring the Law, and leading His people astray. 2 Samuel 7, where God promises David that one of his sons will establish an eternal kingdom, stands in sharp relief from the otherwise negative portrait of monarchy painted throughout the Old Testament. What are we to make of this apparent contradiction?

The writer of Deuteronomy proleptically anticipated Israel's demand for a king and, ironically, the degradation which occurred under Israel's 'like the other nations'-style monarchy. Deuteronomy 17:14-20, channeling 1 Samuel 8 and the behavior of Saul, David, Solomon, and other kings of Israel, outlines exactly what any potential king of Israel ought *not* to do. It's worth quoting in full; notice how well the text approximates what Israel's leaders actually did: "*When you enter the land which the Lord your God gives you, and you possess it and live in it, and you say, 'I will set a king over me like all the nations who are around me,', you shall surely set a king over you whom the Lord your God chooses, one from among your countrymen you shall set as king over yourselves; you may not put a foreigner over yourselves who is not your countryman. Moreover, he shall not multiply horses for himself, nor shall he cause the people to return to Egypt to multiply horses, since the Lord has said to you, 'You shall never again return that way.' He shall not multiply wives for himself, or else his heart will turn away; nor shall he greatly increase silver and gold for himself*"[89]. In other words, Israel's kings should act exactly opposite of how they actually behaved. Modern politicians should take note. Either way, the one who inherits the throne of David is required to perform better than David himself.

After explaining what kings should not do, the writer of Deuteronomy makes a positive case for the God-ordained role of a king: "*Now it shall come about when he sits on the throne of his kingdom, he shall write for himself a copy of this Law on a scroll in the presence of the Levitical priests. It shall be with him and he shall read it all the days of his life, that he may learn to fear the Lord his God, by carefully observing all the words of this Law and these statues, that his heart may not be lifted up above his countrymen and that he may not turn aside from the commandment, to the right or the left, so that he and his sons may continue long in his kingdom in the midst of*

---

89. Deuteronomy 17:14-17

Israel"[90]. A real king *serves* Israel by honoring the Law of God, setting an example for the people, and leading them to keep covenant. There are in this passage none of the trappings of human power, no self-aggrandizement or wealth, and no cult of personality. If Israel is to have a king, he will humbly orient the people towards their God, the only true king over creation. This is, indeed, a far cry from the behavior exhibited by Israel's kings.

It is also perfectly aligned with the prophecies regarding the coming heir of David in Isaiah, Jeremiah, and Ezekiel. The constellation of themes we find in those texts regarding the coming of David, the restoration of Israel, a return to faithfulness, and the knowledge of Israel's God spreading to the nations are entirely consistent with the portrayal of righteous kingship in Deuteronomy 17. Israel's true king, the worthy heir of David, would satisfy the Deuteronomistic pattern of kingship which looks nothing like 'the other nations'. The eschatological Davidic monarchy would not conform to the patterns of pagan rulers but instead rule as God Himself intended. The prophetic hope, based on 2 Samuel 7, envisages God's deliverance of Israel, His second exodus, occouring through the work of His kingly representative. This is the foundation for classic Jewish Messianic theology.

The English word 'Messiah' comes from the Hebrew term '*mashiach*', and the Greek term used when the Hebrew scriptures are translated into Greek is '*christos*', which for perceptive readers should sound an awful lot like 'Christ'. This is because the title 'Christ' is derived from the Greek *christos*, which is itself a translation of the Hebrew *mashiach*. The noun *messiah* and the adjective *messianic*, therefore, are rooted in the Hebrew concept of *mashiach*. Old Testament scholars Andrew Abernethy and Gregory Goswell explain how "*these terms are understood to refer to the hope of the coming of a royal agent who will serve God's kingdom purposes, an expectation that Christians believe finds fulfillment in Jesus Christ . . . a messianic passage or book in the Old Testament is one in which this royal figure is prefigured, anticipated, predicted or described*"[91]. The messiah, then, is a royal figure who will inherit the throne of David and a key component of God's restoration of Israel. Messianism is an extremely important concept in Second Temple Judaism and is also one of the Old Testament's most enduring themes.

The term '*mashiach*', or messiah, means 'anointed one'. This is a person chosen by God for a special purpose and in the Old Testament is granted only to

---

90. Deuteronomy 17:18-20

91. Abernethy, Andrew, and Gregory Goswell. 2020. *God's Messiah in the Old Testament*. Baker Academic. p. 1

prophets[92], priests[93], and kings[94], including in Isaiah 45:1 Cyrus of Persia, the only pagan who received this honor. Contrary to certain strands of western Christian theology, the term 'messiah' itself does not denote divinity but describes someone who is entrusted by God to perform a particular task. Messianic language is first used of kings in 1 Samuel, and the concept is widely evoked throughout 1 and 2 Samuel. Abernethy and Goswell make a few very important points about the concept of messiah in the Old Testament. As a noun, the word is always determined by God. The messiah is never a solitary figure, but 'God's' anointed, the 'Lord's' anointed, or 'His' anointed. Those who are anointed act on behalf of God to carry out his work. As a verb, anointing is done either directly by God or indirectly through a prophetic representative, again demonstrating that God's various messiahs do not act independently of His will. In fact, the term 'the Messiah' is never used in the Old Testament, it is always invoked with reference to God. Messianism as a concept is present throughout the Old Testament even when *mashiach* and its cognates are not present. Many of the prophetic passages which reference a coming Davidic ruler don't use the specific language of anointing even though the concept is still clearly present.[95] It is therefore entirely appropriate to refer to the coming son of David as a messiah or anointed one; whoever this figure may be, he will rule on behalf of God in a manner consistent with Deuteronomy 17, ushering in the restoration of Israel.

Scholar Kevin Chin agrees with Abernethy and Goswell on the pervasive presence of messianic themes in the Old Testament, specifically as it relates to the coming son of David: *"the eschatological Messiah is not only a major theme but the integrative center of the Old Testament . . . since he often appears in compositionally strategic passages . . . as the climactic expression of major Old Testament themes, starting in the Pentateuch and across the Tanakh"*[96]. Whether this is a feature of the traditions (written or oral) which would become the Old Testament or a redactional strategy employed by its finally compilers I will leave up to the textual critics; what is undeniable, though, is how often Old Testament authors envisage an eschatological messiah who will rule wisely on God's behalf. Many Jews in the Second Temple period hoped God would quickly deliver on His promises. When Matthew opens his gospel with *"The record of the genealogy of Jesus the Messiah, the*

---

92. 1 Kings 19:16, Isaiah 61:1

93. Exodus 29:7, Numbers 35:25

94. Saul is anointed in 1 Samuel 10:1 while David receives his anointing in 1 Samuel 16:13.

95. Abernethy and Goswell, *God's Messiah*, pp. 2-3

96. Chen, Kevin. 2024. *Wonders From Your Law*. InterVarsity Press. p. 27

son of David[97], he is deliberately invoking this tradition. The gravity of messianism cannot be ignored.

A handful of passages, chosen somewhat at random, will sufficiently demonstrate just how dominant the theme of a coming messianic king is in the Old Testament. Amos 9:11 states *"In that day I will raise up the fallen booth of David . . . And rebuild it as in the days of old"*. Micah 5:2 reads *"But as for you, Bethlehem . . . From you One will go forth for Me to be ruler in Israel"*. A final example from the prophets is Zechariah 13:1, in which *"a fountain will be opened for the house of David and for the inhabitants of Jerusalem"*. In none of these passages is the language of 'anointing' employed specifically, but they each envisage an eschatological messiah.

Rounding out our exploration of messianic themes in the Old Testament, we turn to the Psalms. Stephen Dempster explains why: *"The Psalter—David's book—shows how David will be the key to God's salvation"*[98]. Psalm 2 explicitly uses the messianic language of 'anointing' in verse 2 before, in opposition to the oppressive nations, God *"installed* [His] *King Upon Zion, My holy mountain"*, refers to this king as *"my son"*, and then promises to give him dominion over the nations, saying He will *"break them with a rod of iron..shatter them like earthenware"*.[99] Psalm 72:1-2 requests *"Give the king Your judgments, O God, And Your righteousness to the king's son. May he judge Your people with righteousness, and Your afflicted with justice"*, revealing how this king will rule the nations, deliver the oppressed, and bring peace.[100] As a result, the Psalmist longs for a day when *"the whole earth* [will] *be filled with His glory"*[101]. Psalm 89:3-4, directly invoking 2 Samuel 7, states *"I have made a covenant with My chosen; I have sworn to David my servant, I will establish your seed forever And build up your throne to all generations"*. Because of David's anointing (note the clear messianic language in 89:20), this coming king is God's firstborn whose descendants will, like the sun, endure forever.[102] The rest of the Psalm recounts Israel's suffering as a result of breaching covenant, ending in 89:49-52 with a request that God remember His commitment to David and the reproach of His people. The request is plain: God must rescue Israel from the covenantal curses by fulfilling His promise to restore the Davidic monarchy.

---

97. Matthew 1:1

98. Dempster, *Kingdom*, p. 137

99. Psalm 2:4-9

100. Psalm 72:3-17

101. Psalm 72:19

102. Psalm 89:19-37

Ezra and Nehemiah didn't inherit a Jewish culture in which all of the ideas expressed in the previous pages were fully developed, but they did help construct a foundation for the long centuries which lay ahead. The exile was not properly over; the pagans, even if benevolent towards Jews, were still in charge, the distinction between Jews and Gentiles was under constant threat, the Law was not well known, and the promises of restoration, including David's house, remained unfulfilled. While Judaism became a complex, dynamic, and variegated phenomenon during this period, intra-Jewish debates were generally about how these various ideas should be implemented or would come to fruition in the future. In order to fully grasp the context of first century Judaism in which the New Testament was written, it is imperative to view, at least broadly, the historical developments which took place between the return from Babylon under Persian rule and the crucifixion of Jesus on a Roman cross.

PERSIA AND GREECE

Persian Benevolence

From 539—332 BCE Jews lived under Persian rule. After the brilliant military campaigns of Cyrus the Great resulted in the overthrow of a seemingly invincible Babylonian empire, the Persians built a sweeping and administratively savvy state which was unrivaled in the eastern Mediterranean. Unlike the Babylonians who had implemented a policy of forced resettlement over those they conquered, the Persians wisely allowed most of their subjects to remain in their ancestral homes. Anticipating Roman imperial rule by half a millennium, much of the administrative minutiae was handled by local leaders. The Persians also allowed Jews to worship their own God instead of converting to Zoroastrianism, the official cult of Persia. As long as the taxes were paid and the peace was maintained, the Persians had little desire to intervene in local politics. While those who governed the region which included Judea were often themselves not Jewish, the high priest of the Second Temple became the de facto head of state for all internal Jewish affairs, yet another reminder that institutions like the temple which moderns interpret as 'religious' were fundamentally political as well. During this period Jews built upon the foundations of Judaism constructed by Ezra and Nehemiah. The Law became the basis for Jewish practice, special emphasis was placed on excluding Gentiles from Jewish society, and synagogues, where Jews gathered in community, were constructed.[103] Persian rule facilitated enough political stability that Judaism could develop in a relatively peaceful manner.

---

103. Bruce, *Nations*, pp. 107-115

Greek Hegemony: The Ptolemies, Seleucids, and Maccabean Revolt

Persian rule over Judea would come to an abrupt end in 332 BCE, when Alexander the Great swept into Judea after conquering Persian holdings throughout the rest of the region. Jews were quick to offer Alexander enough respect for him to leave them mostly alone, and he would in the following decade continue his campaign against the once mighty Persian empire, spreading Greek culture to every region he conquered. By his untimely death in 323 BCE, Alexander had left the Persian empire in ruins and thoroughly Hellenized the eastern Mediterranean. Alexander was, from a tactical standpoint, one of the greatest generals in human history. While his military prowess is undeniable, Alexander was no politician and thought very little about how the massive amounts of territory he had acquired would be ruled. With no succession plan in place, his death brought about civil war between several Greek military leaders and politicians. Alexander's vast empire was parceled up into various kingdoms, two of which had a profound impact on the course of Jewish history. One dynasty, the Ptolemies, ruled out of Egypt and would, from 320—200 BCE, exercise political control over Jerusalem. The Ptolemies wisely extended the same privileges to their Jewish subjects as the Persians, and the greatest challenge Jews faced during this period was preventing the encroachment of Greek Hellenistic culture in Judea. The second Greek kingdom, the Seleucid dynasty, took control of Syria after Alexander's death and rivaled the Ptolemies for control of the eastern Mediterranean.[104]

Around the turn of the second century BCE the Seleucids would wrest control of Judea away from the Ptolemies. While Greek culture had threatened Jewish identity under Ptolemaic rule, the Ptolemies were much more sympathetic to Jewish cultural concerns and never imposed a policy of forced Hellenization. The Seleucids, however, were much less tolerant and aggressively sought to impose what they believed to be their superior Greek culture upon conservative Jewish factions in Judea. The political shift which occurred under Seleucid control after 200 BCE created a rift between Jews who wanted to resist Greek culture and those who desired to embrace it. The conservative faction, taking their cue from Ezra and Nehemiah, believed that strict adherence to the Law and separation from pagan neighbors were essential to Jewish identity and tended to align themselves with the priesthood in Jerusalem. The Hellenizing faction found Jewish cultural distinctions less relevant and sought closer ties with the Seleucid ruling class.[105] For nearly twenty-five years these pressure groups competed for influence while the

---

104. Bruce, *Nations*, pp. 116-123
105. Bruce, *Nations*, pp. 124-130

Seleucids continued to consolidate power in the region, always with an eye to the strategic significance of Jerusalem.

A new Seleucid king, Antiochus Epiphanes IV, came to power. Desiring to strengthen the borders between Seleucid-controlled Syria and Ptolemaic-controlled Egypt, Antiochus sought to bring Jerusalem fully under his control. With the help of sympathetic pro-Hellenistic Jews in Jerusalem, Antiochus conquered the temple in Jerusalem on December 25, 167 BCE. He outlawed the worship of Israel's God, the Jewish Scriptures, Torah obedience, food laws, and circumcision, declaring any practice of them punishable by death. He also erected a temple to Zeus in Jerusalem.[106] A conservative country priest named Mattathias refused to comply with the decrees of Antiochus, and two of his sons, Judas and Simon (given the nickname 'Maccabeus', meaning 'hammer'), marshalled a volunteer army and launched a three-year long guerrilla war against Antiochus and his professional armies.[107] It became one of the greatest military upsets in history; under the leadership of Judas, the Maccabean Revolt successfully purged Seleucid forces from Jerusalem, and on December 25, 164 BCE, exactly three years to the date of Antiochus's desecration of the temple, Judas cleansed and reconsecrated it. Many Jews saw this as a clear vindication of Israel's God and a powerful reminder of the Jewish hope that He would one day rescue His people. In remembrance of this great act of deliverance, Jews added a new holiday, Hanukkah, to their calendar.[108]

While the Maccabean Revolt was indeed seen by Jews as a reaffirmation of the temple, the Law, Jewish separatism, and the hope for a future deliverance, it also raised several questions which remained decidedly unanswered. While the immediate threat of Jewish extinction had been eliminated, the removal of Seleucid forces from Jerusalem was by no means the second exodus foretold in the prophets. The tides in Mediterranean politics had been slowly shifting westward. Rome was steadily consolidating power and had positioned itself to become the dominant player in Europe, northern Africa, and the Middle East. After Judas cleansed the temple, it was the Romans who brokered a peace between the conservative and Hellenistic factions in Jerusalem; while Jewish practices were fully restored there remained a small yet influential contingent of Jewish elites who wanted to blur the hard distinctions between Jew and gentile.[109] The Hasmoneans (the family name of Mattathias and Judas) had slowly transitioned from a policy of restoring Jewish practices and expelling the pagan overlords to forging complete political

---

106. Bruce, *Nations*, pp. 140-143

107. Bruce, *Nations*, pp. 144-148

108. Wright, *New Testament*, pp. 158-159

109. Bruce, *Nations*, pp. 148-149

autonomy, creating a Jewish state which, echoing a faint melody of Israel's dark past, appeared to 'resemble the nations'.[110] Many Jews were thankful for the hard-fought deliverance won by Judas and his successors but rightfully concerned that the Hasmonean dynasty which emerged in its aftermath was not theologically committed to maintaining Jewish boundaries. Wright sums up the Jewish response to the Maccabees nicely: "*It was* [the] *pluriform response to the ambiguities of the second century BC that created the pluriform Judaism known by Jesus and Paul*"[111]. There would be a diversity of responses to the new political realities in Judea which created a diverse array of interpretations regarding how God planned to bring about the restoration of Israel.

Hasmonean Ambiguities, the Pharisees, and the Jerusalem Aristocracy

By 128 BCE the descendants of Judas had successfully negotiated an independent Jewish state in Judea. The Hasmonean dynasty, ruling over Judea from 128-65 BCE, oscillated between pro-Hellenistic and pro-Jewish separatist leaders, high-lighting again the diversity of Jewish thought during this period. Both the Pharisees and the Sadducees would form during this time as political pressure groups, and in many ways they represent the main divisions within Judaism. While the precise meaning of the term 'Pharisee' is hotly debated among scholars, it is derivative of a Hebrew word which means 'separate', and they appear to have become a self-consciously defined group during the period of Hasmonean rule in opposition to the Jewish Hellenizers.[112] Wright explains that while there was diversity even amongst the Pharisees they were active from the Hasmonean period through to the Bar Kokhba revolt in 135 CE and known to be zealous for maintaining legal and ritual purity. The Pharisees saw themselves in the same line as Ezra and Nehemiah; they were calling Israel back to covenant faithfulness, enforcing the boundaries between Jew and non-Jew, and awaiting the restoration of Israel. The Pharisees' beliefs were both eschatological in that they assumed God would act to deliver His people (with fidelity to the Law hastening the day of His return), and ecclesiological in cultivating boundaries which separated the pure, Jewish "us" from the unclean, non- or sub-Jewish "them". When God returned to rescue Israel only the faithful would be vindicated. Many Pharisees, and before the Roman-Jewish war of 66-70 CE likely the majority, believed Israel's liberation would necessitate a military

---

110. Cohen, *Maccabees*, pp. 22-23

111. Wright, *New Testament*, p. 159

112. Bruce, *Nations*, pp. 169-178

conflict between Jews and their pagan overlords, perhaps waged by the rightful heir of David.[113] Pharisees were perceived by the Jewish population as playing an important role in the tumultuous political landscape of Judea. Calling Israel to remain pure, separate themselves from the nations, and await the day of God's deliverance was as much 'political' as it was 'theological', and we shouldn't impose our modernizing dichotomy between politics and religion onto the less taxonomically systematized world of Second Temple Judaism.

The local governing body based out of Jerusalem was called the Sanhedrin, and the faction which exercised the greatest political influence were the Sadducees. While it appears that the Pharisees held widespread popular approval among Jewish commoners, Sadducees represented the upper class. There were important doctrinal differences between Pharisees and Sadducees, including the Sadducees' infamous rejection of the doctrine of resurrection[114]. They were also more likely, during the Hasmonean period, to accommodate the Hellenizers. The high priesthood in Jerusalem, which was, at least nominally, tied to the Levitical line of Aaron, increasingly came under the influence of Hasmonean kings. Since the temple was a political institution in Second Temple Judaism, having an allied high priest was an asset to Hasmonean, and then Herodian, and then Roman rule. There were also thousands of minor priests in Judea who would serve the local population, many of whom didn't come from wealth.[115] The Sadducees, high priests, and Hasmoneans represented the aristocratic elite, and ordinary Jews had, to put it mildly, mixed feelings about their political and theological legitimacy. Since the ruling class was in charge and not as bitterly opposed to Greek culture as their Pharisaic counterparts, the aristocracy had a different conception of eschatology, one which was less pronounced than their erstwhile opponents.

Political, social, and theological diversity would characterize the Hasmonean period, but the core question remained: how would God rescue Israel and fulfill the prophecy of Deuteronomy 30? As the Hasmonean dynasty and the high priesthood continued to slowly compromise their Jewish values, were there any alternatives to the temple and ruling class? How did Jews negotiate the space between their own eschatological hopes and the reality of pagan empire? These questions would continue to be asked, variously answered, and reframed as the region fell under Roman control.

---

113. Wright, *New Testament*, pp. 181-203

114. Mark 12:18-27 and Acts 23:6-10 both testify to these theological differences.

115. Wright, *New Testament*, pp. 209-213

Roman Rule: Herods and Governors

In 67 BCE a civil war broke out between two Hasmonean brothers, Aristobulus II and Hyrcanus II, both of whom claimed a right to the Hasmonean throne. Antipater, a shrewd political maneuverer who governed Idumea, saw in this civil war an opportunity to leverage his political power. In 63 BCE the Roman general Pompey visited Jerusalem and, in complete defiance of Jewish sensibilities, entered the Holy of Holies. He came out entirely unscathed, marking a decisive turning point in the political destiny of Judea: from 63 BCE onwards, the Romans, and not the Hasmoneans, would be the dominant power. Antipater was quick to cozy up with Pompey, and when Aristobulus and Hyrcanus requested of him to settle political disputes in Judea, Pompey installed Hyrcanus as the titular high priest while entrusted Antipater with a much greater degree of power. Aristobulus, balking at his rejection, would mount several unsuccessful revolts against the Roman representatives but proved enough of an annoyance that his estranged brother Hyrcanus was eventually stripped of all civil power. Antipater, along with his sons Phasael and Herod, brilliantly allied themselves with whichever Roman general happened to be winning the various civil wars which shook the late Roman republic. Pompey was assassinated in 48 BCE, handing victory to his opponent Caesar. Despite his victory, however, Ptolemaic supporters cornered Caesar in Alexandria. Antipater, never one to miss an opportunity, sent a contingent of soldiers to help rescue Caesar. This compensated for the initial support Antipas gave to Pompey, and in gratitude Caesar conferred special privileges on Jews in Roman territory and confirmed Antipater's political power. After Antipater's death in 43 BCE, his sons Herod and Phasael were declared tetrarchs (minor rulers) of the region. Conflict between Hasmonean factions, however, created political instability and resulted in the death of Phasael. Little did they know, this conflict would mark the end of the Hasmonean dynasty.[116]

Herod, eventually earning his famous title "The Great", fled to Rome and was declared king of the Jews by the senate in 40 BCE. By 37 BCE Marc Anthony helped him return to Judea and claim his throne. Herod reigned as a client-king on behalf of the Romans from 37-4 BCE. After Augustus declared victory in the Republic's final civil war, Herod offered him allegiance. Augustus accepted, and Herod kept his job. Herod was, by imperial (if not Jewish) standards, an extremely effective ruler. He made the region safe for trade and initiated massive building projects throughout the region. The most famous of these was a complete overhaul of the temple in Jerusalem, making it one of the most impressive structures

---

116. Everett, *Backgrounds*, pp. 411-412

in antiquity. The motivation for the reconstruction of the Jerusalem temple may have been pure political posturing; as an Idumean, his ethnic Jewish heritage was questionable at best. Despite marrying a Hasmonean princess (Mariamne), many Jews, including members of the aristocracy, rightfully saw Herod as an extension of Roman rule, more concerned with pleasing Rome than appealing to Jewish sensitivities. The fact that his building spree extended to gentile cities in the region and included the funding of new pagan shrines didn't help.[117] He levied massive taxes to fund his architectural progress, which, as we discussed in the previous chapter, enabled city leaders to ravish the agricultural countryside, confiscate land, and thrust farmers into abject poverty, further stoking political discontent in Judea and a hope for God's long-awaited restoration. He also murdered many members of the Jewish aristocracy (including his Hasmonean wife) and was known for being merciless towards his political opponents.[118] Herod was the perfect example of everything Hayek found wrong with the political class: the worst people always wind up on top because they are willing to do whatever it takes to get there.

Herod certainly proved to be one of the early Roman empire's most effective client kings. As he facilitated the transition of power from the Hasmoneans to the Romans, little had changed for the average Jew. Despite the title 'king of the Jews', Herod was not the successor of David promised in 2 Samuel 7. Wright aptly describes the result of Herod's rule from a Jewish perspective: "*it was perhaps inevitable that Herod the Great . . . would never be accepted as the genuine king of the Jews . . . The rigorists saw the new Temple as thoroughly ambiguous, and never accepted any of Herod's successors as the genuine heaven-sent leader for whom some of them persisted in waiting . . . A mood of revolt was not far below the surface*". Indeed, on Herod's death in 4 BCE several revolts broke out. Some Jews became tired of waiting for God to act and, like Judas Maccabeus, decided to take matters into their own hands.[119] None were successful, but rebellion against Roman imperial power remained very much a viable option.

After Herod's death the Romans divided his territory up among his sons in accordance with his detailed will. Herod Antipas was made tetrarch of Galilee and Perea where he ruled as Rome's client king until 39 CE. It is this Herod whom Jesus called a 'fox'[120], was responsible for John the Baptist's untimely death[121], and

---

117. Everett, *Backgrounds*, pp. 413-414

118. Cohen, *Maccabees*, p. 5

119. Wright, *New Testament*, p. 160

120. Luke 13:32

121. Mark 6:17-28

assisted in the trial of Jesus[122] since Jesus resided in his region. He was, like his father, a competent ruler, and, also like his father, assessed with well-earned suspicion by his Jewish subjects. He succeeded in maintaining an uneasy peace. His half-brother Phillip effectively ruled a region to the northeast of the Sea of Galilee until his death in 34 BCE. Archelaus was given the status of ethnarch over Judea, Samaria, and Idumea, which came with a great amount of power. He entirely squandered this opportunity and was such a terrible politician that the Romans recalled him in 6 CE. From this time on Judea became an imperial province ruled directly by Roman governors, which were called either prefects or procurators. The governor's residence was located in the coastal city of Caesarea, but they would travel to Jerusalem for special occasions such as Passover. The designation of Judea as an imperial province is telling, because the heavy presence of Roman troops suggests the Romans understood a real potential for violent military conflict.[123] The revolts which occurred after the death of Herod were a sign something was amiss, and the ever-cautious Romans were not willing to be taken by surprise.

JEWISH POLITICAL INSTITUTIONS

From the time of the Hasmoneans through Herod the Great, the high priesthood had always been a mechanism for consolidating power; Herod wanted to ensure that whoever occupied the office was firmly in his camp. The procurators continued this policy. As we discovered in the last chapter, Roman governors usually delegated most of the day-to-day decision making to local governing bodies, and in Jerusalem this council was known as the Sanhedrin. The high priest presided over the Sanhedrin, giving him a relatively large degree of political authority. It was important for the Roman governors of Judea, who were interested in keeping peace and generating personal wealth, to have a high priest which would not imperil those goals. The most significant high priest in the first century CE was Joseph Caiaphas, son-in-Law of Annas. He was in office from 18-36 CE and presided over the trial of Jesus, ultimately bringing charges before Pontious Pilate, who held the imperium.[124] Not only was the high priest seen as a means of facilitating Roman rule, he would have also been an advisor to the governors regarding Jewish customs and affairs, allowing them to make decisions that wouldn't disturb the native population.[125] It also must be said, once again, that the high priest and Sanhedrin

---

122. Luke 23:7-15

123. Ferguson, *Backgrounds*, pp. 414-415

124. See, for example, Mark 14:53-65 and John 18:12-14

125. Ferguson, *Backgrounds*, p. 115

didn't represent 'religious' power as opposed to the real Roman 'political' power; the Sanhedrin and the high priesthood were both political and understood as such by the Jews and Romans.

By far the most significant Roman governor for our study is the aforementioned Pontious Pilate, notoriously known as the Roman which sentenced Jesus to crucifixion. Ruling from 26-36 CE, Jewish historian Josephus portrays Pilate as excessively harsh and unsympathetic towards the Jews, while the gospel writers present him as weak and indecisive, not wanting to disturb the peace. Reconciling these two views, Ferguson explains how *"The general picture that emerges is of a governor loyal to Rome, intent of preserving order, trying to avoid excessive bloodshed, and flexible in the face of demonstrations"*, but was, however, *"the first of the governors seriously to antagonize the Jewish populace"*[126]. Pilate, like most political authorities throughout history, was concerned first and foremost with his own self-interest. His interactions with Jesus will be of great significance in later chapters; suffice it to say for now that Pilate was the face of Roman imperial power in Judea during the ministry of Jesus.

One final comment on the political background of Second Temple Judaism is in order before synthesizing the research presented in this chapter. It is absolutely imperative, and will often stand as an unstated presupposition when I begin interpreting the New Testament, that for however much we as moderns want to relegate Jewish institutions like the priesthood, the Sanhedren, the temple, the Law, and other Jewish practices to the margins of 'religion', this perspective is incompatible with any historically plausible interpretation of the New Testament. Our chronic inability to think through the consequences of New Testament passages on politics and economics is a casualty of modernized assumptions about the dichotomy between religion and politics. As Shaye Cohen deftly articulates in his description of the temple and Sanhedrin, the people who controlled these institutions, including especially the high priest, were political leaders, full stop.[127] The Jewish population would have had varying degrees of respect or loathing towards them, and, as Oakman, Horsley, and others have noted, often viewed them as corrupt and the source of agrarian suffering in the villages of Judea and Galilee. The hope that God would rescue Israel and put the right people in charge was not just a theological aspiration but a political one as well. When John the Baptist appears in the wilderness (and not Jerusalem!) *"preaching a baptism of repentance for the forgiveness of sins"*[128] without reference to the temple, the Sanhedrin, or the high

---

126. Ferguson, *Backgrounds*, p. 116

127. Cohen, *Maccabees*, pp. 99-103

128. Mark 1:4

priest, his followers (and detractors) interpreted his actions as, in part, a political condemnation of the ruling elite. As Jesus proclaimed *"the kingdom of God is at hand; repent and believe in the gospel"*[129], his audience would hear this as a claim to the fulfillment of Jewish hopes which, unbelievably, were coming to fruition *outside the institutional channels of power in Jerusalem*! Jesus announced God's final return to rule over His people, and the aristocratic Jewish power base would not be at the center of God's great liberation.

To round out our study of Judaism and finally begin exploring political and economic texts in the New Testament, I will explain how, based on the historical arguments I have proposed in this chapter, Jews in antiquity (and, by extensions, the earliest followers of Jesus, the Jewish messiah) would have understood their relationship to the wider world and particularly the empires which opposed the universal kingship of God.

SEEK THE WELFARE OF THE CITY GOD WILL DESTROY

Jeremiah 29:7

Shaye Cohen, commenting on the complexities of Jewish attitudes towards gentile culture, notes there are *"three distinct but interrelated themes: political (to what extent should the Jews submit to foreign domination?, cultural (to what extent should the Jews absorb gentile ideas and practices?), and social (to what extent should Jews mingle and interact with Gentiles?)"*[130]. For Jews living in the diaspora, spread throughout the Roman empire, the questions of cultural and social interaction were more pronounced than for those living in Judea and Galilee. We have already seen how Judaism developed a diverse array of addressing these questions, usually based on assumptions about how God was going to bring about the restoration of Israel promised in His Scriptures. Most Jews were concerned about the corrupting influence of Greco-Roman culture but lived in contexts where they regularly interacted with Gentiles. Jews in the diaspora looked to the synagogue where local Jews gathered and the reading of the Torah for guidance, with strict Law observance providing the much-needed distinction between Jews and Gentiles. Diaspora Jews would often congregate in a single part of town, and the maintenance of boundaries, purity, and fidelity to the Law helped Jews conserve their distinct cultural values while living under the reality of pagan rule.[131]

---

129. Mark 1:15

130. Cohen, *Maccabees*, p. 19

131. Cohen, *Maccabees*, pp. 26-50

How Jews generally understood their relation to political authorities in light of the Old Testament promises of God's coming deliverance is of great relevance to this study. Jesus, Paul, Peter, and other leaders of the early church all inherited Jewish traditions about the nature of human authority, and, with the exception of the belief that God had *already* acted decisively in the life, death, resurrection, and ascension of Jesus continued to operate within the same broad political framework of Second Temple Judaism. The intellectual substructure of passages like Mark 12:13-17, Romans 13:1-7, and 1 Peter 2:13-17 are solidly Jewish, and by reading them in light of imprecisely defined modern political categories while ignoring the contexts in which they were written has undermined their original intention completely. The starting point of Jewish political theology during the Second Temple period is found in Jeremiah 29:7.

Jeremiah 30-33 contains, as we reviewed above, some of the most powerful prophetic oracles about the restoration of Israel. God would redeem his people from captivity, defeat the oppressive pagan empires, restore the house of David, issue a new covenant, and pour His spirit upon Israel. The restoration would come in God's good time. Jeremiah understands, of course, that Israel was being punished by the Babylonians and taken into exile because they had failed to follow the Law. Their disobedience, as promised in Deuteronomy 28 and narrated in the Jewish Scriptures, led to an exile from which God had to rescue His people. When Ezra and Nehemiah returned to the land, they were still slaves under foreign rulers. The geographical exile was technically over, but the great deliverance foretold in the prophets, the coming second exodus, had yet to occur. Given this state of affairs, how should Jews think about the nature of pagan rule in light of the eschatological hope for restoration?

In Jeremiah 25:8-14, the prophet explains how God is using Nebuchadnezzar, king of Babylon, to punish Jerusalem for its disobedience. The Babylonians, though, were not to be masters of the world; in just seventy short years, the Babylonians would be overthrown and the Jews would return home. Their empire had no eternal value, Nebuchadnezzar was simply being used by God to uphold his covenantal promises. How, then, should the Jews who found themselves in Babylon act in the meantime? Jeremiah 29:4-7 recounts this command from God: *"Thus says the Lord of hosts, the God of Israel, to all the exiles whom I have sent into exile from Jerusalem to Babylon, 'Build houses and live in them; and plant gardens and eat their produce. Take wives and become the fathers of sons and daughters, and take wives for your sons and give your daughters to husbands, that they may bear sons and daughters; and multiply there and do not decrease. Seek the welfare of the city where I have sent you into exile, and pray to the Lord on its behalf; for in its welfare you will have welfare.'"*. In other words: live life and make peace with the Babylonians. Simple enough.

This would seem to conflict with Jeremiah's message about a coming restoration. In Jeremiah 29:10-14 the Jews are reminded of the promise from 25:11 where they would return to their homeland after seventy years. The following four chapters, as has already been stated, explore in great detail the glory of a restored Israel, taking place through the reestablishment of David's house. Jeremiah 50-51, two climactic prophecies in this long work, are oracles of destruction directed against Babylon. God promises to one day wipe the Babylonian empire off the face of the planet for their sins against His people. There is no turning back; Babylon will be decisively judged, found guilty, and condemned. Jeremiah creates a conspicuous tension between the instructions of Jeremiah 29 and his wider oracles against pagan rulers and the eventual restoration of Israel.

Jeremiah knows his God is in control of history. Any power granted to the Babylonians was temporary and for a particular purpose, in this case dispensing divine judgment against the Southern Kingdom of Israel. The fate of Babylon, however, was predetermined: they would be destroyed, and, after that, Israel would be restored. As Cohen explains, *"In the interim, Jews were powerless to change the divine decree. Let them support their conquers and pray for the welfare of the countries in which they live"*[132]. These ideas would have, in Cohen's words, *"an enormous impact on subsequent Jewish thought and practice . . .* [here are found] *the two basic elements of the political theology of Jeremiah: the Gentiles rule the Jews to punish them for their sins; the Gentiles will continue to rule the Jews until the immutable sequences of empires has run its course and the predetermined day of their destruction has arrived"*[133]. Jews never lost sight of the promises made by God and longed for the future restoration, but rarely in the Second Temple period of Jewish history would they rebel against the state. As long as Jews could maintain their ethnic distinction and practice their Laws, they were generally quite content to pray for, support, and even work under foreign powers. Remain faithful in the present, seek the welfare of the pagans, and await the coming day of God's judgment and restoration. This is the general pattern of non-revolutionary political engagement during the Second Temple period.

---

132. Cohen, *Maccabees*, p. 20

133. Cohen, *Maccabees*, pp. 20-21

Jews Within Babylon: Daniel and Esther

Two post-exilic works included in the Old Testament, Daniel and Esther, perfectly exemplify the Jeremiac nexus between present pagan empire and the future reign of God. Daniel is by far the more significant of the two, and, in order to grasp the political significance of Daniel within its Second Temple Jewish context, I must briefly explain the genre in which it was written: apocalyptic. While I will offer a more detailed analysis of apocalyptic literature when we examine Revelation in Chapter 18, a basic description elucidates the function of Daniel. The great scholar of apocalyptic literature, John Collins, crafted the standard definition of 'apocalyptic' used in biblical scholarship: *"'Apocalypse' is a genre of revelatory literature with a narrative framework, in which a revelation is mediated by an otherworldly being to a human recipient, disclosing a transcendent reality which is both temporal, insofar as it envisages eschatological salvation, and spatial, insofar as it involves another, supernatural world"*[134].

While many modern Christians have (anachronistically) read biblical apocalyptic literature such as Daniel, Revelation, and Mark 13 as if they are codes to be deciphered, the genre itself is a poetic extension of the Jewish hope explained earlier in this chapter: God reveals a message to a human recipient (generally a prophetic figure), using an angelic being, revealing how God is going to rescue his people in the future. While John Walton correctly argues that 'apocalyptic' as a genre is categorically distinct from classical prophecy[135], it is *thematically* identical to the forms of prophecy which preceded it. Like the great prophecies of restoration found in Isaiah, Jeremiah, and Ezekiel, *"Apocalyptic does not have the purpose of foretelling the future. Instead, it reveals how God's plans and purposes begun in the past will find future completion"*[136]. Apocalyptic is characteristically symbolic, but the symbolism refers to the same hopes of a coming restoration consistently found in the Old Testament; apocalyptic literature is an innovation in style, not substance. Wright helpfully summarizes the role of symbol and metaphor in apocalyptic: *"The metaphorical language of apocalyptic invests history with theological meaning"*[137]. It is designed to powerfully evoke the significance of contemporary (for the original audience) events and vividly remind them that God will ultimately make good on His promises. In our short foray through Daniel we must avoid becoming lost in

---

134. Collins, John. 1984. *Daniel with an Introduction to Apocalyptic Literature.* Eerdmans. p. 4

135. Walton, *Prophets*, pp. 127-134

136. Walton, *Prophets*, p. 134

137. Wright, *New Testament*, p. 284

the evocative language and remain focused on the substance, which is Israel's hope for restoration.

Daniel is one of the earliest works of apocalyptic literature. I find the theory of Daniel's composition proposed by John Collins compelling. The book is divided into roughly two halves; the first, spanning Daniel 1-6, are a collection of court stories which most likely circulated as independent oral or written tradition before being compiled in Daniel. The second half, Daniel 7-12, is an extended apocalyptic narrative likely written shortly after the Maccabean Revolt, with the court stories being incorporated and recast to address the themes of the apocalyptic section. It is telling that 1:1-2:4a and chapters 8-12 were written in Hebrew, while 2:4b-7:28 was composed in Aramaic.[138] From the standpoint of Jeremiah 29:7, Daniel could more or less function as an extended commentary on balancing the command to 'seek the welfare of the city' with the prophecies of God's final judgment against Babylon and the future restoration of Israel.

In Daniel 1:1-16, Daniel and his friends Hananiah, Mishael, and Azariah (given the Babylonian names Belteshazzar, Shadrach, Meshach, and Abed-nego, respectively) are brought to Babylon during the exile but, under the auspices of Nebuchadnezzar, commanded to be trained as royal officials. Officials-in-training are offered Babylonian food and drink which Daniel and his friends refuse to consume on the grounds that it might violate their Law. A nervous commander extends a provision for them to eat only vegetables, and they become the strongest and wisest officials in Babylon. Nebuchadnezzar found Daniel and his friends superior to every other official, and they *"entered the king's personal service"*[139]. Rounding out the chapter in 1:21, Daniel remains a top official into the early years of Persian rule. As an introduction to the book as a whole this chapter explains how Jews could faithfully navigate political engagement under pagan rule. Daniel and his friends refuse to disobey God's Law; Jewish values will not be compromised, even under direct commandments from the king. As a result of Daniel's faithfulness, however, the king trusts him more than any other advisors and promotes him to a position of power. The book of Daniel, as we will see, envisions the ultimate defeat of all pagan empires, but until that day comes Jews can faithfully represent their God even at the heights of power.

In Daniel 2, Nebuchadnezzar has a dream which none of his advisors can interpret and in frustration orders them all to be slaughtered.[140] Daniel, however, believes that God will enable him to interpret the dream and requests the king's

---

138. Collins, *Daniel*, pp. 29-33

139. Daniel 1:19; in context see 1:17-21.

140. Daniel 2:1-13

audience. Characteristic of the genre, Daniel 2:17-49 is saturated in the language of 'revelation'; God reveals not only the content and meaning of Nebuchadnezzar's dream but His ultimate plans for creation to Daniel. In language reminiscent of Jeremiah, Daniel affirms with thanksgiving that God *"changes the times and the epochs; He removes kings and establishes kings"*[141], demonstrating that God is ultimately in charge of history and will use political leaders to advance His purposes. In 2:25-45, Daniel relays the dream and its interpretation to the king, which envisions the defeat of all pagan empires by the one God of heaven, summarized in 2:44: *"The God of heaven will set up a kingdom which will never be destroyed, and that kingdom will not be left for another people; it will crush and put an end to all these kingdoms, but it will itself endure forever"*. The echoes of 2 Samuel 7 and the prophecies based upon it are audible. In awe of Daniel's ability to interpret the dream, Nebuchadnezzar praises God and promotes Daniel and his friends to the heights of administrative power.[142] This reworked court story, which reveals several fundamental assumptions about the nature of political power and the proper Jewish response to it, rests upon the same set of themes we have seen repeatedly in this chapter. God is king, He is in control of history, the pagan empires will fall, and God will reign over all creation once again. Like Jeremiah 29:7, Jews can seek the welfare of the city in the meantime knowing that they won't last forever. Daniel is a faithful witness to his God, for which the king praises him and gives him power.

Daniel 3 shifts the focus to Daniel's friends Shadrach, Meshach, and Abednego. In 3:1-12, Nebuchadnezzar orders his administrators to bow down and worship a golden statue. The three Jews refuse to do so. In anger, Nebuchadnezzar orders that they be thrown into a furnace of blazing fire from which no god could possibly rescue them.[143] The Jews stand firm and in 3:12 issue a revealing response: *"let it be known to you, O king, that we are not going to serve your gods or worship the gold image that you have set up"*. While Jews are willing to work in the Babylonian administration, striving for the general welfare, they will refuse to worship pagan gods or compromise Jewish values, even unto death. For their defiance they are cast into the fire, but God sends an angel to deliver them.[144] 3:28-30 closes out the chapter with Nebuchadnezzar again praising God and even protecting the Jews who worship Him. God is once again revealed to pagan kings through the faithful witness of Shadrach, Meshach, and Abed-nego.

---

141. Daniel 2:21

142. Daniel 2:46-49

143. Daniel 3:13-18

144. Daniel 3:19-27

In Daniel 4-5, Babylonian kings are yet again confronted with the power of Israel's God. Daniel 4 begins and ends with Nebuchadnezzar hailing God as the eternal king who will forever rule over all creation[145], a lesson which he apparently forgets due to his arrogance in 4:28-30. As Daniel predicts, Nebuchadnezzar is stricken with a bout of madness until he returns to his senses and acknowledges Israel's God. Daniel foretells this in a vision which concludes with Daniel stating that Nebuchadnezzar's madness will end "*until you* [Nebuchadnezzar] *recognize that the Most High is ruler over the realm of mankind and bestows it on whomever He wishes*"[146]. Pagan empires are used by God for a purpose but will all be undone in the end because God is the only true king. Daniel 5 reinforces this message by showing how the Babylonian empire fell due to the arrogance of subsequent king Belshazzar. God controls the epochs of history, and Babylon is given into the hands of the Medes and Persians.

The infamous story of Daniel and the lion's den is found in Daniel 6, and for all of the popular interpretive abstractions which reduce this narrative to a parable about personal faith the major themes we are discussing all come rushing together in this passage. We can't isolate it from its historical context and ignore the larger point which Daniel's making. King Darius respects Daniel and his God, making the other imperial advisors jealous. They trick Darius into passing an ordinance, irrevocable even by the king, which states that anyone who fails to worship pagan gods shall receive capital punishment. Daniel refuses to comply and prays to his God anyway, after which his opponents expose him to Darius.[147] Darius, who greatly admires Daniel, becomes distressed and hopes that the "*God whom you* [Daniel] *constantly serve will Himself deliver you*"[148]. Daniel is thrown into a den of hungry lions at night but is completely unharmed come morning. Daniel is rescued and Darius throws his opponents in the den where they are promptly eaten alive.[149] In 6:26 Darius issues a decree which bears all the hallmarks of Second Temple Jewish kingdom theology: "*I make a decree that in all the dominion of my kingdom men are to fear and tremble before the God of Daniel; For He is the living God and enduring forever, And His kingdom is one which will not be destroyed, And his dominion will be forever*". Daniel, servant of the king, refuses to compromise, God delivers him, and the pagan king proclaims God's eternal rule. This is what it means to seek the welfare of the city which God will destroy.

---

145. Daniel 4:3, 34

146. Daniel 4:25

147. Daniel 6:1-13

148. Daniel 6:16

149. Daniel 6:16-24

The rest of Daniel (7-12) is a proper apocalypse and develops the themes repeated in chapters 1-6. It speaks of God raising and destroying empires until, finally, the last great pagan empire is no more and God rules as king over the earth. Two passages in particular are relevant for this study. The first is Daniel 7:9-18. After a series of successive empires, God constructs a heavenly courtroom over which he presides as judge. As judge, He condemns the 'bestial' nations who have come against His people. In 7:13-14, God establishes His kingdom: "*behold, with the clouds of heaven One like a Son of Man was coming, And he came up to the Ancient of Days And was presented before HIm. And to Him was given dominion, Glory and a kingdom, That all the peoples, nations and men of every language Might serve Him. His dominion is an everlasting dominion Which will not pass away; And His kingdom is one which will not be destroyed*". After this, God's people will rule over all the earth: "*the saints of the Highest One will receive the kingdom and possess the kingdom forever, for all ages to come*"[150]. This passage was interpreted by Jews in the Second Temple period as messianic[151], and the 'Son of Man', possibly a Davidic figure, would assist in establishing God's kingdom in which His faithful people rule the world. As we will see, early Christians universally associate this Daniellic 'Son of Man' with Jesus. At his trial, Caiaphas asks Jesus if he is the Christ (from *christos*, the Greek word for 'messiah'), to which Jesus quotes Daniel 7, stating in Mark "*I am*"[152]. More on this anon. The final chapter in Daniel is one of the first complete articulations of the doctrine of resurrection, a centerpiece of Jewish eschatological hopes in the Second Temple period. According to Daniel 12:1-2, there will be a great time of tribulation before God finally establishes His kingdom, and at that time those who have died will be awakened to either everlasting life or everlasting contempt. Daniel will not live to see this day but, for his faithfulness, will "*go your way to the end; then you will enter into rest and rise again for your allotted portion at the end of the age*"[153]. Resurrection guarantees that justice will be given to Jews who don't live until the end of the ages when God fulfills His promises to restore Israel. The faithful dead will rise to everlasting life and participate in the kingdom which, according to Daniel 7:18, will endure forever. The empires will be destroyed, and God's people will be vindicated.

The book of Esther is set during the reign of Persian King Ahasuerus (late-to-mid fifth century BCE) and narrates the story of a Jewish girl named Esther

---

150. Daniel 7:18

151. Collins, *Daniel*, pp. 81-83

152. Mark 14:61-62

153. Daniel 12:13

who becomes queen of Persia. She is an orphan raised by her uncle Mordecai[154], and after the king finds his wife displeasing he issues a decree that several beautiful women be presented to him so he might choose from the women a new queen. In Esther 2:17-18 Esther finds favor with Ahasuerus and is crowned the new queen. Mordecai hears of a plot to kill the king and, after revealing it through Esther, saves the king's life.[155] Esther 3, echoing Daniel 3 and 6, portrays a corrupt official, Haman, becoming angry with Mordecai for refusing to bow down and pay him homage. In his fury, he convinces Ahasuerus to kill all the Jews living in Persia. In chapter 4, Esther learns of this plot through Mordecai, who encourages her to share it with Ahasuerus. This would be a clear breach of court etiquette and could result in her death; Mordacai exhorts her to be brave, issuing the most famous line in the book: *"if you remain silent at this time, relief and deliverance will arise for the Jews from another place and you and your father's house will perish. And who knows whether you have not attained royalty for such a time as this?"*[156]. Resolved to save her people, Esther 5-7 narrates Esther valiantly appearing before Ahasurus, revealing Haman's treacherous plot, and saving the Jews. Haman is killed for his treachery, Mordecai becomes the second-in-command, and peace is guaranteed to all Persian Jews.[157]

These are the exact same themes we found in the book of Daniel. Notice that Esther is called to seek the welfare of the city by becoming queen of Persia (a political role if ever there was one) and Mordecai both saves the king's life and with his niece rescues the Jews. He becomes the second-in-command over a pagan empire as a Jew by refusing to pay homage to anyone other than his God. Gleason Archer summarizes the book nicely, highlighting the themes we have explored in this chapter: *"The theme of this short book is an illustration of the overruling providence of the sovereign God who delivers and preserves His people from the malice of the heathen who would plot their destruction . . . nothing could be clearer than the irresistible power of His omnipotent rule, watching over his covenant people"*[158]. This fits well within the Jeremiac framework of Second Temple Judaism that God's people seek peace and prosperity within pagan empires under the knowledge that God will one day destroy them and vindicate his people. Following the path charted by Ezra and Nehemiah, Jews were to remain distinct from their gentile neighbors and follow the Jewish Law, but so long as they did not surrender their unique identity

---

154. Esther 2:5-7

155. Esther 2:19-3:1

156. Esther 4:14

157. Esther 9-10

158. Archer, Gleason. 2007. *A Survey of Old Testament Introduction*. Moody Publishers. p. 395

as God's covenant family Jews were called to live in harmony with the nations. Jeremiah's command to *'seek the welfare of the city'* and his oracles of judgment against Babylon are squared by Jewish ecclesiology and eschatology: we alone are God's people, and he will one day return to fulfill his promise. Until then, we must seek peace.

ANTICIPATING THE NEW TESTAMENT

Jeremiah 29:7 was the cornerstone of Second Temple Jewish political engagement. Some Jews, including several Pharisees, sought to emulate the Maccabees and rebel against their pagan leaders, hoping God would get the message and intervene on their behalf. Revolutionary violence was not the primary Jewish approach to pagan imperialism. The dominant position during the Second Temple period, particularly in the diaspora, mirrored Jeremiah 29:7: live peacefully among the pagans without compromising God's Law. While smoldering revolutionary fires were never extinguished during the life of Jesus (and broke out into a full-fledged conflagration in 66 CE), the ethics of Jesus's kingdom proclamation and Paul's gospel fall within the venerable tradition of Jeremiah. Followers of Jesus were called not to exercise power like the Gentiles but find greatness in serving others, for even the Son of Man (Daniel 7:13!) did not come to be served, but to serve.[159] Before being executed on a Roman cross, Jesus tells Peter not to fight, for *"all those who take up the sword shall perish by the sword"*[160]. God's kingdom was coming, but it would not be established through human violence.

Bruce Winter identifies for the New Testament authors what Shaye Cohen found in Second Temple Judaism: *"a paradigm for the role of the Christian in society . . . can be found in Jeremiah 29:7"*[161]. Referring specifically to 1 Peter, the letter's approach to pagan authorities conforms exactly to the dominant political tradition of Second Temple Judaism. If, as I believe, the letter was genuinely penned by Peter (or conveyed orally through the hand of a scribe), this only further advances Winter's conclusions. In the first line of the letter, Peter refers to himself as *"an apostle of Jesus Christ"*. "Christ" in the New Testament is unambiguously titular and denotes His status as the long-promised Messiah[162], son of David. Peter then describes his audience as 'aliens', the language of exile and diaspora. The recipients of 1 Peter may live in Asia Minor, but they aren't citizens. In 1 Peter

---

159. Mark 10:41-45

160. Matthew 26:52

161. Winter, *Welfare*, p. 15

162. I will capitalize the word 'Messiah' when applied to Jesus.

2:11, just before issuing his audience instructions regarding their relationship to governing authorities, Peter reminds them that they are *"aliens and strangers"* before finally, in 1 Peter 2:13, exhorting them to *"Submit yourselves for the Lord's sake to every human institution"*. When this passage is isolated from its historical and literary context, as it regularly is in Western exegesis by filtering Peter's statements through the predominant political paradigm of authoritarian socialism, it appears to legitimize the inevitability of temporal human power. Read as but one part of an entire letter and within the tradition of Jeremiah 29:7, the text is much more nuanced than authoritarian interpretations would suggest. I will address this formidable passage in a later chapter, but a careful reader can anticipate my conclusion. 1 Peter 2:13-17 does not produce a timeless principle which sanctions believers to justify and impose their favorite political policies on unwilling neighbors through monopolistic state violence. Quite the opposite. Peter's reference to Rome as the new Babylon in 5:13 is no accident. Not all is as it appears.

One final, tantalizing example (which will be the subject of Chapter 16) to round out our study: Romans 13:1-7. Without a doubt the most contentious 'political' passage in the Bible, these seven verses have spawned endless debates, generating political theologies which are used to justify various forms of temporal power and the policy regimes which undergird them. Examining the historical and rhetorical context of the letter, even at a glance, once again complicates what most Christians wish in vain was a clear endorsement of their preferred political values. Paul begins his letter to Rome with an unambiguous statement about the nature of Jesus's identity. He is the Christ promised by Scripture, descendant of David raised from the dead, and one Lord, among whom the Gentiles through Paul are becoming obedient through faith.[163] The final line of the letter in 16:27 repeats the first: Jesus is the Christ, the messiah. Paul argues that both Jews and Gentiles are guilty of sinning against God but are redeemed through Jesus's sacrificial death[164], and that all of those who put their faith in him are now part of the global family of Abraham, thus fulfilling the promise made to him in Genesis.[165] Gentiles are now a part of God's family *without* having to embrace the Law and proselytize to Judaism. Just as in the Second Temple period the Law served an eschatological purpose, marking out those whom God would rescue in the final day, everyone sealed to receive eschatological salvation are now defined by faith in Jesus *as lord*: *"if you confess with your mouth Jesus as Lord, and believe in your heart that God raised*

---

163. Romans 1:1-5

164. Romans 3:21-26

165. Romans 4:13-25

Him from the dead, you will be saved[166]. The confession that Jesus is Lord cannot be detached from the Scriptural narrative, as Paul argues in 1:2. Jesus the Christ, resurrected lord of the world, is the fulfillment of the promises God made in 2 Samuel 7, Daniel 7, and the other prophets: Israel is restored, the nations will be judged, and the true son of David sits on His eternal throne.

The family of Abraham, which now includes Gentiles *as Gentiles*, are, like Ezra, Nehemiah, Daniel, and Esther, "*not* [to] *be conformed to this world, but be transformed by the renewing of your mind*"[167]. They should not emulate the patterns of those who aren't in Christ, the true king. They are, in the tradition of Jeremiah 29:7, to "*be at peace with all men*", leaving vengeance to God, and overcoming evil with good[168]. Immediately after this passage Paul issues his notorious statement on submission to the governing authorities but follows it up with a command to love everyone[169], and, also in the Jeremaic tradition, explains why his audience to follow this advice: "*Do this, knowing the time, that it is already the hour . . . for now salvation is nearer to us than when we believed . . . the night is almost gone, and the day is near . . . put on the Lord Jesus Christ, and make no provision for the flesh in regard to its lusts*"[170]. He closes out the body of his letter with a final ecclesiological exhortation, urging the family of Abraham (now including Gentiles!) to make sacrifices on behalf of one another, just as Christ made sacrifices for them.

Framed this way, it almost appears as if Romans 13:1-7 is practical advice; in light of Jewish ecclesiology and eschatology which has been reworked around the death, resurrection, and ascension of Jesus, Romans 13 can be read as yet another way of appropriating Jeremiah 29:7 in evolving historical circumstances. The authorities are in charge. God is in control of their destiny. They are called to punish bad and promote good. Live in peace with them, knowing that Jesus already sits on the throne and will one day finally bring about an end to the pagan empires. Through faith, God's people are assured of vindication on that day and will share in Christ's eternal reign.

There is, of course, more to the story. By incorporating a small handful of texts from the gospels and epistles at the end of this long review Second Temple Jewish history I hope to demonstrate both how the New Testament stands firmly within that Jewish tradition (instead of radically departing from it) and the value of reading complex texts in their literary and historical contexts. After exploring

---

166. Romans 10:9

167. Romans 12:2

168. Romans 12:18-21

169. Romans 13:8-10

170. Romans 13:11-14

the problem of imprecise political and economic categories in New Testament interpretation, providing consistent, irreducible, and universally applicable categorization of political and economic concepts, considering methodological issues in biblical interpretation, and outlining the Greco-Roman and Jewish contexts in which the New Testament were written, we are now finally in a position to begin exploring the New Testament itself, carefully analyzing what it says about political power and economic exchange. We begin our study with an examination of the gospels.

PART III | New Testament Interpretation

With consistent, irreducible, and universally applicable definitions of political and economic categories in place, a fully-articulated interpretive methodology, and a review of the Greco-Roman and Jewish contexts in which the New Testament was written, we are now in a position to demonstrate my thesis: the New Testament is incompatible with modern authoritarian socialism. The rest of this book, save for the concluding chapter, will review the entire New Testament, contextually examining the most controversial texts which relate to political and economic themes.

With the exception of Romans, I will proceed in canonical order, beginning with Jesus and the gospels. I explore the hermeneutics of gospel interpretation, how the gospels were designed to function as ancient biography, and what they are able to tell us about the historical Jesus. Before turning to the gospels themselves, I describe the main themes which characterize their narratives and which are relevant to our study. I examine the gospels in three broad units, devoting a chapter to the infancy narratives, baptism by John, and temptation, another to the life and ministry of Jesus, and a third to his final week in Jerusalem and beyond. Following my analysis of the gospels, Acts provides a bridge between the gospel narrative and Paul's letters as I navigate the history of Jesus's first followers in Jerusalem and throughout the Roman empire.

I then turn to the letters of Paul, saving Romans for last. As with the gospels, I propose a hermeneutical framework for interpreting Paul's letters, defining the type of information they were intended to provide for their audience, and reviewing the main themes in Paul which impinge upon our study of the political and economic themes in his letters. I move from 1 Corinthians through Philemon, situating each epistle in its historical context before turning climactically to Romans and, of course, the infamous (and notorious) 13:1-7. I move from Paul directly to Hebrews and the Catholic Epistles, spending a significant amount of time with 2 Peter 2:13-17, before concluding with Revelation. Let's get started.

CHAPTER 7 | Jesus and the Gospels

What the Gospels Tell Us About Jesus

Jesus came into Galilee, preaching the gospel of God, and saying, "The time is fulfilled, and the kingdom of God is at hand; repent and believe in the gospel."
Mark 1:14-15

The woman said to [Jesus], "Sir, I perceive that you are a prophet . . . I know that the Messiah is coming (He who is called Christ); when that One comes, He will declare all things to us." Jesus said to her, "I who speak to you am He."
John 4:19, 25-26

THE STORIES OF JESUS

Narrative First

Professional biblical scholars might object to launching a study of New Testament texts and their political and economic consequences with the gospels. Why? If the gospels are first in the New Testament's canonical order, doesn't it make sense to start with Matthew and work our way forward? It is universally acknowledged in scholarship, however, that Paul wrote his letters long before the gospels. In this prevailing theory the gospels were not composed until sometime after the fall of the Second Temple in 70 CE. Tracking the development of ideas in early Christianity must therefore commence with our earliest primary sources (Paul) and move chronologically to later ones (the gospels). Jonathan Bernier has recently challenged this paradigm, arguing persuasively that the Synoptic gospels were likely penned between the early 40s and late 50s CE, making them concurrent with Paul's ministry and therefore his letters.[1] Even if Bernier's argument

---

1. Bernier, Jonathan. 2022. *Rethinking the Dates of the New Testament*. Baker Academic. p. 84

is inaccurate, I still find the gospels to be a better starting point for our study than Paul.

In an attempt to understand how consistent, irreducible, and universally applicable definitions of political and economic concepts can help us think clearly about the principles we draw when interpreting New Testament passages which relate to those concepts, the gospels as narratives offer us a more vivid perspective on political and economic structures than those we receive from Paul's letters. This isn't to say that the letters of Paul are boring or less helpful; quite the contrary! Paul's letters are not narratives. The Pauline epistles were written to particular communities with the goal of addressing very specific questions and challenges relevant to Paul's audience. Paul only explains or elaborates on an issue if he finds it pertinent to his recipients, especially if they fail to comprehend an aspect of his teaching. The gospels, while certainly occasional and composed for specific intended audiences, are also narratives. As stories, they include details which would be superfluous in an epistle. It is a matter of genre, not substance or quality. Letters function differently than formal narratives. In researching this book I debated about placing Paul's letters first and then moving to the gospels, but concluded that, at least for this study, it makes more sense to begin with story before moving to letter.

"Hold Firmly to the Traditions"

The differences between Paul (along with other New Testament authors) and the gospels are, as I see it, entirely stylistic. While this view is controversial in certain quarters of biblical scholarship, I find there to be a great intellectual, thematic, and conceptual consistency between the gospel narratives and the epistles. This case can be compellingly made by appealing to a handful of New Testament texts once they are set in their proper historical context. Those who were fortunate enough to experience the ministry of Jesus in person became the first eyewitnesses, and they immediately formulated traditions that included both sayings of and stories about Jesus which circulated orally prior to written transcription. In a culture where very few people could read or write these stories would continue to circulate primarily in oral form even after the composition of textual gospels. Assuming Bernier is correct that Mark, the first written gospel, was composed sometime between 42-45 CE, this still leaves a twenty-year window between Jesus's ascension and Mark's gospel. Even if some of these traditions were actually committed to parchment, the earliest followers of Jesus, mostly drawn from the lower classes, would have heard them read aloud at their gatherings and disseminated them to others orally.

We know that the gospels include many of these early traditions, reworked of course by the evangelists to meet their personal rhetorical needs. The stories which would ultimately be included in the gospels were also probably well known in the early church, including the Christians to whom Paul and other New Testament authors wrote. Fourth century church historian Eusebius, writing sometime before the Council of Nicea in 325 CE, recounts what an earlier Church Father, Irenaeus, said about the authorship of the gospels: "*Matthew, indeed . . . produced his gospel written among the Hebrews in their own dialect, while Peter and Paul proclaimed the gospel and founded the church at Rome. After the departure of these, Mark, the disciple and interpreter of Peter, also transmitted to us in writing what had been preached by Peter . . . Luke, companion of Paul, committed to writing the gospel preached by him..Afterwards John the disciple of our Lord, the same that lay upon his bosom, also published the gospel*"[2]. While the accuracy of Irenaeus's identification of the gospel writers is debatable, what matters for our purposes is his underlying point: the gospels included material which was taught by the most prominent leaders of the early church.

Paul himself refers to the 'traditions' with which he instructed his congregations. In 1 Corinthians 11:2 he praises his congregations "*because you remember me in everything and hold firmly to the traditions, just as I delivered to you*", and, only a few verses later, explains the origins of these "*traditions*": "*I received from the Lord that which I also delivered to you*"[3]. Blomberg notes that Paul is not claiming Jesus *directly* received instruction about the Lord's Supper (the wider context of the passage) but that he is referring to the traditions handed down from the eyewitness which were transmitted in early Christian communities.[4] Paul appeals to this tradition yet again in 2 Thessalonians 2:15: "*stand firm and hold to the traditions which you were taught, whether by word of mouth or by letter from us*". We see the same dynamic in the epistles of Peter and John. In 2 Peter 1:18, Peter claims that both him and other leaders were eyewitnesses, exhorting his audience in 3:2 to "*remember the words spoken beforehand by the holy prophets and the commandment of the Lord and Savior spoken by your apostles*". 1 John 1:1-4, which opens the letter, makes the same move: "*what we have heard, what we have seen with our eyes, what we have looked at and touched with our hands . . . we have seen and testify and proclaim to you . . . These things we write*". In other words, John, like Peter, is saying "trust us, we were there". Paul, Peter, and John were writing letters to believers familiar with traditions they accepted as derived from eyewitnesses, and it is these same traditions which would be appropriated and reworked into the written gospels.

---

2. Eusebius, *Ecclesiastical History*, 5:8:1-3; in Cruse, C.F. 1998. *Eusebius' Ecclesiastical History*. Hendrickson Publishers.

3. 1 Corinthians 11:23

4. Blomberg, Craig. 1994. *1 Corinthians*. Zondervan. p. 229

We should assume, then, that the traditions taught to the earliest believing communities included many (or perhaps most) of the stories which would later become the four canonical gospels. The notion, popular in some intellectual circles, that Paul was not interested in the 'historical Jesus' is flat-out wrong; in writing letters addressing particular problems, such as 1 Corinthians, he does not need to waste space by reviewing the sayings and stories of Jesus his audience already knew. He simply assumes they are familiar with these traditions and develops his instructions around them. This drives my point home: while Paul, Peter, John, and other early followers of Jesus knew the stories about him and indeed circulated them orally for decades, we actually *have* these traditions, albeit in redacted form, in the gospels, making the gospels a logical starting point for thinking about the New Testament, politics, and economics. We begin with Jesus and build up from there.

Four Gospels, One Gospel

The English noun 'gospel' comes from the Greek word *euangelion*, meaning 'good news'. This term is used to summarize Paul's proclamation[5] and Jesus's message of the kingdom of God[6] and is an extremely important term in early Christianity. *Euangelion* becomes the name given to the four narratives about Jesus found in Christian Scripture. Since the singular noun *euangelion* appears nowhere in the Septuagint, it seems as if the term may have been, as James Dunn suggests, a creation of Paul. Even if 'gospel' is a neologism, Dunn argues that the concept of 'good news' is a common theme in the Old Testament, particularly in Isaiah.[7] Cognates of the noun *euangelion* are used in four passages in the second half of Isaiah, 40:9, 52:7, 60:6, and 61:1, and the rhetorical context of each passage are, unsurprisingly, prophecies about the coming restoration of Israel. God will return, vindicate and rescue Israel, and reveal Himself to the nations. Note that *euangelion* and its cognates (all of which are, in Isaiah, verbal, *'proclaiming'* good news) imply a narrative; they are not general messages about Israel's God making positive statements but assume that Israel has sinned, God will redeem her, and restoration will result in the fulfillment of God's promises. In other words, *euangelion*, a concept central to early Christianity, implies a narrative, particularly the story of Israel reaching its climactic fulfillment in God's great, long-anticipated restoration. It is also important to note that the term was used in the Greco-Roman world. A

---

5. Romans 1:1-5, 1 Corinthians 15:1-4, 2 Timothy 2:8

6. Mark 1:14, Matthew 4:23, Luke 9:6

7. Dunn, James. 1998. *The Theology of the Apostle Paul.* Eerdmans. pp. 166-169

Roman inscription describes the peace brought by Augustus as 'good news' and was also employed in reference to a military victory. Generally the term implied good news of some significance. In the Synoptic Gospels, the word *euangelion* "*refers primarily to the announcement of "good news" associated with the arrival of God's kingdom, particularly in association with Jesus' mission and identity as the Messiah*"[8].

A telling example of this dynamic is found in Luke 4:16-30. Teaching in the synagogue of Nazareth, Jesus quotes directly from one of the 'good news' passages in Isaiah 61:1-2: "*He opened the book and found the place where it was written, "The Spirit of the Lord is upon Me, because He anointed Me to preach the gospel to the poor. He has sent Me to proclaim release to the captives, and recovery of sight to the blind, to set free those who are oppressed, to proclaim the favorable year of the lord*", and concludes, dramatically, by stating "*Today this Scripture has been fulfilled in your hearing*"[9]. Jesus, evoking the narratival implications of *euangelion*, makes the audacious claim that his ministry marks the beginning of the restoration of Israel; it is 'good news' because God is finally, through Jesus, fulfilling the prophetic hope. The thematic statements of Mark 1:14 and Matthew 4:23, which link Jesus's kingdom proclamation to 'good news', demonstrate this point perfectly. The Kingdom of God is 'good news', *euangelion*, because it means God is finally making good on His promises. The time is up, repent and believe the gospel.

Since the term *euangelion* implies a narrative of restoration, it is entirely appropriate that Matthew, Mark, Luke, and John are given the title 'gospel'. In Greek, each gospel includes the preposition *kata* in their titles, which means "*according to*". Scot McKnight explains that when the early Christians chose the title 'gospel' for the four gospels, they were not inventing a new kind of literature or insinuating there were four different versions of the 'good news', "*they didn't call the first four books of the New Testament the "Gospels." Instead, they called each one of them the "Gospel." They were saying there was one Gospel, but it was written down in four versions, the (one) Gospel according to* [thus the Greek *kata*] *Matthew, Mark, Luke, and John*"[10]. They are all making the same claim: Isaiah promised God's restoration of Israel would be 'good news', Jesus is the fulfillment of that promise, therefore the story of Jesus completes the story of Israel.[11] *Euangelion* presupposes a long narrative which finds its denouement in Jesus. This is why Matthew, Mark, Luke, and John all bear the title 'gospel'.

---

8. Schenck, Kenneth. 2013. "*Gospel: Good News*". In *Dictionary of Jesus and the Gospels*, 2nd ed. ed. by Joel B. Green, InterVarsity Press. pp. 342-343

9. Luke 4:17-21

10. McKnight, Scot. 2011. *The King Jesus Gospel*. Zondervan. p. 81

11. McKnight, *King Jesus*, pp. 82-82

One of the persistent themes in the Old Testament was the kingship of God, quite obviously invoked when Jesus proclaims the 'kingdom of God'. In light of the built-in eschatological narrative invoked by the term *euangelion*, this must have a transformative effect on the political and economic institutions of his day, and, as texts which Christians read in search of principles that can be applied today, we must remember that the very title 'gospel' itself can't be extrapolated from its historical context and anachronistically employed to perpetuate the modern distinction between religion and politics, a distinction which exists only as an intellectual construct in the minds of educated Westerners. For those of us who believe the gospels matter, we must pay close attention to how they tell the story of Jesus if we want to understand their political and economic implications. We must now address the kind of information the gospels were designed to communicate about Jesus. How do the gospels work as source material and what impact are they supposed to have on those who read them? There can be no serious commentary on the relationship between the gospels, politics, and economics without discerning how they work as texts. We will now turn to this question.

HOW TO READ THE GOSPELS

The history of gospels scholarship is tortuously complex. Jesus was a historical figure, and no one save for a small number of fringe mythicists would deny his existence. This is one of the very few areas in which New Testament scholars are in complete unanimity: Jesus existed. Beyond this assertion there is scholarly agreement on very little. For most of church history, Christians believed that Jesus as a historical figure was more or less exactly as he is described in the gospels. This paradigm was completely shattered in the modern era. After the Reformation and through the Enlightenment, skeptical intellectuals began to develop theories which suggested that the gospels might not be an accurate reflection of Jesus as a historical figure but instead heavily influenced by the theology of the early church. Albert Schweitzer famously attributes this intellectual iconoclasm to Herman Samuel Reimarus, a late eighteenth century skeptic[12], but Tucker Ferda and other scholars have argued convincingly that skepticism about the gospels accurately representing Jesus preceded Reimarus[13]. Either way it is with the dawn of modernity that the distinction between 'the Jesus of history' and 'the Christ of faith' was first articulated, with a parallel assumption that the gospels were more a product of early Christian belief than an unbiased presentation of Jesus as a historical figure.

---

12. Schweitzer, *Quest*, pp. 13-26

13. Ferda, Tucker. 2024. *Jesus and His Promised Second Coming*. Eerdmans. pp. 7-14

Thus was born what Albert Schweitzer termed the 'Quest for the Historical Jesus', the attempt to separate facts about Jesus from the mythology of the early church which had crept into the gospels. Which parts of the gospels actually go back to Jesus, giving us authentic information about him, and which parts were invented by the evangelists themselves to make a theological point? These questions have dominated modern scholarship, and answers to them are as numerous as the scholars who work on them. On one end of the spectrum are extreme skeptics like D.F. Strauss and Rudolph Bultmann, both of whom argued that the gospels are almost entirely mythological, little more than the doctrines of early Christians cast as story, and that they provide us with very little information about the historical Jesus. On the other side of the spectrum are scholars like Ben Meyer and N.T. Wright. While not denying the gospels were shaped by the theological interests of the evangelists, they have contended that the gospels are generally reliable and provide us with enough information to plausibly reconstruct the historical Jesus. Between these two positions are a myriad of variations, with scholars developing theories, methods, and thousands of books and articles all arguing for their particular perspective on the relationship between the gospels and Jesus as a historical figure. The uninitiated wade into the turbulent waters of Jesus research, fail to find solid footing, and leave the river, never to return. Having spent nearly two decades reading gospels scholarship, I can't blame them.

This book is not designed to settle these questions. I suspect my conclusions will be compatible with a number of theories about the historical Jesus and his relationship to the gospels as source material for reconstructing him. In order to make a compelling case about the interpretation of political and economic concepts in the gospels, however, I must address this question and then make a positive case for how I understand the gospels and the information they provide us about Jesus. Far too many books, articles, and podcasts about the Bible and politics never address the mechanics of the text, which is one of the reasons I believe it is easy for commentators to bring their modernized, unsystematized assumptions about political and economic categories with them when they read the Bible.

There are four methodological issues which are relevant for the reading of the gospels I am proposing in this book, and we will review them in this section. First, I will address the perplexing question of how the gospels relate to one another. Matthew, Mark, and Luke are very similar. John is quite different. Why is this the case, and how might understanding their relationship help us better mine the text for information? Second, I will argue that the gospels are an ancient form of biography and explain how part of the genre's intended effect was insisting that the audience emulate the main character's virtuous attributes. Third, I will explore the gospels as literary works and discuss how story elements shape their presentation of the material, before finally addressing what the gospels can tell us about Jesus as a historical figure and the four main themes which emerge from a historical reading of them. The final section of this chapter will explore these four main themes, all of which have an enormous influence on how the gospels convey information about politics and economics.

The Synoptic Problem and John

Matthew, Mark, and Luke each present traditions about Jesus in which he gives instructions regarding divorce. Matthew 19:3-12 and Mark 10:2-9 tell the same story, but with slight differences. Jesus's instructions are given because the Pharisees test Jesus, asking Jesus if it is lawful to divorce one's wife. Matthew includes the phrase *"for any reason at all"*[14]. In Mark, Jesus asks the Pharisees what Moses says about the issue before quoting Genesis and stating that what God has joined together shouldn't be divided[15]. Matthew flips the order, quoting Genesis first and then explaining why Moses gave the instructions on divorce before declaring divorce is, in most cases, a form of adultery[16]. In Mark 10:10-12, the disciples ask Jesus about his instruction, and he answers them. Matthew recounts the same story but lengthens it in 19:10-12. Luke, on the other hand, omits nearly all of the narrative details found in Matthew and Mark; while Jesus's teaching on divorce is still issued in response to the Pharisees it is reduced to a single verse, Luke 16:18, with no commentary about Moses, Genesis, the Law, or the disciple's questions. The language, however, is so similar to Matthew and Mark it is inconceivable Luke created the story from scratch.

This raises several pertinent questions. First, someone was likely copying somebody else. Was Luke copying Matthew? Was Mark copying Matthew and Luke? How do we account for the literary similarities between these different versions of Jesus's instruction? Why are they different, and what does this say about the historicity of these passages? If the evangelists are all telling the same story, Luke could easily be summarizing Matthew or Mark, but why do Matthew and Mark recount the same story differently? Is one 'correct' historically and the others ahistorical? Are they all wrong? Why is John silent on the issue of divorce if it was such an important part of the Jesus tradition that the other three evangelists included it? These are serious questions which deserve compelling answers. In this section I will discuss how scholars account for the similarities and differences between the four

---

14. Matthew 19:3, Mark 10:2

15. Mark 10:3-8

16. Matthew 19:4-9

gospels and argue for a particular theory I believe adequately solves the problem. Building on this in the following sections, we will explore how the gospels work, why they portray the same stories in different ways, and what this insight tells us about Jesus, all with a view to understanding how the evangelist's presentation of Jesus impacts our study of politics and economics.

I was challenged to read the gospels by someone from my church at the age of fourteen. I took him up on the challenge and stormed through all four of them in about two weeks. While it was a spiritually transformative experience, I also noticed Matthew, Mark, and Luke were similar while John was entirely unique. It doesn't take a scholar to recognize John is not like the others and that the others have a whole lot in common. Augustine, following Eusebius, proposed Matthew as the first written gospel, used by Luke and Mark as a source. John on this theory was written later. Augustine articulated the dominant paradigm for thinking about gospels' authorship and source material for much of Christian history, but as Enlightenment deists began to challenge the idea that the gospels gave us unvarnished information about Jesus, the traditional view of their composition was questioned as well. It didn't take long for intellectual critics to draw a hard line, placing Matthew, Mark, and Luke on one side and John on the other. The former became known as the *Synoptic* gospels, from a Greek term meaning "together seen", and were analyzed independently of John. This hard dichotomy between John and the Synoptics, dubbed the *"Johannine firewall"* by Mark Goodacre[17], shifted scholarly interest to Matthew, Mark, and Luke for much of the modern era. As the historicity of the gospels became fair game for revision, so did the Augustinian view of Luke and Mark's dependence on Matthew. Dubbed the 'Synoptic problem' in the late eighteenth century by scholar J.J Greisbach, the synoptic problem is *"the question of their literary interrelationship"*.[18]

By studying the Synoptic problem scholars were attempting to determine which versions of the stories told in the Synoptics were the most primitive, possibly giving them accurate historical information about Jesus shorn of their mythological dress. Even if certain scholars believed 'getting back' to the historical Jesus hidden behind the embellished gospels was impossible, identifying the earliest traditions would at least allow historians to propose theories about why the church would invent traditions about Jesus in the first place. The quest for the historical Jesus depends upon an answer to the Synoptic problem. While some scholars argue for the inclusion of John in historical Jesus research, the majority either marginalized or outright rejected John as historically viable, even if they valued its

---

17. Goodacre, Mark. 2025. *The Fourth Synoptic Gospel.* Eerdmans. p. 19

18. Blomberg, Craig. 2009. *Jesus and the Gospels.* 2nd ed. B&H Academic. p. 89

literary beauty.[19] The synoptics would take pride of place in biblical scholarship, and, in the words of Alan Kirk, there was *"no more basic question in Christian-origins inquiry than the Synoptic problem"*[20].

This isn't a matter of abstract theory. The infamous exchange between Jesus and the Pharisees in which Jesus utters the phrase *"render unto Caesar"* occurs in all three Synoptic gospels[21] as part of a larger set of traditions which were transmitted as a unit. Like Jesus's teaching on divorce there are minor differences in each retelling. If we want to know why Matthew's version differs from Luke's we must employ a theory of literary dependence. If Luke copied Matthew, why did he rearrange parts of the story? If Mark used Luke or Matthew, why did he make the exchange shorter? While answers to the Synoptic problem are always speculative, interpretive conclusions must account for the literary relationship between the Synoptic gospels. Far too often modern Christians rush to draw exegetical conclusions about controversial passages without thinking about the underlying literary mechanics, all while assuming imprecise definitions of political and economic concepts. Interpretations constructed in this manner will inevitably mischaracterise the Jesus tradition and by extension Jesus himself. What is the most compelling solution to the Synoptic problem and how can we think critically about Synoptic differences? Recent scholarship may have found a way through the maze.

Perhaps the greatest accomplishment of nineteenth-century biblical scholarship is the theory of Markan priority. Now almost universally accepted by scholars, Markan priority asserts that Mark wrote the first gospel and Matthew and Luke used Mark as a source. I entirely agree. As this theory rose to prominence, it was accompanied by a second theory: Matthew and Luke were entirely independent of each other. Even though they both utilized Mark as a source, neither were aware of the other's gospel. This presented another complication: Matthew and Luke both contain material, mostly sayings of Jesus, not found in Mark but so linguistically similar they must have been derived from a common source. Scholars began to develop a theory that there was a second source besides Mark which Matthew and Luke used when composing their gospels, comprised mostly of Jesus's sayings. German scholar Fredrich Schleiermacher, writing in the early nineteenth century, called this document 'Q', from the German word *quelle*, meaning 'source'.[22]

---

19. Blomberg, Craig. 2024. *Jesus the Purifier*. Baker Academic. p. 29

20. Kirk, Alan. 2023. *Jesus Tradition, Early Christian Memory, and Gospel Writing*. Eerdmans. p. 1

21. Matthew 22:15-22, Mark 12:13-17, Luke 20:20-25

22. Blomberg, *Gospels*, pp. 99-103

Markan priority was combined with Q theory, and a new reigning paradigm for the Synoptic problem was born: the Two-Document Hypothesis.[23]

The Two-Document Hypothesis dominated biblical scholarship for over a century. While there were various proposals for refining or nuancing the theory, very few people questioned its basic premise. The Two-Document Hypothesis would meet its greatest challenge in 1955 when Austin Farrer made a radical proposal: perhaps Q didn't exist. While Farrer retained Markan priority he also contended there was no solid evidence for the existence of Q and reformulated the Synoptic problem without it. Mark wrote first, Matthew followed Mark, adding his own traditional material, and Luke knew Mark and Matthew, employing them both as sources for his retelling of the gospel. The so-called 'Farrer Theory' is now the greatest alternative to the Two-Document Hypothesis and has been widely developed, promoted, and popularized by Michael Goulder and Mark Goodacre.[24]

I believe the Farrer Theory is correct. James Barker has written an excellent defense of Farrer in his book *Writing and Rewriting the Gospels*. A glaringly obvious flaw in the Two-Document Hypothesis is the complete lack of any historical evidence for Q, and Barker explains how the Farrer Theory easily accounts for the differences between the Synoptics without recourse to a hypothetical sayings document. He examines 'trajectories' in the development of Synoptic tradition. Mark, the shortest gospel, was the first to be written. Matthew uses Mark as a source and adds his own material, clustering sayings and stories together in large units. Luke, using both of these gospels as sources, rearranges, edits, and omits material to construct his narrative while supplementing it with additional traditions not found in the other two.[25] The Farrer theory is elegant and logically accounts for the Synoptic data. Mark Goodacre, perhaps the most important proponent of the Farrer Theory in recent decades, explains that dispensing with Q and following Farrer allows scholars to take seriously the creativity of the evangelists, giving them the freedom to modify their sources in ways previous generations of scholarship never anticipated. The Farrer Theory also accounts for the flexibility of the oral tradition through which the sayings and stories found in the gospels were primarily circulated in the first century.[26] In my interpretation of the gospels, I accept the Farrer (Goulder-Goodacre) Theory as the Synoptic Problem's solution.

---

23. Kirk, *Jesus Tradition*, pp. 122-150

24. Barker, James. 2025. *Writing and Rewriting the Gospels*. Eerdmans. pp. 56-57; see also Kirk, *Jesus Tradition*, pp. 203-297

25. Barker, *Writing*, pp. 60-63

26. Goodacre, Mark. 2004. *"A World Without Q"*. In *Questioning Q*, ed. by Mark Goodacre and Nicholas Perrin, InterVarsity Press. p. 177

This also has a profound impact on our understanding of John. There are a growing number of scholars arguing in favor of John's historical reliability and attempting to integrate it with data from the Synoptics.[27] Barker believes the Farrer Theory can help. He explores the ancient writing technique *oppositio in imitando*, "*an ancient technique of imitating a classic story while turning elements inside out*"[28]. He provides several examples from Greek, Roman, and Jewish literature, showing it was relatively common for ancient authors to imitate a classic story while changing its major details.[29] Writers who employed o*ppositio in imitando* were showing respect for the works they imitated; Barker explains how this impacts our understanding of the gospels: "*As it pertains to gospel writing, the point is that subsequent authors could be deeply indebted to a source text while creatively rewriting it*"[30]. While the Synoptic authors used this practice with individual stories, Barker argues that following the trajectories of creative rewriting through the gospels leads us to John, who must be familiar with the Synoptics and writing in the technique of *oppositio in imitando*.[31] While John and the Synoptics are *stylistically* different, they are often entirely compatible in *substance*. Goodacre agrees. In his book published after the first draft of this chapter, *The Fourth Synoptic Gospel*, Goodacre conclusively demonstrates that John not only knew the Synoptics but creatively rewrote them. Summarizing his findings, Goodacre contends that the "*Fourth Gospel is at a unique point in history, still inspired by Mark's Gospel yet influenced by the ways that Matthew and Luke retell its stories*"[32]. I agree with Barker and Goodacre; themes which appear in Mark's gospel develop in trajectory across Matthew and Luke and are rewritten in John.

Revealing my methodological cards, I affirm Markan priority, the Farrer Theory, and the thematic compatibility of John with the Synoptics. How does this solution to the Synoptic problem impact my interpretation of the gospels? From this point on I will refer to Mark as the first gospel writer, and my commentary and footnotes will reflect Markan priority. As I explore the differences between the gospels I am operating under the theory that Matthew knew only Mark, that Luke knew both Mark and Matthew, and that John knew all three. While my own study of the gospels places a greater emphasis on the Synoptics, I will show where

---

27. Blomberg, *Purifier*, pp. 179-222; Blomberg's entire book argues in favor of using John for historical Jesus research.

28. Barker, *Writing*, p. 21

29. Barker, *Writing*, pp. 20-25

30. Barker, *Writing*, p. 21

31. Barker, *Writing*, pp. 82-113

32. Goodacre, *Fourth Synoptic Gospel*, p. 162

themes which are critical to the Synoptics are also found and developed in John. Now that I have accounted for the literary relationship between the gospels we must discuss their genre.

The Gospels as Biography

In Chapter 4 I argued in favor of the reliability and authority of Scripture and explained how, in order to do proper exegesis, the Bible must be understood in its historical context. This includes accounting for the various genres of literature found in the Bible and interpreting texts in accordance with the standards of those genres. I briefly commented on the growing consensus in gospels scholarship which assert they conform to the ancient genre of biography, both similar to and dissimilar from modern biographical writing. In order to properly understand how the gospels were designed to work in antiquity, it is worth repeating some of the content from Chapter 4 here and expand upon my initial introduction.

Helen Bond, whose work I previously referenced, has been at the forefront of biographical gospels research. Like modern biographies, those written in antiquity were intended to communicate information about their subject, but ancient biography had two unique characteristics. Bond explains *"all Greek biographies have two things in common: (1) the desire to commemorate a great life (or to occasionally to record a dissolute one); and (2) a hope that their audience would learn from it . . . a person's life was laid out for others to imitate"*[33]. While modern biographies often commemorate a great life and occasionally encourage the audience to learn from its subject, this was *the* main purpose of ancient biographies. They were written to honor the memory of a great figure and intentionally crafted to set an example for readers to emulate.

This means that historical accuracy, the supposed gold-standard of modern biography, was less important than commemoration or emulation. Bond continues: *"while biography was closely related in many ways to history, and often took "historical" subjects as its focus, we need to be careful about assuming that biographers were interested in history for its own sake. Their purpose was not to provide an accurate list of all that their subject did and said, but to lay bare the essence of the man, to re-create a living character"*[34]. Bond is *not* claiming ancient biographers manufactured false narratives regarding their subjects but were more cornered about accurately portraying their character. Representing the subject was more significant than historical accuracy in the narrow modern sense, and ancient biographers selectively

---

33. Bond, *Biography*, p. 65

34. Bond, *Biography*, 69-70

edited, embellished, rearranged, synthesised, or stylized the stories and sayings they told about their subjects as long as it captured, as Bond perfectly expresses, the *essence* of the man.

When the gospels are understood as ancient biographies, it doesn't matter that Mark, Matthew, and Luke all portray Jesus's teaching on divorce in a slightly different manner, or that John eschews it altogether. Each evangelist is constructing a narrative about Jesus in an attempt to commemorate his life and enable their audience to learn from and emulate it. They felt free to edit their source material in an attempt to craft a biographical narrative. Evangelical scholar Mike Licona agrees entirely with Bond's assessment of the gospels as biography, and his commentary deserves to be quoted at length: "*We would be mistaken if we assumed that ancient biography had the same objectives and standards as modern biography . . . Ancient biographers sought to narrate sayings and deeds of the biographee that illuminated his character . . . we should not conceive of ancient biography as the attempt to provide readers with precise reporting and historical descriptions nearing photographic accuracy. Imposing modern expectations on ancient texts and authors is anachronistic since it assumes a standard not aligned with their objectives*"[35]. The differences between the gospels are an example of biographical writing. The objective is to portray the essence of the subject, in this case Jesus, and encourage the audience to learn from his example. The evangelists are crafting their biographies for distinct communities, each of which have different needs, so they naturally borrow from the sources they respect (based on Barker's theory of trajectories) and rework them into a new composition. If we want to read the gospels historically and draw principles from the text we must first accept them as biography. For more theologically conservative Christians, Licona helpfully explains how a biographical interpretation of the gospels is entirely compatible with both inspiration and inerrancy[36], and I encourage skeptical readers to engage with his work.

Not only do the gospels reflect the goals of ancient biography, they also reflect the character of the oral tradition from which they were drawn. Remember that the stories and sayings of Jesus were transmitted and developed *orally* before, during, and even after the gospels were composed, and early followers of Jesus, most of whom were functionally illiterate, would have encountered Him exclusively through oral tradition. In his magisterial book *Jesus Remembered*, James Dunn rightly criticizes biblical scholarship for failing to recognize the impact of orality on the Jesus tradition.[37] Oral traditions are both informal and controlled, meaning

---

35. Licona, Mike. 2024. *Jesus, Contradicted.* Zondervan. pp. 57-58

36. Licona, *Contradicted,* pp. 169-223

37. Dunn, James. 2003. *Jesus Remembered.* Eerdmans. p. 192

that the core of a tradition, its purpose or main point, remains unchanged, but its details may be reworked in subsequent retellings without compromising the tradition's core. Dunn explains how *"in oral tradition one telling of a story is in no sense an editing of a previous telling; rather, each telling starts with the same subject and theme, but the retellings are different; each telling is a performance of the tradition itself. . . oral tradition is typically flexible, with constant themes, recognizable versions of the same story, some word-for-word repetition, and both fixed and variable formulaic elements depending on the content of the performance"*[38]. Dunn goes on to argue that the written gospels, as products of oral tradition, follow the same pattern of informal control as oral retellings. Mark, Matthew, and Luke make the same basic points about divorce but rework them in their own biographical retelling of Jesus's life. Given the biographical nature of the gospels and their reliance on oral tradition, we should expect there to be differences in the tradition, and these differences help us see how each evangelist is accentuating their presentation of Jesus. Even in diversity, a clear picture of the political and economic consequences of Jesus's ministry can be discerned from the gospels once we learn to read them as orally-informed biographies.

Thus far the emphasis has been on how the gospels portray Jesus, the first characteristic of ancient biography. The second, emulation or imitation, is just as significant. The gospel writers intended their biographies of Jesus to elicit a moral, ethical, and behavioral response. Cornelis Bennema, in a recent study of mimesis in antiquity, discusses the complex hermeneutical process of imitation. Bennema explains, *"Mimetic ethics in early Christianity is not about mechanically replicating certain commands or moral principles found in the New Testament but about closely observing an exemplar regarding their character, lifestyle, and conduct"*[39]. While the Synoptic gospels are not primarily composed for memetic instruction, at least when compared to other Greco-Roman sources[40], concepts such as self-denial[41] are obviously exemplified by Jesus with the implication that the audience will imitate Him. This does not mean, quite obviously, imitating Jesus's exact actions (followers are not called to peripatetically preach around Galilee, for instance), but rather to embody his spirit of self-denial in other contexts. Bennema argues that mimesis is central to John[42]. Combining this data with the second function of biography in antiquity, emulating the *ethos* of its subject, the evangelists expected their audience

---

38. Dunn, *Remembered*, p. 209

39. Bennema, Cornelis. 2025. *Imitation in Early Christianity*. Eerdmans. p. 366

40. Bennema, *Imitation*, pp. 150-155

41. Mark 8:34, Matthew 10:38, Luke 9:23

42. Bennema, *Imitation*, pp. 225-227

to find in Jesus an example which those who put their faith in him would embody. The gospels are as much about cultivating discipleship and character formation as they are about conveying the core of Jesus's unique identity.

The implications of ancient biography for our study are extremely important. The gospels are stylized, material is reworked into new narrative forms, and the holistic presentation of Jesus matters more than its constituent parts. I will not waste any time arguing for the historicity of particular sayings or stories in the gospels because, as in oral tradition, ancient biographers were not concerned with perfect historiographical accuracy. They sought a faithful representation of the subject while creatively structuring narratival details. More importantly, the presentation of Jesus in the gospels should shape the lives of believers who read them. We are called to emulate his character, seeking to embody it in historical contexts which are foreign to Jesus's own. Imitation, as Bennema correctly noted, is a hermeneutical process; it requires creative interpretation and application. If, as I will argue in the following chapters, the biographical representation presents Jesus as a man who consistently renounces violence, allows critics to walk away, and personally offers help to those in need, Christians must follow his example. Maybe the political and economic system of authoritarian socialism isn't compatible with the teachings of Jesus after all.

The Gospels as Narratives

In Chapter 4 I discussed the importance of Scripture's literary and rhetorical contexts. Individual words, passages, or units cannot be understood without reference to the larger purpose of the work within which they are included. Nearly all modern discussions about the political and economic consequences of New Testament texts isolate passages from their literary (in the case of stories like the gospels) or rhetorical (as in Paul's letters) contexts and proceed as if they can be fruitfully interpreted independent of contextual considerations. This method doesn't work, as I will explain below. The gospels are biographies, narratives which deserve to be read as literary wholes. No one picks up a novel, reads a few paragraphs from a handful of random pages, and claims they understand the plot. That would be utterly ridiculous. The evangelists each spin their own story of Jesus by including individual sayings and stories from the Jesus tradition to construct a complete narrative.

Speaking of the gospel of Matthew, Jack Kingsbury makes an accurate point about reading narratives: *"approach*[ing] *Matthew's Gospel as a unified narrative . . . is to attend to the very story it tells. When one reads Matthew, one temporarily takes leave of one's familiar world of reality and enters into another world that is autonomous in its own right*[43]. Like any other story, the gospels must be read from start to finish. While it is impossible in a book like this to do justice to the narratival arc of each gospel, I will make reference to how individual passages contribute to their literary contexts when relevant for my exegesis. Although Christians are used to hearing individual passages expounded in sermons, Bible studies, and small groups, we must break our habit of thinking we can derive meaning from an individual unit, especially in a long narrative, without considering how the individual unit functions within the larger story as a literary whole.

Reading the gospels as biographical narratives also requires paying attention to the features intrinsic to any story. Holistically analyzing the gospels involves identifying the narrator, the setting, the plot, the characters, and the rhetoric.[44] Just as we would read a modern novel, we can't ignore these basic characteristics of narrative development. The evangelists employ all of them because they are composing compelling narratives about Jesus. Failing to recognize these textual dynamics will inevitably lead to gross misinterpretations of the gospels. They all have a beginning and an end, and the content which is found in between contributes to a coherent plot headed towards a denouement and conclusion. The gospels are not textbooks. While many, perhaps most, modern readers of the gospels believe they primarily exist to provide us with information about Jesus or abstract moral instruction, this is anachronistically reductive. They creatively retell a story about Jesus, whom they believe is Israel's Messiah, and utilize narratival features common to storytelling in all cultures throughout history. While the methods and functions of ancient biographical narratives differ in many respects from modern biographies, the use of plot features, character development, creative settings, and other storytelling features are essential components of the canonical gospels.

One of the presuppositional flaws in post-Enlightenment biblical scholarship was its assumption that academics studying the gospels nearly two thousand years after their composition could easily separate historical fact from mythological fiction. With the right methodological tools early Christianity theology, which had been woven into the gospel texts by the evangelists themselves, was able to be sifted and separated from the bedrock of historical fact, providing the modern world with a reconstructed Jesus entirely divergent from the Christ of faith. Liberating Jesus from his ecclesiastical constraints empowered scholars to recast Jesus in their own image, making him a spokesperson for their preferred political, economic, and social programs. By ignoring the gospel's narrative structure scholars could

---

43. Kingsbury, Jack. 1988. *Matthew as Story*. 2nd ed. Fortress Press. p. 2

44. Rhoads, David, Joanna Dewey, and Donald Michie. 1999. *Mark as Story*. 2nd ed. Fortress Press. pp. 6-7

selectively employ historical criteria that were congenial to reproducing a Jesus which they found palatable to their personal modern beliefs. From the nineteenth century forward, Jesus became a preacher of technocratic authoritarianism. Schweitzer and Cadbury both warned about the dangers of modernizing Jesus and recreating him in our own image, admonitions which have largely gone unheeded.

Such is the danger of failing to account for how the gospels actually work. For too long the quest for the historical Jesus failed to adequately consider the narratival features of the gospels, which by default do not enable us to separate the 'real Jesus' from his narrative context. Chris Keith correctly advocates for scholars to *"abandon the notion that they can "get behind" the Gospels and embrace a more robust role for the scholarly informed historical imagination of the past"*[45]. This includes taking the gospels seriously as constructed narratives which, in accordance with the standards of ancient biographies, are designed to reproduce the essence of their subjects and set an example for their audience to emulate. Not every detail included in the gospels is historically accurate in the narrow, modern sense of the term, but they all contribute to a composite picture which reliably depicts who Jesus was as a historical figure. So what, exactly, do the gospels tell us about the identity of Jesus?

The Characteristic Jesus

It's a shame Jesus himself never committed any of His teachings to writing. Unlike Paul, for whom we have letters penned directly by him[46], Jesus never personally translated his teachings from the spoken word into written form. In his primarily oral context, particularly in rural Galilee, this was the natural way for a figure like Jesus to communicate with an audience, with no expectation that his words should be immediately transcribed. We have already discussed the exceptionally low (by modern standards) literacy rates of antiquity and shown, through the work of James Dunn, the impact of oral tradition on the final composition of the written gospels. The informal, controlled nature of oral tradition, where the main point of a story or saying was fixed while the details, context, and presentation of the tradition was flexible, is the way in which most information was mediated in the ancient world. It isn't how we communicate, but we shouldn't hold the ancients to our modern standards.

---

45. Keith, Chris. 2024. *"Beyond What is Behind"*. In *The Next Quest for the Historical Jesus* edited by Crossley, James and Keith, Chris. Eerdmans. p. 96

46. Usually, or perhaps always, through the mediation of a scribe; see Romans 16:22.

From the beginning, then, the Jesus tradition was circulated orally. These traditions are rooted in the memories of those who first experienced Jesus, meaning that the earliest stages of the tradition were based on eyewitness testimony. Even though the earliest traditions were developed and circulated by people who saw Jesus and perhaps even had a personal relationship with him, there is still a historical gap between the man himself and his followers who developed the tradition based on memories of their eyewitness encounters with Jesus. To put it bluntly, this means none of our primary sources 'go back' to Jesus as they do with Paul, who is directly responsible for producing his letters. Even if Eusebius is correct in his authorial attribution of the gospels, they were not written by Jesus himself and are based on memories which were first transmitted and conditioned by the process of oral tradition. Does this mean we can know nothing for certain about Jesus? Not at all.

Dunn perfectly explains how memories of Jesus, transmitted through oral tradition, enable us to reconstruct Jesus as a historical figure: "*The primary formative force in shaping the Jesus tradition was the impact made by Jesus during his mission on his first disciples, the impact which drew them into discipleship . . . The Jesus tradition of the Gospels confirms that there was a concern . . . to remember Jesus . . . its character strongly suggests again and again a tradition given its essential shape by regular use and reuse in oral mode . . . [and] the essential shape was given by the original and immediate impact made by Jesus that was first put into words by and among those involved as eyewitnesses . . . the Jesus tradition is Jesus remembered*"[47]. Jesus's followers remembered Jesus and circulated their memories orally; these tradition-shaped memories would eventually produce the New Testament gospels, composed in narrative form as ancient biographies.

The evangelists' goal was to represent Jesus in his essence and encourage hearers to emulate him. The concern is not whether any individual tradition happened exactly as recorded, or whether Jesus used this particular word or perhaps another, but rather the composite picture we can construct of Jesus based on the gospels, which act as primary source material for our reconstruction of Jesus as a historical figure. When analyzing Jesus through the gospels, the details are much less important than the general presentation. Dunn makes the salient argument that we should focus "*on the characteristic motifs and emphases of the Jesus tradition, rather than making findings overly dependent on the individual items of the tradition*"[48]. He is correct. Jesus had an impact on his followers, and the tradition reveals what the evangelists thought characterized him as a subject. This is why, following Dunn's

---

47. Dunn, *Remembered*, p. 882

48. Dunn, *Remembered*, p. 882

terms, it is more helpful to think in terms of the 'characteristic Jesus'; the gospels accurately reveal what *characterizes* Jesus, the essence of the man. Why were some traditions so impactful for Jesus's audience that they were translated from oral tradition to written biography? Returning to our earlier example of Jesus's teaching on divorce, it profits us little to worry about why Matthew reorders Mark's version and Luke truncates both. What matters is that Jesus is remembered as having taught on divorce, and it became such a characteristic part of the tradition that all three Synoptics include Jesus's teaching on the subject, flexibly reworked to fit their larger narratives, exactly as in oral retellings.

Dale Allison is another gospels scholar whose work has had an outsized and significant impact on the field, and his approach is similar to Dunn's. Allison discusses the 'impression' which Jesus made on his first followers and how these impressions would necessarily shape the Jesus tradition which proceeded from them.[49] This means, once again, that details are less relevant than the characteristics of the tradition, and instead of judging each unit of text based on its historiographical accuracy we should instead identify recurring themes which likely reveal the impression Jesus made on those who witnessed him. Allison, reflecting on how memory mediates the past, presciently explains *"that we typically remember the outlines of an event or the general purport of a conversation rather than the particulars and that we extract patterns and meaning from our memories, it makes little sense to open the quest for Jesus by evaluating individual items . . . in the hope that some bits preserve pristine memory. We should rather be looking for repeating patterns and contemplating the big picture"*[50]. While the details matter precisely because they accent what they evangelists found compelling about the characteristic Jesus, we must begin with the themes and motifs that characterised him in the first place, many of which are accurate impressions based on the impact Jesus had on His followers. In his recent work Dale Allison provides a list of themes and motifs that characterize the Jesus tradition, many of which are directly relevant to our study of political and economic passages in the gospels.[51] Summarizing his findings, the gospels characterize Jesus as *"an eschatological prophet who expected God's kingdom in short order . . . a moral rigorist who was nonetheless perceived at times to be compassionate, and . . . a well-known teacher whose miracles prompted many to pay him heed"*[52]. Agreed. Allison's summary of the Jesus tradition includes three of the main themes

---

49. Allison Jr., Dale. 2009. *The Historical Christ and the Theological Jesus*. Eerdmans. pp. 61-66

50. Allison, *Historical Christ*, p. 62

51. Allison Jr., Dale. 2025. *Interpreting Jesus*. Eerdmans. p. 342

52. Allison, *Interpreting Jesus*, p. 343

we will explore in our reading of the gospels, all of which are extremely significant for drawing modern political and economic principles from these ancient texts.

First, Jesus is a classic Jewish prophet. He acted as a prophet and was perceived by his audience as such, and it is critical to study how Jesus's prophetic identity determined his mission. Second, Jesus proclaims the kingdom of God. This is the center of His prophetic proclamation and constitutes the core of His message. Third, Jesus is an eschatological figure. He taught that God was acting decisively to bring about His purposes and that his ministry was bound to the climax of human history. Allison argues that all three of these are foundational to the characteristic Jesus. To this I will add a fourth: every evangelist assumes Jesus is the Christ, the Messiah, in fulfillment of God's promises to David and establishing God's kingdom. If we are exploring themes and motifs in the gospels it is impossible to ignore the unanimity with which the evangelists assert Jesus is the Messiah. I will now offer an analysis of all four themes.

Four Themes: Prophet, Kingdom, Eschatology, and Messiah

A Prophet in Word and Deed

After Jesus was raised from the dead, he appeared to two unsuspecting men journeying on the road to Emmaus, a city outside of Jerusalem. Neither recognized their new travelling partner. The men were discussing events which had occurred the previous week in Jerusalem, shocked and confused by a near-riot which resulted in the crucifixion of a popular Jewish teacher. Feigning ignorance, Jesus inquired about the topic of conversation. Genuinely surprised that someone within the vicinity of Jerusalem hadn't heard the terrible news, the men recounted to Jesus what had happened. Of interest is their description of Jesus, recorded in Luke 24:19: *"Jesus the Nazarene . . . was a prophet mighty in deed and word in the sight of God and all the people"*. The men did not call Jesus 'Messiah' nor did they hail him as God. Instead, the men recited what sounds like a job title: Jesus, the crucified teacher, was *"a prophet mighty in deed and word"*.

The great fourth-century christological debates produced the Niceno-Constantinopolitan Creed (commonly known by its shorter name, the 'Nicene Creed') which delineated the ontological relationship between God, Jesus, and the Holy Spirit. While divine ontology is essential for Christian theology, the creedal affirmations of Nicea have conditioned Christians to think that Christ's ontological divinity is the only legitimate categorical identifier for Jesus. Creedalism unintentionally obscured what should have always been vital to every biblical analysis of Jesus: he was perceived as a prophet. Many believers, however, have read the gospels as if they are exclusively concerned with Nicene christology, allowing fourth-century ontological debates to determine what the gospels do and do not say about the identity of Jesus. The evangelists have more to say about Jesus than reiterating his status as the second person of the Trinity. Mark, Matthew, Luke, and John deliberately portrayed Jesus as a prophet. Why? Because Jesus *was* a prophet.[53]

Those who encountered Jesus certainly thought so. The men travelling to Emmaus in Luke 24 are not exceptional in that respect. Herod Antipas reasoned, based on public opinion, that Jesus must have been a prophet[54], a view also confirmed by Peter[55]. Matthew reports that everyone in Jerusalem was wondering who Jesus was, with multitudes revering him as a prophet.[56] After bringing a widow's dead son back to life, the people of Nain declare that a great prophet had arisen.[57] Nor is this simply a feature of the Synoptics. While John's divine christology is more developed than in his Synoptic counterparts, he has not marginalized the prophetic identity of Jesus. After conversing with Jesus, the famous woman at the well states "*Sir, I perceive that You are a prophet*"[58]. While he will, in John 4:26, reveal himself to be the Messiah, Jesus does affirm his role as a prophet. Prophet and Messiah are not mutually exclusive titles.

The tradition also attests that Jesus self-identified as a prophet. In Mark 6:1-6, Matthew 13:54-58, and Luke 4:14-30, all three Synoptic evangelists recount a story in which Jesus preaches in His hometown of Nazareth and is rejected, prompting him to say (with some variation) "*a prophet is not without honor except in his hometown*". Luke expands the story to include Jesus reading from Isaiah 61:1-2, a 'good news' passage which anticipates God's restoration of Israel, connecting Jesus's prophetic ministry with popular prophecy. Stunningly, this tradition is retained in John 4:44, where the narrator claims "*Jesus himself testified that a prophet has no honor in his own country*". While Christian theology frequently, to its detriment, downplays the gospel's portrayal of Jesus as a prophetic figure, it is foundational to the Jesus tradition itself. Jesus's words and deeds, as the men

---

53. I am absolutely *not* denying the christological affirmations of the Nicene Creed. I am a Trinitarian, period. While I profess Nicea, it is not an exhaustive catalogue of Jesus's identifiers, particularly as he is portrayed by the evangelists in the gospels. In this case we sometimes miss the canonical trees for the Nicene forest.

54. Mark 6:14-16, Matthew 14:1-2, Luke 9:7-9

55. Mark 8:28, Matthew 16:14, Luke 9:19

56. Matthew 21:10-11, 46

57. Luke 7:11-17

58. John 4:19

traveling to Emmaus corroborate, can only be properly appreciated within the context of classical Jewish prophecy.

The strongest and most enduring aspect of N.T. Wright's magisterial book, *Jesus and the Victory of God,* is his analysis of Jesus as a prophet and its utility for biblical interpretation[59]. Wright explains *"that Jesus was modelling his ministry not on one figure alone, but on a range of prophets from the Old Testament"*, particularly Elijah[60]. In the previous chapter we discussed the function of prophecy; while it is in many ways a multifaceted phenomenon, prophets were primarily responsible for communicating a message from God to a group of human recipients, usually the people or leaders of Israel. Prophets rarely make precise statements about future events but speak to what is happening in the present. They were often in the position of speaking difficult truths during times of unfaithfulness, and, following Jeremiah and Ezekiel, generally directed their prophecies towards those with political power.

The gospels unanimously portray Jesus as a prophet, exactly as his first followers perceived him. How would his audience have understood Jesus as a prophetic figure? Wright explains how *"Jesus regarded his ministry as in continuity with, and bringing to a climax, the work of the great prophets of the Old Testament . . . Like Elijah or Jeremiah, Jesus was proclaiming a message from the covenant god, and living it out with symbolic actions. He was confronting the people with the folly of their ways, summoning them to a different way . . . Though all* [prophets] *had followers, all were politically lonely figures. All were accused of troubling the status quo. When people 'saw' Jesus as a prophet, this was the kind of model they had in mind"*[61]. The Synoptic authors introduce Jesus's public ministry with his proclamation of God's kingdom[62], the core of his prophetic message. Matthew makes the connection between the words and deeds of Jesus explicit in Matthew 4:23: *"Jesus was going throughout all Galilee, teaching in their synagogues and proclaiming the gospel of the kingdom, and healing every kind of disease and every kind of sickness among the people"*. Both his words and his deeds would have been interpreted in a first-century Jewish context as an expression of classical prophecy, as did the men in Luke who serendipitously travelled with Jesus to Emmaus. While modern interpreters abstract Jesus's words and deeds into the categories of ethical commandment and miracle, both must be understood as extensions of Jesus's prophetic ministry. In his words and deeds

---

59. Wright, N.T. 1996. *Jesus and the Victory of God.* Fortress Press. pp. 147-197

60. Wright, *Victory,* pp. 166-167

61. Wright, *Victory,* pp. 167-168

62. Mark 1:14-15, Matthew 4:17, Luke 4:14,33

Jesus was working under the umbrella of prophecy and rightly received by his audience as a prophet.

Everything Jesus said and did as a prophet contributed to his proclamation of the coming kingdom. The words of a prophet are, in terms of importance, more significant than his deeds. What matters is the *message* more than anything else, because prophecy itself is an urgent communication from God. Jesus was motivated by the eschatological moment. The expectation that God would restore Israel and establish His rule over creation, usually through the renewed house of David, was common in Second Temple Judaism. The teachings of Jesus delineated the precise contours of God's coming kingdom, in the process subverting many popular eschatological assumptions of his day: *"Jesus announced that the reign of Israel's god, so long awaited, was now beginning; but, in the announcement and inauguration itself, he drastically but consistently redefined the concept of the reign of god itself"*[63]. The kingdom was coming, but it would not look like many first century Jews expected.

The most characteristic element of Jesus's prophetic words were his parables. Derived from the Greek word *parabole*, meaning 'comparison', the parable had roots in Old Testament literature; the Hebrew term used to describe this style of teaching is *mashal*. There are many aspects of parabolic teaching; Robert Stein demonstrates that the genre of *mashal/parabole* can include metaphor, similitude, stories, examples, and allegories[64]. While Jesus utilizes each of these in his own parabolic teaching, they serve a singular purpose: *"Jesus used parables primarily to illustrate his message"*[65]. All of his teaching is tethered to the prophetic proclamation of God's kingdom and cannot be severed from this central theme. The famous Parable of the Sower[66] is in effect a meta-parable which explains Jesus's prophetic ministry. Jesus prophetically announces the kingdom of God. The seed of the kingdom which falls on bad soil will not grow, but seed falling on fertile soil produces a harvest. Like the prophets that came before him, Jesus's message would often be met with rejection. A critical inflection point had been reached in Israel's history, forcing God's people to choose the message of Jesus or utter destruction. The kingdom of God was imminent, and Israel had run out of time. Jesus's prophetic ministry, manifested in word and deed, served as one final warning. Wright helpfully summarizes Jesus's teaching, particularly His parables: *"Jesus*

---

63. Wright, *Victory*, p. 172

64. Stein, Robert. 1994. *The Method and Message of Jesus' Teaching*. Westminster John Knox Press. pp. 33-38

65. Stein, *Method*, p. 38

66. Mark 4:3-25, Matthew 13:3-23, Luke 8:5-18

was articulating a new way of understanding the fulfillment of Israel's hope"[67]. Israel longed for the kingdom of God. Jesus came as a prophet to announce it. His words, often spoken parabolically, both declared and defined God's coming kingdom.

Jesus was also known for his deeds of power, particularly healings, perceived by his Jewish audience as embodying and enacting his prophetic announcement of God's coming kingdom. The prophetic nexus between word and deed is also rooted in the Old Testament. In Exodus 3-4, Moses is called by God to serve as a prophet to the Hebrews enslaved in Egypt. Moses asks God what he should do if the people refuse to listen or believe his words[68]. God provides him with a staff which promptly transforms into a snake before turning back into a staff[69]. This isn't a neat party trick or an arbitrary act of divine power, but provided by God to reinforce Moses's message *"that they may believe that the Lord, the God of their fathers . . . has appeared to you"*[70]. The sign legitimates the message. God repeats Himself in Exodus 4:17: *"You shall take in your hand this staff, with which you shall perform signs"*. This becomes the paradigm for prophetic deeds of power in the Old Testament; prophets are entrusted with a message from God and granted the ability to perform signs, reinforcing and legitimating their message. The signs themselves are not the point, as if the great deeds of power on display throughout Scripture are irrelevant flashes of divine power, but rather buttress the all-important prophetic oracles.

Jesus, standing in this long line of prophets, employs deeds of power to elucidate his message of the kingdom of God. As Wright expounds, *"from the perspective of a follower of Jesus at the time, his mighty works will have been interpreted within the context of his overall proclamation: they would be seen as signs that the kingdom of Israel's god was indeed coming to birth"*[71]. When the disciples of John ask Jesus if he is the Expected One[72], Jesus responds by citing Isaiah 35:5-6 and 61:11: *"Go and report to John what you have seen and heard: the blind receive sight, the lame walk, the lepers are cleansed, and the deaf hear, the dead are raised up, the poor have the gospel preached to them"*[73]. Those following Jesus saw him perform deeds of power which functioned as signs that the kingdom of God was at hand. When people experienced Jesus's great prophetic acts they recognized them as explicating his central

---

67. Wright, *Victory*, p. 176

68. Exodus 4:1

69. Exodus 4:2-4

70. Exodus 4:5

71. Wright, *Victory*, p. 191

72. Matthew 11:2-19, Luke 7:18-35

73. Luke 7:22

message, the kingdom of God, validating that Jesus was indeed a God-inspired prophet firmly within the Jewish prophetic tradition. Jesus the prophet, announcing the kingdom of God, is a characteristic of the Jesus tradition, and his words and deeds must be interpreted within the wider context of Jewish prophecy. This leads naturally to the second important theme embedded in the Jesus tradition: the kingdom of God.

The Kingdom of God

We have already discussed the centrality of both God as king in the Old Testament and the kingdom of God in Jesus's prophetic ministry of word and deed. We must now examine the phrase itself in greater detail, never neglecting just how important it is for the Jesus tradition and Second Temple Judaism generally. There are several related expressions in the gospels which denote the kingdom of God: "*the kingdom, kingdom of God, kingdom of heaven, kingdom of the Father, kingdom of Jesus, and kingdom of the Son of Man*"[74]. Each of these expressions has the same referent, so I will use them interchangeably. Of particular note is the phrase 'kingdom of Heaven', which is found nowhere in Mark or Luke but used almost exclusively by Matthew. The traditional explanation of this variant is compelling: Matthew was most likely composed for a Jewish audience which avoided using the proper name of God when possible out of respect for the Third Commandment.[75] The phrase is directly equivalent, however, to 'kingdom of God'.

The Greek term for 'kingdom' is *basileia*, which can mean kingdom, reign, rule, or domain. While many Christians throughout history have taken the word *basileia* in a geographical sense as denoting a particular place, usually a heavenly afterlife, this doesn't appear to be the primary way in which Jesus uses the term. Jesus envisions the kingdom as a state of God's reign, not confined to a particular location but encompassing all of creation. Joel Green explains this dynamic in the gospels: "*what happens most frequently with respect to God's kingdom is that it is entered . . . with the result that people can be in . . . not far from . . . or out of the kingdom . . . imagine entering a sphere—that is, entering a field of influence, activity and/or operation—in this case, then, experiencing, identifying with, participating in, coming under the influence of, and joining the community formed in relation to God's kingdom . . . God's kingdom cannot be confined to a particular set of borders . . .*

---

74. Green, Joel. 2013. "*Kingdom of God/Heaven*". In *Dictionary of Jesus and the Gospels*, 2nd ed. ed. by Joel B. Green, InterVarsity Press. p. 468

75. Stein, *Method*, pp. 60-65

because God's rule is not subject to any geographical boundaries"[76]. At the creation, God sat as king. Israel's demand for a king was a rejection of the kingship of God. The prophets longed for a day when God would return to rule as king again.

This evidence all suggests that the 'kingdom of God' should be understood as the rule or reign of God. When Jesus speaks of the kingdom, he is making the bold and audacious claim that God is finally coming back to rule, making good on His promises. Because of this we cannot depoliticize *basileia*. When Jesus uses the phrase he isn't proposing a rule of God over individual hearts, facilitating a private 'religious' experience which has no bearing on social, political, or economic realities. While the kingdom does make claims over individual lives, nothing in Second Temple Judaism or the ancient world would suggests this term can be understood in a private, religious sense. That line of interpretation imports anachronistic modern categories into ancient texts. Crossley and Myles, commenting on the kingdom, state "*the kingdom of God referred to an actual kingdom, ruled by God's anointed . . . not a heavenly afterlife or ethereal vision as it has sometimes come to be understood through the Christian tradition*"[77]. God's rule results in concrete consequences for the political loyalties of those who enter it. Only one king rightfully sits on the throne. The entire world must change as a result. Green agrees: "*Jesus' proclamation of the kingdom belonged thoroughly within the complexities of Second Temple Judaism, whose intertwined threads of religious, political and social interest could (and should) never be disentangled. God was coming as king, so the whole world would be set right*"[78].

N.T. Wright summarises the meaning of 'kingdom of God' in the Second Temple period: "*'The kingdom of god', historically and theologically considered, is a slogan whose basic meaning is the hope that Israel's god is going to rule Israel (and the whole world), and that Caesar, or Herod, or anyone else of their ilk, is not. It means that Torah will be fulfilled at last, that the Temple will be rebuilt and the Land cleansed . . . Israel's god will rule her in the way he intends, through properly appointed persons and means . . . it clearly implies a new order in which Israel is vindicated, and then ruled over, by her god—and, by implication, in which the rest of the world is ruled in some way or other, whether for blessing or judgment, through Israel*"[79]. This is the constellation of themes, all informed by the Jewish Scriptures, that those who first heard Jesus would have associated with the coming kingdom of God. While Jesus is offering a new interpretation of the kingdom which challenges several prevailing

---

76. Green, *Kingdom*, pp. 468-469

77. Crossley and Myles, *Class Conflict*, p. 107

78. Green, *Kingdom*, p. 469

79. Wright, *New Testament*, p. 302

first century theories about how God will establish His rule, Jesus retains the essential components of this popular hope.

James Dunn agrees with Wright and Green's assessment of the kingdom of God. Dunn identifies three aspects of the kingdom which most Jews of the Second Temple period would have accepted. First is the fundamental assumption that God is king of the entire world with His rule encompassing all of creation. Second, even though God is the one true king, only Israel presently acknowledges His kingship. The nations have either ignored or rejected Israel's God, a situation which cannot be maintained in perpetuity. Finally, God will one day return to rule from Jerusalem, at which point His kingship would be manifested to the entire world.[80] God's reign, finally revealed through Jesus's prophetic ministry, isn't reducible to a private religious experience. With Judea under the direct rule of Roman governors and Galilee under Rome's client Herod Antipas, the kingdom of God fueled dreams of liberation. The Romans didn't accept Israel's God and Herod was a sell-out collaborator with the pagan imperialists. Oakman convincingly argues that rhetoric of the kingdom betrays a keen awareness of Israel's political situation under Roman rule; this wasn't to be Israel's lot forever, and God would return to do something about it[81]. Jesus, of course, radically redefines *how* God returns to rule and the consequences of restoration for those who hear him, but the political and economic repercussions are unavoidable.

In Luke 13:22-30, someone asks Jesus why only a few people are being rescued. Jesus responds by echoing Matthew 7:13-14, exhorting his interlocutor to enter through *"the narrow door"*[82]. In the kingdom of God many will come from the ends of the earth to recline at the eschatological banquet with Abraham, Isaac, Jacob, and the prophets. This group, however, will include people who were not expected to participate, and many who believe they have a place in the coming kingdom will be cast outside.[83] Jesus concludes his saying with an ominous warning in Luke 13:30: *"behold, some are last who will be first and some are first who will be last"*. Entering through the narrow door means accepting Jesus's redefinition of *basileia*, which unexpectedly fulfills the promises God made to Israel in the Old Testament. Jesus follows this saying with a condemnation of Herod, the Pharisees, and Jerusalem in Luke 13:31-35. Those who hold political power expect to inherit the coming kingdom, but unless they repent and accept the prophetic proclamation of Jesus they won't make it. God is bringing about His *basileia* in unexpected

---

80. Dunn, *Remembered*, p. 390-392

81. Oakman, *Political Aims*, pp. 75-78

82. Luke 13:24

83. Luke 13:26-29

ways: *"when Jesus spoke of the 'reign' or 'kingdom' of Israel's god, he was deliberately evoking an entirely story-line that he and his hearers knew quite well . . . [but] he was retelling this familiar story in such a way as to subvert and redirect its normal plot"*[84]. The world is changing, and those currently in charge won't be for long. God's plans are finally coming to fruition; the dramatic climax of Israel's Scriptures, foretold in the prophets, commences with the ministry of Jesus. The end had arrived. But what do we mean by 'the end'?

Eschatology

"The time is fulfilled", Jesus says at the beginning of his public ministry, *"and the kingdom of God is at hand"*. Mark 1:15 encapsulates Jesus's prophetic message to Israel, framed by a stunning chronological assertion: the time is up. God is inaugurating His kingdom. Before his crucifixion, Jesus in Mark 13:1-27 issues an oracle of destruction against Jerusalem which was fulfilled by the Romans in 70 CE. Jesus promised that the destruction of the temple would vindicate his prophetic message and anticipate his return, perplexing his disciples. Despite his cryptic comments, they were to learn an eschatological lesson from the fall of Jerusalem, which Jesus likened to a ripening fig tree: *"learn the parable from the fig tree: when its branch has already become tender and puts forth its leaves, you know that summer is near. Even so, you too, when you see these things happening, recognize that He is near, right at the door"*[85]. The public ministry of Jesus is bookended in Mark by a conviction that Jesus is initiating the eschatological moment. There is a tension, however, in Jesus's statements. How can 'the time be up' when the fall of Jerusalem is a sign that 'the end' is in some sense still to come? The eschatological dynamic which is characteristic of both the Jesus tradition and early Christianity must be accounted for here. It determines how we think about political and economic arrangements in the time between the arrival of God's kingdom with Jesus and its full future implementation.

Albert Schweitzer is famous for arguing that the Jesus tradition is only comprehensible within an eschatological framework, based on the historical *"assumption that the atmosphere of the time was saturated with eschatology"*[86]. We discussed in the previous chapter how Second Temple Judaism was distinguished by a complex matrix of hopes regarding God's ultimate deliverance of Israel, and even though there was widespread variation on the exact nature of God's future plans most Jews

---

84. Wright, *Victory*, p. 199

85. Mark 13:28-29

86. Schweitzer, *Quest*, p. 350

believed, in complete continuity with the Old Testament, that He would at some point act, forever changing the world as a result. Jesus and his followers inherit this long tradition of eschatological hope from their Jewish context.

The eschatology of the Jesus tradition presupposes something had already begun to happen which would not be completed until a future time. Dunn explains the tension between what has occurred and what must yet occur. The tradition quoted at the beginning of this section from Mark, where Jesus declares the kingdom is '*at hand*', is incorporated in Matthew 4:17, another programmatic introduction to Jesus's prophetic ministry. The same language is used again in Matthew 10:7 and Luke 10:9, and the force of the statement is that something had happened *in history* to bring the kingdom near, identified in the Jesus tradition and the early church as Jesus's public ministry. In fact, the tradition is saturated in eschatology. The so-called 'Lord's Prayer' of Matthew 6:10 and Luke 11:2 recounts Jesus praying "*Your kingdom come*", revealing, in line with Mark 13 and parallels, that even though God's reign was currently 'at hand' it would be worked out into the indefinite future in which, at some point, the kingdom would be fully realized. During this process there would be an 'eschatological reversal', paramount to Matthew's 'Sermon on the Mount' and Luke's 'Sermon on the Plain'[87], in which those who "*hunger now . . . shall be satisfied*" while those who "*are well-fed now . . . shall be hungry*"[88]. The kingdom is both at hand and yet to come; in the meantime the last are slowly becoming first while the first are slowly becoming last.[89] Much like Jesus's oracles of judgment against the rich and powerful in Luke 13, the hopes of Israel were being fulfilled through Jesus in innovative and surprising ways. Given the prevalence of eschatology in Second Temple Judaism, a prophet like Jesus would have naturally amassed a dedicated group of followers (and equally dedicated detractors) by claiming the end had arrived and that God was acting on behalf of the disenfranchised. The work Horsley, Oakman, Crossley, and Myles historically accounts for the discontent many of Jesus's earliest followers felt towards the ruling elite. In the context of rural Galilee, his the eschatological message of Jesus was extremely appealing.

A little problem, though: Jesus winds up dead and his followers remain oppressed. If the kingdom was really 'at hand' as the evangelists claimed, why had almost nothing changed? Every strain of early Christianity believed the Jewish hope was in some ways already fulfilled because the crucified Jesus *had been raised from the dead*! In Paul's words, Jesus is the "*first fruits*" of the resurrection; those who are

---

87. Matthew 5:4-12 and Luke 6:20-26

88. Luke 6:21, 25

89. Dunn, *Remembered*, pp. 406-420

"*in Christ*" will also be raised on the final day when Jesus hands the kingdom over to God[90]. Although the eschaton had already dawned through the resurrection of God's Messiah Jesus, his work was not yet complete.[91] Patrick Schreiner emphasises the ascension as an important aspect of the eschatological hope developed in the Jesus tradition. Since Jesus is God's resurrected Messiah, currently ruling over all creation at the Father's right hand in heaven, the kingdom is a present reality awaiting a future revelation at the return of Jesus.[92] This logic undergirds Paul's instructions in Colossians 3:1 that Christians should "*keep seeking the things above, where Christ is, seated at the right hand of God*", which is precisely the reason why Christians are "*transferred . . . to the kingdom of His beloved Son*"[93] were Jesus sits as "*the head over all rule and authority*"[94]. The author of Revelation portrays kingdom as a present reality; in the throne scenes of Revelation 4-5 Jesus *already* sits at the right hand of God, therefore "*The kingdom of the world has become the kingdom of our Lord and of His Christ; and He will reign forever and ever*"[95] and has "*begun to reign*"[96]. Even though Jesus inaugurated the kingdom and currently sits as king, the final chapters in Revelation envisage the completion of his kingdom when he returns in glory.

This already-but-not-yet eschatology is not an invention of the early church. It is deeply embedded in the Jesus tradition; Jesus was remembered as proclaiming the now-and-future reign of God. Tucker Ferda argues in his book *Jesus and His Promised Second Coming* that Second Temple Jewish eschatology imagined God working through a series of events to bring about His intended purposes; the restoration wouldn't happen instantaneously but sequentially, even if this sequence was chronologically brief.[97] Ferda coins the phrase 'process eschatology' to emphasise the sequential nature of Jewish eschatology, explaining "*It concerns the common expectation that the eschatological fulfillment of God's purposes in history would involve some kind of process, with various events expected to transpire with varied transformative effects . . . the expectation for a radical action of God in history to change it for good can sit with, and alongside, an interest in timelines, sequences, and the expectation of more observable changes, including the ethical labor of persons . . .*

---

90. 1 Corinthians 15:20-24

91. Wright, *New Testament*, p. 459

92. Schreiner, Patrick. 2020. *The Ascension of Christ*. Lexham Press. pp. 88-95

93. Colossians 1:13

94. Colossians 2:10

95. Revelation 11:15

96. Revelation 11:17

97. Ferda, *Second Coming*, pp. 376-422

It was not uncommon . . . to expect a process of inauguration, working towards a more decisive, climactic, and irreversible end"[98]. This is exactly what we see in Mark 13 and parallels; Jesus, suspecting his imminent death, also predicts his own divine vindication. When Romans armies sacked Jerusalem and destroyed its temple in 70 CE, it served as a prophetic sign that God's kingdom had come but would not be fully consummated until his return. It is little wonder that when Jesus foretells his death, resurrection, and vindication earlier in Mark, Peter sharply rebukes him.[99] While Peter as a Jew presumed an eschatological process, the death and resurrection of God's Messiah before the end of history was an unanticipated revision of kingdom theology. It flows quite well, however, within the stream of Jewish process eschatology .

The phrase which best describes the already and still-to-come kingdom portrayed in the gospels and other New Testament literature is *inaugurated eschatology*. Through Jesus the eschaton has already begun but not yet fully realized.[100] Jesus proclaimed the kingdom of God was currently at hand, his prophetic words and deeds powerfully declaring and embodying the arrival of God's kingdom, but his followers were still instructed to pray for its completion. Believers live in the tension between these twin realities. God's restoration was underway but awaiting completion. Inaugurated eschatology is the best historical explanation for the eschatological tension in the New Testament, and the gospels were written in part to help believers emulate Jesus in a kingdom which had arrived but was yet to reach its fulfillment. Jesus's parable of the seed in Mark 4:26-29 captures the essence of inaugurated eschatology: "*The kingdom of God is like a man who casts seed upon the soil; and he goes to bed at night and gets up by day, and the seed sprouts and grows— how, he himself does not know. The soil produces crops by itself; first the blade, then the head, then the mature grain in the head. But when the crop permits, he immediately puts in the sickle, because the harvest has come*". Jesus's followers live between the planting and the harvesting in which the kingdom will grow through the faithfulness of those who follow Jesus. Inaugurated eschatology makes sense of the complex biblical data and is a feature of the characteristic Jesus tradition.

---

98. Ferda, *Second Coming*, pp. 388-389

99. Mark 8:31-32

100. Schellenberg, Ryan. 2013. "*Eschatology*". In *Dictionary of Jesus and the Gospels*, 2nd ed. ed. by Joel B. Green, InterVarsity Press. pp. 234-235

Christ Jesus the Messiah

The Greek word for 'Christ' is *christos*, meaning 'anointed one'. As we discussed in the previous chapter, this word is used in Jewish texts to translate the Hebrew word *mashiach*, from which we derive the English word 'messiah'. It was a term applied to prophets, priests, and kings given a provisional dispensation of God's spirit to bring about His purposes. During the Second Temple Period the title *christos* was often used in reference to the coming Davidic king promised in passages like 2 Samuel 7. The term is used over five hundred times in the New Testament, almost always as a title denoting the fulfillment of God's promises to David in Jesus.[101] The gospels portray Jesus as the Davidic Messiah, bringing about God's kingdom on earth. The gospels themselves unambiguously proclaim Jesus is Christ, the promised Messiah. The gospels as ancient biographical stories were labeled 'gospels' because they narrate the *euangelion* of the Messianic kingdom established by Jesus the king.

The first line of the first written Gospel, Mark 1:1, is unambiguous: "*The beginning of the gospel of Jesus Christ, the Son of God*". Matthew expands Mark's introduction in his own opening line, Matthew 1:1, which reads "*The record of the genealogy of Jesus the Messiah* [a cognate of *christos*], *the son of David, the son of Abraham*", tracing the lineage of Jesus back though the greatest king in Israel's history to the founding father himself, Abraham. While Luke outlines his literary method in the opening lines of his gospel, it doesn't take long until the son of Joseph and Mary is called "*the Son of the Most High; [whom] the Lord God will give Him the throne of His father David; and He will reign over the house of Jacob forever, and His kingdom will have no end*"[102]. No christological subtleties in Luke. John, creatively reworking the Synoptic tradition through the ancient literary technique *oppositio in imitando*, opens his gospel by delineating the relationship between God and Jesus. John is promoting an explicitly divine christology but hasn't abandoned the messianic identity of Jesus; far from it. Jesus is called 'Christ' in 1:17, John explicitly denies himself the title 'Christ' in 1:20, and Andrew's first explanation of Jesus to his brother Simon Peter in 1:41 reads "*We have found the Messiah*", with John adding the editorial line "*which translated means Christ*". All four evangelists are in complete agreement: Jesus is the Christ, the long-promised messiah. The stories they tell are good news because they narrate his coming.

---

101. Bird, Michael. 2013. "*Christ*". In *Dictionary of Jesus and the Gospels*, 2nd ed. ed. by Joel B. Green, InterVarsity Press. p. 115

102. Luke 1:32-33

I explored the diverse array of Jewish eschatological expectations in the previous chapter. The restoration of David's house, a prominent eschatological motif in Israel's Scriptures, was anticipated by many Jews of the period. Although, as Michael Bird argues, not every Jew in the Second Temple period believed in a coming messiah, many did. The beliefs Jews held about the Davidic messiah were predictably diverse; while there was no single paradigm for a Davidic successor, the reestablishment of his line was central to many strands of Jewish eschatological hope.[103] The tense political and economic situation in Palestine no doubt intensified the longing for a God-ordained king. Corroborating the work of Hosley, Oakman, Crossley and Myles, Bird explains why messianism was popular among Jews: "*The sociopolitical context of Palestine in the first century A.D.—domination by the Roman Empire . . . several sporadic and unsuccessful revolts against Rome, turmoil within the Judean ruling class, sectarian rivalries over the proper way to observe the Law of Moses, and speculation on prophetic oracles about Israel's deliverance in the Hebrew Scriptures—created a fertile context in which Jewish messianic hopes could flourish*". Many Jews were dissatisfied with the Romans and Jewish political class and longed for a day when God would finally make good on His promises of deliverance, often conceived as taking place through the mediation of an anointed king from the house of David. The evangelists unequivocally identify this figure as a prophet from Nazareth. Jesus, according to all four gospels, is the long-promised Messiah, announcing and inaugurating God's kingdom on earth.

Other titles given to Jesus in the gospels are also directly related to his status as the Davidic Messiah. 'Son of God', declared of Jesus by God as His baptism[104], acknowledged by "the tempter' when Jesus was in the wilderness[105], spoken by the centurion who crucified him[106], and found in many other passages associated with Davidic messianism in the Second Temple period[107], is one such title. While Christians interpret the title 'Son of God' as denoting Jesus's divine identity, its primary historical referent was messianic, signifying David's son. The evangelists indisputably portray Jesus as more than the Davidic messiah, but 'Son of God' as a title is never disassociated from messianic expectations. There might be more to the story, but there certainly isn't less.

---

103. Bird, *Christ*, p. 116

104. Mark 1:11, Matthew 3:17, Luke 3:22

105. Matthew 4:1-11, Luke 4:1-13

106. Mark 15:39

107. Collins, Adela, and John Collins. 2008. *King and Messiah as Son of God*. Eerdmans. pp. 48-74

Jesus also describes himself as the 'Son of Man'[108]. When asked directly if he is the Christ during His trial, Jesus responds in the affirmative by claiming to be the Son of Man promised in Daniel 7:13[109]. Note the strong correspondence between the Messianic, Davidic christology of Jesus and his self-referential use of 'Son of Man' language; Bird is correct in saying *"Jesus' characteristic designation of himself as the "Son of Man" was pregnant with messianic significance"*[110]. As we learned in the last chapter, the 'Son of Man' in Daniel helps God establish His eschatological kingdom; by applying this language to Jesus the evangelists are affirming his Messianic status. Jesus is the Christ, the Davidic king, therefore the eschatological kingdom of God is indeed at hand. Terms like 'Son of God' and 'Son of Man' must be read in their historical contexts before investing them with the developed Christian theology of subsequent centuries, important as that may be.

The Davidic christology found in the gospels is consistently employed throughout the New Testament. Jesus is hailed as *the* Davidic messiah by every single canonical author. Joshua Jipp, summarizing the New Testament witness to Jesus's Davidic status as Christ, states *"the messianic identity of Jesus of Nazareth is not only the presupposition for, but is also the primary . . . content of, New Testament theology . . . Jesus's messianic kingship is something of a root metaphor, a primary designation and driving image for making sense of NT Christology . . . not only do the major NT compositions presuppose Jesus as the Davidic messianic king but they are also creative expansions upon the earliest Christian confession that Jesus is the Messiah of God"*[111]. The gospel tradition provides abundant evidence of Davidic christology by utilizing a network of related terms to designate Jesus as the *christos*, the anointed son of David promised in the Old Testament. The rest of the New Testament follows suit; in Romans 1:1-5, 1 Corinthians 15:3-5, and 2 Timothy 2:8 the Davidic status of Jesus is central to Paul's gospel, the foundation of his apostolic message. The writer of Hebrews quotes two Davidic messianic texts, Psalm 2:7 and 2 Samuel 7:14, when referring to Jesus in its opening passages[112], James 1:1 begins the letter by referring to Jesus as *"the Lord Jesus Christ"*, Peter uses *christos* and its cognates extensively in both of his epistles, those who deny that Jesus is the Christ are labeled *"antichrist"* in John's letters[113], whereas those who truly follow

---

108. Matthew 8:20 and Luke 9:58, for example.

109. Mark 14:61-62, Matthew 26:63-64

110. Bird, *Christ*, p. 117

111. Jipp, Joshua. 2020. *The Messianic Theology of the New Testament*. Eerdmans. p. 6

112. Hebrews 1:5

113. 1 John 2:22, 4:3; 2 John 1:7

Him believe Jesus is the *"son of God"*[114], Jude ends his short epistle by calling *"Jesus Christ our Lord"* and ascribing Him *"glory, majesty, dominion and authority, before all time and now and forever"*[115], and the entire apocalyptic narrative of Revelation hinges upon the messianic status of Jesus as one who rules over the nations after establishing a kingdom which is already present but yet to be fully consummated[116]. Jesus is the Christ, the son of David, who is currently ruling over an inaugurated kingdom to be fully consummated in the future, and his prophetic ministry of word and deed marked the beginning of God's promised restoration.

It is impossible to overstate just how consequential the Davidic status of Jesus is in the New Testament, particularly for the evangelists. Mark, Matthew, Luke, and John all assume Jesus is the Christ and structure their narratives accordingly. In John 20:31 the author even reveals that he wrote his gospel *"so that you may believe that Jesus is the Christ, the Son of God; and that believing you may have life in His name"*. They thought that Jesus was the Messianic Christ and wanted their audience to believe as well. While Jesus's sacrificial death, resurrection, and ascension will powerfully rework Second Temple Jewish Davidic hopes, the christology of Jesus in the gospels is not metaphorical. Jesus didn't simply come to rule over the hearts of private individuals, completely inconsequential for the political or economic order. The evangelists ardently proclaimed that Jesus was the actual, long-promised Davidic king, the one through whom God would establish His kingdom, restore His people, and overthrow the evil powers which dominated human history. Jesus is not just a real king, he is *the* real king, and those who call him *christos* are obligated to treat Him as such. The evangelists contend that something had changed, was in the process of changing, and would one day be entirely changed because Jesus, the crucified Davidic *christos*, now ruled over all creation. The political and economic message of the gospels are incomprehensible without this basic christological confession. The messianic identity of Jesus forces his followers to rethink the political and economic order of His day, and the principles that we draw from the gospels must shape the way we approach political and economic structures in our day.

THE NARRATIVE STRUCTURE OF EACH GOSPEL

Since the gospels are biographical narratives, they each arrange their source material in a manner which is conducive to their overall rhetorical agenda. While

---

114. 1 John 5:5-20

115. Jude 1:25

116. Revelation 5:1-14

technical gospels scholarship have created myriads of complex theories about the possible intended audiences, theological differences, and redactional motivations of each evangelist, much of this work is admittedly speculative and provides little value for our study, however interesting the academic literature may be. Before closing out this chapter, I want to briefly comment on the narrative structure of each gospel so that readers have a better sense of how the evangelists arranged the Jesus tradition. Instead of wading into literary conjecture, my brief analysis of the four gospel narratives are rudimentary and widely accepted in New Testament scholarship. Nothing I claim is innovative or controversial. Any introductory textbook on the gospels will outline their narrative structure in a manner similar to what I am presenting below, and I will reference these outlines occasionally in the exegetical work which follows this chapter.

Mark is divided into roughly two halves, the first (chapters 1-8) narrates his deeds while the second (chapters 9-16) narrates his death. It would impose an artificial disjunction between the two halves to claim there is a radical break in the narratives between chapters 8-9; rather, Mark tells one long narrative by emphasising Jesus's ministry first and naturally culminating in his death. One of the motifs of Mark is his emphasis on the so-called 'messianic secret'; no one except for the minor characters know that Jesus is the messiah until right before his death, which casts Jesus in narratival form as a *suffering* messiah. Mark intends for his audience to perceive Jesus as such.[117]

Matthew generally follows Mark's outline while adding a plethora of sayings material along with some stories which aren't included in Mark. The bulk of Matthew's gospel is structured around five long discourses (chapters 5-7, 10, 13, 18, and 24) which are generally tied to the narratives which precede them. Mattew alternates between narrative and discourse, uniting them in either theme or topic. The first narratival section is 3:1-4:25, beginning with John the Baptist and ending with Jesus proclaiming the kingdom of God. The discourse which followers in chapters 5-7, the Sermon on the Mount, presents Jesus explaining what the dawn of the kingdom means for his followers. The final set of narrative-discourse begins with Jesus in Jerusalem between Matthew 19:1-23:39, in which Jesus challenges the Jewish political leaders, and ends with a discourse of judgment against Jerusalem in chapter 24.[118] This structure allows Matthew to topically arrange stories and sayings, impacting how individual units in his gospel ought to be interpreted.

---

117. Blomberg, *Gospels*, pp. 131-133

118. Meyer, Ben. 1994. *Five Speeches that Changed the World.* Wipf & Stock. pp. 19-21

Luke opens his gospel with an explanation of his authorial intentions. He notes that *"many have undertaken to compile an account of the things accomplished among us"* which were *"handed down to us by those who from the beginning were eye-witnesses"*[119]. Luke acknowledges his utilization of sources (most likely, following Barker, Mark and Matthew) and that his sources were based on eyewitness testimony. In 1:3 Luke states that he *"investigated everything carefully"* and wrote it out *"in consecutive order"*. The Greek word rendered 'carefully' is the adverb *akribos*, which connotes diligence and accuracy, while the Greek adverb translated 'in consecutive order', *kathexes*, means 'orderly'. While *kathexes* can denote *chronological* order, the genre of ancient biography doesn't require chronological accuracy. I take Luke 1:3 to mean Luke carefully used his source material and then constructed an orderly, comprehensible narrative based on eyewitness accounts which both builds upon and creatively innovates them. While Luke certainly adds sayings and stories which are not included in Mark or Matthew, much of his material is derivative of those gospels. Luke freely rearranges Matthew's highly structured material and reworks it into his own narrative framework, which is indeed carefully ordered in its own right. Blomberg observes how *"Luke grouped his material together in small thematic units, but beyond that there is no overarching pattern"*[120]. Why he chose to arrange Matthew's material into smaller topics while eschewing the narrative-discourse pattern is anyone's guess, but it is nevertheless precisely what Luke does. Since Luke is also responsible for writing Acts, it is possible, as Blomberg and others have suggested, that Luke's narrative moves from the Roman empire to Jerusalem, with Acts mirroring that ordering, moving from Jerusalem out to the Roman empire.[121] Themes which appear in Luke are also prominent in Acts, an important point to keep in mind when reading both works.

As noted above, John writes his gospel to inculcate belief in Jesus as Christ. I find Barker's theory of *oppositio in imitando*, which posits that John knew the Synoptics and creatively rewrote and developed them, extremely compelling. Many of the main Synoptic themes are incorporated in John, even if the style is deliberately different. I will focus on the motifs in John which I find relevant to our study and show in my exegesis how they correspond to similar motifs in the Synoptics. John, like Mark, is structured into two halves. The first, chapters 1-11, recount his deeds of power, while the second, chapters 12-21, emphasise His journey to the cross and beyond. For interpretation the deeds in the first half are contextualized by the narratives in which they are embedded, and the narratives in

---

119. Luke 1:1-2
120. Blomberg, *Gospels*, p. 162
121. Blomberg, *Gospels*, pp. 159-163

the second half are contextualized by Jesus's impending death and resurrection.[122] This is especially important for the "Last Supper Discourse" of John 13-17, in which Jesus is presented as a model for Christian imitation in light of the cross.

This brief overview of the structure of each gospel should be enough to help us navigate the complex narratival context within which each of the individual passages we study are located. While there can never be anything approaching perfect certitude in historical reconstruction, we are indeed in a position to make arguments about these texts which are historically plausible and based on relevant evidence.

Conclusion

In this chapter we have examined the gospels from a macro level. The gospels are ancient biographical narratives which are based on oral traditions that were passed down from those who witnessed Jesus firsthand. They conform to the standards of ancient biography, which are designed to represent the essence of their subjects and encourage emulation. The traditions included in the gospels are both fixed and flexible, reflecting the oral traditioning process in which they were originally transmitted, and we should not expect conformity to modern paradigms of historiographical accuracy. They are entitled 'gospel' because of the fulfillment of promises made by God in the Old Testament through Jesus, which is the 'good news' promised in the work of prophets like Isaiah. There are four main themes found in the gospels which are important for this study: Jesus's prophetic ministry, his announcement of the kingdom of God, the inaugurated eschatology which asserts that the kingdom has been inaugurated in the life of Jesus but will be consummated in the future, and Jesus's identity as *christos*, the Davidic messiah who now rules over all creation. These four themes are interwoven throughout the four gospels, and the messianic identity of Jesus is, as Jipp rightly claims, foundational for the entire New Testament.

The next three chapters will focus on specific episodes in the gospels and follows the Synoptic's broad narratival flow. Chapter 8 will explore the opening chapters of each gospel. Beginning with Mark's assertion that Jesus is Christ, I will move through the birth narratives, investigate the significance of John the Baptist, and examine Jesus's temptation in the wilderness, all of which help construct an edifice upon which the rest of the gospel material rests. Chapter 9 will address a

---

122. Blomberg, *Gospels*, pp. 184-186

number of passages which occur during the ministry of Jesus that are related to political and economic themes, setting them in their historical and narratival context and drawing principles which guide our thinking on complex modern questions. Chapter 10 will round out our study of the gospels by analyzing Jesus's final week in Jerusalem, his crucifixion, and his resurrection. Let's get started.

CHAPTER 8 | Birth, Baptism, and Temptation

The Beginning of the Gospel

Already in antiquity, certain conventions were established for beginning a story. It has therefore long been recognized that "placing an item at the beginning or at the end may radically change the process of reading as well as the final product."[1]

Francis Moloney

The beginning of the gospel of Jesus Christ, the Son of God.

Mark 1:1

IN THE BEGINNING

As we embark on a detailed analysis of the gospels, we must start where the evangelists do: at the beginning of the narratives. The previous chapter attempted to explain how the gospels worked and outlined the dominant themes found within them which impact the political and economic consequences of particular texts. The goal was to establish a set of overarching interpretive principles to guide our exegesis of relevant passages in the gospels. I didn't want to waste any time explaining complex concepts like inaugurated eschatology or messianic christology as I worked through the gospels themselves, and if you are a reader who skipped the methodology in order to dive right into the texts it may help to reference certain sections of the previous chapter if you feel my exegetical judgments are underdeveloped or rushed.

The opening passages of each gospel lay out their main themes, and the Synoptics waste no time letting their audience know Jesus is the Messiah. While John certainly develops Synoptic messianic christology, he does not abandon it;

---

1. Moloney, Francis. 2002. *The Gospel of Mark*. Hendrickson. p. 27

quite the contrary, the evangelist claims in John 21:31 to have written his gospel *"so that you may believe that Jesus is the Christ, the Son of God"*. While his introduction elucidates the divine identity of Jesus in a more nuanced manner than the Synoptics, John still affirms that Jesus is the Davidic king bringing about God's long-promised restoration. Divine christology does not negate Davidic christology, it only enhances it. Framing the gospels as stories about Jesus the Christ, the only rightful king over all creation, grounds our interpretation of other passages in the messianic identity of Jesus, which is precisely how the evangelists intended to portray Him.

Only Matthew and Luke include narratives about Jesus's birth, but each are in their own respect literary expansions of Mark 1:1, which claims Jesus is the Christ, Son of God. The main theme which runs throughout the infancy narratives is the messianic identity of Jesus and the long-awaited fulfillment of Old Testament prophecies, and I will show how these narratives are constructed to portray Jesus as the Davidic Messiah. It has long been noted by scholars that the two accounts are historically difficult to reconcile[2]. I agree with the scholarly consensus that they are designed to advance both Matthew and Luke's larger theological agendas and are therefore not neutral descriptions of 'what actually happened'[3]. While I will happily leave the question of historicity to professional apologists, I do believe the two infancy narratives bear a striking *thematic* similarity; while the stories they tell may be different, both Matthew and Luke craft them to portray Jesus as the Davidic Messiah.

Aside from one unique biographical detail in Luke[4], the evangelists entirely ignore Jesus's childhood and adolescence, moving straight to his baptism by the prophet John. John is a fascinating figure in his own right, and Jesus's baptism shows that the two men stand in continuity with one another. Highlighting John the Baptist's prophetic ministry only further elaborates the christological assertions made in the introductions and infancy narratives: Jesus is the Christ. John is a prophet who announces the impending kingdom of God and prepares Israel for the arrival of their messiah. His baptism of Jesus is Jesus's first public appearance as an adult. Mark 1:12-13 briefly mentions Jesus's wilderness temptation, with Matthew and Luke once again offering an expansion of Mark's truncated narrative. Both evangelists demonstrate that Jesus, unlike Israel, avoids succumbing to temptation in the wilderness and remains faithful to God, and when Jesus is offered all the kingdoms of the world he not-so-politely declines. If only modern politicians

---

2. Brown, Raymond. 1993. *The Birth of the Messiah*. 2nd ed. Doubleday. pp. 32-37

3. Brown, *Birth*, pp. 37-38

4. Luke 2:41-52

would follow his example. The temptation narratives mark the end of the beginning, so to speak, and are the last events to be narrated before Jesus formally begins his public ministry.

It is impossible to avoid the obvious implication of the evangelist's opening sequences. Jesus is the Christ. God is fulfilling His promises. The time is up. While generations of Christian readers have rightfully found these traditions inspiring, reading them for personal edification and worship, it has become easy to miss the point they were intending to make. There is one king, and his name is Jesus. This assertion is incompatible with political authoritarianism, whether ancient, medieval, or modern, and Christians who accept the authority of Scripture, believing it provides us with principles which must shape our lives, need to hear this message loud and clear: no one else shares Christ's throne. The evangelists agree.

INTRODUCING THE CHRIST

The first word of the first written gospel is *arche*, '[the] beginning'. Mark 1:1 reads as follows: "*The beginning [arche] of the gospel of Jesus Christ, the Son of God*". This statement hangs over the rest of Mark's gospel, and indeed the rest of the *gospels*, as a summary of the story which the evangelist is about to unfold. Following the use of *arche*, the 'good news' begins with Jesus Christ, the Son of God. As we learned in the previous chapter, the noun *euangelion*, "good news", denoted in Isaiah the announcement that God was returning to restore His people and was also used to proclaim an event of monumental importance in the Greco-Roman world. The gospels declare the 'good news' of Jesus from the very beginning, and their titles imply the long narrative of Israel which was now reaching its fulfillment in Jesus. We also discussed the significance of both 'Christ' and ' Son of God'; these titles are messianic and clearly refer to the status of Jesus as the anointed Davidic messiah. This will become evident in Mark 1:9-11 when he narrates Jesus's baptism, but this opening passage makes it clear that the "*good news is that Jesus of Nazareth is the Christ, the Son of God*"[5]. Anyone familiar with the story of Israel would immediately understand what Mark was saying: Jesus is the coming King.

By utilizing this charged language, "*Mark is noting the start of the arrival of divine acts of "good news" (gospel) that previously had only been announced in the ancient Scripture*"[6]. This rather obviously brings together two of the major themes we discussed previously, eschatology and christology, and implies the kingdom of God. If Jesus is truly the *christos*, the anointed son of God, an explicitly royal

---

5. Moloney, *Mark*, p. 31

6. Bock, Darrell. 2002. *Jesus According to Scripture*. Baker Academic. p. 78

category in the Old Testament, then the *euangelion* foretold in Isaiah had finally become a present reality. God's plans were no longer a future hope; the intended eschatological 'end' where Israel is restored and God revealed to the world was happening through Jesus. The arrival of the king, of course, establishes the kingdom God promised to David in 2 Samuel 7. This is why Jesus is the *arche*, the beginning, of the good news. The eschatological drama begins with the messiah.

Matthew, Luke, and John will all push this *arche* further into the past, refining and developing Mark's messianic introduction of Jesus. The first verse in Matthew is similar to Mark, but takes it a step further: "*The record of the genealogy of Jesus the Messiah* [a genitive form of *christos*], *the son of David, the son of Abraham*"[7]. Matthew calls Jesus *christos* and names Him the 'son of David', both of which denote Jesus's Messianic identity, and then, taking Mark a step further, connects Jesus with Abraham, the father of Israel. Matthew then outlines the genealogy of Jesus in 1:2-16, beginning with Abraham, moving through David, and ending with Joseph, Jesus's father, who confers upon Jesus the status of son of David, which Matthew explicitly refers to as "*the Messiah*" in 1:16. Matthew himself acknowledges that his genealogy is highly stylized in 1:17, and scholars have endlessly debated the structure of Matthew's genealogy[8]. These debates can obscure the point Matthew is making: Jesus is the rightful Davidic messiah, and his lineage is traceable to the great patriarch himself, Abraham. Darrell Bock explains how genealogies *"are significant because they communicate a person's social standing and status. A person's family line, if it is prominent, conveys his or her importance"*[9]. Whatever scholars argue about the genealogy itself, Matthew wants to connect Jesus to David and, behind him, Abraham, making Him the legitimate king over God's people. Whereas the *arche* for Mark is the announcement of Jesus as messiah, Matthew sees the story as beginning in Genesis 12:1-3 with the calling of Abraham. Jesus the Messiah completes the long, complex story of Israel.

Not to be outdone, Luke sees Matthew's development of *arche* and pushes it back one step further to the creation of all humanity. Luke doesn't open his gospel with a summary statement of Jesus's messianic identity, but he quickly develops it in the infancy narrative which follows the formal introduction in Luke 1:1-4. Luke places his version of Jesus's genealogy after the baptism of Jesus in Luke 3:23-38. Unlike Matthew, Jesus's genealogy begins with His father Joseph and moves backwards through David to Abraham but takes it even further, ending

---

7. Matthew 1:1

8. For a helpful overview of the relevant positions, see Bauer, David. 2013. "*Genealogy*". In *Dictionary of Jesus and the Gospels*, 2nd ed. edited by Green, Joel. InterVarsity Press. pp. 299-301

9. Bock, *Jesus*, p. 55

with "*Adam, the son of God*"[10]. The *arche* has been shifted back yet again, this time to the creation of Adam, the first man. The story of Jesus begins with the creation of humanity, a radical development of *arche* indeed. It is a widely-held position in biblical scholarship that Matthew was likely composed for a primarily Jewish audience (which, as we discussed in the last chapter, explains Matthew's characteristic 'kingdom of Heaven'), and in that context it makes sense for him to connect Jesus not only with David but with Abraham, the father of Israel. Whatever we make of the addressee "Theophilus" in Luke 1:3 (was this a person or a group?), he was writing for a predominantly Gentile audience.[11] Luke is also unique because he is the only evangelist to pen a sequel, Acts, and demonstrates how the gospel of Jesus is for the entire world throughout both of his works. In Luke 24:47 Jesus tells His disciples "*that repentance for the forgiveness of sins would be proclaimed in His name to all the nations, beginning from Jerusalem*", and the book of Acts ends with Paul in the imperial capital of Rome doing just that: "*preaching the kingdom of God and teaching concerning the Lord Jesus Christ with all openness, unhindered*"[12]. By restructuring Matthew's genealogy and tracing His lineage back to Adam, Luke shows how the *arche* of Jesus Christ is for all humanity. The entire world is under the dominion of Jesus, son of Joseph, son of David, son of Abraham, son of Adam, son of God.

How could anyone possibly begin the story of Jesus any further back than Adam? Enter John. Perfectly reflecting Barker's theory of trajectories, the fourth evangelist crafts a prologue which portrays Jesus Himself as having a hand in creation. John 1:1-18 begins with a reappropriation of Genesis 1: "*In the beginning was the Word, and the Word was with God, and the Word was God. He was in the beginning with God. All things came into being through Him*"[13]. Not only was the lineage of Jesus traceable to Adam, Jesus participated in creation! John then narrates that Jesus, creator of the world, became incarnate, donning flesh and dwelling among man.[14] John identifies the incarnate Word as *christos* in 1:17, and after His baptism he is hailed as Messiah by Andrew, Simon Peter's brother in 1:41. While John certainly evinces a divine christology, this in no way compromises the messianic identity of Jesus. It does, however, move the *arche* of the gospel back to creation itself. Andreas Kostenberger comments, "*By linking Jesus' coming into the world to its creation, John signals that the incarnation of the Word . . . culminates a*

---

10. Luke 3:38

11. Stein, Robert. 1992. *Luke.* Broadman & Holman. pp. 26-27

12. Acts 28:31

13. John 1:1-3

14. John 1:14

stream of salvation-historical events that command humanity's utmost attention"[15]. Whatever is happening with Jesus, all of creation is enfolded within his story. John wants his readers to understand that the person he calls *christos* has a legitimate claim over the entire created order. While this idea is certainly present in the Synoptic gospels, John has taken an already high christology and raised it even further.

Our sources unanimously impress upon their readers the messiahship of Jesus. Even though they each develop this concept in their own unique manner, one of the consistent features of the Jesus tradition is the universal affirmation that He is the *christos* who will bring the story of Israel and indeed all of human history to its dramatic conclusion. Even if our study ended with this small number of texts, it would be impossible to claim the evangelists portrayed Jesus as anything less than the Davidic king. It also quickly raises the question, for those perceptive enough to ask it, of what we are to do with worldly political powers. If Jesus is the rightful king, does he share his power with other authorities? And, if so, how should those authorities exercise power? The dominant political and economic paradigm in the post-Enlightenment world is authoritarian socialism of varying degrees. Nearly everyone in the West believes governments should be granted an arbitrary monopoly on violence and afforded the power to regulate exchanges between peaceful producers and consumers. If the gospel writers are correct in their affirmation of Jesus as Christ, however, it casts a long shadow of doubt over our modern authoritarian political assumptions. The infancy narratives in Matthew and Luke will only strengthen the case already made in every gospel that Jesus is the Christ and has an unprecedented claim over creation.

THE BIRTH OF THE MESSIAH

Biblical scholarship is constantly changing, so perhaps one day a precocious young academic will find an innovative way to harmonize Matthew and Luke's infancy narratives. Or maybe, following the Dead Sea Scrolls, there will be another discovery of texts long-buried in the Middle Eastern sands which provide a different perspective on the question of why the two accounts seem so historically divergent. Today, unfortunately, is not that day. I have no new contributions to the conversation regarding the infancy narratives and will not attempt to reconcile them historically. I will argue, however, that they both accomplish the task of further delineating Jesus's status as Christ; Matthew and Luke advance the theme of Jesus's messianic status, portraying him as the rightful heir to David's throne

---

15. Kostenberger, Andreas. 2004. *John*. Baker Academic. p. 19

within the eschatological framework of restoration which blossomed in the Old Testament and Second Temple period. Despite their differing historical details, Matthew and Luke exhibit a nearly perfect *thematic* overlap and care easily harmonized christologically. We can summarize both narratives with a short phrase: Jesus is the Christ.

This does little to resolve the question of divergent detail. We know Matthew and Luke were writing to different audiences, Matthew's being primarily Jewish and Luke's primarily Gentile, and this probably accounts for some of what we see as historical inconsistencies in the texts. We also know that both gospels are structured differently, and it is possible the infancy narratives reflect these structural dissimilarities. The differences were shaped by the agendas of the evangelists, and we may never know precisely what these agendas encompassed. Because of this I find it best to analyze Matthew and Luke's account of Jesus's birth independently, showing how each author presents the Davidic christology of Jesus in their own right. Since I believe Matthew's gospel was composed prior to Luke, we will begin with Matthew.

Born King of the Jews: Matthew 1:18-2:23

Matthew narrates the birth of Jesus immediately following his genealogy, which explicitly links Jesus to David and Abraham through His father Joseph. In case his audience missed the point, Matthew opens the narrative in 1:18 by stating *"the birth of Jesus Christ was as follows"*. Matthew has already connected the phrase *christos* with Davidic sonship in 1:1 and confirmed this connection genealogically. Let's not miss the point: for Matthew, to call Jesus 'Christ' is to grant him the title 'anointed son of David'. 2 Samuel 7 and the prophecies it generated are being fulfilled in Jesus. Matthew 1:18-25 recounts the familiar story told annually in Christmas services around the world. Joseph is engaged to a woman named Mary, who conceived a child by the Holy Spirit, and Joseph seeks to send her away privately, being a righteous man.[16] An angel appears to Joseph in a dream and explains how Mary conceived, exhorting him to *"call his name Jesus, for He will save His people from their sins"*[17]. This second statement needs qualification. The temple in Jerusalem was the mechanism by which Jews were able to atone for their sins, and Joseph would have believed in its efficacy. While the New Testament does envisage Jesus as a the permanent offering for individual sinfulness (see, for example, Hebrews 7:27 which views Jesus's death and enthronement as the final sacrifice

---

16. Matthew 1:18-19

17. Matthew 1:21

given *"once for all when He offered up Himself"*), the angel's assertion that Jesus will save His (God's) people from their sins possesses a very significant historical context.

The Greek root word for 'save' in 1:21 is *sozo*, which can also mean 'rescue', and the following phrases 'His people' and 'their sins' are both plural, meaning Matthew has more in mind than the atonement of individual transgressions. Wright helpfully contextualizes this passage: *"in its first-century Jewish context, this denotes, not an abstract transaction between human beings and their god, but the very concrete expectation of Israel, namely that the nation would at last be rescued from the exile which had come about because of her sins"*[18]. Nehemiah 9 and many other Old Testament passages acknowledge Israel had sinned against God and were under the curse of the covenant because of those sins, and prophecies such as Jeremiah 31:31-34 envisaged the restoration of Israel as a forgiveness of their corporate sins against God, based on the covenantal blessings and curses of Deuteronomy 28-30. By framing the angel's message to Joseph in this way, Matthew signals that Jesus, son of David, is the means by which Israel will be rescued from their sins. It's no coincidence that the prophecy of corporate forgiveness in Jeremiah 33:8 is followed by the restoration of David's house in 33:15-17. Matthew 1:21 evokes the story of Israel by merging eschatology and christology.

Matthew 1:22-25 rounds out the angelic vision to Joseph, with the angel specifically evoking prophetic fulfillment by quoting Isaiah 7:14 in Matthew 1:23. The virgin is with child, a sign that God is at work. Joseph obediently stayed with Mary but kept her a virgin until she gave birth to Jesus. The significance of Jesus's parental heritage is often overlooked. Joseph is from the line of David and legitimates Matthew's claim that Jesus is the son of David. Without the legal inheritance of His father, this claim, essential for the narrative logic of all four gospels, would become much less secure. While the genealogy traces Jesus back to Abraham, thus binding Him to Israel, ethnic Jewish descent was matrilineal. As Adele Reinhartz explains, *"the Jewishness of Jesus's mother establishes her son's Jewish identity . . . A person with a Jewish mother is a Jew, full stop"*[19]. Jesus, by virtue of His mother and father, can rightfully be called the Jewish son of David, precisely what Matthew has been insisting since the opening line of his gospel.

Matthew 2:1-12 recounts the visit of magi from the east who travel to see Jesus. This tradition continues to develop the messianic christology of Jesus. The meaning of the term 'magi' is contested in biblical scholarship, but it appears to

---

18. Wright, *Victory*, p. 561

19. Reinhartz, *Beyond the Jewish Jesus Debate*, pp. 50-51

have Persian roots[20]. Whatever we make of the word's etymology, the Assyrian, Babylonian, and Persian empires had all been from the east and were responsible in part for Israel's current plight. It appears as if Matthew is subtly suggesting that the people who once dominated Israel were now coming to Judea to worship Israel's king. The root word behind the NASB's 'worship' in Matthew 2:2 is *proskyneo*, which can mean 'pay homage' and doesn't necessarily denote the liturgical worship of a god; given the magi's conviction that Jesus is a king, *proskyneo* most likely refers to honoring Jesus as a royal figure. Matthew narrates that the magi visited Herod in Jerusalem and asked him in 2:2 for the location of *"He who has been born King of the Jews"*. Herod, of course, believed that *he* was the king of the Jews, and gathered the chief priests and scribes (both of whom, we must remember, exercised political power) to determine the location of the Messiah's birth. They consult Micah 5:2, a prophetic oracle which announces the future birth of Israel's king, and determine that the messiah must be born in Bethlehem. Herod promptly sends the magi to Bethlehem, hoping for more information.

After following a star to Bethlehem, the magi find Jesus in a house with His mother Mary. In Matthew 2:11 they see Jesus, fall to the ground, and worship (*proskyneo*) him, indicating that they had accomplished their goal and found the king of the Jews. They offer Jesus gold, frankincense, and myrrh. These gifts are not chosen at random. They evoke Isaiah 60:6, a gospel passage announcing the restoration of Israel and the political reversal which occurs as a result: the nations who once dominated Israel were flocking to Jerusalem, bringing their wealth with them. Specifically named are gold and frankincense, another allusion to this prophetic hope fulfilled in Jesus. By contrasting this 'king of the Jews' with Herod, who was given no homage and offered no gifts, Matthew uses the magi as characters to certify Jesus's messianic status. The nations were traveling to Israel, worshiping their king, and offering him gifts, just as prophets like Micah and Isaiah had foretold, but this king wasn't the one currently occupying the throne. The true king of Israel was Jeusus, not Herod. After paying homage to Jesus, the magi are warned in a dream to avoid Herod and they find a road around Jerusalem on their journey home.

In Matthew 2:13, an angel of the Lord appears once again to Joseph, warning him that Herod was going to kill Jesus and commanding Joseph to move his family to Egypt. Joseph faithfully obeys; Mary and Jesus relocate to Egypt. Matthew is evoking the Exodus, and, as Bock argues, *"Jesus recapitulates the history of the nation itself, when it came into Israel by way of Egypt in the original journey of redemption"*[21].

---

20. Bock, *Jesus*, p. 69

21. Bock, *Jesus*, p. 71

Matthew 2:15 quotes Hosea 11:1, "*Out of Egypt I called my Son*". In its original context, Hosea 11:1 recounts the Exodus before rebuking Israel for their unfaithfulness to the God who delivered them from Egypt. It appears as if Matthew is creatively appropriating this text to make two points. First, following Bock, Jesus is reenacting the exodus, demonstrating that the eschatological deliverance of Israel taking place through the Davidic king. Second, since Hosea 11:1 is situated within a context of condemnation, Matthew is likely leveling it against Herod, the false 'king of the Jews' whose murderous policies sent Jesus to Egypt in the first place. In Matthew 2:16-18 Herod slaughters every child in Bethlehem under the age of two, hoping to kill Jesus. Frustrating Herod's plans, Joseph and Mary had already fled to Egypt. Matthew 2:18 quotes Jeremiah 31:15, which is a lament for Israel's captivity but strategically located before the prophetic promise of glorious deliverance in Jeremiah 31:31-34. Matthew's inclusion of Jeremiah 31:15 likely plays on its wider context, implying that Jesus will deliver Israel from bondage to its unrighteous rulers.

Matthew 2:19-23 concludes the infancy narrative. After the death of Herod, Joseph is instructed by an angel to return to the land of Israel, but finds Archelaus, Herod's son, ruling over Judea. As we learned in the previous chapter, Archelaus was such an ineffective leader that the Romans deposed him in 6 CE and substituted the office of client-king for official Roman governors. Joseph, perceptively wary of life under Archelaus, is warned in another dream to live in Galilee. He settled his young family in Nazareth. By the end of Matthew's infancy narrative, the evangelist has conclusively established Jesus as the rightful king of Israel, the son of David who rises to rule the nations, and the one through whom God's people are being delivered. The eschatological moment of restoration is here. Christians should draw an obvious conclusion from this story: if Matthew teaches that Jesus is the one true king, we should believe him. Matthew deliberately constructed his narrative to make a messianic point, and it is one that shouldn't be missed. As we are about to see, Luke reworks Matthew's narrative while making the exact same claim.

His Kingdom Will Have No End: Luke 1:5-2:52

Addressing the main themes of Luke and Acts, Joshua Jipp perceptively writes "*there can be little doubt that for Luke the centrality of Jesus as the promised Davidic Messiah who enacts the kingdom of God occupies the most critical role*"[22]. Luke wastes precious little time arriving at precisely that destination, and his own reinterpretation

---

22. Jipp, *Messianic Theology*, p. 85

of the infancy narratives makes the same point (in perhaps even grander scale) as Matthew's: Jesus is King. It is no surprise then that Luke names both Herod the Great and Caesar Augustus in his version of the story[23]. He wants his audience to compare and contrast the rulers of Judea and the Roman empire with Jesus, whose rule will supplant them both. The lofty language employed by Luke to describe the meaning of Jesus's birth cannot be overstated and should be seen in direct contrast to the so-called political powers of His day.

Surprisingly for some readers, Luke begins his narrative not with the parents of Jesus but instead with those of John the Baptist. Luke 1:5-25 tells the story of a priest named Zacharias and his barren wife Elizabeth, both of whom *"were . . . righteous in the sight of God, walking blamelessly in all the commandments and requirements of the Lord"*[24]. As Zacharias was performing his duties in the temple an angel appeared to him, announcing that his wife will bear a son which is to be named John. In Luke 1:16-17 the angel explains to Zacharias that his son will have an important job: *"he will turn many of the sons of Israel back to the Lord their God. It is he who will go as a forerunner before Him in the spirit and power of Elijah, to turn the hearts of the fathers back to the children, and the disobedient to the attitude of the righteous, so as to make ready a people for the lord"*. The angel alludes to Malachi 3:1-4 and 4:5-6, passages which speak about the purification of Israel before the eschatological restoration. The latter passage envisages a prophetic figure like Elijah who will prepare Israel for this restoration. John, according to the angel, is the prophet foretold in Malachi. The angel describes his message in 1:19 as 'good news' using a cognate of *euangelion*. John initially doubts Elizabeth could conceive, and the angel stays his tongue. Surprising no one save for Zacharias, Elizabeth is shortly found to be with child.

biblical scholarship has tended to overlook the similarities between the parents of John the Baptist and Samuel the prophet. Jipp sets the record straight: *"The incredible amount of parallels between Luke's infancy narrative and 1 Samuel 1-2, centering especially upon the stories of the barren women and their messianic hymns (1 Sam 2:1-10; Luke 1:46-55), draw the reader's attention to both God's promises to Abraham (Gen 12-21), and the origins of the Davidic monarchy (1 Sam 1-2), thereby hinting at God's prophetic plan to finally restore the Davidic kingdom"*[25]. Just as Samuel, the prophet who anointed king David[26], was conceived despite his mother's barrenness, so was John, the prophet who proclaims the coming of David's son

---

23. Luke 1:5 and 2:1, respectively.

24. Luke 1:6

25. Jipp, *Messianic Theology*, p. 86

26. 1 Samuel 16:13

Jesus. The Songs of Mary and Zacharias at the end of Luke 1, which we will examine shortly, are, as Jipp suggests, thematically similar to Hannah's Song in 1 Samuel
1:1-10. Luke is drawing a deliberate line between the prophet of David and the
prophet of Jesus, and the entire narrative may perhaps be an example of *oppositio
in imitando*. Whatever scholarship makes of this claim, Luke is clearly signaling
that God is about to restore Israel. John will prepare the way for God's Messiah.

Whereas Joseph is the main character in Matthew's infancy narrative, Mary
takes center stage in Luke. In Luke 1:26-38, an angel appear to Mary, a virgin engaged to "*Joseph, of the descendants of David*"[27], and promises her she will conceive
a son named Jesus despite her virginity. What the angel says about Mary's son is
consequential: "*He will be great and will be called the Son of the Most High; and
the Lord God will give HIm the throne of His father David; and He will reign over
the house of Jacob forever, and His kingdom will have no end*"[28]. This leaves little
room for interpretation. Jesus is the promised Davidic messiah, He will rule over
Israel forever, and His kingdom will have no end! Once again we see the themes
of kingdom, christology, and eschatology rushing together, signaling the arrival of
God's long-promised restoration and casting into doubt the status of Herod and
Augustus. Only a few verses later in Luke 1:35 Jesus is called "the son of God"
by virtue of both Mary's divine conception and His relationship to David. Luke
wants his audience to know that Jesus is nothing short of God's Messiah.

Luke 1:39-80 is structured around two songs; one sung by Mary and the
other by Zecharias, both of which bear a striking resemblance to Hannah's song
in 1 Samuel. Mary visits her relative Elizabeth in 1:39-45[29], and Elizabeth in 1:43
refers to Mary as "*the mother of my Lord*", yet another reference to Jesus's messianic
status. This prompts the song of Mary in 1:46-55. It begins with a thanksgiving for
God's grace and mercy in 1:46-50, and then in 1:51-55 exemplifies several messianic themes. The passage in full reads "*He has done mighty deeds with HIs arm;
He has scattered those who were proud in the thoughts of their heart. He has brought
down rulers from their thrones, And has exalted those who were humble. He has filled
the hungry with good things; and sent away the rich empty-handed. He has given
help to Israel His servant, In remembrance of His mercy, As He spoke to our fathers,
To Abraham and his descendants forever*". The eschatological reversal, where the
rich and powerful are supplanted by a God who cares for those in need, is already
underway. God will strike down those who rule (Herod and Augustus, perhaps?)

---

27. Luke 1:27

28. Luke 1:32-33

29. Luke 1:36 identifies Mary and Elizabeth as 'relatives', but the Greek word behind it, *syngenes*,
is a general term for relationship. Christian tradition suggests they are cousins.

and exalt those who are humble. Alluding to Psalm 107:9, which praises God for His deliverance of the righteous, Mary proclaims that those who are hungry will be fed while the rich will be sent away empty-handed. This great reversal will occur because of God's mercy and promises to Abraham.

Up to this point we have explored the explicitly political claim m that Jesus is the Christ, a messianic identity which is no mere spiritual metaphor. With Mary's song we must address our first economic question: what does it mean for the poor to be fed and the rich sent away? Scholarship has generally recognized Luke's unique emphasis on the plight of the poor and the concurrent responsibility for those with material possessions to steward them in a way which benefits those in need.[30] In Robert Stein's commentary on Luke, he incorporates this theme within a section on eschatological reversal, stating *"A strong theological emphasis that continually appears in Luke-Acts involves God's concern for the downtrodden and outcasts"*[31]. As we will see, both Luke and Acts express a concern for those in need and encourage (or perhaps even command) those in their audience who are materially prosperous to share with those who have little. Modern western Christians often look to passages like this as a justification for state economic intervention. If Mary says the poor will be fed and the rich will leave empty handed, shouldn't we support policies of authoritarian economic redistribution? Isn't this passage essentially an argument for socialism?

Hardly. Recall from Chapter 2 that a consistent, irreducible, and universally applicable definition of 'capitalism' and 'socialism' divests both terms of their unfortunate popular ambiguity. Capitalism is the absence of arbitrary intervention in economic exchange, particularly by political authorities, and socialism denotes an economic system characterised by arbitrary intervention, where the ruling class coercively confiscates and regulates property to achieve their desired social ends. The root of the Greek word translated 'rich' in Luke 1:53 is *plouteo*, which generally means one is either already wealthy or, since the cognate of *plouteo* in this passage is in verbal form, becoming wealthy. Mary is referencing those who either have or are gaining wealth but will go away empty handed while the poor are fed in the eschaton.

In the previous two chapters we examined how taxation was essential to the Roman imperial order and that local rulers often overtaxed and confiscated peasant land. Richard Horsley, openly critical of what he incorrectly labels 'capitalism', discusses the nature of agrarian economics in Judea and Galilee. *"Those who wielded authority and/or power induced or coerced the productive villagers to yield a*

---

30. See Blomberg, *Gospels*, p. 166

31. Stein, *Luke*, pp. 49-50

portion of their produce to support a more comfortable life for the ruling elite and their retainers and servants in cities"[32] and, with respect to the Roman empire generally, "*The economy of the Roman Empire was not a market economy but a political economy that was based not on "supply and demand" but demand and supply, that is demand by the imperial state and its wealthy urban elites and supply coerced form subject peoples, tenants, and slaves*"[33]. Herod, already name-dropped by Luke, was a poster child for the kind of exploitation which occurred under Roman client-kings which kept the peasantry impoverished, creating a climate which produced numerous Jewish revolutionaries who wanted to overthrow the entire system and usher in God's kingdom. As a historical fact, however, those who became 'rich' off of this system were not doing so by engaging in peaceful, voluntary transactions but through the appropriation of state power, confiscating property which didn't rightfully belong to them and using it to advance their personal wealth and power! If we were to place a modern label on this kind of economic system, it wouldn't be 'capitalism', despite Horsley's protestations. The rich exercised arbitrary power, and in the kingdom this state of affairs would be reversed. By using a cognate of *plouteo* Mary is castigating the rich and powerful who live luxuriously from ill-gotten gain.

Immediately following Mary's song Luke narrates the birth of John. Zacharias is able to speak again and begins praising God.[34] As the people of Judea wonder what all this means, Zacharias issues a prophetic song which perfectly encapsulates the messianic and eschatological themes already articulated in Luke. in Luke 1:67-79, Zechariah praises God for redeeming His people, raising up "*a horn of salvation for us in the house of David*", rescuing Israel from her enemies, "*remembering His holy covenant . . . which He swore to Abraham*", granting Israel "*rescue from the hand of* [their] *enemies*" so that they "*Might serve Him without fear*", declaring, in a quotation from Malachi 3:1, that John will be "*the prophet of the Most High*", and that Israel will be granted knowledge of salvation and the forgiveness of their sins. The song ends in 1:79 with a quotation from Isaiah 9:1-2, which is a prophecy regarding the salvation of Israel through the restoration of David's line. Zacharias's song leaves readers with little doubt that Jesus is the one through whom God is going to restore Israel. Luke concisely describes John's upbringing in 1:80; he grows stronger in spirit, living in the desert until the day of his public appearance. We will return to John below.

Luke 2 narrates the birth of Jesus and provides us with the only direct tradition in the New Testament describing an event from Jesus's childhood. Thematically,

---

32. Horsley, *Bow Down*, p. 46

33. Horsley, *Bow Down*, p. 101

34. Luke 1:64

Luke's account of Jesus's birth is identical to Matthew's despite the differences in detail. In Luke 2:1-7 Joseph and Mary travel to Bethlehem because of a census imposed by Quirinius, governor of Syria. After referencing Augustus in 2:1, Luke portrays the birth of Jesus as occurring in the shadow of empire. 2:4 asserts that Bethlehem is a city of David, Joseph traveled there because he was of the house and family of David. Jesus is born in a manger because the guest room in the house they were staying was full.[35] After his birth an angel appears to shepherds, a profession which, as we discussed in Chapter 5, was often viewed with contempt by the wealthy. This is a narratival enactment of Mary's line in Luke 1:52 about the exaltation of the humble; God appears to shepherds, not kings. Note the messianic themes in the angel's message: "*I bring you good news* [yet another cognate of *euangelion*] *of great joy which will be for all the people; for today in the city of David there has been born for you a Savior, who is Christ the Lord*"[36]. The Christ has been born, and He will rescue Israel. Like the magi, the shepherds visit Jesus, disclose the message they received from the angel, and glorify God God.[37]

After eight days, Joseph and Mary travel to Jerusalem to offer the proper sacrifices for their firstborn son. Luke 2:24 includes a quotation of Leviticus 12:8, which proscribes the appropriate sacrifice for those unable to afford a lamb. Again channeling Luke's emphasis on eschatological reversal, this sacrifice indicates Mary and Joseph are poor.[38] The king of Israel is born into a family of humble means. They encounter a man named Simeon. Luke describes Simeon in 2:25-26 as "*righteous and devout, looking for the consolation of Israel*", a man promised by the Holy Spirit "*that He would not see death before he had seen the Lord's Christ*". Upon glimpsing Jesus, Simeon proclaims "*my eyes have seen Your salvation, Which you have prepared in the presence of all peoples, a light of revelation to the Gentiles* [alluding to Isaiah 42:6 and 49:6, both of which describe the restoration of Israel and the revelation of God to the nations] . . . *Behold, this Child is appointed for the fall and rise of many in Israel*"[39]. Jesus is Israel's Messiah, God will reveal Himself to the nations, and God's people will either rise or fall depending on their response to Him. A prophetess named Anna, upon hearing this, praises God because she was "*looking for the redemption of Jerusalem*", which she recognized was now

---

35. The traditional Christmas story where Mary and Joseph are rejected from an inn is not biblically viable; for an explanation see Bailey, Kenneth. 2008. *Jesus Through Middle Eastern Eyes*. InterVarsity Press Academic. pp. 25-37

36. Luke 2:10-11

37. Luke 2:15-22

38. Stein, *Luke*, p. 114

39. Luke 2:30-34

occurring.[40] After these events, Luke:39-40 explains how Jesus settles in Nazareth, claiming that "*the grace of God was upon Him*".

Luke 2:41-52 cannot technically be described as an *infancy* narrative because the event, according to Luke 2:42, occurs when Jesus is twelve. There are no other New Testament traditions about the childhood of Jesus. Jesus accompanies his family on a pilgrimage to Jerusaelm for Passover but misses the caravan traveling back home. When it is discovered Jesus was left in Jerusalem, they return to find him "*in the temple, sitting in the midst of the teachers, both listening to them and asking them questions*"[41]. When asked why He stayed behind, Jesus responds "*Did you not know that I had to be in my Father's house?*"[42]. Luke 2:50 narrates that His family didn't understand Jesus's words, and New Testament scholarship has followed suit. There are a range of interpretive options nuancing Jesus's precise meaning, but Bock finds a common denominator in the varying exegetical proposals: "*Whatever the reply means exactly, it recognizes that ultimately Jesus' unique relationship to God will be a priority over any familial duty or custom. It is specifying Jesus' unique relationship to "my Father"*"[43] Jesus, however, returns home and remains obedient to His parents. Echoing Luke's description of John, in 2:52 Jesus "*kept increasing in wisdom and stature, and in favor with God and men*".

Between Matthew and Luke the infancy narratives vigorously portray the Jesus tradition's messianic theology. Matthew and Luke have both expanded in narratival form Mark's introduction to Jesus as Christ, the son of God. Although these stories have been used throughout Christian history without reference to their explicit eschatological christology, attentive readers are obliged to deduce that Matthew and Luke both believed Jesus to be the legitimate Davidic Messiah, king of both Israel and the world. Herein lies the actual Christmas story; it isn't merely about good feelings, family, and a general sense of religious sentiment, but a declaration about the one who rightfully rules the world. All four evangelists introduce Jesus as none other than the heir of David's throne, and, once they have established his identity, proceed to narrate how John the Baptist announces the coming king. It is John who prepares the way for the Lord.

---

40. Luke 2:36-38

41. Luke 2:46

42. Luke 2:49

43. Bock, *Jesus*, p. 75

THE FORERUNNER: JOHN THE BAPTIST

Luke's infancy narrative recounts the unusual circumstances surrounding John's birth in order to demonstrate his prophetic credentials. John was granted the unique calling of announcing the fulfillment of Israel's eschatological hope. The Messiah was coming, and God's people needed to be ready. Luke wasn't constructing this profile of John *ex nihilo*; Mark and Matthew had both already made similar claims about the significance of John which Luke expands in chronicling his birth. John (the evangelist) reworks the Synoptic traditions about John (the Baptist) but makes largely the same point. John the Baptist is a herald for the coming king, Jesus, and proclaims to all Israel that they must prepare for His arrival. Time's up.

The four themes we discussed in the previous chapter which characterize the ministry of Jesus, namely, his role as a prophet, the kingdom, eschatology, and messianic christology all run through John, who has the privilege of baptizing Jesus in the Jordan River, marking the beginning of Jesus's public career. Any reconstruction of Jesus must account for John, as James McGrath wisely observes: *"If we do not understand John correctly, we will misunderstand Jesus as well"*[44]. While this is no place to offer a full-scale reconstruction of John the Baptist, a few historical considerations will help us see how the evangelists incorporate traditions about the Baptist as a means of undergirding the unique identity of Jesus. We will follow Mark's abbreviated narrative and show how Matthew and Luke both build upon Mark's foundation.

Mark 1:2-3 introduces John by reference to Israel's Scripture: *"As it is written in Isaiah the prophet: Behold, I send my messenger ahead of You, who will prepare Your way; The voice of one crying in the wilderness, 'Make ready the way of the Lord, make His paths straight"*. Mark interestingly attributes this quotation to Isaiah, but 1:2 is actually a quotation of Malachi 3:1. Mark 1:3 quotes Isaiah 40:3. Both are eschatological prophecies about the return of Israel's God to rescue His people. Interestingly enough, both Matthew and Luke realize Mark has conflated his sources; in Matthew 3:3 the evangelist drops the reference to Malichi altogether and only cites Isaiah, while Luke 3:4-6 actually *expands* the quotation from Isaiah to include Isaiah 40:3-5 but follows Matthew in dropping the citation from Malachi. Both Matthew and Luke think Malachi 3:1 applies to John, but they move the quotation from Mark 1:2 to Matthew 11:10 and Luke 7:27, respectively. These curious textual differences shouldn't obscure the point Mark, Matthew, and Luke unanimously make about John: he is the one who announces the coming Messiah and God's imminent eschatological restoration. Both Malachi

---

44. McGrath, James. 2024. *Christmaker*. Eerdmans. p. 3

3:1 and Isaiah 40:3(-5) are prophetic oracles about the day God finally vindicates His people.

All is not sunshine and roses, though. Mark and Matthew both describe John as one who preached a baptism of repentance in the wilderness, wore a garment of camel's hair, ate locusts and honey, and baptized those who confessed their sins in the Jordan River.[45] Matthew alone explains the specific content of John's preaching: "*Repent, for the kingdom of heaven is at hand*"[46]. All three Synoptic evangelists also agree that John was wildly popular. People traveled to the wilderness to hear John and be immersed by him in the river. While scholars debate the exact meaning of John's baptism, it denotes some sort of purification which occurs *outside of the temple* in Jerusalem: "*Immersion especially could be connected with repentance, forgiveness and conversion; it could take place in rivers, including the Jordan, and in some instances may connote criticism of the temple cult and authorities*"[47]. John strategically positions himself; we discussed in the previous chapter how the temple was a political institution in antiquity, and by calling Israel back to God outside of Jerusalem John mounts a not-so-subtle critique of the Jewish political class. McGrath skillfully explains how John's ministry tapped into popular discontent with the current political regime in Jerusalem: "[John] *challenge*[d] *an institution that stood at the heart of his people's identity and piety, yet from which many felt alienated or at least distant . . . The response that John's message and his proclamation of baptism received from people far and wide shows that it offered something people were longing for*"[48]. The way of the Lord wasn't being prepared in Jerusalem, and many Jews found comfort in John's anti-establishment message.

John was widely perceived as a prophet, likely styling himself after Elijah. Following Elijah, John resides in the wilderness but is deeply critical of Israel's political class, fiercely convinced they were leading God's people astray and failing to honor Him.[49] Not only was John's choice of location an invocation of Israel's long prophetic tradition, his food and dress further validated his prophetic credentials "*John's clothing was reminiscent of what the prophet Elijah had worn (2 Kings 1:8). By dressing as he did, John styled himself as a prophet in the vein of those who shake things up, challenge the status quo, and even bring about regime change*"[50]. Locusts

---

45. Mark 3:4-6 and Matthew 3:4-6

46. Matthew 1:2

47. Cummins, S.A.. 2024. "*John the Baptist*". In *Dictionary of Jesus and the Gospels*, 2nd ed. edited by Green, Joel. InterVarsity Press. p. 437

48. McGrath, *Christmaker*, p. 62

49. McGrath, *Christmaker*, p. 33

50. McGrath, *Christmaker*, p. 2

and wild honey were both kosher and readily available in the wilderness; a Jew who was intensely concerned with ritual purity but had no income would find both a valuable (and ritually safe) source of sustenance.[51] While these habits certainly seem odd from a modern perspective, John's Jewish audience would have quickly apprehended their symbolic meaning. John was one, perhaps the final one, in a long line of Jewish prophets announcing an urgent message from God to His wayward people. With John, however, the message was thoroughly eschatological. Israel was living at the end of history; there would be no more second chances.

In Matthew 3:7, John specifically addresses the Pharisees and Sadducees who were coming to him for baptism, saying to them, "*You brood of vipers, who warned you to flee from the wrath to come*". Luke includes this saying but widens its target to "*the multitudes*" in Luke 3:7. Both Matthew and Luke follow this vicious taunt with a warning. John tells his audience they must bear fruit if they have really repented; no one can claim that having Abraham as their father will vindicate them in the coming crisis because of God's ability to raise up children for Abraham out of the stones. The axe of judgment is laid before the trees of Israel, and those who don't bear fruit would be cut down. Only the truly penitent would avoid cataclysm.[52] Luke alone records a series of questions posed to John from the multitudes about how to bear fruits of repentance. John tells those who have food and clothing to share with those who have none, that tax collectors should take no more than what they have been ordered, and that soldiers should not confiscate money, levy false accusations, and remain content with their wages.[53] His instructions are all addressed towards those with some degree of political power or connection to those in political power; wealth was usually generated by exploitative coercion, and both tax collectors and soldiers represented the Roman occupation.[54] While John's message of repentance was directed at the multitudes, the rich and powerful would be especially vulnerable in the impending crisis.

All three Synoptic evangelists turn their attention to John's relationship with Jesus. In Mark 1:7-8, John predicts that one is coming who is mightier than him, and while John baptizes with water the coming one will baptize with the Holy Spirit. Matthew retains this tradition and adds a warning of judgment: "*His winnowing fork is in His hand, and He will thoroughly clear His threshing floor; and He will gather His wheat into the barn, but He will burn up the chaff with unquenchable*

---

51. McGrath, *Christmaker*, pp. 26-27

52. Matthew 3:7-10, Luke 3:7-9

53. Luke 3:10-14

54. Bock, *Jesus*, pp. 82-83

fire"[55]. Israel is standing on a precipice, and the coming one will bring both salvation and judgment. Luke agrees with Mark and Matthew but introduces this pericope in Luke 3:15 with a comment about the crowds wondering if John might be the Christ. Immediately after this, Jesus presents himself to John for baptism.

While the Synoptic portrayals of Jesus's baptism differ in minor narrative details, the substance of the event is identical. John baptizes Jesus, and as soon as He emerges from the water the Spirit of God descended on Him in the form of a dove, and a voice from heaven declares "*You are My beloved Son, in You I am well pleased*"[56]. Two elements of this tradition are salient for Jesus's identity. Just as Samuel anointed David, who was immediately granted God's Spirit in 1 Samuel 16:13, John's baptism of Jesus should be seen as a major turning point in Jesus's life. While Matthew and Luke both attest to Jesus's divine origins, the descent of the Spirit is both validation of Jesus's identity and the sign that He is God's messiah. It is also the beginning of Jesus's prophetic ministry to Israel which will culminate on the cross in Jerusalem. The Spirit is granted to prophets, priests, and kings, and Jesus's baptism is likely an indication that he holds all three offices. "*This is my Son*" alludes to Psalm 2:7 and Isaiah 42:1. In Psalm 2:7 'God's son' is the king of Israel who defeats the pagan nations and rules the world. It is undeniably messianic, and by employing this tradition the evangelists are unambiguously calling Jesus Israel's king. In Isaiah 42:1, God grants the Spirit to His servant who brings forth justice to the nations and illuminates the way of the Lord. Isaiah 42 is, in context, decidedly eschatological; the baptism signals Jesus as the turning point for all of human history. Also important but often overlooked is that Jesus's baptism by John "*represents Jesus' endorsement of John's message for the nation*"[57]. Jesus will stand in direct continuity with John and affirm his prophetic ministry; the time is at hand, Israel will be judged, and salvation will come through repentance and bearing fruit.

While the fourth gospel's description of John the Baptist is aesthetically different from the Synoptics, it is, much like the birth narratives, thematically identical. Luke raises the question of the Baptist's messianic status, and John also makes it a point to distinguish the Baptist's identity from Jesus. In John 1:6-8, the Baptist testifies to the Light but is not himself the Light. John 1:15-36 is a catena of Synoptic traditions about John reworked into a compressed presentation. John testifies about Jesus Christ, denies that he is the messiah, quotes Isaiah 40:30 to describe his prophetic ministry, reluctantly baptizes Jesus, and announces that Jesus will

---

55. Matthew 3:12

56. Mark 1:9-11, Matthew 3:13-17, and Luke 3:21-23

57. Bock, *Jesus*, p. 86

baptize with fire. He also personally testifies that Jesus is the Son of God. In fact, John's presentation of John the Baptist is an excellent case study in Barker's theory of Synoptic trajectories. It would appear that John knew the Synoptic Baptist traditions and restructured them to fit his narrative. Everything the Synoptics say about John the Baptist is affirmed by John the evangelist. God was, through John, announcing the time of eschatological fulfillment. This would take place through Jesus and as a result the world could never be the same. John sets the stage for the one mightier than him. Before His public ministry commences, however, Jesus must undergo one significant challenge. Jesus, freshly baptized, enters the wilderness to face temptation head-on.

THE TEMPTATION OF JESUS

Mark's temptation narrative is short and sweet: *"Immediately the Spirit impelled HIm to go out into the wilderness. And He was in the wilderness forty days being tempted by Satan; and He was with the wild beasts, and the angels were ministering to Him"*[58]. Despite its brevity, Moloney argues that this passage is theologically rich. The wilderness is simultaneously a place where Israel's great heroes experienced powerful encounters with God but also where Israel was tempted to sin and ultimately failed. Jesus, like Israel, is tempted in the wilderness but, unlike Israel, overcomes. He succeeds where His predecessors failed. There is also an echo of the creation narrative; when the man and the woman give in to the tempter, creation is thrust into chaos. When Jesus defeats temptation, the wild beasts present him no danger.[59] This short passage presents Jesus quite literally defeating the demons that had haunted humanity, and by extension Israel, from the beginning of creation. As the messianic son of God, Jesus is conquering the powers which enslave humanity. Matthew and Luke will both expand on Mark's temptation tradition.

There are very few differences between the temptation narratives in Matthew and Luke. Both agree Jesus was compelled by the Spirit to enter the wilderness, fasted for forty days, and became hungry[60]. Jesus is then tempted by Satan three times. The second and third temptations are flipped in Luke but recounted almost identically to Matthew's. For the sake of clarity, I will follow Matthew's order. Jesus, starving from his fast, is first tempted by Satan, who calls Jesus "the Son of God" in Matthew 4:3 and Luke 4:3. He insidiously suggests Jesus use his power to turn stone into bread. Jesus responds by quoting Deuteronomy 8:3: man doesn't

---

58. Mark 1:12-13

59. Moloney, *Mark*, pp. 37-40

60. Matthew 4:1-2 and Luke 4:1-2

live by bread alone but by the word of God[61]. Because Jesus is God's Son he remains faithful. Satan then takes Jesus to Jerusalem in Matthew 4:5-7[62], places him at the peak of the temple, and quotes Psalm 91:11-12, telling Jesus that if He jumped off the ledge God would rescue him. Jesus responds with yet another quotation from Deuteronomy, this time 6:16: "*You shall not put the Lord your God to the test*". Finally, Satan in Matthew 4:8-10 takes Jesus to a high mountain, showing Him all the kingdoms of the world. Satan promises that if Jesus bows down, all the kingdoms will be His. Jesus quotes Deuteronomy for a third time; Deuteronomy 6:13 shuts down Satan, "*You shall worship the Lord Your God, and serve Him only*". Satan is defeated and finally leaves Jesus alone.

These temptation narratives are of course highly stylized, but they make an emphatic point. Jesus overcomes temptation of the highest order, demonstrating that the claims which the evangelists have been making about him are entirely true. Jesus Christ is the messiah, the son of God, and his defeat over the ultimate powers of evil confirm his identity. Given the widespread discontent towards political authorities both Jewish and Roman in first century Judea and Galilee, this tradition also helps explain what *kind* of messiah Jesus is going to be. He will in fact rule over all the nations, just as the evangelists have hinted, but his dominion isn't temporal. Jesus defeats the cosmic powers which animate the evil empires of this world. The vanquished enemy in the temptation narrative isn't Rome or the political class in Jerusalem but the dark power which stands behind them. Strike the root to fell the tree. While many Jews expected the messiah to mount a violent revolution against the Roman occupation, Jesus is doing something much bigger: defeating the power of evil itself.[63] Bock beautifully summarizes the cosmic scope of Matthew and Luke's temptation tradition: "*Jesus succeeds against Satan where the previous representative of humanity (Adam) failed*"[64]. Jesus will liberate Israel and usher in the reign of God, but in an unsuspected way.

Of particular interest to our study is Matthew's third (and Luke's second) temptation. Matthew 4:8-10 and Luke 4:5-8 contain the grandest offer Satan makes to Jesus. If he would only bow the knee to Satan, Jesus would inherit the entire earth. I detect an echo of Genesis 3:5 in this passage; the man and woman in the garden were promised to become "*like God*" if they consumed the fruit, and Satan seems to be making Jesus a similar proposal. He could quite literally become

---

61. Matthew 4:4; Luke 4:4 abbreviates the quotation of Deuteronomy but makes the same point.

62. Luke moves this to the end of his temptation account in Luke 4:9-12 most likely because he strategically highlights Jerusalem as the place of climactic conflict; see Bock, *Jesus*, p. 90.

63. Wright, *Victory*, pp. 457-459

64. Bock, *Jesus*, p. 90

master of the world. Jesus declines, choosing to honor God instead. The story isn't over. Jesus is the Messiah, and by the end of Matthew *"All authority has been given to Me* [Jesus] *in heaven and on earth"*[65]. Through the life, death, resurrection, and ascension of Jesus, he becomes more than just another human emperor. He is installed as king of all creation. Jesus challenges the very foundation of political power. When God gives dominion over creation to humanity after fashioning them in His image in Genesis 1:26-28, humans are not granted dominion over each other. That is God's prerogative alone. By turning down Satan's offer of global imperialism, Jesus denies that God's coming kingdom will resemble those crafted by fallen human conceptions of power. The kingdom of God will subvert the kingdoms of men once and for all.

Conclusion

As we discussed in the previous chapter the goal of ancient biography was twofold: first, to recount the lives of great men, and second, to encourage the audience to emulate or learn from their example. Since the Bible is a culturally embedded collection of texts, modern Christians must draw principles from these documents which can then be applied in a historical context which is different from our own. Anyone who believes in the authority of Scripture must allow the conclusions we draw from the Bible to shape their theology and practice. This is no less true about the political and economic claims we find embedded in the texts. What light does the opening chapters of the gospels shed on the questions we are addressing in this book?

The first and most obvious conclusion relates to the messianic identity of Jesus. All four evangelists speak in a unified voice. Jesus is the Christ, the son of David, the son of God, the one promised in the Old Testament who brings about the restoration of Israel, the defeat of the evil empires, and ushers in the reign of God over creation, revealing Him to the world once and for all. From Mark's bold opening verse to John's creative christological reworking of Synoptic tradition, it is impossible to deny that the four biographers of Jesus want their audiences to know Jesus is king. Nor is this kingship reducible to personal spirituality; God's kingdom isn't a subjective experience which has no bearing on the 'real' world. It is, quite literally, the exercise of His omnipotent rule over the entire created order through the work of His Davidic representative Jesus. If the evangelists are correct regarding Jesus's identity, as Christians confess they are, then the very notion of human political power where one person or group of people exercises arbitrary,

---

65. Matthew 28:18

coercive dominion over others is entirely subverted. In the kingdom, Jesus the king defines the meaning of power.

Since biographies were written for their audiences to emulate or learn from the subject, the gospels must inform Christian moral character. Much of the material we covered in this chapter was *descriptive*, in that it tells us who Jesus was and why his identity matters. This doesn't mean, however, that there are no ethical consequences in these texts. As we discussed above, Christians who read the gospels *must* allow them to challenge our understanding of political power. Beyond that, the reign of God is urgent and results in salvation for those who accept it and judgment for those who don't; John's warning about the axe being laid at the root of the tree is still prescient. While in its original context these oracles of judgment were directed towards Israel, and particularly their readers, they stand as a testament to the seriousness which the eschatological moment poses for all humanity. If Israel is judged for rejecting John, how much more those who reject the one coming after him? Luke in particular emphasised the eschatological reversal both in his infancy narratives and his unique tradition about the crowds who questioned John. Those who become wealthy through coercion and exploitation will not survive the coming judgment unless they change their ways and are generous with their accumulated wealth. This stands as both a testament against unjust gain and a reminder that those of us who have more than we need are obligated to help the less fortunate. Far from being an affirmation of the predominant modern political and economic theory of authoritarian socialism, the Jesus tradition undermines it. Jesus rejects worldly political power in his temptation and demonstrates an unswerving commitment to God. We must follow his example, which will be further developed in the rest of the gospel narratives.

In Chapter 4 I used the work of scholar Halvor Moxnes as an example of the contradictions which often occur when biblical scholars work with inconsistent definitions of modern political and economic concepts. Moxnes rightly understands the Jesus tradition to be in part a critique of the political and economic structures of his day and correctly argues that nineteenth-century nationalism was influenced and legitimated by false nationalistic readings of the gospels. His proposed alternative, however, is to create a system of global authoritarian socialism where political authorities who think like him have imposed their will on people living thousands of miles away, all in the name of some nebulous conception of 'justice'. This is a shamefully widespread assumption in both conservative and progressive Christianity shared equally by the laity, clergy, and academics. Even in their opening chapters the evangelists have demolished that paradigm of political thought. Christians are presented with two mutually exclusive theological paths. The first is the wide and well-worn path, exemplified in the work of Moxnes:

Christians can weaponize their interpretation of Jesus and attempt to use the levers of state power to impose the values which arise from their interpretations on others. This path leads to destruction. The narrow path is much harder to navigate but exemplified by Jesus: rejecting any offer to rule the world in imperial fashion and instead remaining faithful to God, whose kingdom is coming through the very Messiah that subverts all structures of human power. This path runs through the cross but, paradoxically, ends in life. If I have to choose between Moxnes and Jesus, I'm sticking with Jesus.

It is now time to examine the ministry of Jesus. This chapter attempted to demonstrate how the four themes which are relevant to the study of political and economic texts in the gospels, prophecy, kingdom, eschatology, and messiah, are intrinsic to the evangelist's narratival construction of Jesus from the opening passages of each gospel. In order to accomplish this goal I reviewed most of the material contained in the first chapters of each gospel. The following chapter will be much more piecemeal, examining individual units in the tradition which I believe impact the ways in which Christians understand the political and economic consequences of Jesus's teaching. We will begin with his announcement of the kingdom and end at the walls of Jerusalem before his fateful final week. Let's explore the life of Jesus.

CHAPTER 9 | The Life and Ministry of Jesus

A Prophet in Word and Deed

You know that those who are recognized as rules of the Gentiles lord it over them; and their great men exercise authority over them. But it is not to be this way among you, but whoever wishes to become great among you shall be your servant; and whoever wishes to be first among you shall be slave of all.

Mark 10:42-44

Zacchaeus stopped and said to the Lord, "Behold, Lord, half of my possessions I will give to the poor, and if I have defrauded anyone of anything, I will give back four times as much." And Jesus said to him, "Today salvation has come to this house, because he, too, is a son of Abraham.

Luke 19:8-9

WORDS AND DEEDS OF THE KINGDOM

From the opening lines of each gospel the evangelists firmly establish the identity of Jesus. He is Christ, the son of God, inaugurating God's long-promised kingdom as the culmination of human history. Kingdom, eschatology, and christology are foundational components of the characteristic Jesus shaped by the oral tradition and textualized into the genre of ancient biographical narrative. Jesus is God's Davidic king who comes to judge and save. This is not a 'spiritual' reality but an objective one; God promised a descendant of David would rule over all creation and that through him every knee would bow and tongue confess the Lord God of Israel as the only true God. These promises come to fruition through Jesus.

The evangelists know this is true, and so do their audiences. For the large crowds of Jews which followed Jesus around Galilee, their initial impression of his ministry was not primarily messianic. That realization would slowly dawn on those who remained faithful to him. Jesus was, during his lifetime, popularly perceived as a prophet mighty in word and deed, announcing the arrival of God's kingdom. A feature of the characteristic Jesus tradition, his prophetic ministry provides an explanation of how God's kingdom, which was finally breaking in, actually worked in practice. Now that the final moment of deliverance was at hand, what would change? How should Israel respond? Jesus's prophetic words and deeds define his public career. His message is often met with confusion or resistance. Jewish messianic eschatology, remember, was not a monolithic, systematized set of expectations. There were various interpretations within Judaism regarding how exactly God would bring about the restoration of Israel, and no one was expecting it to happen through someone like Jesus. This chapter will address Jesus' prophetic proclamation to Israel from the beginning of His public ministry until His final trip to Jerusalem.

Space does not permit a detailed exegetical commentary of each gospel. I instead selected a wide number of traditions which provide us, either explicitly or implicitly, with a presentation of Jesus that impacts the way we think about political and economic structures in the modern world. There will no doubt be passages which I omit that could have been profitably included, but by working through the selected texts attentive readers will be able to deduce how material not incorporated into this study should be interpreted. It is also important to remember that the traditions which comprise the written gospels were designed to give us the characteristic Jesus, revealing the impact he had on those who followed him. I will not argue for the historicity of any particular text but rather attempt to explain how they fit into the wider presentation of Jesus offered by the evangelists.

It's nearly impossible to find a coherent order for the texts I am interpreting in this chapter. Since Mark was the first written gospel I will loosely follow his narrative sequence. This immediately raises sequential problems, however, because much of the early narratival traditions in Mark are placed by Matthew *after* Jesus' long Sermon on the Mount in Matthew 5-7. To further complicate matters, Luke 6 offers an abbreviated version of Matthew's famous sermon (often called the 'Sermon on the Plain') but takes several sayings from Matthew 6 and moves them towards the end of his narrative. Many of these sayings address material possessions and wealth, obviously crucial for this study, and Luke adds a wealth of material unique to his gospel which builds upon sayings from Matthew's sermon that Luke chose to rearrange. John includes several traditions which are relevant but have no close Synoptic parallels. How does one possibly manage these divergent traditions? Most of the passages which are common to the Synoptics will be handled in the order in which they appear in Mark. I will examine Matthew's Sermon on the Mount and Luke's Sermon on the Plain as discrete literary units; while Luke will rearrange and expand much of Matthew's sermon, I will first account for how these traditions work within Matthew. Since Luke emphasises the themes of wealth, money, and power in several traditions found only in his gospel, this special material will receive its own section. I will also do the same with passages from John which have no parallels in Synoptic tradition. We will see, once again, that Luke and John develop their source material but do so in a manner consistent with their idiosyncratic authorial interests, a classic example of differentiation in style but not substance. Let's turn to the text.

THE KINGDOM OF GOD IS AT HAND

In Mark 1:14-15, Jesus begins His public career with a dramatic announcement: *"Jesus came into Galilee, preaching the gospel of God, and saying, 'The time is fulfilled, and the kingdom of God is at hand; repent and believe in the gospel.'"*. Every word of this fateful text has been explained above. By invoking the term *'euangelion'*, Mark is connecting Jesus' message with the long story of Israel which had yet to be resolved. By claiming *"the time is fulfilled"*, Mark signals the eschatological significance of Jesus' mission. 'Gospel' in Isaiah refers to the promised restoration of God's people, the decisive moment when He would be revealed to the world and restore His universal reign, and that time had finally come.[1] Mark has already disclosed to his audience Jesus' unique identity as Christ and son of God, both of which were understood with reference to the Davidic monarchy in the first century. In its historical context, Mark couldn't be more direct: God was working through Jesus to bring about His rule over creation. Since this text demarcates the beginning of Jesus' prophetic ministry, His *"characteristic message was the announcement of the kingdom"*[2]. Everything Jesus will do and say following this announcement is an explication of His kingdom proclamation. The gospel, good news, is about the kingdom, as Matthew Bates explains, *"we are compelled to conclude that the gospel Jesus preached is intimately bound up with the kingdom of God"*[3].

I must stress yet again that Jesus' gospel of the kingdom is not a metaphor or a description of a spiritual reality which only impacts the private lives of those who hear it. God created the world and would rule over it once again, this time for good. As in texts like Psalm 2, the nations must finally bow the knee to Israel's God. The phrase *"repent and believe"*, summarizing how those who hear the gospel must respond, further intensifies this point. The root verbs are *metanoeo* and *pisteuo*, respectively, and they denote a radical turning around and committing

---

1. Moloney, *Mark*, p. 49

2. Wright, *Victory*, p. 227

3. Bates, Matthew. 2017. *Salvation By Allegiance Alone*. Baker Academic. p. 48

oneself to Jesus' gospel, the announcement of God's kingdom. We will discuss the significance of *pisteuo*'s cognates in more detail when analyzing Paul, but the term as Jesus uses it denotes more than simply changing one's mind or cognitively assenting to a set of theological propositions. The kingdom is at hand; the only proper response is a complete reorientation of belief and practice while fully accepting the message of Jesus. By opening his public ministry in this manner, Mark is signaling that everything Jesus says and does will explain the good news of God's kingdom; those who put their faith in it must undergo a conversion of assumptions about the kingdom, replacing them with Jesus's teaching. For many in Jesus's audience, this will be a bridge too far.

Matthew incorporates and elaborates on Mark's summary statement. Matthew 4:12-16 serves as an introduction for Jesus's kingdom announcement by placing him in the Galilean city of Capernaum and quoting Isaiah 9:1-2, a passage which introduces a prophecy in Isaiah about the restoration of Israel and the Davidic monarchy. In Matthew 4:17, Jesus finally goes public: "*From that time Jesus began to preach and say, "Repent, for the kingdom of heaven is at hand"*". Matthew punctuates Mark's kingdom announcement with the calling of disciples in 4:18-22 before completing Mark's thematic introduction by stating in Matthew 4:23 that "*Jesus was going throughout all Galilee, teaching in their synagogues and proclaiming the gospel of the kingdom, and healing every kind of disease and every kind of sickness among the people*". In this passage Matthew unambiguously identifies Jesus as a prophet. His words ("*teaching*" and "*proclaiming*") and his deeds ("*healings*") would have been perceived by his original audience as a clear indication of his status as a classical Jewish prophet. Since the primary role of a prophet is to communicate an urgent message from God to His people, in this case "*the gospel of the kingdom*", Jesus's words and deeds elucidate the meaning of that phrase. Jesus proclaims and enacts the kingdom, which is incomprehensible apart from Jesus' prophetic ministry.

Matthew, who constructs his narrative around five major discourses, elaborates this basic point in the following chapters. Matthew 4:23 is the start of a lengthy section which concludes with a rhetorical *inclusio* in Matthew 9:35, reading "*Jesus was going through all the cities and villages, teaching in their synagogues and proclaiming the gospel of the kingdom, and healing every kind of disease and every kind of sickness*". The material which Matthew incorporates between these two passages explain Jesus' teaching and healing in narratival form, revealing what the "*gospel of the kingdom*" actually entails. The first major discourse in Matthew, the Sermon on the Mount (chapters 5-7) delineate Jesus' kingdom teaching, showing his followers the meaning to "repentance" (from 4:17, 'turn around' or 'change'), and the powerful deeds recounted in chapters 8-9 demonstrate how his healings and other deeds of power manifest God's kingdom.[4] The kingdom is here, and Jesus enacts and defines the contours of God's eschatological rule. The only proper response is repentance and following Jesus.

Luke completely reworks Mark and Matthew's introduction of Jesus' ministry but retains their thematic concerns, presenting them in expanded narratival form. Luke 4:14-15 narrates that *"Jesus returned to Galilee in the power of the Spirit . . . And began teaching in their synagogues"*. Luke recalls a Sabbath in Nazareth where Jesus reads from Isaiah 61:1-1, a gospel passage about God's servant proclaiming deliverance to His people.[5] Jesus adds a commentary to this text in Luke 4:21, saying *"Today this Scripture has been fulfilled in your hearing"*. Following this incredible statement, Luke 4:22-30 records Jesus' first public controversy. Many are excited about the words of Jesus but doubt him. Jesus, consciously referring to himself as a prophet, utters the famous line in 4:24 *"no prophet is welcome in his hometown"*, then spends several verses comparing himself to Elijah, another prophet who was also rejected by the people of Israel. The synagogue becomes enraged at Jesus' message and seeks to kill him, but he successfully retreats to Capernaum. While this tradition is radically different from Mark and Matthew in terms of style, Luke makes the same point: Jesus is a prophet who announces that the good news of God's deliverance is at hand, therefore Israel must repent and believe. In Luke 2:34 Simeon claimed Jesus was *"appointed for the fall and rise of many in Israel"*; the people of Nazareth, Jesus's own hometown, are apparently falling. Israel will be judged by their response to Jesus, and all who accept his message must repent and believe.

Luke 4:31-43 chronicles an early trip to Capernaum. Contrasted with Nazareth, the people of Capernaum *"were amazed at His teaching, for His message was with authority"*[6]. He then casts out several demons who ironically call him *"the Holy One of God"*[7] and *"the Son of God . . . Christ"*[8]. Upon experiencing Jesus's power the people of Capernaum quickly connect his words with his deeds, the hallmark classic prophecy. In 4:36 the crowd wonders *"What is this message? For with authority and power He commands the unclean spirits and they come out"*. The words and deeds of a prophet indeed. To round out the start of Jesus's public ministry, Luke has Jesus explain his itinerancy to the listening crowds: *"I must preach the kingdom of God to the other cities also, for I was sent for this purpose"*[9]. Luke, in

---

4. Blomberg, *Gospels*, p. 144

5. Luke 4:16-20

6. Luke 4:32

7. Luke 4:34

8. Luke 4:41

9. Luke 4:43

developed and expanded form, introduces Jesus' ministry in the same way as Mark and Matthew. The kingdom of God is the gospel, the core of Jesus' prophetic ministry, and those who hear him must respond appropriately. The kingdom can only be correctly interpreted through the words and deeds of Jesus.

All three Synoptic evangelists make the exact same claim about Jesus and his message. He is a prophet (and more than a prophet!) who is announcing the coming kingdom of God and calling Israel to repentance, enacting and explaining the kingdom through his words and deeds of power. For Jesus and his earliest followers and detractors his message is no metaphor. Jesus would not have been crucified had he travelled around Galilee and Jerusalem teaching people to cultivate a new sense of inward spiritual piety. He believed God's kingdom was coming and Israel needed to be ready. Following the prophets of old, his message was a direct challenge to the political authorities of his day.[10] His ministry begins in Galilee, not in Jerusalem, and draws huge crowds of peasants who were most likely dissatisfied or suspicious of the Jewish ruling class and found comfort in Jesus's proclamation of impending eschatological reversal. Like John, Jesus worked outside of the official political system, casting judgment on its corruption. In this way both figures imitated the great prophets which came before them. Jesus intended his message to impact the lives of all who heard it and by extension change the fabric of society.

Much like the infancy narratives, modern Christians have been quick to spiritualize or consign to the abstract category of 'religion' the gospel's announcement of the kingdom. This is a massive mistake. The evangelists certainly believed Jesus's teaching was concrete and inaugurated a decisive turning point in history, one where God returned to rule over creation through the work of His messiah and all who follow him. How could the world ever be the same? While Jesus doesn't violently displace the political authorities or economic structures of his day, he certainly calls his followers to stand above them, remembering that God's kingdom has come and arranging their lives accordingly. It is convenient, comfortable, in fact, for modern Christians to ignore Jesus' message of the kingdom. We would much prefer our uncritical commitment to 'democracy', our favorite political parties and politicians, our decadence and entertainment, and the ease of conforming to prevailing systems and thought patterns over the radical announcement that God, and no one else, is in charge. The kingdom of God challenges our political and economic presuppositions to the core. From the outset the evangelists simply assume Jesus is king, a claim which challenges all other authority figures. Famous statements such as '*render unto Caesar*' or Jesus's command to the rich young ruler that he sell his possessions cannot be isolated from the announcement of God's

---

10. Horsley, *Empire*, pp. 73-74

kingdom, and modern applications of particular texts cannot be divorced from their narratival context. The kingdom is here. After his initial announcement of the kingdom, Jesus calls a small group of men to follow him.

CALLING TWELVE DISCIPLES

After Jesus announces the kingdom of God, he invites several fishermen to follow him. In Mark 1:16-20, Jesus meets brothers Andrew and Peter. In Mark 1:17, Jesus requests them to join his movement, saying *"Follow Me, and I will make you become fishers of men"*. Often overlooked is the allusion to Jeremiah 16:16, an oracle of restoration in which God sends fishers and hunters to search for and rescue His scattered people. Jesus' disciples will complete that task. Andrew and Peter follow Jesus *"immediately"*. Jesus meets another set of fishermen brothers, James and John, who leave their father Zebedee's business and accompany Jesus on his journey. Zebedee is presumably a successful fisherman; Mark 1:20 indicates he was at least able to afford *"hired servants"*, indicating that the brothers likely lived above subsistence level, even if the category "middle class" is an inappropriate description of their social status.[11] Why would these fishermen leave their families and professions behind? After all, the brothers possessed great commercial skill and, perhaps more significantly, would abandon the tight-knit web of familial relationships which typified village life in rural Galilee.[12]

The first answer, already apparent from the earliest passages in Mark, is theological. Jesus is the Messiah, but in the narrative logic of Mark no one except his audience knows this yet. The fisherman would have taken Jesus to be a prophet, announcing the coming kingdom of God, and as Jews awaiting the day of God's redemption they were likely motivated by eschatological hopes. While this is pure historical speculation, Zebedee might even have encouraged his sons to follow a prophet mighty in word and deed despite the challenges it would pose for the family business. The kingdom of God was, for these Galilean fishermen, not simply a matter of abstract theology. They believed God was powerfully at work in Jesus and that something was happening which would lead to pronounced changes in society.

The second answer to the question posed above, related to the first, is about the expected political and economic reversal which the fishermen hoped God's kingdom would elicit. Rhodes, Dewey, and Michie helpfully summarize our earlier conclusions about the agrarian economy of regions like Galilee in antiquity:

---

11. Contra Bock, *Jesus*, p. 98; see instead Rhodes, Dewey, and Michie, *Mark as Story*, pp. 65-66
12. Moloney, *Mark*, p. 53

"The rulers, including the high priest, the elders, and other aristocratic landowners, constitute a very small elite group—people of status and wealth—who dominate the populace"[13]. As Crossley and Myles point out, fishermen were not exempted from exploitation at the hands of those who wield political power: *"Fishers and their households were presumably subject to the same excessive taxation, discontent, banditry, warfare, and violent reprisals that implicated the daily life of farmers and other villagers . . . Rome and its client-kingdoms were reliant upon revenue funneled upwards through its taxes and other measures of economic extraction like tariffs, tolls, or tithes . . . The local aristocracy, though constituting a small minority of the population, lived off a share of any surplus produced to sustain their relatively indulgent lifestyle"*[14]. A small group of fishermen, disenfranchised by the political establishment and awaiting the restoration of God's rule, would have many reasons for following an anti-establishment prophet such as Jesus. The concrete political and economic factors animated working-class fishermen to dream of a situation in which the ruling class was supplanted by God's ordained authorities.

Matthew retains the basic contours of Mark's story. Matthew 4:18-22 is situated between two statements which initiate the beginning of Jesus' public ministry, but emphasises, with Mark, the immediacy with which the fishermen left their boats and families to follow him. Luke modifies the story, making Peter the central character. In Luke 5:1-11, Jesus enters Peter's boat and commands him to sail into the sea. Peter, having caught nothing all day, does as Jesus requests. To his great surprise, Peter winds up catching so many fish his boat nearly capsizes. Peter's response, recorded in Luke 5:8, echoes Isaiah's visionary experience in God's courtroom from Isaiah 6:5: *"Go away from me Lord, for I am a sinful man"*. At this point we are introduced to James and John, both of whom, as in Matthew and Mark, will now fish for men. When they return to shore they leave their boats and follow Jesus. Interestingly, John seems to have rewritten Luke's story and incorporated it into the resurrection narratives of Jesus in John 21:1-14. John's calling story occurs in John 1:35-51; presumably Andrew and Peter are already followers of John and upon seeing Jesus Andrew announces *"We have found the Messiah"*, after which John adds an editorial note stating that "Messiah" equals "Christ"[15]. Nathaniel concurs towards the end of the story, saying to Jesus in John 1:49 *"Rabbi, You are the Son of God; You are the King of Israel"*. John distinctively emphasises the messianic christology of Jesus, whereas the Synoptics reveal the disciples didn't

---

13. Rhodes, Dewey, and Michie, *Mark as Story*, pp. 65

14. Crossley and Myles, *Class Conflict*, p. 80

15. John 1:41

acknowledge Jesus as Christ until much later in the narrative[16]. However we understand John's reworking of the Synoptic traditions, all four are in agreement that when Jesus called the disciples, they responded.

It makes perfect historical sense that a prophetic figure like Jesus would appeal to followers who believed they were being oppressed by the political elite and longed for God's deliverance. It is highly historically unlikely, contrary to the way these traditions are interpreted in Western sermons, that among first century Jewish peasants Peter and his associates would be viewed as radical for following Jesus. While discipleship certainly incurred social and economic costs, a direct call from a prophet of restoration might have been perceived as a great honor. More inconceivable, and much less socially acceptable, is the next disciple whom Jesus calls in the Synoptics. In Mark 2:13-17, Matthew 9:9-13, and Luke 5:27-32, Jesus does the unthinkable: he invites a tax collector to follow him. This tax collector, called "Levi" in Mark and Luke and "Matthew" in Matthew[17], accepts the invitation to follow Jesus. All three Synoptic evangelists place this event right after the controversial healing of a paralytic[18] in which Jesus forgives the sins of the paralytic man, is chastised by the scribes who witness it, and then heals him of his affliction *"so that you may know that the Son of Man has authority on earth to forgive sins"*[19]. This tradition places Jesus' authority in opposition to the politically-connected scribal elite who believed themselves to be in a position of influence over their fellow Jews. The calling of Levi/Matthew is connected with other traditions which highlight the authority of Jesus.

Matthew and Luke follow Mark closely, and the story is rather simple. According to Mark 2:13-14, Jesus was headed to teach at the seashore and passed Levi sitting in his tax booth. He implores Levi to follow him, and without uttering a word Levi does as he is told. Luke 5:28 notes that Levi *"left everything"*. What is incredible about this story is its relationship to the calling of the fishermen. Tax collectors were widely viewed as agents or clients of the occupying Romans, even though Levi was likely employed by Herod Antipas. They were still viewed as collaborators with the enemy and a reminder that Israel had yet to be delivered from the hands of evil imperial powers.[20] Not only was Levi a tax collector, he was stationed on the shores of Galilee, meaning *he was the one responsible for taxing the*

---

16. Mark 8:27-29, Matthew 16:13-16, and Luke 9:18-20

17. This certainly refers to the same individual; just as Peter was also called 'Simon' and Paul 'Saul', so was Levi known as 'Matthew'. See Bock, *Jesus*, p. 112

18. Mark 2:1-12, Matthew 9:1-8, and Luke 5:17-26

19. Mark 2:10

20. Bock, *Jesus*, p. 112

fishermen who Jesus had just called! While there is no record of Peter, James, John and Andrew responding to the unexpected invitation offered to a tax collector who extracted money from fishermen on behalf of powerful political authorities, the calling of Levi was scandalous. Whatever Jews thought about the coming kingdom of God, tax collectors were not included.

After being called by Jesus, Levi invites him over for a dinner in which *"many tax collectors and sinners were dining with Jesus and His disciples"*[21]. The Greek noun for 'sinners' is *hamartoloi*, and to understand this passage it is imperative we review how the term was used in Second Temple Judaism. Christians have widely misrepresented Jewish understandings of sin and salvation, a situation only intensified by the soteriological debates of the Protestant Reformation. It has been almost universally assumed within Christianity that Judaism required legal perfection and Jesus came to rescue individuals from the impossible burden imposed upon them by the law. This isn't historically accurate. The law itself assumed Israelites would sin against God and offered provisions for dealing with those sins, exemplified in passages like Leviticus 4:1-6:7. When Paul says in Philippians 3:6 that he was *"found blameless"* according to the law, he is not claiming to have never sinned but rather that when he did he would offer the proper sacrifices to atone for them. *Hamartoloi*, in this context, doesn't refer to 'sin' in general because no one was without sin; if this was the case there would be no provision in the Jewish law to absolve those who sin. When the evangelists note Jesus is dining with tax collectors and *hamartoloi*, this doesn't refer to 'people who sin' as opposed to 'people who don't'.

James Dunn brilliantly argues that the language of 'sinners' is conditioned by Jewish sectarianism in the first century.[22] There were widespread disagreements within Judaism, often extremely hostile, with the term 'sinners' applied by in-groups to other Jews who diverged from their interpretation of the Law. The implications were both ecclesiological and eschatological; groups labeled 'sinners' were functionally equal to pagan gentiles, meaning they were outside of the family of God, and because they were not 'true' Jews they would not inherit the world to come when God finally returned to rescue his Israel. 'Righteousness', which will be discussed in much greater detail when we study Paul, was used to denote those Jews who believed they were in the right before God, while the epithet 'sinner' meant the opposite. 'Sinners' might be Jewish but they were playing for the wrong team.

The presence of the judgmental Pharisees in the tradition of the dinner at Levi's house confirms this reading of *hamartoloi*. Mark 2:15 and parallels portray

---

21. Mark 1:15

22. Dunn, *Remembered*, pp. 281-286

Jesus and his disciples dining with tax collectors and sinners, and in Mark 2:16 the Pharisees twice question why Jesus would eat with 'sinners'. This reveals the factional nature of the term 'sinner'; from the Pharisees' perspective Levi's dinner guests are sinners "*because they fail to observe the doctrine or praxis which is of such self-definitional significance for the group*"[23]. The Pharisees were in the right before God while Levi's dinner guests were not. Why would a prophet announcing the kingdom of God dine with those who are clearly, as the Pharisees would say, outside of God's good graces? If Jesus was really announcing the return of Israel's God, he would certainly align himself with the political authorities. Mark 2:17 records Jesus' response: "*It is not those who are healthy who need a physician, but those who are sick; I did not come to call the righteous, but sinners*". The kingdom of God will incorporate those who the elite consider outsiders. Tax collectors and sinners are repenting and believing the gospel of the kingdom, precisely as God intended.

Not only does Jesus' response call into question the authority of the Pharisees, it also challenges their presuppositions about the dichotomy between those deemed 'sinners' and those deemed 'righteous'. If the *hamartoloi* are positively responding to the message of Jesus, what does that say about Pharisees who reject him? All three Synoptics follow this story with a tradition where Jesus is asked by the Pharisees and the disciples of John why Jesus's disciples didn't fast.[24] Jesus responds with a set of parables: new cloth is not stitched on an old garment, and new wine is not poured into old wineskins. The kingdom has arrived, but Jesus challenges popular conceptions about how it would work in practice. The only way through was repentance, which the most unlikely of people were willing to do.

Jesus is also known for calling twelve disciples to form his inner-circle. This is one of the best-attested features of the characteristic Jesus tradition. Mark, Matthew, and Luke all include a list of Jesus' twelve disciples[25], and Luke even repeats it at the beginning of Acts[26]. Paul also references "*the twelve*" in his summary of the gospel in 1 Corinthians 15:5. Dunn wisely notes that the minor variation between the lists is typical of traditions which were initially transmitted orally.[27] The symbolism of "twelve" is obvious and widely recognized even in popular circles; as Wright helpfully summarizes "*The very existence of the twelve speaks, of course, of the reconstitution of Israel . . . [this] indicates pretty clearly that he was thinking in terms*

---

23. Dunn, *Remembered*, p. 529

24. Mark 2:18-22, Matthew 9:14-17, and Luke 4:33-39

25. Mark 3:16-19, Matthew 10:2-4, and Luke 6:14-16

26. Acts 1:13

27. Dunn, *Remembered*, p. 507

of the eschatological restoration of Israel[28]. Rightly so. The calling of twelve disciples further confirms the rich kingdom theology of the Jesus tradition. God is restoring Israel and is doing so through Jesus. Those who want to enter the kingdom must repent and believe in Jesus' prophetic message.

The list of the twelve reveals one more important insight for our study. It includes, of course, the four fishermen Peter, James, John, and Andrew as well as Matthew, presumably the same Matthew/Levi who was responsible for collecting taxes from the fishermen[29]. The list also includes one Simon the Cananean (in Mark 3:18 and Matthew 10:4) who is called 'the Zealot' in Luke 6:15 and Acts 1:13. While Dunn is likely correct in asserting that the title "Zealot" didn't denote a revolutionary political faction until after the Jewish-Roman war of 66-70 CE, the term itself has an interesting history. The word used in Luke 6:15 is a derivative of *zelotes*, of which Paul employs a cognate in Philippians 3:6 to describe his persecution of the church and another in Galatians 1:14 to express his commitment to the Law. There was a great tradition of 'zeal' (also translated as 'jealousy') in Judaism, beginning with Phineas in Numbers 24:6-13 through to Mattathias, father of the Maccabees, in 1 Maccabees 2:23-26, in which the term describes those willing to maintain Israel's distinctive boundaries through force. If Israel was called by God, who is described as 'jealous' for His people[30], to be separate, those who exercised 'zeal' for God used violence to ensure that Israel didn't compromise its unique identity.[31] This is assuredly what Paul has in mind in Philippians 3:6 when he directly links the term 'zeal' with 'persecution'. By using this word to describe Simon, Luke is claiming that 'the Zealot' stands in a long tradition of Israelites who were willing to employ violence to defend God's Law.

The juxtaposition of four fishermen, a tax collector, and a zealot couldn't be more ironic. While the fishermen and Simon would likely share a similar disdain for the political elite impoverishing the Jewish population and colluding with Roman imperial rule, it is historically likely they expressed their desire for liberation differently. Both parties, however, would have viewed a tax collector such as Matthew/Levi with suspicion and contempt; he was, before following Jesus, on the side of those who oppressed God's people. As Jesus travels around Galilee announcing the kingdom of God, he calls those whom the elite would label 'sinners' to repentance. His inner circle, symbolic of the reconstitution of Israel, included men who may have been natural enemies. All of them follow Jesus, and all of them

---

28. Wright, *Victory*, p. 300

29. Dunn, *Remembered*, p. 509

30. Exodus 20:5, 34:14; Deuteronomy 4:24, 5:9, 6:15

31. Dunn, *Paul*, pp. 350-351

must repent. The Synoptic evangelists recount a tradition at the arrest of Jesus that *"one of"* His disciples drew a sword and severed an ear of the high priest's slave.[32] Readers might understandably assume that this unnamed disciple would be the one labeled 'Zealot'. John reveals that the violent figure is actually Simon Peter[33]. It isn't the one associated by Luke with the violent maintenance of Israel's holiness. The 'Zealot' fails to express his zealotry. This perfectly encapsulates the significance of discipleship in God's kingdom. Israel is being restored, God is calling all, especially the disenfranchised, the social and political power brokers are rejecting Jesus, and sinners are being transformed. The kingdom of God is at hand, and it is arriving in surprising ways.

This extended review of Jesus' disciples illuminates several themes conveyed by the evangelists, all of which challenge the ways in which modern Christians relate to the political and economic structures of our day. Within the narrative logic of the gospels, the traditions about the disciples primarily reinforce Jesus's surprising reinterpretation of the kingdom of God. Like the magi outmaneuvering Herod, the so-called 'king of the Jews', Jesus directs his message not towards the rich and powerful Jerusalem elite but to peasants and laborers in rural Galilee. He also calls those responsible for enforcing the Roman occupation. The kingdom is open to everyone but must result in personal transformation. Answering the call requires repentance, *metanoia*, not simply a recognition of sinfulness but a change of heart and practice. The self-proclaimed 'righteous' may wind up 'sinners', while those labeled 'sinners' become a part of Jesus' inner circle. For Christians today, the kingdom requires us to reframe the way we conceptualize worldly power and personal identity. Cognitive assent to a particular set of doctrines doesn't constitute 'repentance'; while theology is extremely important, it only matters if one properly responds to Jesus, whom all of the evangelist believe is the one true king, calling all to join God's kingdom through repentance and faith like the disaffected disciples. Mark begins to narrate the ministry of Jesus after the calling of Peter and his associates, but Matthew and Luke both include an extended section of Jesus' teaching where he explains what the kingdom of God is like and how those who believe his message must respond if they want to enter it. If the gospels as ancient Greek biography are designed to encourage people to emulate or respond to their subject, Jesus, there is no better place to begin our analysis of the moral transformation which occurs as the result of following Jesus than in Matthew's Sermon on the Mount and Luke's Sermon on the Plain.

---

32. Mark 14:47, Matthew 26:51, Luke 22:50

33. John 18:10-11

THE SERMON ON THE MOUNT

A Constructed but Characteristic Sermon

Perhaps the most famous extended passage in the gospels, Matthew 5-7 is a collection of sayings material which has come to be known as 'The Sermon on the Mount'. Beautifully but somewhat mysteriously ordered, this so-called 'sermon' is the first of five major discourses in Matthew and is designed to explain the implications of Jesus's message about the kingdom of God. If Israel is to, as Jesus commands in Matthew 4:17, *"repent, for the kingdom of heaven is at hand"*, what, exactly, does repentance look like in practice? The Sermon on the Mount contains a series of instructions which should shape the lives of those who accept the kingdom. If one wants to know what following Jesus entails, this is an excellent place to start.

I rarely disagree with the great Ben Meyer, but I find his claim that the sermon was transmitted in its entirety and easily traceable to Jesus as a uniform tradition implausible.[34] Since Matthew is highly structured it seems much more likely that he was familiar with traditions which are largely absent from Mark and reappropriated them for his own gospel, stitching them into a brilliant literary unit for pedagogical reasons. Stylized speeches were a common feature of ancient biography. This doesn't mean that Matthew was simply 'making things up'. Every line of the sermon is consistent with the characteristic Jesus constructed by the evangelist; Wright is correct in criticising scholarship which sees the sermon as little more than a product of early Christian theology, entirely unaffected by the oral Jesus tradition.[35] Matthew is constructing a brilliant speech which further elucidates the kingdom of God, but his construction is consistent with the recurring themes which characterise the gospels.

It is also placed at a strategic juncture in Matthew's gospel. Up until this point, Matthew has expanded upon Mark's brief introduction to Jesus, and in Matthew 4 Jesus announces the kingdom of God and calls his first disciples, following Mark 1:9-20. Mark immediately launches into Jesus' public ministry in 1:21, explaining that Jesus began teaching in the synagogue at Capernaum. Matthew will resume following Mark's narrative structure in chapter 8. This indicates that Matthew felt compelled to summarize Jesus' teaching on the kingdom before representing it in narrative form, and the Sermon on the Mount, despite its rustic setting, could easily have been set in the synagogue at Capernaum. Matthew takes the redactional

---

34. Meyer, *Five Speeches*, pp. 33-36

35. Wright, *Victory*, pp. 287-288

liberty of appropriating Jesus tradition into a stylized speech, consistent with his narratival agenda, and frontloading the ministry of Jesus with a programmatic collection of sayings which delineates the nature of the kingdom, particularly how his hearers should repent and behave in response. This is why Matthew constructed the Sermon on the Mount; the biographical objective of calling the audience to emulate the subject takes center stage. For Christians, Matthew 5-7 is pedagogical and contains implications for our interpretation of and participation in modern authoritarian socialism.

Before looking at the content of the sermon, Luke throws us an interesting interpretive curveball. Luke preserves an abbreviated version of Matthew's sermon, geographically moved to a plain[36], in Luke 6:17-49. Much of Matthew 6 has been removed and relocated to a later point in Luke's narrative. Why would Luke do such a thing? This disjunction between Matthew and Luke's sermon has been used by scholars to advance the Two-Document hypothesis that Matthew and Luke were independent but both relied on Mark and an undiscovered, historically unattested document named 'Q'. The argument is mostly aesthetic; why, scholars ask, would Luke rearrange a sermon so beautifully crafted as the one found in Matthew 5-7?[37]

Mark Matson challenges this scholarly consensus, arguing that Luke's omission and reworking of Matthew's Sermon on the Mount is entirely comprehensible without recourse to Q. Much of the material which is omitted in Luke 6 is grouped in Matthew, particularly Matthew 5:21-37 and 6:1-8[38]. Given that Matthew strongly emphasises Jewish themes in his gospel, Matson notes that what *"is noteworthy is that both sections that are avoided by Luke tend to deal with a reinterpretation of Jewish law or criticism of Jewish practice"*, and, since Luke and Acts characteristically highlights the inclusion of gentiles *"attention to divisive issues such as particular practices might serve to distract from Luke's sense of the synthesis of Jewish practices and Gentile inclusion . . . and the interest in bridging the divide between Jews and Gentiles"*[39]. Just as Matthew creatively clustered traditions to advance his own rhetorical agenda, Luke does the same with material which he omits from the sermon but incorporates at later points in his narrative. Given that Luke's stated

---

36. Luke 6:17, *"level place"*.

37. Matson, Mark. 2004. *"Luke's Rewriting of the Sermon on the Mount"*. In *Questioning Q*, ed. by Mark Goodacre and Nicholas Perrin, InterVarsity Press. pp. 43-48

38. Matson, *Luke's Rewriting*, p. 48

39. Matson, *Luke's Rewriting*, p. 49

goal in Luke 1:3 was to compose an "orderly"[40] account of the Jesus tradition he had every right to rearrange the material as he saw fit. Matson explains *"Luke has engaged in intentional clustering of this material . . . he did not simply disrupt an existing coherent sermon, but rather created his own thoughtful approach to the material by transposing it into his plan"*[41]. Much of Matthew 6 is expanded upon later in Luke with material which is unique to his gospel. Since it deals primarily with the issues of wealth, material responsibility, and financial power, we will explore that material in greater detail below. In the following section, I will mainly work through Matthew's Sermon on the Mount, highlighting Luke as it directly corresponds to or differs from Matthew. As with every tradition we have analyzed up to this point, Matthew and Luke diverge in style, not substance.

Goals of the Sermon

How does the Sermon on the Mount/Plain contribute to the evangelists' overall presentation of Jesus and the kingdom of God? Wright is correct that the sermons aren't an arbitrary assembly of abstract moral ideals: *"The sermon . . . is not a mere miscellany of ethical instruction. It cannot be generalized into a set of suggestions, or even commands, on how to be 'good'. Nor can it be turned into a guidemap for how to go to 'heaven' after death. It is rather, as it stands, a challenge for Israel to be Israel"*[42]. The kingdom of God issues a dire and urgent warning to Israel: repent because the time is up. Repentance, *metanoia* in Greek, means more than simply feeling sorry for personal sins. Dunn rightfully recognizes the importance of repentance for the Jesus tradition and offers and explanation for how the language should be understood historically: *"'to repent' is to change one's mind, often with an overtone of regret for the view previously held"*, and is not reducible to a subjective psychological reordering, *"The call expressed in the Greek term metanoeo [the verbal form, "repent"] . . . would have been heard as a reiteration of the call of the prophets to turn back to God . . . from a life in breach of God's commandments, from a social irresponsibility which should have been unacceptable . . . Its radical quality is indicated quite appropriately by rendering metanoeo as a call to 'convert', that is, for individuals to radically alter the manner and direction of their whole life, in its basic motivations, attitudes, and objectives, for a society to radically reform around its communal goals and*

---

40. The Greek word here is *kathexes* which, as we saw in Chapter 7, is confusingly translated in the NASB as *"in consecutive order"*. The term doesn't necessarily denote chronology; when Luke utilizes it he is most likely referring to an orderly arrangement of the traditions with which he was familiar.

41. Matson, *Luke's Rewriting*, p. 50

42. Wright, *Victory*, p. 288

values"[43]. The implications of this lengthy summary are obvious. Jesus, the prophet of God's coming kingdom, is telling his Jewish audience in classic prophetic form that they must reorient their entire lives, both personally and communally, around the coming kingdom. They need to embrace the identity which God has given them. They will do this, of course, by following Jesus's teaching, and there is no better summary of the ethical and social imperatives of the kingdom of God than in Matthew 5-7.

Richard Horsley also emphasises the social and political dynamics that formed the context in which Jesus would have issued the teachings which were eventually incorporated into the Sermon on the Mount. Jesus was intentionally initiating his ministry in Galilee, away from Jerusalem and other centers of power, and his primary audience was not the Jewish political class but Jews from rural villages. The economic consequences of the political policies enacted by Roman clients on behalf of the world empire had a profoundly negative effect on those living in these villages who were often seen as means to an end by the politically connected elites residing in the region's major cities. Much of the material in the Sermon addresses these problems. Promising blessings for those who are faithful and judgment upon those who exploit, calling for mercy, forgiveness, and charity, and showing respect for others are not abstract values but would enable those living in rural Galilee to support one another in the midst of economic and political instability.[44] Horsley predictably draws all the wrong modern conclusions; he argues for the 'rights' of particular goods and services and an "*end to or perhaps a roll-back of privatization to restore the common good*"[45], which means he wants to give *more* economic and political power to a small handful of politicians and bureaucrats as well as force people to labor without compensation or consent. While Horsley uses the language of 'justice' in service of imperial power, his fundamental historical claim is sound: we must not divorce Jesus's teaching from the concrete social, political, and economic systems of his day.

Nor can we downplay, as Horsley does, the intended effect the Sermon on the Mount/Plain was designed to have on their audiences. Matthew and Luke were likely written for people who didn't live in rural Galilee, but the message was supposed to have a real impact on them. They too, like the crowds to which Jesus addresses his words, are called to repent and believe. There are massive political and economic consequences for Jesus' teaching, but we must never isolate those from the personal and theological summons issued by Jesus. Unfortunately

---

43. Dunn, *Remembered*, pp. 499-500

44. Horsley, *Bow Down*, pp. 33-36

45. Horsley, *Bow Down*, p. 37

many scholars like Horsley who correctly argue that 'religion' can't be separated from 'politics' and 'economics' in the first century tend to ignore everything in the tradition which isn't explicitly 'political' or 'economic'. All of these concepts must be integrated if we are to make sense of the New Testament in its historical context while reflecting upon what it might mean for us today. To that end, Jack Kingsbury elegantly summarizes the effect Matthew's speeches, including the Sermon, were intended to have on his audience: "*Intended to be heard and internalized, the great speeches of Jesus have as their chief purpose to bring the life of the disciple, or the implied reader, into conformity with the shape of Jesus' own life, which is one of single-hearted devotion toward God and loving service towards neighbor*"[46]. The Sermon on the Mount(/Plain) isn't abstract theology, political or economic theory, or a rulebook for getting into heaven. It is a prophetic challenge for Israel and by extension everyone who believes in Israel's Messiah to repent and believe in the kingdom which Jesus is inaugurating. It must transform us, God's family, and the world.

The 'Gospel of the Kingdom' Explained

Matthew's Sermon occurs immediately after Jesus announces the kingdom of God and calls his first disciples.[47] Luke precedes his Sermon with narrative material found in Mark. Both evangelists include a similar proximate introduction to their Sermons. Matthew 4:24-25 explains that news about him was spreading through Syria, and people were coming to him for healing, after which "*Large crowds followed Him from Galilee and the Decapolis and Jerusalem and Judea and from beyond the Jordan*", and Luke 6:17-19 is reworded but includes the same geographic indicators. This is no accident. Matthew, despite composing a gospel characterized by Jewish themes, makes it a point that those who were seeking Jesus and who listen to his teachings aren't just Jewish. The gentiles have heard about Jesus and are giving him a fair hearing. This anticipates the Great Commission in Matthew 28:18-20, where Jesus is given all authority on heaven and earth and tells his disciples to go and baptize the nations. Just as the prophets foretold, the nations would come to Israel and pay homage to her king. Luke, always with an eye to the imminent gentile mission, concurs with Matthew and presents Jesus delivering his Sermon to a mixed audience of Jews and gentiles.

Matthew 5:1-2 formally opens the Sermon. Jesus sees the crowds, goes up to a mountain, sits down, and receives His disciples. He then begins to teach. Matthew

---

46. Kingsbury, *Matthew as Story*, p. 113

47. Matthew 4:17-23

portrays Jesus as a new Moses, which is why mountains are a significant motif in his gospel. By portraying Jesus as teaching on a mountain, Matthew is drawing a parallel between Moses and Jesus's prophetic ministries.[48] In Deuteronomy 17:14-20, Israel's king is given the primary responsibility of leading God's people to follow the law. Matthew has already demonstrated that Jesus is the Davidic king and as such he must lead the people to obedience. Joshua Jipp notes how the restoration of Israel would be accompanied by true repentance and obedience, as Jeremiah 31:31-34, alluding to Deuteronomy 30:11-14, foretold. While Jesus's teaching, particularly on the mountain, is evocative of Moses and the Law, it is also a reaffirmation of his kingship as well. As the true king of Israel proclaiming the restoration of God's people and the inauguration of His kingdom, Jesus will lead not just Jews but the gentiles who follow him into obedience to God.[49] While these overtones are muted in Luke, he has already established the Davidic christology of Jesus and assumes his readers accept Jesus's identity.

Once the setting, crowd, and identity of Jesus are established, Matthew opens his Sermon with the famous Beatitudes in 5:3-12. The word 'Beatitude' is derived from the Latin translation of the Greek *makarios*, "blessed", a cognate of which opens each line. In this context, those described as *makarios* are marginalized people who will receive God's blessing, given assurance from Jesus that the eschatological reversal is at hand.[50] Those upon whom Jesus declares God's blessing are described as poor in spirit, those who mourn, peacemakers, gentle, hungry for righteousness, merciful, pure in heart, peacemakers, and those persecuted and insulted for righteousness. Despite attempts to spiritualize these descriptors, Jesus is not addressing the powerful. Those who will be blessed are both faithful to God and others. Luke truncates the blessings in Luke 6:20-23, and leaves no room for spiritualization. He declares blessing on the poor (not "in spirit") and the hungry (not "for righteousness"), for the kingdom of God belongs to them. He also balances the blessings with oracles of woe: "*Woe to you who are rich, for you are receiving your comfort in full. Woe to you who are well-fed now, for you shall be hungry. Woe to you who laugh now, for you shall mourn and weep. Woe to you when all men speak well of you, for their fathers used to treat the false prophets in the same way*"[51].

The word translated "*rich*" in Luke 6:24 is *plousios*, a cognate of the term used by Mary in Luke 1:53 to describe those who would be sent away "*empty handed*"

---

48. Yang, Seung. 2013. "*Sermon on the Mount/Plain*". In *Dictionary of Jesus and the Gospels*, 2nd ed. ed. by Joel B. Green, InterVarsity Press. p. 846

49. Jipp, *Messianic Theology*, pp. 37-43

50. Seung, *Sermon on the Mount/Plain*, p. 846

51. Luke 6:24-26

as a result of the impending eschatological reversal. As I explained in the previous chapter, those who could be categorized as rich in antiquity very rarely acquired their wealth through voluntary production and exchange. The rich were often politically powerful and sustained their wealth by violence and coercion, primarily through the mechanism of political power. The aggressive accumulation and protection of wealth is precisely how the rural peasants who followed Jesus would have understood this condemnation, and in the kingdom God would finally dispense justice to those who oppressed and impoverished others. This is why the poor are blessed; God, through the inauguration of His kingdom, would finally vindicate them.

It is also crucial, since Matthew spends a large portion of his Sermon addressing the dangers of wealth, to reflect upon how the Jewish tradition thought about poverty and riches. Scholars like Moxnes and Horsley, who would identify themselves as working within the tradition of Marxism, are reflexively antagonistic towards those they deem rich, but within Judaism there is a much more nuanced and complex understanding of wealth. Christopher Hays demonstrates that the Old Testament portrays God defending those who are poor from the wicked who oppress them, citing passages such as Exodus 22:25-27, Psalm 12:5, and Amos 8:4-8, and that texts such as Isaiah 5:8-13 and Jeremiah 5:26-28 threaten the wealthy with divine judgment.[52] All of these writings are critical of those who exploit, defraud, and take advantage of other people. While left-wing scholars are quick to conclude that passages such as these are a critique of capitalism and an endorsement of socialism, they have gotten it exactly backwards. The rich are not becoming rich by providing goods and services on the open market, respecting the property rights of others, and upholding the non-aggression principle, but by weild arbitrary power to take what rightfully belongs to someone else. Wealth is seen as a gift if it is accrued honorably through hard work, as passages like Psalm 112:1-3 and Proverbs 12:27 attest, and there is no sympathetic romanticizing of the poverty which accompanies laziness and irresponsibility in Proverbs 10:4, 12:27, and 13:4.[53] Commenting on how these related ideas developed in Second Temple Judaism, Hayes writes *"Prophetic and apocalyptic books inveigh against the rich for their abuse of the vulnerable to such a degree that affluence and corruption became interchangeable categories"*, again referring to wealth acquired by coercive and non contractual means, while *"Judaism developed legal and voluntary mechanisms*

---

52. Hayes, Christopher. 2013. *"Rich and Poor"*. In *Dictionary of Jesus and the Gospels*, 2nd ed. ed. by Joel B. Green, InterVarsity Press. p. 800

53. Hayes, *Rich and Poor*, p. 801

for the redistribution of goods . . . Judaism valued frequent and voluntary expressions of charitable care for the poor"[54].

The legal mechanism for redistribution was of course written into the Law, given to Israel by God Himself, and was not a command which the Jews delegated to their pagan neighbors. Care for the poor was an in-house responsibility. Following the legal guidelines for helping the poor, voluntary charity was seen as both virtuous and obligatory for those with means. Anyone fortunate enough to acquire wealth peacefully was expected to share with those in need. Everyone would be accountable for what they did with their resources in the great eschatological event. We must keep in mind, as with every other subject broached by Jesus, that his conceptualization of wealth was conditioned by Second Temple Judaism, the political and economic structures of first century Judea and Galilee, and above all else his proclamation of God's kingdom. Hayes rightly summarizes Jesus' teaching on the subject: *"Although Jesus had quite a lot to say about riches and poverty, his mission was not to discuss wealth as such, but rather to proclaim the coming of the kingdom of God. Therefore, any account of the historical Jesus' teaching on money ought to be located within his broader kerygmatic agenda"*[55]. Correct.

Anticipating our findings, Hayes condenses Jesus's teaching on wealth and poverty: *"none of* [Jesus's teaching] *amounts either to a direct critique of rich people qua rich or to a characterization of the wealthy as generally unjust. It should, however, dispel any notion that Jesus saw money as "neutral". Quite the contrary, Jesus thought of money like fire: a useful thing in its proper place, but in abundance ever more likely to leap its bounds and consume its erstwhile master"*[56]. Luke casts judgment on those who have acquired wealth through impious and unjust means, stating decisively that they will receive condemnation on the day of judgment without repentance. The poor who have been oppressed by the rich will be vindicated while the rich themselves judged. None of this, of course, requires modern Christians to accept the absurd notion, advocated by Horsley and Moxnes, that Jesus's judgment on the rich requires us to give even more money and power to a smaller handful of wealthy and powerful politicians so that they can remake the world in the image of two successful, affluent academics living comfortable middle-class lives. Jesus is not advocating for socialism, he is condemning injustice of the type supported by those who believe the state has a right to confiscate from whom it wants and 'redistribute' the illegitimately stolen wealth to those who ally themselves with the state. Wealth is dangerous and must be used responsibly, and the modern nation-state

---

54. Hayes, *Rich and Poor*, pp. 801-802

55. Hayes, *Rich and Poor*, p. 803

56. Hayes, *Rich and Poor*, p. 804

has demonstrated it can't be trusted. Those who follow Jesus, however, must heed this warning: wealth can be a devastating trap and must be both acquired justly and managed in a way which benefits others.

Returning to Matthew's Beatitudes, we must also ask ourselves what it means to be gentle, merciful, pure, and peacemakers. Summarizing the Beatitudes, Bock states *"if you desire to receive God's blessing, then respond to the announcement of blessing, identify with it, and seek to reflect these characteristics . . . they are a part of a spiritual commitment to walk in God's ways in the pursuit of his character . . . children of God will reflect the character of the God they follow"*[57]. Jesus calls all who hear to embrace the character of God and live it out. Those who accept the kingdom seek for peace, mercy, purity, and gentleness, all of which characterize the relationships they have with their neighbors and with God. These qualities must impact *every* area of a disciple's life, not simply their 'spirituality'. As I argued in Chapter 3, the political spectrum in modernity is not between progressive and conservative but rather liberty and authority. Political libertarianism is based on the non-aggression principle and stipulates that no one has the right to initiate aggression against another's life or property. All social interactions must be voluntary and consensual. The only other alternative is authoritarianism, which is the political presupposition of both conservatism and progressivism, where the power of the state is leveraged to control and regulate behavior of which the authoritarian disapproves. I ask the reader a simple question: is peace, mercy, purity, and grace achieved by dominating a neighbor through force or by peacefully interacting with them? If we are to draw a principle from the Beatitudes which influences our understanding of modern political systems, the choice is clear. Our king is Jesus, not the American president, and we are loyal to his kingdom and his values. The Beatitudes call for a radical reorientation towards others and cannot be relegated to individualistic, private relationships.

After the Beatitudes Jesus tells his followers in Matthew 5:13-16 that they are the *"salt of the earth"* and the *"light of the world"*. Both of these are exhortations to set an example for all of those around them, guiding others to a knowledge of Israel's God by following Jesus's teaching. The notion of "light" is rooted in the Old Testament; in passages like Isaiah 42:6 and 49:6 Israel is a light to the nations with the goal of revealing God to a world which had forgotten Him.[58] Jesus is certainly tapping into this tradition because the section ends in Matthew 5:16 with precisely that statement: *"Let your light shine before men in such a way that they may see your good works, and glorify your Father who is in heaven"*. There is an implied

---

57. Bock, *Jesus*, pp. 128-129

58. Bock, *Jesus*, p. 131

ecclesiology in this passage. Israel was set apart as God's chosen nation to be, as promised to Abraham in Genesis 12:3, a blessing to the nations. Abraham's family will be defined by how they respond to Israel's Christ.

Matthew 5:17-20 introduces the so-called 'antitheses' where Jesus explains what it means to obey the Law. It concerns not just outward actions but inward motives. Since the vexing question of the Jewish law in relation to early Christianity is not the subject of this book, I will defer my brief comments on this complex problem to my chapters on Acts and Paul where the issue is more relevant. I have no desire to wade into the quagmire of that theological debate here.[59] Whatever we make of Jesus' claim in 5:17-18 that he *"did not come to abolish the law but to fulfill"*, Matthew's audience is informed in 5:19 that *"whoever keeps and teaches* [these commandments], *He shall be called great in the kingdom of heaven"*. Greatness in God's kingdom comes through following Jesus' commands, not through power, wealth, or prestige.

The antitheses offer politically and economically relevant principles. In Matthew 5:21-26 Jesus quotes Exodus 20:13, the Decalogue's prohibition against murder. Jesus intensifies the command; being angry with or insulting another person violates the Law. Far from being a novel or unique instruction, the Law itself in Leviticus 19:17-18 concurs with Jesus. Anger and wrath are evil, and those who follow Jesus must pursue reconciliation with opponents. In Matthew 5:38-42, parts of which are quoted in Luke 6:27-28, 32-36, Jesus quotes Exodus 21:24 (*"An eye for an eye, a tooth for a tooth"*) and explains his interpretation to the crowd: *"whoever slaps you on your right cheek, turn the other to him also. If anyone wants to sue you and take your shirt, let him have your coat also. Whoever forces you to go one mile, go with him two. Give to him who asks of you, and do not turn away from him who wants to borrow from you"*. Bock contends Jesus is not delineating a comprehensive legal theory but signifying how his followers ought to personally relate to others[60]. Luke appears to agree, and in his version of this tradition Jesus summarizes his statement by saying *"Give to everyone who asks of you, and whoever takes away what is yours, do not demand it back"*[61]. In the final antithesis, found in Matthew 5:43-48, Jesus tells His followers to *"love your enemies and pray for those who persecute you"*, another extension of the command in Leviticus 19:17-18 to

---

59. See Sloan, Paul. 2025. *Jesus and the Law of Moses*. Baker Academic. The book was released after I completed this chapter but argues persuasively that Jesus interprets Israel's Law in light of restoration eschatology. I am consciously avoiding the scholarly debates about Jesus and the Law but find myself in substantial agreement with Sloan's thesis. I would highly recommend this book to any reader interested in exploring this question further.

60. Bock, *Jesus*, p. 136

61. Luke 6:30

"*love your neighbor*"; even the tax collectors and gentiles love those who love them back. Jesus's followers should do better. Note again an implied ecclesiology; by employing the term 'gentile' Jesus is appropriating Israel's set-apart status and applying it to his followers. They must act in accordance with his teaching.

There are several principles embedded in these texts. The Beatitudes demand mercy, gentleness, and peace, and Jesus showing his audience how to embody these attitudes in practice. His followers should suppress anger and work towards reconciling relationships, not seek revenge but sacrifice material possessions for others, and love those who don't love them in return. Political authoritarianism and economic socialism are diametrically opposed to these values. Relying on force and aggression in pursuit of a subjective conception of social good, authoritarian socialism inevitably sows discord and animosity, confiscates what rightfully belongs to others, and creates enemies which must be dominated. Rural Galileans might be tempted to embrace the long-standing tradition of zeal and initiate violent conflict against the rich and powerful who oppress them. Jesus has proclaimed the impending day of judgment, and in the meantime his followers must not travel the path of violent revolution.

Matthew 6:7-15 includes the infamous (and misleadingly titled) "Lord's Prayer", where Jesus teaches His disciples how they ought to pray. Three lines are relevant for this study. In 6:10, Jesus' disciples are to pray "*Your kingdom come. Your will be done, on earth as it is in heaven*". The kingdom of God is at hand. The two verses read "*Give us this day our daily bread. And forgive us our debts as we forgive our debtors*". At the end of the prayer, Jesus warns his audience "*if you forgive others for their transgressions, your heavenly Father will also forgive you. But if you do not forgive others, then your Father will not forgive your transgressions*"[62]. Praying for the kingdom of God, asking God to provide what is necessary for survival, forgiving personal debts and remembering to forgive others are central components of accepting Jesus's teaching on the kingdom of God, further solidifying the main themes of his sermon. Luke 11:2-4, his version of the prayer, is slightly truncated but includes all three of the requests listed above; for Luke these considerations were critical components of the Jesus tradition.

Matthew 6:19-34 is an extended exhortation on wealth and possessions. It largely follows the Jewish tradition of wealth outlined above, where wealth is not a vice in and of itself but must be justly acquired and responsibly managed. Matthew 6:19-24 exhorts the crowd to store up treasures not on earth, but in heaven, where they can't be stolen, "*for where your treasure is, there your heart is also*". It is more valuable to follow Jesus and obey his commands than to acquire

---

62. Matthew 6:14-15

material possessions. His commands include being a light to the nations, showing mercy, and making peace, all as a response to the kingdom which Jesus has inaugurated. Those who place material possessions above building the kingdom are, according to Matthew 6:22-23, "*full of darkness*". The climactic verse is Matthew 6:24: "*No one can serve two masters; for either he will hate the one and love the other, or he will be devoted to one and despise the other. You cannot serve God and wealth*". The Greek word translated "wealth", rarely used in the New Testament, is a cognate of *mammonas*, an Aramaic transliteration which "*is not merely a reference to money; it refers to possessions in any form*"[63]. Also interesting is the root of the Greek word translated "*serve*", *douleuo*, which refers to work performed by a slave. Jesus presents his audience with two options: they can be enslaved to God or enslaved to their possessions. This is, in context, a subtle critique of the wealthy who oppress the rural poor; many of Jesus's followers had few possessions. It is also a warning to readers of Matthew who are materially prosperous. God or wealth?

In Matthew 6:25-34, Jesus utilizes pastoral imagery and encourages his audience to spend little time worrying about the acquisition of wealth. Birds feed without working and flowers grow with toiling, so unlike the gentiles (note again the implied ecclesiology) who eagerly seek these things Jesus's followers are not to worry because their "*heavenly Father knows that you need all these things. But seek first His kingdom and His righteousness, and all these things will be added to you.*"[64] This is not, of course, a command to abandon work, nor is it meant to be a timeless treatise on economics revealing the optimal method of production and exchange. When the crowd returns home, they will continue working. The point Jesus is making here builds on his statement in Matthew 6:24. Instead of serving wealth and continuously worrying about acquiring it, orient your life around the kingdom. God will provide what is needed. While Horsley overstates his case, he isn't wrong: "[Jesus's] *main emphasis is on serving God by seeking the kingdom of God/ heaven and its economic justice, that is, seeking covenantal community and trusting in its cooperative mutual aid as security*"[65]. If the agrarian peasants who were listening to Jesus followed the Sermon's teachings, it would create communities which would alleviate the ravages of poverty. It is entirely plausible that Jesus intended communal renewal to be one effect of his teaching.

Matthew 7 rounds out the Sermon on the Mount, with some of its key components anticipated in Luke 6:37-49. It begins in 7:1-11 with an exhortation to avoid judging others, using discernment, and asking God for provisions. 7:12

---

63. Bock, *Jesus*, p. 143

64. Matthew 6:32-33

65. Horsley, *Bow Down*, p. 34

contains what is popularly known as "The Golden Rule": "*In everything, therefore, treat people the same way you want them to treat you, for this is the Law and the Prophets*". Jesus then tells his audience to "*enter through the narrow gate . . . the way is broad that leads to destruction . . . .the way is narrow that leads to life*"[66], followed in Matthew 7:15-20 with a warning to live in a manner consistent with Jesus' teaching; those who reject Jesus have no place in the kingdom of Heaven and will receive eschatological judgment. In Matthew 7:24-27, those who hear and act upon Jesus' words are compared to a house built on a solid foundation; it is toppled by neither wind nor rain. Those who refuse to listen are likened to a house built on sand which collapses under pressure. Matthew slyly notes, closing his Sermon on the Mount, that "*the crowds were amazed, for He was teaching them as one having authority, and not as their scribes*"[67]. Jesus, not the Jewish elite, had taken charge.

This final chapter of Matthew's Sermon on the Mount is a proper conclusion to the themes Matthew developed in his Sermon, and it raises a few problematic questions for modern Westerners about our political and economic commitments. Starting with Matthew 7:12, Jesus says treating others the way you want to be treated encapsulates the law and the prophets. The politics of authoritarianism is impossible to square with this teaching, even (or perhaps especially) in contemporary democratic societies. While Matthew is not constructing a coherent political theory in this text, both the Christian left and right view voting as a mechanism for imposing their will on the rest of society based upon their own preferential values. Should Christians participate in, much less *celebrate*, a system which enables the domination of others, even if they believe it's in the interest of 'society'?

When Jesus warns his audience not to judge others before first judging themselves, it would seem to forestall Halvor Moxnes's grand plan (which will be deservedly criticized again and again throughout this book, don't you worry) of a one-world government dictating how people in small American towns live. Perhaps academics with little experience in the trades or manual labor have no idea what life is like in those towns and should never be put in the position of asserting political dominance over them, even if elites in European cities believe their monopoly of power will bring about a golden age of human prosperity. Moxnes's blatant authoritarianism captures the essence of political power; those who presume they have the right to rule over others will always find a way to morally justify power, no matter how abhorrently they wield it. Christians must always oppose political authoritarianism. The kingdom of God makes all-encompassing

---

66. Matthew 7:13-14

67. Matthew 7:28-29

claims on those who enter it. Many will fail to take the narrow path, but the few who do will find life. 'Democracy', little more than a cipher for authoritarian socialism, is an unquestioned assumption in the post-Enlightenment west. Perhaps Christians should start asking difficult questions about our political and economic presuppositions. As we turn to Jesus's conflict with the Jewish elite, it will become increasingly evident that no one can match the authority of Jesus.

PREACHING, HEALING, AND CONFLICT WITH AUTHORITY

The gospel of Mark includes no grand sermon. After Jesus calls the first disciples he teaches in Capernaum on the Sabbath.[68] Unlike in Luke 4, where Jesus is met with both wonder and contempt, Mark describes Jesus' positive reception in 1:22, stating they *"were amazed at His teaching; for He was teaching them as one having authority, and not as the scribes"*, the tradition which Matthew used to conclude the Sermon on the Mount. Jesus demonstrates his authority in Mark 1:23-28 by casting out an unclean spirit which recognizes Jesus in 1:24 as *"the Holy One of God"*. After publicly exorcising the unclean spirit, 1:27 records the crowd's response: *"They were all amazed, so that they debated among themselves, saying "what is this? A new teaching with authority! He commands even the unclean spirits and they obey Him.""*. News of Jesus spreads quickly. Mark 1:29-34 is mostly retained by both Matthew and Luke[69]; Jesus heals Simon Peter's mother-in-law and is then presented with diseased and possessed people by *"the whole city"*, whom Jesus heals and casts out many demons. Mark 1:34 adds an editorial comment: Jesus did not permit the demons to speak because *"they knew who He was"*, indicating his authority. Matthew alone quotes Isaiah 53:4, *"He Himself took our infirmities and carried away our diseases"*, at the end of this tradition, only intensifying Mark's claims regarding Jesus' authority. Mark 1:35-38 and Luke 4:42-43 summarize the previous narrative; Jesus *"went into their synagogues throughout all Galilee, preaching and casting out the demons"*[70]. This is a perfect digest of Jesus' prophetic ministry. He proclaims the kingdom of God in both word and deed, becoming a local celebrity.

Mark 2:1-12, Matthew 9:1-8, and Luke 5:17-26 record Jesus healing a paralytic who was dropped through a ceiling and set before Him. Jesus declares that the paralytic's sins are forgiven, and the scribes (Luke adds *"and Pharisees"* in 5:21) balk at this statement, replying that only God alone can forgive sins. Mark 2:10-11, Matthew 9:6, and Luke 5:24 contextualizes his action: Jesus heals the man *"so*

---

68. Mark 1:21-22

69. Matthew 8:14-17, Luke 4:38-41

70. Mark 1:39

that you may know that the Son of Man has authority on earth to forgive sins"[71]. The authority of Jesus, including his proclamation of the kingdom, is revealed through his ability to heal the paralytic. Just as Moses and other Old Testament prophets were empowered to perform great deeds for the purpose of legitimizing their message, Jesus's healings and exorcisms function the same. It is another powerful validation of his authority over and against the Jewish elite. In all three Synoptics this tradition is immediately followed by the call of Levi/Matthew and the dinner he holds for Jesus, his disciples, tax collectors and sinners in which the Pharisees grumble about Jesus consorting with 'sinners'. Jesus again challenged their authority by insisting the Pharisees change their perspective.[72] All of the Synoptic evangelists hold these traditions together, meaning they were likely transmitted together and are thematically unified. Jesus possessed legitimate authority while the Jewish elite did not. It is a classic showdown between God's prophet (who the audience knows is Christ) and the Jewish leadership. These stories echo the clashes between prophetic figures like Elijah, Jeremiah, and Ezekiel and the Jerusalem political establishment.

In both Mark and Luke, this passage is promptly followed by a set of traditions which draw a link between Jesus' teaching and healings and the Jewish authorities.[73] Matthew relocates this tradition to a later point in his narrative[74]. In Mark 2:23-28 and parallels, Jesus and his disciples are walking through a grainfield on Sabbath, picking the heads of grain. The Pharisees observe them and accuse Jesus of breaking the Sabbath. Jesus alludes to 1 Samuel 21:1-6, where David and his companions ate consecrated bread, and then declares in 3:28 that *"the Son of Man is Lord even of the Sabbath"*. Jesus is yet again asserting his authority over that of the Pharisees. He also conflates the messianic categories of David, the 'Son of Man', and 'Lord'. Jesus self-identifies as more than a prophet (though not less). He is the eschatological David, the 'Son of Man' from Daniel 7 who establishes God's kingdom. All three Synoptics follow this tradition with a similar one in which Jesus, still in the presence of Pharisees, heals a man's hand in a synagogue on Sabbath. The Pharisees question him, and Jesus responds by asking in Mark 3:4 *"Is it lawful to do good or to do harm on the Sabbath, to save a life or kill?"*, at which point his opponents are silenced. Jesus proceeds to heal the man's hand in front of the Pharisees. In all three Synoptics this healing initiates a major turning point in the narrative. Mark 3:6 contains a premonition, *"The Pharisees went out and*

---

71. Mark 2:10

72. Mark 2:13-22, Matthew 9:9-17, Luke 5:27-39

73. Mark 2:23-3:12, Luke 6:1-11

74. Matthew 12:1-6

immediately began conspiring with the Herodians against HIm, as to how they might destroy Him". Matthew 12:14 omits Mark's reference to the Herodians but retains the Pharisees's determination to destroy him, while Luke's retelling in Luke 6:11 is more cryptic and ominous, as Jesus' opponents "*discussed together what they might do to Jesus*". Mark's version of the event, revealing the Pharisees and Herodians conspiring together, is all the more curious since the Pharisees, ever-concerned with Jewish national interests, were not natural allies with the Herodians, Rome's clients. Both parties perceived Jesus to be a serious threat to their political power and influence. Bock succinctly summarizes the narratival significance of this story: "*all three Synoptics see a line being crossed for the leadership in this final Sabbath challenge . . . His Sabbath activity is a key turning point in the dispute*"[75]. There was no going back; the Jewish elites had declared war against Jesus.

While Wright observes that the Pharisees, Jesus's main sparring partners throughout the gospels, did not hold any official jurisdiction under Herod, the chief priests, or the Roman authorities, they were extremely influential and motivated by a zealous belief in the coming eschaton for which Jews needed to prepare themselves by following the Law.[76] Individual Pharisees could and often were granted delegated power from the authorities, as in the case of Paul in Acts 9:1-2, but even if they didn't operate in any official political capacity the Pharisees were analogous to political lobbyists or political influencers on social media today. Just because Jesus was arguing with them about the Jewish law doesn't mean these conflicts weren't political; that would amount to reading this story through the facile post-Enlightenment dichotomy between 'religion' and 'politics'. Jesus was ultimately tried and crucified for his efforts, a testimony to the political substance of his ministry.

After the Synoptic evangelists portray the Pharisees decisively turning against Jesus and plotting to destroy him, their debates become even more contentious. Jesus maintains that the Jewish elite are leading the people astray and failing to honor God, dangerously imperiling Israel at the dawn of God's eschaton. The evangelists continue to insist that Jesus, not the Pharisees, scribes, Herodians, or high priests, is the only figure who possesses true authority. In Matthew 12:15-20 the evangelist includes a tradition unique to Matthew in which he narrates that Jesus' ministry, including in context his battle with the Pharisees, is a fulfillment of Isaiah 42:1-4; Jesus is God's spirit-enabled servant who will (intriguingly for the most Jewish gospel) serve as a light to the gentiles, another significant affirmation of Jesus's unique identity and the eschatological moment accompanying

---

75. Bock, *Jesus*, p. 120

76. Wright, *Victory*, pp. 390-396

his ministry. Matthew, Mark, and Luke all include a tradition in which scribes from Jerusalem accuse Jesus of being in partnership with the prince of demons.[77] Matthew 12:23 alone records the crowds asking if Jesus is the Son of David. His response to the Pharisees and scribes underlies the ignorance of their accusation. Jesus is in fact binding the demons, not enabling them. Mark 3:26 portrays Jesus' ministry as the end of Satan's reign, and both Matthew 12:28 and Luke 11:20 connect it to the kingdom of God. If Jesus is casting out demons, God is in charge.

Mark and Matthew follow this tradition by stating the Pharisees are sinning against the Spirit through their rejection of Jesus[78], which Luke moves it to a slightly later point in his gospel[79]. Matthew launches into a tirade against the Pharisees, channeling John the Baptist and calling them a *"brood of vipers"*. Good trees produce good fruit and bad trees produce bad fruit; Jesus implies that he, not his opponents, is producing good fruit and issues a dire warning against the Pharisees regarding the coming day of judgment. Matthew 12:38-42 contains a long condemnation of the Pharisees. Mark and Luke rearrange this material and place it at different points in their narratives[80], so to hear the force of Jesus' words I will examine Matthew's version. The scribes and Pharisees ask Jesus for a sign. The irony in this passage is thick; the reason they want to destroy him is precisely because *they have already seen him perform signs!* He retorts that no sign will be provided to them except the *"sign of Jonah"*, a cryptic prefiguration of his resurrection, and informs the Pharisees that on judgment day they will be found guilty by the Ninevites and the Queen of the South, gentiles who responded positively to Israel's God. The scribes and Pharisees will be left out in the cold. While they view themselves as the vanguard of God's kingdom, zealously following the Law in anticipation of vindication at the eschaton, Jesus thoroughly rebukes them. By refusing to follow Jesus, the Pharisees will not survive the coming calamity. Shockingly, the *gentiles* will have a place in God's kingdom, not the Pharisees.

Matthew appropriates another tradition (found earlier in Mark and Luke[81]) and sets it in the context of Jesus's fight with the Pharisees. Matthew 12:46-50 reveals that Jesus's true family is not defined by blood but *"whoever does the will of My Father who is in heaven, he is My brother and sister and mother"*[82]. The inclusion of gentiles and the exclusion of Pharisees in Jesus's family is scandalous. Jesus is

---

77. Mark 3:22-27, Matthew 12:22-30, Luke 11:14-23

78. Mark 3:28-30, Matthew 12:31-37

79. Luke 12:10

80. Mark 8:11-12, Luke 11:16, 29-32

81. Mark 3:31-35, Luke 8:19-21

82. Matthew 12:50

preaching the kingdom of God, healing and casting out demons, calling the gentiles, and acting like King David. Instead of correctly interpreting the signs, the Pharisees and scribes reject Jesus. One final example is in order before reflecting upon the significance of these traditions. In Mark 7:1-23 and Matthew 15:1-20, Jesus has yet another showdown with the Pharisees and scribes (both evangelists note that Jesus's opponents came *"from Jerusalem"*). The Pharisees ask Jesus why his disciples eat with unwashed hands, a practice which Mark explains to his audience[83], and Jesus responds by calling them hypocrites for withholding financial support from their parents in violation of the Decalogue. Mark 7:6-7 and Matthew 15:8-9 quote Isaiah 29:13, which is an attack on the faithless Jerusalemites in Isaiah's day. Jesus then addresses the crowds and condemns the Pharisees. Matthew 15:13 suggests his opponents, having not been planted by God, will be uprooted. In Mark 7:24-30 and Matthew 15:21-28, a gentile woman asks Jesus to heal her daughter. In Matthew 15:24 Jesus appears to deny her request, replying that he was sent only for the lost sheep of Israel (expanding upon a similar denial in Mark), but the woman responds with humility, pointing out that even dogs eat crumbs which fall from the table. Jesus comments on her great faith and grants her daughter healing. The narratival context of this passage in Matthew and Mark makes it impossible to miss the tradition's function. Unlike the Pharisees, the gentile woman responds positively to Jesus. Like the Ninevites and the Queen of the South, she has encountered Israel's God and responded in faith. The Pharisees and scribes have not and will be judged accordingly.

Jesus' conflict with the Jewish elites over his words and deeds exemplifies the themes of prophecy, eschatology, kingdom, and messianic christology. For our purposes, the conflict narratives reveal the identity of Jesus, whom the evangelist's declare Christ, son of David, God's eschatological messiah. The passages reviewed above all emphasise these characteristics of Jesus which, commensurate with the goals of ancient biography, recount the essence of Jesus. He is God's ultimate authority both as prophet and king. The Jewish elite must either submit to his program or suffer judgment. One consistent principle materializes in the conflict narratives: Jesus is the final authority for all who follow him. Christians are expected to obey his kingdom manifesto, reordering their lives around his teaching. Fidelity to Jesus calls into question Christian devotion to modern political systems. Often characterized by uncritical, toxic admiration or hatred, we place our hope in political leaders ("democractically" elected, of course!) who promise to make the world better, leveraging bureaucracy to impose their will on society. At this point in our analysis of the gospels, Christians should already be skeptical

---

83. Mark 7:3-4

about *any* human claims to power, especially the ability of secular political leaders to implement positive change through force. The technocracy, funded by extorting productive labor, doesn't compete with the authority of Jesus. The evangelists unapologetically present Jesus as the *only* authority worth following. Will we, like the Pharisees, refuse to accept Jesus's radical kingdom agenda? Or will we imitate the gentile woman who approached him with faith and humility? Most Christians would prefer to sit on the fence. Jesus is our king but the political process determines world history. The evangelists force us to pick a side.

PARABLES OF THE KINGDOM: SOWERS, WHEAT, AND THE WORLD

Jesus, prophet mighty in word and deed, was known for issuing parables which explained the kingdom of God, dramatically reframing popular expectations of Jewish eschatological hopes. We discussed the function of parables above; they are challenging anecdotes designed to encourage reflection and moral transformation. Parables vividly portray the kingdom of God as it is coming to fruition in Jesus. There can be no adequate interpretation of Jesus's kingdom proclamation without recourse to his parables. For our study of political and economic themes in the New Testament, several parables are worthy of special consideration.

The Parable of the Sower serves as a paradigm for and prelude to Jesus's other parables. It explains the kingdom of God and, most importantly, why many are rejecting it. In all three gospels this parable follows traditions of conflict between Jesus and the Jewish elite. Mark 4:1-9 and Matthew 13:1-9 are similar, while Luke 8:4-8 omits material which is reincorporated at other places in his gospel. This parable initiates the third of Matthew's discourses and is clustered with material unique to his gospel. All three evangelists agree that Jesus presents this parable to a large crowd; Mark and Matthew portray Jesus issuing this parable near the Sea of Galilee. Christians are familiar with the Parable of the Sower. A farmer sows seed, some of which falls on a path, some of which falls upon rocks, and others among thorns. None of that seed will grow. Some seed, however, falls on good soil and produces a massive crop, much larger than average harvests in the first century[84]. Mark, Matthew, and Luke all conclude the parable with a famous saying of Jesus: "*He who has ears to hear, let him hear*"[85]. The disciples ask Jesus to explain why Jesus spoke in parables.[86] Matthew 13:10-17 contains the most complete response;

---

84. Bock, *Jesus*, p. 200

85. Mark 4:9, Matthew 13:9, Luke 8:8

86. Mark 4:10, Matthew 10:10, Luke 8:9

Mark and Luke rearrange much of this material. In 13:11, Matthew connects Jesus's parables to the kingdom: *"Jesus answered them, "To you it has been granted to know the mysteries of the kingdom of heaven, but to them it has not been granted""*. Some will comprehend the words of Jesus, many will not. Jesus quotes Isaiah 6:10, a passage where Isaiah is informed that his prophetic message to Israel will be met with resistance. Jesus' disciples, however, have not resisted Jesus, as Matthew 13:16 explains, *"blessed are your eyes, because they see; and your ears, because they hear"*. I agree with Stein that this statement should not be understood in a cause-and-effect manner which implies God intentionally obfuscated Jesus's kingdom message but rather works from effect-to-cause; the people (scribes and Pharisees in particular, especially given the narratival context of this passage in both Mark and Matthew) have rejected Jesus and therefore fail to understand his parables.[87] Just as many in Israel refused to heed Isaiah's warnings and as a result suffered catastrophe, so many in Israel were rejecting Jesus.[88]

In all three Synoptics Jesus interprets the Parable of the Sower.[89] The bad soil represents those who have ignored Jesus. Some ignore him because of Satan, some because of tribulation and persecution, and some, reminiscent of Matthew 6, because of the cares of the world and a delight in riches. The good soil, on the other hand, represents those who, from Matthew 13:23, *"hear . . . the word and understand . . . it; who indeed bears fruit"*. Those who not only hear Jesus but respond positively by changing their lives and bearing fruit, demonstrating repentance, are likened to seeds which fall on good soil. There is another subtle reference to Jesus' reframed ecclesiology; the in-group is composed of good soil, and the out-group is composed of bad. The opponents of Jesus are certainly 'bad soil' and despite their high status in society will not inherit the kingdom of God. Mark 4:21-25 and Luke 8:16-18 round out the explanation with a tradition found in Matthew 5:15 about not placing a light under a basket, and then explains how one day everything will be revealed for all to see. Mark 4:26-29 is a parable unique to his gospel. The kingdom is compared to a man who scatters seed which eventually grows. The man doesn't know how it grows, but eventually the plant becomes ripe and ready for harvest. Moloney, commenting on this passage, says the *"kingdom of God is like the mystery of growth, beyond human control . . . the growth is the result of the action of God. There will be a harvest at the end of time"*[90]. God is sovereign over His kingdom, and it will grow until the time of harvest.

---

87. Stein, *Method*, p. 39

88. Kingsbury, *Matthew as Story*, p. 106

89. Mark 4:13-20, Matthew 13:18-23, Luke 8:11-15

90. Moloney, *Mark*, p. 95

Matthew includes several parables which are not found in Mark or Luke. The Parable of the Wheat and the Weeds (sometimes called 'The Parable of the Tares') in Matthew 13:24-30 follows Jesus' explanation of the Parable of the Sower. I must confess that when I began reading the Bible at the age of fourteen, this passage had a profound impact on the way in which I understood my relationship towards other people and played a critical role in sending me down the path to finding a political theory based on peace and non-aggression. A man sows good seed in his wheat field, but an enemy comes when he is asleep and sows weeds. As the wheat sprouts, so do the weeds. His servants notify him and ask if they should remove the weeds. The farmer wisely responds *"No; for while you are gathering up the tares [weeds], you may uproot the wheat with them"*. Instead, they are instructed to allow *"both to grow together until the harvest; and in the time of the harvest I will say to the reapers, "First gather up the tares and bind them in bundles to burn them up; but gather the wheat into my barn""*[91]. Matthew will offer an explanation of this parable in a few passages, but the traditions which he includes between the telling of the parable and Jesus' explanation of it further reinforce its meaning.

Matthew 13:31-32 is paralleled in Mark 4:30-32 and Luke 13:18-19. In this parable the kingdom is compared to a tiny mustard seed which will, when fully grown, become a large tree. Matthew 13:33 and Luke 13:20-21 both follow this with another parable not found in Mark which compares the kingdom of God to leaven which is hidden in flour but causes it to rise. Matthew 13:34-35 and Mark 4:33-34 explain how Jesus teaches the crowds in parables with Mark stating that Jesus habitually explains them to his disciples. For the narrative logic of Matthew, comparing the kingdom to a mustard seed or leaven is a natural continuation of Jesus' Parable of the Wheat and the Weeds. The kingdom must grow; it starts out small but will one day rise to greatness. It is in this context which Jesus explains the parable.

Matthew 13:36-43 is set in a house, away from the crowds. The disciples ask him to interpret the Parable of the Wheat and the Weeds. It's worth quoting in full: *"The one who sows the good seed is the Son of Man, and the field is the world; and as for the good seed, these are the sons of the kingdom; and the tares are the sons of the evil one; and the enemy who sowed them is the devil, and the harvest is the end of the age; and the reapers are angels. So just as the tares are gathered up and burned with fire, so shall it be at the end of the age. The Son of Man will send forth His angels, and they will gather out of His kingdom all stumbling blocks, and those who commit lawlessness, and and will throw them into the furnace of fire; in that place there will be weeping and gnashing of teeth. Then the righteous will shine forth as the sun in*

---

91. Matthew 13:29-30

the kingdom of their Father. He who has ears, let him hear". Jesus is inaugurating the kingdom of God. As in the Parable of the Sower, the good seed represents those who respond positively to Jesus, while the bad seed represents those who reject him. At the end of the age those who reject him will be removed from the kingdom and thrown into the fire. Jesus quotes Daniel 12:3 to explain the reward which awaits those who follow him; Daniel is one of the classic resurrection texts in the Old Testament. Followers of Jesus will be resurrected and participate in the consummation of the eschatological kingdom which has been planted by Jesus and is currently in the process of growing. Note again the us/them dichotomy; Israel is being redefined around Jesus and the reception of his message. Also important are the themes of kingdom, christology, and eschatology, all of which are tightly intertwined in this prophetic parable.

Before I explain the significance of these parables, and particularly the Parable of the Wheat and the Weeds, Matthew concludes his third discourse with three other parables which are distinctive to his gospel. Matthew 13:44-46 compares the kingdom to a man who finds hidden treasure in a field; upon doing so he sells everything and buys the field. A merchant likewise finds an extremely valuable pearl and sells everything he has to acquire it. In Matthew 13:47-50 Jesus likens the kingdom to a dragnet thrown into the sea. At the end of the fishing expedition the fishermen sit down and separate the good fish from the bad. Jesus reveals this will happen at the close of the age. Finally, in Matthew 13:51-52 Jesus asks his disciples if they have understood his teaching. They respond in the affirmative, and Jesus says that those who understand the kingdom are like householders who have both old and new treasures. The kingdom has come, but it wasn't like many expected.

The political, economic, and social consequences of these kingdom parables are enormous. The Parable of the Sower conclusively demonstrates what Jesus' conflict with the scribes and Pharisees hinted at; not everyone is going to accept his kingdom proclamation. There will be many reasons why people reject it, the pursuit of wealth being one significant hindrance, and those who accept it must bear fruit, presumably by following Jesus' teaching. It is notable that Jesus nowhere indicates any plans to force the seeds to grow on bad soil. Quite the opposite, actually. His audience is free to walk away. This is consistent with what Simeon says in Luke's infancy narrative about Jesus being appointed for the rise and fall of many in Israel, and John the Baptist's statement that claiming descendancy from Abraham is meaningless unless coupled with repentance and belief. Those who inherit the eschatological kingdom must follow Jesus, Israel's Messiah. The Davidic line has been reestablished and the end has been inaugurated. This kingdom will grow as people continue to turn towards Jesus and bear fruit until the final, great consummation.

The Parable of the Wheat and the Weeds as well as The Parable of the Net both illustrate an important feature of the kingdom. The righteous and the wicked will only be separated by the Son at the end of the age. Any attempt to draw a hard line between those who follow Jesus and those who don't will result in damaging the wheat, Jesus's followers. This is an instruction which has been left unheeded for most of Christian history. Modern Westerners falsely believe they have liberated themselves from the vestiges of medieval Christendom, but it is still very much alive, concealed under the rhetoric of democracy. Progressives and conservatives alike operate under the modern political presupposition that the role of government is at least in part the enforcement of values which go beyond the Lockean conception of protecting natural rights. Christians both left and right, while disagreeing on specific policy platforms, are nevertheless in complete lock-step about the use of force to impose Christian values, always appealing to the rhetoric of 'justice', 'order', or 'the common good'. Left-wing Christians want to impose taxes, regulate private exchange, suppress speech, and restrict association in the name of a nebulously defined 'social justice'; right-wing Christians also want to tax, regulate, suppress, and restrict, only for different reasons than their left-wing counterparts, justified as 'protecting children' or 'promoting order'. Most American Christians on the left and right happily ignore the never-ending wars, and inflationary monetary regime, the pharmaceutical-industrial complex, and other degrading policies so long as their preferred politicians are in charge. Like Halvor Moxnes, modern Christians believe people living in other towns should be forced to play by a set of rules subjectively imposed from the outside because, for some vague reason, of Jesus.

Jesus's kingdom parables challenge this conception of political power. The great separation between the righteous and the wicked won't occur until the end of the age. Jesus minces no words. Any attempt to uproot the weeds before harvest will damage good wheat. Those who follow Jesus must accept that seed will fall on bad soil, resulting in many turning away from the call. God's kingdom will grow slowly through Jesus's followers faithfully living out his teachings and bearing fruit. We must reject the conventional use of political force, no matter how 'normal' it is for contemporary society, and embrace the kingdom agenda of Jesus. There is a distinction between insiders and outsiders, and on the final day outsiders will be held accountable. These texts present readers with an uncomfortable principle. We must get used to living among those who reject Jesus and faithfully serve him anyway. God will work it all out in the end. Jesus is not the kind of messiah any-one was expecting. Instead of doling out punishment he is crucified on a Roman cross. Christians who endorse authoritarian socialism are taking Rome's side, not Christ's . The kingdom of God is like a treasure in a field or an expensive pearl. It is worth selling everything to own it. This includes, I believe, the way we understand human power. When Peter finally realizes Jesus is the Christ, Jesus teaches him a lesson about power in the kingdom of God.

Peter's Confession and the Transfiguration

The Suffering Christ?

The Synoptic evangelists unambiguously regard Jesus as the Davidic Messiah, God's Christ and king of Israel. As the infancy narratives, the preaching of John, Jesus' temptation, and his prophetic ministry of words and deeds all hint, however, that his messianic identity may not conform to popular expectations. While he is indeed the Messiah, Jesus radically redefines the role. The decisive revelation of Jesus's unique messianic identity occurs with the confession of Peter[92], a major narrative turning point in all three Synoptics.. Jesus is presented with an opportunity to finally explain to his disciples what the messianic vocation entails. They are, needless to say, bewildered by his explanation. In order to grasp the significance of Jesus's messianic identity and the relevance it has for the church today we must assess his dramatic redefinition of messianic christology.

In Matthew and Luke, the question of Jesus's messianic identity and the ambiguity surrounding it is raised before Peter's confession. In Matthew 11:2-6 and Luke 7:18-23, John the Baptist sends two of his disciples to ask Jesus *"Are you the Expected One, or shall we look for someone else?"*[93]. John's question is sincere. Jesus didn't conform to any existing messianic expectations, so it's no wonder that John was uncertain. Stein's analysis of John's concern is correct: *"John experienced real doubt and questioning about whether Jesus . . . was the Christ because Jesus was so unlike what he had expected . . . John, as well as the Twelve, had difficulty adjusting their preconceptions of what the Messiah was to be like with what they saw in Jesus' ministry"*[94]. Jesus' response to John's query utilizes a pastiche of imagery from Isaiah; the blind see, the lame walk, the deaf hear, lepers are cleansed, the dead are raised, and the poor have the gospel preached to them. In other words, Jesus is answering John in the affirmative. Jesus concludes his response to John's disciples by stating in Matthew 11:6 and Luke 7:23 that *"blessed is he who does not take offense at me"*. Jesus' redefinition of messianic hopes will be shocking, indeed scandalous, for many who hear it. Those who accept Jesus as Messiah, however, are 'blessed'. Both

---

92. Mark 8:27-38, Matthew 16:13-27, Luke 9:18-27

93. Matthew 11:3

94. Stein, *Luke*, p. 225

Matthew and Luke follow this tradition with an extended saying of Jesus praising John the Baptist; he came in the spirit of Elijah (both evangelists quote Malachi 3:1) and is therefore the legitimate prophetic forerunner to Israel's Messiah.[95] Jesus uses this as a condemnation of those who heard both John and Himself and yet still refused to accept that the eschatological moment had come.[96] While Jesus will not offer a full-fledged explanation of his messianic identity, he leaves John's disciples with little doubt that he is claiming to be the Messiah.

In Mark 8:11-21 the disciples are having a difficult time understanding Jesus' teaching about the Pharisees, and Jesus asks at the end of this passage *"Do you not yet understand?"*. In the following passage, located before Peter's confession, the evangelist includes a tradition which was not used by either Matthew or Luke. This unique tradition is found in Mark 8:22-26. A blind man is presented before Jesus, who attempts to heal him. The blind man regains partial sight, and Jesus works with him a second time before his sight is fully restored. While interpretations of this passage have often explored the subjective psychological motives of the blind man, concluding that he lacked full faith, there is a much easier narrative explanation at hand. Bock wonders if the *"image may be significant, coming as it does before Peter's confession . . . Does this mirror the two-step development of the understanding of the disciples in Mark?"*[97]. It certainly does. Situated between a passage in which the disciples misunderstand Jesus and Peter's confession, also accompanied by misunderstanding, the blind man prefigures and exemplifies the disciple's incomplete perception of Jesus. Matthew 16:1-12, located right before the confession, is a reworking of Mark 8:11–21, also highlighting the disciple's confusion. Luke has no such tradition of confusion before the confession, consistent with his redaction of Mark and Matthew. Mark and Matthew, though, both highlight the disciple's perceptive deficiencies.

According to Mark 8:27, Jesus was traveling with his disciples to Caesarea Philippi; Matthew 16:13 implies they had already arrived while Luke 9:18 situates the tradition in a context of prayer. The story becomes more consistent after this detail.[98] Jesus asks his disciples what people were claiming about his identity (Matthew asks specifically about *"the Son of Man"*[99]) and the disciples respond by stating that many believed Jesus was John, Elijah, or another prophet, with Matthew adding Jeremiah. Completely consistent with our analysis of Jesus as a

---

95. Matthew 11:7-15, Luke 7:24-30

96. Matthew 11:16-24, Luke 7:31-35

97. Bock, *Jesus*, pp. 226-227

98. Mark 8:27-30, Matthew 16:13-20, Luke 9:18-22

99. Matthew 16:13

Jewish prophet, the people who heard his words and saw his deeds correctly interpreted them within the prophetic tradition. Jesus then asks his disciples who *they* thought he was and Peter responds "*You are the Christ*" in Mark 8:29, "*You are the Christ, the Son of the living God*" in Matthew 16:16, and "*The Christ of God*" in Luke 9:20. In Mark and Luke Jesus immediately commands the disciples to tell no one. Matthew too will silence the disciples in 16:17-19 Jesus commends Peter for his confession and promises that "*on this rock I will build my church*".

Jesus qualifies Peter's confession. While Peter is absolutely correct in identifying Jesus as the Messiah, Peter doesn't yet understand the meaning of Jesus's messianic identity. All three evangelists present Jesus clarifying the consequences of his identity as Messiah: suffering, rejection, dying, and resurrection.[100] Mark 8:31 reads "*he began to teach them that the Son of Man must suffer many things and be rejected by the elders and the chief priests and the scribes, and be killed, and after three days rise again*". This is not what the disciples expected to hear. In Mark 8:32-33 and Matthew 16:22-23 Peter rebukes Jesus; there is no way the Messiah can suffer and die! Jesus tells the disciples plainly that by denying his messianic mission they are opposing God and taking the side of men. Just as Luke includes no traditions about the disciple's confusion before Peter's confession, he also omits the rebuke from his gospel. The force of Peter's confession remains. Jesus is the Messiah, but as the Messiah, the Lord's Christ, Jesus must suffer and die. Jesus is radically reinterpreting the messianic vocation.

All three Synoptics include a saying of Jesus which clarifies what it means to follow him in light of Peter's confession and the way Jesus reframed it.[101] I will quote the Marcan version in full: "*And He summoned the crowd with His disciples, and said to them, "If anyone wishes to come after Me, he must deny himself, and take up his cross and follow Me. For whoever wishes to save his life will lose it, but whoever loses his life for My sake and the gospel's will save it. For what does it profit a man to gain the whole world, and forfeit his soul. For what will a man give in exchange for his soul? For whoever is ashamed of Me and My words in this adulterous and sinful generation, the Son of Man will also be ashamed of him when He comes in the glory of His Father with the holy angels"*". Not only is Israel's Messiah to suffer and die, those who accept Jesus must be willing to follow in his footsteps. The themes of kingdom, messiah, and eschatology are present: the Messiah is here, the kingdom is dawning, and God's purposes for Israel and the world are being fulfilled.[102] None of it will happen as the disciples expected.

---

100. Mark 8:31, Matthew 16:21, Luke 9:22

101. Mark 8:34-38, Matthew 16:24-27, Luke 9:23-27

102. Wright, *Victory*, pp. 650-651

Peter's confession and Jesus's subsequent teaching is the most dramatic and revolutionary statement of what it means for Jesus to be the Messiah and the responsibilities which accompany discipleship. At this point in the narratives the twin goals of ancient biographies, representing the essence of the subject and encouraging the audience to emulate them, come together. Jesus is the king of the world, God's final eschatological agent. The evangelists are in complete agreement. The Jesus tradition twists conventional conceptions of the messianic vocation. Jesus himself teaches that God's Christ, the son of David, will suffer and die prior to vindication. Western Christians, accustomed to privileging atonement theology above other historical considerations, have tended to ignore the explicit critique of human power embedded in the Jesus tradition. Unlike Herod, the scribes and Pharisees, the high priests, the Sanhedrin, or the Roman authorities, Jesus is the true, absolute king of the world. He exercises his power, however, not by waging a violent insurrection or through political force but by enduring a brutal torture and execution at the hands Jewish and Roman aurthorites. This is what it means to be the Messiah and therefore what it means to possess real power. Greatness comes not through dominating others but by sacrificially serving them.

Not only has Jesus reframed the very nature of kingship, he has also redefined what it means to follow Him. Those who 'repent and believe' in Jesus's proclamation of the kingdom are called to emulate his sacrificial disposition. Cornelis Bennema explains how Jesus's summons to the crowd in Mark 8:34-38 and parallels are a call to imitate him: *"Jesus specifies two requisites for, or characteristics of, following him—self-denial and cross-bearing. Jesus himself practices these principles . . . By implication, Jesus suggests that his would-be followers will imitate him . . . the disciple's experience is equated with the death of Jesus, and hence following Jesus involves imitating him"*[103]. Everyone who follows Jesus must deny themselves and carry a cross. The evangelists, by incorporating this tradition, intend to challenge their audience. Obedience to Jesus includes imitating his willingness to suffer.

How can Christians read passages such as Peter's confession and still maintain we have a prerogative to endorse political and economic systems which are predicated on violence? Modern conservatism and progressivism, both of which seek to reform society by leveraging the technocratic power of state violence, are antithetical to the redefined nature of human power which Jesus the suffering Messiah embodies. Not only do the evangelists hail Jesus as the ultimate authority, they present him as the archetype of Christian behavior. Following him *necessarily* entails abandoning human conceptions of dominating power by cultivating an attitude of service towards others. Instead of lobbying to regulate economic exchange,

---

103. Bennema, *Imitation*, p. 112

enforce speech codes, or police non-violent personal decisions, Christians must first seek to follow their king by serving others. For Paul and other New Testament authors, it is the sacrificial death of Jesus which characterises Christian ethics. We ignore the call to emulate Jesus at our own peril. Wide is the path which leads to destruction. Many who profess faith in Christ travel it anyway.

The Transfiguration: A Validation of the Suffering Christ

Immediately following Peter's confession, all three evangelists recount the Transfiguration.[104] Despite minor variations in details, Matthew and Luke retain much of Mark. Jesus, accompanied by Peter, James, and John, travel up a high mountain. Jesus is transfigured before them, radiantly shining, and Elijah and Moses both appear to converse with Jesus. Peter, extremely confused about what to do, suggests erecting a tabernacle for Jesus, Elijah, and Moses. After Peter's proposition a voice says *"This is My beloved Son, listen to Him!"*[105]. When the voice had finished speaking, Elijah and Moses were gone and Jesus was no longer radiant. Jesus then commands the disciples to tell no one about the event until after he was raised from the dead. Mark 9:10 alone recounts the disciples wondering what Jesus meant by appealing to the resurrection. As Wright observes, *"'the rising of the dead'. . . normally referred to the rising of all the righteous at the end of time, not of one righteous person in the middle of time"*[106]. This is the plausible historical context for Mark 9:10. Matthew omits it from his version of the transfiguration but follows Mark by shifting the conversation to the coming of Elijah, an event which was supposed to precede the eschatological kingdom. Mark strongly implies that John the Baptist was the eschatological messiah while Matthew 10:13 makes it explicit: *"Then the disciples understood that he was speaking to them of John the Baptist"*. In both Matthew and Mark Jesus discusses the suffering which will befall him. Luke omits this exchange altogether.

The Transfiguration naturally flows from Peter's confession, the reason why all three evangelists incorporate these traditions together. Bock suggests that Moses and Elijah represent both the Law and the eschaton, with their presence confirming that Jesus is the coming Davidic king promised in the Old Testament.[107] The voice from heaven repeats what was said about Jesus at his baptism. He is God's Son, a term which in Second Temple Judaism denotes messianism and

---

104. Mark 9:1-13, Matthew 17:1-13, Luke 9:28-36

105. Mark 9:7

106. Wright, N.T. 2003. *The Resurrection of the Son of God.* Fortress Press. pp. 414-415

107. Bock, *Jesus*, p. 234

from which Christians construct divine christologies. The transfiguration validates Jesus's claims regarding his own messianic identity. He is the Christ, just as Peter claimed, but must suffer and die on behalf of his people. *Listen to Jesus*, the voice says, *because he is telling you the truth.*

Following the Transfiguration, all three Synoptics have Jesus return from the mountain to find a man with his possessed son.[108] Despite minor differences between the three accounts, the disciples are unable to heal the boy, at which point Jesus asks why that generation was so faithless. Mark 9:24 alone records how the father responds to Jesus: "*I do believe; help my unbelief*". Like the blind beggar before Peter's confession, the father in Mark is implicitly compared to the disciples. He wants to believe, but \isn't there quite yet. Jesus heals the boy. After this healing Jesus takes another opportunity to discuss his messianic fate.[109] The Son of Man will be delivered into the hands of men, killed, and then rise. Mark and Luke comment that the disciples do not understand Jesus's statement, Luke because they were afraid to ask about it, and Matthew because they were "*deeply grieved*". This set of traditions, all of which were transmitted together, only further defines Jesus's messianic status. He is the king, validated by God at the transfiguration, who will rule the nations. The only way for this to happen, however, is through suffering and death. His disciples must emulate Him, following in his footsteps. It is clear, however, that the disciples don't understand what Jesus is saying. Despite their experiences, it was simply too much for them to process. The disciples were trying to pour new wine into old wineskins. Jesus's pedagogical work is far from over; he must instruct the disciples about the precise nature of his mission and the appropriate response to Israel's king.

Greatness in the Kingdom of God

At the end of the Transfiguration and related traditions, Mark, Matthew, and Luke relay another tradition which shows, yet again, that the disciples haven't properly grasped Jesus's messianic identity or the nature of his coming kingdom.[110] Matthew includes a unique story about taxation between the Transfiguration and this tradition which is contextualized by the two; it will be more comprehensible after exploring this passage and will be discussed in its own section below. The evangelists recount the disciples arguing about which of them is the greatest, with Matthew alone revealing the debate was specifically regurding greatness in the

---

108. Mark 9:14-29, Matthew 17:14-21, Luke 9:37-43

109. Mark 9:30-32, Matthew 17:22-23, Luke 9:43-45

110. Mark 9:33-37, Matthew 18:1-5, Luke 9:46-48

kingdom[111]. While the evangelists reorder the sequence of events and sayings, both Matthew and Luke retain the bulk of Mark, where Jesus responds " *"If anyone wants to be first, he shall be last of all and servant of all." Taking a child, He set him before them, and taking him in His arms, He said to them "whoever receives one child like this in my name receives Me; and whoever receives Me does not receive Me, but Him who sent Me."*"[112]. Matthew 18:3 adds another comment from Jesus, *"unless you are converted and become like children, you will not inherit the kingdom of heaven"*.

Moloney correctly identifies the historical reason why Jesus' disciples would debate who was greatest among them: *"they suspect that the Messiah they are following to Jerusalem will establish himself with power. They are concerned about their own respective places in the power structure of the messianic kingdom which Jesus will establish after his victory"*[113]. Given the revolutionary aspirations of many first century Jews, Jesus's disciples presumed his kingdom would look like all the others, only this time with God in charge. The disciples still don't get it. Jesus reveals that greatness comes through serving; in the kingdom it is those who are 'the least' which will be great, a sentiment on full display in both the infancy narratives and the Beatitudes. That Jesus uses a child as an example is telling; children had little social status in Jewish culture.[114] All three evangelists have Jesus say that the disciples must receive children like this in his name; failing to do so is tantamount to rejecting Jesus and the God who sent him. The point is clearly made: the disciples should take care of those whom society deems as inferior. Jesus intends for his followers to serve all, not seek to be served. Matthew adds that his followers *"must become like children"*[115], meaning they should stop worrying about status. In the kingdom, greatness means servanthood. Jesus sets the example. Mark 9:38-50 and Matthew 18:7-35 expand on this teaching, recording sayings of Jesus which speak of servanthood, self-control, forgiveness, and mercy. These are the practices which characterize greatness in God's kingdom.

Jesus will return again to the subject of greatness. In Mark 10:32-34 and Matthew 20:17-19, Jesus, nearing Jerusalem, issues further instructions about the fate which awaits him in the city of David. Referring to himself as *"the Son of Man"*, Jesus reiterates that he will be handed over, tried, killed, and then raised. The disciples are still under the impression that Jesus is inaugurating a kingdom which conforms to their expectations. The disciples are hoping for a Maccabee,

---

111. Matthew 18:1

112. Mark 9:35-37

113. Moloney, *Mark*, p. 188

114. Bock, *Jesus*, p. 140

115. Matthew 18:3

not a martyr. This tradition introduces another question about greatness in the kingdom of God. Mark 10:35-45 and Matthew 20:20-28 are reminiscent of the exchange which took place between the disciples after Jesus was transfigured. In Mark, James and John request to sit at the right and left hand of Jesus when he comes in glory. In Matthew, it is their mother who makes the request; Matthew also uses the term *"kingdom"* instead of glory, adding precision to the petition. Jesus responds by telling the disciples they are ignorant and wonders if they are able to share in his *"cup"* and *"baptism"*. Both 'cup' and 'baptism' are well-attested metaphors of suffering in the Old Testament, making it obvious that Jesus is referring to his imminent demise.[116] Jesus tells them that they will drink from his cup, but that he does not determine who sits at his left and right.

Predictably, the other disciples become indignant with James and John. Jesus' response is consequential, and I will quote Mark 10:42-45 in full: *"Calling them to Himself, Jesus said to them, "You know that those who are recognized as rulers of the Gentiles lord it over them; and their great men exercise authority over them. But it is not this way among you, but whoever wishes to become great among you shall be your servant; and whoever wishes to be first among you shall be slave of all. For even the Son of Man did not come to be served, but to serve, and to give HIs life a ransom for many.""*. The importance of this saying for followers of Jesus cannot be overstated. The disciples were expecting a kingdom in which they would hold great power over others. Jesus challenges this expectation to the core. He begins this saying with an explanation of gentile power; the nations lord it over others and exercise authority. This is the way of the world. The phrase *"are recognized"* includes a cognate of the word *dokeo*, which means 'to suppose' or 'think'. Moloney correctly notes *"The phrase "supposed to be" is subtle irony. In the design of God, their all-powerful and self-sufficient rule is only apparent"*[117]. Jesus is claiming that the gentiles only appear to have power. It is not to be this way with disciples of Jesus. Greatness comes from being a *diakonos* and *doulos*, a servant and slave. In the kingdom of God, *"established patterns of lordship and authority are to be subverted"*[118], and the *"only power that leaders who follow Christ should seek is that which gives of itself to the people they are called to serve"*[119]. Jesus, the Daniellic Son of Man, will be the ultimate example of power in the kingdom of God. He came to serve, not be served, and to give his life for others. Luke moves this saying to his Last Supper discourse

---

116. Bock, *Jesus*, p. 308

117. Moloney, *Mark*, p. 206

118. Moloney, *Mark*, p. 207

119. Bock, *Jesus*, p. 309

in Luke 22:24-27, making the same point. Greatness comes through serving, not through conquering.

Those who follow Jesus are obligated to live like him. Jesus doesn't make an exception for those who wield political power; in fact, he specifically forbids his followers from exercising authority like the nations. Those who want to be great must become slaves, an image not lost on his first century audience. It is also a lesson Christians today are in desperate need of learning. Medieval Christendom was doomed to failure from the start; Christians were never intended to wield violent power, and the long road from antiquity through modernity was paved by abuses of Christian political power in Europe. The post-Enlightenment division between 'religion' on the one hand and 'politics' and 'society' on the other, however, presents yet another problem which the church has failed to solve. By privatizing and spiritualising discipleship, modern Christians are tempted to dichotomize personal faithfulness from political engagement. The nineteenth-century paradigm of technocratic nation-states progressively building a 'better' world through implementing social and economic control over society imposed from the top has been essentially unchallenged by western Christians, many of whom accept this political and economic order as 'the way things have to be'.

This has led to a culture in which Christians on the left and right view it as a responsibility to weaponize state power on behalf of their preferred policy programs. Christians support nationalism, war, corporatization, redistributive welfare, inflationary monetary policy, or any other political and economic control they believe will improve society. As we discussed extensively in Chapter 2 and Chapter 3, all of these policies are based on the use of force or the threat of violence against those who dissent. While Christians justify these policies with rhetorical appeals to 'justice' or 'order', none of them can be implemented without granting men with guns the power to take what doesn't belong to them by threatening punishment for those who refuse to comply. This isn't exactly a new phenomenon; while philosophical justifications for the state have changed in the modern era, the brute implementation of power has not. The rulers of the gentiles, now as always, exercise authority over others under threat of violence. Jesus teaches that all who follow him must fundamentally reject gentile-ish conceptions of power. The kingdom of God is built through sacrificial, humble service, not through dominating others by force. Just as Jesus suffered, so must we. There is no way around Jesus's straightforward commandments. Christians must absolutely reject any system of arbitrary political power. We are not called to be revolutionaries, and, as in Jeremiah 29:7, should seek the welfare of those around us by attempting to live in peace with our neighbors, knowing that no matter what problems we face in the present God will resolve them all in the end. This is the challenge of Jesus: the kingdom has already been inaugurated and his followers must act like it. We leave the path of power untravelled and follow the road walked by Jesus.

This is exemplified in the tradition which follows Jesus' remarkable teaching on greatness. In Mark 10:46-52 and Matthew 20:29-34 (which Luke includes in a slightly different context; see Luke 18:35-43), Jesus is nearly in Jerusalem when he passes two blind men on the road. They hail Jesus as "Son of David" and "Lord", requesting that he restore their sight. Jesus is moved by compassion and heals them. Mark and Matthew, by locating this tradition immediately after Jesus' teaching on greatness and his Triumphal Entry to Jerusalem, are comparing the faith of two blind beggars with the disciples. The blind men approach Jesus with humility, acknowledging his Messianic status. The disciples have work to do. Before concluding this chapter with an examination of material which is unique to Luke and John, there are two more traditions worth examining. The first is the story of Jesus and the fish in Matthew 17. The second is Jesus' interaction with the so-called 'Rich Young Ruler'. This interaction occurs in Mark and Matthew, perhaps intentionally, between the two instructions regarding greatness. We will now turn to these stories.

JESUS, TAXES, AND FISH: MATTHEW 17:24-27

Matthew alone incorporates an interesting tradition about Jesus and taxes. In Matthew 17:24-27, Peter is asked whether Jesus will pay the two-drachma tax used to maintain the temple in Jerusalem.[120] Peter answers in the affirmative. Upon returning to Jesus, Peter is asked by him " *"What do you think, Simon? From whom do the kings of the earth collect customs or poll-tax, from their sons or from strangers?" When Peter said, "From strangers," Jesus said to him, "Then the sons are exempt. However, so that we do not offend them, go to the sea and throw in a hook, and take the first fish that comes up; and when you open its mouth, you will find a shekel. Take that and give it to them for you and Me"'*".

There are several compelling dynamics in this individually attested tradition. The first is its narratival location. Matthew places it between the Confession/ Transfiguration sequence and his teaching on greatness in chapter 18, which is one of Matthew's five discourse sections, sometimes referred to as the 'Ecclesial Discourse'[121]. Jesus introduces the idea of servanthood as the path to greatness which, as we learned above, will be fully developed in Matthew 20. This narrative context is significant because it presupposes what Peter has recently confessed,

---

120. Bock, *Jesus*, p. 238

121. Meyer, *Five Speeches*, p. 21

that Jesus is indeed the Christ, God's Messiah. Jesus has also radically redefined what it means to be the Messiah, which will culminate in his suffering, death, and resurrection. This was not what anyone expected and led to confusion. Greatness, as Jesus is about to explain, means becoming like a child; children had no social status in antiquity, and Jesus' followers must likewise reject all claims to power, authority, and status if they want to follow him.

The story of the fish in Matthew 17:24-27 plays on both the idea of Jesus as king and the nature of political authority. Notably this is not a tax directly imposed by the Romans; Exodus 30:13-16 requires Israel to pay for the temple. The Jerusalem establishment, however, has been roundly condemned by Jesus for refusing to believe his message and are in danger of being excluded from the kingdom. Jesus's point to Peter about the kings collecting taxes from strangers and not their own sons is an obvious allusion to Jesus's messianic status. If he is, as Matthew and now Peter have affirmed, the Christ, then he should be exempt from paying the tax. Jesus will pay anyway, but the reason he gives has little to do with the temple. The tax is paid, as Jesus says in Matthew 17:27, *"so that we do not offend them"*. There is no appeal to the divine authority of Jerusalem's political elite nor a timeless theory of taxation as an inevitable facet of life. Jesus pays the tax so as not to offend the tax collectors.

This is a sentiment which is entirely compatible with Jeremiah 29:7. While Jeremiah speaks of seeking the welfare of Babylon in light of its eventual destruction, Jesus has already hinted (and will openly proclaim before his crucifixion) that Jerusalem will be judged for rejecting his message. The temple, as a result, will be destroyed. In the meantime, Jesus pays the tax so as not to give offense. Jesus called his followers to make peace, and sometimes 'peace' means playing by the rules of a game which is coming to an end. Incidentally this dynamic between the reality of the kingdom and the reality of political authorities is present in the two most controversial 'political' (anachronism notwithstanding) texts in the New Testament, Romans 13:1-7 and 1 Peter 2:13-17. Paul exhorts the Romans to be *"at peace with all men"* and to *"overcome evil with good"*[122] right before admonishing them to submit to the governing authorities, and immediately after he explains that his audience should *"Owe nothing to anyone except to love one another"* while rounding out Romans 13 by stating that the Romans should follow his instruction because the eschatological consummation is soon coming.[123] Peter likewise refers to his audience as *"aliens and strangers"*, clearly evoking exilic language, and prefaces his comments about the authorities with an exhortation to *"Keep your*

---

122. Romans 12:18 and 12:21, respectively.

123. Romans 13:8-14

behavior excellent among the Gentiles, so that in the thing in which they slander you as evildoers, they may because of your good deeds, as they observe them, glorify God in the day of visitation", just before telling them to submit to human institutions "*for the Lord's sake*"[124]. Both Paul and Peter are in harmony with Jesus; their calls to respect authority are pragmatic, not existential. Any attempts to construct a timeless theology of taxation based on this text are doomed to failure from the start. When read historically, contextually, and canonically, Matthew's strange story about taxes and fish makes much more sense. Far from being a justification of modern authoritarian socialism, it reaffirms the central message of the gospels: Jesus is the one true king.

JESUS AND THE RICH YOUNG RULER

In Mark 10:17-22, Matthew 19:16-22, and Luke 18:18-23, Jesus has an exchange with a wealthy person whom he ultimately requests to "*go and sell all you possess and give to the poor*"[125]. The request proves too difficult, and the man walks away. This passage has caused a considerable amount of anxiety for Christians who believe, as I do, that the Bible makes ethical claims on our lives. It has also been uncritically employed by left-wing Christians to justify redistributive programs and a general disdain for 'the rich'. That Western progressives by any global or historical standard should be categorized as 'rich' themselves tends to escape their notice. The Greek root for the word "*all*" is *hosos*, which can mean 'as much as' or, as in the NASB, 'all' is also a problem for left-wing interpreters; everyone who uses this passage as a critique of 'capitalism' continues to own some personal possessions, so they clearly haven't given up 'as much as' they possibly can. This doesn't mean that the anxiety caused by this passage is entirely unjustified. Before deriving a principle from this tradition and applying it to the modern world, we must situate it in its historical and narratival contexts.

The story is a classic example of triple-tradition, included with minor variations in all three Synoptic gospels. It is also flanked on either side by traditions which are similar in either content or theme. This increases the likelihood that these traditions were either transmitted together orally or that Matthew and Luke both believed the story was best understood within Mark's wider narrative context. Either way, the tradition must not be read in isolation; it has to be interpreted within the narratival context of all three Synoptics. Notably, this exchange occurs during Jesus' final trip to Jerusalem. While this journey begins much earlier in

---

124. 1 Peter 2:12-13

125. Mark 10:21

Luke, starting in 9:51, both Mark 10:1 and Matthew 19:2 begin the chapters in which this tradition is included by referencing Jesus' turn towards Judea. He is on the way to meet his fate, and this is intended, at least by Mark and Matthew, to hang over the story of the rich young ruler.

The long chain of triple-tradition begins with a conflict between Jesus and the Pharisees. Mark 10:2-12 and Matthew 19:3-13 present Jesus in a legal debate with his opponents, whom Jesus claims are not correctly following the Law with respect to divorce. The tradition is designed to show Jesus' authority as superior to that of the Pharisees, a common theme in the gospels. Luke incorporates a story which is unique to his gospel but makes the same point. In Luke 18:9-14, Jesus tells a story *"to some people who trusted in themselves that they were righteous, and viewed others with contempt"*. A Pharisee and a tax collector are praying in the temple at the same time. The Pharisee congratulates himself before God for following the Law, contrasting himself with the despicable tax collector. The tax collector, on the other hand, begs God for mercy, acknowledging his sin. After the parable, Jesus tells this audience that the tax collector *"went to his house justified rather than the other; for everyone who exalts himself will be humbled, but he who humbles himself will be exalted"*. Humility before God is what matters; pride is an impediment to faithfulness. Even though this story is different from Jesus's debate regarding divorce, it is thematically similar. The Pharisees who oppose Jesus believe themselves to be superior to others, and they are proven wrong. This is how, in all three Synoptics, the material contextualizing the rich young ruler is introduced.

Following this, the evangelists share the same story of children who were brought before Jesus.[126] The disciples complain about this, and Jesus rebukes them. Mark 10:14-15 records his response: *"when Jesus saw this He was indignant and said to them, "Permit the children to come to Me; do not hinder them; for the kingdom of God belongs to such as these. Truly I say to you, whoever does not receive the kingdom of God like a child will not enter it at all""*. As we have learned about ancient narratives, the minor characters are designed to act as a foil or contrast to the major characters; after humbling the Pharisees, Jesus chastises his disciples and commends them to become more like children.[127] Both this tradition and the ones preceding it further demonstrate that the kingdom of God is either rejected or misunderstood by the major characters and that what constitutes repentance and faith is different from what the Pharisees and disciples thought. These traditions frontload the story of the rich young ruler and serve as its proximate context; the details of that tradition must be read as a continuation of these themes.

---

126. Mark 10:13-16, Matthew 19:13-15, and Luke 18:15-17

127. Rhoads, Dewey, Michie, *Mark as Story*, pp. 129-135

The traditional designation of this tradition[128] as 'The Rich Young Ruler' is actually a composite from all three gospels. Mark 10:22 and Matthew 19:22 use the phrase "*owned much property*"; the Greek root behind "*property*" is *ktema*, which particularly emphasises landed estates. Luke 18:23 uses the term *plousios*, cognates of which we have seen in other Lukan passages such as 1:53 and 6:24, which is a more general term for 'wealth'. Matthew 19:20 identifies the man as 'young', and Luke 18:18 describes him as an *archon*, a ruler or someone with power. Stein suggests he may have been a synagogue official or perhaps even a member of the Sanhedrin[129], and his wealth is a near guarantee that he would have been politically connected and, given the oppressive measures utilized to generate wealth in Roman provinces, was likely viewed with suspicion by many of Jesus' followers, and rightly so. Whatever we make of the details, the man is wealthy and influential.

In Mark 10:17 the man kneels before Jesus, a clear sign of respect, and in all three gospels the man asks a nearly identical question: "*Good teacher, what shall I do to inherit eternal life?*"[130] This question is a loaded one in Second Temple Judaism; those who inherit eternal life will be resurrected in the coming kingdom. As we have discussed previously, the Law in Second Temple Judaism served both an ecclesiological and an eschatological function. Fidelity to Torah was a boundary marker which separated those on the inside from those on the outside and demarcated Jews from gentiles. Those who followed the Law were on the right side of the boundary and would therefore be vindicated when God finally returned to restore Israel. The rich young ruler is asking a question about the kingdom; how can he know in the present that he is properly within the Law and worthy of eschatological vindication?[131] Jesus responds by asking why the man called him good, for only God is good. While this passage has caused endless amounts of christological speculation, Jesus's response is intended to point the man towards God: "*Jesus establishes that only God is good, and thus points to a selection of the Decalogue, the commandments of God, as the way to eternal life*"[132]. If the man will inherit eternal life, then he would have certainly followed the Ten Commandments, the foundation of the entire Jewish Law.

In Mark 10:19 and parallels Jesus lists a set of commandments from the Decalogue, and in 10:20 the man says he has followed all of them. Interestingly, Mark adds "*do not defraud*" to the commandments, which would most likely refer

---

128. Mark 10:17-22, Matthew 19:16-22, Luke 18:18-23

129. Stein, *Luke*, p. 456

130. Mark 10:17, see also Matthew 19:16 and Luke 18:18.

131. Wright, *Victory*, p. 301

132. Moloney, *Mark*, pp. 198-199

to a wealthy person exploiting their hired workers by withholding wages[133], further reinforcing this man's wealth. Equally interesting, especially in anticipation of the man's response, is which commandments Jesus *omitted*: he says nothing about having no other gods, abstaining from idolatry, taking God's name in vain, or following the Sabbath.[134] The man responds to Jesus by stating that he had followed *the commandments Jesus outlined*, not including those which relate to God. There is an interesting irony in his response. A rich Galilean would have almost certainly gained his wealth through unjust exploitation of others, often using the levers of political power. The commandments listed by Jesus are ones *"that a rich man might be prone to violate"*[135]. It appears, however, as if the man had not defrauded others. Jesus believes there is but one thing he lacks. Quoting from Mark 10:21-22 (the parallels are nearly identical), *"Jesus felt a love for him and said to him, "One thing you lack: go and sell all you possess and give to the poor, and you will have treasure in heaven; and come, follow Me." But at these words he was saddened, and he went away grieving, for he was one who owned much property"*.

By omitting the commandments about honoring God, the evangelists have shown that the rich man, even though he may happen to be a rare example of one who generated wealth without oppressing others, has made an idol of his possessions. At this point in all three Synoptic gospels all of the major characters have been told they need to reexamine their understanding of the coming kingdom, repent, and believe Jesus. As the previous tradition demonstrated, even Jesus' inner circle didn't yet comprehend the kingdom. Children, those with no power or social status, were made an example of what it meant to follow Jesus. Even if the rich young ruler had virtuously abstained from defrauding, his possessions were inhibiting him from accepting God's kingdom. His wealth had become an idol; Paul twice connects 'greed', the desire to preserve one's wealth, with 'idolatry'[136], and the rich young ruler had fallen right into the trap. Even if we grant the most generous translation of *hosos*, 'as much as possible', the man is still unwilling to part with his wealth. He cannot accept the kingdom like a child and leaves Jesus dejected. Of critical importance for our study, Jesus permits him to walk away. It can be assumed that eschatological judgment awaits the rich young ruler.

In Mark 10:23-31, Matthew 19:23-30, and Luke 18:24-30, Jesus unpacks to the incredulous disciples his interaction with the rich young ruler. Jesus instructs his disciples that it will be hard for those who have wealth to enter the kingdom

---

133. Crossley and Myles, *Class Conflict*, p. 110

134. Exodus 20:3-11

135. Moloney, *Mark*, p. 199

136. Ephesians 5:5 and Colossians 3:5; we will discuss these passages in detail below.

of God. There was an expectation, based on passages such as Proverbs 10:22, that wealth could be an indication of God's blessing.[137] Even for rural Galileeans who might be naturally suspicious of the rich and powerful, Jesus' intense statement about wealth comes as a shock. Jesus employs the famous image of a camel going through the eye of a needle, an obvious impossibility, to reinforce how difficult it is for a rich man to enter the kingdom of God. Later traditions which postulate that the 'eye of the needle' refers to a hole in ancient city walls has no historical basis[138]; Jesus means what he says. Anyone with the disposition of the rich young ruler will be excluded, not 'saved' on the final day, and therefore outside of God's people in the present. The disciples understandably ask Jesus how anyone can be saved, to which he responds in Mark 10:27 *"With people it is impossible, but not with God; for all things are possible with God"*. Entering the kingdom requires submission to God. Repent, for the kingdom is at hand. Peter reminds Jesus that the disciples had sacrificed much to follow him; Jesus responds by assuring them of the great eschatological reversal. In the age to come everything lost will be restored to those who follow Jesus, and they will inherit eternal life. In other words, those who follow Jesus in the present are guaranteed a place in the consummated kingdom. Mark and Matthew both conclude this tradition with a warning: many who are first will be last, and the last, first.

Matthew 20:1-16 follows this with the Parable of the Laborers in the Vineyard, unique to his gospel. It imitates Matthew 19:30, stating again that the first will be last, demonstrating its thematic unity with the story of the rich young ruler. Mark 10:32-34 and Luke 18:31-34 both include another prediction about Jesus' forthcoming messianic death, which Matthew includes after his parable in 20:17-19. Again, this should be read in contrast to the rich young ruler; as king, Jesus is willing to die. Those who follow him should do likewise. Mark and Matthew, as seen above, follow this with the story of the disciples asking who is the greatest in the kingdom, revealing them to be more like the rich young ruler than the children, and to round out the triple-tradition set Mark 10:46-52, Matthew 20:29-34, and Luke 18:35-43 present a blind beggar (Matthew has two) affirming that Jesus is the son of David and humbling asking for healing. Jesus grants his request. The Pharisees, disciples, and the rich young ruler have all misunderstood Jesus and his kingdom. The children and the blind man, with no social status, are paradigmatic of what it takes to follow Jesus.

---

137. Bock, *Jesus*, p. 304

138. Crossley and Myles, *Class Conflict*, pp. 110-111

What are we to make of Jesus's interaction with the rich young ruler? Remembering that Jesus is a prophet whose words and deeds both explain and enact the coming kingdom, this exchange must be understood within that context. Jesus has radically redefined the restoration of Israel, to the ire of the Jewish elite and the perplexity of his disciples. This exchange demonstrates yet another twist, albeit one for which the evangelists have already primed their audience. Wealth must no longer be considered a reward for following the commandments, and in fact could be more of a liability than an asset. Jesus was, in the insightful words of Myles and Crossley, promising *"to turn the world upside down, punish those who benefited from the world as it was, give all the trappings of wealth to those who had suffered, and urge the rich to mend their ways before it was too late"*[139]. The special Lukan traditions which we will examine shortly make much the same point. Wealth can become an idol, even if it is generated without coercion. Those who are wealthy are obligated to employ their possessions in the service of others.

Moloney correctly observes what many interpreters have noted about this tradition: *"Such a command* [to give all of one's possessions away] *is found only in this story"*[140]. He is correct. Jesus does not expect all of his followers to sell everything they have and give it to the poor. In Luke 8:1-3, there are several women who fund Jesus's ministry out of their private means. They had clearly not sold everything they possessed. Jesus directed this particular command at one particular person, and the traditions are designed to make a larger point about the nature of Jesus's kingdom and discipleship. This doesn't dull the sharp edge of Jesus's instructions. Wealth comes with a massive responsibility and the temptation to use it not for the purposes of building God's kingdom but for personal satisfaction. Those of us who live in the Western world, including affluent progressives who superficially identify with the poor but live lives of material abundance, are called to check our motives. As in Matthew 6:24, it is impossible to serve both God and wealth. Many western Christians, when confronted with this harsh truth, act like the rich young ruler and choose wealth over Jesus. 1 Timothy 6:17-19 captures the essence of Jesus' teaching: *"Instruct those who are rich in this present world not to be conceited or to fix their hope on the uncertainty of riches, but on God . . . instruct them to do good, to be rich in good work, to be generous and ready to share, storing up for themselves the treasure . . . of that which is life indeed"*. The echoes of the Jesus tradition are impossible to miss (and precisely what we would expect if my theory that Paul taught

---

139. Crossley and Myles, *Class Conflict*, p. 111

140. Moloney, *Mark*, p. 200

oral traditions which would eventually become the written gospels is correct) and should serve as a warning to us all. A failure to use our possessions responsibly will result in eschatological judgment.

Those who would celebrate this passage as a triumph of authoritarian socialism are greatly mistaken. Socialism is impossible without political authoritarianism because it relies on the threat of force to confiscate wealth. Those who believe the technocratic socialist bureaucracy mismanages the money which is confiscated from them are unable to do anything about it. This is especially distressing for people like me who find it a grave moral evil that much of my wealth is confiscated in the name of 'justice' and then used to bomb innocent people who have never threatened my life in countries thousands of miles away from my home. This is always and inevitably the long-term consequence of socialism. Some socialists will balk that they simply want to 'tax the rich' and that the story of the rich young ruler provides a convenient theological justification for that policy. They are wrong.

It is imperative to reflect upon how the exchange is terminated: Jesus allows the man to walk away and keep his wealth. Jesus doesn't chase after him, threaten him with physical violence, or petition the Sanhedrin, Herod, or the Romans to pass a new progressive tax law which confiscates his wealth and redistributes it to particular interests groups. Instead, Jesus stands in the long line of God's prophets, announcing that those who refuse to respond to God in the present can expect judgment on the final day. The eschaton is coming and those who refuse to accept Jesus and his kingdom won't make it unless they repent. Jesus refuses to pull up the weeds; instead, he will await the harvest where the weeds can be safely separated from the wheat, bundled up, and thrown into the fire. The rich young ruler, assuming he never repented, will get exactly what he deserves in the end. Jesus, the soon-to-be crucified Messiah, would never condone the use of gentile-ish violence to confiscate wealth. Christian socialists, on the other hand, positively worship the use of violence. Those with abundant possessions run the risk of making their wealth an idol, but those who believe in socialist economic policies idolize political force to achieve their ends. Jesus has redefined power, but few can accept it. Wide is the path which leads to destruction.

There are a handful of traditions found only in Luke and John which highlight and supplement the characteristic Jesus we have been describing thus far. Since these traditions dovetail thematically with the material we have covered above, I will briefly mention and interpret several passages which are unique to those gospels. Their presentation of Jesus and message of the kingdom is entirely consistent with everything we have studied thus far.

SPECIAL LUKE: SAMARITANS, FARMERS, STEWARDS, LAZARUS, AND ZACCHAEUS

The Parable of the Good Samaritan: Luke 10:29-37

All three Synoptic gospels record a story in which Jesus is asked by a Jewish lawyer about which of the commands was the greatest.[141] Both Mark and Matthew place this exchange in a series of traditions which occur just before the Last Supper and will be covered in the next chapter. In Luke, however, the question posed by the lawyer is similar to that of the rich young ruler: "*Teacher, what shall I do to inherit eternal life*"[142]. Jesus responds by asking him what the law says, to which the lawyer replies "*you shall love the Lord your God with all your soul, and with all your strength, and with all your mind; and your neighbor as yourself*"; Jesus responds positively "*You have answered correctly; do this and you will live*"[143]. The lawyer's rejoinder appears to reveal an insincerity[144]: "*But wishing to justify himself, he said to Jesus, "And who is my neighbor?*""[145]. In Luke 10:29-27, Jesus tells the famous Parable of the Good Samaritan in response to this question.

The precise identity of the Samaritans and their relationship to Jews in Galilee and Judea is complex. The Samaritans were in one sense heirs of the Northern Kingdom which fell to the Assyrians in 722 and could trace their roots back to that era.[146] While the Samaritans shared many beliefs in common with Jews, the biggest difference being that their temple was built on Mount Gerizim near the city of Shechem.[147] During the Second Temple period many Samaritans capitulated to Antiochus Epiphanes IV and for a time dedicated their temple to Zeus, earning the ire of the Hasmoneans. This animosity would continue into the time of Jesus and can, from a historical standpoint, be viewed within the overall framework of developing Jewish sectarianism; the Samaritans were a group which was particularly hated by the Jerusalem establishment.[148] Jews generally oscillated between understanding the Samaritans as a rival sect or flat-out denouncing them as

---

141. Mark 12:28-34, Matthew 22:34-40, Luke 10:25-28

142. Luke 10:25

143. Luke 10:27-28

144. Stein, *Luke*, p. 317

145. Luke 10:29

146. Stein, *Luke*, pp. 317-318

147. Ferguson, *Backgrounds*, p. 534

148. Cohen, *Maccabees*, pp. 162-163

foreigners.[149] However we understand this complex group, one point is certain: a Jewish lawyer would not be interested in comparing himself to a Samaritan.

The story is familiar. A man travelling from Jerusalem to Jericho was accosted by robbers who beat him, took his belongings, and left him for dead. A priest and a Levite see this man in distress and choose to ignore him, passing by on the opposite side of the road. A Samaritan has compassion on the man, bandages his wounds, and takes him to an inn for care, paying for the room with his own money. Jesus asks the lawyer which of the three proved to be a neighbor to the man. The parable concludes with an exchange in Luke 10:36: "[The lawyer] *said, "The one who showed mercy towards him." Then Jesus said to him, "Go and do the same."*". The Samaritan, perceived as a sectarian foreigner by the Jewish lawyer, faithfully obeys the command to love one's neighbor. Luke has already recognized Jesus as king over all creation, and in the kingdom of God 'neighbors' aren't simply confined to ethnic Jews. Loving Israel's God means serving everyone and embracing a willingness to cross social lines.

Wright summarizes this parable helpfully: "*Loving Israel's covenant god means loving him as creator of all, and discovering as neighbors those who were beyond the borders of the chosen people. Those who followed Jesus in this way would be 'justified'; that is, they would be vindicated when the covenant god acted climactically within history. 'Go and do likewise.'*"[150] The lawyer's question centered around 'salvation', which as we discussed above contains both ecclesiological and eschatological assumptions in Second Temple Judaism, and knowing in the present that one is 'in the right' before God requires that person to love like the Samaritan. Much like the rich young ruler, it appears as if the lawyer walks away unchanged. Jesus doesn't chase him or petition for a new law, he just lets him walk. Without repentance he will not survive judgment day.

A very important principle located in this text and others which universalize the kingship of Jesus has to do with rethinking our political identities. Jews and Samaritans were in opposition to each other, and yet Jesus presents the Samaritan as a paragon of neighborliness. In the modern world, we tend to privilege our national and cultural identities above all else. The world can be neatly separated into 'Americans', 'Germans', 'Japanese', 'Egyptians', and the like. While Jesus isn't minimizing cultural or ethnic distinctions, in the kingdom of God they bear absolutely no relevance to defining who is or who is not one's neighbor. Following Jesus means learning to love *everyone* in the same way Jesus loves us and should

---

149. Ferguson, *Backgrounds*, pp. 534-535

150. Wright, *Victory*, p. 307

challenge Christians who take pride in national identity. The question of identity will become increasingly prominent as we explore the rest of the New Testament.

The Parable of the Rich Fool: Luke 12:13-21

As Jesus is teaching the crowds, one of those in attendance asks Jesus to arbitrate an inheritance dispute between him and his brother. Jesus refuses and warns the crowd to "*be on your guard against every form of greed; for not even when one has an abundance does his life consist of his possessions*"[151]. Jesus recognizes that the man's request is based on a desire to retain possessions which threatens to damage the relationship he has with his brother.[152] Not only is greed degrading for the individuals, it destroys communities, which Jesus's many rural followers would have attributed to the wealthy urban elites and their oppressive policies.

In Luke 12:16-21, Jesus tells a parable which addresses the question posed by the greedy brother. A rich man (Luke uses a cognate of *plousios*) owns a large tract of productive land, and, reasoning with himself, determined to tear down his barns and build larger ones, laying up goods for many years so that he could live a life of ease. The man perishes that evening, and Jesus compares him in Luke 12:21 to a "*man who stores up treasure for himself, and is not rich towards God*". Kennenth Bailey convincingly argues that the man in this parable, acting on his own behalf, is defying a common Galilean social convention in which decisions about constructing new storage facilities were not made without consulting neighbors[153]. The sharp edge of Jesus's parable is directed at the brother seeking an inheritance; there is no hierarchical prioritization of possessions over people in the kingdom of God.

Luke 12:22-34 follows this parable with material from Matthew 6:25-34 about the dangers of storing up wealth, the need to trust God with possessions, and seeking God's kingdom first. In the final two verses, 12:32-33, Jesus admonishes his audience to sell possessions and give to the poor, because "*where your treasure is, there your heart will be also*". Unlike the rich man in the parable who wanted to store up for himself goods without regard for the concerns of his neighbor, those who follow Jesus are called to reflect upon how their possessions impact other people. Accepting the kingdom means that one must use what they own to serve others, not live luxuriously with complete disregard for the rest of society. Luke will return to themes introduced in this parable in chapter 16.

---

151. Luke 12:13-15

152. Bock, *Jesus*, p. 266

153. Bailey, *Middle Eastern Eyes*, p. 303

The Parable of the Unrighteous Steward: Luke 16:1-13

Luke 15:1-2 introduces a series of parables which are told in response to the Pharisees and scribes complaining about Jesus' association with those they deemed 'sinners'. In Luke 16:1-13, Jesus tells the Parable of the Unrighteous Steward. All of Luke 16 addresses the question of properly utilizing wealth and possessions, and this complex parable introduces the thematic shift.[154] While there are important historical questions about the details of this story[155]Jesus explains its point at the end. In typical Lukan form, a man described as *plousios* plans to fire a servant for "*squandering his possessions*"[156]. After being alerted of his master's intentions, the servant worries about where he will live without employment. He devises an ingenious plan. Calling up his master's debtors, he instructs them to quickly pay a lower sum than what is owed and presents the money to his master, who is impressed with the servant's shrewdness. It is possible that the discount given to the debtors by the servant reflects his commission, meaning he was forgoing his cut to quickly compensate the master.[157]

Jesus explains this parable in Luke 16:9: "*I say to you, make friends for yourselves by means of the wealth of unrighteousness, so that when it fails, they will receive you into the eternal dwellings*". The word for 'wealth' is a cognate of *mamonas*, which denotes all material possessions, not simply money. While the construction is somewhat confusing, in Luke 16:10-13 Jesus further elucidates the parable. Those who faithfully manage their possessions in the present will be entrusted with true riches, and those (like the rich young ruler) who do not manage what they possess will be deemed unreliable. Jesus concludes his instruction with a parallel to Matthew 6:24: one cannot serve both God and wealth. It makes perfect sense given the emphasis Luke places on the use of possessions that he would isolate this saying from Matthew's structured Sermon on the Mount and incorporate it at the end of a unique parable which further develops its theme. The message is direct: those who have possessions must use them faithfully by serving others and building the kingdom.

This parable corresponds thematically to the exchange with the rich young ruler and develops the principle of using resources sacrificially. Bailey beautifully summarizes the challenge of this parable for modern Christians: "*All possessions belong to God because he created matter. Indeed, "The earth is the LORD's and the fulness*

---

154. Stein, *Luke*, p. 410

155. See Bock, *Jesus*, pp. 283-284

156. Luke 16:1

157. Bock, *Jesus*, p. 283

thereof" (Ps 24:1). This basic biblical principle is foreign to the contemporary capitalist West. The car in the driveway, the house I live in, the pen in my pocket, the watch on my wrist, the computer I use to compose these reflections-all belong to God. I am merely a steward of them"[158]. Those who follow Jesus are obligated to use what we have, none of which we would possess without being created by God and placed in His world, to benefit others. While I am not sure if Bailey is using the term 'capitalist' neutrally or critically, capitalism as an economic arrangement based on peaceful, voluntary exchange is entirely compatible with Jesus's teaching, but the wealth it creates places a responsibility upon us to use it wisely or risk eschatological judgment. We should not take this parable lightly. It is an unequivocal summons to use what we own in service of others. In Luke 16:14-18 the Pharisees, identified as *"lovers of money"*, scoff at Jesus' teaching. He launches into a tirade against the Pharisees, calls them *"detestible"*, and implies they fail to live up to the standards of God's Law. This will set the stage for the Parable of the Rich Man and Lazarus.

The Parable of the Rich Man and Lazarus: Luke 16:19-31

The Parable of the Rich Man and Lazarus only further reinforces what the earlier passages in Luke 16 teach. Anyone who accepts the kingdom must use their possessions to benefit others, and the Pharisees have absolutely failed. Luke 16:19-31 continues his beatdown of the Pharisees and issues yet another dire warning about the dangers of wealth for those who follow Jesus. The story is intriguing. A rich man (Luke uses *plousios* again) *"habitually dressed in purple and fine linen, joyously living in splendor every day"* is contrasted to a poor man named Lazarus who sits at the rich man's gate. It is possible that the description of the rich man's dress denotes royalty, with the comment on joyous living suggesting he is perpetually well-fed.[159] Lazarus, by contrast, is described as *ptochos*, which denotes someone who is so poor they must resort to begging. He was longing to be fed by the crumbs of the rich man, who apparently pays him no attention whatsoever in spite of Lazarus's proximity to his property. Both men die; Lazarus is transported to Abraham's side while the rich man is tormented in Hades. The rich man begs Abraham to have mercy on him, but Abraham refuses, saying in Luke 16:25 *"child, remember that during your life you received your good things, and likewise Lazarus bad things; but now he is being comforted here, and you are in agony"*. Many who are first will be last. Some in Israel rise while others fall. The rich man then begs Abraham to warn his brothers so they will avoid his fate. Abraham again denies the rich man's request,

---

158. Bailey, *Middle Eastern Eyes*, pp. 379-380

159. Stein, *Luke*, p. 16:21

telling him that his brothers have Moses and the prophets to warn them. The parable concludes with a foreboding admonition. Sbraham tells the rich man *"If they do not listen to Moses and the Prophets, they will not be persuaded even if someone rises from the dead"*.

While this parable generates a set of curious eschatological questions,[160] the main point of Jesus's message mustn't be overlooked. In direct continuity with his teaching regarding wealth and eschatological judgment, this parable vividly illustrates the fate of those with means who refuse to help those in need. The rich young ruler cannot accept Jesus's injunction to sell his possessions and will receive the same judgment which befell the rich man in this parable. Jesus once again does not endorse a political policy of redistribution or encourage his followers to use violence as a means of confiscating his wealth, but unapologetically announces that the rich man, and the Pharisees who act like him, will reap what they have sown in the end.

Zacchaeus the Tax Collector: Luke 19:1-10

Thus far Luke has presented the rich in an entirely negative light. Accepting that these traditions are legitimately based on memories of Jesus which were preserved and circulated orally prior to written composition, it is fairly easy to see why. As we have discussed several times, the urban elite in Galilee often acquired and maintained wealth through oppression and coercion, a fact not lost on Jesus's original audience. His warnings about the rich were both an oracle of coming judgment for those who failed to repent and comforting to those who had been exploited. Until this point in Luke's narrative, the rich and powerful have either opposed or ignored Jesus. This all changes with the story of Zacchaeus the tax collector.

In Luke 19:1-10 Jesus is passing through Jericho on his way to Jerusalem. Zacchaeus lives in Jericho. Luke describes him as *"the chief tax collector"*, using the Greek term *architelones* which is found in no other extant literature from the time. Since Jericho was a well-known toll center, Zacchaeus was most likely in charge of managing the taxes which were collected in the city.[161] Luke describes him as *plousios*, which generally denotes characters whom Luke regards as deplorable. Zacchaeus wants to meet Jesus and, because of his short height, climbs a tree to get a good look at the prophet. Jesus sees Zacchaeus in the tree, calls him down, and invites himself over for dinner. Those who witnessed Jesus's interaction with Zacchaeus grumble, protesting that Jesus would dare eat with a sinner. While Luke

---

160. Resolved satisfactorily in my view by Wright; see Wright, *Resurrection*, pp. 437-438.
161. Stein, *Luke*, p. 467

doesn't specify the identity of the grumblers, much of the preceding material was directed towards the Pharisees, casting them as the likely critics of Jesus. Zaccheaus is profoundly impacted by Jesus's offer and says *"Behold, Lord, half of my possessions I will give to the poor, and if I have defrauded anyone of anything, I will give back four times as much"*[162]. Jesus responds by saying *"Today salvation has come to this house, because he, too, is a son of Abraham. For the Son of Man came to seek and to save that which was lost"*[163].

If my identification of the grumblers as Pharisees is correct, this tradition is a living example of Luke 18:9-14 in which Jesus tells the parable of a self-righteous Pharisee and a contrite tax collector; the tax collector is justified before God. Despite his wealth, Zacchaeus commits to selling much of it and giving the proceeds to the poor while paying back those he defrauded. Notably Zacchaeus does not, nor does Jesus ask him to, give up all of his possessions. He will nevertheless entirely reform his relationship with wealth, now using it for the sake of others. Zacchaeus becomes a model of repentance and belief in the gospel. The contrition of Zacchaeus also serves as a blistering critique of the Pharisees, whom Luke labeled *"lovers of money"* in 16:14. They are now cast as the ones who act like 'sinners' in the sectarian definition of the term. An evil tax collector meets Jesus and changes his life, while the supposedly 'righteous' Pharisees continue to oppose him. Meanwhile, the disciples remain stuck somewhere in between Zacchaeus and the Pharisees. Luke's audience is encouraged to follow the example of a tax collector, a scandal to the Jewish elite but paradigmatic for the kingdom of God. Many in Israel will rise, and many will fall.

JOHN: PROPHET, MESSIAH, AND AUTHORITY

John's gospel often differs in both style and substance from its Synoptic counterparts. As I argued in Chapter 7, however, I believe that John knew the Synoptics and was creatively rewriting them. There are a growing number of scholars who contend John's gospel may offer more information about the historical Jesus than previously recognized. While I tend to agree with this line of reasoning, our quick foray through John has but one goal: demonstrating the thematic similarities between John and the Synoptics. Space permits but a cursory examination of the characteristic Jesus in the fourth gospel, but we will quickly find the Johannine Jesus consistent with his Synoptic profile

---

162. Luke 19:8

163. Luke 19:9-10

The Woman at the Well: John 4:1-42

John 4:1-42 contains the famous encounter between a Samaritan woman and Jesus. As Jesus and his disciples are passing through Samaria, they stop at a city called Sychar near Jacob's well. While his disciples travel into town to purchase provisions, Jesus stays at the well to relax. A Samaritan woman approaches Jesus, who asks her for a drink. Taken aback, she responds *"How is it that You, being a Jew, ask me for a drink since I am a Samaritan woman"*, with John adding the editorial comment *"for Jews have no dealings with Samaritans"*[164]. As we discussed above, the relationship between Jews and Samaritans was socially, politically, and ideologically fraught. Since some Jews considered Samaritans unclean, accepting a drink of water from the woman might ritually contaminate Jesus.[165] Worse still, initiating a conversation may have been perceived as flirtatious and, to top it all off, she was unaccompanied and drawing water in the heat of the day when most women would have traveled in groups either in the morning or evening when it was cooler. This detail suggests the Samaritan woman was socially disreputable[166]. Echoing Jesus's interactions with 'sinners and tax collectors' in the Synoptic gospels, this story is rife with social scandal.

Jesus responds with a cryptic statement. He will provide the woman with living water, telling her that whoever drinks his water will inherit eternal life. The woman requests the living water, and Jesus instructs the Samaritan to first retrieve her husband. The woman reveals she has no husband. Jesus fills in the missing details of her salacious autobiography. The Samaritan woman has had five husbands and was not married to the man with whom she was currently living. She acquiesces and immediately identifies Jesus's occupation: *"Sir, I perceive that You are a prophet"*[167]. She then reminds Jesus that the Samaritans worship at their own mountain, while Jews ought to worship in Jerusalem. Jesus's response is significant: *"Woman, believe Me, an hour is coming when neither in this mountain nor in Jerusalem will you worship the Father . . . an hour is coming, and now is, when the true worshipers will worship the Father in spirit and truth; for such people the Father seeks to be His worshipers"*[168]. Already in this passage the themes of prophecy and eschatology are prominent; Jesus' reference to the hour being now is certainly a

---

164. John 4:9

165. Bock, *Jesus*, p. 435

166. Kostenberger, *John*, p. 148

167. John 4:19

168. John 4:21-23

Johannine expression of inaugurated eschatology.[169] Jesus is a prophet announcing God's promised restoration. Like the magi at Jesus' birth or the Parable of the Good Samaritan, what God is doing through Jesus will change the entire world. The eschatological framing of Jesus's response to the woman is a rejection of the centrality of the Jerusalem temple. Those who worship God no longer need a special place to do so.[170]

The next part of their exchange hinges upon Jesus's messianic identity: "*The woman said to HIm, "I know that Messiah is coming (He who is called Christ); when that One comes, He will declare all things to us." Jesus said to her, "I who speak to you am He"*"[171]. After this, the woman returns to the city, announcing to everyone that she thinks Jesus is the Christ. He knew her past, after all. This is a classic example of prophetic validation in service of revealing Jesus's messianic identity. The people of Sychar pay Jesus a visit; later in the chapter John discusses the number of Samaritans who believe, "*for we have heard for ourselves and know that this One is indeed the Savior of the world*"[172]. Although John only specifically employs 'kingdom' language three times in his gospel[173], the concept is built into this messianic confession. The Samaritans believe, unlike the Jewish leaders with whom Jesus had been sparring earlier in the narrative, that he is the Christ and will therefore exercise authority over the whole world. The story of the woman at the well is an excellent demonstration of the four major themes relevant to our study of the gospels: Jesus the prophet, Jesus the Christ, the kingdom of God, and eschatology. John is operating within the same conceptual framework as the Synoptics, and the political and economic principles derived from John sit comfortably alongside those found in Mark, Matthew, and Luke.

Questions of Authority

In the gospel of John Jesus is constantly engaged in conflict with a group of adversaries labeled "the Jews". This title for Jesus's opponents has been one of the most widely misunderstood concepts in New Testament interpretation and has unfortunately been used to discriminate against ethnic Jews throughout history. The term first appears in John 1:19 in reference to priests and Levites sent "*from Jerusalem*" to question John. Many Christians have anachronistically understood this language

---

169. Koestenberger, *John*, p. 155

170. A point often ignored by Christian Zionists.

171. John 4:25-26

172. John 4:42

173. John 3:3, 3:5, and 18:36

as a de-Judaising of Jesus, distinguishing the new 'Christianity' of Jesus from the old 'Judaism' of his opponents. This doesn't work historically. In the story of the woman at the well, Jesus self-identifies, and is identified by the woman, as a Jew. He is hailed as the Jewish messiah and savior of the world. John presents Jesus and his followers as Jewish, yet they are never identified with those he labels "the Jews". John uses this term seventy times but never in reference to Jesus or his disciples; rather, as Adele Reinhartz observes, this term is primarily used to describe those who are opposed to Jesus.[174] Koestenberger correctly argues that in John the term is applied specifically to Jewish leaders, perhaps temple authorities or members of the Sanhedrin.[175] Jesus is portrayed as being in constant conflict with the Jewish elite in both the Synoptics and John. Whenever John names "the Jews", he is referring to the same antagonistic leaders we know from the Synoptics.

A brisk stroll through John demonstrates my point. In John 5:24-47 Jesus responds to "the Jews" and their desire to kill him for healing on a Sabbath,[176] precisely what precipitates his conflict with the Pharisees in Mark 3:1-6. John comments in 5:18 that Jesus *"was calling God His own Father, making Himself equal with God"*. A developed christology, perhaps, but entirely congruent with the Synoptic portrayal of Jesus as prophet and Christ. In response, the rest of John 5 is an extended defense of his authority, in which Jesus describes how he was given by God *"authority to execute judgment, because he is the Son of Man"*[177]. In John 5:36, Jesus states that his works *"testify about Me, that the father has sent Me"*, a classic example of the way in which 'deeds of power' function in Jewish prophecy, concluding with an assertion that those who believe in Moses's writings should also believe in Jesus.[178] Jesus heals a man, is criticized by the Pharisees, and then denounces their authority by proclaiming his own. While the style is unique, John is still very much swimming in the same thematic stream as his Synoptics counterparts.

The very next passage is borrowed from a triple-tradition Synoptic story which occurs *twice* in Mark and Matthew![179] Jesus, speaking to a large crowd, multiplies bread and fish, providing them with a meal. The crowd responds in John 6:14 by calling Jesus *"the Prophet"*, and in the very next verse Jesus is forced to leave because the crowd wants to install him as king. The rest of John 6 includes another lengthy, poetic explanation of Jesus' authority, after which *"the Jews were seeking*

---

174. Reinhartz, *Beyond the Jewish Jesus Debates*, pp. 56-57

175. Koestenberger, *John*, p. 108

176. John 5:1-18

177. John 5:27

178. John 5:45-47

179. Mark 6:34-44, Mark 8:1-9, Matthew 14:13-21,Matthew 15:32-38, Luke 9:10-17

to kill him"[180]. In chapter 7, Jesus finds himself in yet another contentious debate with the Jewish authorities, which dominates the entire chapter. The altercation will continue through John 8 and 9, both of which read like an all-out rhetorical war between Jesus and his opponents centering on issues of authority and identity. In John 9, Jesus heals a blind man on Sabbath who is subsequently apprehended and questioned by the Pharisees. The man identifies Jesus as "*a prophet*"[181], with John later remarking that the Jewish authorities would expel anyone from the synagogue who "*confessed Him to be the Christ*"[182]. After being released by the Pharisees, the man finds Jesus and hails him 'Son of Man'.[183]

Jesus self-identifies as the 'good shepherd' in John 1:10-17. Jesus is alluding to Jeremiah 23 and Ezekiel 34, where the 'good shepherd' is the coming Davidic messiah, compared directly to the wicked and unfaithful leaders of Israel who led God's sheep astray. The appropriation of prophetic imagery should not be lost on John's audience; only a few lines later Jesus is asked by the authorities if he is the Christ, to which he answers "*I and the Father are one*".[184] They of course want to kill Jesus, but he appeals to his works as a validation of his message: "*If I do not do them, though you do not believe Me, believe the works, so that you may know and understand that the Father is in Me, and I in the Father*"[185]. The powerful deeds and signs which Jesus performed are a validation of his prophetic message; in this case reaffirming his identity as God's Christ.

One final passage will tie our short examination of John together. After healing Lazarus, the authorities determine it is imperative to kill Jesus. Luke 11:47-53 is quoted in full: "*Therefore the chief priests and the Pharisees convened a council meeting, and they were saying, "What are we doing in regard to the fact that this Man is performing many signs? If we let Him go on like this, all the people will believe in Him, and the Romans will come and take over both our place and our nation." But one of them, Caiaphas, who was high priest that year, said to them, "You know nothing at all, nor are you taking into account that it is in your best interest that one man die for the people, and that the whole nation not perish instead." Now he did not say this on his own, but as he was high priest that year, he prophesied that Jesus was going to die for the nation; and not for the nation only, but in order that He might also gather together into one the children of God who are scattered abroad. So from that day on*

---

180. John 7:1

181. John 9:17

182. John 9:22

183. John 9:35-38

184. John 10:22-30

185. John 10:37-38

they planned together to kill Him". Jesus is performing prophetic signs and many are believing in him. This poses a threat to the authorities; they fear that Jesus might create such a public disturbance the Romans would remove and replace the Jewish authorities. The high priest Caiaphas, wielding considerable political power within the Roman provincial system, argues that Jesus should die for the nation. John editorializes that the death of Jesus would be for all the children of God scattered abroad. Followers of Jesus will apparently worship neither in Jerusalem or any other specified location, but in spirit and truth. It takes little reading between the lines to identify the themes of prophecy, messianic christology, kingdom, and eschatology.

CONCLUSION

All four evangelists are unanimous in their affirmation that Jesus is both a prophet and the Messiah who announces God's eschatological kingdom, calling people to repent and believe. Jesus reveals how his followers should live by appealing to his own impending sacrificial death. Jesus's words and deeds disclose that while he is indeed the Christ, his kingship will not conform to any existing patterns of political domination but is characterized by self-sacrificial suffering on behalf of others. His followers must pick up their cross and follow him, renouncing the power structures maintained by the Jewish elite and gentile authorities. Jesus will demonstrate real power during his final, fateful trip to Jerusalem. True repentance entails faithfully embodying the teachings of Jesus *especially* if they are at odds with prevailing cultural norms. It is impossible to put new wine into old wineskins.

Jesus calls his followers to be peacemakers, offer forgiveness towards those who wrong them, live mercifully, and trust in God for provisions. The rich and powerful who had been exploiting rural Galileans were not, in fact, blessed by God. They must completely reorient their attitude towards wealth and possessions before the impending day of judgment. Failure to do so will end in catastrophe. Like Zacchaeus, those with possessions must willingly use them to benefit others, ensuring that the needs of all are met. Communities damaged by the exploitative economic policies of the elite could be restored through radical, sacrificial charity. Jesus flatly denounces any use of violence or coercion to confiscate wealth from those who are greedy. They will, however, be marked out fo eschatological judgment.

The characteristic Jesus, the impression or gist of his life and identity, is consistent throughout the infancy narratives, his baptism, and his temptation. The words and deeds which were recounted by the evangelists only further developed themes present from the opening lines of each gospel. Jesus's political program of sacrifice over coercion and economic program of radical charity over idolatrous wealth offers us principles which must shape the way we think about politics and economics in the modern world. The passion narratives which depict the last week of Jesus's life will only sharpen the conclusions we have drawn thus far. Jesus is king, but not the kind anyone was expecting. The kingdom of God does not resemble the kingdoms of man. Our story finally reaches the gates of Jerusalem.

CHAPTER 10 | Jerusalem, the Cross,
and the Resurrection

The (Almost) Final Week

Jesus must have known it was possible, if not actually expected outright, that the cost of his activity would be his very life.

Tucker Ferda[1]

So they cried out, "Away with Him, away with Him, crucify Him!" Pilate said to them, "Shall I crucify your King?" The chief priests answered, "We have no king but Caesar."

John 19:15

ALL ROADS LEAD TO JERUSALEM

The ministry of Jesus reaches its climax with his fateful entrance to Jerusalem at the beginning of Passover. By the end of the week he would hang crucified on a Roman cross. All four evangelists have prepared their readers for Jesus' grim fate. From the beginning, Jesus has been in conflict with the Jewish elite, who held real political power and influence, and by the time Jesus arrives in Jerusalem the Jewish establishment wants him dead. After Peter's confession in the Synoptics (and as a recurring motif in John) Jesus has already instructed his disciples that his role as Messiah will culminate with his death and resurrection, a notion fundamentally at odds with Jewish expectations of the Davidic messiah. The prediction of his resurrection, which many (but not all) Jews believed would happen at the consummation of God's eschatological kingdom, made little sense to the disciples. They had no theological category for a suffering Messiah.

---

1. Ferda, *Second Coming*, p. 337

The story of Jesus' final week is chronologically contextualized by the Passover. The event had slowly become formalized over time and was *the* major pilgrimage festival during the Second Temple period. If possible, Jews from all over would travel to Jerusalem and observe the feast commemorating God's deliverance of Israel from slavery in Egypt. As we discussed in Chapter 6, many of the prophets conceptualized the restoration of Israel as a second exodus; as God delivered His people from Egypt, so He would deliver them from whichever power was currently enslaving them, bringing about the kingdom promised to David in 2 Samuel 7. Many Jews would have sympathized with Ezra 9:36, written in Jerusalem during the Persian period, that although the relatively benevolent Persian empire had allowed the Jews to return home it was far from the great final deliverance promised in Isaiah, Jeremiah, and Ezekiel. God had work to do.

Passover was not what we would call a purely 'religious' holiday. Horsley is entirely correct in stating that "*For the people . . . Passover remained a celebration of their formative liberation. Under Roman imperial rule, Passover became the occasion for peoples' protest of their current subjugation*"; the Romans, aware of the political hopes expressed during passover "*Fear*[ed] *that the celebration by crowds who came in from the villages might get completely out of hand . . .* [and] *Roman governors made a practice of bringing their troops into Jerusalem and posting them on the porticoes of the newly constructed Herodian temple*"[2]. Better safe than sorry. John 11:47-53, which summarized our section on John in the previous chapter, attests to the delicate political nature, and potential for revolutionary chaos, which could erupt during Passover. Since many Jews had placed their messianic hopes in Jesus, the Jewish leaders felt it best to dispose of him, lest his followers start a riot and the Romans level Jerusalem.

All four evangelists will, throughout their Passover narratives, continue to affirm that Jesus is the divinely-appointed son of David bringing about the eschatological kingdom and condemning the wicked leaders of Jerusalem. They will also continue to develop the nature of Jesus's messianic identity; expectations of power and violence will be subverted and replaced with a Roman cross and an empty tomb. Jesus is Christ, but not like anyone expected. The themes of prophecy, messianic christology, kingdom, and eschatology all reach their summit in Jerusalem. The great act of deliverance occurs, ushering in the kingdom, and as a result the world would never be the same. The end is inaugurated and a timer is set for the expiration of what Paul in Galatians 1:4 calls "*this present evil age*". Followers and opponents of Jesus alike will get much, much more than they bargained for. Our story begins on the back of a colt.

---

2. Horsley, *Bow Down*, p. 87

THE TRIUMPHAL ENTRY

All four evangelists record what Christians celebrate on Palm Sunday as 'The Triumphal Entry'. Blomberg humorously describes the ironic inaccuracy of that august title: *"It might better be labeled the "a-triumphal entry." This ragtag band of followers accompanying a Galilean peasant riding a donkey would have looked like a parody of the standard welcome and fanfare for governors and generals astride their white horses with a retinue of soldiers"*[3]. Nothing about his entrance to the city would suggest Jesus is the sort of ruler with whom the ancients were accustomed. Nevertheless, Blomberg qualifies his description of the "a-triumphal entry": *"Still, Jesus is making a deliberate messianic claim"*. In fact, the narrative itself testifies to the unique nature of Jesus's messianic identity.

The Synoptic evangelists follow each other closely.[4] Jesus arrives near the villages of Bethphage and Bethany, close to Jerusalem, and directs his disciples to enter one of the cities (Mark and Luke are ambiguous; Matthew seems to suggest Jesus was in Bethphage and sent his followers to Bethany[5]) in search of a colt on which he could ride into Jerusalem. If anyone starts asking questions questions, Jesus instructs his disciples to tell them the *"Lord has need of it"*[6]. In all three Synoptics this happens exactly as Jesus predicted. Central to each narrative is the idea that Jesus is in complete control of his fate; even in death, Jesus is the one directing events. Jesus chooses to ride into Jerusalem on a colt, simultaneously a prophetic act and an allusion to Zechariah 9:9. In that passage, Zechariah announces that God's king will return to Israel humbly, riding on a colt, and deliver Jerusalem from the hands of their enemies, after which Zechariah 9:10 claims *"And He will speak peace to the nations; And His dominion will be from sea to sea, And from the Euphrates River to the ends of the earth"*. This initiates another section in Zechariah about the restoration of Judah. By traveling to the city on a colt, Jesus is declaring that he is the coming king who will rescue Israel, bring peace to the nations, and rule the entire world. Mark and Luke allude to this passage, while Matthew 21:5 quotes it directly.

While the evangelists have creatively incorporated Old Testament passages and themes into the gospels from the very beginning, appeals to Scripture both implicit and explicit will become even more prominent from the Triumphal Entry to the end of the gospels. While some scholars have contended that these narratives

---

3. Blomberg, *Gospels*, p. 366

4. Mark 11:1-10, Matthew 21:1-9, Luke 19:28-40

5. See Moloney, *Mark*, p. 217

6. Mark 11:3

are little more than creative amalgamations of Old Testament interpretation, many scholars have more persuasively argued that the historical events surrounding the final week of Jesus's life influenced early Christian readings of the Jewish Scriptures, which were woven into the traditions that became the written gospels.[7] Joel Green explains how this works: "*In the process of working out the significance of Jesus' death in a narrative context, early Christians employed the OT* [Old Testament] *at a number of levels. In some cases they incorporated direct citations of OT materials into the passion story . . . In other instances allusions to OT texts were woven into the narrative material*"[8]. While Green is specifically referencing the passion narratives, this methodological use of the Old Testament is employed to a greater degree by the evangelists starting with the Triumphal Entry, as Jesus's use of the colt attests.

As Jesus sits atop a colt, headed into Jerusalem, "*many spread their coats in the road, and others spread leafy branches which they had cut from the fields*"[9]. In Mark 11:9-10 and parallels[10] the crowd sings from Psalm 118:26 and acclaims Jesus as king: "*Blessed is He who comes in the name of the Lord; Blessed is the coming kingdom of our father David*". James Crossley perceptively notes that the mention of 'leafy branches' which had been cut in the field implies that those following Jesus were agricultural workers, not anyone from the Jewish elite, consistent with both Jesus' anti-establishment ministry and popular discontent with the Jerusalem establishment. The Maccabees were also celebrated with branches and hymns after delivering the temple from Antiochus, which is probably what the audience expected Jesus to do upon entering the city.[11] The use of Psalm 118 is strategic; this passage is frequently cited in the New Testament, and in context the Psalm describes the establishment of the Davidic king. By applying this Psalm to Jesus, the evangelists (and the crowds they record) are hailing Jesus as the rightful king. It also serves as a dire warning to those who oppose Jesus: they are on the wrong side of God's plans.[12]

By the time Jesus darkens the gates of Jerusalem he has been hailed as king, symbolically associated with the restoration of Israel and the great deliverance for which many Jews hoped, and deliberately evoked the prophet Zechariah. N.T. Wright appreciates the symbolism: "*Within his own time and culture, his riding on*

---

7. Green, Joel. 2024. "*Passion Narrative*". In *Dictionary of Jesus and the Gospels*, 2nd ed. edited by Green, Joel. InterVarsity Press. p. 664

8. Green, *Passion Narrative*, p. 665

9. Mark 11:8

10. Matthew 21:9, Luke 19:38, John 12:13

11. Crossley and Myles, *Class Conflict*, p. 199

12. Jipp, *Messianic Theology*, p. 97

a donkey over the Mount of Olives, across Kidron, and up to the Temple mount spoke more powerfully than words could have done of a royal claim . . . The so-called 'triumphal entry' was thus clearly messianic"[13]. All of the themes so far analyzed in the gospels blend together as Jesus enters Jerusalem. These themes will hang over the rest of the evangelist's narratives. Jesus is the kingdom-bringing Christ, utilizing prophetic symbolism to enact and explain the eschatological moment which is taking place through his ministry. It is impossible to understate how significant the messianic identity of Jesus as king of both Israel and the world is to the evangelists.

The Triumphal Entry is as much a celebration of the coming king as it is a dark omen of what he will endure at the hands of Jerusalem's political authorities. The evangelists know Jesus is going to be rejected and die; part of the point, as Jipp recognizes, of quoting Psalm 118 is the insinuated *judgment* against those who refuse to accept Israel's king. Jesus doesn't come to Jerusalem only to save, he comes to judge. A passage unique to Luke, occurring just after he narrates the Triumphal Entry, envisages the consequences Jerusalem will face for rejecting Jesus. Luke 19:41-44 reads *"When [Jesus] approached Jerusalem, He saw the city and wept over it, saying, "If you had known in this day, even you, the things which make for peace! But now they have been hidden from your eyes. For the days will come upon you when your enemies will throw up a barricade against you, and surround you and hem you in on every side, and they will level you to the found and your children within you, and they will not leave in you one stone upon the other, because you did not recognize the time of your visitation"*. This passage, which could have been lifted directly out of Jeremiah or Ezekiel, is a lamentation over the fate of Jerusalem. The tax collectors and sinners who have repented and believed in Jesus have risen. The Jerusalem establishment who rejects Jesus is about to fall. Jesus issues one final warning.

Jesus Condemns the Temple

Mark is the only evangelist who places Jesus' confrontation with the temple authorities a day after he arrives in Jerusalem. In Matthew and Luke, the showdown begins right after Jesus enters the city. In Mark 11:11, Jesus visits the temple before retreating to Bethany with the twelve. Mark sandwiches his presentation of the temple cleansing between a symbolically-charged story about a fig tree. In Mark 11:12-14, Jesus is walking with his disciples from Bethany to Jerusalem when he wanders upon a fig tree. Hungry, he checked to see if the tree had figs. Since it wasn't in season, there was no fruit for Jesus to eat. In front of his disciples Jesus curses the tree, saying in 11:14 *"May no one ever eat fruit from you again!"*. In Mark

---

13. Wright, *Victory*, pp. 490-491

11:19-26, Jesus leaves the temple. The next morning Jesus passed the fig tree with his disciples, which had withered from the roots up. Peter points this out to Jesus, who responds by saying *"whoever says to this mountain, 'Be taken up and cast into the sea,' and does not doubt in his heart, but believes that what he says is going to happen, it will be granted to him"*[14]. Mark ends the tradition with a statement about prayer and forgiveness.

The fig tree, rather obviously, stands as a symbol of the temple in Jerusalem and the Jewish leaders who oppose Jesus.[15] Because the temple establishment, the local political authorities delegated power under the Roman provincial system, have declined to heed Jesus's (and John the Baptist's!) announcement of the kingdom, they, like the fig tree, will be destroyed, never again bearing fruit.[16] When Jesus tells his disciples that *"this mountain"* could be cast in the sea, he wasn't issuing a timeless theology on the efficacy of prayer. Instead, as Wright observes, *"the fact that someone speaking of 'this mountain' being cast into the sea, in the context of a dramatic action of judgment in the Temple, would inevitably be heard to refer to Mount Zion"*[17]. Mark frames the temple cleansing with a symbolic judgment of the temple and the political authorities it represents. Matthew moves this entire event to the end of his temple incident; in Matthew 21:18-27 Jesus curses the fig tree and instructs his disciples on the same morning. Luke doesn't record this event at all, but includes a unique parable in Luke 13:6-9 regarding a cursed fig tree which is also directed at Jesus's opponents. The cleansing of the temple is a powerful symbol of judgment on the rich and powerful establishment seeking to kill Jesus.

Mark's account of the temple cleansing is found in 11:15-18: *"Then they came to Jerusalem. And He entered the temple area and began to drive out those who were selling and buying on the temple grounds, and He overturned the tables of the money changers and the seats of those who were selling doves; and He would not allow anyone to carry merchandise through the temple grounds. And He began to teach and say to them, "Is it not written, 'My house shall be called a house of prayer for all the nations'? But you have made it a Robber's Den." The chief priests and the scribes heard this and began seeking how to destroy Him; for they were afraid of HIm, for the whole crowd was astonished at His teaching"*. The scene can be divided into two parts, Jesus's actions and his corresponding words.

---

14. Mark 11:23

15. Moloney, *Mark*, p. 227; his statement that the fig tree represents *'Israel and its temple'* is overstated; Jesus is not rejecting *Israel* but the leaders of Jerusalem.

16. Jipp, *Messianic Theology*, p. 83

17. Wright, *Victory*, pp. 334-335

Precisely what Jesus intended to do, and why he intended to do it, when he stopped the money changers, flipped over the tables of those selling doves, and refused to allow anyone carrying merchandise through the temple is hotly debated among scholars. I find Crossley and Myles' account plausible; they argue that many Jews, the same agriculturalists who would have cut down leafy branches and thrown them on the road before Jesus, viewed the temple as a center of political and economic oppression. The priestly class and the Sanhedrin were legitimized in part by their proximity to the temple. Moneychangers were seen as exploitative, charging high prices for sacrifices and accepting payments in Tyrian Shekels, which featured an image of a pagan god.[18] Jesus quotes both Isaiah 56:7 and Jeremiah 7:11 as an indictment against the temple. In Isaiah 56:7, God restores Israel and the nations flock to Jerusalem, worshiping Israel's God and offering Him prayer. This is how the temple was *supposed* to function. Instead, Jesus argues that the temple and the Jerusalem authorities mirror Jeremiah 7:11, a prophetic oracle against the temple and political establishment of Jeremiah's time, eventually destroyed by the Babylonians.

Whatever we make of the details, Jesus is certainly condemning the temple and those who run it. James Dunn's analysis is prescient: "*the act could hardly have been understood by the priestly authorities as other than critical of the Temple in its present form and operation . . . the Temple was the principal focus for economic and political power as well as for religious power. An act seen as critically or prophetically subversive of the priestly power . . . would provide sufficient excuse . . . to dictate Jesus' removal from the scene*"[19]. The characteristic Jesus is portrayed as being in constant conflict with the authorities and the temple cleansing is yet another powerful example of that theme in the Jesus tradition. As we will soon see, all three Synoptic evangelists follow this scene with a long block of triple-tradition material which presents Jesus debating representatives from every authority group in Jerusalem. Jesus's cleansing of the temple serves the narrative function of preparing the audience for the showdown about to occur. Matthew and Luke progressively truncate Mark's story, omitting minor details, but both retain the quotation of Isaiah 56:7 and Jeremiah 7:11. All three evangelists are making the same point: the temple authorities are corrupt and will not escape the judgment of God.

Less pronounced in the temple cleansing tradition is a direct affirmation of Jesus's messianic status. Even though there are no direct christological claims made by the evangelists, every conflict with the Jewish authorities implies the unique identity of Jesus. It is because Jesus is both prophet and Messiah that he possesses a

---

18. Crossley and Myles, *Class Conflict*, pp. 201-207

19. Dunn, *Remembered*, pp. 638-639

unique right to criticize and disrupt the temple establishment. Following straight on the heels of his triumphal entry into Jerusalem, the temple cleansing is another affirmation of Jesus as God's Christ. Even if the majority of his followers would have been rural agriculturalists, anyone observing Jesus disrupt the temple services would no doubt ponder his identity. I am in complete agreement with Dunn: "*it is hard to doubt that among the reverberations set off by Jesus' action in the Temple would be the question, 'Could this be the expected Davidic messiah?'*"[20]. Given the volatile political atmosphere which filled Jerusalem during the Passover, it would be a perfectly natural question for people to ask.

John's version of the temple cleansing is located in John 2:13-22, placed chronologically at the beginning of Jesus's ministry instead of near the end. The parallels between John and the Synoptics are too profound to conclude that John is incorporating a separate tradition, and scholars have put forth various proposals to explain why John would move this tradition to the front of his gospel. Many scholars argue it was rearranged for rhetorical purposes, to emphasise particular features of Johannine interpretation, while others suggest Jesus did in fact cleanse the temple twice.[21] Admittedly I remain agnostic on the question. Either way, John has reworked the synoptic tradition while retaining its most important feature, the question of Jesus's authority. His opponents specifically ask him about it in 2:18: "*What signs do You show us as your authority for doing these things?*". John's sole quotation of Scripture occurs in the previous verse and cites Psalm 69:9 in which the Psalmist expresses admiration for the temple, which John employs to emphasize Jesus's legitimate authority. This is a textbook example of *oppositio in imitando* reflective of the Jesus tradition's oral character. John's account differs in style, not substance.

Mark and Luke conclude the section by explaining how the chief priests, scribes, and, in Luke, "*leading men*" seek to kill Jesus, but cannot because of his popularity.[22] All of these figures hold real political power, even if under the watchful eye of Rome, and are not antagonistic towards Jesus because of a slight religious disagreement. They view Jesus's critique of the temple as an imminent threat to their power and authority, which is exactly how the evangelists framed the narrative. Luke 19:47 adds the Greek phrase *hoi protoi*, literally 'the leaders' (translated "*leading men*" in the NASB); Stein suggests "*This looks like an official delegation representing the leadership of Israel, i.e. the Sanhedrin*"[23], and considering

---

20. Dunn, *Remembered*, p. 640

21. Blomberg, *Jesus*, p. 263

22. Mark 11:18-19, Luke 19:47-48

23. Stein, *Luke*, p. 487

how the extended set of traditions which will follow in both Mark and Luke (and in Matthew as well) portray Jesus in conflict with various Jewish leaders, Stein is likely correct. By condemning the temple, Jesus has struck yet another nerve with the political elite. There is nothing they can do at present, however, because the people are fascinated with Jesus's teaching. They needed to devise a plan to rid themselves of the annoying prophet with illegitimate messianic pretensions. Jesus will continue to be a thorn in their side despite various attempts to publicly undermine his authority. This conflict, much of which is included in an extended set of triple-tradition material, will dominate the Synoptic accounts of Jesus's final Passover week and set the stage for one last great condemnation of the temple, the Last Supper, his arrests and trials, and his crucifixion. We turn to the culmination of Jesus's conflict with the Jewish authorities.

By What Authority Are You Doing These Things?

The final fight between Jesus and the Jewish authorities before his arrest in Gethsemane includes some of the most vicious denunciations of the establishment in the Jesus tradition. All three of the Synoptic gospels have already prepared their audiences for this showdown; Jesus, the eschatological prophet and Messiah versus the Jewish political elites who want to kill him. Coincidently, all three Synoptics are in close alignment when recounting these traditions, meaning that the traditions were likely transmitted and interpreted as a unit. In the middle of these traditions we find the ever-perplexing statement *"render unto Caesar"*, a passage which has precipitated no shortage of debate and dissension between Christians in search of a Jesus who endorses their preferred political theories.

This statement, along with many other less famous (though no less important) declarations, occur within the larger context of this narrative unit which centers on authority. Is Jesus the one in charge, or the Jewish elite? Since Matthew and Luke both preserve Mark's narrative structure, I will lead with his gospel and comment only on significant redactional differences in the other two. There are several different traditions contained within this lengthy unit on authority, each of which will be addressed in turn and showing how they contribute to the debate about who in Jerusalem is truly deserving of honor and power.

Jesus, John, and Authority

This great conflict between Jesus and the authorities starts with a tradition recorded in Mark 11:27-33, Matthew 21:23-27, and Luke 20:1-8. Jesus is teaching in the temple (Luke 20:1 reads *"preaching the gospel"*) and is approached by the chief priests, scribes, and elders. Remembering that these are figures who hold real political power and influence, they ask Jesus a question which serves as an introduction to the following material: "*By what authority are You doing these things, or who gave You this authority to do these things?*"[24]. In Mark 1:21 the people of Capernaum were "*amazed at His teaching; for He was teaching them as one having authority and not as the scribes*". After spending nearly his entire gospel illustrating the basis of Jesus' authority, Mark has come full circle. Jesus is going to prove why he possesses authority and his opponents do not. In typical prophetic fashion Jesus refuses to answer their question directly. He instead asks them if John's baptism was from heaven, or from men. In other words, did John have divine authority to baptize? The elites are rightfully "*afraid of the people*", the crowd listening to Jesus teach and now witnessing the conflict firsthand, "*for everyone considered John to have been a real prophet*"[25]. Trapped, the elites feign ignorance. Mark 11:33 records the exchange: "*Answering Jesus, they said, "We no not know." And Jesus said to them, "Nor will I tell you by what authority I do these things.""*".

Jesus has backed his opponents into an impossible corner. The crowds believed that John was a real prophet whose prophetic ministry of baptism bore eschatological significance. It is a brilliant move on the part of Jesus, one of many recounted in the material which follows. Moloney explains the predicament of the elders: "*The dilemma shows that the leaders of Israel place their concern in their own reputation and status. They are unable to explain why they did not accept John's baptism, and they are unwilling to be badly regarded*"[26]. Jesus is concerned with truth, his opponents with themselves, their power, and their prestige. On its own, this passage appears as if Jesus is playing defense. He could have left the conversation there and resumed teaching the throngs of people clinging to his every word. But Jesus takes the opportunity to go on the defensive. From a literary standpoint, everything else we discuss in this section is impacted by this initial question regarding Jesus' authority. The evangelists will demonstrate, one humiliating story after another, why the so-called leaders of Israel are frauds who have rejected the eschatological moment.

Matthew follows this tradition with a parable unique to his gospel. In Matthew 21:28-32, Jesus tells a story of a man with two sons who owns a vineyard. He instructs one son to go and work in the vineyard. Initially the first son refuses, informing his father he is not interested in working. Later, however, the son changes his mind and tends his father's vineyard. The father asks a second son to go and

---

24. Mark 11:28

25. Mark 11:32

26. Moloney, *Mark*, p. 231

work in the fields; this time, however, the son promises his father he will work but never completes the job. Jesus asks his opponents which son actually fulfilled the will of the father, and they concede it was the first. Matthew provides the punchline: *"Jesus said to them, "Truly I say to you that the tax collectors and prostitutes will get into the kingdom of God before you. For John came to you in the way of righteousness and you did not believe him; but the tax collectors and prostitutes did believe him; and you, seeing this, did not even feel remorse afterward so as to believe him"*[27]. This parable works on two levels; it chastises Jesus's opponents for not believing in John, painting them as the second son who falsely promised to labor, and prepares the reader for yet another parable about a vineyard which predicts that the Jewish elite will not remain in power for long.

The Wicked Tenants

In Mark 12:1-12, Matthew 21:35-46, and Luke 20:9-19, Jesus goes on the offensive. After successfully deflecting his opponent's question about authority, he issues a challenge to them in front of the watching crowds. Jesus delivers a parable often titled 'The Wicked Tenants'. This parable is a creative reworking of Isaiah 5:1-7 and Psalm 80, both of which describe unfaithful Israel as a vineyard which God destroys on account of their wickedness. Jesus appropriates this analogy and reworks it into a parable directed at the Jewish authorities. A man plants a vineyard, lends it out to tenants, and then travels to a distant town. Desiring the fruits of his harvest, the vineyard owner sends several servants to collect the produce. The tenants which occupy his vineyard ignore his request, beating, stoning, and even killing some of his servants. In frustration the vineyard owner sends his own son, whom the tenants kill under the irrational illusion that the son's death would somehow enable them to acquire his inheritance. The owner returns, slaughters the tenants, and rents out his vineyard to others. Jesus concludes his parable with a reference to Psalm 118, quoted in Jesus' triumphal procession. This time Jesus recites verses 22-23: *"The stone which the builders rejected, this became the chief cornerstone; this came about from the Lord, and it is marvelous in our eyes"*. All three evangelists comment that the Jewish leaders understood Jesus directed the parable at them; Matthew 21:43 openly states *"the kingdom of God will be taken away from you and given to a people, producing the fruit of it"*. An axe has been laid at the foot of the tree. The leaders desperately wanted to kill Jesus but were unable to arrest him because they feared the crowds, with Matthew 21:4 adding that the people *"considered Him to be a prophet"*.

---

27. Matthew 21:31-32

Jesus directs this attack at the faithless leaders in the temple precinct, foretelling the judgment that is about to befall them. By appropriating imagery from the Jewish Scriptures related to past judgment on Israel's ruling class, Jesus directs his ire towards those who believe they have a right to rule God's people.[28] According to Jesus, their authority is entirely illegitimate. Jesus's words are not directed at 'Judaism' or 'Jewish people' in general, contrary to a long and unfortunate tradition of this parable's reception in christianity.[29] Consistent with Dunn's analysis of Jewish factionalism, Jesus is proclaiming, in line with the historic prophets of Israel, that the leaders who oppose him have rejected God's commands and will soon be punished. Jesus is Jewish, his disciples are Jewish, and his audience is Jewish. There is no notion of replacement theology or supersessionism in this text; instead, Jesus is making a claim against the rulers and their administration of the temple. Based on their response to Jesus, he lands the punch.

The citation from Psalm 118:22-23 is telling. Psalm 118 was already referenced during the triumphal entry and carried eschatological and messianic overtones. Jesus reworks it to level an attack against his opponents, as Bock explains succinctly: "*now the tables of that psalm's meaning are turned on the leadership. In its original setting, the psalm would have depicted the Gentiles' rejection of the king of Israel in battle, a king who now returns victorious and is welcomed by the nation. But now, tragically, it is the leaders of Israel who are the rejectors*"[30]. Jesus is challenging, to the very core, the Jewish people's (self)appointed political leaders, turning their own Scriptures against them, and revealing they will be judged for rejecting the arrival of God's kingdom. There is no turning back. judgment is imminent, and the Jerusalem establishment has run out of time to repent and change their ways. Wright suggests the use of Psalm 118 implies vindication; just as the owner destroys the wicked tenants for murdering his son, there will be a swift judgment against those who kill Jesus.

Matthew 22:1-14 inserts another parable into the sequence also found in Luke. Typical for Lukan redaction of Matthew, Luke locates the parable earlier in his gospel, in Luke 14:15-24. Contextual variation notwithstanding, the parables have an identical function: demonstrating that Israel's leaders are facing divine judgment. Luke softens the rough edges of Matthew's parable, but the violent nature of Matthew's version flows naturally from the preceding material. A king hosts a wedding ceremony for his son and sends out his slaves, who invite all in the

---

28. Bock, *Jesus*, p. 325

29. See, for example, Kensky, Meira. 2025. "*Gospel of Luke*". In *Judeophobia and the New Testament*, edited by Rollens, Sarah, Eric Vanden Eykel, and Meredith Warren. Eerdmans. pp. 132-134

30. Bock, *Jesus*, p. 327

kingdom to attend. Many invitees decline and make excuses, while others murder the king's slaves. The king's response echoes the parable of the tenants: *"the king was enraged, and he sent his armies and destroyed those murderers and set their city on fire"*[31]. The king sends more slaves out into the streets, gathering both evil and good, inviting them all to the feast. As the king greets those attending the feast, he sees a man wearing improper attire and throws him out into the streets. Matthew 22:14, echoing Matthew 7:13-14, concludes the parable: *"For many are called, but few are chosen"*.

After this, representatives of various powerful interest groups within the Jewish elite attempt to trap Jesus into making self-condemning comments before the crowds. The Synoptics are in near lockstep. First, the Pharisees and Herodians ask Jesus a question about the payment of Roman tribute taxes. The Sadducees will then press Jesus on the doctrine of resurrection. Mark and Matthew subsequently narrate a challenge posed by a lawyer which Luke includes at an earlier point in his gospel. This tradition is followed in all three Synoptics by a set of cryptic statements regarding the relationship between Jesus and David along with a withering condemnation of the scribes and Pharisees. Matthew extends his condemnation with unique material while Mark and Luke incorporate a tradition about a poor woman who serves as a foil for the Jerusalem establishment. All of these traditions are simply carrying on the main theme which has already been established in this long section of material: Jesus is the divinely-appointed authority while the Jewish elites are not. None of the material is comprehensible apart from the narratival intention of this long string of triple tradition. With this contextual boundary marker in place, we now examine perhaps the most controversial political statement in the New Testament outside of Romans 13:1-7.

Render Unto Caesar

During his discussion of the infamous 'render unto Caesar' passage, Christopher Bryan wisely remarks *"Only a fool would claim to be sure about the meaning of a passage that has puzzled exegetes for centuries"*[32]. Indeed. Pretensions to certitude are woefully naive and guarantee misinterpretation. I do maintain, in line with every interpreter who has attempted to grapple with this passage before me, that we can deduce at least some reasonable conclusions about the function of Jesus's exchange and, just as significantly, what Jesus was *not* attempting to communicate when

---

31. Matthew 22:7

32. Bryan, Christopher. 2005. *Render Unto Caesar*. Oxford University Press. p. 44

he enjoins the Pharisees and Herodians to 'render unto Caesar'. In the following paragraphs, I will aim to do both.

Mark 12:13-17, Matthew 22:15-22, and Luke 20:20-26, all of which follow the Parable of the Tenants, narrate the Pharisees and Herodians (Luke 20:20 calls them "*spies*") approaching Jesus with the stated purpose of, as Mark 12:13 puts it, "*trap*[ping] *Him in a statement*". Luke elaborates on what is implied in Mark and Matthew, commenting that the Pharisees and Herodians were sent "*in order that they might catch Him in some statement, so that they could deliver Him to the rule and the authority of the governor*"[33]. Mark records the short exchange: "*They came and said to Him, "Teacher, we know that You are truthful and defer to no one; for You are not partial to any, but teach the way of God in truth. Is it lawful to pay a poll-tax to Caesar, or not? Shall we pay or shall we not pay?" But He, knowing their hypocrisy, said to them, "Why are you testing Me? Bring Me a denarius to look at." They brought one. And He said to them "Whose likeness and inscription is this?" And they said to Him, "Caesar's." And Jesus said to them, "Render to Caesar the things that are Caesar's and to God the things that are God's" And they were amazed at Him*". As with the Pharisees initial question about Jesus's authority, he successfully evades their trap by defeating them at their own game.

As a consequence of the Enlightenment modern Westerners have adopted a rhetorical commitment to the concept of a separation between 'church and state'. While the church-state dichotomy can trace its lineage back to antiquity, contemporary thinkers routinely presume that the church naturally inhabits one sphere of influence while ceding to the state another. Jesus's response to his opponents has been mapped onto that supposed dichotomy, providing biblical legitimacy for an intellectually ubiquitous modern concept. Preston Sprinkle's commentary is on target: "*This scene appears to support a kind of "God and country" ideology, where allegiance to Caesar can coexist alongside one's allegiance to God*"[34]. Various attempts have been made by interpreters on the political left and right to incorporate this passage within their preferred political frameworks. Both Schweitzer and Cadbury's warnings about the dangers of forcing Jesus into a modern paradigm have gone unheeded, and the results of ideologically-driven exegesis have produced modern applications which are often directly at odds with the intended purpose of the text. In order to do the tradition justice, it must be interpreted within its literary and historical context.

Jesus's antagonists are the Pharisees and Herodians. I recall a (now embarrassing) moment in college when, during a lecture on this passage, my professor, Dr.

---

33. Luke 20:20

34. Sprinkle, Preston. 2024. *Exiles*. David C Cook. p. 89

Jon Weatherly, asked the class if anyone wanted to guess why the evangelists specify both the Pharisees and Herodians as Jesus's sparring partners in this tradition. I raised my hand and eagerly answered that the two parties represented the 'religious' and 'political' authorities. He politely accepted my answer as a possibility. My answer, of course, stemmed from a confusion about political and economic categories and my own flawed assumption that the ancients neatly divided the world into separate spheres of religion and politics. The Pharisees and Herodians did not represent the post-enlightenment division between 'religion' and 'politics'. Both groups possessed real political power. The Pharisees were primarily concerned about maintaining ritual purity and were dissatisfied with Roman rule. The Herodians, on the other hand, represented Rome's client king in Galilee, Herod Antipas, and were, for obvious reasons, more positively inclined to Roman rule. The two groups competed for influence and prestige. While the Pharisees and Herodians were not natural allies, Mark 3:6 had already established a common interest between the two groups: a desire to eliminate Jesus.[35] Any answer to their question would naturally offend one of the two parties and possibly implicate himself in a criminally punishable statement. Jesus is forced to choose between angering the Jewish crowds or running afoul of the Roman authorities. It is a brilliant tactic on the part of two groups who want Jesus dead.

The Pharisees and Herodians do not ask Jesus about taxation in general, but about a specific tax, the *kensos*, a poll tax which was paid to Rome known as the *tributum capitis*, was discussed above as a symbol of Roman imperial rule and a mechanism for diverting wealth from rural provincials to politically-connected urban aristocrats. The tribute was deeply offensive to Jewish sensibilities[36], especially Jews longing for independence, and had an interesting history which Jesus's opponents were exploiting. In 6 CE a man from Galilee named Judas recruited a mercenary army to rebel against Rome over the same tribute tax, resulting in his death and the elimination of his army.[37] When Peter is dragged before the Sanhedrin in Acts, a Pharisee named Gamaliel references this event: "*Judas of Galilee rose up in the days of the census and drew away some people after him; he too perished, and all those who followed him were scattered*"[38]. Why would the Pharisees and Herodians inquire about this particular tax? If Jesus says Jews should pay it, the crowd turns against him as a supporter of Roman imperialism. If Jesus says they shouldn't, the Herodians paint him as another revolutionary like Judas the Galilean who must

---

35. Moloney, *Mark*, p. 235

36. Bryan, *Render to Caesar*, p. 44

37. Moloney, *Mark*, pp. 235-236

38. Acts 5:37

be put down before he mounts a violent rebellion. Before we draw any modern principles from this passage, it must be recognized that the question posed to Jesus is not about taxation in general but about this *specific, politically-charged tax* which was designed to trap Jesus in his words.

Of significance is the Greek behind the English word *"pay"*, which the Pharisees and Herodians use three times in reference to the tribute tax. In all three cases they employ cognates of the Greek term *didomi*, *"a word that refers to "giving" in the most general terms and that can be used in a wide variety of contexts and situations, including "giving" as "an expression of generosity"*[39]. Roman imperial propaganda heavily utilized the notion that Caesars were the ultimate charitable benefactors, generosity which their client subjects must reciprocate with gold and honor. Why not pay the tax in honor of Roman rule? Jesus is not amused; Mark 12:15 recounts that Jesus knows his opponents are not being sincere (he uses the word *"hypocrisy"*) and asks them to bring him a denarius, the common Roman silver coin used to pay this tax. The Pharisees and Herodians present a denarius to Jesus. He asks them whose likeness and inscription is on the coin; visible to all, there is only one correct answer: *"Caesar"*. This is a massive tactical mistake. Jesus does not have a Roman coin with an image of Caesar in his possession, but his opponents do. As they stand in the temple before the watching crowd of Jewish pilgrims who came to Jerusalem in celebration of Exodus (with all its eschatological significance of a coming deliverance), the opponents of Jesus, Pharisee and Herodian alike, are carrying a coin with the image of a pagan emperor. This *"places the Pharisees and the Herodians at a disadvantage: they should not have been carrying coins bearing effigies in the temple precincts. Unlike the widely used copper coins of Palestine, the denarius bore the image and inscription of the emperor"*[40]. Seeking to trap Jesus, Jesus has turned the tables and ensnared his opponents: *"Jesus' questioners were thus themselves already heavily compromised by possessing such an object"*[41]. The crowd might now rightly accuse the Pharisees and Herodians of idolatry.

Jesus has the upper hand. His inquiry about the *"likeness and inscription"* of the coin did more than play on Jewish sensitivities to idolatry; in antiquity a ruler's coinage was considered his property. Love Caesar or hate him, the coin, in the ancient mind, belonged to the man whose face was minted on it. While the Pharisees and Herodians pressed Jesus about giving the tax with the Greek word *didomi*, a general term for giving, Jesus' response is more direct. Bryan explains: *"Jesus' statement is, actually, more forceful than his questioners required, since he has*

---

39. Bryan, *Render to Caesar*, p. 44
40. Moloney, *Mark*, p. 236
41. Wright, *Victory*, p. 503

exchanged the rather general word for payment (didomi) that they used for a much more precise word, apodidomi—a word that speaks of payment as "a contractual or other obligation, " or restoration "to an original possessor." The implication is, "Pay up what you owe! Give back to the Emperor what is his!"[42] Jesus views the tribute tax, imposed by Caesar and paid with coins which in the mind of ancients belong to him, as an obligation. This is precisely in line with the tradition established by Jeremiah 29:7 in which Jews are obligated to make peace with the ruling powers under the eschatological hope God will come back, destroy them, and restore His people. The coin is Caesar's, and he happens to represent the current instantiation of Babylon. Return what belongs to him.

The second half of Jesus' statement, receiving far less attention than it deserves, is "[give] *to God the things that are God's*". The statement is phrased as an analogy; if Caesar owns the coin, and it belongs to him, then the Jews are obligated to return it. But what, exactly, is owned by God? From the Jewish perspective, everything! God is the creator of the entire universe, and, at the consummation of the eschatological kingdom now inaugurated through the Davidic king Jesus, the nations would finally recognize Him as the one true God. Jesus is ushering in the restoration, and the Herodians and Pharisees are missing it, as the entire narrative of conflict up to this point has made abundantly clear. Jesus also plays on the idea of "image": "*The basis on which he has said that something is owed to Caesar is that it bears Caesar's image. What then bears God's image, so that it should be owed to God? No Jew, Pharisee, or even Herodian could fail to know the answer to that. They themselves bore God's "image" (Gen. 1.26). They owed a mere head-tax to Caesar, because the coinage was Caesar's. But they owed themselves to God, because they belonged to God . . . [Jesus] challenge[s] them with an altogether deeper and more dangerous question of his own, about their relationship to God*"[43]. And this is precisely what the Jewish elite have refused to do. They had rejected John's proclamation of the imminent kingdom, and they had rejected Jesus as the rightful king of Israel. Far from giving themselves to God, as the tax collectors, prostitutes, and others had, they were actively opposing His reign. The wicked tenants would be purged from the vineyard and the stone they rejected was becoming the cornerstone. Instead of conforming to the image of God, Jesus's opponents carried the image of Caesar right in their pockets, and inside of the temple no less! Jesus has roundly defeated the Pharisees and Herodians, demonstrating that he is in charge while the Jewish elites are not.

---

42. Bryan, *Render to Caesar*, p. 45

43. Bryan, *Render to Caesar*, pp. 45-46

The narratival context is firmly established: this is another example of Jesus flexing his authority against the political establishment, and doing so in a way that evokes the venerable prophetic tradition of Israel's past. It proves that the Pharisees and Herodians have not been faithfully managing God's vineyard and will be removed. Historically, Jesus is able to leverage a question regarding an extremely unpopular tax that represented Roman imperialism and against which Judas the Galilean waged a violent revolt less than thirty years earlier. Jesus' opponents possess a blasphemous coin which ought to be returned to its owner, and Jesus suggests quite forcefully, in front of a large audience, that the Pharisees and Herodians are blaspheming God. This, and this alone, is the purpose of the 'render unto Caesar' tradition in its triple tradition sequence.

There are, of course, principles which can be deduced from this passage, all of which are entirely congruent with the wider Synoptic witness. This passage, despite centuries of abuse and neglect, does not offer us a timeless theology of government, nor does it legitimize taxation as an inevitable and morally justifiable practice. Neither of these popular misinterpretations of this passage make sense of the historical details or its narrative placement. Bock is wrong, then, when he suggests that the tradition includes *"the recognition of different spheres of given relationship and responsibility. Both God and the state need to be properly honored"*[44]. The gospels have, up to this point, been exceptionally unambiguous about the nature of Jesus's Davidic identity, and even a cursory reading of Old Testament texts such as 2 Samuel 7, Psalm 2, and Isaiah 11 reveal how the coming king will rule over all creation. The kingdom of God leaves no room for the kingdoms of men, and Jesus, far from legitimizing the Roman empire, makes the same essential point as Jeremiah 29:7. Get along with empire if you can. Sprinkle correctly recognizes that *"Submitting to the empire does not mean celebrating the empire. It just means that citizens of God's empire recognize an authority much higher and more powerful than the self-proclaimed rulers of the earth"*[45]. Caesar owns the coins. For now. Give them back to him if he asks. But giving to God what belongs to God requires repenting and believing the gospel, the good news that His kingdom is breaking in through the work of Jesus Christ. The end has already begun, and as Jeremiah concludes with an oracle of Babylon's destruction, God's kingdom will actualize it.

This also doesn't mean Jesus is ignoring or has forgotten the oppressive nature of Roman taxation and the local rulers, be it the Herods or the Jerusalem establishment, who wield political power for their own personal gain. As we have seen time and again from the work of Horsley, Oakman, Crossley, and Myles, many rural

---

44. Bock, *Jesus*, p. 329

45. Sprinkle, *Exiles*, p. 91

Galileans followed Jesus because they believed he would deliver them from poverty and deprivation suffered at the hands of the ruling class. Sprinkle perfectly summarizes the nature of taxation in antiquity (and, as I would argue, in modernity as well): "*Taxation benefited the rulers, not the ruled . . .* [they] *were designed to serve the interests of the elite. Taxation was the means by which the rich and powerful maintained their luxurious lifestyle, and it "was required for the maintenance of the Empire's military power and bureaucratic structure." In Jesus' day, taxation was synonymous with exploiting the poor*"[46]. None of this was lost on either Jesus or the watching crowds when he utters the phrase "*render unto Caesar*". His words are obviously not a justification for Roman rule or the oppressive taxation which accompanied it any more than Jeremiah's advice to "*seek the welfare of the city*" was a defense of Babylonian rule. Jesus's statements must be understood in light of Jewish eschatology, which absolutely asserts that no matter how bad it might be in the present God is going to ultimately make it right in the end.

Jesus debates the Pharisees and the Herodians likely knowing he will be killed before the end of the week. All throughout his ministry Jesus has called his followers to renounce power, privilege, and wealth. He has instructed them to be peacemakers, show grace and mercy, take care of those in need, and choose love over violence. His own shocking death, of which he alone understands the significance, will be the epitome of true power. The Messiah, the authentic son of David, must die on a Roman cross. His disciples could not yet understand the logic of christological crucifixion. It was a radical revision of everything they knew about human power and authority. But Jesus was unequivocal. Those who follow him must never exercise gentile-ish power, lording it over their subjects. The greatest in the kingdom of God becomes a slave to all. The first will be last, and the last first.

Jesus's teaching takes violent revolution as an option off the table. Judas the Galilean had tried and failed. The Maccabean revolt, for all its initial success, resulted in a much-compromised Hasmonean dynasty which loved to play imperial politics. The tradition of violent zeal which began with Phinehas ends at the threshold of God's kingdom. New wine must not be placed in old wineskins. Jesus is not endorsing Roman imperialism, the Herodian client-kingdom, the Jerusalem establishment, and the policies of taxation and exploitation that accompany them. But he is unwilling to violently overthrow the system. In fact, as Bryan points out, "*the striking fact is that the gospels do not contain so much as one example of a saying of Jesus that attacks the system as a system*"[47]. All of it is evil, and all of it will come to an end. In fact, the inauguration of God's kingdom through the ministry of

---

46. Sprinkle, *Exiles*, pp. 89-91

47. Bryan, *Render to Caesar*, p. 42

Jesus demarcates the decisive beginning of the eschatological moment. Tearing down the system, however, requires violence. Jesus won't have it. People respond to the kingdom by repenting and believing; God takes care of the rest. The gospel of the kingdom is, in that sense, *supra*-political; it transcends any and every human structure of power, dealing with them as present realities which will not survive the future consummation. Jesus and his followers are participating in a kingdom *beyond* what any political power or economic structure has ever accomplished. Jesus is, as the evangelists all unanimously agree, king of the entire world. From this established fact the powers of the age will continue to slip away into increasing irrelevance until God decisively acts to end them once and for all. This is, following the work of Tucker Ferda, 'process eschatology' at its finest. As God builds out His hoped-for but completely unexpected kingdom, followers of Jesus emulate him, even if it entails taking up a cross.

Christians cannot, and indeed must not, use this passage to legitimize their favorite political policies. Returning to our definitions of political and economic categories, this tradition in context absolutely cannot be forced into a system of authoritarian socialism, whether in its conservative or progressive forms. Socialism requires the coercive and oftentimes violent intrusion by third parties into peaceful, voluntary transactions between consenting individuals. All taxation and economic regulations require either violence or the threat of violence to enforce them. Conservatism and progressivism in their contemporary iterations are both predicated on the assumption that technocratic management of society is necessary for constructing a civilization which is oriented towards the 'common good', defined, as always, by the subjective preferences of whoever happens to employ the phrase. Like the Roman empire, maintaining authoritarian political systems always involves the initiation of force. An apology for violence cannot be inferred either from this passage or the Jesus tradition in general. While followers of Jesus must give Caesar what belongs to him (possibly, as Matthew 17:27 suggests, so as not to offend those in power), their primary responsibility is to give to God what rightfully belongs to Him. Meaning everything. It also necessitates emulating Jesus and his commitment to nonviolence, a principle which modern Christians who are enthralled with the nineteenth century concept of technocratic authoritarian socialism struggle to accept. Wide is the path that leads to destruction. Jesus reminds his followers, however, that the harvest is soon coming. There is no use following the path of Judas the Galilean by attempting to separate the wheat from the weeds before harvest time. The kingdom is here, and God will see it through to the end. After embarrassing the Herodians and Pharisees, the Sadducees step up to take another rhetorical beating.

The Sadducees and Resurrection

As noted above, the Sadducees were another politically influential group. Sadducees were not as numerous as the Pharisees and were mostly confined to Jerusalem, but they were drawn from the highest levels of Jewish society and possessed a significant influence over the Sanhedrin. They are known for rejecting the common Jewish belief in bodily resurrection, the subject of their debate with Jesus. Mark 12:18-27, Matthew 22:23-33, and Luke 20:27-40 recount the tradition. Coming directly on the heels of the Pharisees and Herodians, Jesus is approached, presumably still in the crowds, by Sadducees, whom all three Synoptics comment do not believe in resurrection. They challenge Jesus with the Levirate Law in Deuteronomy 25:5-10, an appropriate tactic for a group who revere the Torah as the only authoritative Scripture for Jews.[48] This prescription in Deuteronomy stipulates that if a married man dies without providing a child for his wife, his brother should marry her to ensure she bears children. The Sadducees run a hypothetical story by Jesus: there are seven brothers, and one of them perishes before impregnating his wife. The woman marries another brother, who also dies without conception. She marries the rest of them in turn, and, as fate would have it, every brother passes away before she bears a single child. The Sadducees then ask Jesus to which of the brothers she would be married in the resurrection.

While Luke records a longer answer than Mark and Matthew, Jesus's response in Mark 12:24 is an excellent summary of his response: *"Is this not the reason you are mistaken, that you do not understand the Scriptures or the power of God?"*. Quoting from Exodus 3:6, Jesus argues that God is the God of Abraham, Issac, and Jacob, and that *"He is not the God of the dead, but of the living; you are greatly mistaken"*[49]. The technical debate about resurrection would take us beyond the scope of this book; suffice it to say, in line with the majority position in Second Temple Judaism, the earliest Jesus followers believed in the resurrection because they maintained that God had already done it once with Jesus and would therefore do it again at the end of the age. For our purposes, Jesus's argument rests on the promise God made to the patriarchs: *"God has made a commitment to the patriarchs as the God of promise. To fulfill that commitment to them, they must be alive to receive what he promises. All of this presupposes resurrection and the capability of God's power to bring it to pass"*[50]. Whatever we make of this argument, the evangelists believe

---

48. Moloney, *Mark*, p. 237

49. Mark 12:26-27

50. Bock, *Jesus*, p. 330

it was successful. Jesus shuts down the Sadducees, demonstrating once again that the authority of Jesus is superior to their own. This is a continuation of the major theme in this section of the gospels, which narrate Jesus openly defying the authority figures in Jerusalem. The crowds are still watching. In Mark and Matthew, a lawyer enters the ring with Jesus for a new round.

The Greatest Commandment

Mark 12:28-34 and Matthew 22:34-40 record another exchange between Jesus and a member of the Jewish elite, this time a lawyer. In characteristic Lukan fashion he shortened the tradition and moved it to an earlier segment of his gospel, Luke 10:25-28. He will rejoin Mark and Matthew's sequence in the following episode. Mark 12:28 casts the person confronting Jesus as a *"scribe"*, with Matthew 22:34-35 adding precision: *"when the Pharisees heard that Jesus had silenced the Sadducees, they gathered themselves together. One of them, a lawyer, asked him a question"*. Jesus's lawyer opponent comes from the ranks of the Pharisees. He asks Jesus the question *"which commandment is the greatest of all?"*[51]; in the Second Temple period there were debates about how to interpret the multitude of Jewish laws and if some of them could serve as an organizing principle for the others.[52] This question, therefore, is not out of the ordinary. Jesus responds by quoting Deuteronomy 6:4-5 and Leviticus 19:18. Love the Lord God with all your heart, and love your neighbor as yourself. Jesus concludes in Mark 12:31 by stating *"there is no other commandment greater than these"*, and in Matthew 22:4 with *"On these two commandments depend the Law and the Prophets"*.

Matthew's version ends with that statement, but in Mark 12:32-34 the lawyer responds positively, repeating what Jesus said and unexpectedly praising Jesus for his answer. In return, *"when Jesus saw that he had answered intelligently, He said to him, "You are not far from the kingdom of God.",* after which *"no one would venture to ask Him any more questions"*[53]. This is not, as many Christian interpreters have suggested, a condemnation of the Jewish Law. It must be seen within the context of an ongoing intra-Jewish debate about how to fulfill the Law, and both Jesus and the lawyer agree that loving God and neighbor is the foundation upon which the rest of the Law is built.[54] This is indeed an excellent summary of Jesus's teaching,

---

51. Mark 12:28, Matthew 22:36

52. Moloney, *Mark*, p. 240

53. Mark 12:34

54. Sloan, *Jesus and the Law of Moses*, pp. 13-40

and the impending crucifixion will be the decisive revelation of how to love both God and neighbor. Mark's version offers his audience a tantalizing and yet tragic possibility: many of Jesus' critics were so close to receiving his message and yet couldn't quite do it. His opponents will not accept the kingdom of God. He will have one final conflict with the Jerusalem elite before directly addressing his disciples and the crowds.

David's Son?

Luke rejoins Mark and Matthew's sequence with a final debate between Jesus and the Pharisees in Mark 12:35-37, Matthew 22:41-46, and Luke 20:41-44. Mark's version is short and sweet: *"And Jesus began to say, as He taught in the temple, "How is it that the scribes say that the Christ is the son of David? David himself said in the Holy Spirit, 'The Lord said to my Lord, "Sit at My right hand, Until I put Your enemies beneath Your feet."' David himself calls Him 'Lord'; so in what sense is He his son?" And the large crowd enjoyed listening to him"*. Matthew 22:46 adds that after this statement, no one dared to ask Jesus another question.

Jesus quotes directly from Psalm 110:1; in doing so, he accepts what many Second Temple readers of the Psalm recognize, namely that it was written by David and refers to the coming Messiah.[55] The question, of course, is why Jesus would seem to be downplaying the connection between himself and David (how can the Christ be David's son?) when the Synoptic evangelists have unanimously presented him as such? Bock correctly argues *"Jesus' point is not to deny that the Christ is David's son but to argue that the key name for him is "Lord" . . . If he is the Messiah, then the authority he possesses is one that David acknowledged to belong to the Messiah as Lord. This ruler is the one to whom God gave the right to sit at his right hand, a picture of sharing rule on a throne and a metaphor for the sharing of his authority"*[56]. Jesus is not denying his Davidic lineage but making a pronouncement about his own authority. Even his father David calls him 'Lord'; a massive assertion of authority in a patriarchal society. Jesus is David's son, but his authority transcends his father's. In context, this is yet another way of stating that Jesus is king and his opponents are not. Jesus uses this as an opportunity to launch an all-out tirade against his opponents.

---

55. Bock, *Jesus*, p. 332
56. Bock, *Jesus*, pp. 332-333

Woe to the Scribes and Pharisees

In Mark 12:38-40 and Luke 20:45-47, Jesus, before the attentive crowds, turns to his disciples and criticises the scribes. Mark, whom Luke follows closely, says *"In His teaching He was saying: Beware of the scribes who like to walk around in long robes, and like respectful greetings in the market places, and chief seats in the synagogues and places of honor at banquets, who devour widow's houses, and for appearance's sake offer long prayers; these will receive greater condemnation.'"*. Jesus's opponents are hypocritical; as the Christ, Jesus will suffer and die, and his followers must do likewise. Greatness is found in serving others. The Pharisees and scribes, however, want only to serve themselves. Jesus even alludes to the popular dissatisfaction with elite wealth; the Pharisees 'devour widow's houses', taking advantage of them for their own benefit. As Moloney notes, *"The woman without a husband was particularly fragile and open to physical, social, and financial abuse"*[57], and the Pharisees are guilty. Mark and Luke will compare the Pharisees with a widow shortly.

Matthew, on the other hand, takes Mark's condemnation of the Pharisees and greatly expands it. In Matthew 13:1-36, Jesus excoriates the Pharisees, showing them to be hypocrites who claim to honor God but instead oppress the very people they are supposed to serve. Jesus's extended tirade conforms to the contours of Mark but stylistically resembles the great oracles of woe against the wicked leaders of Israel found in prophets like Isaiah, Jeremiah, and Ezekiel. The Pharisees have "neglected *the weightier provisions of the law: justice and mercy and faithfulness*"[58]. Jesus also uses his condemnation of the elite as a teaching movement; while the Pharisees love to be called "Rabbi" and enjoy enjoy respectful greetings in the marketplace, a public demonstration of their supposed superiority,[59] it is not to be this way with Jesus's followers. Instead *"the greatest among you shall be your servant. Whoever exalts himself shall be humbled; and whoever humbles himself shall be exalted"*[60]. The implication: the Pharisees and scribes who reject Jesus will be humbled. Matthew 23:29-36 is an oracle of woe against the Pharisees, who would have been complicit in killing the prophets of old. As a result, they will be judged. Matthew 23:37-39 serves as a bridge between Jesus's conflict and his great oracle of destruction; Luke's version is found at an earlier point in his gospel, Luke 13:34-35. For Matthew, the rejection of Jesus by the Jerusalem establishment can only end in disaster. All three Synoptics include a long discourse about the coming destruction

---

57. Moloney, *Mark*, p. 246

58. Matthew 23:23

59. Matthew 23:5-7

60. Matthew 23:11-12

of the temple. Matthew 23 prepares his audience for this oration. Mark and Luke have built a different bridge between the temple conflicts and Jesus's discussion of the temple's demise.

The Poor Widow

While Matthew's transition to what some interpreters have called the 'Eschatological' or 'Olivet' Discourse is an extended condemnation of the Pharisees and scribes, Mark 12:41-44 and Luke 21:1-4, developing their terse critique of Jesus' opponents, tell the story of a poor widow. Readers of both gospels will notice immediately that in the preceding narrative the Pharisees are criticised for "*devour*[ing] *widows' houses*", and this tradition plays on that statement. Jesus sits down next to the temple treasury, noticing that many of the rich (*plousios*, Luke's preferred term; a cognate is also used in Mark) are donating large sums of money. A poor widow puts in two small coins. Jesus addresses his disciples and, according to Mark 12:43-44 tells them "*this poor widow put in more than all the contributors to the treasury; for they all put in out of their surplus, but she, out of her poverty, put in all she owned, all she had to live on*".

In its narrative context, the tradition is one final shot at the Jewish elite, proving them to be without authority and rightfully condemned for judgment. In Luke 16:14 the Pharisees were already accused of being "*lovers of money*" and Mark has implied they were corrupt. I circle back yet again to our analysis of the wealthy in antiquity; very few of the rich acquired their fortunes through voluntary market transactions, and the Jerusalem elite lived lavishly by leveraging the political and economic system against common Jews. While the wealthy were donating out of their abundance, this widow, one of the most financially precarious groups of people in antiquity, gave all she had. Blomberg explains just how small her contribution was: "*Lepta were small copper coins, each worth next to nothing, less than one one-hundreth of a denarius, or one one-hundredth of an average worker's daily wage—that is, about six minutes' work! So on the surface, the woman's gift would hardly be significant*"[61]. Jesus, however, signals her out for greatness because she gave everything she had, risking her livelihood to provide for the temple.

This serves as an incredibly embarrassing example of the selfishness of the Jewish elite; numerically they contributed much more than the widow, but the widow sacrificed everything. Comparing the elites to a poor widow (a woman, no less!) and scandalously suggesting she contributed more than them drives home the main point of this entire section in Mark and Matthew. The emperors have

---

61. Bock, *Jesus*, p. 337

no clothes. Much like Jesus's admonition to the rich young ruler that he needed to give up 'everything', there is nothing in this passage which suggests those who follow Jesus are required to live in abject poverty. It is, like everything the Jesus tradition says about wealth and possession, a painful reality check. Wealth comes with responsibility, and the scribes and Pharisees have been exceptionally irresponsible. Those who follow Jesus should cultivate an attitude of humility and dependence on God. This text, therefore, is not a justification for authoritarian socialism. There is no indication whatsoever that the woman is being coerced by the state into giving over her miniscule amount of money (and every indication that her poverty might be the result of Jerusalem's political establishment) and no suggestion that the peasants should seize the scribes and Pharisees' wealth by force, redistributing it as they see fit. judgment day is coming, and God will right every wrong. Before we look at Jesus's long description of Jerusalem's impending downfall, we will briefly sketch how John narrates the aftermath of Jesus's dramatic entry into Jerusalem.

Challenging Authority in John's Gospel

Before the lengthy upper room discourse in John, Jesus arrives in Jerusalem. In John, Jesus directly teaches the crowd without a series of debates between himself and the Jerusalem elite. While John's version of these events are stylistically different, compressed, and display a developed awareness of Jesus' identity, it is nevertheless entirely congruent with the Synoptic accounts despite Jesus's rhetoric not being levelled directly at his opponents. John has already established that the chief priests and Pharisees want him dead in John 11:47-53, and John's audience is expected to remember this as the context for Jesus's temple sayings. John's shortened version of the triumphal entry in John 12:12-19 ends with the disheartened Pharisees complaining about Jesus's popularity among the common people, whom he will address.

John 12:23 indicates Jesus's discussion is related to his messianic identity by announcing that *"the hour has come for the Son of Man to be glorified"*, followed by a Synoptic-esque saying in 12:26 that anyone who wants to serve Jesus must follow him. In 12:27-43 Jesus proleptically indicates his imminent crucifixion; his audience, "the crowd", draws the connection between his instruction and messianic expectations in 12:36: *"The crowd then answered Him, "We have heard out of the Law that the Christ is to remain forever; and how can You say, 'The Son of Man must be lifted up'? Who is this Son of Man?""*. Jesus responds that he is the light, and John notes that even though he had performed many signs the people still wouldn't believe in him, citing Isaiah 53:1 and 6:10 as examples of Israel's rejection of God's prophets. John 12:42-43 even claims some rulers believed in Jesus but were hesitant to express it for fear of the Pharisees.

John 12:44-50 begins with Jesus stating *"He who believes in Me, does not believe in Me but in Him who sent me"*. This passage encapsulates the essence of Jesus' debate with his opponents in the Synoptics; Jesus derives his authority from God, which is why his is superior to his opponents. Kostenberger aptly summarizes this passage: *"This is why Jesus' words are so definitive in pronouncing judgment on unbelief; in reality, they are words of the Father"*[62]. This is both a legitimation of Jesus as a prophet, speaking on behalf of God, and his own messianic status which will soon be revealed through the cross and resurrection. Just as the Synoptic portrayals of Jesus in the temple illustrate his authority, John follows the Synoptic trajectory in his own idiosyncratic manner. Jesus is the way, the truth, and the life. There is only one path to the Father and it runs through His Son Jesus. John narrates the last supper after this event while the Synoptics incorporate a long speech about the forthcoming destruction of Jerusalem's temple.

NOT ONE STONE WILL BE LEFT UPON ANOTHER

In Chapter 4, I promised to avoid, to the best of my ability, contentious theological debates which divide Christians and generate unnecessary dissension. This book is intentionally ecumenical in scope. Any controversial positions I defend in these pages are directly related to my agenda of analyzing the New Testament in light of stable political and economic categories. There are, unfortunately and unavoidably, passages which relate to my thesis that also happen to intersect with the very theological controversies I am striving to bypass. Mark 13, Matthew 24, and Luke 21, often called either the 'Olivet Discourse' or the 'Eschatological Discourse', named for the location and subject matter of the tradition respectively, is one such example. Even a cursory internet search will yield thousands of books, articles, and videos all advocating for a very particular interpretation of this discourse, and entire theological traditions are contingent upon how one interprets Jesus's prophecies against the temple. I am wading into a quagmire and will do my best to provide a contextual reading of these passages which will transgress the cherished theological dogmas of as few readers as possible. That being said, I believe that my commentary below could theoretically fit into a number of eschatological models.

I will refer to the traditions found in Mark 13:1-37, Matthew 24:1-25:46, and Luke 21:5-36 as the Olivet Discourse for the sake of simplicity. At first glance, Matthew's version appears longer than Mark and Luke's; much like the previous

---

62. Kostenberger, *John*, p. 394

sequence in which Matthew supplemented the triple-tradition material with explanatory parables, he will closely follow the other two evangelists then add an entire chapter of parables which elaborates his point. Since Matthew and Luke follow Mark closely, I will use Mark as my primary text. The setup is simple; Jesus, after defeating his opponents and revealing them to have no real authority, leaves the temple with his disciples. As he debarts, Jesus has the following conversation with his disciples about the temple: *"one of His disciples said to HIm, "Teacher, behold what wonderful stones and what wonderful buildings"*, referring, of course, to the massive reconstruction on the temple mount (which began, by means of increased taxes, with Herod the Great), to which Jesus responds *"Do you see these great buildings? Not one stone will be left upon another which will not be torn down"*[63]. He then leaves for the Mount of Olives, which is situated opposite the temple, and is asked a very specific question by his disciples: *"Tell us, when will these things be, and what will be the sign when all of these things are going to be fulfilled"*[64]. Whatever we make of the following instructions, they are all related to this specific question. The disciples want to know when the temple in Jerusalem will fall, an event which comes to pass in 70 CE. Towards the end of the discourse, in Mark 13:24-32 and parallels, Jesus explains how the fall of Jerusalem is a sign of the coming Son of Man, which his disciples didn't yet fully comprehend. The entire exchange, though, is predicated on their question about the temple.

The narrative context of the Synoptics provides the immediate context for Olivet Discourse. Jesus has entered Jerusalem, been proclaimed as king, and won several public debates against the Jewish establishment, in which all three evangelists present Jesus as condemning them to destruction. The establishment has refused God's kingdom and will not survive the eschaton. Both Matthew and Luke have already specified that Jerusalem's destruction is a consequence of rejection by the Jewish aristocracy[65]. The Olivet Discourse, then, should be read in continuity with the triple-tradition material which preceded it as an oracle of judgment against Israel's wicked tenants. Every condemnation of Jesus's antagonists is an affirmation of his authority. His words have ramifications for our understanding of political power. I will tie these strands together in a few short paragraphs.

The disciples' question is more nuanced in Matthew 24:3, where they ask Jesus to *"Tell us, when will these things happen, and what will be the sign of Your coming and of the end of the age?"*. Bock, acknowledging that their inquiry is directed at the fate of Jerusalem's temple, contends that the disciples are not asking about Jesus's

---

63. Mark 13:1-2; see Matthew 24:1-2 and Luke 21:5-6

64. Mark 13:4

65. Matthew 23:37-39, Luke 13:34-35

second coming but rather "*The reference to Jesus' coming is not really a question about the Lord's return, because these disciples did not yet appreciate or anticipate his resurrection. Without an expectation of resurrection, they would not be raising a question to discuss a return. Rather, the disciples sense a purging of the city for righteousness and probably tied it to the judgment that Jesus had predicted for Jerusalem*"[66]. Given that prior to entering Jerusalem, Jesus's disciples were asking to sit at his left and right hand, intending to wield political power after Jesus entered Jerusalem and became king[67], Matthew appears to be referencing their confusion about the coming kingdom. Matthew may also be adding an interpretive gloss to his source, Mark, where Jesus uses his instruction about the temple's demise to instruct the disciples about his future return. The fall of the temple will mean something, as Moloney argues: "*He tells of the destruction of Jerusalem, but focuses upon how the disciples are to understand that dramatic event*"[68]. Jesus will leverage the coming destruction of Jerusalem to elucidate his unique messianic identity to his disciples.

There are, then, two elements of the Olivet Discourse which are relevant for the question of Jesus's authority. As Ferda explains regarding Mark 13, "*Jesus's discourse in Mark 13 as it now stands predicts two different things: (1) historical and political realities that lead up to the destruction of the temple (if not that destruction itself), some of which were recent history or current events for the original readership of Mark, and (2) another and even more climactic event to follow (the "after" of v. 24): the coming of the son of man from heaven*"[69]. As we will see, the second prediction proceeds quite naturally from the first.

Jesus responds to the disciples' inquiry. There will be signs of the temple's imminent demise. Many will attempt to mislead his followers, conflict will run rampant, and the world will be afflicted with various disasters.[70] In other words, things aren't going to get much better in the short run. Mark and Matthew both end this section of the Olivet Discourse by likening these events to 'birth pangs', a possible allusion to Jeremiah 22:23, in which Jeremiah employs an identical metaphor in an oracle of judgment against Jerusalem. Jesus's followers will be persecuted severely and must endure[71]; but while they suffer the "*gospel must first be preached to all the nations*"[72], which, intriguingly, Paul claims has already happened

---

66. Bock, *Jesus*, p. 340

67. Matthew 20:20-28

68. Moloney, *Mark*, p. 253

69. Ferda, *Second Coming*, p. 189

70. Mark 13:3-8, Matthew 24:3-8, Luke 21:7-11

71. Mark 13:9-13, Matthew 24:9-14, Luke 21:12-19

72. Mark 13:10

in Romans 16:25-27, certainly written before the fall of Jerusalem in 70 CE. Mark 13:14-23 and parallels[73] describes the destruction of Jerusalem's temple in vivid detail. Borrowing the phrase *"abomination of desolation"* from Daniel in Mark 13:14, Jesus describes the desecration of Jerusalem. The phrase is used three times in Daniel[74], all of which likely refer to the profaning of the temple by Antiochus Epiphanes IV in 167 BCE. Jewish readers in the first century hearing the phrase *"abomination of desolation"* applied to the Jerusalem *"would take it to refer to pagan pollution in the Temple, accompanied by tribulation for the true people of YHWH"*[75]. Much like the time of suffering which accompanied the Maccabean revolt, Mark 13:19 states *"those days will be a time of tribulation such as has not occurred since the beginning of the creation"*. Jesus has answered the disciples' question. The temple will be destroyed after all these events take place.

The fall of the temple itself serves as a sign of Jesus's future vindication. In Mark 13:24-27, Matthew 24:29-31, and Luke 21:25-28, Jesus describes the events which will occur *after* the temple is destroyed. Mark's version reads *"But in those days, after that tribulation, the sun will be darkened and the moon will not give its light, and the stars will be falling from heaven, and the powers that are in the heavens will be shaken. They will see the Son of Man coming in clouds with great power and glory. And then He will send forth the angels, and will gather together His elect from the four winds, from the farthest end of the earth to the farthest end of heaven"*. Jesus draws upon a common apocalyptic motif found in the prophets, particularly Isaiah 13:10, Ezekiel 32:7, and Joel 2:10. In each of these passages the prophets describe consequential acts of God by appropriating the rhetoric of comic cataclysm. The language doesn't refer to the end of the world but its radical and eschatological transformation. Jesus quotes the 'Son of Man' passage from Daniel 7:13, referencing the figure who assists in the establishment of God's kingdom. The historical sequence of events is significant; Jesus's disciples will endure great hardship, the temple will fall, and sometime *after* the temple falls Jesus will be vindicated and God's kingdom consummated.

Lest the disciples fail to comprehend the words of Jesus, he qualifies his instruction with a parable about a fig tree[76]. The disciples must learn the lesson, taught in Mark 13:28 and parallels, *"from the fig tree; when its branch has already become tender and puts forth its leaves, you know that summer is near"*. The destruction

---

73. Matthew 24:15-28, Luke 21:20-24, with some parallel material moved to earlier places in Luke's gospel.

74. Daniel 9:27, 11:31, 12:11

75. Wright, *Victory*, p. 350

76. Mark 13:28-32, Matthew 24:32-26, Luke 21:29-33

of Jerusalem proves Jesus's message true and functions as a sign which points to the eschatological consummation of God's kingdom. While Jesus is adamant that no one can know the time or hour of his vindication, the destruction of the temple is a sign that it must come to pass. When his disciples see the destruction of Jerusalem, they can be assured Jesus was correct. In Mark 13:33-37 Jesus exhorts his followers to remain alert; like servants awaiting the arrival of their master, the disciples must be prepared because they do not know exactly when Jesus will return. Matthew 25 contains a series of parables, including the tradition found in Mark 13:33-37, all of which encourage his audience to faithfully await his coming. It is the theme of the entire chapter, built upon the Olivet Discourse in Matthew 24. Of particular interest is Matthew 25:31-33, which envisions the eschatological judgment: *"when the Son of Man comes in His glory . . . He will sit on His glorious throne. All the nations will be gathered before Him; and He will separate them from one another, as the shepherd separates the sheep from the goats; and He will put the sheep on His right, and the goats on his left"*. No matter how much followers of Jesus suffer, either in the run-up to Jerusalem's demise or awaiting the Son of Man, they are assured that justice is coming. The destruction of the temple in 70 CE constitutes a sign for what is to come.

Apart from validating Jesus's authority and final victory, these concluding Synoptic parables (especially in Matthew) encourage those who believe in Jesus to patiently anticipate his return. Jesus never suggests that the character of kingdom discipleship will be altered after the fall of Jerusalem. If anything, it should motivate his followers to increase in love for God and neighbor, knowing that God will make everything right in the end. The passage from Matthew quoted above introduces an instruction about how *"the King"* will sort out the sheep from the goats on judgment day. In Matthew 25:24-46, those who inherit the eschatological kingdom have fed the hungry, given drink to the thirsty, invited in the stranger, clothed the naked, and visited the imprisoned. judgment is distributed on *"the basis of practical compassion . . . for the poor, the miserable, the down and out"*[77]. Those who decline, according to Matthew 25:46, *"will go away into eternal punishment,* [while] *the righteous into eternal life"*. This encapsulates the quintessence of kingdom ethics, from the Sermon on the Mount to the lawyer who challenges Jesus in Jerusalem. Love God by serving others. Radical, sacrificial servanthood mitigates the damage caused by Roman imperialism (and Rome's corrupt clients) while testifying to the world that a new king sits upon the throne. The kingdom of God is at hand.

---

77. Meyer, *Five Speeches*, p. 118

If Christians seek to remain alert and prepared for the return of David's son, the final eschatological consummation signaled by the fall of the temple, we are obligated to serve those in need. Unfortunately for many modern Christians, Western culture has uncritically accepted the nineteenth-century theory that charity must be monopolized by the state, with the funds used to provide charity confiscated under threat of violence from productive people and distributed to others favored by the political class. The task of loving service to neighbors is not, at any point in the gospels, delegated to state actors. The task of helping those in need falls upon the community who now participates in God's kingdom, and on judgment day the church will be held accountable for what *we* did to serve others. Too many Christians are content with voting for politicians who promise to help other people, a complete abdication of our responsibility towards those in need. Jesus won't be asking who you voted for, he will be asking who you served. Jesus commands his followers to diligently await his return, but the Western church has essentially hired the rich young ruler to keep watch for us while we take a long, carefree nap. I think it's about time for the church to wake up.

THE LAST SUPPER

Before Jesus goes to trial he celebrates the Passover with his disciples. Jesus has entered Jerusalem as king, defeated the Jewish elite in the temple, and cast judgment on the leaders who have rejected him. This series of offenses is intolerable for his opponents, and they begin seriously formulating plans to kill him. Mark 14:1-2, Matthew 26:1-5, and Luke 22:1-2, right after narrating Jesus's Olivet Discourse, relay to the audience that Jerusalem's leaders are going to kill him, but this time for real. Two days before the passover, Mark recounts how *"the chief priests and the scribes were seeking how to seize Him by stealth and kill Him; for they were saying, "Not during the festival, otherwise there might be a riot of the people"*. They understand that Jesus is a popular prophet, so they must find a way to dispense of him covertly. Their time is approaching. The evangelists recount the story of a woman who pours expensive oil over Jesus. When the disciples rebuke her for wasting costly perfume, Jesus chastises them, claiming that she has anointed Jesus for burial and will be remembered wherever the gospel is proclaimed. This proves too much for Judas, and the Jewish authorities receive a timely gift: Judas takes leave of the disciples and visits the chief priests, plotting to betray Jesus. They, of course, are more than willing to collaborate with Judas.[78]

---

78. Mark 14:3-11, Matthew 26:6-16, Luke 22:1-6

Jesus procures a room in which his disciples celebrate the passover.[79] As the disciples sit down to eat, Jesus reveals that one of them will betray him.[80] This is inevitable. Jesus knew his trip to Jerusalem would likely be his last. The highlight of their Passover celebration is a statement Jesus makes about the meaning of the meal. After distributing bread and wine to his disciples, Jesus announces in Mark 14:24-25 that "*This is My blood of the covenant, which is poured out for many. Truly I say to you, I will never again drink of the fruit of the vine until that day when I drink it new in the kingdom of God*". Passover, the celebration of Israel's deliverance from Egypt by the hand of God, is rife with eschatological hope in the Second Temple period. By evoking the language of blood and covenant, Jesus is preparing his disciples for the events about to take place. As Crossley and Myles explain, "*Jesus' interpretation of the . . . elements would renew hopes of liberation as the Israelites were once liberated from slavery under the Pharaoh*"[81]. The great act of restoration, the establishment of God's eschatological kingdom, and the fulfillment of prophetic hopes would be sealed by Jesus' blood. The disciples have yet to understand the meaning of this great event, but Jesus, hailed Messiah, prophet of the kingdom, is about to trigger the eschaton. Those who follow Jesus, even to the cross, will inherit the kingdom. By appealing to "covenant", Jesus is evoking prophetic hopes from passages like Deuteronomy 30 and Jeremiah 31 in which God restores His people and establishes a new covenant of faithfulness. The time has come.

In the context of Jesus's temple action and oracles of destruction against it, Jesus's words at his final Passover meal reveal the meaning of his death: "*Jesus intended his death to accomplish that which would normally be accomplished in and through the Temple itself. . . Jesus saw his own approaching death in terms of the sacrificial cult . . . The controlling metaphor that he chose for his crucial symbol was . . . Passover: the one-off moment of freedom in Israel's past, now to be translated into the one-off moment which would inaugurate Israel's future*"[82]. The promised time of restoration had arrived. Israel's sins would be forgiven. Jesus himself would accomplish the task, a Messiah dying on behalf of his people. Jesus's words were a tough pill for the disciples to swallow. In Luke 22:22-30, Jesus again predicts his imminent death, after which Luke incorporates the tradition about greatness from Mark 10:41-45 and Matthew 20:24-28. Jesus then informs Peter that he will deny him three times in 22:31-34. Luke 22:35-38 records a unique exchange

---

79. Mark 14:12-17, Matthew 26:17-20, Luke 22:7-14

80. The Synoptic Last Supper accounts are found in Mark 14:17-25, Matthew 26:20-35, and Luke 22:14-38.

81. Crossley and Myles, *Class Conflict*, p. 219

82. Wright, *Victory*, pp. 604-605

between Jesus and his disciples in which he tells them *"whoever has no word is to sell his coat and buy one"*; but when the disciples present him with two swords Jesus says *"that is enough"*. Jesus is almost certainly signaling, in the symbolic language typical of Jewish prophecy, that a major change is about to occur for which the disciples must prepare themselves. Jesus's comments about the disciples having enough swords likely indicates they misunderstand the metaphorical nature of his instruction and think Jesus is asking them to fight, quite the opposite of his instructions only a few lines earlier regarding greatness.[83] John's gospel is much less ambiguous about how Jesus' disciples should relate to others.

Before the Passover meal in John 13:1-11, Jesus washes the feet of his disciples. Footwashing was a menial task often performed by slaves in antiquity[84]. After he performs the washing, Jesus instructs the disciples: *"You call Me Teacher and Lord; and you are right, for so I am. If I then, the Lord and the Teacher, washed your feet, you also ought to wash one another's feet. For I give you an example that you also should do as I did to you"*[85]. Much like the recurrent theme of servanthood in the Synoptics, the Johannine Jesus is instructing his disciples to serve others. Cornelis Bennema sees this tradition as a clear example of mimesis, in which Jesus' followers are directly called to imitate him: *"An authentic and effective imitation of the footwashing would include the adoption of a slave identity, thereby retaining a countercultural aspect since menial, servile service runs counter to human aspirations . . . the imitator and the mimetic act become a channel through which the beneficiary can experience Jesus and his humble, loving service for himself"*[86]. As an introduction to the long 'Upper Room Discourse' spanning John 13-17, Jesus's example serves a model for his followers to imitate; instead of seeking power and privilege, expecting others to serve them, Jesus's disciples must become like the Messiah and wash the feet of others, sacrificially serving them as a slaves.

Jesus appeals at several points in John's Upper Room discourse to both the sacrificial nature of discipleship and his own authority. A handful of examples will suffice. John 13:34-35 makes love, which John understands christologically as sacrificial servanthood towards others, the center of his ethical program: *"A new commandment I give to you, that you love one another, even as I have loved you, that you also love one another. By this all men will know that you are My disciples, if you have love for one another"*. Jesus boldly declares in John 14:6-7 that he is *"the way, and the truth, and the life"*, claiming that one cannot know the father without

---

83. Stein, *Luke*, p. 555-556

84. Koestenberger, *John*, p. 400

85. John 13:13-15

86. Bennema, *Imitation*, pp. 192-193

Jesus; those who love him, according to John 14:15, will keep his commandments. Anticipating the ecclesiology of Paul, those who "abide" in Jesus, a reference to the community of all who follow him[87], must, according to John 15:12, "*love one another, just as* [Jesus] *has loved you*". While Jesus and those who follow him must endure suffering, in the end they will overcome the world through Jesus's accomplishment.[88]

The question must be asked, once again, about the character of Christian discipleship in the modern world and its relation to political and economic authoritarianism. How can one sacrificially love their neighbor while simultaneously advocating for a cabal of wealthy politicians and bureaucrats to confiscate their property? How can one believe that Jesus is "*the way, and the truth, and the life*" while trusting in the state to manage society through force? If those who follow Jesus participate in his kingdom, why should we compromise our witness by placing our faith and hope in the kingdoms of men, all of which are based on violence, coercion, and selfish power? Jesus is inaugurating the kingdom, the 'new covenant' sealed in his blood, and because of the events which were about to take place the world would never be the same. Unfortunately many Western Christians would rather have their feet washed than wash the feet of others.

ARRESTED AND CONDEMNED BY THE JEWISH AUTHORITIES

After the Passover dinner, Jesus and his disciples travel to a garden called Gesthsemane, on the Mount of Olives, to pray. It is here that Jesus is arrested and tried by the Jewish authorities. This is not, as many popular portrayals would have us believe, a 'religious' trial which occurs before the 'political' one under Pilate. Roman governors, as we discussed above, held the power of *imperium*, the right to kill (or exonerate) any non-citizen accused of a crime. In the provincial system, local political leaders such as the Sanhedrin in Jerusalem were responsible for making day-to-day administrative decisions and possessed real political power. If local authorities considered someone worthy of execution, they had the power to arrest and try the suspect with the purpose of formulating charges which could then be brought before the governor, who would decide if the suspect lived or died. This is exactly how the trials of Jesus work historically.

With minor differences between the Synoptics, Jesus enters Gethsemane and prays while the disciples fall asleep.[89] Mark and Matthew both depict Jesus pre-

---

87. John 15:1-11

88. John 16:1-33

89. Mark 14:26-42, Matthew 26:36-46, Luke 22:39-46

dicting Peter's denial before he prays; for Luke this scene occurs during the Last Supper. John 18:1 abbreviates the entire scene and simply portrays Jesus entering the garden. Mark 14:41 takes a subtle shot at the Jewish authorities; Jesus calls them "*sinners*", an epithet with which they have charged Jesus repeatedly. Given that the term 'sinner' denotes those outside of the will of God and thus outside of His people, Jesus is signaling that his accusers are beyond hope. There are several variations between the scenes of Jesus's betrayal by Judas and arrest, but the gist of the tradition is retained in every gospel.[90] Judas comes to Jesus, accompanied by an armed crowd sent from the "*chief priests and the scribes and the elders*"[91]. These are the very opponents Jesus thoroughly embarrassed in the temple, and they want payback.

One of Jesus's disciples, identified only in John as Peter, draws a sword and strikes the ear of the high priest's slave. Jesus chastises Peter in Matthew, Luke, and John, expressing his disapproval towards the act of violence. In Matthew 26:52, Jesus instructs Peter to sheath his sword, "*for all those who take up the sword shall perish by the sword*". Congruent with Jesus's teaching on nonviolence, this instruction contrasts the actions of the armed men arresting Jesus and challenges Matthew's audience to emulate Jesus by rejecting violence. I doubt Jesus considered a special carveout for followers who hold political power. Jesus responds to the authorities by asking in Mark 14:48-49 and parallels "*Have you come out with swords and clubs to arrest Me, as you would against a robber? Every day I was with you in the temple teaching, and you did not seize Me; but this has taken place to fulfill the Scriptures*". Jesus uses the same Greek root word, *lestes*, "robber", which he used to describe the authorities in Mark 11:17. From this point on, all four of the gospels are heavily laced with irony; the real 'robbers' are not Jesus and his disciples but the men arresting him. Even as he is apprehended, Jesus considers it a fulfillment of Scripture. He is in control of the entire situation. Upon Jesus's arrest, the disciples abandon him.

Mark 14:53 identifies the array of Jewish leaders in attendance at Jesus's hearing: "*the high priest; and all the chief priests and the elders and the scribes*", those who are responsible for sending the armed crowd to arrest Jesus in 14:43. If this scene portrays a 'trial', its purpose is to bring charges before the governor Pilate which would compel him to exercise his exclusive right of *imperium* over Jesus. The Jewish political leaders, led by Caiaphas the high priest, are attempting to build a case against Jesus and transfer him to the governor for execution. Malina and Rohrbaugh argue that this is also an expression of a 'status degradation ritual'

---

90. Mark 14:43-52, Matthew 26:47-56, Luke 22:47-53, John 18:2-12

91. Mark 14:43

in which the Jewish elite engage in a deliberate degradation of Jesus' status, honor, and identity, with the goal of turning the crowds against him.[92] The hearing[93] is recounted by the evangelists in a similar manner, with each successive author redacting their sources to develop its original themes. As the authorities begin testifying against Jesus, Mark twice notes (in 14:56 and 14:59) that their testimony is wholly inconsistent. They accuse Jesus of threatening to destroy the temple *himself* and rebuild it in three days; while Jesus indeed issued prophetic oracles of judgment against the temple, he never claimed it would fall by his own hands. Much like his proclamation of the kingdom of God, the authorities misunderstand Jesus' oracles of woe.[94] All four of the evangelist depict Jesus as an innocent victim, and the purpose of framing the hearing with inconsistent testimony is to develop "*The theme of Jesus innocence* [by opening] *the Jewish hearing . . . with a series of general statements indicating that there is no case against Jesus*"[95]. He is innocent and yet stands accused anyway.

While the elders are deliberating, Jesus remains silent. The Jewish legal tradition, based on passages such as Deuteronomy 17:6 and 19:15, require multiple corroborating testimonies to condemn a suspect; by remaining silent, Jesus is attesting to the contradictory nature of the evidence presented against him.[96] Jesus will break his silence only when the high priest asks him a specific question: "*the high priest was questioning Him, and saying to Him, "Are You the Christ, the Son of the Blessed One?" And Jesus said, "I am; and you shall see the Son of Man sitting at the right hand of power, and coming with the clouds of heaven" . . . the high priest said, "What further need do we have of witnesses? You have heard the blasphemy; how does it seem to you?" And they all condemned Him to be deserving of death. Some began to spit at Him, and to blindfold Him, and to beat him with their fists*"[97]. This is a question about the messianic identity of Jesus. Matthew sharpens the messianic emphasis of the accusation; Caiaphas asks Jesus in Matthew 26:63 if he is "*the Christ, the Son of God*", and Luke's shortened hearing depicts Caiaphas inquiring if Jesus is the Christ and Son of God, to which Jesus responds in the affirmative. Jesus alludes to Daniel 7:13 and Psalm 110:1, both of which envision the exaltation of a messianic figure. Jesus openly declares himself to be the Messiah.

---

92. Malina and Rohrbaugh, *Social-Science Commentary on The Synoptic Gospels*, pp. 271-273

93. Mark 14:53-65, Matthew 26:57-68, Luke 22:66-71, John 18:12-14, 19-24, 28-32

94. Wright, *Victory*, pp. 523

95. Moloney, *Mark*, p. 301

96. Moloney, *Mark*, p. 303

97. Mark 14:61-65

The high priest accuses Jesus of *blasphemia*, "blasphemy", which denotes an offense against God. Jesus has set himself against the temple and the Sanhedrin, considered by the authorities a false prophet leading Israel astray, and claimed to be God's Messianic representative.[98] Whether or not divine christology is implied in the charge of blasphemy, for Caiaphas and his associates, the accusation is good enough. They repudiate Jesus's entire message and mission to Israel, interpreting it as a slander to God's good name (and, of course, their own political power). They all condemn Jesus as being worthy of death, mocking and assaulting him. The hearing ends; Jesus will be sent to Pilate in the hope Jesus will be condemned to death. This exchange is something of a christological denouement; Peter is the first to confess Jesus as Messiah, and Jesus has now openly declared his identity before his opponents. For our purposes, the point made by the four evangelists should be blindingly obvious: Jesus is the Christ. As Jesus is led to Pilate, his messianic identity will be, as it has been throughout the entire gospel tradition, further refined and developed. The trial before Rome's governor and the crucifixion which follows is characterized by a dark, tragic irony. No one expected a crucified Messiah.

TRIAL BEFORE PILATE AND THE CRUCIFIXION

Paul, writing only decades after the crucifixion of Jesus, reminds the unruly Corinthians what he taught them during his stay in Corinth: *"For I determined to know nothing among you except Jesus Christ, and Him crucified"*[99]. No one in Jerusalem at the time of Jesus's trial, except Jesus himself, would have ever thought to associate "Christ" with "crucifixion". While the practice of crucifixion existed in other cultures, the Romans developed it into a form of art. Roman citizens were exempt from crucifixion, which was generally pronounced as a sentence for crimes against the state; treason, revolution, brigandage, and sedition, threatening imperial stability, were all punishable by crucifixion, precisely why the Sanhedrin had to construct a plausible case that Jesus was a threat to Roman imperial rule. The Romans privileged crucifixion as a punishment because of its perceived ability to act as a deterrent. Crucifixions were often performed in public places such as highways and hilltops with the *intention* that others would see the crucified criminals and think twice about challenging Roman hegemony. Crucifixion sent a powerful message: Rome was in charge, and the cross is what happens to anyone who threatens Rome's power. There was no handbook for crucifixion, and Roman

---

98. Wright, *Victory*, pp. 526-527

99. 1 Corinthians 2:2

soldiers found creative and innovative ways to inflict unthinkable agony upon their victims. It was the most violent and shameful way a provincial could die.[100]

The tension between crucifixion and messianic Christology is the defining feature of all four evangelist's portrayal of Jesus's trial before Pilate and subsequent punishment. It was a massive social contradiction in antiquity to insist that the son of David, God's royal representative, would be condemned to a Roman cross. As Paul concludes in 1 Corinthians 1:24, only a few lines before the passage quoted above, "*we preach Christ crucified, to Jews, a stumbling block and to Gentiles foolishness*". Paul's observation is historically correct. No one saw the crucifixion coming, and had anyone accurately predicted what awaited Jesus when he reached Jerusalem they would not have entertained any wild hope that he might be the eschatological Messiah. And yet, as Paul informs the Corinthians, a crucified Christ is one of the defining beliefs of early Jesus followers. The church which emerges in the wake of Jesus is both created and *shaped* by the cross. The cross becomes the centerpiece of Christian ethics; what it means to love God and neighbor will be defined by the cross. Jesus, crucified Christ, forever redefines human power.

From the moment Jesus entered Jerusalem, all four evangelists showed time and again that Jesus is Christ and possesses the divine authority which his opponents lack. From the literal opening line of Mark, the first written gospel, to Jesus's hearing before the Sanhedrin, the gospels have unanimously hailed Jesus as son of David. There is little value, then, in explaining the precise christological affirmations which dominate the trial and crucifixion scenes. We are travelling a well-worn path. The evangelists are at their most creative, theologically rich, and darkly satirical in the trial and crucifixion narratives, and we review them here to show how Jesus is portrayed as the paradoxically crucified Messiah. There is perhaps no better critique of authoritarian political and economic systems than the cross.

As Jesus is taken to Pilate, he is abandoned by his disciples and thrice denied by Peter. He stands entirely alone. In typical fashion, Matthew, Luke, and John have developed Mark's account but are thematically similar.[101] Luke 23:2 recounts the charges brought before Pilate by the Sanhedrin: "*they began to accuse Him, saying, "We found this man misleading our nation and forbidding to pay taxes to Caesar, and saying that He Himself is Christ, a King."*". Their goal has been to present Jesus as a politically subversive revolutionary, and his accusers have deliberately misrepresented Jesus's words to do so. In John 18:29-32, Pilate instructs the council to judge Jesus according to Jewish law, but they protest because it was unlawful

---

100. Dennis, John. 2024. "*Death of Jesus*". In *Dictionary of Jesus and the Gospels*, 2nd ed. edited by Green, Joel. InterVarsity Press. pp. 173-174

101. Mark 15:2-15, Matthew 27:11-26, Luke 23:1-25, John 19:28-38

for them to condemn a man to death. Pilate held the *imperium*, and Jesus's opponents needed Pilate to wield it. In all four gospels Pilate asks Jesus directly if he is the king of the Jews. Jesus provides the same answer in the Synoptics; as the NASB translates Mark 15:2, Jesus responds *"It is as you say"*. The Greek is more ambiguous; Jesus's response is better translated *"You have said so"*, which implies a conditional acceptance of Pilate's question.[102] In Mark and Matthew, Jesus refuses to answer Pilate's follow-up questions; Luke adds that Pilate, after hearing Jesus's response, notifies the council that he found Jesus innocent. The council responds with a claim that Jesus had been stirring up trouble in Galilee, so Pilate sends Jesus to Herod, tetrarch of Galilee, for examination. Even though Herod humiliates Jesus, he too finds Jesus without guilt and returns him to Pilate. Luke 23:12 records that Pilate and Herod became friends that day. Luke 23:13-16 adds a unique tradition where Pilate assembles the Jewish leaders and informs them of his plans to free Jesus. Pilate tried the Messiah and found him innocent.

Jesus has a lengthier exchange with Pilate in John 18:33-38. As in the Synoptic tradition, Pilate asks Jesus, based on the charges brought before him by Caiaphas, if he is the king of the Jews. Jesus characteristically responds with a question in 18:34: *"Are you saying this on your own initiative, or did others tell you about Me?"*. Pilate reminds Jesus that he is not a Jew and is only repeating the charges brought before him by the priests. Jesus then utters what is perhaps one of the most famous (and misunderstood) lines in John: *"My kingdom is not of this world. If My kingdom were of this world, then My servants would be fighting so that I would not be handed over the Jews; but as it is, my kingdom is not of this realm"*. Many interpreters, Kostenberger included, have read this passage as a straightforward rejection of a 'political' kingdom; since Jesus says that his kingdom is not 'of this world' he must be denying any 'political' notions of kingship.[103] I disagree.

Rarely do interpreters who take this approach connect the first half of Jesus's statement to the second. The reason why his kingdom is not 'of this world' is because his disciples were not violently fighting on his behalf! Nonviolence is a ubiquitous component of the characteristic Jesus tradition and marks the kingship of Jesus as distinctive from the kingdoms of man. John also generally uses the term "the world" in connection with evil, as in John 3:19, so what Jesus is denying is not a *political* kingship but one that conforms with worldly evil and violence. This becomes even more significant if, as Marianne Meye Thompson argues, there is a literary (and perhaps even authorial) relationship between the gospel of John and

---

102. Moloney, *Mark*, p. 310

103. Koestenberger, *John*, pp. 528-529

the Johannine epistles.[104] The author of 1 John defines "the world" as "*the lust of the flesh and the lust of the eyes and boastful pride of life . . . The world is passing away, and also its lusts*"[105]. Jesus is inaugurating a kingdom which rejects worldly lusts. The non-political reading of John 18:36 is predicated upon the false Enlightenment division between 'politics' and 'religion' which artificially imposes a distinction between the two. I agree with Sprinkle, who asserts that "*When Jesus said that his kingdom was "not of this world," then, he "does not mean that his kingdom has nothing to do with politics or worldly matters." After all, Jesus' kingdom brought healing to the sick, food for the hungry, justice for the oppressed, radical welcome to the outsider . . . a ruthless challenge to the wealthy and elite, and a whole host of other material matters. All these things were "political"—and, if you were Roman, "politically subversive."*"[106]. John's point is that while Jesus is the Messiah he isn't the violent insurrectionists his opponents paint him to be. Pilate gets the message. In John 18:37-38, Pilate asks Jesus the same question as he does in the Synoptics, and Jesus provides him with the same cryptic but affirmative answer, expanding it slightly by discussing how his words testify to the truth. In John 8:32, Jesus states that those who listen to him "*will know the truth, and the truth will make* [them] *free*". Pilate asks the famous question "*what is truth?*", in my view indicating his personal uncertainty, and then promptly notifies Jesus's opponents that he finds the man innocent.

After Pilate's questioning Mark, followed by the other evangelists, introduces the story of Barabbas. In Mark 15:6-15, Mark informs his audience that Pilate had a tradition of releasing one Jewish prisoner every year during passover. The man in question, named "Barabbas" (literally "*son of a father*"[107]), is described in Mark 15:7: "*The man named Barabbas had been imprisoned with the insurrectionists who had committed murder in the insurrection*". Ironically, this man was guilty of the very same charges which the Jewish leaders were attempting to pin on Jesus. Crucifixion was reserved for violent revolutionaries such as Barabbas, not for non-violent prophets like Jesus.[108] The evangelists are satirically showing the farcical nature of Jesus's trial. Why would anyone consent to release a violent prisoner when Pilate himself seemed to think Jesus was not deserving of death? In Mark 15:9-10, Pilate asks the crowd if they want "*the King of the Jews*" to be released, with Mark editorially commenting that Pilate himself knew Jesus had only been handed over to him because of envy. The chief priests leverage their influence and the crowd

---

104. Meye Thompson, Marianne. 1992. *1-3 John*. InterVarsity Press. pp. 20-21

105. 1 John 2:16-17

106. Sprinkle, *Exiles*, p. 75

107. Crossley and Myles, *Class Conflict*, p. 230

108. Wright, *Victory*, p. 420

request freedom for Barabbas. When Pilate asks what crime Jesus had committed to warrant the death penalty, the crowd demands crucifixion. Pilate, worried about the possibility of a riot, capitulates. He condemns Jesus to crucifixion, as Mark 15:15 puts it, "*to satisfy the crowd*".

Matthew 27:19 includes a brief tradition involving Pilate's wife. Troubled by a dream, she implores Pilate to pardon Jesus. Pilate's intentions to release Jesus are frustrated by the crowd., He washes his hands of the matter and the crowd yells that responsibility for the blood of Jesus rests with them and their children.[109] John briefly mentions Barabbas in 18:39-40 before narrating a longer dialogue between Pilate and the crowds. In John 19:6-7 Pilate advises the Jewish leaders that Jesus is not guilty, but they respond to Pilate by telling him "*We have a law, and by that law He ought to die because He made Himself out to be the Son of God*". Even if John is implying a divine christology, his narration is implicitly messianic. This is confirmed just a few lines later; goading Pilate into sentencing Jesus, the Jewish leaders tell him in 19:12 "*If you release this Man, you are no friend of Caesar; everyone who makes himself out to be a king opposes Caesar*". The scene ends in 19:15 with a wild admission by Jesus' opponents: "*Pilate said to them, "Shall I crucify your King?" The chief priest answered, "We have no king but Caesar."*". This is a breathtaking rejection of Israel's God by the very people who were supposed to represent Him, as Koestenberger explains: "*The OT frequently reiterates that Yahweh alone is the true king of Israel . . . None of the foreign overlords qualified, whether Persian, Greek, or Roman . . . The very Feast of Passover, which the Jews are in the process of celebrating, is built on God's unique and supreme role in the life of the nation . . . Yet here, by professing to acknowledge Caesar alone as their king, the Jewish leaders betrayed their entire national heritage, as well as deny their own messianic expectations based on the promises of Scripture*"[110]. By murdering God's Messiah, the Jewish elite are forsaking their God. The Jerusalem establishment would rather be friends of Caesar than followers of God. Jesus is handed over for crucifixion.

The crucifixion narratives[111] depict the opponents of Jesus making a mockery of his kingship. The irony, of course, is that Jesus is paradoxically revealing the true nature of Messianic kingship. Jesus instructed his followers that his prophetic ministry would result in death and explained how greatness in the kingdom of God comes through servanthood, not domination. Jesus is embodying his kingdom ethic. The texts are rife with royal imagery. The soldiers who crucify Jesus dress him in purple, place a crown of thorns on his head, and sarcastically hail him "King of

---

109. Matthew 17:24-25

110. Koestenberger, *John*, pp. 538-539

111. Mark 15:16-41, Matthew 27:27-56, Luke 23:26-56, John 19:1-37

the Jews". Jesus is tortured so severely that in the Synoptics a man named Simon of Cyrene is asked (politely, I'm sure) by the Roman centurions to bear Jesus' cross. After he is crucified, an inscription is placed above his head which reads "*The King of the Jews*", written, according to John, in Hebrew, Latin, and Greek.[112] In John 19:21-22 the chief priests ask Pilate to reword the sign to read "*He said, 'I am king of the Jews'*", but Pilate refuses to make the change. His cross is raised between two criminals while those witnessing the crucifixion hurl insults at Jesus. If he really is the Messiah, why has God not rescued him? In Luke 23:39-43 one of the thieves realizes Jesus's innocence and asks Jesus to remember him in the kingdom. The thief is informed that he would accompany Jesus in paradise that very day. All four evangelists lace the scene with multiple allusions to Scripture, further reinforcing the messianic identity of Jesus.

In Mark 15:34 and Matthew 27:46, Jesus's final words are "*My God, My God, why have You forsaken Me?*". It is a quotation from Psalm 22:1, brilliantly appropriated for the context of Jesus's crucifixion. Many references to texts from the Old Testament in the New are designed to evoke the entire narratival context of the original passage, and Jesus's words are a textbook example of that hermeneutical phenomenon. Psalm 22, a Psalm of David, begins with a cry of lament which God quickly reverses. Despite the Psalmist's sense of despair, he trusts in the only God of Israel, who will deliver him from trouble.[113] The Psalmist feels alone; there is no one to help him, his enemies have pierced his hands and feet, and they are casting lots for his clothing.[114] All of this, not coincidentally, has already happened to Jesus. The Lord is not far off. He will deliver the Psalmist, and after the dramatic rescue "*All the ends of the earth will remember and turn to the Lord, And all the families of the nations will worship before you. For the kingdom is the Lord's And He rules over the nations*"[115]. The parallels to Jesus' ministry, his crucifixion, and his coming vindication couldn't be more obvious. As Wright comments on this text in the gospel tradition, "*The combination of themes is remarkable*"[116]. By alluding to Psalm 22:1, the entirety of the text is evoked; Jesus is suffering now, but will be vindicated. Through his deliverance the entire world will submit to the kingdom of God, and the nations will finally worship their Creator. Luke 23:46 recounts Jesus's final statement as "*Father, into Your hands I commit My spirit*", yet another

---

112. John 19:20

113. Psalm 22:1-10

114. Psalm 22:11-18

115. Psalm 22:27-28; in context 22:19-31

116. Wright, *Victory*, p. 601

allusion to a Psalm of David (this time 31:5) in which the author is rescued by God. Jesus's last words in John 19:30 are *"it is finished"*, which serves as an announcement that Jesus has completed his mission.[117] His work is finished. The Roman and Jewish authorities killed God's Messiah, just as Jesus said they would.

But the story isn't over. A centurion, witnessing the death of Jesus, declares *"surely this man was the Son of God!"* in Mark and Matthew and attests to his innocence in Luke[118], one final ironic admission of Jesus's messianic status. Even a gentile comprehended the unique identity of Jesus! His death posed a problem for his Jewish followers. It was the day before Sabbath, and Jesus needed to be buried beforehand. In all four gospels a man named Joseph of Arimathea ensures Jesus receives a proper burial.[119] Joseph complicates the rhetorically oversimplified conflict between Jesus and the Jewish elite. In Mark 15:43 Joseph is described as *"a prominent member of the Council, who himself was waiting for the kingdom of God"*. He asks Pilate for the body of Jesus, which he places in a tomb. Joseph comes from the ranks of Jesus's opponents but is apparently sympathetic to his cause. His high status on the Council is the most likely reason Pilate would grant his request.[120] Matthew 27:57 describes him as both a *"rich man"* and a *"disciple of Jesus"*; the term for 'rich' is the same Greek word used in 19:24 when Jesus tells his disciples it is impossible for a rich man to enter the kingdom of God; this linguistic parallel is yet another indication that Jesus's instruction to the rich young ruler was not intended to be normative. Luke 23:50-51 calls Joseph a *"good and righteous man"*, revealing Joseph disagreed with crucifying Jesus, while John 19:38 says he was a secret disciple *"for fear of the Jews"*. Everyone, including the Jerusalem establishment, can respond positively to Jesus if they so choose. While most do not, even a rich Jewish aristocrat like Joseph can inherit the kingdom.

Jesus is laid in a garden tomb hewn out of rock with a large stone door. Matthew 27:62-66 alone narrates how the chief priests and Pharisees gather before Pilate and beg him to provide security for the' tomb. They worry the disciples will steal away the body and claim he was raised from the dead such that *"the last deception will be worse than the first"*. Pilate allows the establishment to secure the grave with their own forces, and they comply. The body of Jesus goes missing anyway.

---

117. Koestenberger, *John*, p. 551

118. Mark 15:39, Matthew 27:54, Luke 23:47

119. Mark 15:42-47, Matthew 27:57-61, Luke 23:50-56, John 19:38-42

120. Bock, *Jesus*, p. 393

THE RESURRECTION OF THE MESSIAH

The four resurrection accounts in the gospels pose significant interpretive difficulties. N.T. Wright's observation is spot-on: *"The resurrection narratives in the gospels are among the oddest stories ever written. At one level they are simple, brief and clear, at others complex and perplexing. Studying them carefully involves almost all the problems of studying the rest of the gospel narratives, with several extra complications added in for good measure"*[121]. While I have tried to account historically and literarily for the differences between the gospels, it will be impossible to do so with the resurrection accounts. The world's greatest professional scholars have sharp exegetical disagreements and I have nothing of substance worth adding to the conversation. My goal in these lengthy chapters on the gospels has been to show that Jesus was clearly portrayed as Israel's king, launching the kingdom of God, as well as the political and economic consequences of following the Messiah. To that extent the evangelists' complex and diverse resurrection accounts are ingenious summations of those very themes. The kingdom has come, the king has been raised from the dead, and his followers will build his kingdom until the end of the age. The resurrection serves as the eschatological turning point in human history; the end has dramatically been inaugurated in the present, awaiting full consummation at the return of Jesus.

As we discussed above, most Jews (but not all, the Sadducees being an excellent example) believed in the bodily resurrection of all God's faithful at the end of the age. Those who served God would finally defeat death in the coming restoration. While the resurrection was expected to be a one-time event for all the faithful at the end of history, early Christians *"believed that this still-future hope had begun to happen already, in Jesus' resurrection, and that this even served as the prototype for others"*[122]. The earliest followers of Jesus quickly made the connection between Jesus's kingship and his resurrection; Paul's three explanations of his gospel in Romans 1:1-5, 1 Corinthians 15:1-5, and 2 Timothy 2:8 explicitly link the two concepts. It is central to the preaching in Acts, typified by Peter's opening speech in Acts 2:22-36, and fundamental to the christology of Revelation, illuminating the power of Jesus over all creation in Revelation 1:1-8. Prophecy, kingdom, christology, and eschatology all reach their logical apex with the resurrection (and subsequent ascension) of Jesus. Regardless of the resurrection narrative's literary complexities, they cannot be accused of making a point that diverges from the Messianic christology which the evangelists laboriously developed. Jesus is king, therefore the kingdom

---

121. Wright, *Resurrection*, p. 587

122. Wright, *New Testament*, p. 460

has come. Because of the wide variation between the gospels' accounts of Jesus's resurrection, it will be helpful to analyze them independently, showing how each of them in their own unique manner explicate the messianic identity of Jesus and its eschatological consequences. We will begin and end with Mark.

Mark is unique because, as the first written gospel, it does not include a direct account of Jesus' resurrection. Mark 16:1-8 concludes the narrative with an empty tomb but no encounter with the resurrected Jesus. Three women, Mary Magdalene, Mary mother of James, and Salome visit the tomb after Sabbath had ended, hoping to anoint his body with spices. When they arrive they find the stone door rolled away and a young man, presumably an angel, sitting in the tomb. The man informs them that Jesus has been risen and they were to go and tell the disciples that Jesus had gone ahead of them to Galilee. The women run away in fear. Thus ends the first gospel. Most English translations include several additional verses, usually numbered 16:9-20, which were not original to Mark. There have been various attempts to make sense of this abrupt ending, such as postulating that Mark died before completing the text or that the original scroll was damaged, but these theories make little sense of the evidence. The additions to Mark were, after all, crafted by a scribe to account for Mark's strange finale.[123] We must accept that, for whatever reason, Mark intended to end his gospel at 16:8, as Moloney argues: "*The original Gospel of Mark ended at 16:8, and the interpreter must make sense of Mark's literary and theological reasons for closing his Gospel with fear, flight, and silence of women*"[124]. Mark, no stranger to irony, reports three women hearing of the resurrection first. A woman's testimony was considered less relevant in antiquity than that of a man; that three women were entrusted with the proclamation of Jesus's resurrection attests to the revolutionary nature of his kingdom.[125] Bock makes a credible case for Mark's ending as the fulfillment of several themes and motifs central to his gospel. Fear is often connected with opportunities for faith in Mark's gospel. Now that Jesus is raised from the dead, the women are still afraid![126] It is also quite plausible that Mark is challenging his audience to do the opposite of the women and proclaim Jesus's resurrection in spite of fear. Given that ancient biographies were designed to inspire emulation, the women may be examples of what *not* to do. It is, predictably, impossible to know for sure, but the literary theories accounting for Mark's ending are the most plausible. Significantly, Mark neither denies his opening claim that Jesus is Christ nor downplays the resurrection.

---

123. Crossley and Myles, *Class Conflict*, pp. 244-245

124. Moloney, *Mark*, p. 341

125. Bock, *Jesus*, p. 394

126. Bock, *Jesus*, p. 395-396

His intended audience already accepts both of these realities. As for the additions to his gospel, we will return to them after examining Matthew, Luke, and John.

Matthew characteristically expands Mark's account, recounting two interactions between the disciples and Jesus.[127] Both Marys arrive at the grave of Jesus. An earthquake has rolled away the stone and the women are greeted by an angel who gives them the same instruction as in Mark: tell the disciples Jesus was raised from the dead and that he will meet them in Galilee. They leave with both fear and joy, telling the disciples what they had seen. Jesus actually meets his disciples, who worship him, and he instructs them to return to Galilee. The guards are bribed by the chief priests to remain silent about the empty tomb while the disciples journey home. In Matthew 28:18-20, Jesus orates the famous Great Commission: *"And Jesus came up and spoke to them, saying, "All authority has been given to Me in heaven and on earth. Go therefore and make disciples of all the nations, baptizing them in the name of the Father and the Son and the Holy Spirit, teaching them to observe all that I commanded you; and lo, I am with you always, even to the end of the age."*. Echoing Daniel 7:13-14, the resurrected Jesus *has been given* all authority in heaven and on earth. The Davidic Messiah now rules the entire world by virtue of his resurrection. His reign will be announced to all the nations through the work of his disciples, who will baptize in his name and teach the nations all of Jesus's commands. Because the end has broken into the present, Jesus will oversee this mission until the end of the age.[128] Bock helpfully summarizes the relationship between kingdom, eschatology, and christology in this passage: *"Jesus' commission notes that he has been given all authority in heaven and on earth. The language is the language of heavenly rule and mediatorial authority. The kingdom is here; Messiah is at work. God is working through Jesus, just as Jesus had claimed in his ministry. The kingdom had arrived. So the call is to make disciples of all the nations. Now God will make his gracious claim on people from every nation. They will become his disciples, followers of God"*[129]. The kingdom of heaven is at hand, and the nations are called to repent and believe in the gospel. Pilate and Caiaphas are no longer in charge, Jesus is. For Matthew and his audience the Great Commission is not a metaphor but an objective reality. The resurrected Jesus is king. The entire world would know soon enough.

Luke expands on Matthew's resurrection account but is in full agreement with the themes presented in the Great Commission.[130] The women, attending Jesus's

---

127. Matthew 28:1-20

128. Jipp, *Messianic Theology*, pp. 55-56

129. Bock, *Jesus*, p. 401

130. Luke 24:1-53

tomb, are met by two angels who refer to Jesus as the *"Son of Man"*, reminding the women how Jesus predicted he would be crucified and raised on the third day. The women leave and inform the disciples, and this time Peter visits the empty tomb himself. The first resurrection appearance is found in Luke 24:13-35, where Jesus joins two men traveling from Jerusalem to Emmaus, both of whom remain unaware of his identity. Jesus asks them what they were talking about, and the men reply *"Jesus the Nazarene, who was a prophet mighty in deed and word in the sight of God and all the people, and how the chief priests and our reuters delivered Him to the sentence of death, and crucified Him. But we were hoping he was going to redeem Israel"*[131], followed by the curious discovery of an empty tomb. Luke is being ironic; Jesus did indeed redeem Israel, although not in the way either man was expecting.[132] Jesus rebukes them: *"O foolish men and slow of heart to believe in all that the prophets have spoken! Was it not necessary for the Christ to suffer these things and to enter into His glory?"*; Jesus further elaborates: *"beginning with Moses and with all the prophets, He explained to them the things concerning Himself in all the Scriptures"*[133]. Jesus refers to himself as "the Christ" and then explains to the men how he fulfills the Old Testament story. Once again, this is an indication of Jesus' eschatological and messianic significance. Jesus accompanies the men for dinner, breaking bread with them. He disappears, and the men realize the identity of the man with whom they had been eating.

Jesus then appears to the disciples in Jerusalem; some of them doubt until they touch Jesus's physical body. Luke insists that Jesus was truly raised from the dead, not as a spectral ghost but an embodied human.[134] Jesus is present with a fish, which he eats. Luke then includes his own version of the Great Commission. Jesus, explaining to his disciples from the Scriptures that everything written about him in Moses, the Prophets, and the Psalms must be fulfilled, says *"Thus it is written, that the Christ would suffer and rise again from the dead the third day, and that repentance for forgiveness of sins would be proclaimed in HIs name to all the nations, beginning from Jerusalem. You are witnesses of these things. And behold, I am sending forth the promise of My father upon you; but you are to stay in the city until you are clothed with power from on high"*[135]. Luke will narrate these events in Acts. Jesus, after offering his final instructions, ascends to heaven. The messianic significance of the ascension will be discussed in the next chapter. Luke, however, leaves his

---

131. Luke 24:19-21

132. Stein, *Luke*, p. 611

133. Luke 24:25-27

134. Wright, *Resurrection*, p. 657

135. Luke 24:46-49

readers with little doubt that Jesus ushers in the eschatological kingdom in fulfillment of Scripture and rules as king over all creation. His disciples carry on his
mission, beginning in Jerusalem, to the ends of the earth.

John devotes two chapters of his gospel[136] to the resurrection narrative. In
typical Johannine fashion, his story differs from the Synoptics in style but not
substance. Themes in the Synoptic resurrection account are woven throughout
John. The women visit the empty tomb with Peter accompanying them. Mary
Magdalene is the first to encounter Jesus, initially mistaking him for the gardner.
Jesus informs her of his coming ascension, and Mary hails him as "*Lord*"[137]. Jesus
appears to his disciples, but Thomas refuses to believe until he touches Jesus's
resurrected body. John then adds an editorial explanation for the purpose of his
gospel: "*but these things have been written so that you may believe that Jesus is the
Christ, the Son of God, and that believing you may have life in his name*"[138]. There
we have it. John wants his audience to accept Jesus as the Messiah, the king over
all creation who is soon to ascend to God's right hand, so that all who believe will
inherit life. John asserts that Jesus is in some sense divine but hasn't forgotten or
marginalized Jesus's messianic identity. Like the Synoptics, John's Jesus is unambiguously king. In John 21 Jesus returns to Galilee, meeting his disciples as they
fish. He eats breakfast with them and instructs Peter three times to tend his sheep,
echoing Matthew 16:17-19. Peter will be a prominent leader in the Jesus movement. John's ending implies that the story of Jesus has not concluded; rather, the
mission of his disciples was just getting started. The outworking of Jesus's mission
will occupy us for the rest of this book.

CONCLUSION

From the opening lines of the four gospels Jesus is hailed as Messiah. His birth,
life, crucifixion, resurrection, and ascension inaugurated the eschatological kingdom of God. Jesus, son of David, will reign over creation as king, a reality to
which the four evangelists all attest. His prophetic ministry explained the radical
implications of God's kingdom. Instead of being shaped by human structures of
power, those who repent and believe the gospel will seek peace, mercy, and justice
by following the example of Lord Jesus. Greatness is measured in service towards
others, not domination. The kingdom comes not through violence or force but
through compassion and sacrifice. All are called, but few will answer. Jesus doesn't

---

136. John 20:1-21:25
137. John 20:17-18
138. John 20:31

force anyone to accept the ethics of God's kingdom but warns those who refuse to heed his call that they will not survive the eschatological judgment. The characteristic Jesus, known through the genre of ancient biography, is an eschatological prophet who both announces and establishes the kingdom of God. He alone will sit at the right hand of God, ruling as king over all creation.

Mark 16:9-20 was added to the gospel no earlier than the second century, after the other works which would become the New Testament were composed. The section appears to be based on the expanded resurrection narratives in Matthew 28, Luke 24, and John 20-21.[139] The risen Jesus is presented to the disciples, whom he calls to preach the gospel among the nations. Those who accept the message will be saved while those who don't will be condemned. Signs will accompany those who preach the gospel, and Jesus ascends to heaven, sitting at the right hand of God. While not original to Mark's gospel, these texts nevertheless reveal how early Jesus' followers understood the consequences of Jesus' mission. The Lord Jesus Christ, the Son of God, will be proclaimed to all the nations. Human history had reached a decisive turning point in the resurrection of Jesus. His followers are given the task of proclaiming him to the nations, necessarily transcending political loyalties. The resurrected one has no competitors.

The cross is without a doubt the source of early Christian atonement theologies and serves as the mechanism by which God deals once and for all with the problem of human sinfulness. Christians throughout history have recognized the salvific significance of Jesus's crucifixion, which is one of the defining characteristics of church doctrine. Every orthodox Christian tradition teaches that God decisively condemns sin on cross. Much less explored, but of equal significance, is how the cross shapes the practice and worldview of those who follow Jesus. Discipleship conforms to the cross; throughout his ministry, Jesus explained to his disciples how to love God and neighbor, and his example culminates with his crucifixion. Followers of Jesus pick up their own crosses and follow him. The cross is also a re-evaluation of true power. Jesus, son of David, God's Messiah, allows himself to be crucified by sinful men for the sake of all creation. Jesus wages no violent battle or terroristic revolt, nor does he threaten to harm or kill his opponents. He proclaims the kingdom, announces the eschatological moment, and dies as a means of bringing it about. The cross is an illustration of kingdom power and a condemnation of worldly power. The age of violence is coming to an end while the age of peace is dawning. Jesus's followers are called to embody his example while they go and make disciples of all nations.

---

139. Moloney, *Mark*, pp. 356-357

The four themes which we analyzed in the Jesus tradition, prophecy, kingdom, christology, and eschatology, reach their climax in Jesus' death, resurrection, and ascension. As a prophet, Jesus announced the kingdom of God was at hand, explaining and enacting it through his words and deeds of power. At the heart of his prophetic proclamation was the kingdom of God, the long-awaited restoration of Israel which inaugurates the 'end of the age' and the revelation of God to the entire world. The reestablishment of David's line was expected to accompany this great deliverance. Jesus is heir to the throne of David. These events all mark the beginning of the end; the eschatological kingdom is a present reality. Jesus had been raised from the dead, a clear sign that last days had dawned, and in his ascension he sits at the right hand of God ruling over all creation. As we explore the rest of the New Testament, we will find that the constellation of ideas present in the Jesus tradition suffuse the entire canon. The book of Acts, to which we will turn shortly, weaves all of these themes together, allowing us to see more clearly the political and economic consequences of following Jesus.

What, then, do the gospels reveal about our political and economic commitments? Believers should take the christological claims of all four evangelists seriously. Jesus is the Messiah who currently rules over all creation. There is, within this framework, no hint that either the Romans or the Jerusalem establishment have some mysterious divine legitimation. Far from it. Jesus predicted what would come to pass only forty years after his death: Jerusalem fell to Roman armies. The fall of Jerusalem was no endorsement of Roman power; kingdoms rise and kingdoms fall, but all who follow Jesus patiently wait for his return and the accompanying consummation of his kingdom. In the meantime, believers live like the Jews in Babylon, following the advice of Jeremiah 29:7 to seek the welfare of those around them while acknowledging that the evil empires will one day fall. God is the creator and Jesus is His Messiah. Followers of Jesus must not travel the path of violent revolution but follow the example of their king by sacrificing on behalf of others. Within this framework all political power is relativized. The church is *supra*political; its commitment to the Lord of the world transcends human political structures. There is no combination of king and country, no hint in the gospel tradition that the kingdom of God has viable rivals. Believers pledge their loyalty to a different king. These truths should automatically make us wary of the modern technocratic state. There can be no proper Christian hope in an institution which seeks to remake society under the threat of violence and coercion. Christians are called to be crucified, not crucify others.

The economic consequences of God's kingdom are also shaped by the cross. In an agrarian society characterized by elite exploitation, sharing resources was essential to survival. While Jesus doesn't condemn the possession of wealth outright, he recognizes that most of the wealthy maintained their prosperity through oppression and force. Moreover, wealth has the potential to become an idol, tempting those who possess it to forsake God. It is impossible to serve God and wealth. The rich young ruler is a perfect example of this paradigm. Jesus asks him to renounce his possessions, and he refuses. Jesus doesn't chase after him or advocate for political policies which will shake him down and confiscate his wealth anyway. He simply warns his disciples of the dangers of wealth and the impending eschatological judgment. No need to pull up the weeds while the wheat is still growing. Both Zacchaeus and Joseph of Arimathea are presented as examples of rich men who use their possessions wisely. Jesus advocates for a radical reassessment of wealth and the absolute responsibility towards others which accompanies prosperity. The teachings of Jesus are completely incompatible with modern conceptions of socialist redistribution which *necessarily* rely on coercion and violence to impose economic control over society. No matter how noble the motives of modern socialists, any economic system which includes forcible redistribution is incompatible with the teachings of Jesus, full-stop. The church should be a prophetic voice against immorally-earned wealth and an example of charitable giving, but it must never trust in the political authorities to leverage violence against those the church deems financially unfaithful. God will deal with them on judgment day. The modern conception of authoritarian socialism is completely incompatible with the kingdom of God, as the rest of the New Testament will also demonstrate. We will now turn to Acts and examine how the earliest followers of Jesus spread his gospel of the kingdom.

CHAPTER 11 | Acts of the Apostles

From Jerusalem to Rome

*When Jesus departed in Acts, a cloud took him out of the disciples' sight . . .
[this] shows how King Jesus was installed as the king in the midst of the broken and chaotic kingdoms of the earth.*

Patrick Schreiner[1]

*They commanded them not to speak or teach at all in the name of Jesus. But
Peter and John answered and said to them, "Whether it is right in the sight of
God to give heed to you rather than to God, you be the judge; for we cannot
stop speaking about what we have seen and heard."*

Acts 4:18-20

FROM JERUSALEM TO ROME

Luke's gospel ends with the resurrected Jesus explaining to his disciples that the
Jewish Scriptures have been fulfilled and commissions them to proclaim his name
to all the nations, starting in Jerusalem. Jesus promises that he will equip them
with the power they need to complete this massive endeavor. Jesus then ascends to
heaven while his disciples continue to worship him and praise God in Jerusalem.[2]
Acts, the sequel to Luke's gospel, tells the story of a small number of Jewish disciples, beginning in Jerusalem, taking the gospel to the furthest reaches of the world.
At the end of the story, a man named Paul is proclaiming the kingdom of God
in the imperial capital of Rome. The story is driven by a single, all-encompassing
conviction that Jesus is king of the world.

---

1. Schreiner, *Ascension*, p. 88

2. Luke 24:44-53

Acts is incredibly important to Christian history because it is the sole extant literary source detailing the first few decades of the Jesus movement. It is, like the gospel which preceded it, theologically rich and creatively written. Nearly every important topic discussed in the New Testament epistles has an analogy in Acts, and without it several significant historical and doctrinal questions related to early Christianity would become nearly impossible to answer. The narrative spun by Luke is bold, provocative, and challenging for the church in all ages. For our study, Acts uniquely portrays the earliest disciples in dialogue with the political authorities and navigating the turbulent waters of Jewish and Roman culture. Acts also provides us with a sense of the economic diversity of the movement, particularly as it relates to charity. There is perhaps no other work in the New Testament, save for Revelation, which elucidates the complex relationship between Jesus followers and the political and economic structures of the early Roman empire.

It is precisely because the church is intimately engaged in world affairs that Acts has served as something of a staging ground for justifying contemporary political and economic theories. The description of the Jerusalem church in Acts 2 and Acts 4 sharing pooled resources is a common prooftext for socialist interpretations of Scripture. Horsley, writing from a self-consciously socialist perspective and in opposition to what he deems the *"socially and politically conservative"* scholarly establishment explicitly refers to the Jerusalem church as participating in a *" "communism" of goods"*[3], and Bird notes that *"passages such as Acts 2:44-45 and Acts 4:32 have contributed to the rise of Christian socialism since the nineteenth century in both Catholic and Protestant texts"*[4]. That Bird's description happens to correspond historically with the rise of Saint-Simonianism in Europe should be of little surprise. biblical interpretation is not immune (and may in fact be exceedingly susceptible) to shifting intellectual trends.

The question, of course, is whether or not any aspect of authoritarian socialism, in either its conservative or progressive manifestations, can be justified by Acts, a work which places the resurrected and ascended son of David at the center of its storyline. There is little need to reiterate the Jesus tradition's messianic christology or the eschatological kingdom which accompanies it. Luke's perspective on Jesus has already been firmly established above, along with his nuanced understanding of wealth and possessions. Nothing he writes in Acts will contradict or challenge his presentation of Jesus from the gospel of Luke. If anything, Luke only augments what he has already written. There is no space for a full treatment or commentary on Acts. I will, as with the gospels, emphasise several passages and

---

3. Horsley, *Bow Down*, pp. 116-117

4. Bird, Michael. 2023. *A Bird's-Eye View of Luke and Acts*. InterVarsity Press. p. 186

themes which relate to our thesis that the New Testament is incompatible with political and economic systems predicated on violence. Acts will also act as a pivot to the rest of the New Testament writings, containing within it themes which are of incalculable significance for our interpretation of Paul and other New Testament authors. Before analyzing the trees, we must first appreciate the forest. How does Acts work?

AN INTRODUCTION TO ACTS

I have up to this point been referring to the author of Acts as 'Luke' and assuming that he is the same person who wrote the gospel which bears his name. From the second century onward Christian scholars have associated Luke with Acts and claimed that both were written by a man named Luke, a traveling companion of Paul. How did interpreters arrive at this conclusion? Luke and Acts are both addressed to the same person (or, less likely but still possible, group), Theophilus, who appears in Luke 1:3 and Acts 1:1 as the addressee. The opening passage in Acts even references "*The first account*", and describes the work as "*about all that Jesus began to do and teach, until the day when He was taken up to heaven, after He had by the Holy Spirit given orders to the apostles who He had chosen*"[5]. This is an apt compact description of Luke's gospel, the first volume, of which Acts is the sequel. The literary relationship between the two works is firmly established. Why the Lukan attribution? There are three passing references to Luke in the Pauline letters[6], all of which portray him as a companion of Paul. In Colossians 4:14, Luke is identified as a "*physician*". There are also several passages in Acts where the narrator slips "*from the third person to the first person plural in his narrative; the three 'we-sections' of Acts are 16:1-17; 20:5-21:18; 27:1-28:16*"[7]. Since Luke, who travelled with Paul, would have had at least a rudimentary education and spoke Greek, it was easy to associate Luke with the 'we-sections' in Acts and attribute authorship of both Luke and Acts to him. I agree with this assessment.

Acts was composed after Luke, since it is unambiguously identified by the author as its sequel, but there is no scholarly consensus regarding the relative date of composition. Bernier argues for an early date, perhaps as early as 62 CE.[8] I personally believe that the gospels could all theoretically predate the fall of Jerusalem

---

5. Acts 1:1-2

6. Colossians 4:14, Philemon 1:24, and 2 Timothy 4:11

7. Bruce, F.F.. 1996. "*Acts, Book of The*". In *New Bible Dictionary*, 3rd ed. ed. by I. Howard Marshall, A.R. Millard, J.I. Packer, and D.J. Wiseman, InterVarsity Press. p. 11

8. Bernier, *Rethinking the Dates*, pp. 66-67

in 70 CE, and if Luke is using both Mark and Matthew as a source both would have been composed sometime in the 50s CE. Since Acts concludes with Paul's imprisonment in Rome, it was possibly written before his death in the late 60s CE. The martyrdom of Stephen is an important turning point in Acts; wouldn't it make sense for Luke to have narrated the death of its two main protagonists, Peter and Paul? I certainly think so. The absence of their executions attests to the plausibility of Bernier's thesis. The evidence remains inconclusive. Both Bird[9] and Dunn[10] propose a date in the 80s or 90s CE. It is safe to conjecture, however, that Acts was composed no later than one generation after the events which it describes, and possibly earlier.

The genre of Acts does not precisely conform to the standards of ancient biography, but neither is it radically different. There is no single main character in Acts. Luke is instead telling the story of the first disciples of Jesus within a narrative framework which presents the message of Jesus spreading among the nations. Bird, commenting on the genre of Acts, argues that it *"is something like an apologetic historical work written up according to Greco-Roman literary conventions, as a conscious extension of Israel's sacred history, with a key focus on the lives of Jesus' followers, especially the apostles Peter and Paul"*[11]. Dunn agrees, maintaining that Acts was intended to be a work of history told within the framework of ancient historical writing, including stylized speeches and regular summary statements. Luke's source material was likely oral tradition, so the same hermeneutical principles applied to the gospels should also be granted to Acts.[12] Luke is neither playing loose with the details nor writing with a modernist concern for historiographical accuracy. He is capturing the essence of the early Jesus movement by stylistically reworking oral tradition to craft a compelling narrative which conveys an accurate gist of the events described and encourages a positive response to the story from his audience.

What motivated Luke to compose Acts? Bruce correctly contends that the Lukan prologue also applies to Acts: *"The preface to the 'first book' (Lk. 1:1-4) applies equally to both parts of the work: the whole work was undertaken in order that one Theophilus might have a consecutive and reliable account of the rise and progress of Christianity—a subject on which he already possessed a certain amount of information"*[13]. As we discussed above, Luke's 'orderly account' conforms to Greco-Roman

---

9. Bird, *Luke and Acts*, p. 22

10. Dunn, James. 2009. *Beginning from Jerusalem*. Eerdmans. p. 67

11. Bird, *Luke and Acts*, p. 25

12. Dunn, *Beginning*, pp. 60-70

13. Bruce, *Acts*, p. 11

standards of order and accuracy. Luke wants Theophilus to understand Jesus and the movement which resulted from his ministry. While Theophilus was the primary recipient, Luke didn't compose his two works to be consumed only by his direct addressee: *"Undoubtedly Luke intended his own circle of fellow believers and like-minded networks of churches to be interested in his literary endeavors"*[14]. While it is impossible to reconstruct the precise intended audience of his work beyond Theophilus, Luke assumes that they would have understood, agreed with, and been edified by his work. He was not writing into a vacuum, and the presentation of Jesus, his followers, and the Jews and Romans with which they interact would have been readily understandable to his first readers. Luke expects his audience will better understand Jesus and the mission of the church. With this in mind, we are now in a position to analyze the main themes of Acts.

THE KINGDOM OF THE RESURRECTED, ASCENDED MESSIAH AND HIS PEOPLE

Acts begins and ends with the kingdom of God. The opening passage, Acts 1:1-11, and the closing passage, Acts 28:23-31, both evoke the proclamation of the kingdom to the nations. Luke narrates in Acts 1:3 that Jesus *"presented Himself alive after His suffering, by many convincing proofs, appearing to them over a period of forty days and speaking of the things concerning the kingdom of God"*. After explaining to his disciples that God will baptize them with the promised Holy Spirit, Jesus informs his disciples in 1:8 that *"you will receive power when the Holy Spirit has come upon you; and you shall be My witness both in Jerusalem, and in all Judea and Samaria, and even to the remotests part of the earth"*. Upon completing his final discourse, Jesus ascends to heaven. Two angels appear and tell the disciples that Jesus will return in much the same way as he left. In the meantime his disciples must proclaim the kingdom of God to all the nations. At the end of the Acts, Paul is imprisoned in a Roman jail cell, still, according to Acts 28:23, *"solemnly testifying about the kingdom of God"*. In the closing lines of Acts Paul *"stayed two full years in his own rented quarters and was welcoming all who came to him, preaching the kingdom of God and teaching concerning the Lord Jesus Christ with all openness, unhindered"*[15]. Paul, living at the center of the world's greatest imperial power, was openly proclaiming the reign of another king. Jesus instructed his disciples to testify *"to the ends of the earth"*, and Paul had accomplished this goal.

---

14. Bird, *Luke and Acts*, p. 22

15. Acts 28:30-31

The language should sound familiar. God's eschatological kingdom had dawned through the work of the messiah, the Lord Jesus Christ, and it was up to Jesus's followers to share the message with the world. The kingdom is foundational in Acts, so important, in fact, that Thomas Schreiner claims *"the theme of the kingdom actually plays a central role in the book"* and, commenting on Jesus' instructions and Paul's preaching which bookend Acts, *"The kingdom frames the entire work"*[16]. Whatever we make of Peter, Paul, and other early Jesus followers' engagement with the social and political order, it must all be interpreted within the context of God's eschatological kingdom inaugurated by Jesus. As in the Synoptics, the gospel which is proclaimed by the disciples of Jesus is closely connected to the kingdom of God; in fact, despite generations of Protestant interpreters insisting that the concept of 'gospel' is reducible to individualistic models of atonement, Acts 8:12 and 20:24-25, following Luke 16:16, demonstrate that, as one would expect from reading the Jewish Scriptures, gospel and kingdom are inextricably linked.

If the kingdom has come, the king must be sitting on his throne. The resurrection and ascension, much neglected in popular Christian discourse, are of central importance to the gospel of God's kingdom. Both of these events are intimately connected to Jesus's Messianic rule over the eschatological kingdom of God. Peter's Pentecost sermon, examined in the following section, is programmatic for the entire book of Acts and centers on Jesus's resurrection and ascension, as Acts 2:32-33 unambiguously narrates. In the opening passage of Acts the resurrected Jesus explains to his followers the kingdom, instructs them to wait for the Spirit who will empower them to share the gospel with all nations, and is taken up into heaven. Brandon Crowe discusses the significance of the resurrection in Acts: *"The kingdom of God is important in Acts, and the resurrection of Christ is foundational to the rationale of the kingdom . . . Luke's presentation of the coming of the kingdom presupposes the resurrection of Jesus"*[17]. Jesus as the resurrected lord who acts as judge over all creation is a major theme in Acts, as evidenced by Acts 3:15, 4:2, 10:42, and 17:31. Returning to the final verse, Acts 28:31, Paul's preaching about the kingdom of God concerns *"the Lord Jesus Christ"* and would have been incomprehensible had Jesus not been raised from the dead.

The resurrection of Jesus is not the only event which legitimizes his Messianic rule. Acts 1:9 narrates the ascension of Jesus: *"after He had said these things, He was lifted up while they were looking on, and a cloud received HIm out of their sight"*, after which two angels inform the watching disciples that Jesus would return just as he left. Peter describes in Acts 2:33 how at the ascension Jesus was *"exalted to the right*

---

16. Schreiner, Thomas. 2019. *Handbook on Acts and Paul's Letters.* Baker Academic. p. 5

17. Crowe, Brandon. 2020. *The Hope of Israel.* Baker Academic. p. 16

hand of God", and just before Stephen is killed Acts 7:55-56 narrates him gazing "*intently into heaven and* [seeing] *the glory of God, and Jesus standing at the right hand of God*", which Stephen describes in messianic language as "*the Son of Man standing at the right hand of God*". This isn't a description of an idle Jesus, casually relaxing beside God in heaven. Far from it. As Patrick Schriner notes, "*At Jesus' ascent, he became the Lord of heaven and earth . . . After he had completed his earthly work, one final act needed to be finalized. Jesus needed to be installed as the king and thereby confirmed and vindicated in his work by the father. At Christ's ascension, he appeared before the Ancient of Days and was given all dominion . . . He also became the ruler of the world and church because he sits in the throne room of God as the one exalted far above every king this world has ever seen*"[18]. The description of Jesus's ascension in Acts is evocative of Daniel 7, where the Son of Man, a self-referential title employed by Jesus, is instrumental in establishing God's universal reign.[19] The prophets foretold of the coming Davidic king ruling over all creation, and Jesus's resurrection and ascension are the means by which that rule is established. In Acts there are several speeches, often delivered by Peter and Paul, which all possess a very important commonality: "*When the apostles went out and preached the message of Jesus, they highlighted the resurrection and ascension*"[20]. The ascension of Jesus isn't a peripheral or marginal doctrine, it is the logic by which Peter, Paul, and the other disciples could proclaim Jesus as *currently* ruling over the kingdom of God, which encompasses all creation. This is not a metaphor or a 'spiritual' analogy. The earliest followers of Jesus believed in the resurrection and ascension, therefore the eschatological kingdom of God has come and the nations would return to the one true God.

In Luke 3:16 (and parallels) John the Baptist promises that the one who comes after him will "*baptize you with the Holy Spirit and fire*", and in Acts 1:5-8 Jesus informs his disciples the fiery baptism will happen soon after his ascension. As Jesus sits at the right hand of God, the Spirit is dispensed upon the church, enabling them to testify about Jesus to the nations. In Acts 1:6, the disciples still seem to be focused on the very specific restoration of Israel, but as Stephen Dempster points out the ascension and Spirit means Jesus has a rightful claim over all creation; the disciples "*are looking for a restored Israel, but Jesus is looking for a restored world*". By empowering his followers with the Spirit, they are able to fulfil the task of building the inaugurated kingdom of God. Bruce rightly acknowledges the Spirit's prominence in Acts: "*the dominating theme of Acts is the activity of the Holy Spirit . . .*

---

18. Schreiner, *Ascension*, p. 95

19. Schreiner, *Ascension*, p. 88

20. Schreiner, *Ascension*, p. 11

The book might indeed be called 'The Acts of the Holy Spirit', for it is the Spirit who controls the advance of the gospel"[21]. It is, as we shall shortly see, poured out on the Jewish disciples in Jerusalem in Acts 2, but, stunningly, also distributed to the Gentiles in Acts 10. The line which demarcated God's people was the Law, but through Israel's Messiah the boundaries are redrawn around faith and the gift of the Holy Spirit. As Peter affirms before the Jerusalem church leaders in Acts 10:17-18, " *"Therefore if God gave them the same gift as He gave to us also after believing in the Lord Jesus Christ, who was I that I could stand in God's way?" When they heard this, they quieted down and glorified God, saying, "Well then, God has granted to the Gentiles also the repentance that leads to life."'*. Through faith in the Jewish Messiah and the gift of the Holy Spirit, Gentiles are incorporated into the family of God *as Gentiles* without having to follow the Law, precisely the conclusion reached by the Jewish leaders of the church in Acts 15. This new ecclesiology is predicated upon both messianic christology and eschatology; Jesus has begun to reign over creation through his death and ascension, the Spirit has been poured out, and the nations are worshiping Israel's God. As Bruce beautifully summarizes, " *The super-natural manifestations which accompany the spread of the gospel signify not only the Spirit's activity but also the inauguration of the new age in which Jesus reigns as Lord and Messiah"*[22]. The main themes of Acts are all interrelated. Jesus is ruling over a universal kingdom through his death and resurrection, the church, beginning from Jerusalem, is empowered by the Spirit to proclaim Israel's Messiah to the nations, and Gentiles are worshiping Israel's God. The eschatological restoration has unmistakably been inaugurated as the church continues to spread the message. These ideas will permeate the book of Acts and must serve as our framework for understanding texts which address political and economic issues.

Besides addressing and explicating these very important themes, it is entirely possible that Acts was composed as a defense of the church. Despite frequent exhortations throughout the New Testament for followers of Jesus to embody the tradition of Jeremiah 29:7 and, as Paul puts in Romans 12:18, *"be at peace with all men"*, there was no shortage of skepticism towards the nascent Jesus movement in antiquity. As Bird explains, *"Luke is aware that many people, Jews, Greeks, and Romans, are speaking against this peculiar sect of Christians for all sorts of reasons . . . Luke, in different ways, tries to deflect these criticisms of Jesus and the early church. The purpose is, in the end, an apologia pro evangelio, a defense of the gospel"*[23]. It is telling

---

21. Bruce, *Acts*, p. 12

22. Bruce, *Acts*, p. 12

23. Bird, *Luke and Acts, pp. 39-40*

that Luke has Pilate declare Jesus innocent three times[24] while Paul is favorably received by several Roman officials including Jewish client-king Herod Agrippa II and governor Festus in Acts 26:31-32. Even the great Pharisee Gamaliel, in Acts 5:33-39, stood in front of the Sanhedrin and cautioned the council against being too harsh towards Peter and his associates. Perhaps God was at work after all? By casting the early church in this light, Luke is deflecting both potential and actual criticisms. The number of positive encounters between Paul and Roman authorities suggests Luke wants the world to know that for however strange they find Jesus followers to be, they were not violent, seditious revolutionaries. As Bruce comments, *"Luke is obviously concerned . . . to demonstrate that Christianity is not a menace to imperial law and order"*[25]. This in no way detracts from the radical, world-transforming messianic eschatology found in Luke-Acts. In Luke 22:24-27 Jesus instructs his disciples *not* to act like worldly rulers and that true power is found in serving others. Jesus isn't a Roman-style king, and Christians aren't Roman-style subjects. Jesus is still in charge, but his followers won't be mounting an insurrection. Now that we have a firmer grasp on the context and objectives of Acts, we are in a position to understand the political and economic consequences of Luke's work.

GOD HAS MADE HIM BOTH LORD AND CHRIST: ACTS 2:14-36

Jesus, moments before he was ascended to heaven and installed as king of the world, revealed to his disciples that the Spirit would soon be poured out, enabling them to proclaim God's kingdom to the ends of the earth. That day would come on Pentecost. The feast, which was originally established in the Law as a celebration of harvest[26], had also become in Jewish tradition connected with the giving of the Law to Moses on Mount Sinai, and, much like Passover, fueled hopes for eschatological restoration.[27] In Acts 2:1-13, Peter and the other disciples were filled with the Holy Spirit. Jews, who had presumably come from the diaspora but were living in Jerusalem, were able to hear the Spirit-empowered disciples speak in their own language, testifying to, as Acts 2:11 says, *"the mighty deeds of God"*. The crowds were divided: some wondered what was transpiring while others accused

---

24. Luke 23:4, 14-15, 22

25. Bruce, *Acts*, p. 12

26. Leviticus 23:15-21

27. Schreiner, *Handbook*, pp. 11-12

the disciples of being drunk. Peter stands up to issue a lengthy response in Acts 2:14-36.

Brandon Crowe identifies the significance of Peter's response: "*Peter's Pentecost sermon (2:14-36) is crucially important for the narrative of Acts and is programmatic for what follows*"[28]. All of the major themes in Acts are embedded in this passage. After assuring the audience his friends have not been drinking, Peter explains that the strange manifestations of the Spirit were in fulfillment of prophecy, quoting Joel 2:28-32 in Acts 2:17-21. The quotation begins with an eschatological indicator ("*in the last days*") and describes how God will pour out His Spirit on all mankind with the purpose of prophesying. Accompanying this dispensation of the Spirit are incredible signs which attest to the coming "*Day of the Lord*". Because God has decisively acted by sending forth His Spirit, "*Everyone who calls on the name of the Lord will be saved*". Joel 2 is a classic restoration prophecy, and the citation employed by Peter from Joel connects several major themes: inaugurated eschatology, Spirit empowerment, and an openness to "everyone". Joel's prophecy was fulfilled at Pentecost.

After quoting Joel, Peter describes how the passage relates to Jesus. Acts 2:22-32 expounds upon the death and resurrection of Jesus. In 2:22-23, Peter presents Jesus as a prophet who was crucified because the "*Men of Israel*", whom Peter is addressing, handed him over to the Romans. God raised Jesus up from the dead, and Peter quotes another Old Testament passage, Psalm 16:8-11, as a justification for God's action. Although Psalm 16 is likely a historical description of David's faith in God amidst opposition, Peter interprets the Psalm as pointing to the resurrection of Jesus, also a fulfillment of 2 Samuel 7.[29] Acts 2:31 is the first appearance of *christos* language in Acts and establishes the tight relationship between christology and resurrection in Luke's narrative. As Crowe puts it, "*the framework for understanding Christ in Acts (in light of the usage of the term in the Gospel of Luke) is the resurrected, Davidic Son who reigns over an everlasting kingdom*"[30] The next two verses, Acts 2:32-33, are the climax of Peter's speech and confirm Crowe's interpretation: "*This Jesus God raised up again, to which we are all witnesses. Therefore having been exalted to the right hand of God, and having received from the Father the promise of the Holy Spirit, He has poured forth this which you both see and hear*". After alluding to Psalm 110, Peter issues a cutting reproof to his audience in Acts 2:36: "*Therefore let all the house of Israel know for certain that God has made Him both Lord and Christ—this Jesus whom you crucified*". Peter's speech leaves little room for interpretation; Jesus,

---

28. Crowe, *Hope of Israel*, p. 19

29. Crowe, *Hope of Israel*, p. 26-27

30. Crowe, *Hope of Israel*, p. 27

according to the apostle, is the crucified, resurrected, and ascended Lord of all creation who has poured out God's Spirit upon his followers on the day of Pentecost. The old age was coming to a close, and the new, long-promised age of restoration had begun. The "*Men of Israel*" listening to Peter need only to heed his message.

Acts 2:37-42 narrates the response of Peter's audience. They were "*pierced to the heart*" by his words and wanted to respond properly. Peter instructs them to repent and be baptized in the name of Jesus Christ for forgiveness, after which they would receive the gift of the Spirit and be "*saved from the perverse generation*". Three thousand people take Peter up on his offer and devote themselves to the apostle's teaching. Throughout the rest of Acts, Luke will continue to draw on the themes found in Peter's speech to explain how the message of Jesus, which was powerfully taking hold in Jerusalem, spreads to the rest of creation. There are hints, in 2:21 and 2:39, that the message wouldn't be restricted to Jews alone. God's kingdom had broken in, and the disciples were empowered by the Spirit, exactly as Joel had foretold, enabling them to spread the message of Jesus to everyone who would listen, rescuing them from the present evil age and building God's eschatological kingdom. The Spirit becomes the sign that one had responded correctly to Israel's Messiah, a response which included both repentance and acceptance of the message. The framework established in this passage is paradigmatic for Luke's narrative. The Spirit will continue to guide Jesus's followers as they testify about his kingdom. Even if Acts is a political defense of the church, designed in part to deflect accusations of insurrection and revolution, Luke refuses to compromise his christology. Jesus is Lord, full stop.

Sharing Isn't Socialism: Acts 2:43-47; 4:36-5:11; 6:1-6

Richard Horsley is far too competent a historian to draw a direct parallel between the sharing of goods among Jesus followers in Jerusalem and modern-day socialist movements. He gives the impression, however, that the early church and socialism are more or less in continuity with one another. Whatever happened in Jerusalem after Pentecost is, in his view, opposed to capitalism and a justification for Christian socialism.[31] Horsley, following the discipline of biblical scholarship in general, never bothers to define capitalism or socialism. In Chapter 2 I argued that the Austrian school of economics provides the only consistent, irreducible, and universally applicable definitions of those terms. Capitalism is an economic arrangement based on private ownership, decentralized decisionmaking, and voluntary exchange. Socialism is its opposite; resources are 'publicly' (i.e. government)

---

31. Horsley, *Bow Down*, pp. 201-204

owned and regulated, economic decision making is delegated to politicians and technocrats, and exchange is not conducted on a voluntary basis.

After Peter's speech, Luke describes the unity which occurred between Jesus followers in Jerusalem. The first passage, Acts 2:43-47, contains two relevant verses which many modern Christians have appropriated to justify socialism. Acts 2:44-45 read as follows: "*And all those who had believed were together and had all things in common; and they began selling their property and possessions and were sharing them with all, as anyone might have need*". Luke returns to this theme again in 4:32-35: "*And the congregation of those who believed were of one heart and soul; and not one of them claimed that anything belonging to him was his own, but all things were common property to them. And with great power the apostles were giving testimony to the resurrection of the Lord Jesus, and abundant grace was upon them all. For there was not a needy person among them, for all who were owners of land or houses would sell them and bring the proceeds of the sales and lay them at the apostles' feet, and they would be distributed to each as any had need*". In the latter passage charity is predicated upon the power of the apostles and their testimony of the resurrected Lord Jesus. Is Luke describing a prototypical socialist community, one which is commensurate with the ideas of Saint-Simon and Karl Marx? Not quite.

In the same passages, referenced above, in which Horsley hints that Luke is a subtle advocate for modern socialism, Horsley rightly identifies how disaffected Jesus followers, many of whom were economically oppressed by the ruling class, were incentivized to create a counter-cultural community of shared goods which operated, as much as possible, outside of the existing economic order in Judea and Galilee. I believe Horsley is entirely correct on this point, as the work of Oakman, Crossley, and Myles also demonstrate. The Spirit-empowered community of Jesus believers, living in the kingdom of God, would not emulate the exploitative economic policies of the Roman and Jewish elite. There was also a precedent for establishing alternative economic arrangements in Second Temple Judaism. Dunn describes two groups, the Essenes at Qumran and Therapeutae ascetic community located outside of Jerusalem, which practiced the common sharing of goods. Certainly many Jesus followers in Jerusalem were familiar with the Essenes, and the seriousness with which both the former communities and the church in Jerusalem took their identity makes the renunciation of property entirely comprehensible.[32] In neither case, however, is there a justification for calling the Jerusalem church 'socialist' or concluding that modern Christians are obligated to support socialist policies.

---

32. Dunn, *Beginning*, pp. 181-183

We have already discussed at length the Jesus tradition's complex and nuanced understanding of wealth. Even within the writings of Luke, who characteristically criticises those he describes as *plousios*, wealth is not inherently evil. While most of the wealthy in antiquity accumulated and sustained their wealth through violent exploitation, some are portrayed as putting it to good use. In Luke 18:18-27, the rich young ruler is commanded to give up his possessions because, as Jesus craftily forces him to acknowledge, the man regarded his wealth as an idol. Both Zaccheaus and Joseph of Arimathea are wealthy men who use their resources in service of the kingdom. While Zaccheaus forfeits his ill-gotten gain, he is not commanded to sell everything. Three women provide for Jesus's financial means in Luke 8, and the Samaritan in Luke 10 uses his resources to help a beleaguered Jew he finds beaten on the roadside. In Acts 9:36-40, Dorcas is known for her generosity while Lydia houses the apostles in Acts 16. No other church is described in Acts as following the pattern of the Jerusalem community either. As in the Jesus tradition, so in Acts: wealth is morally neutral but extremely dangerous. Those who possess wealth must use it in service of the kingdom by providing for the needs of others, which is what the church in Jerusalem is doing. Luke has a much more sophisticated understanding of wealth and riches than many of his modern interpreters who attempt to use his work to promote their political and economic ideologies.

Luke twice uses the Greek phrase *hapanta koina*, "all in common"[33], to describe the culture of charity which characterized the Jerusalem church. Those who had wealth used it in service of the church. Luke never claims that every member of the church sold all of their possessions at once; in fact, believers retained at least some (and probably much more) of what they owned. Acts 2:45 and 4:34-35 suggest that property was sold and the proceeds distributed to the poor with the purpose of meeting specific needs. Luke describes the church in Acts 2:46 as *"breaking bread from house to house"*, implying, obviously, that some members in the community did *not* sell their homes (or perhaps renounce their lease; many urban living quarters were rented in antiquity) since they were being used as gathering spaces. Dunn comments *"Luke does not say that all believers sold off all property and possessions and contributed the proceeds to the common fund . . . Rather his description envisages members of the new sect selling off possessions and goods as need arose for more funds"*[34]. In Acts 4:36-37, Joseph Barnabas sells a tract of land and offers the proceeds to the apostles. He doesn't sell everything but makes a significant financial sacrifice on behalf of the church.

---

33. Luke 2:44, 4:32

34. Dunn, *Beginning*, p. 183

The notoriously perplexing story of Ananias and Sapphira in Acts 5:1-11 is set in contrast to Joseph Barnabas. The couple sells a piece of property (again, not *all* their property) but keeps some of the proceeds for themselves without disclosing it to the apostles. In Acts 5:4, Peter condemns the couple: "*While* [the property] *remained unsold, did it not remain your own? And after it was sold, was it not under your control? Why is it that you have conceived this deed in your heart? You have not lied to men but to God*". Ananias falls dead before the apostles; when Sapphira visits them just hours later, she too lies about keeping the proceeds and also perishes. For our purposes, this story illustrates the absence of an expectation for early Jesus followers to give up *everything* they owned. The Jerusalem church does not abolish private property, but the gospel of God's kingdom transforms their approach to wealth. Both the story of Joseph Barnabas and Ananias and Saphira illustrate this point; the difference between the two is that while Joseph was open and honest about his giving, the couple lied to the apostles. Adding to this point, the phrase "*common property*" or simply "*common*" found in the NASB translation of Acts 2:44 and 4:32 is a cognate of the Greek word *koinos*. It is used several times in Acts to denote that which is profane or unclean according to the Law[35]. We should therefore see the employment of *koinos* in this category within the context of Joseph Barnabas' charity; in light of the kingdom, those who have wealth should use it to meet common needs. Dunn contrasts the church in Jerusalem with the Qumran community: "*the community of goods was much more voluntary than, say, Qumran, and property was sold, apparently, only in order to maintain the common fund, from which the poorer members of the community could be supported*"[36].

The operative word in the quotation of Dunn above is *voluntary*. This alone disqualifies Acts 2 and 4 from being interpreted as an ancient example of early socialism or a justification for authoritarian state control of economic activity in the modern world. None of the believers in Jerusalem were forced to give up their wealth and possessions, nor was there an expectation that believers live in abject poverty. Instead, Jesus followers are radically transformed by the gospel and the Spirit which cause them to reassess their commitment to personal possessions. They were compelled by the Spirit to provide for those less fortunate when the need arose, and they valued the needs of others more than the maintenance of personal wealth. The church in Jerusalem imitated Zacchaeus. Convinced that Jesus was the Messiah who brought about the eschatological kingdom, the church oriented all of their values, including material possessions, around the Messiah's teachings. Peter and the other apostles are not holding a sword to the throats of

---

35. Acts 10:14, 28; 11:8

36. Dunn, *Beginning*, p. 184

believers and demanding they turn over their possessions. The economic arrangement recorded in Acts is entirely voluntary and therefore entirely compatible with capitalism. Socialism, which by definition relies on involuntary confiscation and coercion, absolutely cannot be legitimized by the Jerusalem church.

There is also no attempt by the Jerusalem church to advocate for the political authorities to impose economic policies on non-believers which resemble their community values. In fact, between Acts 2 and 4, Peter and the other associates find themselves in trouble with the Sanhedrin, and Horsley's thesis that the community represents an alternative to 'the system' is ironically proven by Luke. Genuine charity cannot be imposed by force, especially if the ones wielding force don't even believe in Jesus. Had Peter requested the Sanhedrin or the Roman governor to pass a law which confiscated wealth and redistributed it to those Peter thought were deserving then the socialist reading of this passage might have some historical legitimacy. Instead, the Jerusalem church operates outside of the system, motivated by the values of God's kingdom, which cannot be inflicted upon people under threat of violence. An economic arrangement based on coercion, rightfully labeled 'socialism', is entirely antithetical to the teachings of Jesus and the witness of the early church. Even from this early date, Jesus followers believed their movement transcended all temporal political and economic systems because the resurrected and ascended Lord of the world was currently ruling over God's creation. Acts, like the gospels, attests to the *suprapolitical* nature of the kingdom. The church was, quite simply, playing on a higher level than everyone else.

In Acts 6:1-6 a dispute arises between the widows of Hellenistic Jews and native Hebrews; presumably those two groups represent Jews who had returned to Jerusalem from the diaspora and those who were raised in Judea.[37] The dispute was caused by an accusation that the Hellenistic widows were being overlooked in the distribution of food. The twelve disciples thought this a distraction to their ministry and selected seven men to oversee the distribution. Once again, the early church saw an 'economic' problem and just solved it themselves. There was no appeal to the governing authorities, no campaign for equity, no attempt to change the existing economic order, and no hint that this was a matter concerning anyone outside of the church. As a voluntary, self-regulating community, the Jerusalem church embodies the social *ethos* of political philosophers following Murray Rothbard, not Karl Marx.

There is a principle here, though, which should pose a major challenge to modern Western Christians. Luke depicts Jesus followers operating outside of the system and self-identifying as members of God's kingdom. This is the fundamental

---

37. I find the argument in Dunn, *Beginning*, pp. 242-254 persuasive.

starting point. Following the Jerusalem church, kingdom ethics require believers to reevaluate their possessions in light of Jesus's cosmic rule. It is shameful how many Western Christians, including progressives who falsely believe the Bible can be used to justify state economic intervention, do not view their personal belongings and wealth as a conduit to serve others. Many of us are content to give a small amount here and there, and perhaps even contribute regularly to our local church. But many Christians have entirely abandoned the idea that we should wisely steward our resources in a way which is oriented towards the needs of others. Many Christians are content to live like the rich young ruler when we should instead follow the example of Zacchaeus and Joseph Barnabas. This is not an indictment against private property or capital accumulation, both of which are a necessary prerequisite for creating any wealth at all. Rejecting property rights is the trap into which modern socialist authoritarians have fallen, ironically generating the conditions which lead to systemic poverty through the mechanism of state intervention. For the Christ follower, private property and capital accumulation are not ends in themselves but means of building God's kingdom and providing for the material needs of all. That producers who satisfy the most needs are rewarded with profit should not concern us, and perhaps we should see the Christian entrepreneur or businessperson as entrusted by God with a spiritual gift which can be used in the service of others. Christians are called to radical charity, and charity, voluntarily sharing resources, has nothing to do with socialism. In fact, it is socialism's direct antithesis.

The economic arrangement in Jerusalem likely contributed to long-run financial instability in the church. In Acts 11:27-30, a prophet named Agabus foretells a massive famine during the reign of Claudius[38] which would hit Judea particularly hard. The leaders determined to collect money for the Judean Christians and tasked Barnabas and Saul with the collection. In one of perhaps the most neglected New Testament side stories, Paul addresses this collection at several points in his letters. In 1 Corinthians 16:1-4, Paul instructs the Corinthians to set aside money for the collection, and in Romans 15:22-27 he reveals his intended return to Jerusalem for the sake of delivering the collection. Despite the best charitable intentions of early Jesus followers, without capital accumulation it is impossible to meet long-run economic needs. As Dunn notes, *such a policy was hardly a model for the long term; simply to continue to dispense with property holdings and possessions was a recipe for communal poverty in the not-too-distant future*[39]. While all of the additional New Testament evidence, both in Acts and the epistles, demonstrate a consistent

---

38. Emperor of Rome from 41-54 CE.

39. Dunn, *Beginning*, p. 184

commitment to charity and a kingdom-oriented attitude towards goods, no other community is depicted as adopting the same economic arrangement as Jerusalem. Once every property and possession has been sold there is nothing left with which to meet basic needs. Dunn suggests the decisions made in Acts 2 and 4 in all likelihood created the conditions in which an external charitable collection was necessary: "*we certainly cannot exclude the likelihood that repeated sales of property, together with growing demands on the common fund, constituted a major factor in the subsequent relative poverty of the Jerusalem church*"[40]. Even the best of motives result in unintended consequences, a lesson socialists refuse to learn.

At this point in our discussion of Acts we have reviewed the major relevant themes and explained their political and economic implications. The texts I will examine in the rest of this chapter build upon the case I have already made, leaving little need for extended footnotes or detailed academic commentary. Jesus is the only true resurrected and ascended King and his Spirit-empowered community of believers operates in a space beyond and above the kingdoms of the world. Acts will continue to develop these ideas in surprising and creative ways while simultaneously preparing us to engage with Paul and his letters. The rest of this chapter will be a romp through some of the most significant passages in Acts, exploring their political and economic mechanics as well as how we might draw principles from them for the church today.

"We Must Obey God Rather Than Men": Acts 3-7, 12

Not long after Pentecost, Peter and the disciples run straight into conflict with the Jerusalem authorities. Peter's several encounters with the political elites provide ample opportunities to proclaim Jesus, and many of these traditions resemble the conflict Jesus himself had with the Jerusalem establishment before his crucifixion. Acts 3 provides the immediate context for the first showdown. Peter and John heal a man, and the wondering crowds gather at the portico of Solomon, a meeting area which provided temple-goers access to the city[41]. Peter takes the occasion to preach about Jesus, discussing his crucifixion and resurrection. The healing was, according to Acts 3:16, "*on the basis of faith in His name*", which prompts Peter to exhort the crowds to repentance: "*Therefore repent and return, so that your sins may be wiped away, in order that times of refreshing may come from the presence of the Lord; and that He may send Jesus, the Christ appointed to you, whom heaven must receive until the*

---

40. Dunn, *Beginning*, p. 184
41. Ferguson, *Backgrounds*, p. 562

period of restoration of all things"[42]. Thus repentance is framed by the inaugurated eschatological moment; the ascended Lord will return to finally restore all things, and Israel must be ready. Peter promptly attracts attention from the authorities; in Acts 4:1-4 the Sadducees and temple guard arrest the two apostles for "*teaching the people and proclaiming in Jesus the resurrection from the dead*", although many believe the two apostles. The stage is set for Peter and John's showdown with the men who turned Jesus over for execution.

On the following day, Peter and John stand before a cast of characters with whom Luke's audience is familiar. Acts 4:5-8 describes a gathering of the Sanhedrin, the "*rulers and elders and scribes . . . Annas the high priest . . . Caiaphas and John and Alexander, and all who were of high-prestily descent*". Like Jesus, the two apostles must make a defense before the most powerful political leaders in the Jewish world. They specifically ask Peter "*By what power, or in what name, have you done this*", referring to the healing in Acts 3. Peter offers a direct response in Acts 4:8-12, telling them that it was done in the name of Jesus, blaming them for his crucifixion, and testifying that God raised Jesus from the dead. Peter then references Psalm 118:22, the very same passage quoted by Jesus against the authorities in Luke 20:17, informing the Sanhedrin that salvation is found in no one else. The council is flummoxed. In Acts 4:13-18, Peter and John are depicted, correctly, as "*uneducated and untrained men*", but the council is amazed by their confidence and the undeniable presence of the man they had healed. There is no adequate reply to Peter because they cannot dismiss what had happened. The council's only option is to instruct them to stop speaking or teaching in the name of Jesus. Peter, confronted with a direct command by the Jewish political authorities, refuses. Acts 4:19-20 records Peter's response: "*Whether it is right in the sight of God to give heed to you rather than to God, you be the judge; for we cannot stop speaking about what we have seen and heard*". Peter, when confronted with a choice between following the Jewish political leaders or honoring God, chooses God. Following Jeremiah and Daniel, Peter does not call for rebellion nor does he legitimize the Sanhedrin's power. His loyalty and mission transcends the political powers, whom God will deal with on His own time. Peter must obey his God no matter the consequences.

After this exchange, Peter and John are released by the council. Acts 4:23-31 is a strategic selection of Lukan theology. The men return to the other disciples and report what had happened. They praise the God of creation, citing Psalm 146:6 and Psalm 2:1-2: "*Why did the Gentiles rage, and the peoples devise futile things? The kings of the earth took their stand, and the rulers were gathered together against the Lord and against His Christ*". By conflating the Sanhedrin with gentile

---

42. Acts 3:19-21

rulers who oppose God Luke is delegitimizing their authority and placing them in direct opposition to the Messiah Jesus and his people. The dividing line is drawn, and those who oppose Jesus are on the wrong side even if they happen to be the self-proclaimed leaders of Israel. Peter would soon find himself in trouble with the Sanhedrin for a second time. As the message of Jesus continues to increase, *"the high priest rose up, along with all his associates (that is the sect of the Sadducees), and they were filled with jealousy. They laid hands on the apostles and put them in a public jail"*[43]. The Greek word for '*jealousy*' is a cognate of *zelos*, the same term used in Luke 6:15 to describe the other Simon who was in Jesus's inner circle of disciples, and as we discussed above denotes a willingness to use violence against perceived enemies of God. In Acts 5:19-25 an angel rescues Peter and his associates from jail during the night and instructs them to *"Go, stand and speak to the people in the temple the whole message of this Life"*. The following day, they obediently preach in the temple and are once again apprehended and brought before the Sanhedrin.

The apostles are questioned and specifically asked why they had disobeyed the council's previous command to stop proclaiming Jesus. Peter's retort is framed by the resurrection and ascension of Jesus and builds upon his previous statement in Acts 4:19-20 about giving heed to God rather than men: *"Peter and the apostles answered, "We must obey God rather than men. The God of our fathers raised up Jesus, whom you had put to death by hanging Him on a cross. He is the one whom God exalted to His right hand as a Prince and a Savior, to grant repentance to Israel, and forgiveness of sins. And we are witnesses of these things; and so is the Holy Spirit, whom God has given to those who obey Him"* [44]. Why is it that Peter firmly expresses his obligation to obey God rather than the Sanhedrin? Because Jesus is the crucified, resurrected, and ascended Lord of creation through whom forgiveness was accomplished and the Holy Spirit poured out on those who obey him. Luke strongly emphasises the concept of 'obedience' using cognates of the Greek term *peitharcheo* in both 5:29 and 5:32. Interestingly enough, the word *peitharcheo* denotes submission to a ruler or superior and is most likely employed by Luke as a subtle jab at the illegitimate authority of the Sanhedrin in comparison to the real authority held by the ascended Christ. In Acts 5:33, the Sadducee-led Sanhedrin is furious. They want to kill Peter (and his associates) because they know he is speaking against their authority.

Acts 5:34-42 narrates the intervention of a Pharisee named Gamaliel, perhaps the most prominent, influential, and respected teacher of the law in Jerusalem.[45]

---

43. Acts 5:17-18

44. Acts 5:29-32

45. Ferguson, *Backgrounds*, pp. 490-492

Coincidently, Gamaliel just so happens to have instructed the apostle Paul.[46] Gamaliel addresses the Council and reminds them of two revolutionary movements, one led by Theudas and the other by Judas of Galilee, that dissipated after the death of their leaders. Gamaliel cautions against harming the disciples: *"let them alone, for if this plan or action is of men, it will be overthrown; but if it is from God, you will not be able to overthrow them; or else you may even be found fighting against God"*. Peter's speech enraged the Sadducees both because it challenged their authority and also included a defense of Jesus's resurrection, and affront to Sadducean theology. The Pharisee Gamaliel didn't write it off as an impossibility: *"One gets the sense from Gamaliel's response—especially in light of what we know about the Pharisees . . . —that Gamaliel is not a priori against the possibility that a dead man has been raised. Instead, his message is "wait and see""*[47]. The Sanhedrin heeds Gamaliel's advice and frees them.

Peter's words should have a profound impact on the way in which modern Christians think about their engagement with political authorities. Following the longstanding Jewish tradition of Jeremiah 29:7 in which God's people are instructed to be at peace with the authorities without compromising their faithfulness to God, Peter advocates neither violent revolution nor blind submission. Since Jesus is currently sitting on the throne, Peter's loyalties transcend temporal political structures and profoundly relativizes them. The Sanhedrin isn't really in charge. Peter isn't recklessly disobeying the law or advocating that the council be overthrown and replaced with new leaders who are more congenial to the Jesus movement. He doesn't lobby the Jewish elite to impose Christian values on Jerusalem by force of law. He testifies that the crucified Jesus is also the resurrected and ascended Christ who must be obeyed before all worldly leaders. Peter also subtly suggests, just as Jeremiah predicted the fall of Babylon, that the Sanhedrin will not survive the kingdom's consummation. Jesus would return to set the record straight. This is precisely the kind of attitude the New Testament authors encourage their audiences to have towards the governing authorities and is an extension of the Jesus tradition's political ethic. Revolution is off the table. So is compromise. We can seek to live at peace with our neighbors and the authorities without denying that Jesus is the Lord who will soon return. If our choice is between man and God, we must obey God rather than man.

Two more examples illuminate this dynamic. In Acts 6:8-15, Stephen, a man *"full of grace and power, was performing great wonders and signs among the people"*. Several opponents lie about Stephen to the authorities, and he is brought before

---

46. Acts 22:3

47. Crowe, *Hope of Israel*, p. 41

the Sanhedrin. In Acts 7, Stephen explains himself to the authorities by reviewing Israel's long history and condemning them for executing Jesus. The enraged crowd stones Stephen to death. This is an extrajudicial lynching; Luke provides no indication that the Romans were consulted before Stephen's execution. A young man named Saul watches lynching with approval. Stephen dies because of his testimony to the Sanhedrin, the first martyr for Christ. He did not fight back or attempt to replace his opponents, but he also refused to stop speaking about Jesus. Luke narrates in Acts 7:60 that Stephen *"fell asleep"*, an expression which describes the intermediate state between bodily death and bodily resurrection, the fate which awaits those who are faithful to Jesus.[48] Even though Stephen suffered, God would vindicate him. Herod Agrippa, friend of emperors Claudius and Caligula, is given control over Judea in 41 CE and aligned himself with the Pharisees.[49] He executes James in Acts 12:2 and arrests Peter during Passover. Peter is delivered from prison by God who subsequently kills Herod through an angelic intermediary.[50] The gospel continues to flourish despite stiff opposition from the Jerusalem establishment.

GENTILES AT THE ENDS OF THE EARTH: ACTS 8-11, 15

Jesus, in Acts 1:8, envisions a broad trajectory for the gospel's geographical spread. Once empowered by the Holy Spirit, his followers testify about him in Jerusalem, then move into wider Judea and Samaria, and then to the remotest parts of the earth. After Stephen's death an intense persecution breaks out against the church, and Saul, witness to the death of Stephen, is viciously antagonistic towards believers.[51] Acts 8:1 is a fulfillment of 1:8: *"on that day a great persecution began against the church in Jerusalem, and they were all scattered throughout the regions of Judea and Samaria, except the apostles"*. This is, as Schreiner explains, a major turning point in Acts: *"Stephen's speech became the catalyst for propelling the gospel outside of Jerusalem into Judea, Galilee, and Samaria"*[52]. From this point forward the gospel of the kingdom will burst out of confinement in Jerusalem and spread throughout the region.

Phillip is the first believer to preach in Samaria, and he performs, as Jesus predicted in Acts 1:8, signs which convict the Samaritans.[53] Note the cluster of significant themes relayed by Luke in 8:12: *"when they believed Phillip preaching*

---

48. Wright, *Resurrection*, p. 216

49. Ferguson, *Backgrounds*, pp. 418-419

50. Acts 12:6-25

51. Acts 8:1-4

52. Schreiner, *Handbook*, p. 17

53. Acts 8:4-13

the good news [cognate of *euangelion*] *about the kingdom of God and the name of Jesus Christ, they were being baptized, men and women alike*". Following this, Peter and John join Phillip in Samaria and lay hands on believing Samaritans who then receive the gift of the Spirit.[54] In Acts 8:26-40, Phillip is visited by an angel who tells him to travel the road from Jerusalem southwest to Gaza. On his way Phillip meets an Ethiopian eunuch, court official of Ethiopia's queen, who is reading from Isaiah. Phillip seizes the opportunity to preach Jesus, and the eunuch believes and is baptized. Phillip continues to preach the gospel in that region.

In Acts 9:1-30 Saul solicits the high priest for permission to persecute followers of Jesus in Damascus. Saul is promptly granted his request. On the road to Damascus he encounters Jesus, who asks Saul why he is persecuting Jesus himself. Jesus informs Saul that he must go to Damascus where he would be told what to do next. When Jesus departs, Saul is blind and must be led into the city by associates. A man named Ananias reluctantly agrees to host the persecutor after the Lord appears to Ananias in a vision and relays His plans for Saul: "*Go, for he is a chosen instrument of MIne, to bear My name before the Gentiles and kings and the sons of Israel*"[55]. Ananias, after laying hands on Saul, recounts his message from God. Saul is filled with the Spirit and, according to 8:20, immediately proclaims Jesus as Son of God in the Damascus Synagogue. There is an attempt to kill Saul which requires his escape to Jerusalem, only to fall victim to another death plot. The Jerusalem church send Paul to Tarsus for safe-keeping. Little did they know that Saul would become a prominent figure in the early Jesus movement.

Something entirely unforeseen in the mission to the nations occurs in Acts 10, an event with monumental repercussions for the history of Christianity. Cornelius, a Roman centurion stationed in Caesarea and described in Acts 10:2 as "*a devout man and one who feared God with all his household, and gave many alms to the Jewish people and prayed to God continually*", is visited by an angel of the Lord. The angel instructs Cornelius to send men to Joppa and retrieve Peter, who was staying in that city. Cornelius swiftly obeys. On the following day Peter falls into a trance while praying in Joppa. Peter is shown, three times, a heavenly sheet containing numerous animals and is instructed by a voice to kill them and eat. Peter objects; on the sheet were unclean animals, and Peter had never consumed anything unclean. The voice offers a terse response: "*What God has cleansed, no longer consider unholy*"[56]. Peter, bewildered by the vision, ponders its meaning when the men from Cornelius appear for him. The Spirit commands Peter to accompany them, and

---

54. Acts 8:14-25

55. Acts 9:15

56. Acts 10:15

Peter obeys. When he arrives in Caesarea Peter greets Cornelius and a crowd of people eager to hear him speak. At this moment, Peter finally discerns his vision. He promptly explains it to Cornelius and the crowd: *"You yourselves know how unlawful it is for a man who is a Jew to associate with a foreigner or to visit him; and yet God has shown me that I should not call any man unholy or unclean"*[57]. Cornelius shares his own angelic vision with Peter. Dunn expounds the significance of the two visions: *"it is the double testimony of divine approval given by the complementary visions which puts the issue beyond doubt: God approves and wills the next step"*[58]. Cornelius then invites Peter to address the crowd, assured that whatever Peter says reflects God's will.

Peter's speech (and its attending results) in Acts 10:34-48 is one of the most consequential in Acts. As Crowe rightly observes, *"This [speech] marks the gospel's advance among the Gentiles . . . and thus a major turning point in both the narrative of Acts and the history of salvation"*. Peter's opening and closing lines are decisive yet entirely unanticipated: *"I most certainly understand now that God is not one to show partiality, but in every nation the man who fears Him and does what is right is welcome to Him . . . Of Him all the prophets bear witness that through His name everyone who believes in Him receives forgiveness of sins"*[59]. The gospel is not only for Jews but also Gentiles. The heart of Peter's speech revolves around the major themes in Acts, as Crowe summarizes, *"Jesus is universal Lord, a truth demonstrated by his resurrection from the dead and heavenly reign . . . [this] therefore explains in large measure why and how the gospel goes to the Gentiles: Jesus is not only Lord over Israel but Lord over all nations and people"*. Since Jesus rules the world he is available to all who believe in him. What happens next catches Peter by surprise. Acts 10:44-45 narrates this world-changing event: *"While Peter was still speaking these words, the Holy Spirit fell upon all those who were listening to the message. All the circumcised believers who came with Peter were amazed, because the gift of the Holy Spirit had been poured out on the Gentiles also"*. God was accepting the Gentiles *as Gentiles* and giving them the Spirit based on faith. Peter speedily baptizes the Gentiles and stays in Caesarea for a few days.

Word of what happened in Caesarea quickly traveled but was met with apprehension, as Luke explains in Acts 11:1-3: *"Now the apostles and the brethren who were throughout Judea heard that the Gentiles also had received the word of God. And when Peter came up to Jerusalem, those who were circumcised took issue with him, saying, "You went to uncircumcised men and ate with them"*. Their concern is not

---

57. Acts 10:28

58. Dunn, *Beginning*, p. 384

59. Acts 10:34-35, 43

unwarranted; as we discussed above, the Law defined Jewish identity, serving as the boundary which separated God's people from the nations. It was the definitive sign that one was in right-standing with God and an expression of faithfulness. Peter, by that point the most important leader of the nascent church, had eaten with uncircumcised men in violation of the Law.[60] Peter's actions were justifiably disconcerting for the movement's leaders. In Acts 11:4-16 Peter recounts his vision of the sheet, the reception of Cornelius' house to his message, and the impartation of the Spirit to his gentile audience. His message ends with a theological bombshell: " *"Therefore if God gave to them the same gift as He gave to us also after believing in the Lord Jesus Christ, who was I that I could stand in God's way?" When they heard this, they quieted down and glorified God, saying, "Well then, God has granted to the Gentiles also the repentance that leads to life"*[61].

Peter's dramatic rhetorical crescendo marks another decisive turning point in the mission of the early church. The people of God had always been demarcated by His Law. Law adherence was both ecclesiological in that it identified who was a part of Abraham's family and eschatological in that those who kept it were guaranteed (according to the Pharisees and their followers, at least) a place in the world to come. Gentiles were welcome to join Israel, and Leviticus 17-18 outlined legal stipulations for sojourning foreigners[62], but the Law distinguished Abraham's family from the nations. Peter's encounter with Cornelius forever altered the place of Gentiles in God's family. Gentiles who believed in the Jewish Messiah, Jesus Christ, were given the gift of God's Holy Spirit *in the exact same way* as Peter's Jewish, Law-abiding compatriots. Apparently God was now accepting Gentiles based on their response to His anointed king who ruled over the world. The nations would know God, as Jesus promised, but they were not required to proselytize and adopt the Law in order to do so. This question of the relationship between Jews, Gentiles, and the Law will dominate much of the New Testament including three of Paul's most famous letters, Romans, Galatians, and Ephesians. Much like Jesus radically redefined the nature of God's eschatological kingdom, the Spirit radically redefined the nature of God's family. Schreiner summarizes the

---

60. A crucial caveat is offered in Sloan, *Jesus and the Law of Moses*, pp. 216-221. Sloan points out that the actual objection to Peter had nothing to do with the menu; the vision was not an abrogation of the food laws for Jews but rather, as Luke indicates, a call to accept uncircumcised Gentiles through faith and the Spirit. The Jerusalem church leaders objected to Peter dining with uncircumcised men, even if Peter consumed kosher food during the meal. The Law itself does not restrict foreigners in Israel's midst from eating unclean food (Leviticus 11:2, Deuteronomy 14:21), only those who are circumcised. Acts 10-11 should not, therefore, be interpreted as a repudiation of Jewish identity but rather an *inclusion* of the Gentiles into God's family.

61. Acts 11:17-18

62. Sloan, *Jesus and the Law of Moses*, pp. 221-226

narrative succinctly: "*The story of Cornelius and his friends clarifies that Gentiles are equal members of the covenant community and equal recipients of the Spirit*"[63].

Subsequent Christian theology and biblical scholarship has mostly learned the wrong lesson from this account. Many non-Jewish Christians have supposed this story as explicitly proving that 'Judaism' and its bad Law were being replaced (or perhaps superseded) by 'Christianity' and its good 'grace'. Our review in Chapter 6 dispelled the myth that Jews were seeking to earn God's favor by following the Law. There is nothing in the text of Acts which suggests that Peter or any of the other Jewish leaders ceased following the Law, renounced their Jewish identity, and became Gentile. Jews who believe in Jesus are given the Spirit, and Gentiles who believe in Jesus are given the Spirit. The presence of the Spirit is the sign that one is a part of God's family and becomes the new boundary marker which defines the church. Paul addresses this issue at length in Romans while affirming both that the gospel is for "*the Jew first and also to the Greek*"[64] and that Gentiles "*were grafted among them* [Jews] *and became partakers with them of the rich root*"[65]. Jesus the Jewish Messiah didn't create a new religion which excluded Jews. His sacrificial death, resurrection, and ascension as king became the mechanism by which Gentiles can join the Jewish family *by faith in him without becoming themselves Jewish!* This is the logic at play in Acts 10-11, the same logic which characterizes Pauline ecclesiology. Peter and the Jewish leaders remain Jewish while Gentiles who believe in Israel's Messiah remain Gentiles and are under no obligation to follow the Law. This is revolutionary but also anticipated by several prophets, especially Isaiah, who envisioned Gentile submission to Israel's God in the eschaton.[66] By dispensing the Spirit to Gentile believers through faith, God had fulfilled another promise.

We find in the story of Cornelius and Peter a connection between three related concepts which also permeate Paul's letters: faith/belief, Jesus as Messiah, and the Holy Spirit. The terms translated "believed", "beliers", and "believing" in Acts 10:43, 10:45, and 11:17 respectively are derived from the Greek root *pist-* and are cognates of the nominative *pistis* and verbal *pisteuo*. While we will discuss these related terms more fully in the next chapter, the *pist-* family of words is often translated with cognates of "faith" or "belief". Belief is placed "*in the Lord Jesus Christ*"; the messianic titles need no further explanation. Placing one's 'faith' or 'belief' in king Jesus results in the gift of the Holy Spirit. The presence of the Spirit becomes

---

63. Schreiner, *Handbook*, p. 25

64. Romans 1:16

65. Romans 11:17

66. For one random example, see Isaiah 2.

the sign that one has been accepted by God and thus incorporated into his family. Jews and Gentiles alike must believe in the Messiah and receive God's Spirit. The gospel of the kingdom is preached, hearers believe (place faith in) the king, and are given the Spirit. Ephesians 1:13-14 is the classic Pauline example of this dynamic: *"after listening to the message of truth, the gospel of your salvation—having also believed, you were sealed in Him with the Holy Spirit of promise, who is given as a pledge of our inheritance; with a view to the redemption of God's own possession".* When Paul says in Romans 1:16 that *"the gospel is the power of God for salvation to all who believe"* he is in complete harmony with Peter's explanation to the skeptical Jerusalem church leaders in Acts 11. A new paradigm for membership in God's family is established. Jesus is proclaimed (the gospel of the kingdom), faith is placed in him, and the Spirit is dispensed. Those who possess the Spirit are in good standing before God regardless of Jewish or Gentile identity. God's kingdom was spreading to all the nations through the announcement of Jesus.

Despite the manifest working of God's Spirit, the inclusion of Law-free Gentiles in the kingdom of Israel's Messiah would be an understandably tough pill to swallow for some Jewish believers. The issue is raised yet again in Acts 15:1, this time against Paul and Barnabas, when *"Some men came down from Judea and began teaching the brethren, "Unless you are circumcised according to the custom of Moses, you cannot be saved".* Gentile inclusion became such a contentious issue that a council was scheduled in Jerusalem, and as Paul arrived and began explaining what God was doing among the Gentiles, Jesus-believing Pharisees opposed him, saying *"It is necessary to circumcise them and to direct them to observe the Law of Moses"*[67]. Acts 15:6-21 records the debate. Peter wisely responds to the Pharisees, recounting his experience and arguing in favor of Gentile inclusion: *"Brethren, you know that in the early days God made a choice among you, that by my mouth the Gentiles would hear the word of the gospel and believe. And God, who knows the heart, testified to them giving them the Holy Spirit, just as He also did to us; and He made no distinction between us and them, cleansing their hearts by faith . . . we believe that we are saved through the grace of the Lord Jesus, in the same way as they also are"*[68]. Paul and Barnabas then continue to explain their successful ministry among the Gentiles with James affirming their testimony by quoting Amos 9:11-12, a prophetic passage which envisions the eschatological inclusion of Gentiles. James instructs the Gentiles to abstain from idols and fornication (following the resident foreigner laws of Leviticus 17-18[69]) after which a letter is drafted and sent to Antioch af-

---

67. Acts 15:5; for full context read 15:1-5.

68. Acts 15:7-11

69. Sloan, *Jesus and the Law of Moses*, pp. 221-226

firming Gentile inclusion. While the Gentile question is never fully suppressed, Acts 15 is monumental. From this point forward, the official position of the Jesus movement is full Gentile inclusion through faith and the Spirit without adoption of the Law. The gospel continues to spread, and Luke turns his attention away from Peter and the Jerusalem leadership to the tumultuous Mediterranean excursions of a man who once tried to destroy the church.

PAUL AND THE MEDITERRANEAN MISSION: ACTS 13, 17-19

When Saul, commissioned by the Sanhedrin to imprison Jesus-believers, appeared shell-shocked and blind in Damascus, the man commanded by the Lord to greet him had some serious questions. Ananias knew Saul's reputation and wanted nothing to do with him, but God had other plans. God directs Ananias to pay Saul a visit for *"he is a chosen instrument of Mine, to bear My name before the Gentiles and kings and the sons of Israel"*, adding, ominously, *"for I will show him how much he must suffer for My name's sake"*[70]. This Saul, commonly known as Paul, believed himself to have a divine calling from birth: *"God . . . set me apart even from my mother's womb and called me through His grace"*[71]. Luke concurs; in Acts 13:2, after Paul has spent time in Tarsus and Jerusalem, the leaders at Antioch receive a message from the Holy Spirit: *"Set apart for Me Barnabas and Saul for the work to which I have called them"*. The gospel had flowed out of Jerusalem and swept through the region like a flood and Paul would take it beyond the confines of the eastern Mediterranean, becoming the most influential writer in Christian history. While a full analysis of Paul awaits us in the next chapter, our present focus is on Paul's journeys throughout the Roman empire preaching Jesus, interacting with political authorities, and establishing churches. Paul's engagement with the Roman imperial powers offers us a model for how we might engage with the American imperial power many Western Christians desperately wish was on their team. Since we will in the near future examine each of Paul's letters, our analysis of Paul in Acts is but a foretaste of things to come.

Paul and his traveling companions are, according to Acts 13:4, *"sent out by the Holy Spirit"*, yet another example of how Spirit empowerment leads to the spread of God's kingdom, exactly as Jesus said it would in Acts 1:8. Paul sails to Cyprus[72], a senatorial province under the administration of proconsul Sergius Paulus[73], de-

---

70. Acts 10:15-16

71. Galatians 1:15

72. Acts 13:4-12

73. Dunn, *Beginning*, p. 437

scribed by Luke in Acts 17:7 as *"a man of intelligence"*. Paul first proclaims the word of God in Jewish synagogues, his habit when entering a new city[74], and ultimately develops a positive relationship with Sergius Paulus which is almost thwarted by a magician named Elymas. Paul chastises Elymas and then temporarily blinds him as a sign. Luke records Sergius Paulus' response in Acts 13:12: *"Then the proconsul believed when he saw what had happened, being amazed at the teaching of the Lord"*. This is a significant yet often overlooked exchange in Acts. Paul the Jew is presented with an opportunity to proclaim the gospel to a man who has attained the heights of power in Roman politics. While Paulus (and the many other Roman officials Paul confronts in Acts) aren't quite sure what to make of Paul, nearly all of them have a positive or sympathetic response to his preaching.

There is an obvious apologetic value in Luke's framing of Paul's relationships with the Roman authorities; as I mentioned in the introduction to Acts above Luke intends to neutralize any concerns that the Jesus movement is an imminent material threat to Roman power. Paul serves as a model of Christian political engagement. He is not shy about preaching the gospel of God's kingdom to those in power, nor does he obscure the universal lordship of Jesus. He is neither 'for' nor 'against' Roman officials, tacitly endorsing their power or fomenting revolutionary fervor. He simply preaches the gospel. This, as I have been suggesting all along, is yet another example of the Jeremiah 29:7 standard contextualized for the Roman Mediterranean mission. Paul does not compromise his message or his values and maintains, as we will see from his letters, that God has the final say. His mission is to proclaim the gospel and allow the Spirit to operate. He respectfully engages with political authorities and even shares the gospel with them without compromising his core conviction that Jesus is the Messiah. In this sense Paul is a suprapolitical figure; while he has no choice but to live within the political order, his mission transcends it. God's kingdom is bigger than any human empire.

Paul leaves Cyprus and travels to Antioch where he delivers his first sermon in Acts, an exemplary oration which serves as a foundation for the Pauline narratives which comprise the second half of Luke's work. Acts 13:16-43 is a deliberate parallel to Peter's opening sermon in Acts 2:14-39[75] in both form and content, serving the purpose of introducing a new direction in the narrative arc of Acts. It is also *"the first opportunity for readers to see the type of scriptural argument Paul will make to demonstrate that Jesus is the Son of God and Christ"*[76]. Indeed the Messianic status

---

74. Acts 13:5; Paul's strategy revolved around connecting with the synagogue and then, oftentimes after opposition, preaching to the Gentiles.

75. Dunn, *Beginning*, p. 427

76. Crowe, *Hope of Israel*, p. 50

of Jesus is the central theme of Paul's speech which is delivered in the synagogue after a reading of the Law and Prophets. The first section, Acts 13:16-25, is a brief review of Israel's history emphasising king David who *"from the descendants of this man, according to promise, God has brought to Israel a Savior, Jesus"*[77]. Paul then contends his message is from God and makes several appeals, both historical and Scriptural, to the resurrection of Jesus, a clear legitimation of his messianic identity. Paul, like the evangelists, believes Jesus is the culmination of Scriptural hopes: *"we preach to you the good news* [a cognate of *euangelion* of the promise made to the fathers, that God has fulfilled this promise to our children in that He raised up Jesus, as it is also written in the second Psalm, 'You are My Son; Today I have begotten You'"*[78]. His speech culminates in Acts 13:38-41 with a direct appeal to his audience, exhorting them to believe his words: *"Therefore let it be known to you, brethren, that through HIm forgiveness of sins is proclaimed to you, and through Him everyone who believes is freed from all things"*. Paul will continue to proclaim his message of the crucified, resurrected, and ascended Messiah throughout his life. Paul's sermon is initially well-received, and the following Sabbath nearly the entire city shows up to hear him speak. Some of the Jewish leaders become jealous and stir up the crowd against Paul, who then declares *"we are turning to the Gentiles . . . when the Gentiles heard this, they began rejoicing and glorifying the word of the Lord; and as many as had been appointed to eternal life believed"*[79]. Paul will travel around the Mediterranean sharing the gospel with Jews and Gentiles, often harassed by some Jewish opponents.

In Acts 14, Paul departs Antioch and travels to Iconium, where he again preaches in a Jewish synagogue, is rejected by some of the Jewish leaders, and turns to a receptive Gentile crowd.[80] They then travel to Lystra where the locals confuse Paul and Barnabas for the Greek gods Hermes and Zeus. Once the pair realized what was happening, they preached the gospel to them by specifically explaining how their God had created the entire world. Jews from Antioch and Iconium traveled to Lystra and stirred up the crowd against Paul, who was subsequently stoned and dragged out of the city, assumed to be dead. Paul survives the incident and continues to travel and preach amidst fierce opposition, resigning himself to a life of constant conflict: *"Through many tribulations we must enter the kingdom of God"*[81]. Acts 13-14 offer readers an insight into the life of Paul. He preaches the

---

77. Acts 13:23

78. Acts 13:32-33

79. Acts 13:46-48; for context see 13:42-52.

80. Acts 14:1-7

81. Acts 14:22; for context 14:8-23.

gospel to both Jews and Gentiles, often being persecuted by Jewish leaders but accepted by pagans. He is unwaveringly committed to the gospel of God's kingdom and the belief that Jesus is Messiah while also tailoring his message to fit the needs of his audience; to Jews Paul appeals to Scripture, and to Gentiles creation. Paul does not stir up dissension or sedition and does not seek to directly confront either the synagogue or the Roman imperial order as institutions. It is the opponents of Paul rather than Paul himself who create social discord. The entire ministry of Paul both in strategy and message are introduced in these two chapters. We will quickly highlight his career before being arrested in Jerusalem and will, in the following section, provide a more detailed explanation of his fateful stay in Philippi.

After participating in the Jerusalem Council recorded in Acts 15, Paul befriends Timothy, *"the son of a Jewish woman who was a believer, but his father was a Greek"*[82]. Timothy becomes an integral component of the Mediterranean mission and one of Paul's closest associates. In Acts 16:6-10 the Spirit directs Paul to travel through Macedonia, confirmed by a vision in which *"God has called us to preach the gospel to them"*. According to Acts 17:1-9 Paul finds himself in Philippi, and after much tribulation moves on to Thessalonica. He immediately visits the synagogue and begins preaching Jesus as Christ; some of the Jews forcibly bring him and Jason, the man presumably hosting Paul in his house, before the city authorities. Their charge is similar to the one leveled against Jesus by the Sanhedrin in Luke 23:2 which presented him as an anti-Roman revolutionary: *"they all act contrary to the decrees of Caesar, saying that there is another king, Jesus"*[83]. The strong christological and eschatological emphasis of the gospel was certainly exploited against Paul, which seems to be precisely what his opponents were hoping to accomplish even though Paul's own behavior suggested nothing of the sort.[84] Paul is then sent to Berea, where he receives a more favorable hearing from the *"noble-minded"* Bereans who *"received the word with great eagerness, examining the Scriptures daily to see whether these things were so"*. Paul's opponents soon stir up trouble in Berea as well, which prompts him to travel to Athens.

Paul's response to the city, recorded in Acts 17:16, is one of contempt: *"his spirit was being provoked within him as he was observing the city full of idols"*. As Dunn explains, Paul's response *"was characteristically Jewish; the verb is strong— paroxyneto, 'outraged' . . . Nothing aroused Jewish contempt for the other religions of the Mediterranean and Mesopotamian world so much as idolatry"*[85]. While debat-

---

82. Acts 16:1

83. Acts 17:7

84. Dunn, *Beginning*, pp. 678-679

85. Dunn, *Beginning*, p. 685

ing Jews in the synagogue and Greeks in the marketplace, some Epicurean and Stoic philosophers, representing the two most important philosophical schools in Hellenistic thought[86], asked Paul to speak about his strange teaching before the Areopagus, the council which oversaw the affairs of the city.[87] In Acts 17:22-31 Paul delivers what has been in New Testament scholarship perhaps the most discussed speech in Acts.[88] Instead of appealing to the Jewish Scriptures, which would have little meaning to his Athenian audience, he discusses creation. Paul recounts witnessing an alter to an unknown God and uses the altar as a starting point for his sermon, revealing to the Areopagus that their 'unknown God' was actually the creator God of Israel, a God who cannot be contained in a shrine because He made the world without help from human hands and is the source of all life. Paul is brilliantly addressing both Epicurean and Stoic concerns: "*The line of argument would have been meaningful both to Epicureans (God needs nothing from human hands) and to Stoics (God as the source of all life)*"[89]. Paul wisely presents the gospel in a manner that is palatable to his audience but never compromises its core content, which is the identity of Jesus. He closes out his amicable sermon with a point which would surely be contentious to his Greek audience: "*Therefore, having overlooked the times of ignorance, God is now declaring to men that all people everywhere should repent because He has fixed a day in which He will judge the world in righteousness though a Man whom He has appointed, having furnished proof to all men by raising HIm from the dead*"[90].

The crowd's mixed response is recorded in Acts 17:32-34; the resurrection is a bridge too far for many philosophically-oriented Greeks, but some wish to hear him speak again and a few even accept Paul's gospel. The point which shouldn't be missed for our purposes is this: Paul is yet again in front of a Gentile audience in the Areopagus, the political body of Athens. In this sense, Paul 'confronts' the political authorities with his gospel. Knowing, however, that many of them are aligned with either Stoic or Epicurean philosophy, Paul adapts his presentation of the gospel to their sensibilities without denying or downplaying its major sticking point: the resurrection. This is a model for Christian engagement with the outside world. When given an opportunity to speak with those who hold political power or who are outside of the church, believers should seek to wisely communicate the gospel with them in a way they can understand. Paul does not directly confront

---

86. Ferguson, *Backgrounds*, p. 354

87. Jeffers, *Greco-Roman*, pp. 261-262

88. Crowe, *Hope of Israel*, p. 65

89. Dunn, *Beginning*, 687

90. Acts 17:30-31

the political structure of the Athenian Areopagus but his eschatological gospel logically entails its temporary arrangement. Paul is not intentionally hostile towards the pagans whose gods *"provoke"* him but confronts them with the truth of his gospel. Instead of wielding authoritarian power over others, modern Western Christians find in this story a different principle. Preach the gospel to all who will hear, and let God take care of the rest.

In Acts 18:1-17, Paul travels to Corinth, capital of the senatorial province of Achaea. The proconsul of Achaea, Lucius Junius Gallio, assumed his position in Corinth in 51 CE.[91] Paul's Jewish opponents brought charges against him before Gallio. As Paul is about to speak, Gallio denies their claim: *"If it were a matter of wrong or of vicious crime, O Jews, it would be reasonable for me to put up with you; but if there are questions about words and names and your own law, look after it yourselves; I am unwilling to be the judge of these matters"*[92]. This story attests to the decentralized nature of Roman rule; Gallio did not find the case against Paul to be a matter which violated Roman law and believed it should be handled by the Jews themselves. It also shows, even more significantly, that Paul is absolutely *not* perceived by the Roman authorities as an imminent threat to their power. From Gallio's point of view, Paul's gospel was little more than an inter-Jewish debate. Gallio dismisses the case.

Paul would be accused before the political authorities once again in Ephesus only a few years after his public exoneration in Corinth. When Paul arrives in Ephesus he meets several disciples who were only familiar with John's baptism and had never heard of the Holy Spirit. Paul lays hands on them and they receive the Spirit. After this Paul spends nearly two years in Ephesus preaching *"the kingdom of God"*[93]. Located in Ephesus was the temple of Artemis, one of the ancient world's most celebrated buildings and a source of great pride for Ephesian citizens. The cult of Artemis pervaded Ephesian culture and drew many annual visitors from all over the Greek world.[94] Aside from the cultic worship of Artemis as a god, there was an enticing financial incentive to perpetuate the Artemis cult. It was a major sector of the Ephesian economy. In Acts 19:23-40, a silversmith named Demetrius, who specialized in manufacturing silver shrines of Artemis, realized the growing Ephesian church might be bad for business: *"he gathered together with the workmen of similar trades, and said, "Men, you know that our prosperity depends upon this business . . . this Paul has persuaded and turned away a considerable number*

---

91. Jeffers, *Greco-Roman*, p. 164

92. Acts 18:14-15

93. Acts 19:10; for context see 19:1-20

94. Dunn, *Beginning*, pp. 763-764

of people, saying that gods made with hands are no gods at all. Not only is there danger that this trade of ours fall into disrepute, but also that the temple of the great goddess Artemis be regarded as worthless'"[95]. The crowds, worked up in a fury, drag some of Paul's traveling companions into the theater. Paul, wanting to enter the theater and defend his friends, is warned not to do so by *"Asiarchs"*, local Greek political leaders who were often responsible for promoting the imperial cult.[96] It is notable that Paul had befriended Greek leaders and how, even as representatives of the imperial cult, they respect him.

Once the crowds discovered Paul's companions were Jewish they shouted in praise of Artemis for nearly two hours, teetering on the edge of a full-blown riot. In the Roman provincial system political unrest led to Roman intervention, a situation which local authorities wanted to avoid at all costs. Anyone who couldn't manage their people on Rome's behalf would be out of a job, and often painfully so. That is precisely why the Sanhedrin handed Jesus over for crucifixion. The town clerk, elected head of the city officials[97], recognized the gravity of a potential riot. He stands before the unruly crowd defending Artemis but maintains thatDemetrius and his associates had no legitimate grievance against those preaching Jesus: *"you have brought these men here who are neither robbers of temples nor blasphemers of our goddess. So then, if Demetrius and the craftsmen who are with him have a complaint against any man, the courts are in session and proconsuls are available . . . if you want anything beyond this, it shall be settled in a lawful assembly"*[98]. After reminding the crowd that Roman wrath would accompany a riot, the clerk dismissed the crowds. Once again, Paul and his companions have unwaveringly proclaimed the gospel and been brought before political officials only for the authorities to decide they haven't done anything illegal. Not only did Paul befriend those responsible for maintaining the imperial cult, his companions had not physically threatened the temple of Artemis. Yet they still tried to convince anyone who would listen that Jesus was the crucified, resurrected, and ascended king.

In the long run Jesus *would* actually destroy the cult of Artemis, but not through violence or political action. As the gospel spreads, pagan cults become redundant. In the marketplace of ideas, Christianity proved the superior product. Paul's Mediterranean mission reveals a posture towards politics which appears counterintuitive but wholly in line with the teachings of Jesus. Jesus was, in an objective, historical sense, king of the world, and belief in Jesus as king resulted

---

95. Acts 19:25-27

96. Dunn, *Beginning*, p. 775

97. Jeffers, *Greco-Roman*, p. 163

98. Acts 19:37-39

in the Spirit's indwelling. Paul, however, does not challenge the Roman political structure or the rule of local authorities *as such*. He does not specifically attack systems, advocate for the replacement of political leaders, or lobby the authorities to impose the kingdom of God upon others using the force of law. He instead proclaims the gospel. Paul is willing to befriend, respect, and show honor towards those in positions of power who do not agree with his message. The gospel is revolutionary, but it is a revolution which ascends from the ground up and cannot be won with coercion or violence. The modern authoritarian socialism which frames the worldview of Christians both conservative and progressive is entirely incompatible with the witness of Acts. Christians who are seeking to draw principles from these authoritative biblical texts should take note. Paul is masterfully strategic; his every action is intentionally designed to promote the gospel, the only way of transforming this world and building God's kingdom. We will now explore one particular example of Pauline pragmatism which challenges modern Christian political commitments.

Leveraged Citizenship: Acts 16

As Paul, a Jew, is penning instructions to the church in Ephesus, he makes a passing comment about their identity which is easy to overlook. Ephesians 4:17 reads: *"walk no longer just as the Gentiles also walk, in the futility of their mind"*. The Gentiles? Isn't Paul the apostle to the Gentiles? And isn't the church to which he is writing composed of both Jews and Gentiles alike? After his theologically dense introductory statement connecting the gospel, faith, and the Spirit[99], Paul spends the second half of Ephesians 2 revealing how the Gentiles in his audience have, in Christ, become *"fellow citizens with the saints, and are of God's household"*[100]. Their identity has been so thoroughly transformed that in Ephesians 4:17 Paul can apply the term which traditionally distinguished Jews from everyone else to those who are outside of the church, regardless of ethnicity. In the kingdom of God, the term 'Gentile' refers to those who do not follow Christ. Clearly the language of identity, and the meaning of identifiers, has been shifted. Paul's boldest statement regarding the realignment of identity for those in Christ occurs in Galatians 3:28-29: *"There is neither Jew nor Greek, there is neither slave nor free man, there is neither male nor female; for you are all one in Christ Jesus. And if you belong to Christ, then you are Abraham's descendants, heirs according to promise"*. This revolutionary pronouncement deserves, and will receive below, a substantial exposition. Even

---

99. Ephesians 1:13-14, discussed above.

100. Ephesians 2:19

without consulting the commentaries and monographs, Paul obviously asserts that identity markers are relativized in Christ. Abraham's family is defined by those who have faith in his seed[101], the Jewish Messiah.

It should come of little surprise, then, that when Paul writes a letter to the Roman colony of Philippi he informs his audience of their real citizenship, one which cannot be conferred by Rome: *"For our citizenship is in heaven, from which also we eagerly wait for a Savior, the Lord Jesus Christ"*[102]. Aside from the sweeping christological and eschatological language in this short passage, Paul uses the Greek term *politeuma*, 'citizenship', the significance of which was not lost on his audience: *"This must have evoked the idea of Roman citizenship that was held by many of the people of Philippi, including, no doubt, a significant number of the Christians"*[103]. If Jesus relativizes the social status of Jews and Gentiles, slavery and freedom, and men and women, why not add Roman citizenship to the list also? Paul's audience believes in, as he affirms in the same passage, *"the Lord Jesus Christ"*, which presumably precludes investing emotional attachment to any worldly political status. There is a catch, though. When Paul himself was in Philippi, he seemed to take his status as a Roman citizen very seriously, using it to get himself out of legal trouble in Acts 16:38-40. He also appeals to his citizenship several more times in Acts. How can someone composing an instruction like Philippians 3:20, who generally argues that status symbols are irrelevant, possibly fall back on a major source of status when he finds himself in trouble? It doesn't appear characteristically Pauline. There is, I believe, a completely plausible historical solution to this problem.

Acts leaves little room for doubt: Paul was indeed a citizen of Rome. Besides the aforementioned appeal to Roman citizenship in Philippi, Paul reaffirms his citizenship in Tarsus[104] and again, just before his flogging in Jerusalem, reveals his citizenship to a Roman centurion and explains that he had held it since birth[105]. The Roman government promoted a strategic policy of dual citizenship, allowing provincials to retain ties to their ancestral lands while also being incorporated into the Roman system, assuring stronger bonds of loyalty to the imperial order. This is precisely why Paul appeals in the passages cited above to his birth in Tarsus and as a Roman citizen. There were several means of earning citizenship in the first century, including being born of a citizen, being released from slavery by a citizen, for providing special services to the empire, or upon being discharged from

---

101. Galatians 3:16

102. Philippians 3:20

103. Oakes, *Empire*, p. 192

104. Acts 21:39

105. Acts 22:25-29

the auxiliaries. While we know almost nothing of Paul's parents except that they also bore a daughter[106], it is likely his father received citizenship through imperial service of some kind. Citizens were spared from humiliating and degrading punishments, specifically crucifixion, and could not be scourged or flogged without a conviction. They also reserved the right of appeal to Rome[107]. In Acts Paul availed himself of both benefits, which would seem to contradict, or at least stand in tension with, his contention that real citizenship can be found only in Christ.

One thing is certain about Paul: he is a pragmatist. In 1 Corinthians 9:19-23, Paul discusses his flexibility in proclaiming the gospel to different groups of people, adapting his message to their individual needs as in his Areopagus speech. Paul had, in his own words, *"become all things to all men, so that I may by all means save some"*, which he qualifies with a statement about his ultimate purpose: *"I do all things for the sake of the gospel"*. Paul the pragmatic preacher is willing to subvert his own interests and adapt to the needs of others insofar as he believes it will further the gospel. This was, after all, the mission Jesus entrusted to the church in Acts 1:8. Paul takes the mission seriously. As he says in the opening to his most influential letter, *"the gospel is the power of God for everyone who believes"*[108]. Nothing less than the salvation of humanity was at stake. Paul will do whatever it takes to announce that Jesus is now king of the world. In the city of Philippi, his gospel will land him in a lot of trouble.

Acts 16:11-40 narrates his stay in that fateful city. As Paul, who was being housed by a wealthy woman named Lydia (apparently she was not convicted to sell all her possessions), testifies about Jesus in the city, he is harassed by a slave girl who made her masters money by fortune-telling. In somewhat comical fashion, Luke narrates that Paul became annoyed with the girl and cast out her evil spirit, preventing her from telling any more fortunes and denying her masters a lucrative stream of revenue. Enraged, the masters seized Paul and his associate Silas, dragging them in front of the city authorities and accusing them of transgressing Roman customs. They are beaten with the approval of the authorities and thrown in jail without a trial, but a fortuitous earthquake opens all the cell doors. The jailer, in both shock and shame, is about to commit suicide when Paul informs him no one has left. Paul takes the opportunity to proclaim Jesus to the bewildered jailer, who allows Paul and Silas to stay in his house. The next morning the Philippian authorities find Paul and order the jailer to release him. Paul objects, and offers an explanation: *" "They have beaten us in public without trial, men who are Romans, and*

---

106. Acts 23:16

107. Ferguson, *Backgrounds*, pp. 62-63

108. Romans 1:16

have thrown us into prison; and now are they sending us away secretly? No indeed! But let them come themselves and bring us out." The policemen reported these words to the chief magistrates. They were afraid when they heard that they were Romans, and they came and appealed to them, and when they had brought them out, they kept begging them to leave the city. They went out of the prison and entered the house of Lydia, and when they saw the brethren they encouraged them and departed[109]. Not only has Paul brazenly flaunted his Roman citizenship, which would seem to contradict Philippians 3:20, he also deliberately disobeys the authorities by making a stop at Lydia's house before finally complying. What about the almighty Romans 13? Why didn't Paul just *"submit to the authorities"* and leave Philippi without mentioning his citizenship when asked to do so? The answer to all these questions is, of course, the gospel of Jesus.

While modern Christians rightly valorize imprisonment for the cause of Christ, Greco-Roman thinkers interpreted incarceration differently. As James Smith explains, the acquisition of honor was a major value in Roman society, especially among the upper classes, and one of the fastest ways in which someone could lose honor was through imprisonment. Not only did incarceration degrade the prisoner's honor, it negatively impacted the perception of those associated with the prisoner: *"not only is honor removed from the subject of a prison sentence, or beating, or some other humiliating punishment, those closely associated with the subject were in danger of losing honor as well"*[110]. Paul's beating and imprisonment would have consequential social repercussions and possibly driven a wedge between him and the other Philippian believers. Most importantly, *"Paul's public and thorough humiliation also publicly disgraces the gospel that he had been preaching, along with those with whom he had associated"*[111]. For Paul, a man who does *"all things for the sake of the gospel"*, this was an entirely unacceptable situation. By discrediting him and those who believed in his teaching, Paul's shameful beating and imprisonment imperiled the gospel message itself, the very mechanism by which God rescues humanity. Paul was walking a social tightrope.

In defense of his gospel and the honor of the Philippian church, Paul leverages his citizenship against the Philippian authorities who beat and imprisoned him. Their arrival in the morning, which included a request for Paul to depart the city quietly, would have crystallized in the public mind Paul's desecrated honor and prevented the gospel from spreading. Paul, however, had the upper hand. As a Roman citizen he had been beaten and imprisoned without trial, a clear

---

109. Acts 16:37-40

110. Smith, James. 2005. *Marks of an Apostle*. Society of biblical Literature. p. 60

111. Smith, *Marks of an Apostle*, p. 61

violation of Roman law which could potentially threaten the status and power of Philippi's authorities. They were the ones who would, at least in theory, be charged for violating Roman law. Paul wasn't about to let his honor be unfairly tarnished, casting his gospel in doubt, and demanded a public escort out of the city. The authorities, now themselves publicly shamed by Paul's request, had no other alternative: "*rather than risk a challenge and then possible failure and subsequent personal condemnation under Roman law, they were willing to shame themselves to some lesser degree by agreeing to the demands of Paul, the previously shamed prisoner. Paul and his entourage now get a public escort by the city magistrates, yet Paul is not so easily dispatched. He uses this honor-building process to its fullest and goes to Lydia's house to meet the church before he leaves. The honor-shame struggle is over*"[112]. While Paul by no means leaves Philippi unscathed, his tactical appeal to citizenship went a long way in restoring his own honor, the honor of his associates, and, most importantly, the credibility of his gospel. While his real citizenship was sealed in heaven with Christ, his earthly citizenship could be leveraged to announce that Jesus was Lord.

While Paul sees worldly status and boundary markers as arbitrary, aspects of the old creation which are passing away in light of the inaugurated kingdom of God, he realizes that they still retain social currency. The New Testament writers unambiguously announce the reign of king Jesus, which they believe is an objective, historical fact sealed by his death, resurrection, and ascension, reaching its ultimate conclusion when he returns to judge the world and consummate the eschatological kingdom. Those who believe in him, from every tribe, tongue, and nation, are a part of the family of Abraham, incorporated into Israel by virtue of their faith in Israel's Messiah. Within this framework, it doesn't really matter on which side of imaginary lines drawn on a Roman map a believer happens to have been born. What matters, the *only* thing that matters, is God's gospel of the kingdom. Unfortunately, Paul and the other early Christians inhabited a world, much like our own, where the vast majority of people did not share their eschatological assumptions. In certain situations, particularly those where the integrity of the gospel is threatened, it makes perfect sense for Paul and other believers to insist that their earthly identities be respected, even if they place little theological value in them. Paul's trip to Philippi is a perfect example of this dynamic and does not in any way contradict his statements about citizenship in Philippians 3:20.

I refer to this biblical principle as *leveraged* citizenship, which involves using the privileges which are conferred by political status for the cause of building God's kingdom. Leveraged citizenship does not see the status of 'citizen' as an end in itself or as having any enduring value, but is rather concerned with using

---

112. Smith, *Marks of an Apostle*, p. 61

citizenship to advance the message of Jesus. Paul doesn't care if his congregations are Roman or not, and he certainly doesn't see himself as superior to those who were not granted citizenship. If Paul lived in the modern era of nineteenth-century nation-states, he would regard national identity and the citizenship which it entails as peripheral. Who cares if someone is from Canada, Nigeria, Japan, or Australia? Do they believe that Jesus is king or not? If the answer is 'yes', then they are a part of the global kingdom of God, full stop. If, however, a Christian's citizenship can be leveraged to advance the kingdom, then it is perfectly acceptable to appeal to the rights of citizenship.

We must be careful and discerning, however, to remember that our modern political systems, and the moral assumptions which accompany them, are radically different from those in antiquity. Our world is not the same, and therefore leveraging citizenship will look different for us than it did for the apostle. For Paul, he used his citizenship to restore his personal honor and defend the gospel. In an American context, an excellent example might be our use of the First Amendment right to free speech. Without engaging in the hyperbolic (and oftentimes flat-out false) rhetoric of religious persecution, we could imagine a scenario in which a government official asks a Christian to stop speaking publicly about their faith. In this instance, it would be entirely permissible for that Christian to appeal to their Constitutional rights as an American citizen to speak freely. While we realize that our American citizenship doesn't really matter in light of the kingdom, leveraging it to proclaim the gospel freely is consistent with Paul's example in Philippi. Christians are allowed to hold governments accountable to their own standards, which, as I will argue in my analysis of Romans 13, is in part what Paul is doing in that infamous passage.

Speaking of Romans 13, we must also account for Paul's deliberate disobedience of the authorities in Philippi. When they ask him to immediately leave the city, he makes it a point to stop at Lydia's house first, in open defiance of their request. While this move is about the restoration of honor, it does, on the surface, contradict his instructions in Romans 13:1 to *"be in subjection to the governing authorities"*. Paul, at least in this case, absolutely *refuses* to subject himself to the Philippian magistrates. Submission at that moment would have left the gospel's honor in doubt, threatening the viability of its message. The authorities had dug themselves into a hole, and Paul wasn't about to help them climb out without ensuring the respectability of his gospel. Paul is not denouncing the tradition of Jeremiah 29:7 nor is he privileging his citizenship. It was critical that Paul and his churches were perceived as good citizens, not as violent revolutionaries or insurrectionists who wanted to burn all Roman institutions to the ground. Sometimes maintaining this public persona and honoring God required challenging those in power. Paul truly does want the Christian community to be at peace with the Roman authorities and their pagan neighbors but is also aware that peace isn't always a possibility. Without compromising his moral values, Paul is able to leverage a citizenship which is irrelevant in the kingdom against political leaders who threaten the gospel's integrity. While modern Christians must be extremely cautious in how we apply this principle today, we must learn to think of our own citizenship as a means to an end. Acts 16 also cautions us against reductionistic readings of Romans 13, slavishly following the dictates of every government official 'because the Bible tells me so'. Paul himself is much more nuanced in his approach to political power, and I suggest we ought to follow his example.

From Jerusalem to Rome: Acts 20-28

At this point in the chapter we have already highlighted the main themes of Acts and explored some of the political and economic consequences of Luke's narrative. There is little in Acts 20-28 which isn't directly related to what has come before. Luke has proven to be an excellent storyteller, creatively chronicling the unfolding promise which Jesus made to his disciples at the beginning of Acts. The gospel has been proclaimed in Jerusalem, Judea, Samaria, and the eastern Mediterranean. Paul will carry it to the imperial capital of Rome. The final chapters of Acts tell an enthralling tale, but space permits us only a brief walkthrough, highlighting the presences of motifs which have already been addressed above.

In Acts 20, Paul resolves to travel to Rome. After *"solemnly testify*[ing] *to both Jews and Greeks of repentance towards God and faith in our Lord Jesus Christ"*[113], the Holy Spirit leads Paul to Jerusalem. Paul knows the journey will not be easy and likely end with suffering and death. As he reveals his plans to the church elders in Ephesus, Paul very intriguingly describes his attitude towards work in Acts 20:33-35: *"I have coveted no one's silver or gold or clothes. You yourselves know that these hands ministered to my own needs and to the men who were with me. In everything I showed you that by working hard in this manner you must help the weak and remember the words of the Lord Jesus, that He Himself said, 'It is more blessed to give than to receive"*. Paul paved his own way, working to provide for himself and help others. He intends to set an example for the Ephesians; apparently selling everything is not an option for the church in Ephesus. They should imitate Paul and work hard. Paul will himself testify to his work ethic, and promote it as an example, in his letters. He then embarks on his journey to Jerusalem, arriving in Acts 21:17.

---

113. Acts 20:21

It doesn't take long for Paul's opponents to notice him. Despite his best attempt to appease their sensibilities, Paul is accused of violating the Law and beaten by a mob who seeks to kill him. The commander of the Roman cohort in Jerusalem hears of the uproar and takes action to break it up. The mob stops beating Paul when the commander arrives, intending on taking Paul to the barracks. Paul speaks to the him in Greek, informing the commander that he is *"a Jew of Tarsus in Cilicia, a citizen of no insignificant city; and I beg you, allow me to speak to the people"*[114]. His request is granted. Paul, turning to the crowd and speaking in a Hebrew dialect, recounts his upbringing, his vision near Damascus, and his mission. The crowds were unsatisfied and the Romans chained him up, planning to scourge him for information. Paul, just as in Philippi, informs the closest centurion of his Roman citizenship, causing fear among the Roman officials. They release Paul but bring him before the Jewish Council on the following day in an attempt to understand why Paul was such a problem for the Jewish elite.[115]

Paul, in a scene reminiscent of Jesus's final week in Jerusalem, speaks to the council and is struck in the face at the command of the high priest. Paul protests before realizing that he is standing before a mixed crowd of Pharisees and Sadducees. He appeals to another identity and leverages it against the Sanhedrin: *"perceiving that one group were Sadducees and the other Pharisees, Paul began crying out in the Council, "Brethren, I am a Pharisee; a son of Pharisees; I am on trial for the hope and resurrection of the dead!""*[116]. Paul's words have their intended effect. The crowd is bitterly divided and begins arguing about resurrection. Paul is taken back to the Roman barracks while several of his opponents plot to ambush and kill Paul. Fortunately Paul's nephew hears of this plot and informs the Roman commander and Paul is safely transferred by a contingent of Roman soldiers to Caesarea.[117]

Paul faces trial before Felix, governor of Judea from 52-60 CE and freedman of Emperor Caligula. This is the only proper trial Paul receives in Jerusalem, and the high priest Ananias, accompanied by an attorney named Tertullus, must come to Caesarea and plead their case against Paul.[118] After Ananias charges Paul for being *"a real pest and a fellow who stirs up dissension among all the Jews throughout the world, and a ringleader of the sect of the Nazarenes"*[119], Felix grants Paul a response. Paul explains how his conduct is *"in accordance with the Law and . . . the Prophets"*

---

114. Acts 21:39

115. Acts 21:17-22:30

116. Acts 23:6

117. Acts 23:1-35

118. Dunn, *Beginning*, p. 979

119. Acts 24:5

and pleads his innocence. Felix has mixed feelings about Paul but continues to listen to him. Paul was kept in jail, albeit with many privileges, for two years until Felix was succeeded by Porcius Festus as governor. Although Paul is not formally charged, Felix does the Jews of Jerusalem a favor and leaves him incarcerated.[120]

Porcius Festus, governor of Judea for but a few short years (probably 60-62 CE)[121], asks Paul if he is willing to stand trial in Jerusalem. Paul, yet again leveraging his Roman citizenship, appeals to Caesar. Herod Agrippa arrives with his wife Bernice to discuss the case of Paul with Festus. They agree that Paul has done nothing wrong, and Paul is given an opportunity to defend himself before Agrippa. Paul recounts his personal story, including the transformation in Damascus, and concludes with a defense of his message in Acts 26:22-23: "*I stand to this day testifying both to small and great, stating nothing but what the Prophets and Moses said was going to take place; that the Christ was to suffer, and that by reason of His resurrection from the dead He would be the first to proclaim light both to the Jewish people and to the Gentiles*". Festus jokes that Paul's great learning was driving him mad, and Agrippa (in jest?) tells Paul that he might soon be persuaded to become a Christian. Both agree that Paul is worthy of freedom but honor his appeal to Caesar. Paul is headed for Rome.[122]

Paul's arduous journey to Rome is narrated in Acts 27:1-28:15. An interesting dynamic in the text, but one for which Luke has prepared his readers, is the altogether positive response Paul receives from Roman authorities. Paul never compromises his message or his belief in Jesus, but he interacts with the Romans in such a way that they are almost presented as admiring Paul. He is certainly given much better treatment than the average Roman citizen, and, even if it happens to be a thick slice of Lukan propaganda, Paul is portrayed as respectfully interacting with every authority, earning their trust by his honesty and integrity. While Paul is certainly willing to leverage his citizenship in pursuit of the gospel, he does not make it his official policy to offend Roman sensibilities. Paul's radical gospel is not incompatible with seeking the welfare of the city. Because of his reputation among the Romans, when Paul "*entered Rome, Paul was allowed to stay by himself, with the soldier who was guarding him*"[123]. Paul spends his time in Jerusalem debating with Jews and preaching to Gentiles. The closing verses in Paul show how far the gospel had come: "*he stayed two full years in his own rented quarters and was welcoming all*

---

120. Acts 24:1-27

121. Ferguson, *Backgrounds*, p. 419

122. Acts 25:1-26:32

123. Acts 28:16

who came to him, preaching the kingdom of God and teaching concerning the Lord Jesus Christ with all openness, unhindered"[124].

CONCLUSION

The kingdom had come a long way since Luke 2:1, where Caesar Augustus issued his declaration which forced Jesus's parents to travel to Bethlehem. The baby born in that small Jewish city had ascended to the heights of heaven, far above all imperial powers, and sat as king over all creation. Against massive odds but empowered by the Spirit, Peter, Paul and other early believers had laboriously forged a path for the message of God to reach the heart of Rome's vast empire. Ironically, Paul the prisoner proclaimed another king and another kingdom under the protective supervision of Rome herself. There is no better image representing the radical, paradoxical kingdom inaugurated by Jesus than a Jewish Pharisee testifying to Jesus's messianic rule in the imperial capital. All along,the disciples walked a fine line between resistance and accommodation, rebellion and submission. The death, resurrection, and ascension of the Messiah changed everything and precipitated a movement which would continue to grow. Two thousand years later, it's still growing.

Peter and Paul exemplify the Christian response to human political power. Following the teachings of Jesus eliminates the option of violent revolution. Until the great eschatological consummation believers must continue to follow the tradition established in Jeremiah 29:7 of living at peace with their neighbors in anticipation of the coming cosmic deliverance. There is no greater assurance of the future hope than God's indwelling Holy Spirit. If possible, Christians were to live at peace with all men and accommodate the gospel message to meet their needs. When asked to compromise our faith before the political authorities, we must have the attitude of Peter and the action of Paul. If we are faced with a choice between obeying God or men, we always choose God. If the authorities dishonor our gospel, we must hold them to account. If at all possible, we should seek to walk in integrity and respectability, testifying to the world that Jesus followers are different. Jesus is Messiah, but kingship is characterized by peace, mercy, and compassion. Because of this, our possessions should be used in service of others. We do not seek the abolition of private property (which only transfers ownership to a small handful of oligarchical politicians who use it as they see faith) but rather its creative utilization as instruments for building the kingdom and serving others. Those who follow Christ are one family, relativising social, political, and ethnic identities, and

---

124. Acts 28:30-31

are given the same task of spreading the gospel to all nations. Acts serves as a model for this task, providing us both examples to emulate and principles to enact.

We have only been introduced to the most influential writer in Christian history. The apostle Paul, persecutor turned proclaimer, is man most responsible for the spread of Christianity and its enduring theological legacy. His letters address a wide array of topics, always beginning with the gospel and working outward. There are several passages in Paul outside of Romans 13 that are consequential for modern Christian engagement with contemporary political and economic structures. Many of them have been chronically ignored in the history of biblical interpretation. It is time that we give Paul and his letters the justice they deserve. Paul's gospel has the potential to thoroughly reframe our political and economic assumptions.

CHAPTER 12 | Paul and His Letters

Set Apart for the Gospel of God

For I am not ashamed of the Gospel, for it is the power of God for salvation to everyone who believes, to the Jew first and also to the Greek.

Romans 1:16

I do all things for the sake of the gospel.

1 Corinthians 9:23

INTRODUCTION

Besides Jesus himself, there is no figure which has played a greater role in shaping the course of Western Christianity than the apostle Paul. While the New Testament contains four gospels which creatively recount the life of Jesus, they weren't actually written by Jesus himself. Jesus didn't pen a single word in the Christian canon. This isn't to deny his fundamental significance; Jesus is without a doubt the most influential and important person in world history, an impressive feat considering we don't possess a single primary source composed by the man himself. It's an un-contestable fact of history: Jesus left us with no autobiographical writings or any textual manifestations of his words and deeds. The Christian literary tradition was, somewhat necessarily, placed in the hands of others. The most towering character in that respect is Paul, the man responsible for thirteen of the twenty-seven works included in the New Testament, all of which are letters written to churches located in various cities scattered around the Roman empire. For the last two millennia, and becoming increasingly significant after the Protestant Reformation in the six-teenth century, Paul's letters have been perhaps the most important source material for constructing Christian theology and determine in large part how millions of believers around the world understand their faith. Love him or hate him, Paul's impact cannot be overstated.

Before analyzing the man himself, we need to address the authenticity of his epistles. There are many New Testament scholars who would balk at my claim that Paul actually wrote all thirteen letters attributed to him. From modern biblical scholarship's inception, the Pauline authenticity of several epistles has been challenged. In fact, the scholarly consensus generally issued the label of 'undisputedly Pauline' to only seven letters, including Romans, 1 and 2 Corinthians, Galatians, Philippians, 1 Thessalonians, and Philemon. Endless debates rage on about the authenticity of the other six, with scholars establishing various proposals for or against their direct composition by Paul. Frank Thielman includes an excellent review of the discussion in his book *Paul, Apostle of Grace*, and I largely agree with his conclusion that the arguments against Pauline authenticity are weak.[1] Despite protestations to the contrary, I affirm the authenticity of all thirteen Pauline epistles and will not waste any time arguing for Pauline authorship below. Even if some of the letters were written pseudonymously, I find such a rich ideological consistency among them that any authorial differences are essentially irrelevant for reconstructing Paul's thought.

Paul's career, recounted by Luke in Acts and outlined in the previous chapter, was shaped by his Mediterranean mission and the establishment as well as continuing pastoral care of churches throughout the Roman empire. Paul's letters are written to encourage faithfulness and address the very real-world problems facing these young communities of Jesus believers, and the ideas he expresses in them have profound repercussions for how we understand the worldview of early Christianity. Since Paul is writing to ordinary people living in the Roman empire, working various jobs and engaging with Greco-Roman culture, Paul's letters necessarily relate to the political and economic structures of his day and at several points are explicitly intended to help his audience navigate the complexities of first-century politics and economics in light of the Jewish messiah.

In this chapter we will explore the background information needed to fruitfully interpret Paul, his letters, and his teaching in order to provide us with a basis from which we can analyze texts that relate to political and economic issues in Paul's letters. The rest of this chapter will be divided into three sections. In the first I discuss Paul's identity by examining autobiographical statements in his letters and the witness of Acts to locate Paul in his historical context and reflect upon what it might mean to be a Jewish apostle in a Gentile world. In the second section I will explain why Paul wrote letters, how they were intended to function in antiquity, and what kind of information interpreters should expect to derive from them.

---

1. Thielman, Frank. 2022. *Paul, Apostle of Grace*. Eerdmans. pp. 337-345

In the final section I will address four major sets of themes in Paul which contextualize our understanding of his political and economic instruction, including gospel and faith, church and spirit, ethics and identity, and kingdom and empire. We will then be in a position to read through Paul's letters with historically-attuned eyes and sharpen our perception of political and economic texts in Paul's letters.

WHO WAS PAUL?

Paul loves talking about himself. In nearly every letter, Paul recounts his personal experiences and convictions to an audience which he hopes will accept his testimony. No one has ever accused Paul of being shy. Although Paul often describes events which occur during his ministry we possess precious little autobiographical information about his upbringing and life before Damascus. There are only a few fleeting references in Paul's letters to his own past, but when read carefully and historically the letters offer us a wealth of information regarding the beliefs and motives of the fabled apostle. An analysis of these texts is critical for locating Paul in his historical context and reconstructing his worldview.

In Philippians 3:4-6, Paul discusses the "*confidence in the flesh*" he legitimately held before God: "*circumcized the eighth day, of the nation of Israel, of the tribe of Benjamin, a Hebrew of Hebrews; as to the Law, a Pharisee; as to zeal, a persecutor of the church; as to the righteousness which is in the Law, found blameless*". Even though he will spend the next several verses explaining how these status symbols are relativized in Christ, he doesn't deny that this description represents his identity. While Paul does not believe that his identity grants him special favor before God, his words are nevertheless an accurate personal analysis. In Romans 9:3-5 Paul laments the rejection of Christ among "*my brethren, my kinsmen according to the flesh, who are Israelites*". Paul then outlines the gifts which God has graciously bestowed upon Israel, "*to whom belongs the adoption as sons, and the glory and the covenants and the giving of the Law and the temple service and the promises, whose are the fathers, and from whom is the Christ according to the flesh*". Paul, by extension, believes himself to stand firmly among the people through whom God had acted to send his Messiah. Paul will make the same claim about himself later in the argument, stating in Romans 11:1 that "*I too am an Israelite, a descendant of Abraham, of the tribe of Benjamin*". The implication, of course, is that Paul's mostly non-Jewish audience cannot claim this venerable inheritance but were, by God's grace, "*grafted in among them* [the Israelites] *and became a partaker with them of the rich root of the olive tree*"[2]. As he is defending his apostolic bonafides in 2 Corinthians

---

2. Romans 11:17

11:22, Paul writes acerbically *"Are they Hebrews? So am I. Are they Israelites? So am I. Are they descendants of Abraham? So am I."*, claims which Paul definitely intended to be taken at face-value.

What do we make of Paul's personal revelations in these passages? Paul assuredly sees himself as a Jew, an Israelite from the tribe of Benjamin, and a Law-abiding Pharisee who zealously persecuted the church. This confirms the evidence from Acts we reviewed earlier; in Acts 23:6 Paul declares himself to be a Pharisee, and we learn from Acts 22:3 that he was educated under Gamaliel, the teacher who wisely counseled the Sanhedren against persecuting Peter and his associates in Acts 5:33-39. Acts 23:6 also reveals that Paul was born in Tarsus, and Luke frequently references Paul's Roman citizenship throughout Acts, where Paul leverages it to advance the gospel in several precarious situations. For completion's sake we might also add that Paul has, according to Acts 23:16, a sister and a nephew. Using these data points, it is possible to sketch a composite picture of Paul's personal identity. He believed himself to be a Jew within the Pharisaic tradition who was born and granted citizenship in Tarsus. How do these insights enable us to better understand Paul?

We will begin with his birth in Tarsus. According to Acts 21:39, Paul holds citizenship in this city alongside his status as a Roman citizen. In Acts 9:30 he is sent to Tarsus not long after his Damascus road experience, and even as an adult Paul *"seems to have considered Tarsus in some sense his home, and perhaps he still had relatives there"*[3]. There is little doubt that Paul's connection with Tarsus influenced his intellectual formation. Strabo, an ancient geographer, wrote extensively about Tarsus and the city's academic pedigree. It was widely known for its schools of philosophy and rhetoric, particularly within the Stoic tradition, and provided citizens with a plethora of educational opportunities not available in many cities around the Mediterranean. Several men educated in Tarsus would go abroad and complete their studies elsewhere, but there were few places where one could become deeply acquainted with the venerable Greek intellectual heritage.[4] Paul, fluent in the Greek language and able to utilize Greek rhetorical conventions in his letters, was likely privileged to the educational opportunities available in Tarsus. Following the pattern of many fellow Tarsians, Paul would complete his education in another city. This explains how he wound up studying under Gamaliel in Jerusalem.

Gamaliel was known for his tolerance, as Acts 5 indicates, and represents one particular side of an intra-Jewish debate about Law observance and community boundaries. As we discussed in Chapter 6, Judaism constituted a diverse array

---

3. Theilman, *Apostle of Grace*, p. 2
4. Theilman, *Apostle of Grace*, p. 3

of beliefs and led to the formation of various sects which argued for particular readings of the Jewish Law, and even within Pharisaism there were few areas of unanimous agreement. Christians have ironically downplayed these differences and traditionally understood Judaism as a theologically monochromatic 'religion'; anyone familiar with the intense factionalism of western Christianity should not be surprised that Jews in antiquity didn't all share the exact same set of beliefs. In the early first century, Pharisaic Judaism was roughly divided into two camps, the radical Shammaites who were extremely strict about purity while simultaneously open to political violence and the moderate Hillelites who had a more relaxed understanding of purity and were less inclined to rebellion.[5] Paul, who described himself as 'zealous' and persecuting followers of Jesus whom he believed were compromising the Law, was almost certainly aligned with the Shammaite party while his teacher Gamaliel perfectly represented the Hillelite tradition. Since Gamaliel was so thoroughly respected even an extremist like Paul found value in studying under him.[6] Not only was Paul steeped in one of the best Greek educations available to a Roman citizen, he also learned from one of the greatest Pharisees of his generation. Paul was in a unique position to become the Jewish apostle to a gentile world.

Paul's self-description as a zealous Pharisee is an excellent if subtle insight into his personal understanding of the Law and other related beliefs. We have already discussed several basic Pharisaic beliefs above and it is essential to remember that Pharisees generally placed a high value on proper Law observance. There were both ecclesiological and eschatological reasons for this; the Law demarcated the people of God and was therefore an indication that one was in the right before God, a member of Abraham's family in good standing. It is these people who would surely be vindicated in the eschaton when God finally returned to rescue his people and raise up from the dead those who had perished beforehand. Before Damascus, Paul adamantly held these beliefs. 'Zeal', in the Jewish tradition, had a long pedigree denoting a willingness to violently defend God and his Law and exemplified by Phinehas in Numbers 25, who slaughtered a disobedient Jew and his Gentile courtesan in a successful effort to stay God's wrath. Given the connection between 'zeal' and violence it is of little surprise that Paul in Philippians 3:6 recalls how his zeal manifested itself in persecuting the church. Paul initially thought that Jesus-believers were compromising the integrity of God's people and responded as any zealous radical Pharisee might. Paul freely admits this much in Philippians.

---

5. Wright, N.T. 2013. *Paul and the Faithfulness of God.* Fortress Press. pp. 85-86

6. Wright, *Faithfulness of God*, p. 86

Paul's willingness to use violence against the church helps explain an often-times misunderstood statement found in Galatians 1:13-14: *"For you have heard of my former manner of life in Judaism, how I used to persecute the church of God beyond measure and tried to destroy it; and I was advancing in Judaism beyond many of my contemporaries among my countrymen, being more extremely zealous for my ancestral traditions"*. Paul again appeals to zeal and connects it with both his persecution of the church and his defense of Israel's "ancestral traditions", including, of course, the Law. Many Christians have capitalized on the phrase *"former manner of life in Judaism"* and assumed Paul was somehow abandoning his Jewish identity, perhaps exchanging it for a new identity as a Christian. It can sound, to ears attuned to modern conceptions of 'religion', as if Paul is 'converting' from one set of beliefs to another. Judaism, from a Christian point of view, is a false religion and so in Galatians 1:13-14 Paul abandons his false religion, jettisons his Jewish heritage, and embraces the true Christian faith. This line of argument is, in popular Christian discourse, extremely common. It is also entirely false.

There are exegetical and historical considerations that help us understand the Greek term *ioudaismos* which stands behind the English translation 'Judaism' in Galatians 1:13-14. It may appear to modern readers as if Paul is renouncing his Jewish identity, relegating it to the period of his life before Damascus. Only a few lines later in Galatians 2:15 Paul has no reservations whatsoever about identifying himself as a Jew: *"We are Jews by nature and not sinners from among the Gentiles"*. Referring to a debate with Peter over Law observance, Paul states using a first-person plural that he and Peter are indeed both Jews. Whatever he means by *"my former manner of life in Judaism"* it isn't a rejection of his personal Jewish identity. *Ioudaismos* appears only two times in the New Testament, both in the Galatians passage quoted above, and is an extremely rare term in antiquity. Its first extant appearance is in 2 Maccabees 4:13 where it is used to describe armed resistance against the armies of Antiochus Epiphanes IV by Jewish rebels and seems to be coined as a title which expresses opposition to Greek culture and imperialism.[7]

Dunn explains the significance of *ioudaismos* in a passage which deserves to be quoted at length: *"the term "Judaism" seems to have been coined as a means of giving focus to the determination of the Maccabean patriots to defend the distinctive national identity given them by their ancestral religion. It was not simply a neutral description of "the religion of the Jews," as we might wish to use it today. From its earliest usage it carried overtones of a religious identity shaped and hardened in the fires of persecution, of a religion which identified itself by its determination to maintain its distinctiveness and to remain free from the corruption of other religions and peoples . . . In other*

---

7. Dunn, *Apostle Paul*, p. 347

words, "Judaism," as we find it in our sources, defined itself by separating itself from the wider world and understood the Torah in part at least as reinforcing and protecting that separateness"[8]. It makes perfect sense given Paul's self-description as a zealous Pharisee that his rejection of *ioudaismos* is not a repudiation of his Jewish identity but rather a turning away from violently persecuting the church. Paul himself uses this term twice as he describes in Galatians how he persecuted the church and became "*more extremely zealous*" than other Jews. There is simply no evidence to support the claim that Paul is somehow denying his Jewish identity or claiming that being Jewish makes one inferior. Galatians 2:15 probably indicates the opposite, suggesting that Paul even as a follower of Jesus still sees Jews as occupying a special place in human history. Even though it scrambles our beloved modern categories we must acknowledge, if we want to read Paul faithfully and thereby attempt to understand his letters, that he sees himself standing firmly within the Jewish tradition *as a Jew* and not something else.

Matthew Thiessen, making a similar argument to the one outlined above in his appropriately-titled book *A Jewish Paul*, excellently summarizes the argument advanced in the previous paragraph: "*Paul did not cease to be a Jew, either in his mind or in the minds of others, even those who disagreed with him. Rather, Paul had become a messianic Jewish follower of Jesus. For some, this change meant that Paul had become a bad or a misguided Jew. For Paul, this change meant that he was being faithful to the eschatological revelation of God's son, the Messiah*"[9]. Paul's transformation and disavowal of *ioudaismos* is categorically distinct from his Jewish identity. Given that the Jesus tradition, in which Paul was certainly steeped, emphasized the coming of the eschatological kingdom through the death, resurrection, and ascension of God's messianic son of David and Jesus's overwhelming rejection of violence as a means of building the kingdom, Paul seems to be reframing (but not rejecting) his identity in light of Jesus. Just as we must read the gospels under the assumption they portray Jesus as a Jew, we are historically obligated to do the same with Paul.[10] He was a Jewish Pharisee, educated in the Greek city of Tarsus and the Jewish capital Jerusalem, who zealously persecuted the church before meeting Jesus. After Damascus, Paul came to believe that Jesus was the Messiah and therefore repented

---

8. Dunn, *Apostle Paul*, p. 348

9. Thiessen, Matthew. 2023. *A Jewish Paul*. Baker Academic. p. 42

10. A brilliant example of this line of thinking is found in Novenson, Matthew. 2004. *Paul and Judaism at the End of History*. Cambridge University Press. pp. 29-49. Unfortunately I didn't read Novenson's provocative and insightful book until after I had completed this chapter, but his take on the *ioudaisoms* debate is, in my view, nearly flawless. Although not himself a libertarian, many of Novenson's arguments in *Paul and Judaism at the End of History* intersect perfectly with my interpretation of Paul.

of his zealous violence, which he publicly renounces in 1 Corinthians 15:9: "*For I am the least of the apostles, and not fit to be called an apostle, because I persecuted the church of God*". Paul remains a Jew, charged with announcing Jesus to the Gentile world.

There is one label, however, which Paul does innovatively apply to himself after Damascus. Following his dramatic encounter with Jesus, Paul now considered himself to be an 'apostle'. The title 'apostle' becomes foundational to Paul's sense of vocation and appears as a self-referential description in most of his letters. Paul introduces himself to the church in Rome in the first line of Romans: "*Paul, a bond-servant of Christ Jesus, called as an apostle, set apart for the gospel of God*"[11]. Paul believes God called him to the role of apostle which obligates him to share the gospel. Galatians 1:1 also stresses the connection between apostleship and God's calling: "*Paul, an apostle (not sent from men nor through the agency of man, but through Jesus Christ and God the Father, who raised Him from the dead*". A few verses later in Galatians 1:15, Paul argues that God had "*set me apart even from my mother's womb and called me though His grace*", echoing the calling of Jeremiah in Jeremiah 1:5 and the role of God's servant in Isaiah 49:5. Paul believes he was called by God, like the prophets of old, and given the responsibility of proclaiming an urgent divine announcement. This was God's will for Paul's life, as he comments in 1 Corinthians 1:1: "*Paul, called as an apostle of Jesus Christ by the will of God*". Paul is an apostle because God wanted him to complete a specific task. What does Paul mean when he calls himself an apostle?

The Greek term behind the English 'apostle' is *apostolos*, which in the New Testament refers to a messenger. While the word can sometimes be used in an informational context to denote a generic message, when Paul applies it to himself or the evangelists apply it to Jesus's disciples, *apostolos* designates a messenger whose words are divinely authorized; like the prophets, apostles have been entrusted with the task of communicating a message from God.[12] By appropriating this term Paul evokes his sense of divine mission and legitimizes his message. When Paul is preaching the gospel or writing to churches, he is doing so because God had called him to the task. His allusions to passages in Jeremiah and Isaiah are not accidental; Paul believed himself to be in the prophetic tradition of proclaiming an urgent message from God containing world-changing truths to which people

---

11. Romans 1:1

12. Barnett, Paul. 1993. "*Apostle*". In *Dictionary of Paul and His Letters*, edited by Hawthorne, Gerald; Martin, Ralph; Reid, Daniel. InterVarsity Press. pp. 45-51

must respond.[13] Paul believes that his experience with the ascended Jesus on the road to Damascus qualified him to be an apostle, as he expresses in passages like 1 Corinthians 9:1, 15:8, and Galatians 1:11-17.[14] This encounter with Christ confirmed his calling as an apostle and conferred upon him the status of *apostolos* which could only be shared with others who were directly commissioned by Jesus. For Paul, his identity as an *apostolos* animated him: "*the office of apostle, by which Paul pointedly referred to himself, is of singular importance in the appreciation of his life and ministry*"[15]. God tasked Paul with a specific apostolic mission: preach the gospel of Jesus to the Gentiles. Luke portrayed Paul fulfilling this task in Acts and it is the fundamental objective which lies behind his letters. Paul caps off a summary of his apostolic responsibility in 1 Corinthians 9:1-23 with a terse mission statement: "*I do all things for the sake of the gospel*", exactly what someone called as an *apostolos* by God would be expected to say.

We are now in an excellent position to synthesise our analysis of Paul's identity. We learned in the last chapter that Paul was called as an apostle to the Gentiles specifically; before Ananias meets Paul God tells him in Acts 9:15 that Paul was chosen "*to bear My name before the Gentiles*", and Luke spends the second half of Acts narrating Paul's ministry among Gentiles. Obtaining a quality Greek education in Tarsus *and* studying the Law as a Pharisee in Jerusalem made him uniquely qualified for the task of proclaiming the Jewish Messiah to a Gentile world. Even as a zealous Pharisee, Paul was intellectually positioned, perhaps uniquely so, to engage with Gentiles. A Galilean Jew such as Peter was much less equipped for the task, which is why, in Paul's own words, "*James and Cephas* [Peter] *and John . . . gave to me and Barnabas the right hand of fellowship, so that we might go to the Gentiles and they to the circumcised*"[16]. Paul states in Romans 1:5 that he "*received grace and apostleship to bring about the obedience of faith among all the Gentiles*", and his educational pedigree enabled him to work among Gentiles in a way that other church leaders simply could not. Paul was the right man for the job. As Luke portrays in Acts 15, the relationship between Jews and Gentiles is perhaps the most contentious issue in the early church, the controversy which prompted Galatians, Ephesians and (at least in part) Romans, and which Paul is in a perfect position to address. Paul believes that

---

13. Theilman, *Apostle of Grace*, pp. 21-26; Although I do object to Theilman's characterization of Paul's Damascus experiences as a 'conversion' he nevertheless captures the prophetic essence of the title 'apostle'.

14. Barnett, *Apostle*, p. 50

15. Barnett, *Apostle*, p. 45

16. Galatians 2:9

the Jews in some sense own the gospel, that it belongs to them and was delivered primarily to them, but that as a result the Gentiles were obligated to respond, as he states in Romans 1:16: "*I am not ashamed of the gospel, for it is the power of God for salvation to everyone who believes, to the Jew first and also to the Greek*".

By orienting his mission towards a Gentile audience, the Greek-educated Paul was not renouncing, repudiating, or replacing Jews or Judaism with something called 'Christianity'. Not once does the term 'Christian' appear in any of Paul's letters. He believes, as the prophets foretold, that when Israel's Messiah arrived the nations would finally know and worship the one true God of Israel. His apostleship was a fulfillment of that promise. The incorporation of gentiles into the family of Abraham will have a profound impact on Paul's worldview, as Krister Stendhal, a brilliant scholar who was in many ways years ahead of his time, argued: "*Paul lived his life among Jews and Gentiles . . . In Acts Paul is programmatically portrayed as a Jew . . . who brings the gospel to the Gentile world and that book does not end until Paul has made it all the way to Rome, the seat of power in the Gentile world . . . one of the most basic of the questions and concerns that shaped Paul's thinking in the first place* [was] *. . . the relation between Jews and Gentiles*"[17].

Paul sees himself as standing within the diverse range of Jewish beliefs in the first century, arguing that Israel's God had fulfilled His promises by sending a Jewish Messiah who now rules over all creation. Because Jesus has inaugurated the eschaton and sits at the right hand of God, the Gentiles must now learn the truth: "*there is only one God. the Father, from whom are all things . . . and one Lord, Jesus Christ, by whom are all things*"[18]. This statement is only comprehensible within the matrix of Second Temple Judaism. Paul's sole innovation is that he asserts the Messiah has already come. I agree wholeheartedly with Theissen, who "*categorically reject*[s] *one conclusion at which* [scholars] *frequently arrive: that Paul must have thought something was inherently flawed with, wrong about, or absent from Judaism*"[19]. Jesus was the fulfillment of Jewish hopes, not an abandonment and replacement of them, and Paul's position as a Greek-educated Jew proclaiming Jewish Messiah must be the hermeneutical lynchpin for interpreting his letters. Theissen is again correct when he states that "*Historically, Paul would have been surprised by the later Christian claim that he was rejecting Judaism and founding a new religion*"[20]. Far from it. Paul, called as an apostle by God to proclaim the Jewish Messiah to a Gentile world with which he was intimately intellectually familiar,

---

17. Stendhal, Krister. 1976. *Paul Among Jews and Gentiles*. Fortress Press. p. 1
18. 1 Corinthians 8:6
19. Theissen, *A Jewish Paul*, p. 9
20. Theissen, *A Jewish Paul*, p. 21

would always conceptualize his mission as happening from within Judaism. The nations would be incorporated into the family of Abraham through the reign of Israel's Messiah.

Now that we have established the central elements of Paul's identity we are in a position to analyze some of the core beliefs which shaped his understanding of political and economic structures. Before turning to these themes, however, it will be helpful to analyze the significance of the medium Paul used to communicate with his churches. What is the significance of Paul's letters, why did he write them, and how should we read them?

LETTER WRITING

Writing a Greco-Roman Letter

We all know social media isn't real life. Or at least I hope we do. I didn't touch it until 2022 when I realized how effective it can be for networking, and while social media has helped me meet so many incredible people I am grateful to know, I sometimes wonder if my life would be better had I never created an account. Time will tell. Occasionally, despite all of social media's drawbacks, I have an exchange which helps me appreciate how Christians who don't read books on biblical studies think about the Bible. I made a fairly innocuous post about Paul, echoing the quote from John Walton found in Chapter 4, in which I stated that Paul's letters were not written to us. My seemingly uncontroversial statement was met with a hostile response from one reader, who told me I was wrong and implied I was either a heretic or not really Christian. I rarely argue online, but I thought there was an easy way to address his concern and perhaps change his mind. I opened my Bible app and took a screenshot of 1 Corinthians 1:1-2, which reads (in short) *"Paul . . . to the church of God which is at Corinth"*. It was right there in the Bible; 1 Corinthians was written to the Corinthians, and therefore not to us. I posted the screenshot and explained how my position was, indeed, 'biblical'. Unsurprisingly my interlocutor never bothered to respond.

This is indicative of a larger hermeneutical deficiency in the modern church. Many Christians read the Bible as if it was written directly to us, designed by God Himself to specifically answer our twenty-first century questions. I address these interpretive concerns at length in Chapter 4, but this paradigm of placing our generational concerns above the original intention of the text collapses in the first lines of Paul's letters. Romans was written *"to all who are beloved of God in Rome"*[21],

---

21. Romans 1:7

Galatians "*to the churches of Galatia*"[22], and 1 and 2 Thessalonians "*To the church of the Thessalonians*"[23]. Paul's first letter to Timothy was written "*To Timothy*"[24], and Philemon "*To Philemon our beloved brother and fellow worker, and to Apphia our sister, and to Archippus our fellow soldier, and to the church in your house*"[25]. None of these people lived in the twenty-first century, and none of them were from the United States. While the Bible, both reliable and authoritative for Christians throughout the ages, was written *for* us, it was not written *to* us. If our interpretation of Paul begins with the expectation that he will answer all of our pressing modern questions, we will at best be disappointed and at worst distort his words.

One trio of New Testament scholars put it nicely: "*These letters from Paul were not written to us. When we read them, we are initially prying into someone else's business. Yet we also believe that God continues to speak to us through these old letters*"[26]. I agree wholeheartedly with this statement. Our reading of Paul's letters must take into account the historical contingencies of his original audience, as their problems and questions will necessarily be those to which his letters are responding. The Bible cannot mean anything for us unless we grapple with what it meant for them, and if we take the authority of Scripture seriously then we have to contend with what Paul unambiguously says in the opening of every letter he ever wrote: the people to whom he was writing were not us. When we read Paul's letters, we are in a sense eavesdropping on a two-thousand-year-old conversation between two parties who don't look, think, or act in exactly the same way that modern Western Christians do. I think Michael Bird puts it best: "*When we read these letters, it is like reading someone else's mail*"[27]. If you were to violate federal law and steal a personal letter out of a random person's mailbox, it would be impossible to fully comprehend the conversation unless you knew something about the two people involved in the exchange. This is exactly the same challenge we face with Paul's letters, except for a two-thousand year time gap, a fundamentally different social and cultural context, and the baggage of two millenia's worth of theological traditions. Answers don't come easy, and maybe we shouldn't expect them to.

Like the synoptic evangelists and every other biblical author, Paul's letters are occasional. They were written to a particular group of people, addressing a

---

22. Galatians 1:2

23. 1 Thessalonians 1:1, 2 Thessalonians 1:1

24. 1 Timothy 1:2

25. Philemon 1:1-2

26. Capes, David, Rodney Reeves, and Randolph Richards. 2007. *Rediscovering Paul.* InterVarsity Press. p. 54

27. Bird, Michael. 2008. *Introducing Paul.* InterVarsity Press. p. 57

particular set of problems, within a particular historical context. Paul's letters have a significant historical advantage over other canonical texts in that Paul informs us of his intended audience. When he writes a letter to the church at Corinth, for instance, we know that it would have had to make sense to the Corinthians. Even a slight engagement with historical information about Corinth and its culture enables interpreters to make a more informed decision about what Paul intended to communicate to his audience. Historians also have a basic understanding of how and why letters were composed during this period and the rhetorical techniques which were employed by an author to transmit their message. On the one hand, Paul's letters were some of the first writings ever composed by Christians; Ulrich Mell, who argues 1 Thessalonians was the earliest document included in the New Testament canon, rightly says *"Paul succeeded in the process of transforming the oral Gospel into a written form"*[28]. Even if one is inclined to challenge the literary primacy of 1 Thessalonians, Mell's point stands: in Paul, we have one of the first examples of the oral Jesus tradition committed to parchment. That is indeed revolutionary. Yet Paul's letters still follow the conventional arrangement of Greco-Roman epistles, and in this regard Paul is no different than any of his contemporary authors. Letter writing conforms to a particular set of conventions in antiquity, and a few comments are in order on how this applies to Paul.

Greek and Roman letters differ little in style by the first century, so it is entirely appropriate to speak of a "Greco-Roman" letter.[29] Greco-Roman letters generally followed a three-part structure, with an opening, body, and closing. The opening section often hints at what will be discussed in the body, and Paul usually included thanksgivings in his openings which performed this function. In 1 Corinthians 1:4-9, Paul thanks God for the Corinthian's knowledge, and then spends much of the letter chastising them for using their knowledge improperly. Since letter writing was expensive in antiquity, they were rarely written without an intended purpose, either to address a matter of business or convey important information. Paul's letters do both. Most Greco-Roman letters end with a series of greetings, demonstrating that they were often intended to be read by more than one person. Romans 16 is an excellent example of this convention and even concludes with a summary of Paul's main points in 16:25-27. Paying diligent attention to the beginning and ending of Paul's letters often elucidates his reason for writing and the material contained in an epistle's body.[30]

---

28. Mell, Ulrich. 2025. *Gospel as Letter.* Fortress Press. p. 53

29. Capes, Reeves, and Richards, *Rediscovering Paul,* p. 56

30. Capes, Reeves, and Richards, *Rediscovering Paul,* pp. 56-60

Paul also employs several Greco-Roman rhetorical techniques in his letters which are obscured for modern readers but entirely comprehensible to his original audience. Paul's Greek education in Tarsus no doubt included training in popular rhetorical techniques, and although scholars debate how Paul employed them in his letters they are in complete agreement that he uses them when constructing his arguments. An excellent example of a Greco-Roman rhetorical convention is found in Romans 2:1-11. Gorman explains that Romans 2 *"begins with a direct address, "you have no excuse," that indicates Paul's adoption of a rhetorical strategy called the diatribe, a method of argumentation and instruction using an imaginary conversation partner (the 'interlocutor')"*[31]. When Paul opens this section of the letter in 2:1 saying *"Therefore you have no excuse, everyone of you who passes judgment, for in that which you judge another, you condemn yourself"*, it is entirely possible that he didn't have an individual from the Roman church in mind but was rather constructing an imaginary debate partner which serves as a foil for his ideas. While this technique is perplexing to a modern audience, Paul assumes that his Roman audience would understand his rhetoric. Oftentimes appeals to 'plain readings' gloss over crucial literary nuances, and in order to appreciate Paul and his writings readers must be open to textual features which are foreign to modern literary conventions.

In the modern world most written documents, whether letters, emails, text messages, academic articles, or social media posts, are composed by individuals with little to no collaborative input. By contrast, *"writing in the Greco-Roman world often involved significant collaboration between an author and a number of individuals, each of whom served a specific role during the compositional process"*[32]. As Benjamin Laird explains, nearly every literary work in the first century was composed by a trained secretary, called an amanuensis, who was trained in writing, maintained the necessary writing materials, and could compose documents in a variety of literary genres which would allow the dictating author to most effectively communicate his ideas with their intended audience.[33] In Romans 16:22, Paul's secretary Tertius personally greets the Romans, and in several places in his letters such as 1 Corinthians 16:21 and Galatians 6:11 Paul himself picks up the pen and addresses his audience.[34] While someone with Paul's education would have certainly had a significant impact on the finished product, his secretary was responsible for its composition.

---

31. Gorman, Michael. 2004. *Apostle of the Crucified Lord.* Eerdmans. p. 354

32. Laird, Benjamin. 2023. *Creating the Canon.* InterVarsity Press. p. 15

33. Laird, *Creating the Canon*, pp. 15-16

34. Capes, Reeves, and Richards, *Rediscovering Paul*, pp. 56-60

There are two other historical complications which must be accounted for when reading Paul's letters: the lack of effective postal services and the extraordinarily (by modern standards) low literacy rates of antiquity. Given the amount of effort it took to compose a letter, "*we may safely assume that authors such as Paul relied primarily and possibly even exclusively on trusted colleagues and associates to deliver their writings to their intended recipients*"[35]. This method of delivering a letter was the safest and most reliable way of ensuring a letter was delivered in antiquity.[36]

Based on our analysis of Roman house churches in Chapter 6, few people in Paul's congregations would have been literate. Paul expected his letters to be read aloud: "*a significant number of early Christians would have encountered Scripture primarily through public-reading events rather than from reading texts in private settings*"[37]. Laird further elaborates: "*Because illiteracy was rather high in the first century and access to written texts was often limited, we can safely assume that it was customary for the New Testament writings to be publicly read to the original recipients and other audiences shortly after their initial composition*"[38]. Occasionally the letter carrier would have been involved in explaining Paul's letters upon delivery and perhaps even reading them orally. While it is impossible to know what additional explanations would have been provided during public readings, there was undoubtedly more commentary and discussion about the letters during and after a public reading. In Colossians 4:7-9, Paul lets his audience know that the letter carrier, Tychicus, and his associate Onesimus would offer them additional information beyond what was written in the epistle.[39] While Paul's letters are theologically and pastorally rich we cannot limit his intellectual horizons to the written text alone. Paul was a significant player in the early Jesus movement and it is a safe assumption that he had many beliefs that are only tangentially addressed in his letters. This is particularly true for the churches he founded; when Paul exhorts the Corinthians to "*hold firmly to the traditions just as I delivered them to you*" in 1 Corinthians 11:2, we can be certain that these 'traditions' include information which was never communicated in the letter because Paul would already expect his audience to be familiar with it. With Paul's letters we only have one side of a two-sided conversation which was never purely textual and involved many shared assumptions between both parties to which we as modern readers are not privy.

---

35. Laird, *Creating the Canon*, p. 19

36. Capes, Reeves, and Richards, *Rediscovering Paul*, pp. 80-81

37. Laird, *Creating the Canon*, p. 21

38. Laird, *Creating the Canon*, p. 20

39. Laird, *Creating the Canon*, p. 21

'Function' Before 'Meaning'

Christians have long supposed Paul's letters are repositories of timeless theology, a collection of abstract doctrinal statements which were self-evidently meant to be read and integrated into a larger systematic whole. Our brief historical analysis of Paul's letters complicates this narrative. As Paul explicitly states at the beginning of each epistle, they are all written to specific congregations to answer specific questions or address specific problems. Since we only have one side of the conversation, we must infer from Paul's sometimes opaque rhetoric the situation which prompted him to write in the first place. We cannot escape the historical fact that Paul's letters were occasional and often offered advice which was tailored for whichever church he happened to be writing. Paul is a man of conviction who believed he was teaching and writing the truth, but we must be careful to avoid decontextualizing Paul's letters and forcing them to say that which Paul never intended. He was aware that a letter like Philippians, for instance, included material which he thought to be foundational and true while also directing it specifically to the church in Philippi. The letter simply cannot be interpreted properly without reference to the historical context in which it was produced, and any attempt to do so, particularly under the assumption that Paul is writing a treatise on systematic theology, will inevitably result in distorting Paul's message by forcing it to conform to later theological constructions. Interpreters of Paul must be ever vigilant to avoid the quagmire of modernization lest they undermine the authority of Scripture by substituting its message with one of their own making.

One might naturally wonder, then, what we are supposed to do with Paul's letters and whether they provide anything of value for us at all. Paul does indeed write to individual churches and crafts his rhetoric to best meet the needs of his audience, and there is no abstract 'meaning' to Paul's epistles outside of their specific context. James Smith has identified this problem in Pauline interpretation: "*There has been a fundamental hermeneutical failure to recognize the difference between function and information in the writings of Paul* . . . [there] *is a preoccupation with arriving at theology, or "information," and not with what Paul might actually be trying to achieve through his rhetoric*"[40]. Paul's letters are designed to perform a particular function, to have an intended impact on his audience, and his rhetoric is the vehicle by which Paul accomplishes this task. We cannot understand anything Paul says in his letters without recourse to Paul's larger agenda. While Paul does indeed incorporate a wide range of theological insights in his letters, they must be understood within the context of each letter as an independent literary unit in

---

40. Smith, *Marks of an Apostle*, p. 19

which Paul has a narrow set of objectives. In order to assess what Paul's letters *mean* for us or our theology, we must contend with what Paul was attempting to *do* for his audience by writing them in the first place.

I believe that Smith has perfectly articulated the divide between 'function' and 'meaning' in Paul while exposing a seriously flawed set of hermeneutical assumptions. His insights into this problem warrant extended quotation; according to Smith, we must shift *"the emphasis from product to process . . . from a focus on the traditional search for pure information to a focus on how that information is produced . . . we must continue along the lines established by those who see Paul as a "theologizer" rather than a theologian, but not stop with that observation. That is, when Paul's "activity" comes to the fore of our analyses, our attention is naturally drawn to what he sought to achieve by virtue of that activity; furthermore, only by incorporating the goals of Paul's "theologizing" may we understand more fully the content of that "theologizing". In other words, if we are to be concerned about theology, then let us be concerned with a theology that arises out of the functional effectiveness of a text rather than amputating the rhetoric at the level of the text. It is the preoccupation with "theological doctrine" that has clouded the fact that Paul was a man in history trying to achieve a very specific set of goals and that his writings were written as a means of reaching those goals"*[41].

Smith is not denying that Paul has a theology, nor is he denying that Paul does indeed at many points in his letters intended to communicate information to his audience which is based on his theology. Smith's contention is that far too many interpreters, and I would add that this is an almost *universal* phenomenon among lay readers of the Bible, completely ignore how Paul's rhetorical agenda and wider literary context shapes the actual language of his letters. We simply cannot divorce these contextual considerations from our analysis of Pauline theology. Smith, bringing his argument to a conclusion, rightly contents *"that it is only after we discern the function of Paul's texts can we even begin to consider issues of significance or "theology." . . . a glaring problem in contemporary hermeneutics is the lack of appreciation for what the writers of antiquity were thinking when they themselves put texts together. It appears that ancient writers may have been more attuned to what their texts were intended to do as opposed to what they were intended to mean"*[42]. Smith's hermeneutical analysis is directly on target, as his is prescient warning of the interpretive distortions which occur when interpreters fail to take into account Paul's rhetorical goals.

---

41. Smith, *Marks of an Apostle*, p. 20-21

42. Smith, *Marks of an Apostle*, p. 21

Some might find the preceding paragraphs depressing; a cynic may well make the accusation that all readings of Paul are therefore doomed to fail, and that we are forever trapped in a sort of intellectual nihilism. I don't see it this way. An argument that I have been making throughout this book is how New Testament passages are often employed in modern political and economic conversations in a way which completely isolates them from their historical and literary context. Even professional scholars who are aware of the complex hermeneutical problems proposed by Smith and perhaps agree with his position are prone to ignore his warnings when the interpretive stakes are high; Romans 13:1-7, as we shall see, is an excellent example of this phenomenon. Many interpreters, including several with which I am in broad agreement, jump straight to the question of *meaning*, asking, in effect, *"what does Paul say about government in this passage?"*. This is an inherently theological question; it assumes that the text is designed to provide us with a timeless statement about the nature of political power which can be abstracted and applied in every historical context. I would argue that the question of *meaning* is the wrong place to start our interpretation. Instead, we should ask the much more fundamental question about what the text is intended to *do*, a question which centers on what Paul is trying to accomplish within Romans without assuming that he was intending to communicate timeless theological information about political power.

This dovetails perfectly with the hermeneutical model I proposed in Chapter 4. Before making any determinations about the *meaning* of Romans 13, including what it might "mean" for us today, we must first attempt to grapple with what Paul is *doing* there, and why he included it at that point in his letter. How does Romans 13 *function* with the letter as a whole? What is its immediate rhetorical context, and how does it relate to the material surrounding it? Is he appropriating ancient rhetorical or writing techniques? How does Paul address questions of political power in other passages? Are there other elements of Paul's thought, such as his understanding of eschatology and ecclesiology, which would influence our reading of that passage? How does it map on to Jewish and Greco-Roman conceptions of government? All of these fairly basic questions of historical analysis must be foregrounded if we want to apprehend the functional intention of Romans 13, and we absolutely cannot sidestep these questions if we ever hope to interpret the text as faithfully as possible. In the chapters on Paul's letters which follow this one, I will always attempt to anchor my interpretation of his letters to their historical context and place the question of function before meaning. The self-evidently and indeed biblically authoritative occasional nature of Paul's letters, written to particular churches to address particular problems, must shift the starting point of Pauline interpretation.

Pauline Influences

Paul did not compose his letters in an epistemological vacuum. While Paul is certainly a competent rhetorician and passionate preacher, his letters are not solely, or even primarily, the product of his own mind. Paul brilliantly synthesises discussions which were developing around the early Jesus movement, and as he addresses new challenges within his congregations Paul has a unique propensity to innovate and expand existing ideas in challenging and oftentimes unforeseen directions. He doesn't, however, invent them from scratch. Paul inherited a wide and diverse array of beliefs, teachings, and concepts from his historical context, both in Tarsus and Jerusalem, all of which impact his preaching and teaching. There are a number of external factors which influenced his thinking and it is imperative we account for them before outlining the major relevant themes in his letters.

Bird identifies three intellectual currents within which Paul was deeply influenced, and all of them had an effect on the shape of his occasional letters. Despite appearing under a section heading which problematically describes Paul as a 'theologian', there can be little doubt that Bird has correctly highlighted several sources from which Paul drew: "*1. The Jesus tradition, or the body of Jesus' teaching transmitted in the early church, which informs significant parts of Paul's exhortations. 2. The Jewish Scriptures and Paul's reading of them through a Christocentric grid, which provides the substructure of his theology. 3. Paul's consistent application of the gospel to the situations he faces in order to ensure the vitality and integrity of the churches*"[43].

At several points in Paul's letters, including 1 Corinthians 11:2 and 2 Thessalonians 2:15, Paul appeals to the traditions with which he instructed his churches. As I have articulated at several points in this book, I believe the oral Jesus tradition most likely serves as the basis for Paul's own 'traditions' and that both he and his churches would have known many of the traditions which would eventually be compiled in the written gospels. Paul seems to assume that his audience knows much more about Jesus than he explains in his letters, and his supposed disinterest in the Jesus of history is a mirage; he doesn't need to instruct the churches about the Jesus tradition in his letters because he has already recounted it to them in person. Despite a popular stream in New Testament scholarship which places, often for purely ideological reasons, a solid partition between Paul's letters and the Jesus tradition, it appears to me that the two are exceptionally compatible. Paul's knowledge of the oral Jesus tradition bridges the supposed gap. Bird's second source, the Jewish Scriptures themselves, need little explanation. Paul was trained as a Pharisee in Jerusalem and his letters are shot through with references

---

43. Bird, *Introducing Paul*, p. 21

and allusions to the Old Testament. While the messianic moment precipitated a hermeneutical revolution for Paul, Israel's Scriptures were still the solid foundation upon which his thinking about Jesus was built. Bird's third point, that Paul is constantly applying and reapplying the gospel, which will be discussed in more detail below, to the various situations in which his churches happened to find themselves is one of the reasons why we must first appreciate the function of Paul's letters before searching for their abstract meaning. The gospel is at the heart of Paul's thinking, but he is able to adapt it and refine it in different contexts.

In 1 Corinthians 15:8, Paul recounts how Jesus appeared to him *"last of all"*, after he first appeared to the other apostles. In other words, they were there before Paul and had been transmitting ideas about Jesus longer than Paul himself. Paul will adopt this apostolic tradition and rework it in his letters. In his book *Stewards of God's Mysteries*, scholar Jerry Sumney argues that at several points in his letters Paul explicitly draws on convictions, often in the form of summary statements, hymns, or aphorisms, which were already in circulation before the composition of his epistles. Summarizing his thesis, Sumney explains: *"The amount of quoted or cited tradition in Paul's letters will demonstrate that he remained dependent on the theological ideas and developments that were in the church before he joined and that developed in parallel streams of the church during his ministry. He was not a Lone Ranger creating doctrines no others in the church had thought of; rather, he stayed connected to the wider church—and did so with intentionality . . . We will see Paul's creativity in his use of preexisting traditions to address new questions and situations more than in the creation of new doctrines or doctrinal standards"*[44]. Not only are texts such as Philippians 2:6-11 preformed units which Paul appropriates wholesale to advance his rhetorical agenda[45], even concepts like the title 'Christ', which so thoroughly suffuses the earliest canonical literature, were embraced by Paul in a manner completely consistent with its use in the pre-Pauline church: *"The absence of any defense of its use indicates that Paul thinks the claim that Jesus is Christ is a given in the church"*[46]. While Paul is not a systematic theologian composing abstract theological treatises, his letters are thoroughly shaped by the theological milieu of the early church. As he attempts to accomplish very specific goals in his functional letters, Paul freely draws on traditions which were also accepted by his audience. Paul is definitely a contextual innovator, but he is not a theological inventor.

---

44. Sumney, Jerry. 2017. *Steward of God's Mysteries*. Eerdmans. p. 19

45. Sumney, *God's Mysteries*, pp. 28-31

46. Sumney, *God's Mysteries*, pp. 42-44

After reviewing Paul's personal profile, we have explored how Paul composed letters, why he decided to write them, what they were designed to accomplish, and how they intersect with the wide intellectual currents of the Jesus movement. While Paul is not a systematic theologian, he has well-formed beliefs that shape the contours of his instructions. There are major themes, several of which dovetail exactly with what we have explored in the gospels and Acts, which serve as recurring motifs in Paul's letters. Four sets of related themes directly pertain to our analysis of political and economic concepts in the New Testament. We will examine those in detail presently.

Major Themes in the Pauline Epistles

Although Paul is not a theologian in the proper sense of the term, and even though his letters are occasional, designed to address a very specific set of issues raised by individual churches, there are several major themes that condition his thinking which recur throughout his epistles. Some of these themes are directly relevant to our study of political and economic concepts in the New Testament, and I am deliberately choosing to highlight them in this section. While a case could correctly be made that other Pauline themes which I do not explore below have a bearing on these issues as well, I believe that the following selection of themes are foundational for our reading of Paul and provide a substantial framework through which we may better understand Paul's thinking on politics and economics. None of these themes are unique to Paul; he is influenced both by his upbringing and by the wider theological context of the early Jesus movement, and several of these themes have already been explained in detail or at least alluded to in our study of the gospels and Acts.

Every thematic review of Paul's letters must arbitrarily divide aspects of his thought into discrete categories for independent analysis. I maintain that Paul is an integrative thinker and that all of these concepts are intrinsically connected in his writing. Dividing them into separate units is a heuristic device which enables us to see how the parts contribute to the whole, and I do not want to leave readers with any impression that Paul somehow thought of these themes as independent entities. As a reflection of my assertion that Paul is a holistic thinker, the themes I explore below are separated into sets of two which strongly reinforce each other in the Pauline literature. I hope that by the end of this chapter the logical process of organization will become apparent to my readers. The four sets of themes are gospel and faith, church and Spirit, identity and ethics, and kingdom and empire. We will explore each in turn.

Gospel and Faith

It is worth quoting 1 Corinthians 9:23 again: "*I do all things for the sake of the gospel*". Paul believes, as we also discovered above, that God "*set* [him] *apart for the gospel*", a claim he makes explicit in Romans 1:1. It is impossible to ignore the gospel's centrality in Paul's thought. He was beyond confident that God had called him for the specific task of preaching the gospel to the nations, bringing about the "*obedience of faith*"[47] among those who hear it. In fact, concepts which are associated with the *pist-* root in Greek, often translated in the nominative as "faith" or "belief", are the *only* proper response to hearing the gospel. Romans 1:16-17, the cornerstone of Martin Luther's reformational awakening, draws a straight line between gospel and faith: "*For I am not ashamed of the gospel, for it is the power of God for salvation to everyone who believes* [*pist-* root], *to the Jew first and also to the Greek. For in it the righteousness of God is revealed from faith to faith* [both *pist-* roots]; *as it is written, "But the righteous man shall live by faith* [*pist-* root]*"*". The intrinsic link between belief/faith is also clearly articulated in Ephesians 1:13: "*after listening to the message of truth, the gospel of your salvation—having also believed, you were sealed in Him*". There is, of course, much more which could profitably be said about faith, and we will develop the concept in further detail below, but from the start it must be recognized that faith and gospel are inseparable. Paul's message will either be accepted with faith or not. There is no other option.

We have already discussed above the meaning of *euangelion*, gospel, and its central place in the thinking of the early church. The term is rooted in the second half of the Greek translation of Isaiah and is associated with God's eschatological deliverance of Israel, which early followers of Jesus claimed came to fruition through his life, death, resurrection, and ascension. Paul's frequent use of the term to describe the core of his message is consistent with the way in which *euangelion* and its cognates are used throughout the New Testament and intimately linked with eschatological and christology. Likewise, *pist-* language is, as I argued in the previous chapter on Acts, connected to the proclamation of the gospel as a response which is accepted by God and results in God's gifting of His Spirit. It is important that we reflect on the specific content of the gospel and the nuances of faith/belief language in Paul without isolating him from the wider witness of other New Testament authors.

Before proceeding, a word of caution is in order. In Chapter 4, I stated my sincere intention to avoid as many controversial theological concepts as possible in the hopes of appealing to an ecumenical audience. While many Christians will

---

47. Romans 1:5

have no theological objection to the arguments I am about to advance regarding the gospel and faith below, there are some adherents to particular strands of Reformed and Lutheran theology who strongly maintain that the word 'gospel' means 'justification by faith' with 'faith' denoting something like 'cognitive assent to a specific set of doctrinal propositions'. Those readers may immediately reject my interpretation of the gospel and faith because they don't explicitly conform to their traditional ways of articulating those categories. Such is life. If you find yourself in large agreement with the thesis of this book but theologically committed to the Lutheran or Reformed view, please do not allow one plank of my argument to dissuade you from reading further. I am attempting to make a historical case for both concepts which is firmly rooted in Paul's letters, and I hope that, even if one disagrees with my conclusions, they will see it as an honest attempt to grapple with two monumental pillars of Pauline thought. Those of us who believe in biblical authority must always allow our cherished doctrines to be refined by Scripture. As fate would have it, Paul actually delineates the content of his gospel at several points in his epistles, and we will explore them presently.

Thiessen correctly argues that *"at the center of Paul's message lies not a proposition but a person: Jesus"*[48]. Paul summarizes his message with the term *euangelion* and at three points in his letters he articulates the content of that message. The first is in Romans 1:1-5: *"the gospel of God, which He promised beforehand through his prophets in the holy Scriptures, concerning His Son, who was born of a descendant of David according to the flesh, who was declared the Son of God with power by the resurrection from the dead, according to the Spirit of holiness, Jesus Christ our Lord"*. Jesus is indeed the central figure in Paul's gospel. He describes the gospel yet again in 1 Corinthians 15. As Paul opens the chapter, he presents his first topic of discussion: *"Now I make known to you, brethren, the gospel which I preached to you"*[49], which he expounds upon further in 1 Corinthians 15:3-4: *"For I delivered to you as of first importance what I also received, that Christ died for our sins according to the Scriptures, and that he was buried, and that He was raised on the third day according to the Scriptures"*. Once again, Jesus takes center stage. Paul even ends the section by connecting his gospel with *pist-* language: *"so we preach and so you believed"*[50]. Paul's gospel, with Jesus fixed in the spotlight, is something which the Corinthians have already accepted. Paul's shortest summary of his gospel comes in 2 Timothy 2:8: *"Remember Jesus Christ, risen from the dead, descendant of David, according to*

---

48. Thiessen, *A Jewish Paul*, p. 71

49. 1 Corinthians 15:1

50. 1 Corinthians 15:11

my gospel". Paul condenses his statements from Romans and 1 Corinthians but doesn't deviate from their content.

In all three texts Jesus is the unambiguous core of Paul's gospel. Without Jesus there is no good news. But Jesus isn't simply portrayed by Paul as one particularly good individual among others. He believes that Jesus is the Messiah and draws on christological language which evokes the promises made to David. Jesus is exactly who the evangelists claimed he was, the long-promised Son of David who sits as king over all creation by virtue of his death, resurrection, and ascension. This all takes place, as Paul says in Romans and 1 Corinthians, in accordance with the Scriptures. God had made good on his promises in Jesus. Paul's messianic christology, then, is identical to that portrayed in the gospels and Acts. McKnight helpfully summaries the royal significance of Paul's gospel: *The gospel Story of Jesus Christ is a story about Jesus as Messiah, Jesus as Lord, Jesus as Savior, and Jesus as Son. It is sometimes forgotten that "Christ" is the Greek translation of the Hebrew word Messiah. The word Messiah means "anointed King" and "Lord" and "Ruler." Lord means, well, "Lord," and the word Son here certainly means the anointed king of Israel, as in Psalm 2. So the emphasis here in the gospel is that Jesus is Lord over all*"[51]. It is surprising that some Christians balk at the Messianic significance of the Gospel, because McKnight is simply summarizing exactly what Paul says in Romans, 1 Corinthians, and 2 Timothy. Paul's gospel is the announcement that Jesus is the resurrected king whose enthronement is a fulfillment (not a rejection or cancellation) of Israel's Scriptures. Bates encapsulates it perfectly: "*The gospel centers on Jesus the king*"[52]. Indeed it does. Paul uses the name of Jesus over two hundred times in his letters and the word *christos*, "Christ", over 300.[53]

At this point, there is little more which needs to be said. Throughout the gospels and Acts Jesus is unanimously, unequivocally, and universally regarded as the Davidic Messiah who rescues Israel, ushers in the eschaton, and currently sits at the right hand of God. He will, as Paul vividly illustrates at several points in 1 Thessalonians[54], return to rescue his people and judge the unrighteous. Paul's inaugurated eschatology is in perfect alignment with the New Testament witness, which is why he can speak of Jesus followers "*awaiting eagerly the revelation of our Lord Jesus Christ, who will also confirm you to the end, blameless in the day of our Lord Jesus Christ*"[55]. Twice he speaks of Jesus as Lord and Christ, presupposing his

---

51. McKnight, *King Jesus*, p. 55

52. Bates, *Allegiance Alone*, p. 44

53. Theissen, *A Jewish Paul*, p. 71

54. 1 Thessalonians 1:10, 2:19, 3:13, 4:13-5:11, 5:23

55. 1 Corinthians 1:7-8

Messianic rule over creation in the present as a guarantee that he will return to rescue his people. When Paul references Jesus, he always hails him as Lord. For Paul, to preach 'the gospel' is to proclaim Jesus as the Messiah. Jesus Christ, Son of David, resurrected Lord of all creation, is at the center of Pauline thought. When Paul says in 1 Corinthians 9:23 that he does *"all things for the sake of the gospel"* he is in essence stating what Luke narrates in the second half of Acts: all of the challenges, struggles, and hardships Paul faces are worth it because he was entrusted with taking the gospel of king Jesus to the nations. If Jesus is objectively the world's true king, Paul *must* tell the truth no matter what it costs him: *"I am under compulsion; for woe is me if I do not preach the gospel"*[56].

Not only did Paul feel compelled to preach the gospel, he sincerely hoped that many people would accept it and turn to Jesus. In two critical passages at the opening of Romans and Ephesians (and remembering that in Greco-Roman letters material which appears in the introduction often foreshadows the content of the epistle as a whole) Paul connects 'gospel' with *pist-* language. When Paul says *"the gospel . . . is the power of God for salvation to everyone who believes"*, he means it. God rescues people who hear the gospel and place their faith in it. There is, however, an important translation issue which must be addressed in order to properly understand Paul's conception of *pist-* language. The first should be evident to any reader who has been perceptively following my line of thinking in this chapter. Greek words in the *pist-* family do not have an exact English parallel. Many modern translations (including the NASB) will sometimes render *pist-* language as either 'fath/faithfulness' or 'belief/believe' depending on the context. In the NASB translation of Romans 1:16 the *pist-* root is rendered *"believes"* while in Romans 1:17 it is thrice translated *"faith"*. Both English terms denote slightly different (yet sometimes overlapping) categories and the translational variations mask the shared root, making it appear as if Paul is alluding to two entirely different concepts. Given that there are no perfect semantic equivalents between different languages, no English translation of the New Testament will be able to fully capture the sense of a Greek word group. The translators are not attempting to conceal Paul's original intended meaning but rather finding an adequate way of expressing it in English. Knowing, however, that words like 'faith' and 'believe' share a common root and are conceptually similar in Greek, we must ask how the root '*pist-*' would have been understood in antiquity and, most importantly, what Paul is attempting to communicate by using it extensively in his letters.

While words like 'faith' and 'believe' are deeply personal in English, often denoting an subjective state of interior feelings, Teresa Morgan explains how *pistis*

---

56. 1 Corinthians 9:16

is primarily a relational term in Greek: "*Pistis and* [its Latin equivalent] *fides are fundamentally relational concepts and practices, centering on trust, trustworthiness, faithfulness, and good faith . . . Relational meanings also dominate uses of the lexica across the range of written sources from the first century BCE to the second century CE, describing social interactions of all kinds and the interactions of people with institutions*"[57]. *Pistis* language, therefore, should not be understood as primarily a personal, internal disposition which one privately holds but rather a *relational* category which always implies interconnectivity with another person or group of people. As Morgan elucidates, "*pistis/fides . . . is one of those qualities that can only be practised socially: it is inherently relational and characteristically expressed in action towards other human beings (or, occasionally, animals). As such, though they acknowledge its interiority, neither Christian nor other writers of the early principate make it the focus of their interest*"[58]. When Paul uses *pist-* language, it is inherently relational. This already makes perfect sense in light of Paul's close association between the gospel, which is about Jesus the Messiah (a person, of course), and 'faith' or 'belief'. Paul's use of that terminology implies relationality. Morgan has already hinted at several English concepts which may be related to *pistis*, and the Greek conceptual range can be nuanced even further.

Nijay Gupta justifies the NASB translation of *pistis* as either "belief" or "faithfulness" in his book *Paul in the Language of Faith*: "[*pistis*] *can have at least two distinct (but related) meanings in Paul's letters: belief and faithfulness*"[59]. He argues that it can be understood as either believing faith (denoting a correct perception), obeying faith (perhaps best translated as "faithfulness"), or trusting faith (simply rendered "trust")[60]. The referents of *pistis* are fairly wide, and Gupta contends it "*is a remarkably dynamic word that can move along a spectrum of meaning such that one can use a number of words to translate it depending on the context . . . [and a] set of meaning such that can neither be exhausted nor adequately expressed by any one referent*"[61]. Since the word "faith" "*has certain connotations in modern English that ought not to be read into Paul's letters*"[62], Gupta suggests that *pistis* and cognates be translated with respect to three categories. The English word "faith" is appropriate when Paul is making a particular claim about Jesus in which his audience "believes", the word "trust" is an accurate translation when Paul is writing about how a

---

57. Morgan, Teresa. 2015. *Roman Faith and Christian Faith*. Oxford University Press. p. 503

58. Morgan, *Roman Faith*, p. 472

59. Gupta, Nijay. 2020. *Paul and the Language of Faith*. Eerdmans. p.

60. Gupta, *Language of Faith*, pp. 9-13

61. Gupta, *Language of Faith*, pp. 180-181

62. Gupta, *Language of Faith*, p. 181

believer's relationship with God results in trusting Him to fulfill His promises, and "faithfulness" or "loyalty" is proper when Paul describes commitment to Jesus.[63]. All three cases are intrinsically relational; even the English word "believe" presupposes a referent, something in which the subject places belief.

When Paul employs *pistis*, then, he is certainly thinking of it as a relational term which can be shaded with meaning and employed in a wide variety of contexts. If I was writing a monograph on Pauline language I would no doubt have a difficult road ahead of me. Untangling the various ways in which Paul uses *pist-* language is a daunting task and well beyond my ability level. Fortunately the guiding question of this section is the relationship between faith and gospel, and Matthew Bates has proposed an intriguing solution for how Paul's use of *pistis* correlates with his understanding of the gospel, one which takes Morgan's relationality and Gupta's dynamic interpretation of the term into account.

The gospel is about a person, Jesus, who Paul repeatedly asserts is ruler over all creation. Any use of *pistis* must establish some kind of relationship with the Lord Jesus Christ, David's long-promised son. To have *pistis* in the gospel denotes both a particular understanding of and response to Christ as king. It is about the establishment of a relationship with him which cannot be separated from his Messianic identity. Bates, drawing on the dynamic nature of *pistis*, claims the *"gospel reaches its zenith with Jesus's installation and sovereign rule as the Christ, the king. As such, faith in Jesus is best described as allegiance to him as king"*[64]. "Allegiance" is an excellent English expression of the Greek *pist-* language when used in relation to a person's response to Jesus. If Paul's gospel centers on Jesus as king, those who place their faith in him are declaring their allegiance to his hegemonic rule over all creation, established according to the Jewish Scriptures. This is a more precise, politically-oriented understanding of the "faithfulness" or "loyal" qualities of *pistis* which Gupta argued for above. The gospel of Jesus results in faithfulness on the part of those who believe in him, and political faithfulness or loyalty is conveyed accurately with the English word "allegiance" which captures the full royal significance of Paul's gospel. I am not arguing that the concept of allegiance exhausts Paul's use of *pistis* and cognates; it is a dynamic term with a wide semantic range. It makes sense, however, in the specific contexts in which Paul invokes the term as a response to his royal gospel, as Bates explains, *"since "Jesus is Lord" is at the heart of the gospel, not only does pistis (and cognates) probably shade towards the meaning of allegiance in relevant texts in the New Testament; this meaning also fits contextually*

---

63. Gupta, *Language of Faith*, pp. 181-182

64. Bates, *Allegiance Alone*, p. 77

into Paul's Letters and makes excellent sense within the larger Greco-Roman imperial world"[65].

Paul absolutely believes, along with the other New Testament writers, that Jesus is the promised son of David, king of Israel, who now rules over all creation at the right hand of God by virtue of his death, resurrection, and ascension, and that the enthronement of Jesus inaugurates the eschatological age foretold in the prophets which will be fully consummated upon his return. The idea that allegiance, faithfulness, or loyalty describes an appropriate response to the gospel of king Jesus is both linguistically and historically justifiable, and the evidence presented by Morgan, Gupta, and Bates points definitively in that direction. Those who accept the gospel have given loyal, faithful allegiance to king Jesus. The political implications of this confession are undeniable. If Jesus is king, as Paul rightly hails him, then all other political allegiances or loyalties are relativized. One simply cannot place their hope in Caesar and in Jesus; believers are unable to serve two masters. The witness of Acts demonstrates the *suprapolitical* nature of the early church and is contingent upon inaugurated eschatology. The end has already begun but has not yet reached fulfillment. Worldly powers still exist, but followers of Jesus are called to serve as a witness to them by embodying the message and ethic of king Jesus. Paul's infrequent advice regarding the relationship between the church and political authorities can only be understood properly within the framework of his gospel and the allegiant, faithful response to Jesus.

Understanding faith/belief in the gospel as a form of loyalty, faithfulness, or allegiance also helps elucidate Paul's several references to the 'obedience' which *pistis* will naturally manifest in the lives of those who place their faith in Jesus. At several points in his letters Paul draws a connection between faith(fulness) and obedience, epitomized in Romans 1:5: "we have received grace and apostleship to bring about the obedience of faith among all the Gentiles". Paul closes his letter to Rome by stating that his gospel *"has been made known to all the nations, leading to obedience of faith"*[66]. The generosity of the Corinthians will cause other believers to *"glorify God for your obedience to your confession of the gospel of Christ"*[67]. Conversely, Paul warns in 2 Thessalonians 1:8 that when Jesus returns he will deal *"out retribution to those who do not know God and to those who do not obey the gospel of our Lord Jesus"*. For Paul, obedience is an inseparable aspect of faith. One cannot be faithful to Jesus, believe that he is the Messiah, and give him allegiance without obeying him. Followers of Jesus must actually obey his commands. Since *pistis* is relational

---

65. Bates, *Allegiance Alone*, p. 89

66. Romans 16:25-27

67. 2 Corinthians 9:13

and can encompass the English categories of faithfulness, loyalty, or allegiance, it should be of little surprise that Paul expects those who place their *pistis* in the gospel to obey the Lord Jesus Christ. He is, after all, king.

Paul's gospel, the announcement that Jesus is the resurrected Messiah in fulfillment of Jewish Scripture, must be proclaimed to the nations. The eschaton has been inaugurated and the gentiles will finally come to worship Israel's God. Jews and gentiles alike respond to the message of Israel's Messiah through *pistis*, which in the particular context of Paul's Gospel is equivalent to the English concepts of faithfulness, loyalty, and allegiance. This is an act of political fidelity that *transcends* earthly categories of human power; Jesus is not only the king of individual hearts but the ruler of all creation. How could anyone respond to that message with anything less than faithful obedience, which is precisely what Paul is attempting to convey with his use of *pist-* language. The political consequences of the gospel and faith are staggering. Taking the two categories seriously means reframing our entire understanding of political power around the eschatological Messiah and walking in accordance with this new reality. Christians are called to be suprapolitical, obediently serving another king of a better kingdom. We are, as Paul says in 1 Corinthians 10:11, those *"upon whom the ends of the ages have come"*. There is no going back.

Faith in the gospel has massive implications for the character of the church. Israel's Messiah had come, Gentiles were placing their faith in him, and God was giving all believers the gift of the Spirit. In Acts 15 the Jewish leaders in Jerusalem determined that Gentiles were incorporated into the family of Abraham *by faith and the Spirit* and did not need to become Jewish in order to follow Jesus. Paul wholeheartedly agrees: *"if you confess with your mouth Jesus as Lord, and believe [pist-*root] *in your heart that God raised Him from the dead, you will be saved"*[68]. While centuries of Western theological interpretation have resulted in many Christians reading passages like this individualistically, as if they were intended to address the subjective feelings of a single person's heart, Paul's scope is much wider. The gospel message of the enthroned Lord is not just about individuals. Speaking in Ephesians 1:20-23 of what God has done in Christ, Paul demonstrates that the gospel has a much wider scope: *"[God] raised Him from the dead and seated Him at His right hand in the heavenly places, far above all rule and authority and power and dominion, and every name that is named, not only in this age but also in the one to come. And he put all things in subjection under His feet, and gave Him as head over all things to the church, which is His body, the fullness of Him who fills all in all"*. Individuals place their faith in the gospel of Christ Jesus but then become a part of

---

68. Romans 10:9

his church. Incorporation into the family of God is a critical component of Paul's thinking.

Spirit and Church

In Acts God dispenses the Spirit, enabling His followers to proclaim the gospel of the Lord Jesus Christ to the ends of the earth. Taking everybody by surprise, God even poured out His Spirit upon gentiles *without them adopting the Law,* leading to the conclusion that gentiles were a part of God's family on the basis of faith and the Spirit. Paul explains the relationship between gospel, faith, and Spirit in (the now oft-quoted) Ephesians 1:13: *"after listening to the message of truth, the gospel of your salvation—having also believed, you were sealed in HIm with the Holy Spirit of promise".* The sign that someone has placed their faith in Jesus through the gospel is the gift of God's Spirit. Paul makes the exact same point in Galatians 3:1-5 when writing to Gentiles who are tempted to think that God's Spirit isn't enough: *"did you receive the Spirit by the works of the Law, or by hearing with faith? Having begun by the Spirit, are you now being perfected by the flesh . . . does He who provides you with the Spirit and works miracles among you, do it by the works of the Law or by hearing with faith?"* When Jews and Gentiles hear the gospel and place their faith in Israel's Messiah, God provides them with the Spirit.

As in Acts, the Spirit leads to an unexpected incorporation of Gentiles in the family of Abraham *as Gentiles,* and the dispensation of God's Spirit does not create a loosely connected network of individuals but the Jew-plus-Gentile eschatological community of God which was promised in the Scriptures. Paul makes precisely this point in Galatians 3:6-9 as he elaborates on the bond between faith and Spirit: *"Even so Abraham believed God and it was reckoned to him as righteousness. Therefore, be sure that it is those who are of faith who are sons of Abraham. The Scripture, foreseeing that God would justify the Gentiles by faith, preached the gospel beforehand to Abraham, saying, "All the nations will be blessed in you." So then those who are of faith are blessed with Abraham, the believer".*

He will spend the rest of Galatians 3 explaining his logic relates to the Law, arguing in essence that the position taken by the Jerusalem church in Acts 15 that Gentiles are not obligated to follow the Law is correct. The denouement of Galatians 3, and in my opinion one of the most important passages in the entire Christian Bible, is found in Galatians 3:26-29: *"For you are all sons of God through faith in Christ Jesus. For all of you who were baptized into Christ have clothed yourself with Christ. There is neither Jew nor Greek, there is neither slave nor free man, there is neither male nor female; for you are all one in Christ Jesus. And if you belong to Christ, then you are Abraham's descendants, heirs according to the promise".* Faith in Jesus results in the Spirit. Everyone who possesses the Spirit is now a part of Abraham's family. Gorman helpfully summarizes Paul's argument: "*Christ's cross has inaugurated the age of the Spirit, in which Jews and Gentiles alike inherit Abraham's blessing and are justified by believing the gospel of Christ crucified and thereby being incorporated into the covenant people who exist now in Christ*"[69].

What is the logic behind Paul's rhetoric in Galatians 3? While we explore the purpose of Galatians (and thus its functional significance) in a later chapter, Galatians 1-2 addresses perhaps the most significant controversy in the earliest Jesus communities, the relationship between Gentiles and the Law. Acts conclusively settles the question: Gentiles are incorporated into the family of Abraham by faith and the Spirit, not through Law. The letter of Galatians is addressing this vexing question and coming to the same conclusion as Luke. This is not a rejection of Paul's Jewish heritage, a denigration of Jews, or even a suggestion that Jews should not follow the Law. In line with the promises to Abraham, David, and the prophets, God's Messiah has come, inaugurating the world to come, therefore the Gentiles are now called to worship Israel's God. When they place their faith in Jesus, God seals Gentiles with the Spirit and they become full members in Abraham's family. A Pharisaic Jew like Paul separates humanity into two categories, those who are in God's family and those who are not. Gentiles who believe in Israel's Messiah are now a part of the 'in' group by virtue of the Spirit. God's family, the true church, is defined by faith and the Spirit. Paul will continue this line of thinking in Galatians 4:6, where he again argues that "*Because you are sons, God has sent forth the Spirit of His Son into our hearts*". Thiessen explains the relationship between faith and Spirit: "*It is not faith itself but what faith brings that makes one Abraham's son. Faith brings the pneuma* [the Greek term for 'Spirit'], *and it is the pneuma that creates a connection between Abraham and the gentile believer*"[70]. Because of the Spirit, Paul can close out his letter by referring to the Jew-plus-gentile church as the "*Israel of God*"[71], the family of Abraham now extended to the nations through faith and the Spirit.[72] Paul's ecclesiology, his conception of the church, is a redefinition of Israel's boundaries through the Spirit. There is no community of believers without God's Spirit.

Paul's Abraham theology isn't simply a rhetorical device employed to solve a particular problem in Galatia. It is deeply embedded in his thought and shapes

---

69. Gorman, *Crucified Lord*, p. 208

70. Theissen, *A Jewish Paul*, p. 104

71. Galatians 6:16

72. For a compelling case that Paul does *not* refer to a Jew and Gentile community in Galatians 6:16 but rather only ethnic Israel, see Novenson, *End of History*, pp. 166-167.

his entire post-Damascus worldview. Paul makes the exact same statement about Abraham in Romans 4, that Gentiles are incorporated into his family on the basis of faith, and in Paul's exposition of the Spirit in Romans 8 he argues *"all who are being led by the Spirit of God, these are the sons of God"*[73]. As he reflects upon the plight of unbelieving Jews in Romans 9-11, Paul vividly describes gentiles as being *"grafted in"* to God's family, presumably through faith and the Spirit.[74] Just as the Law defined Israel and demarcated them out for eschatological salvation, the Spirit performs the same function. After delineating the relationship between gospel, faith, and Spirit in Ephesians 1:13, Paul says in the following verse that the Spirit *"is given as a pledge of our inheritance, with a view to the redemption of God's own possession, to the praise of His Glory"*. In Ephesians 2:11-22, Paul asserts that Gentiles are now part of God's family through faith, stating in 2:18-19 that *"through Him we both have our access in one Spirit to the Father. So then you are no longer strangers and aliens, but you are fellow citizens with the saints, and are of God's household"*.

Paul also uses temple language at several points in his letters to describe the church. As Philip Comfort argues, *"The Temple of Jerusalem was one of the principal symbols of the Jewish faith and worldview . . . It was perhaps inevitable that when Paul spoke of God's new work in Christ, he would appropriate temple imagery in some way"*[75]. At four points in Paul's letters, 1 Corinthians 3:16-17, 6:19, 2 Corinthians 6:16, and Ephesians 2:21, Paul refers to either the church as a whole or individual believers as "temples" of God. He does this by virtue of the presence of God's Spirit among believers, perfectly exemplified in 1 Corinthians 3:16: *"Do you not know that you* [plural] *are a temple of God and that the Spirit of God dwells in you?"*. Paul employs two different Greek words for "temple" in his letters, *naos* and *hieron*. Comfort explains *"In terms of the Jerusalem Temple, naos refers to the building, the place of God's dwelling, and hieron refers to the entire area, or precincts, including the sanctuary . . . Generally speaking, naos was used to designate the inner section of the Temple known as the holy place and the holy of holies, whereas hieron designated the outer court and the Temple proper"*[76]. *Naos* is the term used to describe God's dwelling place in the Temple, the holiest area in the most important building ever constructed. In all four passages where Paul refers to the church as a temple he uses the term *naos*, precisely because *it is within the church that God's Spirit resides!*

---

73. Romans 8:14

74. Romans 11:17-24

75. Comfort, Phillipl. 1993. *"Temple"*. In *Dictionary of Paul and His Letters*, edited by Hawthorne, Gerald; Martin, Ralph; Reid, Daniel. InterVarsity Press. p. 923

76. Comfort, *Temple*, p. 924

The Spirit is dispensed upon Jews and gentiles who place their faith in Jesus the Messiah. Because the Messiah rules over creation, the people of God are demarcated by the Spirit, set apart from those who do not believe. God lives within and among His people.

The indwelling Spirit is also why Paul refers to his churches as *hagios*, generally translated either 'holy' or 'saints'. In the opening of nearly every epistle, Paul uses *hagios* language in reference to his audience, as in, for example, Romans 1:7, 1 Corinthians 1:2, and Ephesians 1:1. It is noticeably absent in the introduction to Paul's angriest letter, Galatians, perhaps for rhetorical effect. The concept of holiness is central to Israel's self-conception in the Old Testament as a people set apart by God in witness to the nations. A classic text is Leviticus 19:2: "*You shall be holy, for I the Lord your God am holy*". Paul's holiness language denotes the unique, set apart identity of God's people and is applied to all of those who place their faith in Jesus. As Theissen notes, "*when Paul calls believers "holy ones," he signals that they are a people set apart for God*"[77]. It is little surprise that Paul refers to the Spirit-filled church as the *naos*, the Holy of Holies, and declares them to be set apart for God's purposes. Holiness has massive implications for Pauline ethics, as we will discuss below, but Paul's ecclesiology is entirely framed by the Spirit, given to both Jews and Gentiles through faith in God's Messiah Jesus who is proclaimed in the gospel. Those who are *hagios* in the present will be vindicated by God on judgment day, set apart not only in the present but in the future, as Gorman explains "*the Spirit marks and protects believers as God's possession. As "the pledge . . . of our inheritance," the Spirit is the "deposit . . . or "first installment" . . . of future redemption. The experience of redemption is real, but not yet complete*"[78]. God will finish what he started.

Paul's understanding of the church and the Spirit are inseparable. There is no church without the Spirit and the Spirit doesn't operate outside of the church. Paul's ecclesiology is intrinsically pneumatic. All of this arises naturally out of Paul's Jewish worldview and is in fact only comprehensible within the broad contours of Second Temple Judaism. Paul is not rejecting the calling of Israel or the promises made to the Patriarchs; instead he believes the promises have been unequivocally fulfilled in the Christ who inaugurated the eschaton. Gentiles are now incorporated into Abraham's family through faith and become members of the exclusive, holy, set-apart community of God. Paul does not in any way revoke the Jewish us-and-them dichotomy but expands it to include Gentiles who pledge allegiance to Jesus. In Paul's mind, there are only two types of people: the church, defined by the Spirit, and the world. N.T. Wright's massive book *Paul and the*

---

77. Theissen, *A Jewish Paul*, p. 126

78. Gorman, *Crucified Lord*, p. 507

Faithfulness of God, includes a 268-page *chapter* entitled '*The People of God, Freshly Reworked*'. While I don't agree with every aspect of his argument, Wright does provide an excellent summary of how Paul's ecclesiology is related to other aspects of worldview: "*Here the major themes of Paul;'s thought meet and merge: Israel's God, coming back to rescue his people and the world and to dwell with them for ever; Israel itself, God's people, redefined around the Messiah and spirit who were themselves the means and mode of that dwelling*"[79]. The Christian identity is necessarily rooted in the corporate community of Abraham, defined by the Holy Spirit given through faith in the Messiah.

The political and economic implications of Paul's ecclesiology are often missed. I take Paul's sweeping statements in Galatians 3:26-29 seriously. The social status of those who have faith in Christ is irrelevant. What really matters is faith, and all those who have faith are a part of Abraham's *exclusive* family by virtue of the Spirit. If modern Christians are to infer any principles from this passage, we must surely arrive at the conclusion that our own identity markers mean very little in light of the gospel. Those who believe in Christ are a part of his worldwide eschatological family, irrespective of nationality or any other political boundary. Since the church constitutes the true family of God, why would it care about pleasing politicians or empowering them to make decisions which negatively impact the lives of other people? Is it even rational for a child of Abraham to endorse aggressive military campaigns against other children of Abraham who happen to live on a different side of an imaginary line? Should we outsource *any* community decisionmaking to the political class? If Peter and Paul's witness in Acts are any indication, the answer is a solid 'no'.

Richard Horsley, for all his anti-capitalist and pro-ruling class rhetoric, come dangerously close to realizing the consequences of Pauline ecclesiology: "*Paul's urging the communities of subject peoples to persist in their loyalty (pistis/fides) to Christ, mean that they could no longer maintain loyalty to Caesar. It seems evident from Paul's letters that the assemblies of Christ-loyalists were forming communities that Paul, at least, understood as an alternative, inter-people society who politeuma (social-political order), already established in heaven with/by their Lord, would descend with him from heaven in the final retaliation of the kingdom of God*"[80]. How then does it logically follow that Horsley's modern solution to the problems which plague us always include giving more money and power to a tiny oligarchical ruling class so they can manage the world based on their subjective values? It seems to me that if we are supposed to be faithful or allegiant to Christ alone while seeing ourselves as

---

79. Wright, *Faithfulness of God*, p. 1041

80. Horsley, *Bow Down*, p. 130

operating outside of the temporal political order that we should absolutely reject Horsley's authoritarian socialism. Who are they, the non-Jesus followers, to make decisions on our behalf? Shouldn't we hold *them* accountable instead of, as Horsley repeatedly advocates throughout his work, asking them to hold *us* accountable? If Christian participation in nationalist projects compromises the holiness of Abraham's family, endorsing globalism is even worse. We must begin to see ourselves as Paul says that we are: the *naos* of God, the restored Israel, who faithfully follow the one true king and are united to each other through God's Spirit. This insight alone should challenge all Christian pretensions of acquiring human power, including arbitrarily regulating voluntary economic exchange. Gospel, faith, Spirit, and church lead quite naturally to our next set of Pauline themes: identity and ethics.

Identity and Ethics

When Paul conceptualizes *pistis*, especially in the context of his gospel, that dynamic term naturally connotes English categories such as faithfulness, loyalty, or allegiance. For Paul, the gospel is something that people must *obey*, and obedience is political because the one whom believers are obeying is the exalted Messiah. In order to avoid a theological landmine, I gently suggest that perhaps there the hard dichotomy between 'faith' and 'works' is a theologized construction of the Western mind and not reflective of Paul's actual thought. If *pistis* and cognates are relational terms which presuppose obligations between two parties, obedience is necessarily built into the concept of faith. Since *pistis* in the gospel is the condition under which God grants the Spirit to both Jews and Gentiles, incorporating the latter into Abraham's eschatological family, the identity of those who are in Christ entails an ethical responsibility. The Spirit, God's empowering presence which binds the church and, ala Acts 1:8, enables the community of faith to spread the gospel to the ends of the earth, is also responsible for moral transformation. In Paul there is a tight connection between identity and ethics which will influence his understanding of Christian political and economic engagement.

Towards the end of Galatians, a letter in which Paul contends that Abraham's family is defined by faith and the Spirit instead of the Law, he addresses the moral character of those who follow Jesus. Noting the prominent role of God's Spirit, Paul makes the following argument: "*But I say, walk by the Spirit, and you will not carry out the desire of the flesh. For the flesh sets its desire against the Spirit, and the Spirit against the flesh; for these are in opposition to one another, so that you may not do the things that you please. But if you are led by the Spirit, you are not under the Law. Now the deeds of the flesh are evident, which are: immorality, impurity, sensuality, idolatry, sorcery, enmities, strife, jealousy, outbursts of anger, disputes, dissensions, factions, envying, drunkenness, carousing, and things like these, of which I forewarn you, just as I have forewarned you, that those who practice such things will not inherit the kingdom of God. But the fruit of the Spirit is love, joy, peace, patience, kindness, goodness, faithfulness, gentleness, self-control; against such things there is no law. Now those who belong to Christ Jesus have crucified the flesh with its passions and desires*"[81]. Paul, contrasting the 'flesh' and the 'Spirit', explains how those led by the Spirit will embody "*fruit of the Spirit*", manifesting in concrete ethical behavior in the lives of believers. That these fruits bear a remarkable similarity to the Sermon on the Mount may (or may not) be a curious coincidence, but his use of "*kingdom of God*" is certainly a nod to the Jesus tradition. Also of note is Paul's ecclesiological qualification at the end of this passage: his exhortation is directed to "*those who belong to Christ Jesus*". Christology and pneumatology shape Paul's understanding of the church's identity and the ethical fruits which the Spirit will bear.

These themes of the Spirit-driven identity and corresponding ethical obligations of the church are even more pronounced in Romans 8:12-17 which, like Galatians 5:16-24, is part of a much longer argument about the identity of believers: "*So then, brethren, we are under obligation, not to the flesh, to live according to the flesh-for if you are living according to the flesh, you must die; but if by the Spirit you are putting to death the deeds of the body, you will live. For all who are being led by the Spirit of God, these are sons of God. For you have not received a spirit of slavery leading to fear again, but you have received a spirit of adoption as sons by which we cry out, "Abba! Father!" The Spirit Himself testifies with our spirit that we are children of God, and if children, heirs also, heirs of God and fellow heirs with Christ, if indeed we suffer with Him so that we may also be glorified with Him*". The relationship between identity and ethics couldn't be more apparent. Those who have the Spirit are "*sons of God*", "*children of God*", and "*heirs with Christ*". Since they live by the Spirit, they must kill the flesh.

Some Protestants might worry that the way in which I am framing this passage suggests we are somehow expected to 'earn' or 'perform' our way into God's good favor. Paul's own logic in 8:13 undercuts the case for a 'works-righteousness' reading of this passage: "*by the Spirit you are putting to death the deeds of the flesh*". Those who have faith in Jesus are indeed obligated to obey, but they do so by the power of the Spirit. The ethical responsibilities which accompany our faith are driven by the Spirit, not our own self-righteous effort. God works through the gospel to empower those who respond. As Paul transitions from his extended explanation of the identity of the church into a more concrete moral exhortation,

---

81. Galatians 5:16-24

he issues the following instruction: *"Therefore I urge you, brethren, by the mercies of God, to present your bodies a living and holy sacrifice, acceptable to God, which is your spiritual service of worship. And do not be conformed to this world, but be transformed by the renewing of your mind, so that you may prove what the will of God is, that which is good and acceptable and perfect"*[82]. After spending eleven chapters explaining the identity of the church, Paul's conjunction *"therefore"*, introducing specific ethical instruction, bears an immense theological weight. It is only *because* the family of Abraham has been reoriented around the Spirit that they are able to offer themselves to God for transformation. Without the gospel, faith, and the Spirit, which define the identity of God's family, authentic moral transformation is impossible. There is, in Paul's mind, a tight, inseparable bond between the identity of the church and its moral character.

Since ethics are for Paul a natural extension of identity, from where did he derive his ethical values? Unsurprisingly for a Pharisaic Jew educated in Tarsus, Paul was influenced by both Hellenistic and Jewish conceptions of morality. James Thompson notes that *"Paul's moral instruction is especially noteworthy within the context of the ethical teachings of the ancient moralists-which would have influenced the communities he established-and that of the Jewish heritage based on Scripture. Both traditions offered coherent approaches to moral instruction"*[83]. Paul, along with the communities to which he wrote, would have been familiar with Greco-Roman moral philosophy, particularly the Stoic tradition which stresses that proper knowledge was able to overcome destructive behaviors. They would also have been heavily influenced by Jewish ethical reflection which undoubtedly shaped Paul's moral reflection.[84] Essentially all of Paul's ethical instructions were in conversation with Hellenistic and Jewish moral philosophy.

Paul believes that the community of Jesus followers is in direct continuity with Israel, not a replacement or supersession of it. His understanding of community ethics are thoroughly Jewish: *"As in ancient Israel, the identity of the community is the presupposition for its conduct"*[85]. The people of God ought to act like it. Since Gentiles are now included in Abraham's family through faith, the social status and communal ties of Jesus followers are relativised. Paul's *"first task, therefore, was to maintain a group not bound by familial or ethnic ties as a minority community within a larger society. This group would inevitably be confronted by the religious, social, and philosophical values of the majority culture. Thus, like all minority communities, Paul's*

---

82. Romans 12:1-2

83. Thompson, James. 2011. *Moral Formation According to Paul.* Baker Academic. p. 7

84. Thompson, *Moral Formation*, pp. 7-9

85. Thompson, *Moral Formation*, p. 67

churches would survive only if they distinguished themselves from the larger society by a group identity and shared ethos. Paul created a "group ethos" to unite the community"[86]. Even though Paul draws heavily on the best of Hellenistic and Jewish moral philosophy, his churches would adhere to an innovative set of ethical standards. The trigger for this new ethical reflection was, of course, their identity of faith and the Spirit: *"Paul's "ought" is thus based on the "is" of theological reflection"*[87]. The "theological reflection" which prompted Paul's reevaluation of Hellenistic and Jewish values was, of course, Jesus himself.

One of the aspects of Hellenistic morality that Paul appropriates is *mimesis* or imitation of ethical figures. As Bennema explains, *"Paul's ethics [are] to a large extent mimetic ethics. This is not to say that all of Pauline ethics is about mimesis, but that personal example and imitation are key aspects in Paul's ethical thought"*[88]. Who would Paul expect his audience to imitate other than Jesus himself, the Messiah at the center of Paul's gospel? It is the christological interpretation of mimesis which foregrounds Paul's ethical innovation: *"the concept of Pauline mimesis reflects largely the Greco-Roman mimetic traditions in terms of language and workings . . . but is uniquely Christ-centered . . . for Paul, Christ is the sole exemplar"*[89]. The believing community is called to imitate the one in whom they believe. The moral life of those who have faith and are given the gift of God's Spirit must reflect Jesus; his followers are called to live like him. Paul himself serves as an example of christological mimesis: *"Be imitators of me, just as I also am of Christ"*[90]. This isn't a general call to act like Jesus, nor is it like the vague "What Would Jesus Do?" slogan which allows modern Christians to project all of their contemporary ethical assumptions onto the man from Nazareth. Paul is not calling his followers to become radical Jewish eschatological prophets engaged in a direct critique of the Jerusalem establishment. Paul's charge to imitate Jesus is based primarily on one particular event in the life of Jesus: his crucifixion.

In his letter to the Philippians, Paul encourages them to remain united: *"Therefore if there is any encouragement in Christ, if there is any consolation of love, if there is any fellowship of the Spirit, if any affection and compassion, make my joy complete by being of the same mind, maintaining the same love, united in spirit, intent on one purpose. Do nothing from selfishness or empty conceit, but with humility of mind regard one another as more important than yourselves; do not merely look out*

---

86. Thompson, *Moral Formation*, p. 19

87. Thompson, *Moral Formation*, p. 43

88. Bennema, *Imitation*, p. 313

89. Bennema, *Imitation*, pp. 313-314

90. 1 Corinthians 11:1

for your own personal interests, but also for the interests of others"[91]. Easier said than done. Fortunately for the church in Philippi, Paul provides an example for them to imitate as they strive for the lofty goal of unity. Philippians 2:5-11 may be the single most significant ethical text in the entire New Testament. Paul writes: "*Have this attitude in yourselves which was also in Christ Jesus, who, although He existed in the form of God, did not regard equality with God a thing to be grasped, but emptied Himself, taking the form of a bond-servant, and being made in the likeness of men. Being found in appearance as a man, He humbled Himself by becoming obedient to the point of death, even death on a cross. For this reason also, God highly exalted Him, and bestowed on Him the name which is above every name, so that at the name of Jesus every knee will bow, of those who are in heaven and on earth and under the earth, and that every tongue will confess that Jesus Christ is Lord, to the glory of God the Father*".

Gorman calls Philippians 2:6-11 Paul's "master story", and rightly so.[92] In this breathtaking text Paul presents Jesus as the ultimate example for his followers to imitate. The bridge between Philippians 2:1-4, where Paul exhorts his audience to maintain unity by placing the needs of others before their own ,and the example of Christ in 2:6-11 is 2:5: "*Have this attitude in yourselves which was also in Christ Jesus*". Gorman argues convincingly that the Greek behind this passage is best understood in communal terms and that the mindset of Christ's people, the church, is rooted in Christ himself and therefore his people must adopt his mindset.[93] The strategic location of 2:5 is a call to imitate Christ, which Paul will elucidate shortly. Sumney argues that Philippians 2:6-11 bears all the hallmarks of a traditional hymn which predated Philippians. It is a theologically rich passage which Paul doesn't feel the need to justify, and the lyrical quality suggests his audience would have already been familiar with it.[94] Paul adopts this preformed tradition to make a larger point about Christian morality. Gorman identifies several characteristics of this text which have a bearing on Pauline ethics. The tradition reflects a pattern of reversal where Christ is first humiliated and then exalted. Intrinsic to the passage is Jesus's possession of status: he existed in the form (*morphe* in Greek) of God but gave it up. Jesus twice abases himself, first by humbling himself through becoming a man and then again by dying on the cross. Gorman expresses this as a form of *kenosis*, self-emptying, whereby Jesus possesses great status but willingly renounces it for the sake of others. It is because Jesus was prepared to empty himself, rejecting the trappings of power and privilege which were rightfully his on the

---

91. Philippians 2:1-4

92. Gorman, Michael. 2001. *Cruciformity*. Eerdmans. p. 88

93. Gorman, *Cruciformity*, pp. 40-43

94. Sumney, *God's Mysteries*, pp. 28-31

basis of his *morphe* in God, that he has been highly exalted above all names. In the end, every knee will bow and every tongue confess that Jesus Christ is Lord. The attitude which Paul wants the Philippians to cultivate, sustaining the unity of the Jew-plus-gentile family of Abraham, is the sacrificial, self-emptying model of Christ.[95]

The prefigured hymn, which likely predates every written document included in the New Testament, contains every christological element in the gospels, Acts, and Paul. Jesus is in reality the exalted Messiah who bears a unique relationship with God, but he willingly sacrifices himself for the sake of the world. This sacrifice results in resurrection and exaltation, inaugurating the eschatological age which will be fully consummated upon his return and at which everyone will finally be forced to acknowledge Jesus as Lord. Philippians 2:6-11 is a perfect example of the tight relationship between these themes. The ethical consequences are massive. The Philippians, and by extension all who put their faith in Christ, are called to imitate his attitude of sacrifice on behalf of others. This is the fundamental ethical posture of believers. To fully obey God, honoring the gospel and serving Jesus, means that Christians must be willing to sacrifice themselves for others. The incarnation and cross are Paul's ethical starting points; although he agrees with many aspects of Hellenistic moral philosophy and Jewish ethical reflection, both traditions are reinterpreted through Jesus's sacrificial life and death. Imitating Jesus means picking up a cross and following him.

The term Gorman coins to describe Paul's foundational ethical insight is *cruciformity*, which I will use as a shorthand to describe the moral posture of Christians throughout the rest of this book. Gorman explains his use of the word 'cruciformity': "*The process of "imitation" is therefore better called Christ's formation in believers . . . and the result, believers' conformity to Christ, especially his cross . . . Cruciformity, I therefore suggest, is a term more appropriate for what has often been referred to as the "imitation" of Christ. Cruciformity is an ongoing pattern of living in Christ and of dying with him that produces a Christ-like (cruciform) person. Cruciform existence is what being Christ's servant, indwelling him and being indwelt by him, living with and for and "according to" him, is all about, for both individuals and communities*"[96]. For Paul, the ethical standard was set by Jesus. When Paul in 1 Corinthians 2:2 "*desired to know nothing among you except Jesus Christ and him crucified*", he was not concerning himself with abstract theological pontification. Paul was embodying a new way of living, shaped by the example of Jesus's own sacrificial death. As the Messiah himself said: "*For even the Son of Man did not come*

---

95. Gorman, *Cruciformity*, pp. 88-92

96. Gorman, *Cruciformity*, pp. 48-49

to be served, but to serve, and to give his life as a ransom for many"[97]. Those who claim to follow Jesus must follow him to the cross.

Cruciformity is also the context within which Paul understands 'love'. The concept of love in modernity is unfortunately freighted with emotional baggage and in popular usage denotes a subjective feeling of positivity towards other people. Emotivism is absolutely not the basis for Paul's cruciform ethic. The famous 'love chapter' of 1 Corinthians 13, often read (entirely out of context, I might add) at weddings is one important example of cruciform love. The crucial passage is 1 Corinthians 13:4-7: *"Love is patient, love is kind and is not jealous; love does not brag and is not arrogant, does not act unbecomingly; it does not seek its own, is not provoked, does not take into account a wrong suffered, does not rejoice in unrighteousness, but rejoices with the truth; bears all things, believes all things, hopes all things, endures all things"*. For Paul, love is entirely people-oriented, an expression of concrete actions and behaviors towards others which places their needs before one's own. As Gorman puts it, *"love does not "insist on its own way" . . . in this broader sense of not seeking self-benefit and self-edification"*[98].

Just as Jesus's incarnation and crucifixion were expressions of his *kenotic* disposition towards us, believers are called to love others by sacrificing for them and seeking to meet their needs. Paul expresses this idea succinctly earlier in the letter: *"knowledge makes arrogant, but love edifies"*[99]. Jesus himself said there were no greater commandments than loving God and neighbor[100], and through Jesus's sacrificial death his followers learn what love truly means. For Paul, loving one's neighbor entails building them up and making sacrifices for them when necessary. Christian love is cruciform love. Obedience to king Jesus requires an attitude of sacrificial, self-emptying love for other people. This is why, shortly before the Christ hymn in Philippians 2:6-11, Paul says *"Do nothing from selfishness or empty conceit, but with humility of mind regard one another as more important than yourselves; do not merely look out for your own personal interests, but also the interests of others"*[101]. This is precisely what Jesus did for us. It is also why he sits enthroned as king over all creation.

Many biblical scholars assent, either implicitly or explicitly, to modern authoritarian socialism and maintain that it is somehow endorsed or legitimated by the Bible. Moxnes affirms the view that a small cabal of European politicians

---

97. Mark 10:45

98. Gorman, *Cruciformity*, p. 159

99. 1 Corinthians 8:1

100. Mark 12:30-31

101. Philippians 2:3-4

should have absolute control over the economic affairs of small-town Americans. Horsley, Wright, and Gorman in their own ways reject the concept of free-market exchange. We will discuss the unfortunate political and economic shortsightedness of these otherwise brilliant scholars in the final chapter of this book, but a brief reflection on how Paul's ethic of cruciformity informs our political and economic decisions is in order. The problem with authoritarianism and socialism, whether in their conservative or progressive forms, is that they rely on the arbitrary use of coercive force to achieve particular political and economic ends. No matter how much the ends are perceived as noble, the only way to realize them is through raw, violent power. Christians are supposed to love others like Jesus, sacrificially serving rather than expecting to be served. In every case and despite their real political differences, the scholars mentioned above willingly resort to secular state power as a means of imposing their subjective political preferences on society. They would, like most Westerners, appeal to the rhetoric of justice, peace, and truth as a legitimation of their position while criminalizing consensual behavior they find objectionable.

The logic of cruciformity, in contrast, is terminal. Following Jesus means seeking the good of all people and, like the man himself, renouncing the use of aggressive violence. It is better to serve than to be served, and the political process only creates conditions in which one group of people benefit at the expense of everyone else. While Christians navigate the complex world of earthly power we must think and act differently. Instead of celebrating violence as the only means to construct a just society, Christians should instead follow the cruciform example of the ascended Messiah and choose sacrifice over domination. Rothbard got it right; the laws of morality are not somehow magically suspended when an individual acquires political power. For Christians, the principle of cruciformity isn't magically suspended when participating in the political process. We serve a different king of a superior kingdom, and he calls us to follow after him. This leads us naturally to our final set of themes, which is the relationship between kingdom and empire.

Kingdom and Empire

"Paul's writings represent a pattern seen in the New Testament as a whole: a pattern of fundamental tension inherent in early Christian attitudes towards Rome"[102]. Based on our reading of the gospels and Acts, Oakes is assuredly correct. The strain, of course, is eschatology. God's kingdom *has already come* and the real king, Jesus, is sitting at the right hand of the father, ruling over all creation. This no doubt sat

---

102. Oakes, *Empire*, p. 165

awkwardly beside Roman claims of world domination. Paul's gospel is uncompromisingly Messianic, leaving no space for anyone else to share the throne, his
ecclesiology is driven by the divine indwelling of the Spirit, incorporating gentiles
into the Jewish family of Abraham through faithfulness to Jesus, and his ethics are
shaped by the sacrificial example of a crucified Christ. It's hard to reconcile Paul's
gospel with Caesar's empire.

The question remains, however: is Paul in any meaningful way "anti-imperial"? Paul's gospel and the wider New Testament witness is, as Oakes perfectly
describes it, in tension with the political, economic, social, cultural, and theological values of the Roman imperial order. Of this we can be certain. But was
Paul in active opposition to Roman rule? The question is complicated. When I
was working on my undergraduate degree in Biblical studies in the late 2000s
and early 2010s, anti-imperial readings of Paul were all the rage. The most famous expression of Paul as a full-throttled critic of Roman imperialism (at least
in evangelical circles) was N.T. Wright's essay *Paul's Gospel and Caesar's Empire*[103].
Upon reading the essay I was convinced that Paul's letters included a direct critique of Rome. Fortunately there were many scholars promoting anti-imperial
readings of Paul, including John Dominic Crossan[104] and Richard Horsley, whose
books I purchased and read. The essays included in Horsley's *Paul and Empire*[105]
had a profound influence on my thinking, particularly Neil Elliott's contribution
Romans 13:1-7 in the Context of Imperial Propaganda[106], in which Elliott argued
that Romans 13 contained language that Paul's audience would have understood
as a coded subversion of Roman imperialism. Anti-imperial scholarship felt exciting and transgressive while appealing to historical data. I was hooked; Paul in my
mind was a vocal critic of empire.

Time has a strange habit of challenging our assumptions. As the years went
on I began to see several cracks in the edifice of anti-imperial readings of the New
Testament. The first was my own political and economic awakening; it became
apparent that these scholars were not agenda-neutral and often used anti-imperialism to promote political policies which gave modern politicians more money and
power. The second was developing my thinking on Paul himself, particularly the
role of eschatology and cruciformity as models for reading his letters and Luke's

---

103. Wright, N.T.. 2000. *"Paul's Gospel and Caesar's Empire"*. In *Paul and Politics*. ed. by Richard
Horsley, Trinity Press International. pp. 160-183

104. Crossan, John, and Jonathan Reed. 2004. *In Search of Paul*. HarperSanFrancisco.

105. Horsley, Richard. 2004. *Paul and Empire*. Trinity Press International.

106. Elliott, Neil.. 2004. *"Romans 13:1-7 in the Context of Imperial Propaganda"*. In *Paul and
Empire*. ed. by Richard Horsley, Trinity Press International. pp. 184-204

presentation of his engagement with Roman authorities in Acts. Paul is certainly no apologist for Rome, nor did he believe it to have any eternal value, but his words and actions (if Acts is even somewhat reliable historically) seemed more nuanced than the claims made in anti-imperial scholarship. The final fissure for me was my continued reading of the Old Testament and general historical works on the Roman empire and early medieval Europe. My own historical awareness was more rich, dynamic, and complex than it was during my formative years in college. I became increasingly open to alternative readings of Paul vis-a-vis Rome and started reassessing my intellectual commitments. I think there is great wisdom in framing the question, as Oakes does, with the concept of 'tension'. Perhaps Paul was neither 'pro-' nor 'anti-' imperial and the story is actually much more complex.

A central theme, perhaps *the* central theme, in the gospels and Acts was the arrival of God's kingdom. It is impossible to comprehend the Synoptics or Luke's second volume without it. Scholars, however, have often downplayed the role of 'kingdom' in Paul's thinking; as Dunn argues, much New Testament scholarship can be summarized as *"Jesus proclaimed the kingdom of God; Paul preached Jesus"*[107]. Our analysis of Paul's gospel above directly challenges that popular assertion. The core of Paul's proclamation and the mechanism by which God saves is Jesus Christ, son of David, ruler of creation. Even if Paul never once used the term 'kingdom' in his letters, the Davidic insight alone would demonstrate that Paul held to something like a kingdom theology. Fortuitously Paul does at several points in his letters use the phrase "kingdom of God" or a close equivalent[108], signaling a more significant engagement with the concept of kingdom than the 'Jesus preaches kingdom, Paul preaches Jesus' crowd would concede.

As I have argued, Paul and his audience are most likely familiar with the oral tradition which eventually produced the gospels. On this theory the Pauline communities would have known the characteristic Jesus constructed by his earliest biographers and been cognizant of the main contours of his teaching, including the kingdom of God. Even if one finds my theory unsatisfactory they would be forced to grapple with the fact that Paul never felt the need to explain to his audience what 'the kingdom of God' entails. He references it without ever explaining it, and often does so in surprising contexts. Paul simply assumes his audience knows how kingdom-language functions and works it into his letters strategically. Paul's christology, eschatology, and ecclesiology are entirely compatible with the kingdom theology of the gospels and Acts, and his own Pharisaic Jewish background would

---

107. Dunn, James. 2011. *Jesus, Paul, and the Gospels*. Eerdmans.

108. Romans 14:17; 1 Corinthians 4:20, 6:9, 15:50; Galatians 5:21; Ephesians 5:5; Colossians 4:11; 1 Thessalonians 2:12; 2 Thessalonians 1:15

suggest that God's great act of deliverance at the end of history be interpreted through 'kingdom' categories. I agree entirely with Larry Kreitzer: *"while the explicit expression "kingdom of God/Christ" is not widespread within the Pauline letters, the idea is a fundamental component of Paul's eschatological perspective and underlies the whole of his teaching. The same tension between the present and future dimensions of a kingdom theology found to be present in the teaching of Jesus within the Synoptic Gospels is also contained within the Pauline materials"*[109]. Paul has a kingdom theology, and it is consistent with the one proclaimed by Jesus. Jesus preached the kingdom, and Paul preaches Jesus as the one who brought the kingdom. There is little need to add to my analysis of the kingdom above; God has fulfilled his promises through the death, resurrection, and ascension of Jesus. The kingdom has been inaugurated. Rome has been, in one sense, transcended. Perhaps Paul isn't so much *against* the Roman empire as he is moving his churches *beyond* it. A kingdom greater than Rome's has dawned for those that have eyes to see.

How does this fit within the Paul and empire debate still raging within certain quarters of New Testament scholarship? Christoph Heilig offers an extensive review of the debate in his book *The Apostle and the Empire*[110]. The classic anti-imperial reading of Paul is based on the subtext theory, namely that Paul uses coded language and other rhetorical devices to communicate his dissatisfaction with Rome in order to avoid attracting the ire of Roman authorities. By properly understanding Paul's language, scholars discover a window through which they can determine what he thought about the empire outside the text. Paul engages in "hidden transcripts", private, subversive, and dangerous conversations between members of the ingroup which must be coded in public settings. N.T. Wright is the classic example of this approach, but scholars such as John Barclay, with whom Wright debated the issue, argue instead that Roman imperialism is either on the margins of Paul's thought or entirely irrelevant to him. Pushing the conversation forward, Heilig proposes that Paul is more openly critical of the Roman empire while scholars such as Laura Robinson have followed Barclay in denying anti-imperialism as central to Paul's thinking.[111]

Heilig identifies a flaw in Wright's methodology, particularly the idea that Paul's critique was necessarily hidden. Paul can be brash and confrontational, so why assume his attitude towards Rome would be any different? Heilig sees this at play in 2 Corinthians 2:14: *"But thanks be to God, who always leads us in triumph*

---

109. Kreitzer, Larry. 1993. *"Kingdom of God/Christ"*. In *Dictionary of Paul and His Letters*, edited by Hawthorne, Gerald; Martin, Ralph; Reid, Daniel. InterVarsity Press. p. 526

110. Heilig, Christoph. 2022. *The Apostle and the Empire*. Eerdmans.

111. Heilig, *The Apostle and the Empire*, pp. 5-34

in Christ, and manifests through us the sweet aroma of the knowledge of Him in every place". Paul is appropriating imagery of the Roman triumph, a very public celebration of military victories, and applying it to his own ministry. This would have been, according to Heilig, extremely controversial, portraying Israel's God as both mimicking and surpassing a deeply symbolic Roman celebration.[112] Instead of reading Paul as a veiled critic of Rome, Heilig suggests that passages such as 2 Corinthians 2:14 expose Paul's 'unease' with Rome: *"It might be less misleading to speak of insights into Paul's "unease" with respect to certain aspects of Roman propaganda"*[113]. Perhaps Paul's engagement with Roman power is more complex than the hidden criticism model of scholars such as Wright and Horsley. If Paul is willing to publicly play with Roman imperial propaganda, reworking into a letter which he knew would be read out loud to an audience in Corinth, his critique may be more public than the anti-imperial camp has traditionally allowed. I laud Heilig's choice of terminology: *"unease"*. As with Oake's use of the word *"tension"*, it leaves open the possibility that Paul's perspective on Rome can't be neatly placed into an either anti- or pro-Roman dichotomy.

Anti-imperial scholars have also appealed to the ubiquity of a quickly-growing imperial cult during the ministry of Paul. Words such as *euangelion*, obviously central to Paul's ministry, were a part of the imperial cult's rhetoric and when employed by Paul would have been understood as a challenge to the divine pretensions of Roman power. Since Paul wrote to churches scattered throughout various Roman cities, every member of his audience would have surely felt immense pressure to conform to these Roman cults. Paul's letters, and the veiled critiques of Rome contained therein, were a powerful motivation to hold strong in the midst of a powerful cultic lure. Or so the story goes. Clint Burnett doesn't see any historical evidence for this line of interpretation: *"there was no uniform, centrally controlled "imperial cult" in the Roman Empire, much less one in which provincials were required to participate. Rather, like the cults of the gods, individuals, groups, cities, and provinces worshiped the Julio-Claudians according to their local customs"*[114]. This is the crux of Burnett's argument in his book *Paul and Imperial Divine Honors*. The Roman cult was not monolithic, and in many places followers of Jesus may not have been required to participate. Instead of assuming a hegemonic imperial cult which used language subversively mirrored by Paul, careful historical research is needed to analyze how the cult would have functioned in

---

112. Heilig, *The Apostle and the Empire*, pp. 55-101; the chapter, entitled *Reconstructing Unease*, is well worth a read.

113. Heilig, *The Apostle and the Empire*, p. 137

114. Burnett, Clint. 2024. *Paul and Imperial Divine Honors*. Eerdmans. pp. 12-13

individual cities before drawing overgeneralized conclusions and applying it to Pauline exegesis. As Burnett rightly argues: *"if one wishes to understand imperial divine honors in Philippi, Thessalonica, and Corinth* [the three cities Burnett investigates in his book], *one must do the hard work of delving into the particulars of such honors in these cities and building contextualized profiles of them . . .* [many scholars] *wrongly assume the presence of a uniform centrally controlled Julio-Claudian "imperial cult" in the Roman Empire, and some scholars even contend that emperors desired, even demanded, their subjects sacrifice to them"*[115].

An excellent example of this phenomenon occurs in Paul's letter to Philippi. Many scholars have contended that the word *euangelion* was universally understood as a reference to the imperial cult. When Paul writes that the Philippians are involved in *"participation in the gospel"*[116] they would have unquestionably interpreted his words as a challenge to the *euangelion* of imperial cultic rhetoric. Burnett identifies an acute problem with this thesis: there is no hard historical evidence that the term *euangelion* was used of the cult in Philippi.[117] In fact, on page after page of Burnett's book he demonstrates that many of the sweeping historical claims bolstering anti-imperial scholarship are not at all justified by the available evidence. Cultic pressures were definitely prevalent in some parts of the empire but not in most, particularly in several of the cities to which Paul wrote. We are not, therefore, justified in assuming that Paul's language, even if it bears striking resemblance to imperial rhetoric used in certain contexts, is universally directed against the imperial cult or the Roman empire. For some of his churches there may have been little conflict between them and their pagan neighbors, at least not with respect to politics or theology.

Summarizing his views, Burnett states *"Because of the contextual nature of imperial divine honors in Philippi, Thessalonica, and Corinth and the uniqueness of the Christian communities in these cities, the relationship between Christianity and the honors in questions different from city to city . . . These above conclusions differ markedly from some Pauline interpreters who contend that the relationship between early . . . Christianity and imperial divine honors was one of conflict mainly between Christ and Caesar"*[118]. The evidence for a grand Pauline showdown between kingdom and empire doesn't exist. Even if Paul was deeply antagonistic towards Rome it would be almost impossible to reconstruct it historically from his letters. Oakes and Heilig are correct in their assessment that Paul's gospel stands in tension or

---

115. Burnett, *Imperial Divine Honors*, p. 13

116. Philippians 1:5

117. Burnett, *Imperial Divine Honors*, pp. 106-109

118. Burnett, *Imperial Divine Honors*, pp. 230-231

unease with Roman rule, which is precisely the witness we see in Acts. Defiant opposition, though? It's impossible to prove. On the other hand, Barclay's claim that Roman imperialism was irrelevant for Paul also seems at odds with the evidence. Paul has very strong feelings about Messianic kingdom eschatology and appropriates, perhaps polemically, imperial rhetoric in 2 Corinthians 2:14. The fact that he needs to provide the Romans with instructions on how they should relate to the state is another indication that, despite the much overstated case made in anti-imperial scholarship, Paul does actually reserve some mental bandwidth for the problem of Roman imperialism.

One of the most powerful critiques of anti-imperial readings of Paul is found in the work of Najeeb Haddad. In his monograph *Paul, Politics, and New Creation* he demonstrates how many of the supposed rhetorical techniques Paul employs to express his veiled criticism of Roman power can't be justified by the texts of Paul's letters.[119] Instead of working to fundamentally restructure Roman society, which Haddad suggests is an expression of the modern political biases of anti-imperial scholars, *"Paul structured his communities in such a way that complemented Greco-Roman society, while remaining distinct in its call to all peoples, regardless of their race, sex, or creed. Most especially is his call to follow Jesus Christ in the midst of the world"*[120]. I think Haddad is correct. Besides the intentional call to Gentiles, Paul's churches replicate the experience of diaspora Jews. They are called to live amongst the Gentiles (note Paul's application of the term *"Gentile"* to those outside the church in Ephesians 4:17) while not conforming to Gentile practices and maintaining a unique identity. Paul appears to have adopted the Jeremiah 29:7 model for his own churches. They are to faithfully await the coming of Jesus who will consummate the kingdom and finally, once and for all, transform creation. The Romans, like the Babylonian empire of old, will come crashing down. In the meantime, God's family must attempt to live at peace with their neighbors and, as an innovation of diaspora Judaism, preach the gospel of Jesus to all nations. This makes perfect sense given Paul's background; his message does engender tension with Roman ideology and he likely feels a profound sense of unease with the imperial order, but he remains faithful to the nonviolent witness of the Jewish king who is already the true ruler over all creation. This is why Paul naturally prefaces his infamous Romans 13:1-7 passage with a statement which sounds remarkably similar to Jeremiah's: *"If possible, so far as it depends on you, be at peace with all men"*[121].

---

119. Haddad, *New Creation*, 43-70

120. Haddad, *New Creation*, p. 70

121. Romans 12:18

There are two passages in Paul where he refers to the eschatological event as inaugurating "new creation". In Galatians 6:15 Paul claims, in references to the Jew and Gentile church, that *"neither is circumcision anything, nor uncircumcision, but a new creation"*. Speaking again of the church, Paul says in 2 Corinthians 5:17 that *"Therefore if anyone is in Christ, this person is a new creation; the old things passed away; behold, new things have come"*. Haddad explains how Paul's eschatological reflection relates to his thinking on Roman imperialism. For Paul the eschaton has already been inaugurated by Jesus but the final consummation is yet to come. Christians are, therefore, living in a time where the old creation is passing away and the new creation has already been initiated. The problem, of course, are the many remnants of the old creation with which believers must contend. The Roman empire is consigned to the old creation and, like the Babylonian empire in Jeremiah, will not endure forever. History has already moved beyond Roman imperialism due to the death, resurrection, and ascension of the Jewish Messiah, and those who are "in Christ" are called to live in light of the "new creation", the inaugurated eschatological kingdom of God.[122] The power of Rome has been marginalized: *"Though Paul was not counter-imperial in a strict sense, he did not suggest that the civic authority was saved. Paul relativizes the place of the Roman Empire and includes it, although not in any explicit terms, in his critique of the physical kosmos. For Paul, the death and resurrection of Chrst was the pivotal moment in time that changed the course of history. The Christ-event in Paul's theology is the inaugural event for what he calls a "new creation" . . . Ultimately, sin and death reign over humanity and over creation. It is the Christ-event that has given hope to fallen humanity and, subsequently, to all creation"*[123].

Paul is neither "for" nor "against" the Roman empire in the technical political sense which many modern interpreters (freighted with their biases in favor of authoritarian socialism) would prefer him to be. Paul's gospel stands in tension with Roman imperialism and his letters evince an unease with the character of Roman rule. In this regard Paul is no different than his Jewish contemporaries who do not advocate violent rebellion against the state. Seek the welfare of the city, knowing that God will ultimately vindicate his people and punish the wicked pagans. This is, in essence, Paul's theology of empire. It cannot be disconnected from his Messianic, eschatological ecclesiology. The church, those who have faith in the Messiah and receive the gift of the Spirit, are citizens of the real kingdom. The Roman kingdom is passing away. In another monograph Haddad summarizes his perspective on Paul and empire, and I agree with much of what he says.

---

122. Haddad, *New Creation*, pp. 139-165

123. Haddad, *New Creation*, pp. 139-140

This lengthy quote is relevant to our discussion: *"Considering empire criticism, I understand Paul's theology of new creation, in part, a response to empire. It is neither a direct response to empire nor a veiled one. Rather, it seems Paul is quite broad in the way he categorizes humanity. There are those who are perishing and those who are being saved by means of the Christ event . . . To make such a point, considering Paul's Hellenistic Jewish background, is not the encouragement of active political subversion. Furthermore, it is not a full-on appreciation of the gentile civic authority. It is a very real understanding that everything not in Christ will fade away. As it has been seen, Paul as a Jew could see aspects of the Roman Empire and Greco-Roman religion as directly opposed to God. And yet, Paul was within his Jewish worldview with an overall general appreciation of the stability offered by the civil authority . . . Paul's technology of new creation is a beckoning to those outside of Christ to come into Christ. It is also a beckoning to those who are already in Christ to remain in Christ, lest they should fade away with the world. It is Paul's understanding of new creation and transformation in Christ that colors the entirety of his letters"*[124].

As with the gospel and Acts, the kingdom of God transcends the kingdoms of men, which will all meet their decisive, predetermined end when Jesus returns to finally set the record straight. In the meantime, Paul's churches must embody the spirit of Jeremiah 29:7, seeking the welfare of the city God will destroy by living peacefully with yet in distinction from their non-believing neighbors. Jesus followers must resist the allure of Roman imperialism and imperial propaganda by embracing the values of a crucified Messiah. In this sense, as in Acts, the church is neither "non-", "pro-", nor "anti-" political. The kingdom of God is suprapolitical, transcending and moving beyond the power structures of earthly kingdoms. A new age has dawned and a new kingdom has arrived; those who accept the gospel are bound to another king. Oakes correctly describes the various attitudes of believers towards the Roman empire in the first century: *"awe, appreciation, resentment, contempt, denial of ultimate authority, and expectation of overthrow"*[125]. Tension. Unease. New creation. All of these categories make sense of the complex, nuanced response believers have towards Rome, and all of them have presidents in Jewish attitudes towards pagan rule generally. Paul is tapping into this tradition. He believes that the gospel of Jesus is the power of God for salvation to all who have faith, and he does all things for the sake of the gospel. He desires to know nothing except the crucified Christ. There is no place within this framework for active rebellion against Rome, nor for uncritical acceptance or endorsement of imperialism. *"The time is up"*, Paul might say, *"the kingdom of God is at hand; repent*

---

124. Haddad, Najeeb. 2023. *Paul and Empire Criticism.* Cascade Books. pp. 85-86

125. Oakes, *Empire*, p. 158

and believe the gospel". Paul is playing a bigger, much more urgent game than petty human power-politics. He exhorts his audience to do the same.

CONCLUSION

We are now in a position to better analyze the political and economic implications of Paul's letters. Paul, Jewish Pharisee with a Greek education from Tarsus, had the optimal profile for an apostle to the gentiles. He believed sincerely that God had called him to preach the gospel to all the nations, incorporating gentiles into the family of Abraham. Paul's core proclamation is the gospel, and at the center of Paul's gospel is the crucified, resurrected, and ascended Davidic Messiah Jesus who fulfilled the promises God made to his people in the Jewish Scriptures. Paul communicated with his churches both in person and through letters. Paul's letters reflect Greco-Roman epistolary structures and rhetorical techniques. All of Paul's letters are occasional, written to specific churches and addressing specific questions, concerns, or problems. Since Paul has a particular intention when composing his letters, we must first attempt to discern their function, what they were intended to do for their original audience, before drawing abstract theological conclusions. Paul's thinking is influenced by the Jesus tradition, the Jewish Scriptures, and the application of his gospel to the unique circumstances faced by each of the churches to which he wrote.

There are four sets of dominant themes in Paul's letters which cannot be isolated from one another. Paul is an integrative thinker and our analysis of Pauline themes in discrete categories is a pedagogical technique, not an attempt to silo various aspects of his thought. The first set is gospel and faith; Paul proclaims the message of Jesus and people believe it by becoming faithful, loyal, and allegiant to Jesus the king. The second set is Spirit and church; when people believe in the gospel God gives them His Spirit. Through faith and the Spirit Gentiles are incorporated into the family of Abraham, and Paul divides the world into two groups: the church and everyone else. The third category includes identity and ethics; the identity of the church as the set-apart, holy family of God presupposes a moral transformation. Believers are called primarily to imitate the sacrificial death of Jesus by cultivating a cruciform ethic of servanthood towards other people. The final category is kingdom and empire. Paul believes that the kingdom of God transcends the Roman imperial order. As in Jeremiah 29:7, Christians are neither "for" nor "against" the empire but called to live beyond it, transcending human structures of power.

With our Pauline profile clearly established, it is time to analyse political and economic concepts in his letters. I will tackle his letter in canonical order with the notable exception of Romans. Chapter 13 will cover 1-2 Corinthians, Galatians, and Ephesians. Chapter 14 examines Philippians, Colossians, and 1-2 Thessalonians, Chapter 15 explores the Pastoral epistles and Philemon. I decided to save the most controversial passage, Romans 13:1-17, for last. Chapter 16 will offer an analysis of Romans, emphasizing of course Paul's so-called theology of the state. There are several reasons for ordering the following chapters this way. First, scholarly debate about the exact dating of Paul's letters, especially in relation to each other, is unsettled. I am more interested in reconstructing plausible historical backgrounds for each of Paul's letters and interpreting passages in relation to those backgrounds than I am in offering hypothetical dates for their composition, as important as that work may be. I affirm that Paul wrote the majority of his letter between the late 40s and 50s CE (the general scholarly consensus) and will only comment on dates when relevant to my argument at hand. I also strongly believe that Romans 13:1-7 is much less challenging when set against the backdrop of his other letters and will make interpreting that contentious passage in light of my larger thesis much easier. With these considerations in mind, let's begin our exploration of Paul's letters.

CHAPTER 13 | 1-2 Corinthians, Galatians, and Ephesians

The Rulers of this Age are Passing Away

[T]he rulers of this age . . . are passing away.

1 Corinthians 2:6

[God] *raised* [Jesus] *from the dead and seated Him at His right hand in the heavenly places.*

Ephesians 1:20

INTRODUCTION

The goal of this chapter is simple. Following our analysis of Paul, we will work through passages in 1-2 Corinthians, Galatians, and Ephesians which are relevant to the discussion of political and economic themes in the New Testament. Like our study of the gospels it is impossible to provide a line-by-line commentary on each of Paul's letters. Although that work would be incredibly illuminating (and perhaps one day a competent scholar will attempt this lofty endeavor) space does not permit us to analyze every word in the epistles. There will be some texts which might have contributed to my overall thesis that will be marginalized or ignored, and I apologize for any lacunae in advance. I will begin each of the four works with an overview of the plausible historical circumstances which necessitated the letter in question before working through selected passages. Let's begin our exploration of Paul's letters with 1 Corinthians.

1 Corinthians

Background: Pagan Values and Worldly Division

According to Acts 18:11, Paul stayed in Corinth for nearly a year and a half. Some Corinthians Jews leveled charges against Paul before Gallio, proconsul of Achaia, who promptly rejected their case on the basis that it was a matter of Jewish scruples and not Roman law. After this incident Paul left.[1] Roman Corinth was no ordinary city. Situated atop the tiny isthmus which connects mainland Greece to the Peloponnese, Corinth had the privilege of adjoining harbors, making it a major hub for trade. The Romans had burned the old Greek city to the ground in the second century BCE and it remained in ruins until Julius Caesar rebuilt it as a Roman colony in 44 BCE. Corinth was populated primarily with people from the lower classes but as a thriving trading center the city enabled hardworking residents to succeed in business and improve their social standing. By the time Paul visited Corinth it was one of the most significant economic centers in the Roman empire. Corinth was also a place where people from various cultures intermingled, and the city had a reputation for vice and immorality. The sex trade was a major industry in the city. Its residents had a thoroughly cosmopolitan outlook and believed themselves to be at the forefront of business and culture.[2] Corinth presented a preacher like Paul with a whole host of potential complications.

As Gorman puts it, "*The Corinthian community was Paul's problem child*"[3]. By the time Paul wrote 1 Corinthians, the church was already being compromised by social divisions and the (re)introduction of worldly "Corinthian" values which were at odds with Paul's teaching. Paul is honest about this in his letter, revealing to his audience that their fighting led to divisiveness.[4] Alan Johnson explains the issue: "*Instead of being transformed by Christian values and viewpoints, they were behaving like their counterparts in the pagan society around them. Status seeking, self-promotion, a competitive drive for adulation and success, even use of the Christian church as a means of self-promotion and advancement are themes that reoccur throughout the letter*"[5]. Paul deals with more individual issues in 1 Corinthians than in any of his other letters, and it is the divisiveness and worldliness of the community which fuels their problems. Social pressures from within the city were having a

---

1. Acts 18:1-17

2. Gorman, *Crucified Lord*, p. 228

3. Gorman, *Crucified Lord*, p. 227

4. 1 Corinthians 1:11 and 11:18-19, respectively.

5. Johnson, *1 Corinthians*, p. 22

decidedly negative impact on the believing community, and Paul wrote to address the moral, philosophical, and theological distortions which were deforming the Corinthian church.[6]

The opening passages of 1 Corinthians, in good Greco-Roman epistolary style, introduce the main themes of Paul's letter. In 1 Corinthians 1:1-10, Paul greets his audience, addressing them as *"saints"*, holy ones, with *"all who in every place call on the name of our Lord Jesus Christ, their Lord and ours"*[7]. Because of their unique identity, bearing the status of "holy" and members of God's family, Paul informs the Corinthians that through the grace of God they were enriched with all speech in knowledge, will be sustained by God until the final day, and participate in fellowship with God's Son, the Lord Jesus Christ. Paul refers to Jesus as both "Christ" and "Lord" several times in the opening lines of 1 Corinthians. Already the major themes of Paul's thinking are at play as he moves towards addressing the first major issue in 1 Corinthians. He sets up the particular problem in the first four chapters of the epistle in 1:10-12: *"Now I exhort you, brethren, by the name of our Lord Jesus Christ, that you all agree and that there be no divisions among you, but that you be made complete in the same mind and the same judgment. For I have been informed concerning you, my brethren, by Chloe's people, that there are quarrels among you. Now I mean this, that each one of you is saying, "I am of Paul," and "I of Apollos," and "I of Cephas* [Peter]*," and "I of Christ.""*. Paul launches into a sustained argument about why these divisions were harming the church and how the Corinthians should overcome them.

He does this in response to the cause of divisions, which he outlines in 1:10-17. The Corinthians had each chosen a different leader to follow (Paul, Apollos, Peter, or Christ) and were dividing themselves based on their association with their preferred leader. Paul must explain why these divisions are incompatible with the message of Jesus. In 1 Corinthians 1:13, Paul contends that Christ cannot be divided, and from 1:18-2:16 demonstrates how God's wisdom and the message of the cross are incompatible with Greco-Roman cultural values. 1 Corinthians 3-4 is an extended clarification of apostolic authority; while there were indeed many leaders in the church, God was using them all to build up the Corinthians, who are described in 3:16-17 as a temple of God (using the term *naos* in reference to the "Holy of Holies") in which the Spirit dwells. Because of this, Paul argues in 4:1, all leaders are nothing more than servants of God. Even though God had enriched the church in everything, they were still *"walking like mere men"*[8]. What would cause

---

6. Winter, *After Paul Left Corinth*, p. 27

7. 1 Corinthians 1:2

8. 1 Corinthians 3:3

the Corinthians to choose sides based on preferred leaders, and why would they elevate some leaders over others to begin with?

Bruce Winter provides a plausible historical explanation for the Corinthian divisiveness. In the first century traveling philosophers, known as "sophists", would move from city to city and attract large followings. They would occasionally establish schools in which their disciples would learn to imitate both their philosophy and their manner of life. The sophist teacher became a model for those who followed them. There was often a very pronounced degree of competition between the various popular sophist philosophers. Schools attempted to discredit other sophists and, by extension, anyone who followed them. Debates between sophists and their followers were characterized in terms of *eris*, "strife", which is exactly the word Paul uses in 1 Corinthians 3:3 to describe the behavior of Corinthian believers. Under the influence of popular sophist philosophers, the Corinthians had allowed themselves to be shaped by the values of this prominent cultural trend, assuming that they needed to choose a leader and divide based on that choice.[9] Paul's blistering critique of worldly wisdom in this passage is a direct attack on the factionalism and strife characteristic of the sophists. The cross serves as the ultimate foil to worldly wisdom, because through it *"God has chosen the foolish things of the world to shame the wise, and God has chosen the weak things of the world to shame to things which are strong"*[10]. Unlike the sophists, Paul, Apollos, and Peter share the common goal of preaching a crucified Christ. Believers are united through faith and the Spirit; division only compromises the message and witness of the church.

While there will be various manifestations of factionalism throughout the Corinthian correspondence, they all share a common root with the sophist problem addressed by Paul in 1 Corinthians 1-4. The Corinthian church is allowing themselves to be influenced by pagan values. Instead of following the teachings of their leaders and being transformed in Christ, they are acting exactly like their pagan counterparts. The Corinthians, transformed through the Spirit, should stand out both in belief and behavior. The burden of Paul's first Corinthian epistle is to help his audience understand where they went wrong and encourage them to reject the deficient values of a culture which is passing away in light of the eschaton. Paul's audience has misunderstood Christ, the Spirit, the apostle's teaching, and their own unique identity as believers, and he makes it his goal to clarify these various misunderstandings with an audience that believes themselves to be at the apex of Roman culture. Paul must remind them that the way of Jesus is markedly

---

9. Winter, *After Paul Left Corinth*, pp. 31-43

10. 1 Corinthians 2:27

different. It is within this framework that Paul makes several statements which are of interest to our political and economic analysis of the New Testament.

The Rulers of This Age are Passing Away: 1 Corinthians 2:6-13, 3:16-17, 4:20

In contrast to the sophists, Paul adamantly reminds the Corinthians in 2:1-5 that when he was with them he *"determined to know nothing except Jesus Christ, and Him crucified"*, not conveying a message with sublime sophistic rhetoric but rather with the Spirit and power. Paul is quick to point out that his preaching contains *true* wisdom, a wisdom which is from God and not comprehended by any of his pagan contemporaries: *"Yet we do speak God's wisdom among those who are mature; a wisdom, however, not of this age nor of the rulers of this age, who are passing away; but we speak God's wisdom in a mystery, the hidden wisdom which God predestined before the ages to our glory; the wisdom which none of the rulers of this age has understood; for if they had understood it they would not have crucified the Lord of glory"*[11]. After quoting Isaiah 64:4, Paul claims that God has revealed this message through the Spirit in 2:10-14, and then chastises the Corinthians for acting like *"natural men"* instead of *"spiritual men"* in 1 Corinthians 2:14-3:4.

It's easy to miss the implicit political claim Paul makes 2:6-13. The rulers of this age are passing away. The Greek term behind *"are passing away"* is a form of *katargeo* in the present tense. The rulers of this age are, according to Paul, *currently* in the process of passing away. He does not relegate this event to the future, it is something Paul argues is happening in the present. This is entirely explicable within Paul's inaugurated eschatology. The Lord Jesus Christ, as Paul is fond of putting it in 1 Corinthians 1, is currently ruling over creation, therefore the rulers of this age are passing away. The Corinthians are those, as Paul says in 1 Corinthians 10:11, *"upon whom the ends of the ages have come"*. There have been several interpreters throughout the ages who have suggested that in this passage Paul is referring to spiritual or immaterial rulers, dark cosmic forces which reside just beyond human perception, but not political authorities. That line of argument doesn't work. Paul states in 2:7-8 that these rulers who are passing away do not understand God's wisdom, real wisdom, because if they had they wouldn't have crucified Jesus. As Johnson argues, *"While rulers of this age could refer to the demonic principalities and powers . . . it is better in this instance to see them as the Roman political (Pilate and Herod, etc.) and Jewish religious-political (Caiaphas, Sanhedrin, etc.) leaders. Had they known who Christ was and what great eternal consequences*

---

11. 1 Corinthians 2:6-8

follow rejection of him, they would not have crucified the Lord of glory"[12]. As we will see below, Paul does seem to think that there are malevolent powers imposing themselves upon human institutions, but in this particular passage it is impossible to get around the concrete claim that the political authorities are passing away and do not understand the wisdom of God.

Not only are they passing away, but they cannot comprehend God's wisdom. For Paul, God's wisdom was made manifest in the crucified Messiah, *"to Jews a stumbling block and the Gentiles foolishness, but to those who are the called, both Jews and Greeks, Christ the power of God and the wisdom of God"*[13]. By imitating the values of pagan sophists and their disciples the Corinthians are demonstrating that they themselves have not understood Paul and therefore do not possess the very wisdom they seek to acquire by emulating worldly values. The rulers of this age might have missed the memo, but Jesus believers shouldn't have. In 1 Corinthians 2:10-13 Paul argues that it is the Spirit, operating in both the individual lives of believers and in the entire community of faith, which reveals the real wisdom of God: *"Now we have received, not the spirit of the world, but the Spirit who is from God, so that we may know the things freely given to us by God"*. Christians should conform to the pattern of Christ, not the world.

In 1 Corinthians 3 Paul discusses how, in contrast to the sophists, the leaders of the Corinthian church worked together with God to build up the Corinthians. For the sake of unity, Paul's audience must begin to see themselves as the temple of God. He issues a stark warning in 3:16-17 against those who sow division in the church: *"Do you not know that you are a temple of God and that the Spirit of God dwells in you? If any man destroys the temple of God, God will destroy him, for the temple of God is holy, and that is what you are"*. This is a classic example of Pauline Jewish ecclesiology; there are only two types of people, those who have been granted the Spirit and those who don't. Possession of the Spirit makes one a member of God's family, His holy temple, and they should therefore think and act differently than those who are not animated by the Spirit. Gorman puts it bluntly: *"God not only owns the church, God inhabits the church"*[14]. Why would the Corinthians be shaped by pagan values, indeed *divided* by pagan values, if they are a united family indwelt with the very Spirit of God? The rulers of the world are passing away because they rejected God's wisdom, and the Corinthians are in danger of suffering the same fate.

---

12. Johnson, *1 Corinthians*, p. 66

13. 1 Corinthians 1:23-24

14. Gorman, *Crucified Lord*, p. 244

As Paul concludes the section (or perhaps transitions to the next) in 4:14-21, he admonishes the Corinthians to accept his rebuke and change their ways. Some have arrogantly assumed that Paul would not return, most likely those who associated themselves with either Apollos or Peter in opposition to Paul.[15] They speak arrogant words against Paul, but he cautions against arrogance in 4:20: *"For the kingdom of God does not consist in words but in power"*. Unlike the sophists, the rulers of this age, or those agitating against Paul, power speaks louder than words and the kingdom of God consists of power. Much like 2:6-8, it is easy to gloss over 4:20. Paul appeals to the kingdom of God and its power but doesn't without explaining it to his audience. He simply assumes they would know what he meant by 'kingdom'. It is quite a powerful way of concluding a lengthy argument against worldly values and divisiveness. The kingdom of God once again transcends the kingdoms of man.

Based on our analysis of Paul in the preceding chapter we should expect to see this combination of themes in a discussion about the values and unity of the Corinthian church. Paul asserts that the Corinthians are a part of God's universal church, the family of Abraham, through faith and the Spirit. There can be no compromise with prevailing cultural values which stand in contradistinction to the message of Christ's cross. It can be easy to miss the political ramifications for modern Christians who are attempting to derive political principles from Scripture. By claiming that the rulers of this age are currently passing away, Paul is contextualizing their power. There is nothing timeless or eternal about human rulers, and since they are passing away now Paul implies there will be a time when the authorities will have passed away fully. Worldly power won't last forever and believers shouldn't pretend like it will. The rulers have rejected the wisdom of God but the Spirit-filled community of believers in Corinth have access to real wisdom if only they stop capitulating to pagan values. The church possesses God's Spirit and the rulers do not, therefore the Church transcends the rulers of the age. They belong to the powerful kingdom of God and should start acting like it. Paul makes these statements off the cuff in an argument which isn't directly about political authorities, suggesting his words are fundamental consequences of his gospel which the Corinthians are expected to accept. We can't read Paul without taking him seriously at this point; there can be no interpretation of Romans 13:1-7 which doesn't account for 1 Corinthians 2:6-13, 3:16-17, and 4:20. The Corinthians must remain distinct from their pagan neighbors and must regard themselves as categorically distinct from those without faith, including the rulers of this age who are passing away.

---

15. Johnson, *1 Corinthians*, p. 85

Sleeping With Stepmothers: 1 Corinthians 5:1-13

While interpreters have generally considered 1 Corinthians 5:1 as the start of a new conversation, Kenneth Bailey argues that 4:14 actually represents the transition from Paul's discourse on division to the next topic of controversy.[16] He points out linguistic and thematic parallels between 4:14-21 and the proceeding material in chapter 5, suggesting that 5:1 should not be considered the shift to Paul's next concern. His theory holds water. There are, as I argued above, enough links between 4:14-21 and the rest of 1 Corinthians 1-4 to justifiably see it as a summary of what Paul wrote before. It may be prudent to take a mediating approach; perhaps 4:14-21 is a transitional passage, wrapping up Paul's previous discourse on division while preparing his audience for the next exhortation. Either way, readers shouldn't forget that 1 Corinthians is designed to be read as a unified whole and that in Paul's mind the points he makes in 1 Corinthians 1-4 apply to the rest of his letter as well.

The issue at hand is addressed bluntly by Paul in 5:1: "It is *actually reported that there is immorality among you, and immorality of such a kind as does not exist even among the Gentiles, that someone has his father's wife*". While there have been many reconstructions of Paul's phrase "*has his father's wife*", the most plausible is that the man's birthmother either died or divorced, at which point his father remarried.[17] The verb 'to have' (translated "*has*" in the NASB) means 'to have sexual intercourse' with another person, and the present tense implies the behavior was continuing to happen.[18] So a member of the Corinthian church was sleeping with his stepmother. Gross. While the man's behavior is detestable across cultures, in Roman Corinth a perverse relationship with one's stepmother was more than a matter of transgressing delicate social mores. It was illegal. Roman law punished adultery and incest, and the criminal consequences of engaging in such behavior included banishment, the revoking of citizenship, and the confiscation of property.[19] When Paul says in 5:1 that "*immorality of such a kind as does not exist even among the Gentiles*", he is likely referencing the Roman legal precedent condemning such behavior.

---

16. Baily, Kenneth. 2011. *Paul Through Mediterranean Eyes*. InterVarsity Press Academic. pp. 155-159

17. Baily, *Mediterranean Eyes*, pp. 167-168

18. Winter, *After Paul Left Corinth*, p. 48

19. Winter, *After Paul Left Corinth*, pp. 47-49

Not only have the Corinthians tolerated this man's behavior, they had become arrogant and were boasting about it![20] The precise reason for the Corinthian boast is unclear; Bailey suggests that the Corinthians were celebrating their new-found freedom and grace in Christ by disregarding immoral behavior as if they had somehow overcome it[21], while Winter argues that the man was probably a member of the upper class and the church, proud of his presence in their community, was willing to overlook his indiscretions[22]. Either way, Paul thinks this kind of behavior is intolerable and chastises the church for failing to address it. In 5:6-8, Paul compares the man to old leaven which corrupted the dough; the church needed to clear out the old leaven and become *"the unleavened bread of sincerity and truth"*.

Paul's solution, outlined in 5:9-13, holds the church accountable for ignoring abhorrent behavior in the believing community: *"I wrote to you in my letter not to associate with sexually immoral people; I did not at all mean with the sexually immoral people of this world, or with the greedy and swindlers, or with idolaters, for then you would have to leave the world. But actually, I wrote to you not to associate with any so-called brother if he is a sexually immoral person, or a greedy person, or an idolater, or is verbally abusive, or habitually drunk, or a swindler—not even to eat with such a person. For what business of mine is it to judge outsiders? Do you not judge those who are within the church? But those who are outside, God judges. Remove the evil person from among yourselves"*. The issue is not the immorality of those outside the church, which Jewish Paul takes as a given, but the allowance and approval of immorality *within* the church. Paul commands the Corinthians to take action. The man must be removed from the community. While God alone judges those outside of the church, it is the responsibility of those inside of the church, whom Paul has already labeled "holy" to hold this man to account. Paul isn't just being punitive, however. The removal of this man from the congregation is justified by Paul in 5:5: *"I have decided to deliver such a one to Satan for the destruction of his flesh, so that his spirit may be saved in the day of the Lord Jesus"*. By doing so the moral integrity of the church is preserved, freeing it from the potentially corrupting influence of the man's detestable behavior, while the man himself might repent of his deeds and be saved on the final day.

What does an illicit sexual affair with one's stepmother have to do with politics or economics? Quite a lot, actually. As we learned in the previous chapter, Paul sees the church as its own suprapolitical entity, demarcated by faith and the Spirit, with Jesus ruling over it as king. Within this framework believers must handle

---

20. 1 Corinthians 5:2, 6

21. Bailey, *Mediterranean Eyes*, p. 167

22. Winter, *After Paul Left Corinth*, pp. 53-57

their own internal affairs. The call to holiness, set-apartness, means that the church should not conform to the values of pagan society. If someone within the church is threatening its integrity, they should be judged by the church. On the other hand, the church should not be in the business of either acting against the behavior of those outside the church or refusing to associate with unbelievers. Paul assumes the world is immoral but maintains that salvation comes only through faith in the gospel, and it is the role of God's family to reveal the gospel to the world. A church that refuses to engage with those who don't share their values is a church which has abdicated its mission.

Modern Christians on both the political left and right seek the passage of legislation to impose, under threat of violence, their preferred moral and theological preferences on society. I doubt, based on 1 Corinthians 5:9-13, that Paul would approve of this inclination. While political authoritarianism may be the prevailing secular (dare I say 'pagan'?) political value of our time, those following a crucified Messiah should think twice before proposing political solutions to theological problems. Conversely, problems which arise within the church should generally be handled by the church. The man sleeping with his stepmother should be shamed and removed from the church *by the church*. Paul quotes Deuteronomy 13:5 and 17:7 in 1 Corinthians 5:13. In contrast to those outside the church who are judged by God, the Corinthians should *"Remove the wicked man from among yourselves"*. Christians regulate their own internal behavior instead of seeking to pass some law which regulates the behavior of non-Christians. We should stop acting like worldly people. The contrast between insiders and outsiders, us and them, is sharp, and Paul's instructions about accountability and purity are prescient for Christians today.

There is also an interesting economic principle at play in this passage which might be easily glossed over by readers still feeling queasy about the thought of romancing their father's wife. In 5:11, Paul presents a list of behaviors that disqualify a *"so-called brother"* from participation in the church. Of interest are the words *"covetous"*, *pleonektes* in Greek, and *"swindler"*, which is *harpax* in Greek. The term *pleonektes*, a nominative form of the *pleone-* word group, can mean either "sexual greed" or "avarice", both of which connote an insatiable desire to acquire more, either physical intimacy or property. Given the context, *pleonektes* might refer to an illicit desire for sex, but as scholar Brian Rosner points out, the *pleone-* word group is more commonly used to describe the drive for more possessions in the New Testament and Patristic literature.[23] While we will discuss this term (and Rosner's work) in more detail when we turn to Ephesians later in this chapter, it's a safe

---

23. Rosner, Brian. 2007. *Greed As Idolatry*. Eerdmans. pp. 103-111

exegetical bet to assume Paul has avarice in mind in 1 Corinthians 5:11, since the list is designed to supplement the kinds of behavior which are incompatible with faith. Cognates of the Greek term *harpax* occur in Matthew 7:15, Luke 18:11, and 1 Corinthians 6:10 and are probably best understood as 'extortion', the acquisition of possessions through unjust means. Real "*brothers*" are neither covetous nor swindlers in the full Greek sense of those terms.

Here we stand again on the same solid ground as the Jesus tradition. The gospels didn't criticise the possession of wealth as such but presented unjust accumulation of wealth and the internal dispositions which fueled it as grave moral problems. Those very few who did possess wealth were expected to share, and those who did not faced eschatological judgment. Wealth is morally neutral but often leads to idolatrous corruption. Paul seems to be suggesting by his choice of terminology a similar moral outlook on wealth. Avarice and extortion are, like sexual immorality, incompatible with faithful obedience to Jesus. The church should not entertain those who claim to follow Jesus while participating in avaristic extortion. The condemnation of ill-gotten wealth in the church is a church problem which should be handled within the church.

Paul's teaching is in no way incompatible with capitalism, the private ownership and management of the factors of production. Under capitalism, wealth can only be accumulated through consensual, contractual transactions. Both the buyer and the seller benefit from market exchange. While believers who engage in business for the sole purpose of becoming wealthy must check their motives and are obligated to voluntarily share their wealth, nothing Paul says here is incompatible with market freedom. It is, however, irreconcilable with authoritarian socialism. Paul, envisioning a hard line between insiders and outsiders, does not suggest the Romans step in to confiscate and redistribute wealth. He doesn't lobby for a law, nor does he advocate for the community to forcefully confiscate and redistribute the property of those who are wealthy. Modern Christians expect the state to solve these theological problems by empowering a small oligarchy of wealthy politicians to seize the factors of production and all personal wealth. Paul would have none of it. Any "*so-called brothers*" of means who refuse to share should be held accountable by the church. The church completely compromises its identity when it asks the rulers of this age who are passing away to intervene and violently confiscate from the wealthy. Like the rich young ruler, the wealthy can walk away. Judgment day awaits. The church must follow the path of Israel's crucified Messiah and patiently wait for God's righteous vindication without resorting to coercive force. This is a fundamental New Testament economic principle which modern Christians desperately need to learn.

Believers Before the Courts: 1 Corinthians 6:1-11

Paul continues to argue that intra-believing conflict is an in-house affair. The case in question regards believers taking each other to court. For Paul, the answer is a resounding no: "*Does any one of you, when he has a case against his neighbor, dare to go to law before the unrighteous and not before the saints? Or do you not know that the saints will judge the world? If the world is judged by you, are you not competent to form the smallest law courts? Do you not know that we will judge angels? How much more matters of this life? So if you have law courts dealing with matters of this life, do you appoint them as judges who are of no account in the church?*"[24].

Winter argues that what Paul has in mind here are cases of 'vexatious litigation'. While the courts often legitimately arbitrated cases regarding property rights, contracts, and violence, Romans, usually from the upper classes, could leverage civil litigation to bring dishonor or shame against their opponents. The label 'vexatious' implies that these cases had nothing to do with the restoration of justice but discrediting opponents, not unsimilar to the case made against Paul by the mob in Philippi. Since the Corinthians had emulated the practices of the sophists and their disciples, some were likely going to court in an effort to discredit those who associated with a different leader. Once again the Corinthians embraced pagan values at the expense of their faith.[25] Winter summarizes the conflict neatly: "*The civil courts by convention provided another appropriate arean to conduct a power struggle within the church as it would in any association. The same struggle had moved from the meetings of the Christian community to a session of the civil court*"[26].

Paul is rightly incensed at this behavior. He appeals to eschatological judgment. The church will judge both the world and angels. Paul frames this rhetorically ("*Do you not know*") assuming that the Corinthians are already aware of their participation in final judgment. Paul's logic is tight; if Christians are going to judge the world, why can't they even adjudicate problems within their own community?[27] In 1 Corinthians 6:4-8, Paul shames the Corinthians for daring to air out their dirty laundry before "*judges who are of no account in the church*", "*brother* [going] *to law against brother, and that before unbelievers*". The church is not only embarrassing itself by refusing to resolve conflict between members but is tarnishing its witness before unbelievers. How can believers remain distinct if they act like everyone else? And, more importantly, why would they go before unbelievers "*who*

---

24. 1 Corinthians 6:1-4

25. Winter, *After Paul Left Corinth*, pp. 64-67

26. Winter, *After Paul Left Corinth*, p. 66

27. Johnson, *1 Corinthians*, p. 94

are of no account in the church"? Johnson explains Paul's language: "*Paul is referring sarcastically to the pagan judges as those of little account; from Paul's viewpoint they do not have importance in God's kingdom, and the church should view them the same way (not only as of little account but as nonstatus person). He wants to shame them for taking their ordinary disputes before secular judges and juries who for those in Christ have no real importance, no status*"[28].

Paul's use of familial language is another key to interpreting this passage. Paul believes, as he articulates in Galatians 3 and Romans 4, that all those who have faith in Jesus are incorporated into Abraham's chosen family, the real people of God. This logic has been a hidden substructure of Paul's response to the Corinthian church; there should be no divisions, compromise with pagan culture, or celebrating immorality for those in the family. In 6:6, Paul shames the Corinthians for "*brothers*" taking other brothers to court before unbelievers, those who are not in the family. The Corinthians think themselves to be so wise, so cultured, and yet they can't even solve very basic problems which arise in the community. He then argues in 6:7-8 that it would be better for the Corinthians to be wronged and defrauded than to pursue lawsuits against each other, and, even worse, the Corinthians are the ones wronging and defrauding their own brothers! As Winter notices, "*It is easy to overlook the significance of the highly unusual way in which Paul used a familial term here and elsewhere . . . No Roman would have used the term 'brother' of another person except one who shared the same bloodline or a male who had been formally adopted into the family. When Paul used this term he indicated that the Christian community is 'family' and, as such, it would be unheard of for its members to engage in litigation. It was the role of the paterfamilias to rule in disagreements among blood or adopted brothers . . . [even the] Romans considered it highly inappropriate to engage in intrafamily litigation . . . initiating legal proceedings against a Christian brother was seen as a sign of defeat long before the case was heard by the magistrate and the jury*"[29]. Vexatious civil litigation was unbecoming, indeed unacceptable, for members of God's family. Believers must learn to address these problems from within, not through the civil authorities who have no standing in the kingdom of God and are passing away. Paul's instructions are, yet again, a classic example of the suprapolitical kingdom to which those who believe in Jesus now belong. The church must strive to overcome the trappings of pagan culture and its political and economic assumptions.

Paul puts a fine point on the argument in 6:9-11, reminding his audience that "*the unrighteous will not inherit the kingdom of God*". In context this likely refers

---

28. Johnson, *1 Corinthians*, p. 95

29. Winter, *After Paul Left Corinth*, pp. 70-71

to believers who wrong and defraud their brothers. As in 1 Corinthians 5:11, Paul lists the behaviors of those who will not inherit the kingdom. Included are cognates of *pleonektes* and *harpax*, as well as a new term, *kleptai*, "theives", which is a general reference to those who steal.[30] As in 5:11, Paul is not articulating a macroeconomic theory and certainly not advocating for economic intervention by the pagan state. Like Jesus with the rich young ruler, he warns of the eschatological judgment which accompanies these behaviors: they will not, he says twice in this passage, inherit the kingdom of God. He reminds the Corinthians in 6:11, perhaps to their shame, that many of them formerly practiced these immoral acts, but "*you were washed, but you were sanctified, but you were justified in the name of the Lord Jesus Christ and in the Spirit of our God*". Messiah, Spirit, church, and kingdom. These themes, as well as their social and political consequences, are impossible to deny.

Sacrificial Love Edifies: 1 Corinthians 8:1-11:1

1 Corinthians 8:1-11:1 is a sustained argument which makes one major point: believers must be willing to sacrifice for one another. There are few passages in the New Testament which perfectly articulate the ethic of cruciformity, and this is one of them. Instead of getting bogged down in the details, I will make a few brief contextual comments and explain Paul's reasoning. This passage, particularly 1 Corinthians 9, is crucial for understanding Paul's instructions regarding work and charity in 1 and 2 Thessalonians. I offered a short interpretation of this passage in Chapter 4. Paul opens the conversation in 8:1: "*Now concerning things sacrificed to idols, we know that we all have knowledge. Knowledge makes arrogant, but love edifies*". The issue at hand revolves around the eating of meat sacrificed to idols and the edification of others in love. Paul affirms, along with a group from the Corinthians he labels 'strong', that there is only one God and one Lord Jesus[31]. That would seem to settle the issue. Idols aren't gods, so who cares if one eats meat sacrificed to them?

Apparently many do. In 8:7-13, Paul explains that not all men have this knowledge and when they see believers consuming meat sacrificed to idols they might be tempted to partake in honor of the gods to which the meat was sacrificed. Some, maintaining they have the right (*exousia* in 8:9) to consume sacrificial meat, have exercised this *exousia* in a manner which harms other believers. Winter suggests that *exousia* refers to a handful of socially privileged members in the Corinthian

---

30. Johnson, *1 Corinthians*, p. 97

31. 1 Corinthians 8:4-6

church who were participating in feasts honoring the nearby Isthmian Games[32]. Winter's analysis fits the wider context of division addressed by Paul throughout the letter. This 'right' had become a stumbling block to the 'weak' (those tempted to respect idols) and Paul argues that wounding the conscience of another believer is a sin against Christ. In 9:13 Paul posits a hypothetical: if eating sacrificial meat causes a brother to stumble, it is better to never eat meat again.

Paul has set himself up to make a significant rhetorical move. His solution to this problem is creative. Having already established in 1 Corinthians 8 that there is only one God and one Lord, so therefore idols aren't real, he nevertheless encourages the Corinthians to make sacrifices for each other by abstaining from idol-feasts. The *exousia* of one believer should not compromise the faith of another.[33] Paul will spend all of chapter 9 showing how his own personal conduct as an apostle is an expression of cruciform love for others. His opening salvo in 8:1 frames the entire conversation: knowledge makes arrogant but love edifies. If one must choose between a knowledge-based right and sacrificial love, they must pick love.

In 1 Corinthians 9:1-18, Paul argues that apostles have a right (*exousia* again) to earn a living from their apostolic work, going so far in 9:14 to argue that it is a commandment of Jesus: "*the Lord directed those who proclaim the gospel to get their living from the gospel*"[34]. The other apostles have availed themselves of this right, and it is, according to Paul, entirely appropriate for them to do so. As he says in 9:11, "*If we sowed spiritual things in you, is it too much if we reap material things from you?*", with the obvious answer being, of course, "no". Paul and his associates, however, took a different path. In 9:12 he presents himself as an example: "*If others share the right [exousia] over you, do we not more? Nevertheless, we did not use this right [exousia], but we endure all things so that we will cause no hindrance to the gospel of Christ*". Paul has *not* used his right to receive financial benefits from the Corinthians, and, by implication, if he has denied himself rights for the sake of others then the strong meat-eaters must do the same. Anything that could potentially harm the gospel of Christ and the church must be avoided at all costs. He will spend the rest of chapter 9 (9:19-27) describing his approach to others: "*I have become all things to all men, so that I may by all means save some*"[35]. Paul is not advocating for some kind of moral or theological relativism; the function of 1 Corinthians 9 is exhorting the meat-eaters to deny their rights for the sake of others, and Paul uses his own rights-renouncing, cruciform practice of refusing

---

32. Winter, *After Paul Left Corinth*, pp. 280-286

33. Gorman, *Crucified Lord*, p. 256

34. See Mark 6:10, Matthew 10:11, and Luke 10:7

35. 1 Corinthians 9:22

to rely on the Corinthians for financial support as an example. If Paul can make a monetary sacrifice, surely the 'strong' within the Corinthian church can abstain from dining in the temple.

Paul brings this section of the letter to a close in chapter 10. In 1 Corinthians 10:1-22, Paul nuances the so-called 'knowledge' of the strong. While idols don't exist, demons certainly do, and in 10:19-20 Paul informs the Corinthians that the meat offered to idols is actually sacrificed to demons, and believers should have nothing at all to do with demonic entities. Whatever we make of the *daimonion*, Paul thinks that they are real and very much opposed to God,[36] therefore the eschatological community of believers avoid them, looking to Israel as an example of the dangers inherent in idolatry.[37] Summarizing his argument in 10:23-11:1, Paul constructs a general principle of Christian relationships: "*All things are lawful, but not all things edify. Let no one seek his own good, but that of his neighbor*"; meaning in the specific context that if a believer is aware meat has been sacrificed to an idol they should abstain from consuming it. He caps off the instruction in 10:32-11:1: "*Give no offense either to Jews or to Greeks or to the church of God; just as I also please all men in all things, not seeking my own profit but the profit of the many, so that they may be saved. Be imitators of me, just as I also am of Christ*". Cruciformity characterizes the attitude of believers towards one another; they are to imitate the sacrificial Paul, who is himself imitating the sacrificial Messiah. It is better to serve than to be served.

There are two points which are relevant for our analysis of political and economic principles. First is Paul's own christological attitude towards others. Not wanting to place an obstacle before the Corinthians, Paul renounces his right to receive compensation from them in exchange for preaching the gospel. Instead of encumbering the Corinthians with the burden of funding his ministry, Paul makes a sacrifice on their behalf and pays his own way. He does this in imitation of Christ. We will return to Paul's disposition in this passage when we analyze 1 and 2 Thessalonians, but for our immediate purposes modern Christians can deduce an economic principle from this text: believers should not, if possible, be a financial burden to others. The logic is simple. If we are supposed to imitate Paul who imitates Christ, then we should seek to love and serve others even if it makes our lives more difficult. Paul would (and indeed *does* in 2 Thessalonians 3:6-13) reject the notion that Christians who are able to financially support themselves should rely on the charity of others. There are, as we will see even later in 1 Corinthians,

---

36. Johnson, *1 Corinthians*, pp. 167-168

37. 1 Corinthians 10:1-11

plenty of cases in which charity is both legitimate and necessary, where the giving Christian is providing for the real needs of others. We are called to radical generosity. Conversely, though, we shouldn't expect to live permanently off of the generosity of others. The attitude that others ought to work to meet my needs while I contribute nothing in return is antithetical to the principles Paul outlines in 1 Corinthians 8:1-11:1.

This should cause us to reflect on our economic and political commitments. Centralized welfare is a cornerstone of modern political arrangements, and both the progressive left and conservative right believe in the moral necessity of transfer payments. Taking money from the productive class and distributing it (as the politicians and bureaucrats see fit, of course) to the nonproductive class is assumed to be a necessary component of state power. Often ignored in the conversation is the moral agency of those who receive 'entitlement' benefits, many of whom would consider themselves Christians, as well as the deleterious economic effects of redistribution on working-class families. Is it appropriate, given Paul's instructions, for those who imitate Jesus to support policies where an oligarchical class of wealthy politicians is given the power to take from one group and redistribute to another at will? Should Christians, who are supposed to seek the welfare of others first, expect to receive indefinite transfer payments and even consider it a 'right' to the non-contractually, coercively taken wealth of others? It doesn't follow that supporting state redistributive welfare programs is really 'seeking the good of your neighbor' because a different neighbor must suffer to pay for them. Christians are called to radical, voluntary charity and radical personal responsibility. Outsourcing charity to the state is an abdication of our duty and ensures that an increasing number of economic transactions are conducted under the threat of violence.

It must also be noted that Paul's argument in 1 Corinthians 8-10 is unrelated to the classical liberal conception of natural rights and shouldn't be read as an expression of that modern category. Christians are sometimes called to renounce their right to liberty, property, and sometimes even life, but the renunciation is committed voluntarily for the sake of others. Asking a secular politician to violate the rights of another person to achieve a particular social end is not a virtue. It is a form of theft which is inconsistent with faith in Jesus and membership in the church. The rulers of this age who are passing away are in no position to dictate how and when Christians serve their neighbors, and modern attempts of weaponizing state power to achieve kingdom ends compromises the unique identity of God's family. We all called to imitate Jesus, and our relationships with others must be characterized by cruciformity. Paul makes no exceptions for political and economic arrangements.

The Greatest of These is Love: 1 Corinthians 12-14

A brief comment on one of Paul's most famous passages is in order, only further advancing the thesis proposed in the previous section. 1 Corinthians 12-14, in which the so-called 'love chapter' often read at weddings is contained, is another summons to cruciform love. This section of Paul's letter addresses the use of Spiritual gifts, particularly the gift of tongues.[38] In chapter 12, Paul discusses the variety of Spiritual gifts which God bestows upon the church; everyone receives a different gift for the edification of the community. Paul compares the church to a body, with every member possessing a different function (gift) which contributes to the working of the whole.[39] It is a classic example of Pauline ecclesiology and one of the many places in Paul's letters where the themes of Christ, Spirit, and church are inextricably linked. Because all believers have been granted a unique gift, all must work to build up the body.

Paul transitions seamlessly into chapter 13 by revealing *"a still more excellent way"*[40] than possessing Spiritual gifts. He elaborates on the primacy of love; the possession of gifts, knowledge, or prophecy is worthless without love, and love is always oriented towards the needs of others.[41] Paul ends the chapter in 13:13 with a powerful statement about the value of love: *"But now faith, hope, love, abide these three; but the greatest of these is love"*. The functional value of Paul's teaching about love becomes apparent in chapter 14; Paul places limits on the use of tongues in church and establishes the proper role of Spiritual gifts in general: they must be used for edification. The concept of 'edification' anchors this section of Paul's letter: *"so that the church may receive edifying"*[42], *"seek to abound for the edification of the church"*[43], *"Let all things be done for edification"*[44]. Believers must use whatever God has given them to build up the church, lovingly seeking to serve others instead of dominating them. 1 Corinthians 12-14 is Paul's ethic of cruciformity applied to the specific issue of Spiritual gifts, a principle which was already at work in the previous issues Paul seeks to remediate in his letter. I highlight this passage to drive home a particular point: Christians must always seek to love and serve their neighbors, particularly within the church, and they do so by emulating the

---

38. Gorman, *Crucified Lord*, pp. 270-277

39. 1 Corinthians 12:12-26

40. 1 Corinthians 12:20

41. 1 Corinthians 13:1-7

42. 1 Corinthians 14:5

43. 1 Corinthians 14:12

44. 1 Corinthians 14:26

sacrificial disposition of Jesus the Messiah. There is no carve-out for political and economic action.

He Must Reign: 1 Corinthians 15:20-28

1 Corinthians 15 is one of the greatest texts in the entire Pauline corpus. A full-throttle defense of the resurrection, Paul is at his best: witty, passionate, sarcastic, and exacting. There are many mysterious elements in Paul's prose which theologians have and will continue to debate for centuries. For our purposes we must concern ourselves with one short passage in this section of Paul's letter. The Corinthians were, in the words of Michael Gorman, *"eschatologically challenged"*: *"some of them, likely the most influential, denied the resurrection in any meaningful sense, including Paul's belief in its future, bodily character. Theologically then, they were functionally pagans in their denial of bodily resurrection, following in the footsteps of Plato, the Epicureans, and the man on the street"*[45]. Because of this denial, Paul must elaborate on the nature and significance of resurrection. He begins the chapter with an articulation of the gospel, centered on the crucified and resurrected Messiah, reminding the Corinthians that Jesus appeared to more than five hundred people, including Paul, after he was raised from the dead.[46] The rest of chapter 15 addresses questions relating to the bodily resurrection, and it is within this rhetorical context we find a passage regarding the universal lordship of Christ.

1 Corinthians 15:20-23 compares Adam to Christ.[47] Jesus is the *"first fruits of those who are asleep"* (a Pauline euphemism for death), the one through whom came the resurrection of the dead. As Adam brought about death, Christ brings true life: *"by virtue of his resurrection, Christ, the "new Adam," stands at the head of the new creation, and he remedies the problem of death set in motion by the first Adam"*[48]. This is new creation eschatology; through the resurrection of God's Messiah the age to come has been inaugurated. Since Christ has already been raised, believers can also expect a bodily resurrection at his return. 15:24-26, describing what happens *after* Jesus returns and the general resurrection begins, is a lucid description of Christ's universal rule: *"then comes the end, when He hands over the kingdom to the God and Father, when He has abolished all rule and all authority and power. For He must reign until He has put all his enemies under his feet. The last enemy that will be abolished is death"*. In the end, Jesus will declare victory over all his enemies. As James Ware

---

45. Gorman, *Crucified Lord*, pp. 277-278

46. 1 Corinthians 15:1-11

47. Paul provides an expanded elaboration of the Adam/Christ dichotomy in Romans 5:12-21.

48. Capes, Reeves, and Richards, *Rediscovering Paul*, p. 158

explains, the Greek terms translated *"authority"* and *"power"* in the NASB are used frequently in Jewish literature to denote angelic and supernatural beings, and Paul seems to be adding 'death' to the list of malevolent beings which are coming to an end.[49] Ware attributes the phrase *"rule"* to evil supernatural powers, but Paul's use of a cognate to describe the *"rulers of this age"* in 2:6-8 suggests otherwise. The most likely reading of this passage naturally flows from Paul's use of christological and kingdom language within the text itself. Jesus, resurrected and ascended Lord, is king over all creation, both human rulers and suprahuman forces.

15:25 is a decisive description of inaugurated eschatology: that Jesus *"must reign until"* implies that Jesus is reigning already, and his work will be completed upon his return and through the resurrection of all, finally conquering death: *"The reign of Christ as king . . . here is his present reign at the right hand of God . . . The reign of Christ must culminate in the defeat of all his enemies . . . The last of these enemies to be abolished will be death"*[50]. Paul will argue in 15:27-28, immediately following this provocative declaration, that all will ultimately be subjected to God, after which *"God may be all in all"*. Many interpreters have seen in this passage a sort of subordinal christology where Jesus will submit himself to God at the eschaton. Ware provides an excellent critique of that position[51], but whatever we make of the relationship between Jesus and his Father at the end of history Paul has unambiguously pronounced the universal rule of Jesus *in the present*, which culminates in the eventual defeat of all his enemies (including human rulers) at the consummation of the eschatological age and the resurrection of all believers. Vindication will come for the faithful because Jesus has already been raised from the dead, the first fruits of the general resurrection and the beginning of the age to come. None of Paul's rhetoric was intended to be read metaphorically and the political consequences are easily deducible. Jesus is king. No one else, neither earthly ruler nor supernatural power, has been raised from the dead. In the end, they will all fall to ruin.

The Collection: 1 Corinthians 16:1-4

One criminally neglected aspect of Paul's ministry is his collection for the impoverished Jerusalem church. The collection occupied at least several years of his missionary travels and mentioned, often only briefly, in several of his letters. In 1 Corinthians 16:1-14 Paul issues the following instruction: *"Now concerning the*

---

49. Ware, James. 2025. *The Final Triumph of God*. Eerdmans. pp. 222

50. Ware, *Final Triumph*, p. 225

51. Ware, *Final Triumph*, pp. 211-244

collection for the saints, as I directed the churches of Galatia, so you are to do as well. On the first day of every week, each of you is to put aside and save as he may prosper, so that no collections need to be made when I come. When I arrive, whomever you approve, I will send them with letters to take your gift to Jerusalem; and if it is appropriate for me to go also, they will go with me". Collecting money *"for the saints"*, the 'holy ones' in Jerusalem, was an important Pauline objective. The historical specifics of his collection are somewhat obscure, but between Acts and the epistles there is enough evidence to posit a plausible historical reconstruction. In Acts 11:27-30 a prophet named Agabus predicted a great famine would occur (and did in fact occur) throughout the empire during the reign of Claudius (41-54 CE), hitting Judea particularly hard. Barnabas and Saul are tasked by the elders to collect a contribution from the believing gentile churches, providing relief for the poverty stricken Judeans. During his final visit to Jerusalem, Paul stands before Felix and describes his reason for returning to Judea: *"Now after several years I came to bring alms to my nation and to present offerings"*[52], signaling that he had accomplished the goal given to him in Acts 11.

Paul subtly hints at his motivation for diligently overseeing the charitable collection in Galatians and Romans. In extended argument about Gentile Law observance, Paul discusses his collegial relationship with James, Peter, and John. They had been tasked, according to Galatians 2:9, with ministering to the Jews, while Paul had been called to preach among the gentiles. These pillars of the Jerusalem church endorsed Paul's Law-free gentile mission, making only one request, recounted in Galatians 2:10: *"They only asked us to remember the poor—the very thing I also was eager to do"*. Paul, apostle to the gentiles, was honoring his pledge to provide for the needy Jewish believers in Judea, a sure sign of goodwill between two potentially adversarial factions in the early church. At the end of Romans, Paul expresses his desire to meet the church in Rome, a city which he had never personally visited. Paul intends to preach the gospel in Spain and will pass through Rome on his way. He must first take the collection to Jerusalem, however, as he reveals in Romans 15:24-28: *"whenever I go to Spain—for I hope to see you in passing, and to be helped on my way there by you, when I have first enjoyed your company for a while—but now, I am going to Jerusalem serving the saints. For Macedonia and Achaia have been pleased to make a contribution for the poor among the saints in Jerusalem. Yes, they were pleased to do so, and they are indebted to them. For if the Gentiles have shared in their spiritual things, they are indebted to minister to them also in material things. Therefore, when I have finished this, and have put my seal on this fruit of theirs, I will go on by way of you to Spain"*. Paul assumes that Gentile

---

52. Acts 24:17

believers are obligated to serve the Jewish church in Judea because of their shared spiritual blessing. The context matters; as in Galatians, Romans directly addresses the relationship between Jews, Gentiles, and the Law. Paul's collection must be, in some way, connected to that question.

Scot McKnight illustrates the complexity of Paul's collection: *"Involved in Paul's collection were the credibility of his apostolic mission and the legitimacy of the Gentile mission . . . the recognition of the priority of Israel in God's redemptive plan . . . the goodwill of Christian communities . . . as well as the need for individual Christians to trust in God to supply their needs if they were to give generously . . . It is likely that the collection itself gained different theological arguments as Paul's ministry developed"*[53]. McKnight, reviewing the scholarly work, identifies four theorized motives for Paul's collection: helping the poor, unifying the church, a Gentile substitution for Jewish initiation rites, and eschatological provocation. As a Jew and a follower of Jesus, Paul is concerned for the poor and wants to help them. He also deeply invested in the unity of the church and spends much of his career attempting to cross the treacherous social chasm between Jew and Gentile; as he puts it in Romans 15:27, the collection is an expression of gratitude from the Gentiles for incorporation into the Jewish family of God. Since Paul is an advocate of Law-free Gentile inclusion, a financial gift could possibly be perceived by the Jews in Judea as a metaphorical alternative to circumcision, and, following his dismay in Romans 9-11 that many Jews were rejecting the gospel, Paul may hope that the collection would spur apprehensive Jews to repentance and faith in Jesus.[54]

While the last two suggestions are certainly within the realm of probability, Paul is undoubtedly motivated by the first two. There is no hierarchy or division between helping the poor and unifying the church; for Paul, they are but two sides of the same coin. He offers an extended justification for the collection in 2 Corinthians 8-9, which I will interpret in detail below, but already the cumulative evidence of Acts, Galatians, and Romans, as well as Paul's concern to bridge division in the Corinthian church through cruciform love, provides us with enough information to make sense of 1 Corinthians 16:1-4. Paul, who identified the Corinthians as *"saints by calling, with all who in every place call on the name of our Lord Jesus Christ"* (including, presumably, Jewish believers in Judea), is asking that they put aside money in an orderly manner to meet the needs of Jewish family members in an impoverished corner of the Roman empire. Pauline ecclesiology continues to inform Pauline practice, and those who are in Christ

---

53. McKnight, Scott. 1993. *"Collection for the Saints"*. In *Dictionary of Paul and His Letters*, edited by Hawthorne, Gerald; Martin, Ralph; Reid, Daniel. InterVarsity Press. p. 923
54. McKnight, *Collection*, pp. 144-146

have a responsibility to provide for those in need, especially other believers. Paul's hope, of course, is that his offering heals any divisions between Jew and Gentile believers while edifying the people of God. Just as the Corinthians were instructed to employ their Spiritual gifts on behalf of the church in 1 Corinthians 14, Paul admonishes them to do the same with material gifts in 1 Corinthians 16.

There is little hard evidence identifying how the Judeans became brutally impoverished. The economically exploitative Roman provincial system to which the Jesus tradition responded is certainly at play, and the massive famine predicted by Agabus in Acts 11 would have contributed to worsening conditions. It is possible that persecution also played a role. McKnight, following Dunn, delicately suggests that the brief experiment of communal living by the Jerusalem church in Acts 2-5 may have played a role[55], and the principles of Austrian economics corroborates that tantalizing possibility. Whatever the specific factors, if few in the Corinthian church were wealthy the Jerusalem believers must have been even worse off. Paul uses the Greek term *euodoo* in 1 Corinthians 16:2, translated in the NASB as "*he may prosper*". Paul exhorts believers to contribute as they are able without thrusting themselves into poverty. Those who are able to contribute should contribute, and those who are able to contribute much should contribute much.

Paul must ensure no new divisions are formed on account of the collection. In the patron-client system, gifts were exchanged between social unequals. The collection might provide the well-to-do in Corinth with an opportunity to flagrantly flaunt their possessions while manufacturing the impression that the Corinthian church was offering benefactions to the Jerusalemites and tipping the balance of power in Corinth's favor. Johnson explains Paul's deft handling of this problem in 1 Corinthians 16: "*Paul exercises wise pastoral steps in this whole process of the special offering. First, the process is highly participatory and democratic. Everyone, young and old, wealthy and poor, slave and free, Jew and Gentile, male and female, educated and illiterate, can have a part. This defuses the motives of those who wanted to be recognized as the patrons of benefactors of the poor and thus increase their status with their "clients." Second, giving according to one's ability, in private, eases the competitive spirit and puts all on an equal footing, something the Corinthians needed desperately*"[56]. The collection, theologically rich and pastorally brilliant, exhibits Paul at his best.

Modern Christians should take note. Christians who hold to the authority of biblical principles cannot afford to overlook Paul's instructions in 1 Corinthians 16. Paul believes in the unity and exclusivity of the eschatological church, the family of Abraham defined by faith in Christ Jesus. Faith transcends even the deep

---

55. McKnight, *Collection*, p. 144

56. Johnson, *1 Corinthians*, p. 313

divide between Jew and Gentile, showing the world that God has made the two into one while acknowledging that He first worked through the Jews. The nations owe Israel a debt of gratitude. Paul also avoids the pitfalls of benefaction and conspicuous displays of wealth, encouraging all to contribute without shaming lower-class Corinthians into poverty. Paul's solution to the Jerusalem contribution does not include state welfare programs, coercive confiscation, or threats of violence. He recognizes that the church is distinct and the goal of charity is always edification. We find ourselves again confronted with a modern economic dilemma: is Paul's collection compatible with socialism? The answer is, as always, a resounding 'no'. Conversely, Paul's call to radical charity, directly addressing a specific problem faced by a specific group of people, is entirely compatible with free-market capitalism in which voluntary economic transactions are the only morally consistent norm. As we will see in just a few short pages, Paul makes an even stronger case for voluntary Christian charity in 2 Corinthians 8-9.

One final note before transitioning to the second Corinthian epistle. Our old friend Richard Horsley wrote an excellent essay, originally published way back in 1997, where he argues that 1 Corinthians is an example of Paul constructing an alternative society. Commenting on 1 Corinthians 16:1-4, he comes tragically close to articulating the truth: *"Paul's instructions about the collection in 1 Cor 16. 1-4 (and 2 Cor 8; 9) indicate that the network of assemblies had an 'international' political-economic dimension diametrically opposed to the tributary political economy of the empire . . . The purpose and rhetoric of 1 Corinthians itself . . . indicates how Paul is attempting to 'build up' his assemblies as independent communities over against the dominant society"*[57]. Despite the indulgently Marxist-ish rhetorical glossing, Horsley is correct. Paul was building up an international community of believers who lived in opposition to the dominant economic structures of their day. While working so hard to conform Paul with modern authoritarian socialism, Horsley accidentally makes the case for Christian libertarianism. This is yet another case where contemporary political and economic categories, nebulously defined, lead professional biblical scholars to draw imprecise exegetical conclusions. It is the perennial inability of academics to make the distinction between voluntary (peaceful) and involuntary (violent) economic transactions that produces an intellectual environment in which scholars correctly identify Paul's vision of an alternative society in the first century while simultaneously endorsing the global oligarchical dominion of authoritarian politicians and bureaucrats in the twenty first. The church can do better.

---

57. Horsley, Richard. 2004. *"1 Corinthians: Paul's Assembly as an Alternative Society"*. In *Christianity at Corinth*, edited by Adams, Edward; Horrell, David. Westminster John Knox Press. pp. 236-237

2 CORINTHIANS

Background: All Is (Still) Not Well

2 Corinthians is, as should be expected, written to the same congregation as the first Corinthian epistle. Divisions still plague the church, particularly from a faction opposed to Paul, and many are continually tempted to concede to cultural pressures from without. In other words, not much has changed. In 2 Corinthians 2:1-4 Paul acknowledges that his previous letter caused the Corinthians much sorry, and he writes in part to effect reconciliation between himself and the church.[58] In 2 Corinthians 10-13 Paul goes on the offensive, castigating those in Corinth who oppose him by defending the sincerity of his ministry. While it is difficult to determine with exact precision Paul's antagonists, he seeks to delegitimize their position and demonstrate his personal apostolic credentials.[59] Between his plea for reconciliation in the opening chapters and his assault against opponents in the closing chapters, 2 Corinthians 8-9 addresses the Corinthian contribution to the Jerusalem collection, offering us a rather large window into Paul's perception of charity.

2 Corinthians, then, is divided into three sections; chapters 1-7, 8-9, and 10-13. These somewhat hard divisions have led many scholars to conclude that 2 Corinthians is not a unified letter but rather a collection of smaller letters sent by Paul to Corinth over an extended period of time, with each section representing an individual epistle only later stitched into a unified whole.[60] While this hypothesis is certainly plausible, Gorman offers a compelling theory for the literary unity of 2 Corinthians. According to Gorman, chapters 1-7 are conciliatory in tone, gently clarifying the legitimacy of Paul's ministry and his concern for the Corinthian church. Chapters 8-9 are more motivational and direct as Paul implores the Corinthians to make good on their promised contribution. Chapters 10-13 are polemical and aggressive, intended to shame his opponents and restore his good standing before the Corinthians.[61] Within this historical and literary context there are a few points at which Paul makes statements which are directly relevant to our study of political and economic concepts in the New Testament.

---

58. Gorman, *Crucified Lord*, p. 287

59. Gorman, *Crucified Lord*, pp. 289-290

60. Gorman, *Crucified Lord*, p. 288

61. Gorman, *Crucified Lord*, pp. 290-292

The Triumph of God: 2 Corinthians 2:14

Paul, defending his obedience to God, makes a seemingly innocuous statement in 2 Corinthians 2:14: *"But thanks be to God, who always leads us in triumph in Christ, and manifests through us the sweet aroma of the knowledge of HIm in every place"*. Paul employs the language of 'triumph' again in Colossians 2:15. It is easy for English readers to glance over this passage, assuming that Paul is using a generic term for 'victory' and attributing this victory to God in Christ. A closer examination of this passage, however, reveals a subtle political insight.

Heilig argues that the verb *thriambeuo* used by Paul in 2 Corinthians 2:14 has a very specific historical referent. The word denotes a ceremonial Roman military procession which was hosted in celebration of a great victory in battle, often including a parade of captive soldiers and slaves before the appreciative applause of spectating Roman citizens.[62] Interestingly enough, the Roman emperor Claudius hosted a triumphal procession for himself through the streets of Rome in 44 BC, the only such triumph which occurred during Paul's life. He meets Priscilla and Aquilla, two Jews expelled from Rome by Claudius in the early 50s CE, in Acts 18. Heilig plausibly suggests that Paul would have heard about this rare Roman ceremony from his two companions and works the imagery of the triumphal procession into 2 Corinthians 2:14.[63] What is unique about Paul's use of triumph-language is that he casts God as the victorious military leader and himself as the prisoner of war being paraded through the streets.[64]

The contextual impact of Paul's triumph imagery at this point in his letter is sublime; Paul, attempting to justify his apostolic credentials and effect reconciliation between him and his problematic Corinthian church, portrays himself as the captive of a God who conquered through Christ. God is portrayed as a victorious general with Paul serving as the visual proof that God has won the great battle. This is what makes Paul's ministry unique; it was given to him specifically by a victorious God and is conducted entirely in His service. Paul finishes his thought with a comparison between himself and other would-be leaders in Corinth: *"For we are not like many, peddling the word of God, but as from sincerity, but as from God, we speak in Christ in the sight of God"*[65]. Paul's rhetorical flourish perfectly punctuates his argument. The function of his reference to the Roman triumph is a defense of his legitimacy. From this angle, Paul is not making a direct point about

---

62. Heilig, *The Apostle and the Empire*, pp. 55-60

63. Heilig, *The Apostle and the Empire*, pp. 63-70

64. Heilig, *The Apostle and the Empire*, pp. 59-60

65. 2 Corinthians 2:17

Roman political power. Heilig suggests that there may be more going on in this passage than meets the eye.

Within the proposed framework of Paul's general unease with Roman rule, Heilig argues that Paul's triumph-language operates on several levels. Rhetorically it demonstrates that Paul is working on behalf of an omniscient God who is in charge of everything, therefore if the Corinthians have a problem with Paul they also have a problem with the triumphant God.[66] Paul is the only first century writer to use the term *thriambeuo* in reference to a deity; all other literary attestations of *thriambeuo* refer to humans. More scandalously, Paul appropriates a term associated with Roman honor and power to describe *the Jewish God*, a move bound to offend pagan sensibilities.[67] Heilig also proposes that the employment of triumph-language hints that Paul is not uninterested in the pagan political order but rather an active observer (and occasional commentator) on Roman rule.[68]

Heilig's approach to 2 Corinthians 2:14 is equal parts creative and innovative, and he may well be correct. Based on what we know about Paul's worldview it is entirely conceivable that he would appropriate political imagery to make a wider point about the nature of his ministry and the ultimate sovereignty of the Jewish God. Reading Paul as a strictly 'religious' figure, working in a historical vacuum where he travelled around a Roman world of which he was entirely disinterested, is an anachronistic modern myth. Paul maintained Jesus was ruling over creation, the eschaton had been inaugurated, and the rulers of this world were passing (and would soon pass) away. While he may not have been actively *opposed* to Roman rule, following the paradigm of pagan engagement set by Jeremiah 29:7 he knows Rome has no eternal value and would one day disappear forever. God has and will again triumph. Paul is a part of His public procession, testifying to the creator God's cosmic. 2 Corinthians 2:14 indicates that for Paul the gospel is suprapolitical, calling Jews and Gentiles to push beyond the narrow confines of a human power system which is doomed to failure.

Paul Isn't Always Political: 2 Corinthians 6:11-7:4

In 1 Corinthians Paul twice comments on the relationship between insiders and outsiders. In 2 Corinthians 6:14, Paul tells the Corinthians that they should *"not be bound together with unbelievers"*, seemingly contradicting his previous statements in 1 Corinthians 5:9-13 and 7:12-16 regarding those outside the church

---

66. Heilig, *The Apostle and the Empire*, p. 77

67. Heilig, *The Apostle and the Empire*, pp. 93-98

68. Heilig, *The Apostle and the Empire*, p. 55

and marriages to non-believers respectively. How can Paul claim on the one hand that it is impossible (and indeed undesirable) to avoid contact with outsiders while arguing on the other in 2 Corinthians that they shouldn't be *"bound together"* with them. The answer is simple. Paul isn't talking about outsiders in 2 Corinthians. In the immediate rhetorical context, Paul exhorts the Corinthians to reconcile with him instead of siding with his opponents. 2 Corinthians 6:11-13 and 7:2-4 fit well together, and Paul's instruction in 6:14 is grounded in that context. Paul's *"unbelievers"* are the false teachers who oppose him, whom the Corinthians should denounce in favor of Paul. This isn't a passage about insiders and outsiders with political implications, it is a personal plea to choose Paul over his opponents.[69] Why comment on this section of 2 Corinthians? To demonstrate that there are passages in the New Testament which may, on their face, *appear* to address political and economic questions when in context they do not. Since we are still in the early phases of our analysis of Paul's letters, this text is a helpful reminder that we must be sensitive to the function of a text lest we impose our false assumptions on it. I avoid commenting on several passages in Paul for this reason.

God Loves a Cheerful Giver: 2 Corinthians 8-9

We turn now to the most extensive directive regarding giving and charity in the entire New Testament. The context, unsurprisingly, is the collection referenced in 1 Corinthians 16:1-4 for the impoverished Judean community of believers. Paul's rhetorical agenda, the function of the text, is primarily motivational; the Corinthians must follow through on their previously promised gift. The tone of 2 Corinthians 8-9 suggests Paul was worried his audience might retract their commitment to the collection, shaming both themselves and Paul. He says as much in 2 Corinthians 9:4: *"if any Macedonians come with me and find you unprepared, we—not to speak of you—will be put to shame"*. Paul's conciliatory temperament carries into this section of 2 Corinthians. Gorman identifies a clustering of words in 2 Corinthians 8-9 which emphasise fellowship, sharing, and partnership, as well as the pervasive use of *charis* or 'grace' language: *"These . . . words carry the weight of Paul's message: that joining in the Jerusalem collection is a way for believers to share in earnest their material abundance as an expression of gratitude for, and participation in, the abundant grace of God offered in Christ. To do so is to prove the reality of God's love and grace in their lives"*[70]. Situated in this context 1 Corinthians 8-9 is

---

69. Schreiner, *Handbook*, pp. 204-207

70. Gorman, *Crucified Lord*, p. 313

exegetically straightforward. The implications for modern Christian conceptions of charity and wealth are likewise easily deducible.

In 2 Corinthians 8:1-6, Paul's opening salvo of the section, he commends the Macedonians, a province situated north of Achaia, for their generous contribution to the collection. One of the Macedonian churches, based in Thessalonica, is praised by Paul in his letter to them for practicing *"love for the brethren"*, quite possibly a reference to their generosity.[71] The Philippian church is likewise commended in Philippians 4:15-20 for their generosity towards Paul and his ministry. The impoverished Macedonians all contributed well beyond their means. Not only this, Paul didn't even expect them to give at all; the Macedonians begged Paul to donate and *"gave of their own accord"*. The Macedonians were not coerced or shamed into giving, and their motivation is essentially cruciform. They *"first gave themselves to the Lord"*, manifested in their gift of charity to the Jerusalem collection. Paul, implicitly urging the Corinthians to emulate the Macedonians, proceeds to build his case in 2 Corinthians 8:7-15. God has already enriched the Corinthians in every way, therefore they should seek to abound in generosity as well. Paul is quick to mention he isn't commanding the Corinthians to give, but requesting they follow through on their previously-promised pledge. In 8:9, Paul appeals again to cruciform christology: *"For you know the grace of our Lord Jesus Christ, that though He was rich, yet for your sake He became poor, so that you through His poverty might become rich"*. In imitation of Jesus the Corinthians are obligated to give what they had originally vowed. Paul's goal isn't to cause suffering: *"For this is not for the ease of others and for your affliction, but by way of equality—at this present time your abundance being a supply for their need"*. Believers that have should naturally share with believers who don't. The chapter concludes in 8:16-24 with a recognition of Titus, who will oversee the Corinthian collection, which is *"the proof of your love and of our reason for boasting about you"*. Paul has been bragging about Corinthian generosity, and it would be embarrassing for everyone if they backed out.

It is very easy to see how Paul's teaching corresponds with the larger New Testament witness of charity and giving. There are a consistent set of principles which run through the gospels, Acts, and Paul. No one, neither the Macedonians nor the Corinthians, are being forced to contribute. Giving is a cruciform imitation of Jesus, whose personal sacrifice for the sake of others becomes the model of Christian charity. As Christ sacrificed for us, so we ought to sacrifice for others. The goal is not to impoverish the giver, but rather equality (which must not be modernized into the progressive ideal of social egalitarianism) between Christians.

---

71. 1 Thessalonians 4:9-10

Paul presents the Macedonians as a shining example of Christian charity; begging to participate in the Jerusalem collection despite having little themselves, the Macedonian churches imitate the sacrificial disposition of their crucified Lord. Paul's collection is a decentralized charitable initiative meeting specific needs in a particular church. Paul doesn't lobby the Romans to levy higher taxes and redistribute wealth as they see fit. Paul instead encourages believers to give like Jesus, sharing their possessions with those who are less fortunate. There is a severe disjunction between the coercive nature of modern authoritarian socialism and New Testament charitable principles. Socialism is incompatible with the teachings of Paul.

2 Corinthians 9 follows Paul's line of thought from chapter 8. In 9:1-5, Paul reassures the Corinthians that he believes in their willingness to give and wants the collection organized before he returns to Corinth. Paul worries that their *"previously promised bountiful gift"* might be *"affected by covetousness"* and encourages the Corinthians to prepare their contribution accordingly. 2 Corinthians 9:6-15, rounding out Paul's instructions for the collection, describes both the attitude of those who give and the blessings which flow from giving. Paul summarizes much of what he said in 2 Corinthians 8: *"Now this I say, he who sows sparingly will also reap sparingly, and he who sows bountifully will also reap bountifully. Each one must do just as he has purposed in his heart, not grudgingly or under compulsion, for God loves a cheerful giver. And God is able to make all grace abound to you, so that always having all sufficiency in everything, you may have an abundance for every good deed"*[72]. God desires cheerful giving, therefore giving must not be done grudgingly or under compulsion. As Schreiner states, *"Giving that pleases God comes from a joyful heart, representing the glad and authentic will of the giver. Paul had no desire to compel or force someone to give so that they end up giving reluctantly. Generosity is a response to the grace of God . . . [and] believers [will] stand out for their good works"*[73]. Paul goes on to describe how those who give will be enriched in everything because God supplies for the needs of His saints. Paul does not, as many modern prosperity preachers have falsely proclaimed, state that giving automatically results in material blessings from God. By lending to Christians in need, God is glorified while His church is edified: *"Because of the proof given by this ministry, they will glorify God for your obedience to your confession of the gospel of Christ and for the liberality of your contribution to them and to all, while they also, by prayer on your behalf, yearn for you because of the surpassing grace of God in you. Thanks be to God for His*

---

72. 2 Corinthians 9:6-8

73. Schreiner, *Handbook*, p. 211

indescribable gift"[74]. God is glorified, those in need receive material support, and the giving Corinthians obtain the blessing of prayer. Generous, voluntary charity to worthy causes benefits all parties involved. This is, in essence, the Pauline position on Christian charity.

Paul's instructions could not be more at odds with the socialist ethos. Charity is always a gift, given in response to the sacrifice of Jesus. Paul is not attempting to establish a permanent welfare program where the Achaeans and Macedonians are expected to indefinitely fund their Judean brothers and sisters. The objective is to meet a short-term need with Gentile believers providing for Jewish believers. If the family of Abraham has been expanded to include everyone who calls Jesus 'king' then there is a familial responsibility to help one another and renounce the selfish accumulation of possessions. Giving must be performed with a sincere heart, cheerfully, and not under compulsion. A failure to give is indicative of a weak faith and carries negative eschatological consequences, but Paul never once suggests that if the Corinthians fail to provide their promised gift they should be taken to court and thrown in prison. Like the rich young ruler, people are allowed to walk away from their commitments. Paul also doesn't think the pagan Roman government should come and confiscate Corinthian possessions if the church refuses to give. How could outsiders possibly be allowed to intervene in the internal matters of God's church? Unfortunately most modern Christians would rather outsource charity to the violent, monopolistic state than follow Paul in embodying radical, cruciform giving. It's much easier if the government does it, and two hundred years of political philosophy which assumes the inevitability and superiority of the nineteenth century nation-state has blinded modern Christians to the principles of charity which naturally arise out of texts such as 2 Corinthians 8-9. The modern church prefers the violent coercion of socialism to the peaceful cooperation of capitalism. Christians who wield the cross instead of bearing it are rejecting the crucified Messiah.

As we bring our analysis of the Corinthian epistles to a close, we are in a much better position to understand Paul's attitude towards what we would consider 'political' or 'economic' concepts going forward. In order to avoid repetition, our analysis of several Pauline texts will be more succinct and build upon the evidence I have presented thus far. There are texts which deserve closer analysis and will rightfully receive it, but many of Paul's letters need little extended explanation, especially when Paul's purpose only tangentially relates to politics and economics. We turn now to one such text, Paul's letter to the Galatians.

---

74. 2 Corinthians 9:13-15

GALATIANS

Background: Abraham's Family, the Israel of God

Galatians is a theologically contentious letter. Since the Reformation, theologians and biblical scholars have endlessly (and oftentimes viciously) debated the complex matrix of ideas found in Paul's Galatian epistle, including salvation, justification, the Law, Judaism, and other related concepts. I have taken a hard position in this book on only the topics which I find immediately relevant to political and economic concepts. As I have already argued at length, I'm trying my hardest to avoid the major theological trip wires that offend readers who are passionately committed to a particular tradition's interpretation of Paul. While entirely avoiding sensitive issues is impossible, my goal from the beginning includes appealing to an ecumenical audience. Paul makes this noble objective difficult to accomplish. He is an integrative thinker, and his commentary on power, civil authorities, and the church are inseparable from his teachings on justification and salvation. As promised, I plan on staying the course and will refrain from taking a hard stand on as many theological debates as possible. This isn't a cop-out. The aim of this study is fairly narrow and I plan on staying within clearly-defined parameters. As I move through letters such as Galatians, Ephesians, and Romans, I will keep my eye on the exegetical ball and examine Paul's letters strictly for the impact they have on our understanding of politics and economics.

Galatians is Paul's angriest letter. As Dunn observes, Paul replaces the typically cordial epistolary introduction with incendiary rhetoric in 1:6-9, is brash and dismissive towards his opponents throughout the letter, makes a blistering (and honestly hilarious) joke about his opponents castrating themselves in 5:12, and concludes his letter with one final knock-out blow to his enemies in 6:12-13.[75] What could make Paul so furious? According to Paul himself, there were some in the church, whom he labels *"false brethren"*[76], which were encouraging Gentile Jesus believers to follow the Jewish Law, particularly circumcision and food regulations, as Paul explicates in 2:1-14. The function of Galatians, and the reason for Paul's rhetorical rage, is fairly straightforward: *"Paul didn't want his converts to be circumcised, because they already belonged to Christ. That is the essence of Paul's argument in his letter to the Galatian Christians"*[77]. Paul himself says as much throughout the letter.

---

75. Dunn, James. 2006. *The New Perspective on Paul.* Eerdmans. p. 227

76. Galatians 2:4

77. Capes, Reeves, and Richards, *Rediscovering Paul*, pp. 106-107

Galatia was, in the time of Paul, a relatively new Roman province. Caesar Augustus had expanded the territory of the Galatian people and incorporated under the provincial boundaries the major cities of Iconium, Lystra, and Derbe, administered from the provincial capital of Pisidian Antioch. According to Acts, Paul visits several cities in Galatia between Acts 13-16.[78] Paul's first trip to Pisidian Antioch, recorded in Acts 13:13-52, ends with Jews in the city instigating a persecution against Paul and his associates. Paul was concerned enough about the scruples of his Jewish adversaries in the region that he had Timothy circumcised in Acts 16:1-5 to avoid deliberately offending his opponents.[79] It is impossible to tell which cities in Galatia were the intended recipients of Paul's letter, but it was written to be read by more than one congregation. Equally problematic is the vexing question of Paul's opponents; we know, because Paul informs us in Galatians 2:11-13, that they are *"certain men from James . . . the party of the circumcision"*, and that Peter, Barnabas, and other Jews began separating themselves from Gentile believers because of the *"men from James"*. Whether they came directly from Jerusalem, were diaspora Jews living in Galatia, or even had direct contact with James are all open questions which cannot be settled here.[80] Paul's opponents are encouraging Gentiles to live like Jews, presenting a problem for Paul.

Paul contends, by virtue of faith and the Spirit, that Gentiles are now included in Abraham's family through the Messiah. The social status of believers are relativised in light of their incorporation into the people of God. To this end, it is worth quoting Galatians 3:26-29 another time: *"For you are all sons of God through faith in Christ Jesus. For all of you who were baptized into Christ have clothed yourselves with Christ. There is neither Jew nor Greek, there is neither slave nor free man, there is neither male nor female; for you are all one in Christ Jesus. And if you belong to Christ, then you are Abraham's descendants, heirs according to promise"*. This is the burden of Paul's argument in Galatians. In the first two chapters Paul is aghast that there are agitators attempting to convince Gentile believers that they should follow the Law. Paul foregrounds this critique within the framework of inaugurated eschatology in 1:3-4: *"Grace to you and peace from God our Father and the Lord Jesus Christ, who gave Himself for our sins so that He might rescue us from this present evil age"*. Those who are in Christ, both Jews and Gentiles, are in some sense already rescued from the current age of evil which is passing away.

---

78. Gorman, *Crucified Lord*, pp. 184-186

79. Timothy's mother was Jewish according to Acts 16:1, therefore Timothy himself, based on matrilineal descent, was also Jewish.

80. Gorman, *Crucified Lord*, pp. 186-189

Paul's opponents are not only wrong but preaching a different gospel entirely[81]. The leaders of the Jerusalem church had already agreed Paul's gospel to the gentiles doesn't require them to receive circumcision, so what give?[82] Peter and other Jewish leaders were pressured by Paul's antagonists to separate themselves from the Gentiles, and Paul exposes their hypocrisy[83]. This prompts his sharp response in Galatians 3, reviewed last chapter, where Paul argues that the Spirit was given by hearing with faith, not through Law-observance, and therefore *"it is those who are of faith who are sons of Abraham"*[84]. Abraham's family is defined by faith and the Spirit through the Messiah. The redemption of the nations comes through Christ[85], and while the Law played an essential role in God's plans for the world Gentiles are not obligated to follow it because the Law's goal has been fulfilled[86]. Gentiles are now incorporated into Abraham's family, as Matthew Thiessen explains: *"Gentiles need to become connected to Abraham so that they can inherit God's promises to him and his seed. Paul argues against gentile circumcision . . . because he does not think that circumcision has the power to bridge the genealogical gap between Abraham and the gentiles. For Paul, only the divine power of the* [Spirit] *. . . can truly connect gentiles and Abraham"*[87]. As Paul creatively argues in Galatians 4:1-31, those who place their faith in Christ, Jews and Gentiles alike, receive the Spirit are members of Abraham's family in good standing.

Paul will discuss Gentile freedom from the Law in chapter 5, but he punctuates his argument at the end of the letter in 6:16 by referring to the Jew and Gentile family of Abraham as *"the Israel of God"*. While some interpreters have suggested that Paul here is referring either to ethnic Jews who are *not* Jesus believers, the contextual case for that position is weak.[88] The entire purpose of Galatians, its primary function, is to counter Paul's opponents who argue that Gentiles must become like Jews. As Wright points out, Paul refers to *"the household of faith"* in 6:10 and *"new creation"* in 6:15; both categories inform Paul's ecclesiology, which is that Israel, the family of Abraham, has now been opened through Israel's

---

81. Galatians 1:6-9

82. Galatians 2:1-10

83. Galatians 2:11-21

84. Galatians 3:7; in context 3:1-9

85. Galatians 3:10-14

86. Galatians 3:15-25

87. Thiessen, *A Jewish Paul*, p. 101

88. Although Novenson makes a compelling argument in favor of *"the Israel of God"* in reference exclusively to ethnic Jews; see Novenson, *End of History*, pp. 166-167.

Messiah to the incorporation of Gentiles *as Gentiles* through faith.[89] 'Israel', the one people of God, now includes faithful, Spirit-empowered Gentiles. A political principle justly derived from Galatians, already argued before (and due to the nature of Paul's letters soon to be argued again), is that Paul contends the world can be divided into two categories: those in Christ and those outside of Christ. This is an essentially Jewish way of dichotomizing humanity and comprehensible only if Paul, as a Jew, continues to analyze human relationships in fundamentally Jewish ways. The family of Abraham, Israel-plus-faithful-Gentiles, sits on one side of the dividing line while everyone else sits on the other. Our modern political labels, along with our national and ethnic identities, are relativized in Christ. There is no pledging allegiance to a country, a political party, or a politician for those in the Messiah. Either our identity is in Christ, sealed by faith and the Spirit, resulting in a new familial tie with Abraham's family, or it's not. Unfortunately, most modern Christians have implicitly, perhaps unwittingly, chosen the latter.

Galatians 5: Freedom in Christ

In Galatians 2:4, Paul accuses *"false brethren"* of *"spying out our liberty which we have in Christ Jesus"*. The word for *"liberty"*, *eleutheria* in Greek, cannot be divorced from its immediate rhetorical context. Paul is not mysteriously foreshadowing a Lockean conception of natural rights, nor is he speaking of *eleutheria* as a political value. The 'liberty' to which Paul refers is that of the Gentiles from adopting Jewish legal practices. Although it istempting for an author such as myself who values political liberty to wrest Paul's use of *eleutheria* from its context and apply it to modern intra-Christian political debates, that would distort Paul's use of the term and compromise my commitment to biblical authority. I would be doing with liberty precisely what I argue many biblical scholars have done with socialism. We won't fall into the same trap. When considered against the backdrop of Paul's ecclesiology, however, it does have an implication for the political nature of our membership in Abraham's family.

Paul uses the word *eleutheria* (or cognates) several times in Galatians. In Galatians 4:21-31, Paul develops an interesting allegory in which he compares those who are in Christ by virtue of faith and the Spirit with Sarah's children. Unlike the children born to Hagar, Abraham's bondservant (i.e. 'slave'), those who possess the Spirit are born "of the free woman". Paul declares emphatically in 5:1 that *"It was for freedom that Christ set us free; therefore keep standing firm and do not be subject again to a yoke of slavery"*. Paul's use of *elutheria* (translated by the

---

89. Wright, *Faithfulness of God*, pp. 1142-1151

NASB in this passage as 'freedom') denotes liberty (for Gentiles) from the Law. Paul discusses the proper use of *eleutheria* in Galatians 5:13-15: *"For you were called to freedom, brethren; only do not turn your freedom into an opportunity for the flesh, but through love serve one another. For the whole Law is fulfilled in one word, in the statement, "You shall love your neighbor as yourself." But if you bite and devour one another, take care that you are not consumed by one another"*. Genuine *eleutheria* manifests itself in serving one another. Paul ironically quotes Leviticus 19:18 to demonstrate that those who use their freedom in service of others and not the flesh are actually fulfilling the Law, unlike his Gentile-agitating opponents.

Paul then contrasts the fruits of the flesh with the fruits of the Spirit in Galatians 5:16-26. Gentiles who *"live by the spirit"* must *"also walk by the Spirit"*, using their freedom from the Law to honor God and serve others. Those who live in the flesh *"will not inherit the kingdom of God"* and are outside the boundaries of Abraham's family. In Galatians 6:2, Paul instructs the congregation to *"Bear one another's burdens, and thereby fulfill the law of Christ"*. Freedom from the Law does not result in fleshly indulgence and does not seek one's own interest. Instead, being guided by the Spirit, the church directs its liberty in service of others, *"especially . . . those who are of the household of faith"*[90]. Modern Christians are yet again faced with a political dilemma. We are the true family of Abraham, therefore we must serve others. Does this service happen by weaponizing the monopolistic power of state violence to enact policies against unwilling citizens who don't share our theological views, or does it happen by sacrificially (and voluntarily, *cheerfully*, perhaps) renouncing our own self-interest? I think the answer is self-evident. Paul mounts a similar argument in Ephesians.

Ephesians

Background: One Lord, One Faith, One Baptism

According to Acts 19, Paul stayed in Ephesus for two years before nearly triggering a major riot. He was opposed by many Jews and a silversmith named Demetrius who crafted shrines of the goddess Artemis. Demetrius stirred up much of the city before Paul was acquitted by a town clerk who promptly dismissed all accusations against him. Ephesus, the Roman capital of the province of Asia, served as the homebase for Paul's Asian mission. The city was home to the goddess Artemis, and the temple dedicated to her was one of the seven wonders of the ancient world. While the cult of Artemis was a major pillar of the Ephesian economy,

---

90. Galatians 6:10

its location on the western coast of Asia Minor also made Ephesus a center for trade and commerce, attracting traders from all over the Mediterranean world to its harbors. Paul's letter to the Ephesians, which in the best, earliest manuscripts lacks the phrase *"in Ephesus"* in 1:1, was most likely composed as a circular letter which would have been read in several churches throughout the province of Asia. The circular nature of Ephesians explains the apparent lack of a specific problem addressed by Paul, its commentary on Jesus in relation to other divine beings, and the extended explanation of the relationship between Jews and Gentiles. All of these issues were, as we saw in Acts 19, relevant to Paul's Asian audience.[91]

Ephesians is structurally similar to Colossians but outlines the same ecclesiology Paul developed in Galatians. Although Paul accentuates his exposition of the church differently due to the problems posed by his opposition in Galatia, he nevertheless maintains the same perspective on the unique identity of God's family in Christ. Paul's messianic christology is on full display in Ephesians, where Christ is portrayed as Lord of all creation and head of God's church. Although the division is an arbitrary scholarly construct, Ephesians 1-3 explicate the identity of the church while Ephesians 4-6 reveals how that identity manifests itself in concrete action.[92] When viewed as a whole, Ephesians demonstrates the tight connection between identity and ethics; in fact, it is impossible to separate the two.

A brief glance at Ephesians is enough to illustrate its ecclesiological consistency with Galatians. Paul's opening salvo in Ephesians 1:3-14 expresses the eternal plan of God to choose the church, adopted *"as sons through Jesus Christ"*, the revelation of a *"mystery"* worked out in the *"fullness of times"*. As in all of Paul's letters, ecclesiology is flanked by christology and eschatology. The passage ends with the oft-quoted (in this book, at least) summary of family membership in 1:13-14: those who believe in the gospel are sealed with the Holy Spirit. Paul contextualises the church in relation to the exalted king Jesus who rules over all creation in 1:15-23. Ephesians 2 could be a creative reworking of Galatians 2-4 as Paul explains how the dividing wall of the Law has been broken down through Jesus, erasing the dichotomy between Jew and Gentile *"so that in Himself He might make the two into one new man, thus establishing peace, and might reconcile them both in one body to God through the cross"*. Jews and gentiles are now together in Christ *"fellow citizens with the saints, and are of God's household"*, with Paul again identifying the united church as God's temple to conclude the chapter.

Paul returns to the theme of "mystery" in Ephesians 3; the revealed mystery, according to 3:3-6, is *"that the Gentiles are fellow heirs and fellow members of the*

---

91. Gorman, *Crucified Lord*, pp. 498-502

92. Schreiner, *Handbook*, p. 273

Body, and fellow partakers of the promise in Christ Jesus through the gospel". God had always planned to reveal himself to the world because it is from Him that *"every family in heaven and on earth derives its name"*. Ephesians 4 opens with something of a topic statement for the rest of the epistle; the Ephesians are to *"walk in a manner worthy of the calling with which you have been called, with all humility and gentleness, with patience, showing tolerance for one another in love, being diligent to preserve the unity of the Spirit in the bond of peace"*[93]. He qualifies his exhortation with one of the most powerful declarations on eclessial unity in the entire Pauline corpus: *"There is one body and one Spirit, just as also you were called in one hope of your calling; one Lord, one faith, one baptism, one God and Father of all who is over all and through all and in all"*[94]. The church is called to live in unity. Paul perfectly encapsulates Galatians 3 without specifically invoking Abraham. The church must be united under one Lord and one God through the Spirit. The rest of Ephesians is essentially a commentary on 4:1-6; in a creative inversion of his *"Israel of God"* identification of the church in Galatians 6:16, Paul even refers to those outside of the church as *"Gentiles"* in Ephesians 4:17. Taken as a whole, Ephesians beautifully presents the universal church serving under the universal Lord.

Ephesians 1:15-23: Far Above All Rule and Power and Authority and Dominion

In Ephesians 1:15-23 Paul celebrates the great love which the Ephesians have for each other and prays they will continue to grow in their knowledge and understanding of the Lord. He caps off his prayer with a sweeping statement about Jesus and the church in 1:19-23: *"These are in accordance with the working of the strength of His might which He brought about in Christ, when He raised Him from the dead and seated Him at His right hand in the heavenly places, far above all rule and authority and power and dominion, and every name that is named, not only in this age but also in the one to come. And He put all things in subjection under His feet, and gave Him as head over all things to the church, which is His body, the fullness of Him who fills all in all"*. Paul first chronicles the absolute power Jesus exercises over all creation. The resurrected Lord has been installed above every other competitor. Paul uses four terms (or cognates thereof) to describe what exactly Jesus is *"far above"*: *arche*, translated *"rule"*; *exousia*, translated *"authority"*; *dynamis*, translated *"power"*; and *kyriotes*, translated *"dominion"*. He also throws in the phrase *pantos onomatos*, *"every name"*, for good measure.

---

93. Ephesians 4:1-3

94. Ephesians 4:4-6

It is easy for Christian readers to gloss over these terms and spiritualize them; *certainly*, the logic goes, *Paul isn't referring to earthly political leaders*. Before analyzing the terms themselves, the immediate context in which they are used already exposes a deficiency in the spiritual reading. Schreiner detects in this passage an allusion to Psalm 110:1, a messianic Psalm in which the Davidic king overcomes all his enemies by the hand of God (which, in its own historical context, *clearly* denotes hostile human political rulers), and Psalm 8, which describes the rule of humanity over all creation.[95] These allusions fit perfectly within the broad rhetorical function of the text which celebrates the hegemonic rule of Jesus and his leadership over the church. Even taking the text at face value Paul seems to presuppose that Jesus has superseded all human authorities. He is also asserting that Jesus sits above *more* than human authorities, to be sure, but the spiritualized reading is an insufficient analysis of Paul's linguistic and literary presentation of Jesus's reign.

The words Paul utilizes in Ephesians 1:21 demonstrate the totality of Jesus's Messianic dominion. Daniel Reid's compact study of the words in this passage reveals the breadth of Paul's sweeping christological rhetoric. In Greek the *arch-* prefix was primarily used with reference to human power; Paul employs a cognate of the term in 1 Corinthians 2:6-8 when he names and shames the human authorities who crucified Jesus. Paul's use of *arche* (in the plural) should be interpreted to denote earthly political leaders. *Exousia* generally describes the rights possessed by a person in authority, and Paul uses the same term in Romans 13:1-3 with reference to human political authorities. Both *dynamis* and *kyriotes*, however, are often used in Jewish literature written or translated into Greek with reference to evil spiritual forces which are opposed to both God and His people.[96] By appropriating Greek words signifying both human and, for lack of a better term, 'spiritual' powers, Paul portrays Jesus as ruler over everything, both in the heavens and on earth. The expression *pantos onomatos*, translated *"every name"*, ensures that even unknown forces are included in Paul's list of defeated powers, as Reid explains: *"as the conclusion to a list of four names of evil powers, we find a global reference to "every name named, not only in this age but in the age to come"* . . . *Against a cultural backdrop in which the successful magical manipulation of evil powers was commonly believed to be predicated on the knowledge of the powers name, Ephesians emphasis the sovereignty and triumph of Christ over every power—known or unknown, real or imagined,*

---

95. Schreiner, *Handbook*, pp. 276-277

96. Reid, Daniel. 1993. *"Principalities and Powers"*. In *Dictionary of Paul and His Letters*, edited by Hawthorne, Gerald; Martin, Ralph; Reid, Daniel. InterVarsity Press. pp. 748-749

present or future[97]. Or, as Paul phrases it, God *"put all things in subjection under His feet"*, including human authorities.

Not only does Jesus rule over all creation, he is the head of God's church. The corporate identity of believers (as well as their individual identities) are rooted in the power, authority, and sovereignty of the crucified, resurrected, and ascended king over all creation who is *presently* sitting on the throne and will one day finally vanquish every enemy. As members of God's kingdom, the church already in the present shares in his reign. Gorman is right to point out that this should not lead to Christian triumphalism. Paul is operating within a framework of inaugurated eschatology where the rulers of this age are passing away but not yet abolished. The church is empowered by the Spirit and tasked with taking the gospel to all nations, and God will sustain his church until the end, but believers still reckon with powers which are in opposition to God.[98] Paul explicates this in Ephesians 6, which will be dealt with below, but until the eschatological consummation the church is *"His workmanship, created in Christ Jesus for good works, which God prepared beforehand so we would walk in them"*[99], and *"so that the manifold wisdom of God might now be made known through the church to the rulers and the authorities in the heavenly places"*[100]. The latter quotation, Ephesians 3:10, utilizes the plural form of *arche* and *exousia*; while the qualifier *"in the heavenly places"* could imply both are used with reference to celestial powers, Paul may also be delineating two separate spheres of power, *"rulers"* and *"authorities in the heavenly places"*. Either way, Jesus rules over everything and the church participates in his reign. Paul's high christology and ecclesiology should inoculate modern Christians from placing their hopes in human authorities.

Ephesians 5:5: Greed as Idolatry?

In Ephesians 5:5 and Colossians 3:5 Paul issues a brief yet dire warning to his addressees. In no uncertain terms, Paul claims in Ephesians that *"the covetous man . . . is an idolater"*. When writing to the Colossians he is even more blunt: *"greed . . . amounts to idolatry"*. I have been a Christian for my entire adult life and never once witnessed either of these passages quoted in a sermon. I don't mean this as an indictment of the many fine preachers I've had the privilege of hearing; that a brief, almost off-the-cuff comment has been deeply neglected should come

---

97. Reid, *Principalities and Powers*, p. 749

98. Gorman, *Crucified Lord*, pp. 508-509

99. Ephesians 2:10

100. Ephesians 3:10

as no surprise. The infrequency with which Ephesians 5:5 and its counterpart in Colossians 3:5 are ignored doesn't soften Paul's ethical directive. Greed is idolatry, full stop. In Ephesians 4-6 Paul outlines the ethical consequences of membership in God's family, and Ephesians 5:5 is included in a list of behaviors which disqualify one from inheriting the kingdom of God. The verse in full reads: *"For this you know with certainty, that no immoral or impure person or covetous man, who is an idolater, has an inheritance in the kingdom of Christ and God"*. Quite a provocative argument.

I have already made a fleeting comment on this passage above, but it deserves a more robust exposition here. The Greek word Paul uses in this passage is *pleonektes*, translated *"covetous man"* by the NASB, which has a general semiotic resemblance to the English term 'avarice', excessive greed. Rosner devoted an entire book to these two passages in Ephesians and Colossians. While some interpreters have suggested that *pleonektes* and cognates could mean something akin to 'sexual immorality', a vast amount of literary evidence, not to mention Paul's references sexual immorality (*pornos*) *in the same verse* in both Ephesians and Colossians, points to the best translation being either 'avarice' or 'greed'.[101] It makes sense of the context and bears a striking moral resemblance to the tradition of Jesus and the rich young ruler. Rosner, summarizing his findings, offers an explanation of Paul's teaching: *""greed is idolatry" may be paraphrased as teaching that to have a strong desire to acquire and keep for yourself more and more money and material things is an attack on God's exclusive rights to human love and devotion, trust and confidences, and service and obedience"*[102]. I agree with every word. Greed is a form of idolatry.

Many modern Christians, including the much younger version of myself, believe that 'capitalism' is virtually synonymous with 'greed'. It would follow, based on this logic, that the consequence of 'greed as idolatry' would naturally entail a rejection of capitalism and, to take it one step forward, a tacit endorsement of socialism, which of course is about sharing, charity, and being nice to other people. We already know that logic is fatally flawed. Capitalism simply denotes the decentralization of economic exchange based on private property and peaceful, voluntary transactions. While the material prosperity which results from capitalism certainly creates a greater *temptation* for greed, capitalism itself cannot be conflated with greed. As Mises perceptively observed, in a truly free-market economy the *only* path to satisfying greed is by serving consumers who ultimately direct the market's course. If producers stop providing goods and services which are demanded by

---

101. Rosner, *Greed as Idolatry*, pp. 103-111

102. Rosner, *Greed as Idolatry*, p. 173

consumers they cease to earn a profit and are thus forced out of the market.[103] In Mises's own words, "*Capitalists, entrepreneurs, and landowners can only preserve and increase their wealth by filling best the order of consumers*"[104]. Christian entrepreneurs should not be motivated by avarice and produce only to consume at a higher rate than others. Wealth brings not only temptation but responsibility. The possession of wealth is morally neutral; it is in the motives and process of acquisition as well as what one does with what they own which matters before God. The desire to selfishly possess and hoard is an idol which Christians must avoid. Confusing 'greed' with peaceful, voluntary market production and exchange is a category mistake, but one which benefits the subjective desires of authoritarian socialists.

Conversely, very few modern progressive Christians ever question the motives of bureaucrats, politicians, and other public intellectuals who confiscate and redistribute to achieve their preferred social ends. Does 'greed' not apply to those unproductive members of society who parasitically take through violent coercion and transfer to others who have not earned the confidence of consumers through voluntary production and exchange? Why is it that the honest businessperson is treated as a pariah while the lobbyist-enriched politician is hailed as a messianic savior? Passing through the fog of moralizing rhetoric and walking in the sunlight of reality reveals how 'greedy idolatry' is pervasive in the minds of those who wish to confiscate and redistribute, a hallmark of the socialist ethos. Nothing in Ephesians 5:5 legitimates violent state action or Christian support for socialist economic policies. Authoritarians who only take without themselves producing are guilty of avarice. Socialist redistribution inevitably makes an idol of the state. Christians must take Paul's teaching on 'greed as idolatry' seriously regardless of political persuasion. It's a condition of the heart from which most affluent modern Christians on the left and right suffer.

Ephesians 6:10-17: Not Against Flesh and Blood

Believers are called to imitate the crucified Christ, particularly his rejection of violence. In Ephesians, Paul portrays Jesus as the king over all creation. In Ephesians 6:10-17, Paul implores believers to stand firm in the fight against God's enemies. The passage opens as follows: "*Finally, be strong in the Lord and in the strength of His might. Put on the full armor of God, so that you will be able to stand firm against the schemes of the devil. For our struggle is not against flesh and blood, but against the rulers, against the powers, against the world forces of this darkness, against the spiritual*

---

103. Mises, *Human Action*, pp. 270-273

104. Mises, *Human Action*, p. 271

forces of wickedness in the heavenly places"[105]. In 6:12 Paul uses the familiar terms *arche*, "*rulers*", and *exousia*, "*powers*", which he employed earlier in the letter in his lists of forces over which Jesus reigns. To this he adds the term *kosmokrator*, "*world forces*", a word occasionally used with reference to pagan gods in magical texts.[106] The term *arche* is ambiguous in this context; while it generally refers to political powers in Greek texts Paul wants to emphasise that the church is standing firm not against flesh and blood but spiritual powers. Attempts to politicize this passage cut against the evidence, as Schreiner wisely comments, "*Paul clearly believed that there were invisible demonic powers and beings that oppress and stand against believers*"[107].

Paul instructs believers on how to fight against these powers in 6:13-17: "*Therefore, take up the full armor of God, so that you will be able to resist in the evil day, and having done everything, to stand firm. Stand firm therefore, having girded your loins with truth, and having put on the breastplate of righteousness, and having shod your feet with the preparation of the gospel of peace; in addition to all, taking up the shield of faith with which you will be able to extinguish all the flaming arrows of the evil one. And take the helmet of salvation, and the sword of the Spirit, which is the word of God*". The church is to stand against evil forces, but not with physical weapons. Paul's imagery reflects the equipment of a Roman soldier which the Ephesians wield in defense against enemy powers. The church isn't portrayed in this text as waging a military offensive, as Jipp notes: "*There is no need . . . for the church to triumph over its enemies—simply a need to resist them . . . given that they are the same enemies the Messiah has already defeated*"[108]. There is an ongoing war between God's enemies and the church which will culminate in the final eschatological victory of Christ over all enemies forever, in language reminiscent of 1 Corinthians 15:24-26.[109] The church, over whom Christ is the head, must resolve not to give in to the forces of darkness.

It is also quite possible that Paul issues this instruction to circumvent a revolutionary reading of Ephesians. It might be tempting for some of Paul's audience, particularly those facing social ostracization, to hear Paul proclaiming the glorious reign of the ascended Lord as a warrant to take matters into their own hands and fight against other humans. Jesus isn't that kind of Messiah, and Paul's engagement with political authorities follows the pattern of Jeremiah 29:7. God will one day vindicate his people, but until the end believers are called to live at

---

105. Ephesians 6:10-12

106. Reid, *Principalities and Powers*, p. 749

107. Schreiner, *Handbook*, p. 291

108. Jipp, *Messianic Theology*, p. 224

109. Gorman, *Crucified Lord*, pp. 526-528

peace with non-believing neighbors. The church must embody the cruciform ethic of their Messiah and reject violence as an expression of honoring God. Whether this was on Paul's mind when he wrote or not, modern Christians seeking to draw principles from this text are greeted with familiar themes. Jesus is king. We are his people. God will rescue us in the end. We must obediently imitate Jesus by sacrificing for others, not by fighting. In resisting the evil forces which lurk just behind the veil, we must not allow ourselves to pick up arms and fight against other flesh-and-blood humans, even if they are the rulers who are already passing away which Jesus has already begun vanquishing.

CONCLUSION

1-2 Corinthians, Galatians, and Ephesians, despite their diverse contexts and intentions, offer a remarkably similar perspective on politics and economics which dovetail perfectly with Paul's thinking and the witness of other New Testament writings. Jesus is Lord over the faith-and-Spirit sealed church of Jews and Gentiles who are called to imitate the sacrificial model of their king. All rulers, both political and spiritual, are being defeated by a Messiah who already sits enthroned as Lord of all creation. Christians are to use their material possessions in service of others, sacrificially meeting real needs, and avoid the trappings of greed, a subtle form of idolatry. Radical generosity is the Christian standard. In the next chapter we will examine Philippians, Colossians, and 1-2 Thessalonians.

CHAPTER 14 | Philippians to Philemon

Exaltation, Glory, and Work Ethic

Our citizenship is in heaven, from which also we eagerly wait for a Savior, the Lord Jesus Christ.

Philippians 3:20

But if anyone does not provide for his own, and especially for those of his household, he has denied the faith and is worse than an unbeliever.

1 Timothy 5:8

INTRODUCTION

In Chapter 12 we analyzed Paul, his letters, and the ideas which animated him. In Chapter 13 we examined 1-2 Corinthians, Galatians, and Ephesians, taking a slower walk through the Corinthian epistles as an example of how our analysis of Paul works itself out in his letters. The baseline for understanding Paul has already been firmly established and from this point forward in our study of I have but one objective: review passages in his letters which are directly related to political and economic interpretations of the New Testament. We can now proceed at a much faster pace, stopping only to comment upon relevant texts. Philippians, Colossians, 1-2 Thessalonians, 1-2 Timothy, Titus, and Philemon contain several such passages of interest and, as we shall see, are all in complete continuity with the rest of Paul's epistles. While the various contexts of each letter give rise to differing political and economic questions, Paul's underlying responses to each are built upon the same foundation. Paul still believes that Jesus is Messiah, the church is God's family, the eschaton has been inaugurated, and God will ultimately vindicate his people. Paul says precisely this in Philippians, to which we will turn first.

PHILIPPIANS

Background: Friendship Amidst Opposition

In 31 BCE, Augustus refounded the city of Philippi as a Roman colony placed directly under his personal patronage. Many military veterans and other Romans were added to the colony, and many of its citizens received special rights and privileges due to the colony's close association with Rome. An important city in the Macedonian province, many gods and goddesses were worshipped in Philippi. Because of its status as a Roman colony, honors were also bestowed upon Roman emperors. Interestingly, Acts 16:13-16 suggests there may not have been a synagogue in the city due to its relatively small Jewish population. While not as large as Corinth, Philippi was located along the Via Egnatia, the most important road between Rome and the Greek east, and was but a few short miles away from the harbor city of Neapolis. Because of its strategic location, Philippi was an important and relatively prosperous Roman-facing colony.[1]

Acts 16:11-40 recounts Paul's stay in Philippi. Paul is hosted by a wealthy purple-fabric dealer named Lydia and manages to find himself in a lot of trouble after exorcising a spirit of divination from a slave girl. Her owners didn't appreciate Paul's deliverance and brought him before the courts, resulting in a beating and imprisonment. God rescues Paul and his associates from jail and, leveraging his citizenship against the Philippian authorities, restores his honor by having them escort him throughout the city. What is unique about Paul's time in Philippi is not the riotous response which accompanies it, which happened almost everywhere Paul went, but that it was not instigated by a single Jewish opponent. Paul runs afoul of the Philippian citizens and city officials, not his Jewish countrymen. When Paul encourages his audience to endure suffering at the hands of their opponents in Philippians 1:27-20 he likely has Roman colonists in mind.

At the end of a long chapter discussing the relationship between imperial divine honors and the Philippian church[2], Clint Burnett suggests the social dynamic behind the conflict between the Philippian church and the city's citizens: *"it was the Jewish countercultural or better non-Roman nature of the gospel—with its call for the abandonment of all forms of tradition and imperial divine honors and acceptance of the God of Israel and his Son Jesus the Messiah—and not its suffusion of supposed anti-imperial rhetoric that caused the suffering of Paul's converts in the colony"*[3].

---

1. Gorman, *Crucified Lord*, pp. 413-414

2. Burnett, *Imperial Divine Honors*, pp. 58-105

3. Burnett, *Imperial Divine Honors*, p. 104

While the church was not actively anti-imperial, publicly rejecting and antago-
nizing the imperial cult, its commitment to Jesus resulted in the withholding of
honors, a socially insensitive (from the perspective of non-believing Philippians)
and unacceptable practice. While abstaining from divine honors might certainly
be interpreted as a 'political' act, it was more likely understood as a betrayal of
Philippians colonial culture. The modern distinction between politics, religion,
and society fails to account for the socio-cultural dynamics at play in Philippi. For
our purposes, we must not see the conflict between the church and the community through the lens of anti-imperialism; that conception is much too broad and
imprecise. The beliefs and practices of the church are simply in tension with the
prevailing culture and they suffer persecution as a result.

Paul's letter to the Philippians is written to encourage the young church in
the midst of social opposition. To accomplish this task, Paul writes a 'friendship
letter', an epistolary style common in antiquity which was designed to strengthen
a friendly relationship *in absentia*.[4] Friendship was serious business in the Greco-
Roman world, and many philosophers wrote on the topic. As Gordon Fee explains, the highest form of friendship was "*true friendship between virtuous people,
whose relationship is based on goodwill and loyalty (including trust)*"; this came with
mutual, almost contractual obligations between friendly parties, including the
sharing of common enemies.[5] Paul's references to opponents in 1:15-17 and 1:28
is a rhetorical strategy intended to solidify the bonds of friendship between himself and the Philippian church. The letter both begins and ends with a statement
of mutual solidarity; in 1:12-26, Paul appeals to his current imprisonment. Just
as the Philippian church is under social duress, Paul is sitting in a Roman prison.
While the exact time and location of Paul's incarceration is debated by scholars[6],
Paul's captivity is an illustration of the shared struggles both him and his audience
are experiencing as a result of the gospel. In the same way that Paul's imprisonment has "*turned out for the greater progress of the gospel*"[7], the Philippians will be
proven right on the day of Christ's return[8]. As friends Paul and the Philippian
church not only share in suffering but also in material resources. Paul praises the
Philippians in 4:15-20 for financially assisting him above and beyond any other
church. They were one of the generous Macedonian communities Paul references

---

4. Fee, Gordon. 1999. *Philippians*. InterVarsity Press. pp. 13-15

5. Fee, *Philippians*, pp. 15-17

6. Gorman, *Crucified Lord*, pp. 417-418

7. Philippians 1:12

8. Philippians 1:28

in 2 Corinthians 8:1-6 and their openhanded expression of friendship towards Paul did not go unappreciated.

Despite the rosy tone of Paul's Philippian correspondence, genuine problems lurk just below the surface. The first major issue is, quite obviously, the challenge of persecution. Paul repeatedly discusses the final trump of God's people throughout the letter in passages such as 1:27-30, 3:20-21, and 4:19-20. The infamous (and pre-Pauline) Christ hymn in 2:6-11, discussed extensively above and given a brief contextual treatment below, is incorporated into Philippians as a calculated attempt to remind the church that Jesus is already Lord of all, including their opponents.[9] Paul is also aware that persecution might lead to internal divisions. While it is difficult to tell if there was active dissension in the church or if Paul, perhaps reflecting on the Corinthian correspondence, is worried about potential division, much of the letter, particularly 1:27-2:1,8 serves as an exhortation to unity. This is accomplished by emulating the sacrificial attitude of Christ.[10] Within this context there are two passages in particular which are of interest for our analysis of political themes in the New Testament.

God Highly Exalted Him: Philippians 2:5-11

Without a doubt one of the most powerful passages in the Pauline corpus, Philippians 2:5-11 includes a hymn which most likely predates his letter. We have already spent a considerable amount of time on this passage, detailing its radiant christological and ethical ramifications. The preformed hymn itself comprises 2:6-11 with 2:5 serving as an introductory statement, contextualizing it within the rhetorical flow of Philippians. The immediate literary context is Philippians 1:27-2:18 where Paul exhorts the church to maintain unity by serving one another. The cruciform communal bonds of the Philippian church enables them to overcome external pressure and avoid internal fragmentation. Jesus is presented as the sacrificial king who because of his humility was exalted to rule over creation. Christians are to imitate Christ; the NASB translation of 2:5 reads: *"Have this attitude in yourselves which was also in Christ Jesus"*, and the Greek can literally be rendered *"have the mind of Christ"*[11]. The mind of Christ is known through his double condescension in the first half of the hymn found in 2:6-8. Not only did Jesus exist *"in the form of God"* and yet did not *"grasp"* or hold on to it by *"Being found in appearance as a man"*, he also *"humbled Himself by becoming obedient to*

---

9. Fee, *Philippians*, pp. 28-31

10. Fee, *Philippians*, pp. 31-33

11. Fee, *Philippians*, pp. 91-92

the point of death, even death on a cross". Possessing the divine status, Jesus empties himself, becomes a man, and dies a shameful death on a Roman cross.[12] Believers, according to Paul, should have this attitude or 'mind' towards one another.

Christ's humiliation seems like a defeat but is in fact a prerequisite for his glorification. 2:9-11, beginning with *"For this reason"*, portrayed the humiliated, self-emptying, crucified Jesus being exalted above all creation. The passage is worth quoting again: *"For this reason also, God highly exalted Him, and bestowed on Him the name which is above every name, so that at the name of Jesus every knee will bow, of those who are in heaven and on earth and under the earth, and that every tongue will confess that Jesus Christ is Lord, to the glory of God the Father"*. The hymn's logic is that of revolutionary reversal. The phrase *"highly exalted"*, including the Greek preposition *hyper*, is often used by Paul to express magnification and excess; in this passage Paul is quite literally saying that Jesus was exalted by God to the highest degree possible.[13] Paul also alludes to Isaiah 45:23 (*"every knee will bow"*), a passage which in context refers to the restoration of Israel and the submission of all nations to Israel's God. The implication of Philippians 2, especially considering Paul's exalted christology, is that Christ is currently highly exalted over all creation and, in the end everyone, including those who are persecuting the Philippians, will be forced to bow the knee and confess Jesus as Lord.[14]

The hymn must not be divorced from its epistolary context. While the content of the hymn is about the humiliation and exaltation of Jesus Christ, its *function* within Paul's rhetorical agenda is to address the two main concerns of his letter, namely persecution without and (potential?) conflict within. The exhortation to cultivate the mind of Christ, framing the hymn, presents Jesus as an example for believers to imitate. Those in Christ must sacrifice for others and, like Jesus, willingly embrace humility. This strengthens the church in the midst of persecution and ensures that the unity of God's family won't be compromised by division. The hymn also offers encouragement to the Philippians; even though they are being humiliated God will rescue them in the end. Because of Jesus's ascension and the inauguration of the eschatological age, the Philippians are already winning.

We have seen this logic straight through Acts and Paul. As in Jeremiah 29:7, the Philippians are not to take up arms against unbelievers but wait patiently and faithfully for the day of the Lord. The modern church, slavishly devoted to the political paradigm of authoritarian socialism, should look to Jesus as the exemplar for moral behavior. In a position of colossal power, Jesus humiliated himself for

---

12. Gorman, *Crucified Lord*, pp. 435-437

13. Fee, *Philippians*, p. 99

14. Fee, *Philippians*, pp. 98-102

the sake of others instead. Is it possible to have *"this attitude in yourselves which was also in Christ Jesus"* while advocating for secular politicians and bureaucrats to confiscate wealth and regulate behavior at the point of a gun? Paul seems to think Jesus will win even if the church has no political power or influence. Those who live by the sword will die by the sword. Believers can either lord it over others like the gentiles or follow the Lord of all creation who through his incarnation and crucifixion became the archetypical model for human behavior.

Our Citizenship is in Heaven: Philippians 3:20-21

Writing to a Roman colony where citizenship conferred special civic privileges and obligations, Paul's instruction to the Philippians in 3:20-21 might raise a few eyebrows: *"For our citizenship is in heaven, from which also we eagerly wait for a Savior, the Lord Jesus Christ; who will transform the body of our humble state into conformity with the body of His glory, by the exertion of the power that He has even to subject all things to Himself"*. For the Philippian church, their citizenship, *politeuma*, is in heaven, not granted by the Roman state. This isn't the first time Paul has addressed the question of citizenship in Philippians; in 1:27 Paul instructs the congregation to *"conduct yourselves in a manner worthy of the gospel of Christ"*. The Greek verb translated *"conduct"* is *politeuesthai*, which means to *"live as a citizen"*[15]. Victor Furnish argues that Paul's use of this public-facing verb is intentional: *"The apostle's choice of a recognizably political term points specifically to the civic, public context in which believers are called to live in a way that is appropriate to the gospel they have embraced"*[16]. Believers should not fear civic engagement so long as they don't compromise their values, a sentiment very much congruent with Jeremiah 29:7 and the concept of leveraged citizenship modeled after Paul in Acts. While I think Furnish posits an excessively robust model of civic engagement he rightly refutes any notion that Paul expects his congregations to withdraw from the world.[17] This doesn't dull the sharp edges of Philippians 3:20, however. Colonial citizenship is nothing compared with heavenly citizenship.

While the immediate context of 3:20-21 is 3:17-4:1, it fits tightly within the flow of thought in Philippians 3. The precise identity of Paul's circumcision-advocating opponents, the controversy which instigates Paul's response in Philippians 3, has come under debate in recent years. The traditional reading of 3:2-11 assumes that Paul is responding to Jews trying to impose circumcision upon Jesus-believing

---

15. Furnish, Victor. 2009. *The Moral Teaching of Paul.* 3rd ed. Abingdon Press. p. 143

16. Furnish, *Moral Teaching*, p. 143

17. See the discussion in Furnish, *Moral Teaching*, pp. 142-145

Gentiles. Novenson has persuasively argued, following the work of Mark Naos and others, that Paul actually has in mind Gentile agitators who are attempting to convince *other Gentiles* to embrace circumcision.[18] While I find Novenson's reasoning extraordinarily compelling (as I do with the many other provocative theories proposed in his book *Paul and Judaism at the End of History*), for our purposes it makes little difference. Paul fires back against the agitators, launches into a pronouncement on endurance in 3:12-16, and then asks his audience to *"follow his example"* in 3:17, imitating those who walk like Paul. In 3:18-19 Paul castigates *"enemies of the cross of Christ"*. Representative of the rhetoric one would expect in a friendship letter, Paul calls out his and the Philippian's common enemies. Whether these enemies are Philippian citizens persecuting the church or Paul's circumcision-agitating opponents from earlier in the chapter (even the accomplished exegete Fee is agnostic on the question[19]), the Philippians are to follow Paul's example, not their opponent's.

This leads directly to Paul's contention that the believer's true *"citizenship [politeuma* in Greek] *is in heaven, from which also we eagerly await a savior"*. Oakes perceptively connects Paul's use of *politeuma* with the ethical and communal questions addressed in Philippians: *"This must have evoked the idea of the Roman citizenship that was held by many of the people of Philippi, including, no doubt, a significant number of the Christians. Roman citizenship was supposed to define one's ethics. Paul proclaims heavenly citizenship that implies different ethics. For Christian Roman citizens this relocates their place of primary allegiance . . . This could itself help Paul's call for unity in the church"*[20]. As Oakes argues, the Philippian church included both Roman citizens and non-citizens, and, ala Galatians 3:28, Paul is showing how the identity of 'citizen' is relativized in Christ; those with Roman citizenship are in no better position than those without.[21] The eschatological element of Paul's words, already preemptively staged in 2:9-11, is predicated on the return of Jesus. It is in effect a very real critique of those persecuting the church: *"It means the final subjugation of all the "powers" to him as well, especially those responsible for the present affliction of God's people"*[22]. Because Jesus is in control and the Philippians have a citizenship which is in heaven, Paul can confidently ask them to *"stand firm in the Lord"*[23].

---

18. Novenson, *End of History*, pp. 91-96

19. Fee, *Philippians*, p. 163

20. Oakes, *Empire*, p. 192

21. Oakes, *Empire*, p. 192

22. Fee, *Philippians*, p. 166

23. Philippians 4:1

The Philippians are commanded to be good citizens. Their words and actions should reflect the cruciform Lord who rules over all creation. They are not expected to refrain from social interactions or civic engagement; as Paul modeled *in the city of Philippi* in Acts 16 believers may sometimes need to leverage their citizenship in order to advance the gospel. But just like the status of Jew and Greek, male and female, or slave and free, Roman citizenship is divested of its social significance. Believers may suffer at the hands of political authorities and the citizens who support them, but God will put everything right in the end. Nationalism as we know it today is a product of the nineteenth century and many western Christians place national identity above Christian identity. There is no reading of Philippians 3:20 which legitimates our obsession with nationality. Christians must learn to see themselves as members of Abraham's global family, independent of any particular state. Nor would Paul endorse world government, an arrangement which only escalates the problems of nationalism to a global scale. He is admonishing Christians who serve Jesus to reassess the value of their national identity. If Jesus is king and we are his people, the political details will take care of themselves.

Colossians

Background: Some Kind of False Teaching

The city of Colossae, unlike Corinth or Thessalonica, was not a Roman colony. Situated in the Lycus River valley in the province of Asia, a major east-west trade route ran through the city, which was also surrounded by fertile farmland. Its population consisted of Phrygian natives, Greeks, and a large population of Jews whose ancestors had been relocated to the city by the Seleucids in the 200s BCE. Because of Colossae's cultural diversity, "*The possibility of religious syncretism—the fusion of beliefs and practices from diverse traditions—was perhaps even stronger here than elsewhere in Paul's polytheistic world*"[24]. It appears that Paul himself had never personally visited Colossae (in 2:1 he writes "*for all those who have not personally seen my face*", a likely reference to the local believing assembly) and that the church was established by Paul's associate Epaphras, who receives credit for founding the church in Colossians 1:7 and 4:12.

The occasion of Paul's letter seems to be the rise of false teachers in the church, perhaps from some in the community who were promoting ideas which were antithetical to the gospel. Colossians 2:8-23 is an extended critique of false teaching in which Paul warns the Colossian church about those peddling false ideas: "*See to

---

24. Gorman, *Crucified Lord*, p. 472

it that no one takes you captive through philosophy and empty deception, according to the transition of men, according to the elementary principles of the world, rather than according to Christ". What, exactly, were these false teachers propagating? We have no idea. In his introductory section Schreiner includes a humorous anecdote in which one biblical scholar suggested that there were forty-four different views on the identity of the false teachers in the secondary literature. While Schreiner himself leans in the direction of misguided Jewish mysticism, he acknowledges that the precise identification of this group is an open question.[25] I offer no answer to this complex exegetical conundrum which makes little difference for our political reading of Colossians anyway.

Gorman's general take on the purpose of Colossians is apropos: "[Colossians] *appears to have been written for one purpose: to convince its recipients that Christ is sufficient for their spiritual liberation and life. They should therefore resist that temptation to engage in practices that purport to supplement, but actually supplant (as far as Paul is concerned), their participation in Christ's death and resurrection*"[26]. Good enough for me. As a part of Paul's rhetorical strategy he reassures the Colossians that Jesus is already enthroned over all creation and is head of the universal church. To this end, the language of Colossians is reminiscent of Ephesians, so much so that Paul even describes the eschatological incorporation of Gentiles as a "*mystery*" revealed in Christ.[27] As we will see, the very language of Jesus's authority Paul employs in Colossians is directly paralleled in his Ephesian epistle. The political consequences of both letters are identical.

Disarming the Rulers and Authorities: Colossians 1:15-20 and 2:8-15

Within the context of opposition to false teaching, the function of Colossians, Paul issues two profound comments regarding the universal Lordship of Christ, each worthy of a monograph in their own right. Unfortunately space allows us but a few short paragraphs. Colossians 1:15-20 and 2:18-15 are two of the richest, most theologically intricate passages in the Pauline corpus. I will fail to do them adequate justice here. In Colossians Paul is absolutely certain about two truths: Jesus rules over everything and believers are inextricably connected to him through the church. Our lamentably fleeting romp through these elegant christological

---

25. Schreiner, *Handbook*, pp. 317-318

26. Gorman, *Crucified Lord*, pp. 471-472

27. Colossians 2:26-27

masterpieces will at least enable us to understand how Paul formulates these fundamental realities.

Paul twice mentions the kingdom of God in Colossians, once in 2:13 (leading into 1:15-20) and again towards the end of the letter in 4:11. The former, 2:13-14, reads as follows: *"For He rescued us from the domain of darkness, and transferred us to the kingdom of His beloved Son, in whom we have redemption, the forgiveness of sins"*. The liberation from darkness and the transference to the kingdom is something Paul claims *has already happened*, not an event which lays ahead somewhere in the hazy future. This is a classic example of inaugurated eschatology; the end has already broken into the present. Believers are *"transferred . . . to the kingdom of His beloved Son"*, a statement which would have fit comfortably within the Synoptic tradition. Robert Wall detects allusions to both the exodus and the restoration of the Davidic monarchy in this passage, and I think his argument is sound[28]. As Wall puts it, *"the church's entrance into God's kingdom has already taken place. The verb translated* rescue *(rhyomai) echoes the Old Testament stories of God's intervention to deliver an embattled Israel from its enemies, especially the master story of the exodus"*[29]. The people of God have been delivered by the son of David. Lest anyone think Paul had a different kingdom in mind, he refers to his Jewish associates as *"fellow workers for the kingdom of God"* in 4:11. The kingdom has already come, therefore the king must sit on the throne.

And so he does. Colossians 1:15-20 is an absolutely loaded passage. Like the remarkably similar declaration in Ephesians 1:20-23, Paul begins with a reflection of Jesus and ends with its implications for the church. Colossians 1:15-17 reads *"He is the image of the invisible God, the firstborn of all creation. For by Him all things were created, both in the heavens and on earth, visible and invisible, whether thrones or dominions or rulers or authorities—all things have been created through Him and for Him. He is before all things, and in Him all things hold together"*. The allusions to Genesis 1-2 are undeniable. The categories of creation (obviously), image, and authority are all present in the creation narratives, particularly Genesis 1:27-28. There is also a tradition in Judaism, derived from passages like Proverbs 3:19-20, that depict the personification of God's wisdom as playing a role in creation. Paul is no doubt appropriating these traditions and applying them to Jesus. Christ is over everything because he had a hand in creating it.[30] Everything, heaven and earth, visible and invisible, were created by Jesus. This immediately short-circuits

---

28. Wall, Robert. 1993. *Colossians and Philemon*. InterVarsity Press. pp. 58-61

29. Wall, *Colossians*, p. 59

30. Bruno, Chris, John Lee, and Thomas Schreiner. 2024. *The Divine Christology of the Apostle Paul*. InterVarsity Press. pp. 142-144

a spiritualized reading of the text which would reduce Christ's rule to a subjective metaphor. He created everything, and he is king over everything. The list of institutions which Jesus created should sound familiar to readers of Ephesians; forms of *kyriotes* (dominion), *arche* (rule), and *exousia* (authority) are used in both Colossians 1:16 and Ephesians 1:21. Added to this list is the plural form of *thronos*, "thrones", a reference to monarchical power predictably used to refer to God and the Messiah throughout the New Testament[31]. Jesus created everything and therefore has a right to rule over all, which has already begun to happen by virtue of his death, resurrection, and ascension.

In fact, the logic of new creation, fundamental to Paul's conception of inaugurated eschatology, is the presupposition of the hymn's second half, 1:18-20: "*He is also head of the body, the church; and He is the beginning, the firstborn from the dead, so that He Himself will come to have first place in everything. For it was the Father's good pleasure for all the fullness to dwell in Him, and through Him to reconcile all things to Himself, having made peace through the blood of His cross; through Him, I say, whether things on earth or things in heaven*". This text bears all the hallmarks of Pauline thought; eschatology, christology, and ecclesiology. The repetition of "*firstborn*" language, applied to Christ's hand in creation earlier in the hymn and his resurrection later, marks the transition from creation to new creation. He has "*first place in everything*" by virtue of his creative capacity and resurrection from the dead. As Bruno, Lee, and Schreiner put it, "*the repetition of the firstborn theme indicates a focus on new creation. Christ is not only the architect of the first creation, but through his resurrection from the dead, he is also the originator of the new creation*"[32]. "Christ" has lost none of its Messianic significance in Colossians; in fact, Paul seems to be amplifying it, as "*the fullness . . . dwell*[s] *in Him*" signifies Jesus's identification with Israel's God. While the thesis of this book does not hinge upon divine christology, it sure does seem like that's the direction Paul takes in Colossians 1.[33] Paul's main point, regardless of the christological particularities, is that Jesus is preeminent over creation.

This includes especially the church. Paul characteristically refers to the church as "*saints and faithful brethren*" in Colossians 1:2, and will follow 1:15-20 with an exposition of the identity of the church in 1:21-29. Christ, rescuing all from the domain of darkness, has brought believing Jews and Gentiles into his family. As "*head of the body, the church*", the community is in a privileged relationship with the one true King. As Paul exhorts the community to faithful practice in

---

31. See, for example, Luke 1:32, Acts 2:30, Matthew 23:22, Hebrews 12:2, and Revelation 3:21.

32. Bruno, Lee, and Schreiner, *Divine Christology*, p. 148

33. See the helpful discussion in Bruno, Lee, and Schreiner, *Divine Christology*, pp. 150-155

Colossians 3, he describes the renewed church as one *"in which there is no distinction between Greek and Jew, circumcised and uncircumcised, barbarian, Scythian, slave and freemean, but Christ is all and in all . . .* [you are] *those who have been chosen of God"*[34]. Both inaugurated eschatology and exalted christology shape the way in which the church engages with the outside world. Wall's observations are assuredly correct: *"As God's new creation, the faith community forsakes the old order but does not live in isolation from it. Rather, believers are called to live in the cultural mainstream as a new humanity and to call into question the old structures of "this present evil age" by its life with Christ and its proclamation of him. The church's incarnation of God's truth in deed and word would have absolutely no effect on other people if believers separated themselves from the lost"*[35]. The church is, in essence, embodying the spirit of Jeremiah 29:7 in light of eschatology and christology. Members of the kingdom must testify to the rule of their king.

Paul will soon revisit the universal lordship of Christ in Colossians 2:8-15, a passage in which he begins directly challenging false teachers. No one should be deluded by these false teachers because they contradict Christ, in whom *"all the fullness of Deity dwells in bodily form"*[36]. Paul applies this christological insight to the church in the next verse, Colossians 2:10: *"and in him you have been made complete, and He is the head over all rule and authority"*. Those who are faithful to the Messiah are complete precisely because their Messiah is over all rule and authority. Again we find Paul using forms of *arche* and *exousia*, demonstrating his reign over *all* other authorities. Just a few verses later, in Colossians 2:15, Paul will yet again assert the all-encompassing authority of Christ: *"When He had disarmed the rulers and authorities* [forms of *arche* and *exousia*, unsurprisingly], *He made a public display of them, having triumphed over them through him"*. While Wall interestingly suggests Paul's words may be a jab at the false teachers he is opposing in Colossae[37], the tight linguistic affinity with Ephesians, Colossians 1:16, and Colossians 2:10 suggest that Paul has all of creation in mind. Conceptually and linguistically Colossians 2:15 is strikingly similar to 1 Corinthians 2:6-8 and 2 Corinthians 2:14. In the former passage Paul denounces the *"rulers of this age, who are passing away"* because they didn't understand the wisdom of God. If they had, they wouldn't have crucified Jesus. I find it difficult to see the referent in 1 Corinthians 2:6-8 as anything other than political authorities, and the allusion to resurrection combined with triumph over rulers suggests Paul's logic is directed at least in part against political leaders in

---

34. Colossians 3:11-12

35. Wall, *Colossians*, p. 72

36. Colossians 2:9

37. Wall, *Colossians*, p. 118

Colossians 2:10 as well. Outside of 2 Corinthians 2:14, Colossians 2:10 is the only other place in Paul's letters where he uses the language of *thriambeuo*, the technical term for a Roman military parade. He employs the term in 2 Corinthians to describe the supremacy of God's victory in Christ (and perhaps parody the pretensions of Roman power) and in the context of Colossians it appears Paul is making a similar point. Anyone who would perpetuate false teachings which denigrate Christ and *"the word of truth, the gospel"*[38] must be roundly refuted. The church derives its identity from the man who through resurrection and ascension disarmed the rulers and powers of the domain of darkness. Because of his victory, believers have *in the present* been transferred to the kingdom of light.

Paul expects believers to accept his exalted christology. The universal Lordship of Jesus, including his status as head of the church, is not a theological option. Those who would seek to undermine Paul's exalted, Messianic christology are accused of peddling the *"traditions of men"*, and there are few 'traditions of men' which have a more powerful and perverse hold on the church than modern authoritarian socialism. Christ disarmed the rulers and authorities not by taking up arms, lobbying for state intervention, or holding 'democratic' (irony intended) elections. Although he possessed the fullness of God Jesus willingly accepted crucifixion and by doing so overthrew every power in the heavens and on the earth, established God's kingdom, and inaugurated the new creation. There can be no biblical political theology which doesn't reckon with Paul's eschatological, christological, or ecclesiological logic, and Colossians is a pristine example of the categorical confluence of these critical concepts. How biblical scholars such as Horsley and Wight read texts like these and come to the conclusion that more money, power, and, of course, monopolistic violence should be ceded to the secular state is beyond me. When Paul claims Jesus is above all authority and believers belong to him, I take Paul at his word. Philippians and Colossians have the potential to correct deficient modern conceptualizations of political power. We now turn to the Thessalonian epistles, two texts which challenge our comfortable contemporary economic presuppositions.

1 THESSALONIANS

Background: Persecution and Eschatology

There are two passages in the Thessalonian letters, 1 Thessalonians 4:9-12 and 2 Thessalonians 3:6-13, which serve as the driving force of our analysis. These are,

---

38. Colossians 1:5

in my view, two of the most significant yet underappreciated 'economic' texts in the New Testament. Paul assumes his exalted christology, exclusivist ecclesiology, inaugurated eschatology, and cruciform ethic throughout the letters, and his instructions on work and charity must be understood within that context. Thessalonica, named after Alexander the Great's half sister, was capital of the province of Macedonia and the only port city built on the Via Egnatia, making it a major center for trade and travel. It was not a Roman colony and had its own government, based on the city's Greek heritage. Thessalonica hosted temples to many gods, including the imperial cult, and was a culturally diverse city.[39] It was precisely the sort of place an apostle like Paul might run headfirst into trouble.

According to Acts 17:1-15 that is more or less exactly what happened. Paul enters the city and begins proclaiming his gospel in the Synagogue, convincing many and enraging others. Some of the Jews formed a mob and physically hauled certain believers before the city authorities, accusing them of acting *"contrary to the decrees of Caesar, saying that there is another king, Jesus"*[40]. The authorities are unconvinced and release them. Paul then travels to Berea where he receives a much warmer reception, but some of the Jews from Thessalonica show up in Berea and begin harassing him there. Paul leaves Berea and heads to Athens, away from the irate Jewish mob. While Paul's flight to Athens may have temporarily spared him from trouble, it appears from the text of 1 Thessalonians that the angry opponents of Paul promptly directed their fury at the nascent believing community established by Paul and his associates during their short stay in Thessalonica.

Two themes take center stage in 1 Thessalonians: persecution and eschatology. Paul commends the Thessalonians for receiving *"the word in much tribulation with the joy of the Holy Spirit"* in 1:6. Just as Paul and his associates had faced stiff opposition in Thessalonica and the Judean churches to which the Thessalonians had (or would, depending on the letter's dating) contribute a substantial gift[41], Paul's audience *"endured the same sufferings at the hands of your own countrymen"*[42]. Paul's tone throughout the letter, in spite of the circumstances, remains optimistic. He assumes the Thessalonians are staying faithful to the gospel despite suffering as a result of proclaiming it. He opens the letter with a proud thanksgiving for their endurance: *"We give thanks to God always for all of you, making mention of you in our prayers; constantly bearing in mind your work of faith and labor of love and*

---

39. Gorman, *Crucified Lord*, pp. 146-147

40. Acts 17:7

41. 1 Thessalonians 2:1-16; see also 2 Corinthians 8:1-6.

42. 1 Thessalonians 2:14

steadfastness of home in our Lord Jesus Christ in the presence of our God and Father"[43]. Fortitude under duress shapes Paul's rhetorical strategy, as Karl Donfreid explains: "*1 Thessalonians is about a God who is present among his elect and suffering people and about a God who is leading them to their promised salvation. The theological themes found in the letter are a response to situations created by persecution and martyrdom as well as to the problem of living the Christian life in the midst of a pagan culture*"[44]. It is within this context that Paul's frequent appeal to the return of Jesus functions.

Some in the Thessalonian church had unfortunately misunderstood Paul's teachings regarding the second coming of Jesus. The famous eschatological passage of 1 Thessalonians 4:13-18 (which really continues through 5:11) begins with a recognition of confusion: "*But we do not want you to be uniformed, brethren, about those who are asleep, so that you will not grieve as do the rest who have no hope*". Implied in Paul's rhetoric is uncertainty about the return of Christ. Numerous theories have been proposed regarding the precise dynamics of this misunderstanding, and entire eschatological systems have been constructed upon suggested answers to those questions.[45] Little of that conversation concerns us here. Paul is still operating within a framework of inaugurated eschatology, and he concludes his eschatological instruction with an exhortation to encourage one another. Jesus will return, no need to worry about that. Besides this section of 1 Thessalonians, Paul constantly reminds his audience that Jesus will soon return, providing them with hope in the midst of persecution. Although chapter divisions are artificial impositions on the text, every chapter concludes with a reminder that Christ will return. 1 Thessalonians 1:9-10 is paradigmatic: "*For they themselves report about us what kind of a reception we had with you, and how you turned to God from idols to serve a living and true God, and to wait for His Son from heaven, whom He raised from the dead, that is Jesus, who rescues us from the wrath to come*". Paul's subsequent appeal to the return of Jesus in 2:19, 3:13, 4:13-5:11, and 5:23 all follow the same script. The final reference to Christ's return in 5:23 is a beautiful encapsulation of Paul's objectives in 1 Thessalonians: "*Now may the God of peace Himself sanctify you entirely; and may your spirit and soul and body be preserved complete, without blame at the coming of our Lord Jesus Christ*". The Thessalonians must, and indeed will by the power of God, continue to persevere through intense social opposition knowing that Jesus will soon return. Gorman summarizes 1 Thessalonians perfectly: "*the sure hope of the Lord's coming provides the context within which the countercultural ('holy', 'sanctified,' or 'set apart') life of faith and love that has led to persecution makes*

---

43. 1 Thessalonians 1:2-3

44. Donfried, Karl. 2002. *Paul, Thessalonica, and Early Christianity*. Eerdmans. p. 120

45. Schreiner, *Handbook*, pp. 347-348

sense. Hope makes holiness worthwhile"[46]. There is one specific ethical injunction which frames Paul's commentary on work in 1 Thessalonians 4:9-12. It is the command to imitate him.

You Became Imitators of Us: 1 Thessalonians 1:6-7 and 2:9-12

We have already discussed the mimetic dimension of Greco-Roman ethics adopted and reworked by Paul. Cornelis Bennema, correctly explaining Paul's primary objective in the Thessalonian epistles as "*how to live in view of persecution and the Parousia* [second coming]", makes the statistical observation that half of Paul's uses of the Greek term for mimesis (*mimestha*) and a quarter of his references to the Greek word translated 'example', 'pattern', or 'model' (*tupos*) occur in 1 and 2 Thessalonians.[47] Imitation, then, is the key to unlocking Paul's ethical framework in the Thessalonian correspondence. Two passages in particular, 1 Thessalonians 1:6-7 and 2:9-16, are particularly significant for interpreting Paul's memetic ethics in the letter. Although 1 Thessalonians (and perhaps 2 Thessalonians as well) were likely written before 1 Corinthians, there is a striking parallel between the two Thessalonian texts and 1 Corinthians 9:1-18. In that passage Paul holds himself up as an example of cruciform sacrifice to the Corinthians. Although Paul, as a minister of the gospel, has a right to make his living from his ministry, he made the choice to continue in his trade so as not to be a financial burden on the Corinthian church. Paul sacrifices his right and chooses work as an expression of self-emptying love, emulating the disposition of Christ. While the specific functional context of the 1 Corinthians 8-10 is the eating of meat sacrificed to idols (and subsequent temptation of 'weak', idol-wary believers), Paul in 1 Thessalonians presents himself maintaining theological and moral integrity in spite of resistance.

Paul writes in 1 Thessalonians 1:6-7 that the church is already following his example and are, in fact, serving as an example to others: "*You also became imitators of us and of the Lord, having received the word in much tribulation with the joy of the Holy Spirit, so that you became an example to all the believers in Macedonia and in Achaia*". Just as Paul and the Lord Jesus himself endured suffering and hardship, the Thessalonians received Paul's word (the gospel) under duress but with joy, setting a precedent for other believers in the region. Paul's reference to the province of Achaia is most likely the basis of 2 Corinthians 8:1-6. Carrying on the same line of thought in 1 Thessalonians 2:9-16, Paul reminds the Thessalonians of the high moral standard set by him and his associates, serving as a model by the the church

---

46. Gorman, *Crucified Lord*, p. 151

47. Bennema, *Imitation*, p. 240

would "*walk in a manner worthy of the God who calls you into His own kingdom and glory*"[48], resulting in an imitation of the Judean churches who also suffered on behalf of the gospel. Of interest to our study, Paul chooses to emphasise one specific decision, echoing (or foreshadowing) 1 Corinthians 9, namely his own work ethic: "*For you recall, brethren, our labor and hardship, how working night and day so as not to be a burden to any of you, we proclaimed to you the gospel of God*", and, because of Paul's willingness to work, he can claim the moral high ground: "*You are witnesses, and so is God, how devoutly and uprightly and blamelessly we behaved towards you believers*"[49].

A curious practice to highlight. Paul's point is that he was willing to laboriously provide for his own needs so as not to be a financial impediment to the generous Thessalonian church; not only were they persecuted and impoverished, they also desired to give. Paul honors their charitable disposition by paying his own way, an example which he hopes will motivate the Thessalonians to continue persevering in faithfulness. This strikes at the core of Paul's mimetic instruction in the Thessalonian epistles: "*the actions of the Thessalonians involve the acceptance of the gospel, the observance of the life of Paul and the Judean churches, and the emulation of their lifestyle, corporately and publicly resulting in persecution . . . If we remember that Paul's purpose in writing to the Thessalonians is a moral one, we start to see that imitation is in service of Paul's ethics. In this case, example and imitation are vital aspects of Paul's strategy for the moral formation of the Thessalonian church, and Paul's ethics here is specifically mimetic ethics*"[50]. Paul, boisterous and confident as he was, isn't blowing smoke or showing off. Paul genuinely asserts that his example should serve as a concrete ethical model for the church, and by providing himself as a moral exemplar he is attempting to either maintain (where the Thessalonians are already emulating him) or modify (where they fall short) the community's morality. Whatever Paul says about work, he without question portrays himself as the gold standard of a cruciform laborer. His personal behavior is a crucial subtext for the instructions he issues in 1 Thessalonians 4:9-12.

Work With Your Hands: 1 Thessalonians 4:9-12

Paul expects his communities to work, as he states plainly and without qualification in 1 Thessalonians 4:9-12: "*Now as to the love of the brethren, you have no need for anyone to write to you, for you yourselves are taught by God to love one another;*

---

48. 1 Thessalonians 2:12

49. 1 Thessalonians 2:9-10

50. Bennema, *Imitation*, pp. 248-249

for indeed you do practice it toward all the brethren who are in all Macedonia. But we urge you, brethren, to excel still more, and to make it your ambition to lead a quiet life and attend to your own business and work with your hands, just as we commanded you, so that you will behave properly toward outsiders and not be in any need". Paul isn't speaking into a vacuum; this terse yet dense exhortation is set within a tight rhetorical context. Between 1 Thessalonians 4:3-5:11, Paul addresses three discrete issues. 4:3-8 is a commentary on purity, most likely with respect to sex, 4:9-12 relates to work, and 4:13-5:11, in many ways the denouement of Paul's epistle, deals with eschatological misconceptions. For our exegetical purposes, the specifics of Paul's instructions about sex and eschatology are mostly irrelevant, with one small exception. Paul frames this paranetic section, introducing the underlying themes of the rhetorical unit, in 3:12-13: *"may the Lord cause you to increase and abound in love for one another, and for all people, just as we also do for you; so that He may establish your hearts without blame in holiness before our God and Father at the coming of our Lord Jesus with all His saints"*, and in 4:1-2, Paul states that these instructions will further enable to the church to *"walk and please God"*, following *"commandments [issued] by the authority of the Lord [!] Jesus"*. Paul elucidates the function of each proceeding question in 4:3-5:11. This should cause the church to increase in love for each other, as well as *those outside the church* (*"all people"*), just as Paul has done for them (note the subtle allusion to mimetic ethics) so that they will be established in holiness (*hagiosyne*, of course) before Jesus returns. Put simply: Paul is talking about eclessial ethics in light of eschatology. As Schreiner rightly notes, Paul isn't unhappy with the Thessalonians; they are already faithful. Paul is hoping they will grow even further.[51]

This brings us to Paul's injunctions about work in 1 Thessalonians 4:9-12. Paul begins his exhortation with a positive affirmation of the Thessalonians' love for others, stating at the end of 4:10 that he wants them *"to excel still more"*. The crux of this passage is 4:11-12, which is worth repeating in full: *"make it your ambition to lead a quiet life and attend to your own business and work with your hands, just as we commanded you, so that you will behave properly towards outsiders and not be in any need"*. There are three practices Paul encourages here: leading a quiet life, attending to one's own business, and working with one's own hands. This is based on what Paul has *already commanded*, with the outward-facing goal of social propriety and the internal goal of poverty avoidance. Gorman recognizes the potential threat to integrity associated with occupational idleness: *"When believers deliberately do not work, they fail to love both outsiders and fellow believers by bearing poor witness to outsiders and imposing a burden on those within the church who would*

---

51. Schreiner, *Handbook*, p. 345

feel responsible for them. The church's practical assistance should go only to the truly needy, while idlers should get a job"[52]. I agree with every word, and even Gorman's surface-level analysis fits nicely within the New Testament's larger framework of radical, cruciform charity and personal moral responsibility. In theory we could cap our analysis here, but the social dynamics at play in this passage are vitally important for drawing modern principles.

In Chapter 5 I discussed the prevalence of the patron-client system in Roman society. Characterized by 'benefaction', gifts of money and food were bestowed upon lower-status 'clients' by higher-status (usually *much* higher status) 'patrons' with the goal of producing a tight connection of social obligations which primarily benefited the patron. Houses and even entire cities were constructed to accommodate the daily distribution of benefaction and ensure that high-status patrons always had a faithful (and financially dependent) social following. The patron-client system and its distribution of benefactions is the social context informing Paul's instructions on work in 1-2 Thessalonians. Given Paul's exclusivist ecclesiology where the family of Abraham is defined by faith and the Spirit, Paul would naturally reject the Thessalonian believer being tied as a client to a non-believing benefactor. Apparently there were some in the Thessalonian church caught in the web of patron-client obligations as clients: "*This relationship would have been the one reason why some citizens apart from the rich in the city of Thessalonica, or in any other city in the empire, did not have to work*"[53]. Paul is commanding the Thessalonians to work, implying that some are not. Historically this passage has been interpreted within the context of eschatological misunderstanding; the supposed imminence of Christ's return compelled some to stop working. Bennema, following John Barclay, suggests that patronage is not the context for idleness but rather an abandonment of labor to preach the gospel ahead of the parousia.[54] I do not think, however, that eschatological readings (whatever we make of how eschatological misunderstandings translated to unemployment) are in conflict with patronage readings and that the two together likely contributed to the situation Paul is addressing in the Thessalonian epistles.

Winter's thesis corresponds perfectly with our analysis of Pauline ecclesiology: "*Paul would not endorse a Christian continuing as the recipient of private benefactions by way of the parasitic client relationship with a patron . . . even though it was widely accepted in the secular world as an important element in the social fabric of*

---

52. Gorman, *Crucified Lord*, p. 159

53. Winter, *Welfare*, p. 42

54. Bennema, *Imitation*, pp. 250-252

public life"[55]. How could a person who placed their allegiance in the Lord Jesus Christ possibly be in a dependent relationship with a non-believing, wealthy patron, perhaps someone who would even endorse the social policies which led to the Thessalonian persecution? As we learned from the Corinthian correspondence, Paul draws a hard line between insiders and outsiders; Christians cannot (and absolutely should not) abandon relationships with non-believers but neither should they be dependent upon them, either financially or politically. Paul also expects, short of sporadic bouts of extreme poverty such as faced by the Judean community, that Christians place themselves in a position to provide for those who are in need. In the believing community, Paul flips the patron-client dynamic entirely on its head: *"Paul set out to change the established convention of the . . . relationship between a patron and his client. In doing this he was initiating in Gentile regions a radical social ethic which he regarded as binding on Christians. The secular client must now become a private Christian benefactor"*[56]. As Paul himself says in Acts 20:35, *"It is more blessed to give than to receive"*. By working, believers are not a burden on others (which is completely antithetical with Paul's cruciform ethic of sacrifice) and can place themselves in a position to provide for those who are truly in need.

The language Paul employs in 1 Thessalonians 4:11 of *"lead*[ing] *a quiet life and attend*[ing] *to your own business and work*[ing] *with your own hands"* all have parallels in Greco-Roman texts which discuss patronage and related institutions. Clients often had their own ambitions which were satisfied by the benefaction of patrons, usually in exchange for political support, and noisy enterprise which would have certainly compromised the commitment to Jesus as universal Lord and freighted the church with unnecessary political baggage. Minding one's own business includes *not* minding the business of patrons (or anyone outside of the church for that matter), and working with one's hands is contrasted with receiving handouts.[57] That benefactions were often dispensed for the purpose of procuring political support from patrons should certainly not be overlooked; it is hard to see Paul endorsing a tight political alliance between those within and those outside of the believing community. For Paul, believers must find their identity in the church and concern themselves primarily with the health of God's family. As Mell comments, *"the ethical exhortation gives the believing householder the household goal of concentrating solely on the (daily) necessary tasks of his own household to secure the sustenance of its members"*[58]. Jesus must come before any political loyalties, espe-

---

55. Winter, *Welfare*, p. 42

56. Winter, *Welfare*, p. 42

57. Winter, *Welfare*, pp. 48-51

58. Mell, *Gospel as Letter*, p. 252

cially parasitic client relationships, and by rejecting benefactions, taking up work, and minding their own business the Thessalonian church will *"behave properly towards outsiders and not be in any need"*, the goal, according to 1 Thessalonians 4:12, of Paul's instructions. Furnish understands the positive social consequences of Christian labor: *"extending love (practicing "good") towards outsiders means taking responsibility for one's needs without burdening others"*[59].

Paul himself has already set an example of working hard so as not to be a burden to the Thessalonians (2:9-12 is certainly the pretext for 5:9-12) and likely assumes that a properly ordered, independent church will avoid the ire of those seeking to persecute believers. Patronage comes with strings attached and believers, the family of Abraham, must not be connected through complex webs of social loyalty to those outside of the church. Even though the Greco-Roman elite looked down on manual labor as unbefitting for the upper classes, it was much more preferable than accepting benefactions. The principle writes itself: if at all possible, Christians should work and provide for themselves instead of relying on the charity of others. While this may be a temporary necessity (and unaccompanied by shame), any believer who makes it a permanent goal to live off of the productivity of others is living in direct contradiction of biblical teaching. Paul will make the point even more forcefully in 2 Thessalonians, to which we will now turn. Even after Paul's first letter, there are some in the Thessalonian community who simply didn't get it.

2 THESSALONIANS

Background: New Letter, Same Problems

It would appear as if the Thessalonians needed more of the same instruction. Paul opens the letter with a warm introduction, praising the church *"because your faith is greatly enlarged, and the love of each . . . towards one another grows ever greater . . . for your perseverance and faith in the midst of all your persecutions and afflictions which you endure . . . so that you will be considered worthy of the kingdom of God"*[60]. 2 Thessalonians 1:6-12 is a fiery reminder that God will punish those who are afflicting the church when Jesus returns, at which point all who obey him (including the longsuffering Thessalonian church) will be dramatically vindicated. Following this, Paul swiftly transitions to a new round of instructions about eschatology in 2:1-12, building upon what he said in his first letter to the church. He will turn

---

59. Furnish, *Moral Teaching*, p. 136

60. 2 Thessalonians 1:3-5

once again to the subject of work in 2 Thessalonians 3:6-13, encouraging, yet again, those who are not working to get a job. Everything in this passage logically follows 1 Thessalonians 4:9-12, and like the rest of 2 Thessalonians Paul is simply picking up where the first epistle left off and explaining his logic to them one more time. In fact, the problem surrounding work is already hinted at in 1 Thessalonians 5:14.

No Work, No Food: 2 Thessalonians 3:6-13

In 2 Thessalonians 3:10, Paul makes a bold statement: "*if anyone is not willing to work, then he is not to eat, either*". Talk about offending modern progressive sensibilities. The politically incorrect Paul, however, isn't having second thoughts about charity. In 1 Thessalonians 5:14, Paul asks the community to "admonish *the unruly*". The Greek term translated "*unruly*" is the plural adjective *ataktos*, which "*has a general sense of "disorderly, undisciplined" and occurs in the New Testament only in the Thessalonian correspondence and always in the context of work*"[61]. Bennema, after the quotation just cited, argues that in context it probably refers to frenzied activity which causes the Thessalonians to be dependent on others for a living. While he rejects the patron-client thesis, his analysis of *ataktos* is a fair description of the obligations which attend benefaction. Some in the congregation can correctly be described as *ataktos*, and Paul wants the church to hold them accountable. Apparently they weren't.

Paul will raise the issue again in 2 Thessalonians 3:6-13. His instructions are framed by the preceding material, which enables Paul to transition from his teachings about eschatology to his directives regarding work. In 2:13-15 Paul appeals to holiness language, reminding the Thessalonians that they are set apart by the Spirit, called through the gospel, and ought to stand firm to the traditions which were taught by Paul and his associates either in person or through letters; this passage yet again demonstrates the tight connection between faith and Spirit in Paul's mind. Paul will return to these 'traditions' in 3:6. 2:16-3:5 is a classic Pauline setup; Paul prays that God will "strengthen [the Thessalonian's] *hearts in every good work*" and "*direct your hearts into the love of God and the steadfastness of Christ*", Paul being assured "*that you are doing and will continue to do what we command*". What a polite way to tell someone they better listen or else. Paul's positive, nearly conciliatory tone will become much more direct and serious as he introduces his instructions on work.

---

61. Bennema, *Imitation*, p. 250

Paul uses the verbal and adverbial forms of *ataktos* at several strategic points in this passage. In 3:6 and 3:11 the NASB translates Paul's negative description of those who have elected not to work as "*unruly*" and "*undisciplined*" respectively. Even after Paul's first letter, some in the Thessalonian community were electing not to work. It is possible that those who were in parasitic patron-client relationships returned to their patrons (perhaps in response to an economic crisis), or, due to a misconception of eschatology, believers who were accustomed to unemployment were waiting for the return of Jesus and living off the charity of working Thessalonian Christians.[62] Either way, voluntary unemployment is the major issue Paul addresses in this passage. In contrast to the "*undisciplined*", Paul uses *ataktos* language in 3:7 to refer to himself as an example of someone who "*did not act in an undisciplined* [verbal form of *ataktos*] *manner among you*". How, exactly, did Paul avoid "*undisciplined*" behavior? By working. He becomes the model which those in Thessalonica should emulate. Instead of refusing to work, the undisciplined should imitate Paul and get a job.

The first half of Paul's exhortation reads as follows: "*Now we command you, brethren, in the name of our Lord Jesus Christ, that you keep away from every brother who leads an unruly life and not according to the tradition which you received from us. For you yourselves know how you ought to follow our example, because we did not act in an undisciplined manner among you, nor did we eat anyone's bread without paying for it, but with labor and hardship we kept working night and day so that we would not be a burden to any of you; not because we do not have the right to this, but in order to offer ourselves as a model for you, so that you would follow our example*"[63]. The Thessalonians are instructed to "*keep away*" from those described as *ataktos*, commanding them in the name of the Lord Jesus Christ. They are not following the "*tradition*" which they received from Paul, echoing Paul's previous instruction in 2:15 that they "*stand firm and hold to the traditions which you were taught*". Paul prefaces his argument with an appeal to tradition and describes the "*unruly*" as those who stand outside of the tradition.

Paul of course has in mind 1 Thessalonians 4:9-12, his discourse on work from the previous epistle, but the appeal to his own behavior in 2 Thessalonians 3:7-9 is also a part of the received tradition. In 1 Thessalonians 2:9-12 Paul recounts his own behavior among the Thessalonian church, "*working night and day so as not to be a burden to any of you*". This is clearly paralleled in 1 Corinthians 9:1-14 where Paul presents himself as a model of cruciform work. He sacrificially provides for himself so as not to be a burden on others. By appealing to the tradition and his

---

62. Winter, *Welfare*, pp. 53-57

63. 1 Thessalonians 3:6-9

own example, Paul is making a decisive point: the *ataktos* must find a job. Paul is putting his memetic teaching to work: "*Paul's lifestyle of self-giving (modeled on that of Christ) is the ethical template for mimesis in 1-2 Thessalonians . . . they should imitate the principle that one should work for a living and avoid becoming a burden to others, and this will, of course, look different for different people*"[64]. Whatever the *ataktos* do to support themselves, they must no longer live off the benefaction or charity of others. They are parasites, compromising the integrity of the church and refusing to sacrificially consider the needs of others. Their behavior is the reason for Paul's sharp warning to keep away from them.

Paul reaches the logical conclusion of his exhortation in 2 Thessalonians 3:9-13: "*For even when we were with you, we used to give you this order: if anyone is not willing to work, then he is not to eat, either. For we hear that some among you are leading an undisciplined* [adverbial form of *ataktos*] *life, doing no work at all, but acting like busybodies. Now such persons we command and exhort in the Lord Jesus Christ to work in quiet fashion and eat their own bread. But as for you, brethren, do not grow weary of doing good*". The climax of Paul's argument, based on previously given orders, is simple: no work, no food. Far from being callous to the plight of the poor, Paul envisions anyone engaged in parasitic financial relationships as both morally and theologically compromised, abandoning the principle of cruciformity and the sound instruction of Paul and his associates. Their behavior is anathema to Paul's entire gospel-centered, christologically-based conception of the people of God. Instead of seeking to benefit others, edifying the church and wisely witnessing to the pagan world which is persecuting them, they choose to impose a burden on other believers and should be held accountable. While Paul's sentiment is deeply offensive to moderns who are committed to a state monopoly on charity, it makes perfect sense within his own worldview. Not everyone deserves charity and believers should work to both support themselves and help others during genuine times of need.

What if some members of the Thessalonian church refuse to heed Paul's instructions? In 3:6 he asks the community to "*keep away*" from the *ataktos* brother, and he repeats this commandment even more forcefully as he concludes his exhortation in 3:14-15: "*If anyone does not obey our instruction in this letter, take special note of that person and do not associate with him, so that he will be put to shame. Yet do not regard him as an enemy, but admonish him as a brother*". The Greek word behind the NASB's "*admonished*" is the same Paul uses in 1 Thessalonians 5:14 when he says to "*admonish the unruly* [*ataktos*]" and brings his argument full-circle.

---

64. Bennema, *Imitation*, p. 254

The Thessalonians should shame anyone who refuses to work, not associating with them or providing them food. If they don't work then they don't eat, and no one should feel sorry for them. Paul's instructions on work are, of course, rooted in his Jewish worldview. Contrary to the scorn with which the Greco-Roman elite viewed manual labor, the Jewish tradition, particularly in Proverbs[65], placed great value in work, an essential component of a life honoring God. The *ataktos* Gentiles to which Paul is writing must embrace the Jewish value of hard work, honoring the community of faith and setting a good example for outsiders. James Thompson, summarizing Paul's instructions regarding labor in 2 Thessalonians, deftly ties the strings of Paul's logic together: "*Having instilled in his new converts a corporate consciousness as a family, Paul indicates that the practice . . . requires members not to burden the family, but to contribute to its well-being . . . By their conversion the Thessalonians . . . have provoked hostility from the larger society . . . and been prompted to create an alternative family of those who care for each other and adopt moral conduct that distinguishes them from . . .* [those] *whom Paul describes as "outsiders" . . . Here Paul insists that philadelphia* [love for brothers, i.e. the church], *expressed by living quietly and working with the hands, will correspond to values that the outsiders will approve*"[66]. The community offers support for one another based on the mutual identity they share as members of Abraham's family through faith and the Spirit. They must avoid the dangers of parasitic entanglement with outsiders and testify to God's wisdom by behaving wisely towards outsiders, which includes self-supporting labor.

For believing Christians, we cannot escape Paul's views on work. Jesus is king and following him will oftentimes result in social ostracization. God's family must persevere knowing that Jesus will ultimately vindicate them, and they must live in accordance both with the eschatological inauguration and their new identity as believers. Modern Christians must take Paul's teachings here seriously. If, as I have argued, Paul is critiquing the patronage system, with its ties of political and economic loyalty to those who are not a part of the church, how can Christians possibly support a state monopoly on charity which guarantees that recipients of government entitlement programs will be dependent upon unbelieving politicians. Aside from the fact that the entire welfare state is funded through violent, confiscatory taxation, dependence on the state compromises the integrity of the church and the command that we should strive to be charitable instead of relying on the charity of others. In all of our modern debates about entitlement programs,

---

65. Proverbs 6:6-11, 24:30-34, and 28:19, for example.

66. Thompson, *Moral Formation,* p. 83

few people ever discuss the moral agency of welfare recipients. No Christian able to work should expect to live at the expense of other people for an extended period of time; it is, as Paul says, a grave moral issue to engage in economic parasitism. Christians should try, to the best of their ability, to impose no burden on others and instead be willing (and, able, when possible) to provide for the temporary needs of those who find themselves in disadvantageous economic circumstances which are out of their control. All of this should happen within the church, outside of the tethers which attend benefaction, be it the patron-client system of Roman antiquity or the contemporary welfare states of modernity.

Sheldon Richman, in his book *Tethered Citizens*, provides an excellent analysis of the dependency culture created by so-called "public" entitlement programs that I believe Paul, with his classically Jewish distinction between insiders and outside, would be in wholehearted agreement: "*It is possible that some welfare-state programs, looked at in isolation, have benefited you. But it is misleading to look at them in isolation. All together they have cumulative moral and economic effects that must not be ignored or underrated. The system binds you and makes you dependent on power. It encourages you to look at government as your protector, implying that, first, you are too frail to look after yourself and, second, that a free, self-regulating society would be full of peril and without its own forms of protection. And unless you are immune from the welfare-state ideology, the handouts also tend to make you concerned about cutbacks in government spending. Most people don't want to lose their government benefits. They have developed a stake in their own continued dependency. They have developed the fateful "entitlement" mentality*"[67]. Paul would rather believers pledge their allegiance only to Jesus, not to secular political authorities, and the outsourcing of charity to patrons or politicians compromises the unique integrity of the Messiah's family.

Paul's model of decentralized charity, where the church supports other believers who are in need *only so long as they are actually in need*, should be the goal of Christian generosity in the modern world. While it sounds insensitive to contemporary ears attuned to the ubiquitous (and almost universally unchallenged) pretensions of egalitarian redistribution inherent in authoritarian socialism, those who through their own volition elect to abstain from work should be admonished, shamed, and, if necessarily, dissociated from the community until they come to their senses. Both those who give and those who receive possess moral agency, and Paul deftly balances both positions in the Thessalonian correspondence. The same church whom Paul brags about to the Corinthians also includes several members

---

67. Richman, *Tethered Citizens*, p. 12

who are a net drain and a horrible witness towards outsiders. For Paul, this intolerable situation can only be remedied by withholding aid from believers who don't deserve it. No work, no food, no apologies. Within Paul's framework of cruciform ethics, *all* believers are held morally accountable, and no appeals to the lazy, unsophisticated oppressor-oppressed dynamic of critical theory can rob a person of their moral agency. Just as clients must sever their opportunistic relationships with secular patrons, the church must learn to dissociate itself from systems which enable degenerate dependence. The church can never outsource the responsibility of charity, which it has been given by God, to any other authority.

I will conclude this section with one more longer quote, this time from Bruce Winter, which perfectly encapsulates Paul's thoughts about work in 1-2 Thessalonians. Paul's social ethic is an eschatological reappropriation of Jeremiah 29:7; we are to seek the welfare of the city which God will ultimately destroy and which is being run by rulers who are, at this present moment, already passing away. There can be no eternal, transcendent hope in anyone other than king Jesus, and no identity which supersedes membership in Abraham's family through faith and the Spirit. It's why, as Winter explains, the Thessalonians need to work: "*Given [Paul's] commitment to social ethics which aimed to bestow help and blessing on the everyday life of other citizens, his deep worry about some Thessalonians' welfare syndrome is explicable. Christians were not only to command the respect of outsiders by being self-sufficient, but they were to seek the welfare of their city by having the wherewithal to do good to others. Paul perceived that this involved sharing self-generated financial resources . . . It was not possible for some of the Thessalonians to opt out of work simply because others would support them. While in secular society 'it was less disgraceful to depend idly on the state or on a patron for subsistence than to earn it by sordid labor', it was not to be so in the Christian community—those who did not wish to work were not permitted to be supported by their fellow-Christians acting as patrons . . . One of the tasks of Christians was to go beyond their own needs to the needs of others. It constituted the most visible signal to the society of its day of a new community in which a function of all able-bodied members of this new community was to do good. This created a whole new class of benefactors. They did good because good needed to be done, and did so without expectations of reciprocity or repayment*"[68]. That is, of course, a revolutionary idea, one almost entirely missed by modern Christians enthralled with the quasi-soteriological posturing of the modern, nineteenth century welfare state. I think it's time Christians start taking Paul seriously.

---

68. Winter, *Welfare*, pp. 58-60

1 TIMOTHY

Background: Godly Living and False Teaching

In 1 Timothy 3:15, Paul informs his good friend why he wrote him a letter: "*I write so that you will know how one ought to conduct himself in the household of God, which is the church of the living God, the pillar and support of the truth*". While Timothy himself was an exemplary model of faithfulness, not everyone in Ephesus, where he was ministering, was quite as honorable. Timothy has his work cut out for him by Paul: "*As I urged you upon my departure for Macedonia, remain on at Ephesus so that you may instruct certain men not to teach strange doctrines, nor to pay attention to myths and endless genealogies, which give rise to mere speculation rather than furthering the administration of God which is by faith*"[69]. Anticipating 3:15, Paul reminds Timothy in 1:5 that their instruction to the church has a purpose: "*the goal of our instruction is love from a pure heart and a good conscience and a sincere faith*". Paul, away from the church, has placed Timothy in a supervisory role until his return, and some people are already turning away from sound teaching[70], which Paul addresses head-on in 1:6-11 and 4:1-5:2. It is quite possible that several of these false teachers had arisen *from within the church*[71] and had, much like the *ataktos* in Thessalonica, tarnished the reputation of the community in Ephesus. Gorman helpfully summarizes the letter's purpose: "[1 Timothy's] *emphasis on the ordering of belief, behavior, and leadership that flows from this governing metaphor for the church is due in large measure to the presence of false or 'unhealthy' teachers and to a related concern for the reputation of the church and its leaders*"[72]. It is within this broader context that Paul makes several interesting comments relevant to our study of politics and economics.

The Only King . . . and the Other Kings: 1 Timothy 1:17, 2:1-7

In case Timothy forgot, Paul reminds him that Jesus is the only true king: "*Now to the King eternal, immortal, invisible, the only God, be honor and glory forever and ever*"[73]. Not subtle. Only a few verses later, just after excoriating the blasphemers Hymenaeus and Alexander by name, Paul provides a brief instruction about

---

69. 1 Timothy 1:3-4

70. Gorman, *Crucified Lord*, p. 552

71. Towner, Philip. 1996. *1-2 Timothy & Titus*. InterVarsity Press. p. 23

72. Gorman, *Crucified Lord*, p. 553

73. 1 Timothy 1:17

worldly rulers in 2:1-2: "*First of all, then, I urge that entreaties and prayers, petitions and thanksgiving, be made on behalf of all men, for kings and all who are in authority, so that we may lead a tranquil and quiet life in all godliness and dignity*". In other words, follow Jeremiah 29:7. The purpose of honoring worldly rulers is not to validate them nor seek their benefaction, nor is it an attempt to qualify his lofty christological praise in 1:17. As Paul says, it is so the church may be at peace and live godly, dignified lives. Within the context of 1 Timothy, where Paul is concerned about the perception of the church by outsiders, "*a submissive posture towards the state would lend the church credibility in the eyes of the world*"[74], a pragmatic, not theological, respect for human authority. Paul's own, shall we say, 'eventful' trip to Ephesus, recorded in Romans 19, also lies behind this statement.

Paul, ever concerned about the advance of his gospel, hopes that peace with the authorities will bring about knowledge of the truth, including salvation, which is why God expects his followers to live, as best as possible, tranquil and quiet lives: "*This is good and acceptable in the sight of God our Savior, who desires all men to be saved and come to the knowledge of the truth. For there is one God, and one mediator also between God and men, the man Christ Jesus, who gave Himself as a ransom for all, the testimony given at the proper time*"[75]. Seeking peace with the authorities is for a purpose. God wants all to be saved, to encounter Him and recognize Jesus as Christ. Paul twice uses the word "*all*"; God desires *all* to be saved and come to his knowledge and offers Christ as a ransom for *all*. Presumably this includes the non-believing authorities whom Paul exhorts Timothy to respect. Towner perfectly articulates the crux of Paul's logic in this passage: "*What is sought is the best of conditions for expanding God's kingdom, not simply a peaceful life. The context determines the overriding interest in salvation . . . Furthermore, the description of the manner of Christian living (in all godliness and holiness) contains hints of witness . . . The manner of life here described has the evaluating eye of the observer in mind . . . and is meant to recommend the gospel to those who look on it*"[76]. Pragmatic Paul always has his mind set on the global proclamation of Christ, and making peace with non-believing authorities is simply a means to that particular end.

This is, as I will argue, pretty much exactly what Paul does in Romans 13:1-7. That great letter, bookend by two of Paul's most sweeping declarations of the universal Messianic reign of Jesus and offering an extended explanation of what it means to be a member of God's family, includes instructions about submitting to authorities. Paul is in no way backing down from his unwavering christological,

---

74. Towner, *1-2 Timothy & Titus*, p. 64

75. 1 Timothy 2:3-6

76. Towner, *1-2 Timothy & Titus*, pp. 64-65

eschatological, and ecclesiological teaching. The center of his salvation-inducing gospel, Jesus the Christ, is in no way diminished, threatened, or marginalized by his political pragmatism. Paul's political philosophy, if we can without anachronism speak of such a category, is essentially an eschatological reappropriation of Jeremiah 29:7; instead of the restoration being a distant, future hope, God has already begun delivering His people and installed the Davidic king on a cosmic throne. Followers of Jesus are awaiting his return, the eschatological consummation, and are tasked with the mission of faithfully representing the one true king to all the world, including Roman authorities. By quietly living in peace, believers are effecting the greatest political revolution in human history without, following the example of their Messiah, shedding a single drop of enemy blood. In fact, the great enemy, death itself, has already been conquered. One man, at the end of history, found his way through death and came out on the other side. The church is responsible for letting the world know that the time is up, the kingdom of God is at hand, and all should repent and believe the gospel.

Widows Indeed: 1 Timothy 5:3-16

There are apparently many widows in the church who require financial support, and Paul suggests that their families should be the first people to provide it: "*Honor widows who are widows indeed; but if any widow has children or grandchildren, they must first learn to practice piety in regard to their own family and to make some return to their parents; for this is acceptable in the sight of God*"[77]. Widows, who were in antiquity at an extreme economic disadvantage, needed care. Instead of delegating this responsibility to the state or even non-related believers, Paul argues that a widow's family should be the primary providers of financial aid. There is a long-standing tradition within Judaism of helping widows and orphans, two categories of vulnerable people, and Paul is doing little more that applying this tradition to a concrete situation in Ephesus: "*From the time of Israel's inception, God has been known as the defender of widows (Deut*[eronomy] *10:18; 24:17). "Justice" among God's people was measured in part by the treatment of widows (Is*[aiah] *1:17). God's compassion for the widow became the covenant community's responsibility, which the early church naturally took up*"[78]. Instead of dispersing the cost of widow-care to the entire community, Paul insists that family members should first step in to provide support, demonstrating an authentic care for those in need without placing an unnecessary burden on financially-strapped believers. Paul's language sounds,

---

77. 1 Timothy 5:3-4

78. Towner, *1-2 Timothy & Titus*, p. 115

from the vantage point of welfare-paradigmed modern authoritarianism, excessively harsh: "*But if anyone does not provide for his own, and especially for those of his household, he has denied the faith and is worse than an unbeliever*"[79]. Echoing 1 Thessalonians 4 and 2 Thessalonians 3, believing relatives of widows have a moral obligation to provide for their needs. Anyone who refuses to help their own needy family members is rejecting God's call to sacrificial charity and worse than an unbeliever.

The unbelievers had their own solution to the widow problem. Although philosophically venerating women who remained faithful to their husbands even after death by remaining unmarried, Roman politicians were less noble-minded: "*Legislation by the emperor Caesar Augustus . . . required every woman between twenty and fifty to be married or lose her rights of inheritance and other privileges. Augustus was seeking to stem the tide of childless aristocrats that threatened many old aristocratic families with extinction. Those who were widowed or divorced were to remarry and bear children*"[80]. While it is unclear how (or even if) this policy was enforced on a wide-spread basis, particularly in eastern cities such as Ephesus, it clearly demonstrates how the provisioning of widows was very much a part of the cultural conversation in the Roman world. Paul, in his typically nuanced manner, distinguishes between two types of widows in 1 Timothy 5:5-7, the woman who is a "*widow indeed*" by fixing her mind on God and the woman "*who gives herself to wanton pleasure*". After his admonition that family members must be the first to take care of widows, he then offers instructions in 5:9-16 regarding which widows should be eligible for charitable assistance from the church.

Apparently there were some who, like the *ataktos* in the Thessalonian congregation, were parasitically abusing the benefaction of others: "*The passage* [1 Timothy 5:3-16] *reflects a fairly advanced system of care—a "roll" or "list" of widows eligible for support (v. 9). But the system was being abused; families of widows were not shouldering their responsibility, thus placing financial strain on the church . . . good stewardship of the church's limited resources and protection of its reputation required the leadership to decide who the "real" widows in the church were, and whether other means of support were available*"[81]. By framing the conversation with a charge for familial assistance to be provided before relying on the church, Paul is placing reasonable restrictions on charitable eligibility: "*The church . . . should not be the first line of support for widows. Family members of the widows are obligated to provide for the needs of widows before turning to the church . . . Circles of responsibility*

---

79. 1 Timothy 5:8

80. Jeffers, *Greco-Roman*, p. 250

81. Towner, *1-2 Timothy & Titus*, p. 116

are established so that a family with sufficient funds cares for the widows instead of absolving themselves of responsibility and transferring the widow to the church's care. If a family has the funds, they should not pawn off care for their own family circle to the church"[82]. Paul's requirements for support from the church is fairly strict according to 5:9-10: they must be sixty, the culturally recognized age after which remarriage was unlikely[83], the wife of one man, having a good reputation, a wise mother, and charitable to others. These are the conditions under which a widow could receive charity from the community in Ephesus.

Younger widows, those who were to not to be placed on the list, are described in 5:11-15. Because of their sensual desires, Paul argues, they will want to get married, revoking their widowhood, and are much more likely to be *"gossips and busybodies"*. Paul, ironically (or perhaps intentionally if he has the outward-facing witness of the church in mind), proposes a solution to the financial quandary of younger widows with which the emperor Augustus would have been in hearty agreement: *"I want younger widows to get married, bear children, keep house, and give the enemy no occasion for reproach, for some have already turned aside to follow Satan"*. The church will provide for those widows who need and deserve it, family members should provide for their own widows first, and some widows don't actually require any charity at all and should simply get remarried. To ensure Timothy doesn't miss the point, Paul rounds out the section with one final instruction in 5:16: *"If any woman who is a believer has dependent widows, she must assist them and the church must not be burdened, so that it may assist those who are widows indeed"*. *Widows indeed.* Paul, with a wisdom far exceeding many of his modern interpreters, correctly attributes moral agency to everyone involved in the question of widowhood. Families, the church, and widows themselves must take responsibility for their own actions and seek to live in a manner honoring Christ. This means that some people should receive support and others should not.

We find ourselves once again repeating a principle Paul has articulated at several places in his epistles, particularly the Thessalonian correspondence. The church has a responsibility to help those in need, and believers are called to radical generosity, but charity has its limits. The dehumanizing welfare mentality of modernity denies moral agency to those deemed impoverished, no doubt due to political philosophies which always attribute the success of one group to the suffering of another. While that analysis isn't always incorrect by default, Paul has a much more nuanced, realistic, and theologically rich conception of charity. There are boundaries placed around charitable eligibility, ensuring that giving meets real

---

82. Schreiner, *Handbook*, p. 389

83. Towner, *1-2 Timothy & Titus*, p. 116

needs without enabling degeneracy, exacerbating sin, or tarnishing the reputation of God's church under the watching eyes of unbelievers. Believers have an obligation to support needy family members before tapping into the limited resources of the church, and the non-believing authorities aren't even in consideration as a source of charity for those in God's family. Modern Christians who want to outsource poverty to the state have, to quote Paul, *"denied the faith and* [are] *worse than an unbeliever"* precisely because they, like the Pharisees who oppose Jesus, aren't willing to lift a finger themselves to help others who are in need. The church can do better. In light of the eschatological moment, we are not obligated to accept the nineteenth century nation-state model of planned, centralized welfare which only empowers politicians and bureaucrats while validating dependence and moral degradation. Paul's model of charity is, in every way, superior to our own.

The Love of Money: 1 Timothy 6:6-10

One of the most famous and also most misquoted statements on money in the New Testament is found in 1 Timothy 6:10. Often repeated as *"money is the root of all evil"*, Paul is characteristically much more precise: *"the love of money is a root of all sorts of evil"*. Not all of the problems in our world stem from the love of money, as certain politicized readings of the New Testament might lead us to believe, but it certainly motivates many people to engage in evil behavior. Interestingly enough, this isn't the first time Paul refers to the love of money in 1 Timothy. Hidden within a list of qualifications for church leaders in chapter 3, those in positions of authority in the church must be *"free from the love of money"*[84]. No one who leads the church can also orient their lives around the acquisition of money, channeling the words of Jesus in Matthew 6:24: *"You cannot serve God and wealth"*. The context of Paul's famous statement about money and evil is related to false teaching; in 1 Timothy 6:3-5, Paul critiques those who advocate *"a different doctrine"*, creating *"constant friction"* and *"suppos*[ing] *that godliness is a means of gain"*.

Paul, countering the factionalists, responds as follows in 1 Timothy 6:6-9: *"But godliness actually is a means of great gain when accompanied by contentment. For we have brought nothing into the world, so we cannot take anything out of it either. If we have food and covering, with these we shall be content. But those who want to get rich fall into temptation and a snare and many foolish and harmful desires which plunge men into ruin and destruction"*. It's almost as if Paul had been exposed to the same oral Jesus traditions which would eventually become Matthew 6, but I digress. The same principles which were at play in the Synoptic tradition underlie

---

84. 1 Timothy 3:3

this text as well. Paul is absolutely not constructing a socialistic case against voluntary market transactions, nor is he making the equally dubious claim that wealth *in and of itself* is a grave moral evil. Instead, Paul wants followers of Jesus to be content with the basic necessities and avoid the "*temptation*" and "*snare*[s]" which accompany the service of wealth. Paul does, after all, believe, ala Ephesians 5:5 and Colossians 3:5, that greed is idolatry. Avarice will bring a man to ruin, and believers should avoid it at all costs. This explains his logic in 1 Timothy 6:10, the capstone of this short exhortation: "*For the love of money is a root of all sorts of evil, and some by longing for it have wandered away from the faith and pierced themselves with many griefs*".

Yes. I agree, unsurprisingly, with every word Paul utters in 1 Timothy 6. The pursuit of wealth is idolatry, the placing of one's hope in something other than the love of God and neighbor. Not only is avaristic desire an evil, it will almost inevitably produce other forms of vice and licentiousness which destroys faith and supplants loyalty to God. How this leads modern Christians to the political and economic conclusion that markets and money should be placed in the hands of a small number of oligarchical, ultra-wealthy politicians and bureaucrats who generally have little experience in business or production is a mystery which can only be explained by the dominant ideologies of our day. Just as consumerism and materialism cannot with any degree of precision be correlated to capitalism, which is nothing more than the voluntary, contractual, and decentralized production and exchange of goods and services between non-coerced parties, a skepticism towards greed and avarice must not be conflated with socialism. In fact, the entire socialist project, wherein one group of people are granted the power to determine through threats of violence what another group of people may produce and consume is, at its core, "*the love of money*" projected upon the whole of society, with the same calamitous, immoral, and anti-Christian results which befall those individuals who long for wealth, wander away from the faith, and pierce themselves with many griefs. There is, for those who sincerely search for it, always a better way.

The Rich Must Be Rich in Good Works: 1 Timothy 6:17-19

Apparently there were some people in the Ephesian church who could be characterized as "rich", and Paul doesn't seem to think they have fallen into "the love of money" as a trap. In 1 Timothy 6:17-19, Paul feels the need to provide Timothy with advice about how to approach the rich, which, it would seem, Paul assumes applies to some members of the community: "*Instruct those who are rich in this present world not to be conceited or to fix their hope on the uncertainty of riches, but on God, who richly supplies us with all things to enjoy. Instruct them to do good, to be rich in good works, to be generous and ready to share, storing up for themselves the treasure of a good foundation for the future, so that they may take hold of that which is life indeed*". Once again Paul seems to be channeling Jesus in Matthew 6: "*Do not store up for yourselves treasures on earth . . . but store up for yourselves treasures in heaven*"[85]. We are confronted with an inconvenient truth for contemporary Christian leftists: the possession of wealth isn't itself necessarily a moral evil. It can also be, if acquired justly, considered a blessing, but one which must be used in the service of others. Those who are rich must focus not on their riches, but on God, and be ready to generously share.

The "*enjoy*[ment]" of riches has a particular purpose, as Towner explains: "*Gifts from God are things to be "enjoyed", for Paul states clearly that God gives richly for this reason. But the gift is not to be confused with the Giver; it is rather to point the recipient back again to hope in God. Hope, which acknowledges the Giver, releases the recipient of the gift to "enjoy" or make use of it in ways that mirror the divine Giver*"[86]. Wealth must be subject to the same cruciform standard as all other Christian behavior; if one is in the position of possessing resources, they must be used in the service of others. This should not, of course, be confused with the confiscation and redistribution policy of authoritarian socialism. Paul does not hint that the possessions of the rich should be seized, *especially* by non-believing political authorities, and given indiscriminately to those whom the confiscatory class deem worthy. Paul certainly does not want the rich giving to young, unworthy widows. Not everyone deserves charity, and everyone does possess moral agency. Paul's instructions towards the rich are entirely congruent with the Jesus tradition and, as we will see in a later chapter, a nearly perfect distillation of James. Whatever has been given must be used in the service of others, a moral imperative which is binding on all followers of Jesus who possess riches, including modern socialists.

2 TIMOTHY

Remember Jesus Christ, Descendant of David: 2 Timothy 2:8

Paul writes another letter to Timothy, although perhaps this time with a sense of his imminent demise. Some scholars have suggested that 2 Timothy reads like a last will and testament of Paul, who, upon realizing that his ministry was quickly coming to an end, is handing the reins over to his trustworthy friend and

---

85. Matthew 6:19-21

86. Towner, *1-2 Timothy & Titus*, p. 147

colleague.[87] In my view this theory has some weight to it, but Gorman identifies an even more fundamental function of Paul's second epistle to Timothy: "*The theme of the letter, then, is the charge to guard and suffer for the truth of the gospel in imitation of Paul*"[88]. Suffering for the sake of the exalted Messiah, proclaimed in the gospel, is indeed central, as Paul himself articulates in 2 Timothy 1:8-10: "*Therefore do not be ashamed of the testimony of our Lord or of me His prisoner, but join with me in suffering for the gospel according to the power of God, who has saved us and called us with a holy calling, not according to our works, but according to His own purpose and grace which was granted us in Christ Jesus from all eternity, but now has been revealed by the appearing of our Savior Christ Jesus, who abolished death and brought life and immortality to light through the gospel*". Paul, imprisoned for the gospel, is a model of suffering for the truth. Oftentimes, as Acts accurately portrays, following Jesus leads to trouble. The truth is worth more than the suffering.

From this perspective 2 Timothy provides readers with a powerful political principle: Jesus is king and we must sometimes suffer when proclaiming his kingdom. This is classic Pauline christology; Jesus is in charge, and he has no competitors. While Christians must submit to the powers of this age who are passing away, including, as in Paul's case, accepting imprisonment without violent resistance, in the end Jesus has the final word. Modern Christians, therefore, should not place their hope in secular government. It was never built to last. For our study there are no specific passages in 2 Timothy of which a detailed analysis might substantially contribute to our study outside of the cumulative case I have presented thus far. Two, however, are worthy of an all-to-brief comment.

First, 2 Timothy 2:8 is one of the three places (along with Romans 1:1-5 and 1 Corinthians 15:3-4) where Paul provides a concrete definition of his gospel, and the messianic identity of the risen Lord is at its very core: "*Remember Jesus Christ, risen from the dead, descendant of David, according to my gospel*". Whatever confessional Protestants say about the relationship between gospel and soteriology, it simply cannot be divorced from the messianic, Davidic identity of Jesus. God made promises which he fulfilled in David's son Jesus, and any analysis of the gospel which doesn't include the messianic dynamic is sub-biblical and unworthy of Christian theology. Because of Paul's beliefs about Jesus, presented in his gospel, Paul must "*suffer hardship even to imprisonment as a criminal; but the word of God is not imprisoned. For this reason I endure all things for the sake of those who are chosen, so that they also may obtain the salvation which is in Christ Jesus and with*

---

87. Gorman, *Crucified Lord*, pp. 537-538
88. Gorman, *Crucified Lord*, p. 537

it eternal glory"[89]. In light of the eternal glory of Messiah Jesus, Paul's suffering is barely worth consideration. God's apostle to the Gentiles is playing a bigger game than his opponents, one which he will win in the end. In 2 Timothy 2:24-3:9, Paul contrasts the virtuous and God-centered behavior of church leaders who serve God with those who have gone astray. One of the characteristics of those who have rejected God, reminiscent of 1 Timothy 6:10, includes being *"lovers of money"*[90]. Men such as this are described by Paul as *"always learning and never able to come to the knowledge of the truth"*. Those who believe Jesus is king must never fall to the temptation of greed and avarice.

Titus

Be Subject to Rulers and Be Peaceable: Titus 3:1-2

Like 2 Timothy, Paul's brief letter to Titus contributes little to our conversation about political and economic concepts in the New Testament save for one brief but extremely revealing comment about submission to rulers. Also like 2 (and 1) Timothy, Titus is written to a trusted associate from whom the letter derives its name. Paul at some point traveled to Crete, a large island in the Mediterranean, with Titus, established a community there, and, upon Paul's departure, left Titus in charge of the church on Crete.[91] In the letter, Paul issues Titus several instructions "regarding *church leadership, opposition to false teachers and their controversies, and the general conduct of believers in the world*"[92]. For this reason, Titus obviously bears striking similarities to 1-2 Timothy.

Using language found in Romans 13:1-7, Paul encourages Titus to issue instructions about the relationship between believers and Roman political authorities in Titus 3:1-2: *"Remind them to be subject to rulers, to authorities, to be obedient, to be ready for every good deed, to malign no one, to be peaceable, gentile, showing every consideration for all men"*. This passage must not be read in isolation. Paul prefaces his comments in 3:1-2 with a sweeping statement of the absolute power and glory of God revealed through the Savior Christ Jesus in 2:11-15; as in all of Paul's instructions about political authorities, they are not in competition with Jesus. He is above and beyond all of them, and only Jesus will remain in the eschatological consummation. Paul uses forms of the same verb, *hypotasso*, *"be subject"*, in Titus

---

89. 1 Timothy 2:9-10

90. 1 Timothy 3:2

91. Schreiner, *Handbook*, p. 409; see Titus 1:4-5.

92. Gorman, *Crucified Lord*, p. 572

3:1 and Romans 13:1 (translated *"be in subjection"* in the NASB) as a description of how believers ought to respond to *"rulers"* and *"authorities"* (forms of *arche* and *exousia*, respectively). I think Paul means exactly what he says: with respect to rulers, subject to them. The purpose, as we have seen before, is essentially pragmatic; the force of verse two is that Christians should *"be peaceable . . . showing every consideration for all men"*. That Paul, in Romans 12:18, a mere *four verses* before he begins chapter 13, says *"If possible, so far as it depends on you, be at peace with all men"*, should also come as no surprise.

This is, in essence, the logic of Jeremiah 29:7, with the attendant eschatological orientation that God will honor peace in the present and vindicate believers in the future. Paul won't remain in a Roman prison for the rest of eternity, after all. Immediately after issuing a proclamation on submission to authorities, Paul reminds Titus (rhetorically, given Paul's rather high self-estimation of his life before Christ) how many believers engaged in evil deeds until *"the kindness of God our Savior and His love for Mankind appeared"*[93]. Instead of behaving in an unprincipled, undisciplined, and unfaithful manner, believers, who are called by God to live at peace with all men and proclaim the gospel of Messiah Jesus, are able with a good conscience to submit to governing authorities and maintain, as best they can, social harmony. The irony, of course, is that Paul is in prison *precisely because* of his ministry. Paul causes numerous headaches for political authorities throughout his life, narrated brilliantly in Acts, and yet willingly, without calls for violence or revolution, submits himself to the legal consequences of his actions. As with Jeremiah 29:7, Jesus followers must never compromise their beliefs and values. Sometimes it is impossible to be at peace with all men, and in those cases Christians must live in imitation of the *crucified* Messiah which they worship, including the acceptance of suffering. Violent rebellion is not an option.

Paul is articulating a general principle of the relationship between Abraham's family and worldly empires. It is not, as his own example and theology attests, meant to be a timeless, rigidly applied political theory, equally applicable in all places and situations. But it should be the default position of believers towards secular authorities. What 'submission' looks like in a society where, at least nominally, the government is constrained by a written constitution and citizens are, at least nominally, bearers of rights which exist prior to government is an open question. I suspect our engagement with political authorities ought to more closely resemble the way Paul leverages his citizenship in Philippi. The church must carefully reflect upon what it means to apply this principle in a political context which is dramatically different (in many ways, but perhaps not in others) from the Roman

---

93. Titus 3:3-4

imperial order. Christians are called to be suprapolitical, members of a kingdom beyond empire, and consistently apply the values of love, peace, and mercy in all social relationships, including with people who just so happen to occupy positions of power.

PHILEMON

No Longer a Slave, but a Brother

I quote, once more, Galatians 3:28-29: "*There is neither Jew nor Greek, there is neither slave nor freeman, there is neither male nor female; for you are all one in Christ Jesus. And if you belong to Christ, then you are Abraham's descendants, heirs according to the promise*". This is Pauline ecclesiology in a nutshell; in a brief, breathtaking passage Paul relativizes the status symbols which define the social boundary markers of antiquity. Anyone who "*belong*[s] *to Christ*" by virtue of the faith and Spirit are incorporated, as members, into Abraham's family. In the eschatological kingdom of God, everyone possesses equal value. Paul also expects Jesus-followers to act that way. There is no room in the church for petty division over irrelevant identity hierarchies. Herein lies the burden of Paul's shortest letter, Philemon.

Written to Philemon and the church which meets in his house (including a few individuals mentioned in 1:1-2), the letter is actually about one of Philemon's slaves, Onesimus. As I discussed at length earlier in the book, slavery was a critical and unquestioned component of the Roman economy. Virtually no one in antiquity questioned the validity of slavery *as an institution* in antiquity. Paul is, in this sense, a radical. While he doesn't call for the outright abolition of slavery, which perhaps never even crossed his mind as a possibility, he definitely thinks the institution has lost its social relevancy in light of Christ. The slaveowning follower of Jesus and the enslaved follower of Jesus are on equal footing. How Onesimus meets Paul is an open question, and there are several theories which have been proposed by scholars over the years.[94] Capes, Reeves, and Richards suggests Onesimus may have been following the Roman law of *amicus domini*, "friend of the master", in which a slave, fearing for his life because of the anger of his enslaver, could temporarily run away to a friend of his master. The legislation was not passed out of kindness to the slave, it was meant to protect the slaveowner's property in times of irrationality.[95] Given Paul's direct rhetoric and the public nature of his letter it is quite likely that Onesimus and Philemon had a strained relationship which Paul

---

94. Capes, Reeves, and Richards, *Rediscovering Paul*, pp. 238-239

95. Capes, Reeves, and Richards, *Rediscovering Paul*, p. 238

was hoping to smooth over with a little social and theological accountability.[96] Onesimus had come to Paul, and Paul was sending him back to Philemon not, following the law of *amicus domini*, as property but as an equal.

The relevant passage for our purpose is Philemon 1:15-16: "*For perhaps he was for this reason separated from you for a while, that you would have him back forever, no longer as a slave, but more than a slave, a beloved brother, especially to me, but how much more to you, both in the flesh and in the Lord*". There we have it. Paul's social revolution, millennia ahead of his time, is on full display in this short passage. The eschatological age has been inaugurated through king Jesus and all must now respond to Israel's God. In His kingdom, under the crucified Messiah, the slave and slaveowner are brothers. Paul can't do anything about the institution, but he can fix the relationship. No longer does Philemon occupy a position of arbitrary power over Onesimus; they are now on equal footing before the judgment seat of king Jesus. This is, from the Roman perspective, patently insane. But so is following, indeed worshiping, a crucified Jewish prophet.

There is one political lesson to learn from Paul's shortest letter, and it's that status simply does not matter in the kingdom of God. Rich or poor, politician or citizen, employer or employee, pastor (or priest!) or layperson: all of these distinctions are real, and institutions would not be able to function without them, but regardless of where one falls all stand shoulder-to-shoulder together in God's kingdom. Abraham's family has but one Father, and even though believers are different (channeling 1 Corinthians 12, where the body can only function because of diverse gifts) they are not superior nor inferior in status. In our time this principle must be applied to one of the most fundamental boundary markers in modernity: national identity. Abraham's family is transnational; it doesn't matter if an individual happens to be born on one side of an imaginary line. Political boundaries are almost entirely artificial, and the universal church, regardless of nationality or cultural practices, are called to see each other as family. American Christians must not privilege the priorities of our government over building the kingdom of God. That many American believers are comfortable with the secular government dropping bombs on Christians (and other non-combatants made in God's image) in places like Afghanistan and Iraq while ignoring the death and devastation it causes to people who are faithful to Jesus is an outrage and the great theological crime of our times. We must play the Onesimus to their Philemon by learning to accept believers beyond our borders as siblings, not as inferiors. Taking Paul seriously means holding our nationality at arms-length and refusing to endorse or condone the narrative which implies America has a special right to do harm or that American

---

96. Capes, Reeves, and Richards, *Rediscovering Paul*, p. 239

citizenship somehow confers upon the citizen rights which transcend the responsibilities God has placed upon members of his kingdom. Our political identities can be pragmatically useful, but they mean nothing in the family of Abraham.

CONCLUSION

We have now explored twelve of Paul's thirteen letters. Just as Jesus said that the first will be last and the last first, we turn at last to the first (canonical, not chronological) letter, and perhaps the most influential, which Paul ever wrote: Romans. In some sense, the next chapter is bound to be anticlimactic. There is nothing within that daunting letter which, after reviewing the rest of Paul's epistles, will appear as new. Romans 13:1-7 sits atop the summit of the New Testament's political mountain, but perhaps unjustifiably so. As we approach the top, we may in fact realize that there were shorter, more efficient, and less arduous paths we could have taken to reach the peak. Even so, we *"press on towards the goal"*, as Paul says in another context in Philippians 3:14. Let's climb just a little bit further.

CHAPTER 15 | Romans

Submit to Authorities?

Romans 13:1-7 is among the most difficult and potentially disturbing of all Pauline texts.

Michael Gorman[1]

Paul wasn't writing a treatise on government here!

Thomas Schreiner[2]

INTRODUCTION

We've finally made it to Romans. It will be helpful at the outset of this chapter to quote Romans 13:1-7 in full: *Every person is to be in subjection to the governing authorities. "For there is no authority except from God, and those which exist are established by God. Therefore whoever resists authority has opposed the ordinance of God; and they who have opposed will receive condemnation upon themselves. For rulers are not a cause of fear for good behavior, but for evil. Do you want to have no fear of authority? Do what is good and you will have praise from the same; for it is a minister of God to you for good. But if you do what is evil, be afraid; for it does not bear the sword for nothing; for it is a minister of God, an avenger who brings wrath on the one who practices evil. Therefore it is necessary to be in subjection, not only because of wrath, but also for conscience' sake. For because of this you also pay taxes, for rulers are servants of God, devoting themselves to this very thing. Render to all what is due them: tax to whom tax is due; custom to whom custom; fear to whom fear; honor to whom honor".* The most hotly contested passage on politics in the New Testament, encased in the

---

1. Gorman, *Crucified Lord*, p. 394

2. Schreiner, *Handbook*, p. 104

most controversial letter in the New Testament. It's no wonder readers of Romans find themselves unsettled with the notorious thirteenth chapter.

Much of this consternation is undue. While Michael Gorman, quoted above, refers to Romans 13:1-7 as "*the most difficult and potentially disturbing of all Pauline texts*", Thomas Schreiner wisely turns down the heat: "*We need to recognize, however, that Paul wasn't writing a treatise on government here! We have only a few lines of brief advice, and Paul's counsel has to do with what is ordinarily the case. Typically believers should obey the government and pay their taxes, even if the regime is evil*"[3]. We could end the conversation here. The function of Romans 13:1-7, and indeed the letter as a whole, has nothing to do with constructing a timeless political philosophy, meticulously addressing every potential situation in which believers might find themselves confronted with governing authorities. Completely consistent with the long, venerable tradition of Jeremiah 29:7 which conditioned Paul's thinking on political authorities throughout his letters, Paul's brief commentary in Romans can be fruitfully understood along the lines proposed by Schreiner: most of the time Christians should go along to get along. Everyone can calm down. There is no need to think Paul is doing more (or less) than offering practical advice to a particular congregation about their relationship with political leaders.

We also need to be honest: almost nobody takes Romans 13 seriously anyway. Pretty much everyone recognizes, either implicitly or explicitly, that there are limits to political submission. The book of Daniel serves as the exemplar *par excellence* of the faithful Jewish adherence to Jeremiah 29:7, and Paul himself in Philippi submits only insofar as it doesn't compromise the gospel. The second Daniel or Paul are confronted with a choice between honoring God and submitting to the authorities they follow Peter's defiant rebuttal to the Sanhedrin in Acts 5:29: "*We must obey God rather than men*". The question of Romans 13:1-7, then, is a matter of degree. When must Christians submit to political authorities and when does political compliance become an act of rebellion against God? These are not easy questions to answer, and for most Christians the answer is something like "*it depends*". Left, right, center, or libertarian, very few Christian political philosophies endorse complete moral surrender to the state, and rightfully so. Paul himself doesn't believe it, based on his own example, and neither should we.

Let's work through a hypothetical thought experiment. While appeals to Hitler and Nazi Germany are often little more than a cheap tactic to undermine arguments which those who employ the analogy are unable to counter, the Nazi regime is certainly one of the most evil in human history. Imagine yourself as a German citizen in 1943. A Jewish woman has escaped from a concentration camp and is

---

3. Schreiner, *Handbook*, p. 104

apprehended by a lone SS guard in your presence. The German soldier hands you a pistol and demands that you show allegiance to the Fuhrer by executing the poor woman in his presence. What is the Christian to do in that situation? Romans 13:1-7 tells us to submit to authorities because, after all, they were established by God in order to reward the good and punish the bad. Is taking the life of an innocent Jewish woman at the request of an SS guard morally obligated by Romans 13? Most Christians would emphatically say "*no*"! Some, however, did in fact interpret Romans 13:1-17 in absolute terms. Paul Achtemeier provides one prominent example from Nazi Germany: "*That is the interpretation given to* [Romans 13] *in the late thirties and early forties of* [last] *century by a group within the Protestant church in Germany, who for nationalistic reasons called themselves "German Christians." By means of this passage they justified their claim that Christians owed allegiance to Adolf Hitler*"[4]. This would be a bridge too far for most Christians, and rightly so. If the state commands a believer to murder an innocent person in cold blood, then the believer has a theological obligation to refuse.

Achtemeier poses a series of questions regarding the scope of Romans 13:1-7 which are all worth pondering: "*Does Paul here place on Christians the obligation to obey all edicts of whatever government happens to hold civil power over them? Is the ability to take over governing power, by whatever violent means some group is willing to employ, sufficient demonstration that the governing power they have assumed has been granted by God? Does every government, however established and however maintained, have equal claim to the divine sanction these verses confer on governing authorities?*"[5] The answer is, of course, no. The prophets constantly defied Israel's political leaders, Daniel refused to bow down and worship the Babylonian idols, Peter stood up to the Sanhedrin, and Paul humiliated the Philippian authorities. Based on the biblical witness itself, Paul cannot be read as saying that anyone who happens to be in a position of political power must be unquestionably obeyed. This is why Schreiner's succinct commentary on Romans 13 must be the starting point for any historically and canonically legitimate reconstruction of the passage; Paul isn't writing a comprehensive political philosophy, and to take his rhetoric as such is to misread him from the start. Context, in this case as in all others, is king.

This is also precisely why reflexively anti-imperial readings of Romans 13 are historically unjustifiable. Setting aside the fact, which stems from an imprecise categorical conceptualization of political and economic terminology, that "anti-imperial" readings always result in modern conclusions which aggrandize state power and ironically work in the service of imperialism, they also absolutize

---

4. Achtemeier, Paul. 1985. *Romans*. John Knox Press. pp. 203-204

5. Achtemeier, *Romans*, p. 204

resistance to the political order as the primary function of Romans 13.[6] This isn't to say that anti-imperial scholars are entirely wrong about Romans 13; far from it. We have reviewed the work of Wright, Horsley, and Elliott, as well as the more nuanced perspective articulated by Heilig, in Chapter 13, and found that they make some compelling arguments. Burnett and Haddad, however, have decisively demonstrated that the veiled criticism of Roman imperialism is often dramatically overstated and lacks the robust historical evidence necessary to substantiate anti-imperial claims. Many anti-imperialists have a decidedly modern political axe to grind and their methodological approach to Romans 13 provides a convenient legitimation for their preferred version of contemporary authoritarian socialism. They are correct, however, that the so-called "German Christians" of Hitler's Third Reich, as well as those who, less destructive their application of Romans 13 may be, uncritically appeal to the passage as a casual endorsement of their favorite political policies are misreading Paul. Paul is not affirming the validity of Roman imperialism or any other human government and there is a sense in which the anti-imperial reading, for all its epistemological shortcomings, is helpfully pushing back against facile readings of Romans 13. Its downfall, however, is being equally uncritical in its assumptions about Paul's 'hidden criticisms' of Rome. Romans 13 is much more dynamic than the "pro-" or "anti-" imperial labels would suggest.

One of my favorite quotes by the late great Lutheran biblical scholar Krister Stendhal explains why Western Christians are so obsessively concerned with personal forgiveness at the expense of other, equally important theological concepts: *"we happen to be more interested in ourselves than in God or the fate of his creation"*[7]. While Stendhal is absolutely correct in his context, I think this insight could also easily apply to our analysis of Romans 13. Interpreters, including lay readers, are so often more interested in forcing Romans 13:1-7 to affirm our preferred political arrangements than in understanding what Paul is actually claiming about the relationship between God and government. People love to appropriate Romans 13 when it suits their political interests, using it as a cudgel to beat their opponents into submission, while finding convenient ways to dismiss it when others use it against them in ways they find objectionable. How do we bridge this impasse? By locating Romans 13 in both its historical context, particularly with respect to Paul's general worldview (which has been extensively examined in the past several

---

6. In practical terms, 'resistance' is, ala Horsley, directed at contemporary political leaders they find repulsive and never at the political system itself, which scholars almost universally intend to empower and expand. Horsley's repetitive use of "anti-capitalist" rhetoric, which is entirely void of anything resembling linguistic precision, is a left-wing chimera; Horsley wants his political team to dominate others, and the Bible is but a theological justification for his personal will to power.

7. Stendhal, *Jews and Gentiles*, p. 24

chapters), and its rhetorical context within the epistle to Rome itself. The distinction between *function* and *meaning* is of particular significance here. Instead of beginning with the theological question of what Romans 13 *means* for an analysis of government, we should first ask how it was designed to *function* for Paul's original audience in Rome. Only then can we fruitfully draw principles from a text which was composed in a social and political milieu which differs extensively from the modern Western world.

This chapter will unfold in a fairly straightforward manner. Nothing Paul says in Romans, particularly 13:1-7, contradicts what he claims in his other letters. We already know what Paul thinks about christology, eschatology, ethics, and ecclesiology, and Romans isn't a refutation of Paul's earlier work. We will proceed through Romans as we have done with every other work in the New Testament. I will examine the background of Paul's letter, specifically his intentions in writing it and what he hoped to accomplish after its reception, and then explore how two relevant themes, christology and ecclesiology, are expressed within Romans. We will then explore the location of Romans 13:1-7 within its immediate context of Romans 12-15 and especially 12-13, showing how it relates to the rest of Paul's rhetoric in that section of the epistle. Finally, we will examine the passage in question itself, contextually analyzing Paul's instructions and providing a plausible historical reconstruction. I will conclude the chapter with a summary and synthesis of our findings before turning to the back half of the New Testament.

BACKGROUND: JEWS, GENTILES, THE SPANISH MISSION, AND PAUL'S GOSPEL

Paul himself had never visited Rome, which is in part the occasion of his longest epistle. In Romans 1:8-15, Paul introduces himself to an audience which he had yet to meet in person, praising them for their faith and ensuring them of his constant prayers on their behalf. His inability to drop in wasn't for lack of trying, as he explicates in 1:11-13: *"For I long to see you so that I may impart some spiritual gift to you . . .* [but] *I have planned to come to you (and have been prevented so far)"*. He feels optimistic about his prospects: *"So, for my part, I am eager to preach the gospel to you also who are in Rome"*[8]. In Romans 15:14-29, Paul explains the factors which have prevented his much-desired journey to the imperial capital. First, he wanted to visit places where there were not already established communities of believers: *"I aspired to preach the gospel, not where Christ was already named, so that I would*

---

8. Romans 1:15

not build on another man's foundation"[9]. Paul, believing he has done everything he can in the eastern Mediterranean, has one more task to complete before traveling into uncharted territory: bring the collection to Jerusalem.

He explains his mission in 15:25-26: "*But now, I am going to Jerusalem serving the saints, For Macedonia and Achaia have been pleased to make a contribution for the poor among the saints in Jerusalem*". Once Paul has completed this goal, he plans to travel to Spain, presumably where the gospel has not yet been preached, and on his way he intends to visit the church in Rome: "*with no further places for me in these regions, and since I have had for many years a longing to come to you whenever I go to Spain—for I hope to see you in passing, and to be helped on my way there by you, when I have first enjoyed your company for awhile . . . Therefore when I have finished* [delivering the collection to Jerusalem] . . . *I will go on by way of you to Spain*". Why does Paul write Romans? To introduce himself to an audience with which he is largely[10] unfamiliar and who he hopes to visit (and receive support) en route to Spain in the western Mediterranean. It's also possible, especially given the contents of the epistle, that he hopes his collection for the Judean church will inspire the Romans to support him and further his agenda of uniting the disparate community of Jew-and-Gentile Jesus followers.[11]

While Paul's practical, missional introduction to the Roman church is a primary concern, it is not the only item on his agenda. Paul's appeal to the Jerusalem collection in 15:25-28 isn't just a boast or a matter of autobiographical curiosity, it is likely central to a perennial problem facing the early Jesus movement: the proper relationship between Jews and Gentiles. The infamous opening passage of the letter's body in 1:16-17, the foundation of Luther's great reformational awakening, makes this abundantly clear: "*For I am not ashamed of the gospel, for it is the power of God for salvation to everyone who believes, to the Jew first and also to the Greek. For in it the righteousness of God is revealed from faith to faith; as it is written, "But the righteous man shall live by faith."*". It is important to note what many interpreters have missed: Paul is not, in Romans 1:16-17, defining the gospel, which he has already articulated in 1:1-5, but rather the gospel's *consequences*, what happens *as a result of the gospel being preached*. God saves those who believe (Paul uses the verbal form of the *pist-* word group) through the preaching of the gospel, to the Jews first and also to the Gentiles. I agree with Novenson that Paul, unsurprisingly given his Jewish background, privileges Jewish identity[12], a point confirmed by

---

9. Romans 15:20

10. Although not entirely; Romans 16 reveals Paul has several friends in the city.

11. Gorman, *Crucified Lord*, pp. 342-343

12. Novenson, *End of History*, pp. 138-143

Paul in Romans 3:1-2; Jews have an advantage because they were entrusted with God's oracles. However, consistent with the witness of Acts and the Pauline corpus, Paul maintains that Gentiles are incorporated into the family of Abraham through faith.

I promised to avoid as many contentious and divisive theological debates as possible, and Romans is absolutely rife with controversial material. I will lay down but one hermeneutical marker which might give us pause for reflection: following Krister Stendhal, who was speaking directly about justification (seriously, I'm not going there, I swear!), I believe it is imperative that any reading of Romans must take into consideration the dynamic between Jew and Gentile, already boldly stated at the outset of the letter and the explicit hinge upon which the entire letter swings.[13] Summarizing Pauline scholarship in the twentieth century, and equally applicable in the twenty-first, Zetterholm is spot-on: "*With regard to Pauline scholarship it is probably no exaggeration to suggest that Paul's relation to Judaism aptly frames the most important discussions of the twentieth century*"[14]. No reading of Paul in general or Romans in particular can ignore the Jew-Gentile dynamic at play in the text. Even Achtemeier, in his extremely conventional Protestant commentary on Romans, acknowledges the significance of this theme.[15] In Romans 1-4 Paul discusses the universality of God's judgment; Jews and Gentiles "*all have sinned and fall short to the glory of God, being justified as a gift by the redemption which is in Christ Jesus*"[16], are of the same God ("*is God the God of Jews only? Is He not the God of Gentiles also?*"[17]), and are a part of Abraham's family by faith (the crux of Romans 4). Paul discusses the Law and transformation through the Spirit in Romans 5-8, concluding that children of God are defined by the Spirit (see particularly 8:12-17), and then spends Romans 9-11 discussing (in a spirit of ecumenicism, I am being deliberately vague) the plight of ethnic Israel, reminding the Gentiles not to be arrogant because God graciously grafted them into the root of Israel[18]. He gives advice about how Jews and Gentiles can live in harmony in Romans 14-15, and includes both people with Jewish and Greco-Roman names in the greetings of Romans 16. Romans 12-13, the section which includes Paul's instructions on government, is, as we will see, not itself magically isolated from the Jew-Gentile dynamic which pervades Romans. This sprint through Romans powerfully illustrates

---

13. Stendhal, *Jews and Gentiles*, pp. 1-7

14. Zetterholm, *Approaches to Paul*, p. 1

15. Achtemeier, *Romans*, p. 3

16. Romans 3:23-34

17. Romans 3:29

18. Romans 11:11-24

a major background issue: Paul is concerned about the relationship between Jews and Gentiles, and whatever we make of the theological controversies (justification, sin, grace, Law, gospel, ect.) ignoring Paul's overarching concern with Jews and Gentiles will all but guarantee we never even approach understanding what the apostle intended to communicate.

This isn't just an abstract issue for Paul, either. Despite centuries (and indeed millennia) of interpretative assumptions, Romans is not reducible to a sterile systematic presentation of Paul's 'theology', whatever commentators might mean by that oftentimes nebulous term. As Schreiner himself notes, there are many aspects of Paul's theology which remain underdeveloped in Romans, particularly the role of spiritual gifts, eschatology, and even christology.[19] While these themes are absolutely essential for Paul's underlying logic, they are not expounded in the same detail as in his other letters which were written to different communities dealing with different sets of questions and problems. Yes, by introducing himself to the Roman congregation Paul does provide an expansive explanation of thinking on several other important issues, and to that extent Romans lends itself particularly well to theological exposition. I am not arguing there is no place for theological exegesis in Romans. But in order to properly understand the background of the letter, and thus Paul's intention in writing it, and thus its individual parts (with Romans 13:1-7 always on our mind), we must ask ourselves why Paul felt the need to address the Jew-Gentile issue in particular. It appears as if no less than Roman emperor Claudius is to blame.

In 49 CE there arose a dispute in Rome among Jews about a man named "Chrestus", most likely a reference to Jesus (as Paul's controversial eastern Mediterranean mission would attest). Fed up with the infighting, Claudius found an inelegant solution to the conflict: he expelled all Jewish residents from the city of Rome, including believers Aquila and Priscilla, according to Acts 18:2. This had a profound effect on the Jesus-believing community in Rome; for the first time a congregation was composed entirely of Gentiles, including the leadership. At the death of Claudius and accession of Nero in 54 CE, the Jews were once again allowed to return to Rome (which is why Paul greets Aquila and Priscilla by name in Romans 16:3), but Jesus-believing Jews were coming home to a thoroughly Gentile church which had five full years of social and theological development *without any Jewish participation* behind them. This created a situation in which the division between Jew and Gentile was particularly pronounced.[20] While it is impossible to tell if Paul is addressing an actual conflict between Jewish and

---

19. Schreiner, *Handbook*, pp. 53-54

20. Gorman, *Crucified Lord*, pp. 340-342

Gentile Jesus-believers or forestalling a potential division, Romans addresses the split head-on. Paul's letter is not therefore an abstract treatise on theology but a concrete exposition of the consequences of his gospel on the relationship between Jew and Gentile, which characterizes every aspect of Paul's logic in Romans. As in Galatians and Ephesians (and, for a different set of reasons, 1-2 Corinthians), Paul is promoting the unity of the church by theologizing his way through a discreet problem. This is, in short, one of the primary functions of Romans. A divided, unhealthy church would not be able to support Paul in any future missions to Spain and is anathema to his ecclesiology. It is little wonder, then, that Paul references his collection in Romans 15; if the Macedonian Gentiles can support the Judean Jews, then the Gentiles and Jews in Rome can learn to get along too.

Schreiner accurately summarizes the purpose of Romans: "*It is likely that divisions plagued Jews and gentiles in the churches . . . Furthermore, Paul himself was a polarizing figure, especially among Jews and even Jewish Christians, as Acts 21:20-25 attests. Paul wanted the Roman Christians to be the launching pad for his mission to Spain, but they could hardly function as his base if they were divided over the role of the law, particularly when that was the very issue that raised concerns about Paul. Paul, then, in the letter gives a full explanation of his view of the law and the place of Israel and gentiles in God's plan. His aim was that they would embrace the gospel he proclaimed and support him as he took that same gospel to Spain*"[21]. It is within this framework that we will analyze two themes in Romans which directly impact our study of Romans 13:1-7. Fortunately we are already familiar with both: christology and ecclesiology.

The Christology and Ecclesiology of Romans

Christology: Jesus Christ, Son of David

Paul strategically places three sweeping christological affirmations at key points in his letter. In Romans 1:1-5, the epistle's introduction, Paul briefly explains his gospel which is, as we have already seen, centered on the objective messianic identity of Jesus, son of David, Son of God. As Paul concludes the body of his letter, Romans 15:7-13 draws on a catena of passages from the Old Testament which prophesy about the submission of Gentiles to Israel's God, concluding with Isaiah 11:10 where the messianic son of David rules over the nations. Paul asserts this has already come to pass through the life, death, resurrection, and ascension of Jesus. The final passage of the letter, Romans 16:25-27, forms a doxology. While some

---

21. Schreiner, *Handbook*, p. 54

early manuscripts of Romans lack this passage[22] it is an appropriate finale which includes many of the main ideas in Romans, centered upon the messianic rule of Jesus proclaimed to the nations through Paul's gospel. These three texts form the christological substructure of Romans and are worth considering in more detail.

Arguably the greatest of Paul's great three gospel texts, Romans 1:1-5 is an appropriate introduction to an unfamiliar Roman audience. While we reviewed Paul's exposition of *euangelion* in Chapter 12, it is relevant to revisit it here: "*Paul, a bond-servant of Christ Jesus, called as an apostle, set apart for the gospel of God, which He promised beforehand through His prophets in the holy Scriptures, concerning His Son, who was born of a descendant of David according to the flesh, who was declared the Son of God with power by the resurrection from the dead, according to the Spirit of holiness, Jesus Christ our Lord, through whom we have received grace and apostleship to bring about the obedience of faith among all the Gentiles for His name's sake*". There is no way around Paul's bold definition of *euangelion*: Jesus, son of David, son of God, promised beforehand in the Scriptures, and raised from the dead is king of the world. Paul absolutely, positively does not believe that the messianic identity of Christ is either a 'spiritual' reality or a metaphor. Jesus is king. Period. The fulfillment of Israel's story, a narrative which concluded with the eschatological restoration of Israel and the universal rule of the Davidic Messiah has broken into the present through Jesus himself. The gospel is inseparable from eschatology and messianic christology, and, as Bates correctly highlights, Paul deliberately opens his letter to Rome with a sweeping statement of Jesus's decisive victory.[23]

I don't need to retread a well-worn path. We already know what Paul thinks about *euangelion*, *christos*, and *pistis*, which is, right there in Romans 1:5, the proper response to the message of Jesus fulfilling Israel's Scriptures. What primarily interests us here is the strategic announcement of Jesus at the beginning of Romans. Wright thinks it's intentional, and I, at least in part, would agree: "*part of the point of Romans is that it is written to Caesar's city but with a message very different from that of Caesar himself . . . part of its aim is to challenge, at several levels, the ideological foundations of Caesar's empire*"[24]. Paul's gospel is, as I have been arguing all along, *supra*political, with the reign of Jesus transcending the reign of any earthly rulers who are, as a result of the inaugurated eschaton, currently passing away. Wright, correctly in my view, nuances his views on Paul and empire in his 2013 book *Paul and the Faithfulness of God* ("*Paul's teaching and theology cannot, then, be reduced*

---

22. Gorman, *Crucified Lord*, p. 406

23. Bates, *Allegiance Alone*, pp. 30-35

24. Wright, N.T. 2011. *Justification*. InterVarsity Press. p. 177

to some kind of 'anti-imperial' rhetoric"[25]), but I accept that Paul's opening lines in Romans do have something of a political bent to them. How does it work?

Romans 1:1-5 is a perfect example of Heilig's argument that Paul, brash, bold apostle he was, doesn't resort to any sort of 'hidden criticism' when confronting Roman imperialism. While Paul is nuanced and careful in his rhetoric about Rome, he has no compunction about his position towards the empire.[26] As Heilig puts it: "*one cannot escape the impression that in their reading Paul is in the end quite blunt . . .* [Paul is probably] *more open* [to] *criticism of the Roman Empire than has been recognized so far*"[27]. Is Paul then opening the letter which includes Romans 13:1-7 with a critique of the Roman empire? Perhaps. Bryan, nuancing the conversation further, argues that Paul's language is characteristically Jewish and wouldn't have been perceived by the Roman authorities as explicitly 'anti-imperial'. The Romans made many claims, including political ones, to which Paul as a Jew would naturally object, but this was from the Roman perspective an extension of the monotheistic Jewish refusal to worship pagan gods. Paul might well be somewhat explicitly critiquing Roman rule by delineating the messianic backbone of his gospel in Romans 1:1-5, but no politician in Rome would view him or his message as an imminent political threat.[28] Both Heilig and Bryan make great points, and both are, in their own way, congruent with my thesis of a suprapolitical, christological, ecclesiological, and eschatological reading of Paul's political and economic rhetoric. Paul is against Roman rule and expresses his discontent, but not in the way many anti-imperial scholars have suggested.

Oakes, I believe, offers an excellent synthesis of the two positions which correspond with my analysis: "*To honor Rome while dishonoring Rome's gods was a contradiction in terms. Paul inherited this contradiction as part of his Judaism. For gentile converts to Christianity it must have seemed very strange . . . There is a tension in early Christian thought there. There is, of course, a biblical pattern to all this. Figures like Nebuchadnezzar could be seen as God's instruments even though Babylonian religious beliefs were still attacked. Something of the tension that was present in early Christian attitudes to Rome was also present in earlier Israelite attitudes to other dominant political players*"[29]. This is the Jeremiah 29:7 paradigm applied to the eschatological reign of Israel's Messiah. Jeremiah can exhort the exiles in Babylon to seek the welfare of the city while *in the next three chapters* prophesying about the restoration

---

25. Wright, *Faithfulness of God*, p. 1299

26. Heilig, *The Apostle and the Empire*, pp. 44-54

27. Heilig, *The Apostle and the Empire*, p. 47

28. Bryan, *Render to Caesar*, pp. 90-92

29. Oakes, *Empire*, p. 173

of Israel and, in Jeremiah 33:14-22, foretell the restoration of David's royal lineage! And, to top it all off, two of the final chapters in Jeremiah, 50-51, are oracles of destruction against Babylon, the very imperial capital which Jeremiah has instructed his audience to bless! "*Tension*" is right; that Paul applies this classic Jewish conceptualization of faithfulness in the midst of pagan rule, perfectly exemplified by the book of Daniel, should only come as a surprise to modern Westerners who need the Bible to legitimize their modern social and political projects. To hail Jesus as the one true king while requesting his audience to "*submit to authorities*" isn't a contradiction in terms or a flaw in Paul's logic, it is the very feature which had ensured the survival (and, in many places, relative peace) of God's people. The dawn of the eschaton and accompanying enthronement of Jesus only means the world must now be confronted with the truth. There is no place in the kingdom of a crucified Messiah for a violent rebellion against the pagan rulers. In the end, as Paul says *exactly* in Romans 12:19-21, God will vindicate his people. All they need to do is faithfully, obediently wait.

As Paul begins his letter with an affirmation of Jesus's lordship, so does the letter end. Romans 1 and 15 form an *inclusio*, a literary bookend which frames the rest of Paul's letter, with another explicit reference to the Davidic identity of Jesus.[30] Romans 15:7-13 is a fitting transition out of the body of Romans. In 15:8-9, Paul explains what Jesus Christ has done for both Jews and Gentiles: "*For I say that Christ has become a servant to the circumcision on behalf of the truth of God to confirm the promises given to the fathers, and for the Gentiles to glorify God for His mercy; as it is written*". He follows this up in 15:10-12 with a series of Old Testament citations, concluding with Isaiah 11:10: "*Again Isaiah says, "There shall come the root of Jesse, and He who arises to rule over the Gentiles, in Him shall the Gentiles hope"*". As Jipp notes, the *inclusio* makes a decisive rhetorical point for Paul. The resurrected Jesus rules, *currently*, over all, Jews and Gentiles alike, and Paul, apostle to the Gentiles, has been tasked with proclaiming his name to all the nations in fulfillment of Scripture.[31] I will repeat myself: this is not a metaphor or mere 'spiritual' reality. Paul really means it. The only proper political conclusion one should draw from these texts is that the Messiah which believers worship has transcended any and all earthly competitors, including the Roman empire. Romans 8:34 must be read in this light: "*Christ Jesus is He who died, yes, rather who was raised, who is at the right hand of God, who also intercedes for us*". Romans 16:25-27, which may or may not have been an original part of the letter, is a conceptual representation of Romans

---

30. Thiessen, *A Jewish Paul*, p. 73

31. Jipp, *Messianic Theology*, pp. 161-163

1 and 15: *"Jesus Christ . . . has been made known to all the nations"*. There is no carveout for Roman politicians.

Every serious commentator knows that one of the main themes in Romans is related to *pist*-language, translated either 'faith' or 'belief', and that through *pistis* God grants the Holy Spirit resulting in incorporation into His people, the family of Abraham. As I discussed at length in Chapter 12, *pist*-language is dynamic, having multiple possible English referents, including belief, trust, faithfulness, or, as Bates contends, allegiance. The conceptual advantage of translating *pistis* (and cognates) as 'allegiance' in Romans is its ability to draw out the political implications of Paul's gospel which, undeniably in my opinion, places Messiah Jesus at the center. Paul clearly, unambiguously asserts, along with the gospels and Acts, that Jesus is the son of David, the one true king. All the world now owes him allegiance. This insight also helps explain the close relationship between 'faith' and 'obedience' in Romans. Faith-language isn't reducible to a cognitive exercise, the mere intellectual assent to individual doctrinal propositions, but rather an active, verbal disposition which *necessarily* results in particular actions and behaviors towards the object of *pistis*. It should come as no surprise that in all three passages about the universal lordship of Jesus in Romans Paul discusses the fundamental significance of obedience.

The Greek noun obedience, *hypakoe*, is found in Romans 1:5, 15:18, and 16:26. In 1:5 and 16:25 it is directly connected with the faith (*pist*- language) of Gentiles, *"obedience of faith"*. In 15:18 Paul doesn't directly appeal to faith but has the nations clearly in mind; his gospel has brought about *"the obedience of the Gentiles"*. In all three passages *hypakoe* is associated with both *euangelion* and the Gentiles. This is no accident. Paul, apostle to the Gentiles, believed he was called by God to enact the great eschatological ingathering of the wayward pagans, drawing them into the worship of Israel's God, the only true God. Commenting on the *inclusio* formed by Romans 1 and 15, Thiessen connects the dots: *"not only do both passages connect the Davidic Messiah to the gentiles, but they also connect the gentiles to obedience: in Romans 1:5 the "obedience of faith," and in 15:18 obedience in word and deed. The message that the Messiah's herald* [Paul] *brings should be submitted to or obeyed . . . something that Paul's readers in Rome have done"*[32]. Paul draws on Psalm 18:49 in Romans 15:19, a passage which, of course, is about the Gentiles praising Israel's God, showing Him honor and obedience, all of which is brought about by Paul's gospel to the nations.

Once we understand the Messianic, eschatological significance of Paul's gospel, the relationship between *euangelion*, *pistis*, and *hypakoe* becomes crystal clear:

---

32. Thiessen, *A Jewish Paul*, pp. 73-74

"If we recognize that the climax of the gospel is Jesus's enthronement and that pistis is predominately allegiance, then Paul's point is lucid: the gospel is purposed toward bringing about the practical obedience characteristic of allegiance to a king . . . The gospel and Paul's mission are aimed at bringing about embodied allegiance to Jesus the king among the nations"[33]. Jesus, Israel's king, is also king of the nations, and through faith in the gospel both Jews and Gentiles live in obedience to him alone. The *inclusio* between Romans 1 and 15 marks these themes as a (or maybe even *the*) critical subtext of Paul's letter. With an eye to Romans 13, does that text somehow negate Paul's gospel of the Davidic Messiah? To quote Paul himself in Romans 6:1 and 6:15, *"May it never be"*! Although generations of interpreters have read the passage in isolation from the larger christological context of Romans, failing to balance what Paul says about government with his much more fundamental convictions about the messianic reign of Jesus will result in exegetical conclusions which confuse both. The solution is Jeremiah 29:7, in which the temporary submission to rulers for the sake of peace can sit (with some tension, of course) alongside eschatological hopes which include the destruction of all pagan empires. This leads us quite neatly to the second major theme in Romans which must condition our reading of 13:1-7. Those who faithfully obey the gospel of king Jesus are the people of God, and they are distinguished by incorporation from those who do not follow Jesus. Paul's ecclesiology provides us with yet another piece to the puzzle of God and government in Romans.

Ecclesiology: Abraham, Father of Jew and Gentile

"The gospel", as Paul says in Romans 1:16, *"is the power of God for salvation to everyone who believes, to the Jew first and also to the Greek"*. Paul, like many Jews in his day, perceived the world in binary terms. There were Jews, the chosen people of God, and a basically undifferentiated mass of others which Paul refers to as *"Gentiles"* in the plural and *"Greek"* in the singular, due to his Tarsian upbringing in the very Greek eastern Mediterranean. This was, as Novenson powerfully demonstrates, just the way things were from a Jewish perspective; it is us, God's chosen, upright people living in distinction from the unrighteous pagans.[34] While Paul maintains the Jews occupy a special place in world history (Romans 3:1-2 is illustrative: *"What advantage has the Jew? . . . Great in every respect . . . they were entrusted with the oracles of God"*), the shocking, dramatic eschatological dispensation of the Spirit upon even believing *Gentiles* forever changed the dynamics

---

33. Bates, *Allegiance Alone*, p. 86

34. Novenson, *End of History*, pp. 138-143

of God's people. This is, as we learned from Acts, Galatians, and Ephesians, an unexpected surprise which befell the early Jewish church leaders: God had granted the Spirit to all who have faith, Jews and Gentiles alike, and, perfectly summarized in Galatians 3, the family of Abraham is now defined by faith and the Spirit as the Gentiles are incorporated into the people of God *as Gentiles* through *pistis*. It is God's Spirit, His *pneuma*, which enables the eschatological ingathering of the nations, as Thiessen helpfully summarizes Galatians 3: "*If Jesus is the Messiah, then he is not only the seed of David but also the seed of Abraham, whom God promised in Genesis 15. And if gentile believers have the Messiah's pneuma, then they have his material in them and are, at the same time, clothed in the Messiah. They are in the Messiah, and the Messiah is in them*"[35]. This is exactly the ecclesiology of Romans, Paul's letter to a church uniquely burdened with the question of Jews and Gentiles, and must play a key role in any analysis of Romans 13.

Paul opens the body of his letter in 1:16-17 by appealing to the power of God through the gospel for both Jews and Gentiles. While Romans 1-4 is sometimes interpreted as an abstract commentary on the universal power of sin and grace, Paul in context is attempting to answer the Jew-Gentile question, as Gorman rightfully frames this section of the epistle.[36] In the broadest (and least controversial) possible terms, Romans 1-3 is an indictment against the sin of pagan Gentiles[37], the impartiality of God in judging sin[38], and the deliverance of all humanity through the sacrificial death of Jesus[39]. God will dispense either judgment or vindication on the Jew first, but also the Greek in the final judgment (the thrust of 2:5-11), culminating in the climactic claim of 2:11 that "*there is no partiality with God*", a reference not to general partiality among the human race but between Jews and Gentiles in particular. While, according to Paul in 3:1-2, Jews have an advantage (a position I believe, following Novenson, Paul holds with full sincerity), all are equally under sin: "*for all have sinned and fall short of the glory of God*", with "*all*" meaning "both Jews and Gentiles", whom are equally "*justified as a gift by His grace through the redemption which is in Christ Jesus*"[40]. This is why Paul asks the rhetorical question "*is God the God of Jews only? Is He not the God of Gentiles also?*", answering in the affirmative: "*Yes, of Gentiles also, since indeed God who will justify the circumcised by*

---

35. Thiessen, *A Jewish Paul*, p. 110

36. Gorman, *Crucified Lord*, p. 351

37. Romans 1:18-32

38. Romans 2:1-3:20

39. Romans 3:21-31

40. Romans 3:23-24

faith and the uncircumcised through faith is one"[41]. Nothing here hinges upon any tradition's interpretation of 'justification'; what matters instead is Paul's emphasis on Jews, Gentiles, and the centrality of *pistis*.

Paul has set himself up for Romans 4 in which his basic argument is analogous to Galatians 3. Abraham's family has been redefined by *pistis*, which was, all along, how the people of God should have responded to their creator anyway. The climactic passage occurs in 4:13-16: *"For the promise to Abraham or to his descendants that he would be heir of the world was not through the Law, but through the righteousness of faith. For if those who are of the Law are heirs, faith is made void and the promise is nullified; for the Law brings about wrath, but where there is no law, there also is no violation. For this reason it is by faith, in order that it may be in accordance with grace, so that the promise will be guaranteed to all the descendants, not only to those who are of the Law, but also to those who are of the faith of Abraham, who is the father of us all"*. Without taking a position on the vexing "Paul, the Law, and Romans" question, it is easy to see how Paul is making the same argument, albeit in a different context, that he did in Galatians 3. It's imperative to remember that the "*all*" is not a reference to our common humanity but rather a declaration that Gentiles as well as Jews are "*all*" a part of Abraham's family through *pistis* in the Messiah. While I don't agree entirely with Wright's analysis of Romans 4, he accurately encapsulates the gist of Paul's argument: *"The flow of Paul's thought from Romans 4:9 onward indicates that the question towards which Paul is working in the opening verses is rather the question—much as in Galatians 3!—who are the family of Abraham? Who are his "seed" (Romans 4:16)? Is this a family of Jews only[?] . . . the promise is valid for "all the seed," that is, for the entire family, for Jews and Gentiles alike, because Abraham is the father of us all"*[42]. In the eschatological, messianic age, Jews and Gentiles alike are incorporated into Abraham's family through faith and the Spirit, and, for Paul, the world can be neatly divided into those who are "in Abraham" and those who are not. It should go without saying that the authorities to which Paul requests the Romans submit are on the outside.

Paul's analysis of the Jew-plus-Gentile church doesn't conclude with Romans 4. The next section of Romans, chapters 5-8, also culminates in an affirmation of the unique family of God as defined by the Spirit. As Paul works with concepts such as sin, the Law, grace, and baptism in Romans 5-7, his universalisation of the human condition cannot be detached from the wider context of his letter. In 5:12-21, all, Jew and Gentile alike, were "in Adam" but can now be freed through Christ. Believers should not continue in sin because they are all "*slaves of obedience*

---

41. Romans 3:29-30

42. Wright, *Justification*, pp. 217-218

resulting in righteousness", as Paul claims in 6:15-19. Romans 7, where Paul's rhetoric has been intensely debated, reflects upon the relationship between the Law and Christ, both of which can only be properly analyzed within a Jewish framework. The opening salvo of Romans 8, where Paul will ultimately describe in masterly eloquence the *pneuma*-filled glory of God's people, contrast the Law with the Spirit: "*Therefore there is now no condemnation for those who are in Christ Jesus. For the law of the Spirit of life in Cherist Jesus has set you free from the law of sin and death . . . so that the requirement of the Law might be fulfilled in us, who do now walk according to the flesh but according to the Spirit*"[43]. Paul will then contrast the "*flesh*" with the "*Spirit*" in Romans 8:5-17.

The highlight of this section for our purposes is found in 8:14-17: "*For all who are being led by the Spirit of God, these are sons of God. For you have not received a spirit of slavery leading to fear again, but you have received a spirit of adoption as sons by which we cry out, "Abba! Father!" The Spirit Himself testifies with our spirit that we are children of God, and if children, heirs also, heirs of God and fellow heirs with Christ, if indeed we suffer with Him so that we may also be glorified with Him*". This outlines, following Acts, Galatians, and Ephesians, a familiar set of concepts. God's family is defined by those who have received the promised eschatological Spirit, poured out upon those who place their faith in Jesus, for the Jew first but also for the Greek. The Spirit is what binds the family of Abraham together; the "sons [and daughters, by implication] of God" are "all who are being led by the Spirit", both Jews and Gentiles. As Thiessen explains, "*The creation of new sons of God explains Paul's pervasive use of familial language . . . he addresses them throughout . . . [his] . . . letters in fraternal terms. Why? Because they truly are brothers, a new genus of humans who are sons of God, related to one another through their pneumatic connection to God's son and ultimately to Israel's God*"[44]. And, as we have seen before, Paul envisions this family in characteristically Jewish exclusivistic terms. It's us, those who have faith in the Jewish Messiah and possess God's Spirit, and them, those who have neither. In Romans 8:18-39 Paul maps this onto the entire created order with the promise that God will never abandon the family of Abraham forged by faith and the Spirit: "*But in all these things we overwhelmingly conquer through Him who loved us. For I am convinced that neither death, nor life, nor angels, nor principalities, nor things present, nor things to come, nor powers, nor height, nor depth, nor any other created thing, will be able to separate us from the love of God, which is in Christ Jesus our Lord*"[45]. That Paul uses plural forms of *arche* and *dynamis* in this

---

43. Romans 8:1-4

44. Thiessen, *A Jewish Paul*, p. 124

45. Romans 8:37-39

passage is certainly not accidental. No power can separate God's people from His love, and one day His family will be fully vindicated over and against all of the fleshly powers which war against them in the present.

This takes us into Romans 9-11, which Stendhal (among others) has dubbed *"the climax of Romans"*[46]. Whether this is true or not, Wright correctly identifies the lack of attention this passage has received compared to other Pauline texts: *"Romans 9-11 itself, of course,* [has been] *for so long treated as essentially irrelevant . . . except as a happy hunting ground for theories about predestination"*[47]. Wright isn't wrong. For better or for worse, the purpose of Romans 9-11 is often either ignored or distorted by the need to make it conform to an idiosyncratic theological system. This section of Romans, however, addresses an issue which is near and dear to Paul's heart, as Novenson perfectly summarizes: "[Paul] *undertakes to explain to himself the strange spectacle of gentiles thronging to the Christ sect while Jews, by and large, ignore or reject it"*[48]. A relevant question considering the Edict of Claudius and subsequent return of Jews to the Gentile-led community in Rome. Romans 9-11 is complex and replete with thorny exegetical dilemmas, but the Jew-Gentile dynamic is central to Paul's argument. The section begins with a lament (*"I have great sorrow and unceasing grief in my heart"*[49]) regarding ethnic Israel's rejection of the Messiah in 9:1-5 and ends with great hope that *"all Israel will be saved"*[50], praising God in 11:33-36 for his *"wisdom and knowledge"*, assured in the hope God will ultimately bring his plans for ethnic Israel to fruition. Just as Romans 1 and 15 serve as bookends for the entire letter, christologically conditioning the rest of Paul's argument; the opening passage in Romans 9 and the closing passage in Romans 11 form an *inclusio* around the section which conditions the rest of Paul's thinking in 9-11.

While I don't agree with every aspect of Wright's analysis of Romans 9-11, he correctly calls attention to the section's tight rhetorical structure, climaxing in Romans 10:9.[51] Again practicing self-restraint in a spirit of ecumenicism, I only want to highlight the ecclesiological features of Romans 9-11. I will select a passage on either side of 10:9 before reflecting on its significance in the logic of Paul's argument. In Romans 9:24, Paul discusses the church *"whom He also called, not from among Jews only, but also from among Gentiles"*. This is, of course, what the

---

46. Stendhal, *Jews and Gentiles*, p. 4

47. Wright, *Justification*, p. 179

48. Novenson, *End of History*, p. 143

49. Romans 9:2

50. Romans 11:26

51. Wright, *Faithfulness of God*, pp. 1162-1164

Jerusalem leaders decide in Acts 15 and the foundation of Paul's own discussion in Romans 4 (as well as Galatians 3 and Ephesians 2, for that matter). In Romans 11:11-24, Paul warns Gentiles not to be arrogant against Jews because they were *"grafted contrary to nature into a cultivated olive tree"*[52] on account of *"God's kindness"*[53]. Jews are the natural heirs of God's promises, but through the eschatological rule of Israel's Messiah the Gentiles are incorporated into God's family through faith. This leads us to the rhetorical (and theological) center of Romans 9-11, 10:9: *"if you confess with your mouth Jesus as Lord, and believe in your heart God raised him from the dead, you will be saved"*. Paul prefaces this claim with a brief exegesis of Deuteronomy 30 in Romans 9:5-8; the point, of course, is that the restoration promised to Israel in Deuteronomy 30 results in the blessing of *all* nations, which is why the Gentiles can inherit salvation by proclaiming the Jewish Messiah as their Lord.[54] Contrary to many popular interpretations, the question Paul is addressing in Romans 9-11 is not *"how can Jews become Christian?"* but rather *"how are the Gentiles being incorporated into Abraham's family?"*. The answer is straightforward and in complete harmony with the New Testament witness: faith in Israel's Messiah. We find ourselves right back to Paul's ingroup-outgroup ecclesiology which, of course, places the Roman political authorities squarely on the outside. Romans 13 must be read within the context of Romans 9-11.

Romans 14-16 is, in the words Gorman, *"the goal towards which the theme of Jew and Gentile has been incessantly driving"*[55]. Romans 14:1 begins with the word *"Now"*, marking the transition to a new theme. Although in broad thematic continuity with Romans 12-13, Paul does clearly turn to another set of issues. Similar to 1 Corinthians 8-10, there are some in Rome, whom Paul labels *"weak"*, that have chosen to only eat vegetables and abstain from wine while others have no dietary restrictions.[56] Given the broader historical context of Romans and the rift (actual or potential) between Jews and Gentiles in the church, Gorman's suggestion that this division probably approximates the Jew-Gentile divide is persuasive.[57] Paul's solution to the problem is rather simple. No one, according to Romans 14:3-23, should judge another believer for their dietary preferences, and, in a spirit of unity, the church must determine *"not to put an obstacle or a stumbling block in a brothers way"* but instead *"pursue the things which make for peace and the building up one*

---

52. Romans 11:24

53. Romans 11:22

54. Wright, *Faithfulness of God*, pp. 1172-1176

55. Gorman, *Crucified Lord*, p. 397

56. Romans 14:1-4

57. Gorman, *Crucified Lord*, p. 398

another", not "*tear*[ing] *down the work of God for the sake of food*"[58]. Abraham's eschatological family of Jews and Gentiles under the rule of Israel's Messiah must maintain unity by showing deference to one another, accepting differences and placing the interests of other believers before their own.

Leading up to the great catena of Old Testament citations in Romans 15:9-12, Paul in 15:1-6 argues that "*Each of us is to please his neighbor for his good, to his edification . . . be of the same mind with one another according to Jesus Christ*". Jews and Gentiles must learn to get along, as Paul argues in 15:7-9: "*Therefore, accept one another, just as Christ also accepted us in the glory of God. For I say that Christ has become a servant to the circumcision on behalf of the truth of God to confirm the promises given to the fathers, and for the Gentiles to glorify God for His mercy*". One family, under Christ, indivisible. Romans 16, a greeting to the congregation in Rome, is a fitting conclusion to Paul's long epistle. The list of names includes, echoing Galatians 3:28, Jews and Gentiles, slaves and free, and males and females. As Gorman argues, Romans 16 "*illustrates how the several house churches of Rome embody the Pauline vision of an inclusive community: Gentiles and Jews, slave, free, and freedpersons; elite and nonelite; men and women; from all corners of the empire*"[59]. Paul's letter to the Romans, functionally composed to address the Jew-Gentile division, reveals Pauline ecclesiology at its finest. Abraham's family cannot allow itself to be divided. It is the one true kingdom community, the eschatological family of God, called to testify about the universal reign of Christ to an unbelieving world. Paul's words from Ephesians 4:4-6 works well a summary of Romans: "*There is one body and one Spirit, just as also you were called in one hope of your calling; one Lord, one faith, one baptism, one God and Father of all who is over all and through all and in all*".

Just as Paul does not hold a metaphorical interpretation of Jesus's Messianic identity, his Abrahamic ecclesiology of a church defined by faith and the Spirit is also not metaphorical. Paul believes in an objective, universal Messiah who has ushered in the end of history by defeating death and taking his rightful place on the cosmic throne and that the faith-plus-Spirit family of Abraham are the true people of God, set apart from the world and allegiant to a suprapolitical, transcendent kingdom. This is the context of Paul's wider thought and the subtext (sometimes made explicit) of Romans as an epistle. There can be no fruitful, contextually accurate exegesis of Romans 13:1-7 which doesn't take Paul's christology and ecclesiology into consideration. It would also appear that Paul's logic runs precisely parallel to Jeremiah and Daniel. While for the prophets God's eschatological plans

---

58. Romans 14:13, 19-20

59. Gorman, *Crucified Lord*, p. 405

(including the restoration of Israel and the reign of Messiah) were still entirely *future*, the idea that Jews were God's chosen, set-apart people who would one day be vindicated when the pagan empires were finally, once and for all dismantled by God determined social and political engagement in their present. Neither Jeremiah nor Daniel assumed peace and prosperity, including within the Babylonian (and Persian) imperial orders, to be an inappropriate goal for God-honoring Jews. They should, in fact, strive to be respected among the pagans. Jeremiah, however, declares that Babylon will one day fall to ruin, while Daniel, the wisest imperial advisor in Babylon, never bows down and worships their gods, even if he must spend the night with a few hungry lions. Jeremiah, Daniel, and Paul all have this in common: they live in the real world which has yet to be (fully, in Paul's case) transformed by God. In general, God's set apart people should seek peace so long as it doesn't compromise theological beliefs and values. There is no reason to think Romans 13:1-7 deviates in the slightest from this fundamentally Jewish perspective on Abraham's family in the midst of pagan empire.

THE IMMEDIATE CONTEXT: ROMANS 12-13

Much to the detriment of interpretations which isolate the passage from its rhetorical context, Romans 13:1-7 cannot be detached from its context. Too many readers of Romans, wanting to quickly construct a timeless theology of government which legitimates their preferred political arrangements while denigrating those of others, fail to see how the passage works within the framework of either Romans as a whole or its immediate context. Both considerations necessarily shape the exegetical contours of Paul's most controversial passage about believers and government. An analysis of the surrounding material and rhetorical context of Romans 13 necessarily conditions the parameters of possible interpretive conclusions, including the principles which we in the modern world, enthralled to the theory of authoritarian socialism, may validly draw from the text. Romans 12:1-2 marks a decisive shift in Paul's letter, while the use of "*Now*" in Romans 14:1 serves as a transition to another issue, which is why the immediate context is reducible to Romans 12-13. Once we understand the function of the section as a whole, we will be in a position to soberly assess its constituent parts, including, of course, Paul's instructions regarding the authorities.

The section opens with Romans 12:1-2: "*Therefore I urge you, brethren, by the mercies of God, to present your bodies a living and holy sacrifice, acceptable to God, which is your spiritual service of worship. And do not be conformed to this world, but be transformed by the renewing of your mind, so that you may prove what the will of God is, that which is good and acceptable and perfect*". The conjunction "*therefore*" is of massive significance; Paul has spent 11 chapters passionately delineating the consequences of his gospel and the Jew-plus-Gentile church it generates, precisely *"by the mercies of God"*. God has rescued Abraham's family, *therefore* they must act accordingly.[60] It is also a proleptic summary of the material which will follow it in 12:3-15:13, an explanation of how Romans 1-11 is put into action by the community in Rome. Believers are to be *"a living sacrifice"*, imagery which draws upon the temple. Paul refers to the church as the *naos*, the inner sanctum of God's temple, in 1 Corinthians 3:16-17[61], and by offering themselves as a *"living sacrifice"* believers are orienting their lives around God. Paul's use of the word *logikos*, translated *"spiritual"* in the NASB, can also be justifiably rendered "rational" or "reasonable", making the offering of one's life to God the logical response to His mercies recounted in Romans 1-11.[62]

Believers must be transformed *"by the renewing of your mind"* to understand the will of God, which is contrasted with conformity *"to this world"*. The Greek translated *"world"* in the NASB is a form of *aion*, the same term Paul uses in 1 Corinthians 10:11 when he declares that the Corinthians are those *"upon whom the ends of the ages* [a form of *aion*] *have come"*; as in 1 Corinthians, *"ages"* is the natural translation because Paul is operating within a framework of inaugurated eschatology. Tellingly, and with significant implications for our interpretation of Romans 13, Paul uses *aion* in 1 Corinthians 2:6 and 2:8 to describe the *"rulers of this age* [another form of *aion*], *who are passing away"*; the wisdom of God *"none of the rulers of the age* [yet another form of *aion*] *has understood; for if they had understood it they would not have crucified the Lord"*. Believers are not to be in conformity with the *aion* (and its rulers) who are passing away. The ends of the ages have befallen the Jew-and-Gentile family of Abraham because the Davidic Messiah has been raised from the dead and sits on his cosmic throne. Believers must logically offer their lives as a living sacrifice to God and renew their minds, not conforming to the *aion* but discerning the will of God. Schreiner wisely reflects on this passage: *"True worship means that God's rule is reinstated in the lives of his people. Believers are not to be shaped the the present evil age . . . but the minds of believers are reoriented and recalibrated, and as a consequence they are enabled to carry out God's good and pleasing will"*[63].

Romans 12:1-2 is the foundation for the rest of his exhortation in Romans, with the goal of helping them discern *"the will of God . . . that which is good and*

---

60. Gorman, *Crucified Lord*, p. 390

61. See also 2 Corinthians 6:16 and Ephesians 2:21.

62. Gorman, *Crucified Lord*, pp. 390-391

63. Schreiner, *Handbook*, p. 101

acceptable and perfect". It does not conform to, as Paul argues in 1 Corinthians 2:6-8, the wisdom of the rulers of this *aion*. Is unconditional support for a pagan government, defining oneself by relation to that government, or uncritically accepting the inevitability of pagan rule compatible with Romans 12:1-2? Of course not. Carrying that logic forward, Paul's instructions about authorities *must* take into consideration nonconformity with the *aion* and the absolute surrender of one's life to God, all of which is predicated on the new identity conferred by membership in the family of Abraham through faith and the Spirit. How exactly this is accomplished is Paul's objective beginning in 12:3.

Echoing 1 Corinthians 12 and Ephesians 4, Paul explains in Romans 12:3-8 that no one should "*think more highly of himself than he ought to think . . . because God has allotted to each of measure of faith*" because "*we, who are many, are one body in Christ*" and have been given various gifts which must be used to build up the church. The one family of God should use their God-given gifts in service of others, edifying the church. Paul is then able in Romans 12:9-13 to encourage the church to love one another, hating evil but "*devoted to one another in love*", "*contributing to the needs of the saints*", and "*practicing hospitality*". He hints at external trouble in 12:12 ("*persevering in tribulation*") and is likely preparing his audience for the following set of instructions in 12:14-21. The fine point of Paul's exhortation in this section is that the family of Abraham must learn to treat one another as family members. Everyone has something to contribute in a community which can only be established by Christ-like love for one another. Instead of conforming to the *aion*, believers conform to Christ and the identity they have as a community.

The final section of Romans 12, 12:14-21, presumes hostile external pressure: "*Bless those who persecute you; bless and do not curse*"[64]. It would seem odd for Paul to issue this specific instruction unless he was aware of persecution, and his own personal experiences during the Mediterranean mission provided him with ample opportunities to suffer at the hands of outsiders. His solution, of course, does not conform to this *aion*. Paul, channeling the Jesus tradition in this passage (particularly Matthew 5:43-48), encourages believers to bless those who persecute them, following the example set by Jesus himself.[65] The communal love and support of a united Roman church will enable the community to endure any and every threat posed against them from the outside. As in Philippians and the Thessalonian epistles, the church must maintain its cruciform witness to an outside world that doesn't (yet) know the gospel. Paul's response to persecution is indispensable for contextualising Romans 13. The key statement occurs in Romans 12:17-18:

---

64. Romans 12:14

65. Schreiner, *Handbook*, p. 103

"Never pay back evil for evil to anyone. Respect what is right in the sight of all men. If possible, so far as it depends on you, be at peace with all men". Gorman hits the nail on the head: *"When evil comes . . . the community must respond as its Lord did and taught"*[66]. No matter what outsiders do to the community they must not respond in turn, maintaining respectability before others.

Paul then drops a line which could have been taken directly out of Jeremiah: *"If possible, so far as it depends on you, be at peace with all men"*[67]. Paul might as well have said *"seek the welfare of the city"*. Paul recognizes that peace isn't always possible. Those persecuting the church certainly aren't interested in making peace themselves. Yet he places the responsibility of maintaining peace squarely on the shoulders of believers, *"so far as it depends on you"*. This is, once again, *exactly* the attitude taken by the author of Daniel. The great Jew-in-exile Daniel sought peace with his pagan neighbors, and when the pagans turned on him Daniel refused to compromise his commitment to the God of Israel. Daniel did, as far as it depended on him, attempt to live in peace with all men. Paul is, as we have seen time and time again, tapping into this long Jewish tradition of balancing peace with non-Jews (including their political leaders) and fidelity to God. Yes, Paul has refracted this teaching through a new christological prism (he was, after all, familiar with the Jesus tradition) but his response to a hostile outside world would make Jeremiah and Daniel proud. Might, I suggest with trepidation, this be the authentic Pauline justification for his instructions in Romans 13:1-7? Might that entire contentious passage be summarized by the phrase *"if possible, live at peace with all men"*? Or, even better, *"seek the welfare of the city"*? And might Paul, in fact, understand, as Jeremiah and Daniel both did, that there are real limits to political submission? That when one was forced to choose between God and government there really wasn't any choice to make at all? I certainly think so.

Romans 12:19-21 offers another interesting ideological parallel with Jeremiah.[68] Believers must never pay back evil for evil and seek to live in peace with those who hate them. Why? Because ultimately God will settle the score: *"Never take your own revenge, beloved, but leave room for the wrath of God, for it is written, "Vengeance is Mine, I will repay," says the Lord. "But if your enemy is hungry, feed him, and if he is thirsty, give him a drink; for in so doing you will heap burning coals on his head." Do not be overcome by evil, but overcome evil with good"*.

---

66. Gorman, Crucified Lord, *p. 393*

67. Romans 12:18

68. To be clear, I am *not* claiming Paul's instructions are textually dependent on Jeremiah, only that Jeremiah offers us an insight into a popular Jewish paradigm for political engagement within which Paul must be located to make any historical sense of his approach to the governing authorities.

Paul quotes Deuteronomy 32:35 ("*vengeance is Mine, I will repay*") and Proverbs 25:21-22 ("*if your enemy is hungry feed him . . . for in so doing you will heap burning coals on his head*") as Scriptural justification for his teaching. Deuteronomy 32:35 is, tellingly, set within the context of Israel's rejection and God's eschatological restoration; those who oppose God will be judged but for those who are faithful, "*the Lord will vindicate His people, and have compassion on His servants*"[69]. Paul, deft interpreter of Israel's Scriptures who often alludes to the context of the passages he cites is deliberately invoking the context of eschatological restoration, and his choice of Deuteronomy 32 in light of his appropriation of Deuteronomy 30 only a few passages earlier in Romans 10 is certainly curious. If there is a central theme in Deuteronomy 27-32, it is that God will judge the wicked and vindicate the righteous, which is *precisely* what Paul is arguing in Romans 12:19-21. The reference to Proverbs 25:21-22 is consistent with the common Old Testament motif of describing God's judgment with fiery imagery and signifies the judgment of God.[70] Judgment is God's prerogative alone. There is, as Gorman correctly asserts, an intrinsic connection between Christian peace and God's wrath: "*For believers, retaliation not only violates their Lord's teaching and example but also usurps the future judgment of God that is central to the Scriptures . . . This certainty of divine wrath—since in biblical though the enemies of God's people are ultimately God's enemies—frees believers to deal in goodness with enemies*"[71].

How do these instructions relate to Jeremiah? Immediately after exhorting the exiles to "*seek the welfare of the city*", Jeremiah 27:10-14 promises that God will restore the fortunes of his people and return them to the land. Jeremiah 30-33 is a prophetic expansion of the hope for restoration, including covenant renewal and the permanent establishment of David's line. Because of this, Israel will "*be to Me a name of joy, praise and glory before all the nations of the earth which will hear of all the good that I do for them, and they will fear and tremble because of all the good and all the peace that I make for it*"[72]. The nations will see God's glory when Israel is restored, an event which Paul believes *has already begun to take place* through Jesus and the incorporation of Gentiles ("*all the nations*") into Abraham's family. As Jeremiah draws to a close in 50-51, God promises to destroy the wicked Babylonians. Among vivid imagery employed in these oracles is that of fiery judgment: "*The broad wall of Babylon will be completely razed And her high gates will be set on fire; So the peoples will toil for nothing, And the nations become exhausted only*

---

69. Deuteronomy 32:36

70. Schreiner, *Handbook*, p. 103

71. Gorman, *Crucified Lord*, p. 393

72. Jeremiah 33:9

for fire"[73]. There are similar motifs of judgment and vindication throughout the prophets, all of which call for present faithfulness in light of future vindication. Daniel 12, to pick one example, foresees a great global catastrophe which will engulf all of humanity but is tempered with the promise of resurrection *"at the end of the age"*[74]. Romans 12 adopts the same political paradigm as the Old Testament prophets. Conceptually Paul's only innovation is his eschatological and christological reworking of these basic prophetic themes. He is not singing a new song, only accenting a familiar melody.

Passing by, just for the moment, Romans 13:1-7, Paul builds on these ideas in 13:8-10: *"Owe nothing to anyone except to love one another; for he who loves his neighbor has fulfilled the law. For this, "You shall not commit adultery, You shall not murder, You shall not steal, You shall not covet," and if there is any other commandment, it is summed up in this saying, "You shall love your neighbor as yourself." Love does no wrong to a neighbor; therefore love is the fulfillment of the law"*. Theologically this is a very intriguing comment considering Paul's discussion of the Law earlier in Romans, but its relevance to the immediate context of Romans 12-13 should be apparent. This passage, building upon Leviticus 19:18 and the teachings of Jesus, explains how to live at peace with all men. Nothing is owed except love for one another, and love does no wrong to a neighbor. The Jesus tradition, particularly Luke 10:25-37, expands (or perhaps simply clarifies its original intention) the commandment *"love your neighbor"* to include all people, and the church in Rome is called to *"prove what the will of God is"* by loving their neighbors.

Paul draws this section of his letter to a close by appealing to eschatology, a rhetorical move which would have fit comfortably within the prophetic literature. Believers in Rome should be at peace and show love to all men because the great day of vindication soon approaches, as Romans 13:11-12 illustrates: *"Do this, knowing the time, that it is already the hour for you to awaken from sleep; for now salvation is nearer to us than when we believed. The night is almost gone, and the day is near"*. Or, as Jeremiah might put it, seek the welfare of Babylon because God will soon deliver you. That, I submit, is the basic lesson which both Paul and the prophets are seeking to teach. In case the Roman church hadn't been paying attention, Paul delivers one more set of instructions by which believers could *"be transformed by the renewing of* [their] *minds"*. As Romans 12:12-14 states, *"Therefore"*, because of the impending eschatological consummation, *"let us lay aside the deeds of darkness and put on the armor of light. Let us behave properly as in the day . . . put on the Lord Jesus Christ, and make no provision for the flesh in regard to its lusts"*. One

---

73. Jeremiah 51:58

74. Daniel 12:13

more reference to the Lord Jesus Christ and the future vindication of all believers (christology, eschatology, and ecclesiology tightly bound together) seals Paul's argument. If Paul had written a modern paraphrase of Romans 12-13, it might read something like this: Instead of conforming to the *aion*, offer yourselves as a living sacrifice and transform your mind, as a result of which you will, if possible, live at peace and through love with all men. When life gets hard remember God will judge your enemies and liberate you in the end. They won't win. God will.

Romans 13:1-7 is in many ways a cruel twist of exegetical fate. Had Paul not decided to insert his comments about the governing authorities in the middle of Romans 12-13, generations of interpreters would have found very little objectionable in the preceding summary. From the Garden of Eden to our present day, however, humanity has had an unhealthy obsession with the intoxicating allure of power. A comparatively sizable block of teaching addressing the question of political authority was bound to draw undue attention, and much as the gravity of a black hole consumes any ray of light attempting to escape, Romans 13:1-7 casts a dark shadow in the galaxy of Pauline interpretation. I don't think it has to, though. Let's perform one more thought experiment before moving to the text itself. Romans 12:1-21 flows naturally into 13:8-14. If 13:1-7 *wasn't* a part of the letter, the context of Romans 12-13 wouldn't be affected in the slightest. In other words, it's clear that the agenda Paul sets in 12:1-2 conditions this section of the letter irrespective of the inclusion of 13:1-7. Therefore 13:1-7 isn't a Pauline slip of the pen or an artificial insertion by a secretary of a statement Paul didn't dictate to be included at that point in his letter. The context of Romans 12-13 flows naturally and as a result Romans 13:1-7 must be intrinsically related to its surrounding context; isolating the text as if it can be analyzed without reference to the entire passage is a grave exegetical mistake. We won't fall for the trap. Paul's worldview (informed by the prophets, the church, the eschaton, and, most importantly, the Messiah), the function and intention of Romans as a whole, and the rhetorical context within which Romans 13:1-7 is located have all been established. We have but one more objective: interpret Romans 13:1-7.

ROMANS 13:1-7

I quote again, before we analyze the text in full, Romans 13:1-7: *"Every person is to be in subjection to the governing authorities. For there is no authority except from God, and those which exist are established by God. Therefore whoever resists authority has opposed the ordinance of God; and they who have opposed will receive condemnation upon themselves. For rulers are not a cause of fear for good behavior, but for evil. Do you want to have no fear of authority? Do what is good and you will have praise from the same; for it is a minister of God to you for good. But if you do what is evil, be afraid; for it does not bear the sword for nothing; for it is a minister of God, an avenger who brings wrath on the one who practices evil. Therefore it is necessary to be in subjection, not only because of wrath, but also for conscience' sake. For because of this you also pay taxes, for rulers are servants of God, devoting themselves to this very thing. Render to all what is due them: tax to whom tax is due; custom to whom custom; fear to whom fear; honor to whom honor"*. Read in isolation from its historical and rhetorical context, it's easy to see how this text could be used to legitimize, justify, or endorse nearly any employment of political power. As Achtemeier points out, there were several German Christians during World War II who appropriated this text in support of, to borrow a phrase, "literally Hitler". Apparently they forgot to read the gospels, or even the rest of Romans. Any discerning believer should with little effort demolish the pro-Nazi reading of Romans 13, but the question still stands: what are we to do with this text?

Heilig has a lengthy and productive conversation regarding the difficulties of interpreting Paul's commentary regarding authorities, and even though I don't agree with all of Heilig's conclusions he masterfully identifies the perplexing challenges with which readers must grapple.[75] He lays out three questions in particular which demonstrate the futility of facile, decontextualized readings of Romans 13: "*Is Paul really (a) demanding complete submission to governing authorities and (b) encouraging the Roman Christians to seek out recognition within society, grounding all this in (c) divine legitimation of state authority, including brutal force?*"[76] To arrive at this conclusion, Heilig argues that Paul would have to be both hopelessly naive and completely ignorant about how Roman power was actually deployed against imperial subjects.[77] Considering Paul was a well-traveled citizen of Rome who often wound up on the wrong side of justice, arguing that Paul was naive is unsustainable based on the evidence. Paul was under no illusion that the propagandized *Pax Romana* was wholly benevolent. Oakes asks rhetorically "*has [Paul] forgotten what happened to Jesus?*"[78]; could the man who confidently described himself to the Corinthians as desiring to know nothing "*except Jesus Christ, and him crucified*"[79] not view the cross as anything less than an egregious miscarriage of justice? Paul certainly reflected on the crucifixion and was fully aware of its political (and imperial) symbolism. All four evangelists, in their own idiosyncratic narratives, go

---

75. Heilig, *The Apostle and the Empire*, pp. 103-116

76. Heilig, *The Apostle and the Empire*, p. 107

77. Heilig, *The Apostle and the Empire*, p. 109

78. Oakes, *Empire*, p. 25

79. 1 Corinthians 2:2

to great lengths to prove Jesus was innocent of the charges brought against him by the Sanhedrin and carried through by Pilate, so the Jesus tradition itself is not oblivious to the corruption of Roman rule. There is more to Romans 13 than meets the eye.

We already know this. Paul believes Jesus is the Messiah, the end has already begun, and that Abraham's family belongs to the kingdom of God. Paul holds to a suprapolitical understanding of the rulers of this world who are passing away, consistent with the Jewish tradition of living peacefully (when possible) under pagan rule embodied in Jeremiah 29:7. The immediate rhetorical context itself, Romans 12-13, is about nonconformity to the *aion* and the transformation of the mind for the purpose of becoming a living sacrifice to God. As Sprinkle accurately remarks, there are no chapter divisions within Paul's original letter, and any reading of Romans 13 must be incorporated into the themes which Paul addresses in Romans 12.[80] The church is to embody a cruciform witness to the world in light of the impending eschaton, and, as Gorman argues, Romans was designed to address how the gospel impacts Jews and Gentiles in Rome, how it should be applied to particular circumstances, and to solicit support for Paul's mission in the western Mediterranean. Nothing Paul says in Romans 13 undermines these objectives, and in fact his thoughts about the governing authorities must *contribute* to the overarching function of Romans, which, it must be stated again, is not intended to construct a timeless political theology.[81] We are right back to the quote from Schriner included at the beginning of this chapter: Paul is not writing a treatise on government. Gorman concurs: "[Romans 13 does not] *create a political theology, especially not one for all times and circumstances*"[82].

The question, then, is why Paul decided to give instructions about the governing authorities at this point in his letter. It conforms to his advice about political engagement in his other epistles as well as the general witness of Acts, but was there, other than the usual external social pressures which afflicted Paul's churches, a concrete situation for which Paul was providing the Romans guidance? Perhaps. Bryan tentatively suggests that Paul, writing at the beginning of Nero's reign, was hopeful the new emperor would prove to be a wise and enlightened leader and was encouraging the Romans to give him a chance.[83] I remain unconvinced. More plausible is Bryan's proposal about growing social discontent with Roman taxation. Many within the Roman empire were frustrated with the burdensome taxes

---

80. Sprinkle, *Exiles*, pp. 164-165

81. Gorman, *Crucified Lord*, p. 394

82. Gorman, *Crucified Lord*, p. 396

83. Bryan, *Render to Caesar*, p. 79

levied by imperial authorities (a sentiment with which Jesus's Galilean audience would have sympathized) and led to sporadic outbreaks of social unrest. These complaints became so commonplace that Nero himself considered abolishing all forms of indirect taxation. Since Paul tells the church in no uncertain terms to pay their taxes in Romans 13:6, perhaps Paul was worried that believers in Rome would participate in socially contentious tax protests.[84] Gorman concurs, arguing that participation in tax protests would be a form of retaliation, which Paul's gospel prohibits.[85]

By the mid-50s CE Palestine was subject to increasing political instability, with tax protests and threats of revolt becoming more common. Events in Palestine could easily shift popular perception across the empire against Jews, which would have a deleterious effect on Jewish Jesus-believers throughout the Mediterranean.[86] Since Jews had only recently been allowed to return to Rome, Elliott argues that tax revolts could easily be turned against them, who from the earliest days of the Roman imperial period had received special political concessions not offered to other people groups. In Alexandria Jews had been persecuted by native Greek residents for exactly the same reason in the late 30s CE, a tragic event which Paul would have certainly remembered and found relevant to the political climate in Rome. Not only would Paul's advice in Romans 13 discourage Jesus-believers from participating in public unrest and thereby threatening the peace, it may also protect Jews both within and outside of the church against social agitators who, channeling their resentment about taxation, might resort to anti-Jewish violence.[87] Each of these theories is plausible, and whatever conclusions one draws about the precise situation in Rome, Romans 13:1-7 has a particular function which is not intended, as every scholar quoted above has correctly observed, to provide a timeless theology of government. Paul wrote Romans 13 for a reason, and that reason can't be reduced to a particular theological abstraction.

My point has been made. Romans 13:1-7 is, like all Pauline texts, intended to *function* as an integrative part of the rhetorical whole. Paul is *theologizing* in Romans 13, not writing a systematic theology. Now that we have established the limited goals of Paul's famous passage on governing authorities, there are, I think, four relevant questions about the text itself which must be addressed. First, what is Paul attempting to communicate when he says believers are *"to be in subjection to governing authorities"* in 13:1? Following this, why does Paul think the authorities

---

84. Bryan, *Render to Caesar*, pp. 80-81

85. Gorman, *Crucified Lord*, p. 395

86. Gorman, *Crucified Lord*, pp. 394-395

87. Elliott, *Romans 13:1-7*, pp. 191-196

are *"established by God"*, a theme which runs through the entire passage, and how might that concept work historically for a Jew who believes the Messiah is ruling over all creation? Third, and related in some sense to the previous question, why does Paul claim the authorities *"are not a cause of fear for good behavior, but for evil"*? How do the categories of 'good' and 'evil' government function historically and why does Paul employ them? Fourth and finally, we return to the question of taxation in 13:6-7, which may (or may not) be the reason Paul composed Romans 13 in the first place. What does this tell us about the proper response to governing authorities? Answering these questions won't solve every exegetical problem. History is always a matter of probability, not certainty. It will enable us, however, to better understand the limits of Romans 13:1-7, how it can be integrated into Paul's historical context and Jewish worldview, and which principles modern believers can derive from the text as we seek to navigate the complex world of modern, (supposedly) "democratic" government.

Paul leaves little room for believers to engage in political unrest: *"Every person is to be in subjection to the governing authorities"*. The Gerb verb *"is to be in subjection"*, also used in 13:5 (*"it is necessary to be in subjection"*), is a form of *hypotasso*, which often denotes the placing of one's self below another. Someone reading an English translation of Romans might understandably presume that the *"to be in subjection"* one offers towards governing authorities is different from the *"obedience of faith"* one offers to Jesus. The NASB passively implies this distinction, and while it would support my thesis the evidence does not corroborate the claim. The noun *hypakoe*, cognates of which are used in Romans 1:5, 15:18, and 16:24 with reference to Jesus bears a semantic relationship with the verb *hypotasso*, as the English transliteration of each term suggests. Paul uses variants of *hypotasso* in 1 Corinthians 15:27 and Ephesians 1:22 to describe the rule of Christ, so any reading of *hypotasso* which relegates it to political authorities alone (and in stark contrast to *hypakoe*) is linguistically flawed. As with all language, the precise meaning of *hypotasso* in Paul's thought is conditioned by the context in which it is used, and from this vantage point we must fix our eyes once again on Paul's Jewish context, as Gorman recognizes: *"General statements about authorities (13:1-4) and about submission/subjection to them (3:1,5) should be understood primarily as providing the Jewish theological foundation for the concrete conclusion"*[88].

As always, context is king. Paul would without question deny that *"the obedience of faith"* which one renders to Israel's Messiah is morally or theologically equivalent with *"subjection to the governing authorities"*. In Paul's eschatological cosmology, Jesus sits at the right hand of God, ruling over his church and the

---

88. Gorman, *Crucified Lord*, p. 395

world. Jesus has no political competition. The *"subjection"* of which Paul encourages his audience to show the governing authorities is, both contextually within Romans and as an aspect of Paul's Jewish worldview, an extension of obedience to Jesus. Believers are to offer themselves as living sacrifices to the one true God, particularly by seeking to live at peace with all men. As the universal Lord himself said, *"blessed are the peacemakers, for they shall be called sons of God"*[89]; coincidentally, identifying the *"sons of God"* is a major theme in Romans: *"all who are being led by the Spirit of God, these are sons of God"*[90]. God's family, defined by faith in the Messiah and the indwelling Spirit, are called to make peace. This peacemaking extends to the governing authorities, and if Bryan, Gorman, and Elliot are correct in identifying the potential dangers of social unrest as a possible historical context for Romans 13, being *"in subjection to the governing authorities"* might have been the only possible way for the church at Rome to maintain social and political peace. For Paul, submitting to the rulers of this world who are passing away is nothing more than honoring God and his Messiah Jesus, who has already taken his seat upon a throne which is higher than any earthly political authority.

Instead of functioning as a convenient legitimation of authoritarian political systems, Romans 13:1 fits neatly into the framework of Jewish political engagement which Paul inherited from his ancestors. The prophet Jeremiah openly condemns Babylon as an evil, idolatrous empire and yet for the Jews in exile faithfulness to God was expressed in part by seeking the welfare of the city and living, insofar as it was possible, in peace with their pagan neighbors, knowing that one day God would deliver them and burn Babylon to the ground. For contemporary readers of Paul, accustomed to political systems which promise (but always fail to deliver) political leaders who will take "their side", the tension between evil empire and peaceful submission is incomprehensible, but for ancient Jewish thinkers like Paul there was no other alternative. The pagans weren't on their side, but they were in charge anyway. God would ultimately exact vengeance against His wretched opponents, as Jeremiah 50-51 and Romans 12:19-20 promise, but judgment was an eschatological hope which could only be realised by God himself (and his Messiah) at the end of history. While the end had already begun, Paul's rules for political engagement hadn't changed. Live at peace with the governing authorities by submitting to them, exactly as Jeremiah taught and Daniel exemplified. Believers are obedient and allegiant to Christ first, and as long as the governing authorities aren't commanding believers to compromise their values they are to submit.

---

89. Matthew 5:9

90. Romans 8:14

One common thread which runs through Romans 13:1-7 is the establishment of authorities by God: *"For there is no authority except from God, and those which exist are established by God . . . for [they] are a minister of God to you for good . . . a minister of God . . . for rulers are servants of God"*. It would surely seem, if Romans 13 was unhitched from its historical context, that Paul is advocating a divine sanction for the worst excesses of human political violence. This would be a severe mischaracterization of Pauline thought, as Sprinkle explains: *"the phrase "God's servant" isn't as positive as it may sound. It actually comes from the Old Testament Prophets, who often talked about God working through some rather evil people to carry out his will"*[91]. God directly appointed kings such as Saul[92] and David[93], but they aren't the only political leaders to be described as servants of God.

A telling example is Nebuchadnezzar, king of Babylon. In Jeremiah 27:6-8, only a few short passages before the all-important 29:7, the prophet makes a few intriguing comments about Babylon's pagan ruler: *"Now I have given all these lands into the hand of Nebuchadnezzar king of Babylon, My servant . . . it will be that the nation or the kingdom which will not serve him, Nebuchadnezzar king of Babylon, and which will not put its neck under the yoke of the kings of Babylon, I will punish that nation with the sword, with famine, and with pestilence"*. Coincidently, these punishments befall Judah in accordance with Deuteronomy 27-30 because Israel failed to maintain its commitment to their covenant with God. Nebuchadnezzar, a pagan imperialist, is God's servant, executing judgment against *God's own people* and any other nation which stands in his way! Is this what Paul means in Romans 13:6 when he says *"rulers are servants of God"*? Yes and no. The quotation above is from Jeremiah 27:6 and 27:8. The prophet adds a provocative qualifier in 27:7: *"All the nations shall serve him and his son and his grandson until the time of his own land comes; then many nations and great kings will make him their servant"*. Wait, what? Nebuchadnezzar and his descendants are God's servants *until the time comes when they will serve others*. God is using them for a specific purpose, but that purpose will one day run its course. In Jeremiah 50:17-18, Nebuchadnezzar will get exactly what he deserves: *"Israel is a scattered flock, the lions have driven them away. The first one who devoured him was the king of Assyria, and this last one who has broken his bones is Nebuchadnezzar king of Babylon. Therefore thus says the Lord of hosts, the God of Israel . . . Behold, I am going to punish the king of Babylon and his land, just as I punished the king of Assyria"*. This sounds an awful lot like *"vengeance is mine, I will repay"* and *"for now salvation is nearer to us than when we believed"*,

---

91. Sprinkle, *Exiles*, pp. 166-167

92. 1 Samuel 9:15-10:8

93. 1 Samuel 16:1-13

doesn't it? Perhaps *"rulers are servants of God"* isn't as prestigious an assertion as Christian interpreters have made it out to be?

The king of Assyria, mentioned by Jeremiah, is another excellent test case of a ruler who was used by God to serve His purposes and then discarded. In Isaiah 10:5, Assyria is destined for judgment *because* it serves God: *"Woe to Assyria, the rod of My anger And the staff in whose hands is My indignation"*. Only a few short verses later, in 10:12, Isaiah says *"it will be that when the Lord has completed all His work on Mount Zion and on Jerusalem, He will say, "I will punish the fruit of the arrogant heart of the king of Assyria and the pomp of his haughtiness""*. If that wasn't enough, Isaiah returns to the destruction of Assyria in 14:25: "[God will] *break Assyria in My land, and I will trample him"*. Isaiah 30:27-33 describes the destruction of Assyria with fiery metaphors (as in 30:27, *"the Lord comes from a remote place; Burning is His anger and dense is His smoke)* while Isaiah 31:8 envisions the death and destruction which will befall the once-great empire: *"the Assyrian will fall by a sword not of man, And a sword not of man will devour him. So he will not escape the sword"*. Assyria is both God's servant and destined for destruction. The prophet Daniel says of God *"It is He who changes the times and the epochs; He removes kings and establishes kings"*[94] and of Nebuchadnezzar, who was fatefully destined for judgment, *"You, O king, are the king of kings, to whom the God of heaven has given the kingdom, the power, the strength and the glory"*[95]. In Daniel 5, the Babylonian empire comes to an end, replaced by the comparatively benevolent Persians, and Daniel 12 envisions the ultimate victory of God at the end of history. Cyrus, the Persian pagan ruler who receives good press in Ezra and Nehemiah, is even called *"anointed"* (Christ!) in Isaiah because he afforded the Babylonian exiles a return to Judea[96]. Schriner summarizes the Old Testament data: *"The* [Old Testament] *consistently teaches that God appoints rulers . . . and it is clear from the book of Daniel alone that many of the rulers were evil"*[97].

This is the theology of government which undergirds the Jewish apostle Paul's rhetoric in Romans 13. Referring to pagan political authorities as "God's servant" isn't exactly a compliment. Sprinkle, discussing God's use of evil rulers, accurately summarizes the Old Testament evidence as it relates to Romans: *"God wasn't praising them. Rather, he was asserting his sovereignty over them. Romans 13 is situated in this prophetic tradition. Therefore, the phrase "God's servant" refers not to Rome's sanctified service to God but to God's sovereign ability to use an evil empire as an*

---

94. Daniel 2:21

95. Daniel 2:37

96. Isaiah 45:1

97. Schreiner, *Handbook*, p. 104

instrument in his hands"⁹⁸. As Wright correctly observes, claiming the Roman authorities are servants of God "*constitutes a major demotion*"⁹⁹, especially given the nature of Roman imperial propaganda. Far from condoning Roman imperialism and the political authorities which are tasked with implementing it, Romans 13 emphasises the sovereignty and rule of God over every kingdom which opposes His rule. They exist only to fulfill His purposes and will all one day fall to ruin. The kingdom of God, a present reality in which Jesus has already been installed as the world's true king, is neither supplanted nor complimented by Rome. Believers belong to a suprapolitical kingdom which will one day be made fully manifest over all creation, and in the meantime are called to submit for the sake of peace. Paul deftly balances Jeremiah 27:6-8 and Jeremiah 29:7, both of which condition Christian political engagement in light of the inaugurated eschaton. Romans 13 isn't technically 'subversive' because Paul's claims about the Roman empire are no different than what many first century Jews would have said. As Haddad questions, "*Why would Paul, or any Jew for that matter, regard the emperor or any civil authority as a deity? It would not be shocking to the emperor, or any other Greco-Roman person for that matter, that a Jew would not recognize the divinity of the emperor*"¹⁰⁰. True. Paul also cannot be read as assuredly pro-imperial either. There are different ways of thinking about political engagement than the stale anti- or pro-imperialist dichotomy. That Paul is more nuanced than many of his modern interpreters would prefer him to be is our problem, not his.

Paul's call to submit and his assertion that the authorities are established by God are firmly embedded within Paul's Jewish worldview and the means by which believers can demonstrate faithful allegiance to king Jesus while also creating the conditions which make for peace. We are now in a position to shed some much-needed light on our third question, how Paul understands the categories of 'good' and 'evil' with respect to the pagan authorities, which he addresses in Romans 13:3-5: "*For rulers are not a cause of fear for good behavior, but for evil. Do you want to have no fear of authority? Do what is good and you will have praise from the same; for it is a minister of God to you for good. But if you do what is evil, be afraid; for it does not bear the sword for nothing; for it is a minister of God, an avenger who brings wrath on the one who practices evil. Therefore it is necessary to be in subjection, not only because of wrath but also for conscience' sake*". As both Heilig and Oakes discern, Paul has not forgotten what the Romans did to Jesus. Nor has he suffered a sudden lapse in memory, disregarding his own experiences on the wrong side of Roman

---

98. Sprinkle, *Exiles*, p. 167

99. Wright, *Faithfulness of God*, p. 1303

100. Haddad, *New Creation*, p. 65

justice, or the social persecution which many of his churches had faced, nor the entire frustrating Jewish experience of living under pagan rule. Paul is under no delusion; he knows that the pagan authorities do not always, or even usually, uphold what is 'good'.

The opening clause is revealing: *"rulers are not a cause of fear for good behavior, but for evil"*. The Greek adjective behind the word *"good"* is *agathos*, which Paul uses three times in Romans 12. In 12:2, a transformed mind will *"prove what the will of God is, that which is good"*, in 12:9 believers must *"Abhor what is evil; cling to what is good"*, and in 12:21 the church must *"not be overcome by evil, but overcome evil with good"*. Paul reasons that rulers are not to be feared by those who do *agatha*, but only who engage in evil. In Romans 12, Paul explains to his audience how to embody *agatha*, including honoring others, living at peace with all men, and not seeking revenge, all attitudes which, according to Paul's logic in Romans 13:3-4, the governing authorities should praise. The artificial chapter division between Romans 12 and Roman 13 obscures his continuity of thought; Paul has already encouraged the Romans to do *agatha*, which should result in praise from the authorities. Daniel would agree. If Paul is worried about the witness and safety of Roman believers, the strategy of seeking peace with the political authorities by doing *agatha* might just work. His logic is deceptively simple: do *agatha* and you shouldn't have to worry about the authorities. Do evil and you will get what you deserve. Not only is this excellent practical advice, a principle with universal applicability, it makes perfect contextual sense. Paul genuinely wants the Romans to do what is *agatha*, and by doing so they maintain their outside witness and limit (but not eliminate) the probability of political persecution.

Bryan detects a relationship between Paul's use of 'good' and 'evil' and the theme of God's sovereignty over political authorities. Paul uses the noun *diakonos*, translated *"minister"* in the NASB, to describe the authorities: *"it is a minister of God to you for good"*. Bryan argues that the application of this term to Roman authorities should be read in the sense of "representative" or "agent", and when the political authorities uphold the good and punish evil they are enacting justice on behalf of God. Bryan is quick to add, in congruence with the Old Testament example of divine sovereignty over pagan powers, that Paul's use of *diakonos* relativizes their political power and should not be read as implying blind obedience to evil political actors.[101] Elliott argues that Paul's use of *"fear"* in 13:3 and *"conscience"* in 13:5 mirrors conversations in Roman literature regarding the proper methods for maintaining social order, with fear often being the preferred means of

---

101. Bryan, *Render to Caesar*, pp. 79-80

keeping ignorant lower-class plebeians in check.[102] While Roman political propaganda claimed Augustus ushered in an era of peace, the Mediterranean was ruled at the point of a sword. By appealing to 'fear' and 'conscience' in a context where he is urging believers to do good and thereby receive praise from the authorities, Paul is neither conceding the inevitability of Roman rule nor justifying the violence by which it is maintained but rather cultivating the conditions for peace.[103]

On a more fundamental level the idea that civil authorities were responsible for rewarding good and punishing evil was a well-established political theory in the Greco-Roman world, rooted in the work of Aristotle and seen even in the works of intellectuals like Philo.[104] Many writers believed that the purpose of government was to honor good conduct and promote public morality. Deviations from the good were, quite understandably, seen as a dangerous evil with the potential to corrupt society and therefore warranted legal punishment. Without the preservation of morality, society would collapse. This legal and political philosophy, Haddad explains, lies behind Paul's rhetoric in Romans 13:3-5: *"When Paul says that "rulers are not a terror to good conduct, but to bad"... he is only affirming a positive theory of civil authority that ancient society already subscribed to"*[105]. Paul is asserting, in effect, *"this is the standard by which the authorities judge public conduct, seek after good and you won't run into trouble"*. Not only will striving after *agathos* enable the church to honor the one true God, it will keep them (at least in theory) safe from the Roman sword. There may even be, if Paul's witness in Acts is any indication, a slight polemical edge to his words. In Paul's trial before Festus and the Jerusalem establishment, Paul offers his own defense: *"I have committed no offense either against the Law of the Jews or against the temple or against Caesar"*[106]. By cultivating the good, believers in Rome could say with a clear conscience to the political authorities that they had done nothing wrong, and since the authorities existed to uphold the good and punish evil there was no just reason for the Romans to take punitive action against the church. Paul has already set his audience up for this instruction in 12:17: *"Respect what is right in the sight of all men"*. *"All men"* would obviously include the political authorities.

In Daniel 6:1-3, the king planned to appoint the exceptionally effective Daniel as commissioner over the entire kingdom. The other commissioners and political authorities became enraged with Daniel and endeavored to sabotage his

---

102. Elliott, *Romans 13:1-7*, pp. 196-201

103. Elliott, *Romans 13:1-7*, pp. 200-202

104. Haddad, *New Creation*, pp. 66-69

105. Haddad, *New Creation*, p. 67

106. Acts 25:8

promotion: "*Then the commissioners and satraps began trying to find a ground of accusation against Daniel in regard to government affairs; but they could find no ground of accusation or evidence of corruption, inasmuch as he was faithful, and no negligence or corruption was to be found in him*"[107]. They were left with only one option, recounted in Daniel 6:5: "*Then these men said, "We will not find any ground of accusation against this Daniel unless we find it against him with regard to the law of his God"*". Paul knows that believers will suffer because of their faith in Jesus, but any persecution brought upon believers by the state should not be the result of failing to do good. The cross is foolishness to the world, and sometimes the world treats those who bear the cross foolishly. Paul knows good and well that the Romans punish people who don't deserve it. Jesus, for instance. Loyalty to Jesus must manifest itself neither in rebellion nor worship of the state, and, just like Daniel and Jeremiah, it is possible to honor God and respect authorities "*so far as it depends on you*". Paul's prescient wisdom is on full display in 13:5; it is "*necessary to be in subjection, not only because of wrath, but also for conscience' sake*". Believers are called to avoid the wrath of political authorities (who should, by their own standard, praise good and punish only evil) and maintain a clear conscience, because, ultimately, they are to offer themselves as living sacrifices to God, the theme of this entire section in Romans.

This brings us to Paul's concluding statement on the political authorities in Romans 13:6-7: "*For because of this you also pay taxes, for rulers are servants of God, devoting themselves to this very thing. Render to all what is due them: tax to whom tax is due; custom to whom custom; fear to whom fear; honor to whom honor*". Withholding taxes, especially in a politically-charged environment where dissatisfaction of Roman taxation was in the air, was a guaranteed way to break the peace and bring about Roman wrath. It would also be a terrible look for the Roman church, the exact opposite of Paul's instructions in Philippians 2:15 "*that you will prove yourselves to be blameless and innocent, children of God above reproach in the midst of a crooked and perverse generation, among whom you appear as lights in the world*". In letter after letter Paul is constantly concerned with how outsiders perceive the church. They are representing the exalted Lord and, as in Romans 12:1-2, allegiance to him must result in moral transformation. The church is a witness to the gospel, which is God's power to save, and if that witness is endangered then so is the effectiveness of Paul's gospel. Paying taxes and showing honor to authorities is a manifestation of the believing community's faithfulness to God for the purpose of peace. If the Roman church is to be in subjection to the authorities which are under the sovereignty of God and tasked with promoting good and punishing evil

---

107. Daniel 6:4

then the church must pay taxes and show honor. Failing to do so would actually dishonor God and blunt the message about the real king, Jesus.

Winter advances a compelling proposal regarding the concept of civic honor and the praise of "good" in Romans 13. Although I don't agree with every aspect of his analysis, Roman social relationships were regularly secured through benefaction, and wealthy Romans often donated large sums of money to complete construction projects or host games which benefited the residents (not to mention the political class) of individual cities.[108] As Winter explains, "*The welfare of the city in the Graeco-Roman world depended on the ongoing contributions of civic-minded benefactors . . . Rulers praised and honoured those who undertook good works which benefited the city. At the same time they made the conventional promise to honour publicly those who in the future world undertake similar benefactions . . . the praising of rulers referred to in Romans 13:3 . . . was related to [the] specific area of public benefactions. Christians of substance were taught to seek the welfare of the city in the public domain by undertaking benefactions as part of their responsibilities in accordance with the will of God*"[109]. While it is unclear if Paul has financial benefaction in mind (which would depend upon the socio-economic status of the Roman church, a speculative historical judgment at best), he certainly expected believers to pay their taxes and honor the authorities, fulfilling their civic duties. By doing good and (perhaps) financially contributing to civic projects, the community in Rome would receive public honor from the authorities, solidifying the social perception of the church as a law-abiding, legitimate association of public-peace oriented people. All political authorities, and therefore the taxation which supports them, are passing away, but believers should not withhold payment before the end for the sake of peace, knowing God will have the final word.

The Jesus tradition itself bears a curious similarity to Romans 13. The Greek word behind "*render*" in 13:7, *apodidomi*, is the *exact same term* Jesus uses in Mark 12:17[110] to tell off the Pharisees and Herodians who are trying (and failing) to catch him in a trap. As we learned in Chapter 10, *apodidomi* generally refers to a contractual exchange, with the implication that the coin, which bore Caesar's image and therefore belongs to him, should be returned to its rightful owner. Paul, perhaps under the influence of the oral Jesus tradition, is making the same point as his Messiah. In 13:7 believers are to "*Render* [a form of *apodidomi*] *what is due*"; the Greek word behind "due" is a form of *opheile*, which he will employ in the very next verse: "*Owe* [variant of *opheile*] *nothing to anyone except to love one another*". As

---

108. Winter, *Welfare*, pp. 25-40

109. Winter, *Welfare*, p. 26

110. Paralleled in Matthew 22:21 and Luke 20:25

Bryan explains, the commandment in Leviticus 19:18, quoted by Paul in Romans 13:9, has been expanded to include not only fellow countrymen but the entire world, including, of course, the Roman political authorities.[111] What is owed to the authorities? Precisely the same cruciform love which is owed to everyone, contextualized by a relationship of submission for the sake of peace which includes paying taxes and showing honor to those in power. In many ways, Romans 13:1-7 can be summarized by the words of Jesus in Matthew 17:24-27. When asked to pay a tax, Jesus acknowledges that he should be exempt but pays up anyway *"so that we do not offend them"*. The goal of Paul's instruction is neither legitimation nor affirmation of political authorities, but the more noble goal of helping believers in Rome offer themselves as living sacrifices to God by the renewing of their minds, following the example set by Jeremiah and Daniel of living at peace with all men in light of God's promised eschatological vindication.

Oakes accurately summarizes the function of Romans 13: "*This* [set of instructions] *makes sense in a house-church context. Their remapped universe removed the emperor from his place of divinity. It also prophesied the future supplanting of all earthly authority by Christ and God. However, here and now, the Christians can accept the empire and live within its authority structures obediently and quietly. Paul's attitude and teaching in 13:1-7 makes good sense if his horizon of view is the daily life of house churches. He legitimates their approach to empire and reinforces it with a theology, of governments serving God, that has a pedigree going back to Babylon (and, as in that case, is not incompatible with expectation of their ultimate overthrow)*[112]. Echoing Schriner, Paul has not constructed a timeless treatise on government nor deviated from his christological, ecclesiological, eschatological, and ethical commitments. Paul remains firmly committed to the ascended Lord and his universal church, who will continue to honor God while awaiting the return of the king.

CONCLUSION: MODERN PRINCIPLES FROM ANCIENT TEXTS?

Romans 13:1-7, like every other text in the New Testament surveyed thus far, cannot justify modern authoritarian socialism. Paul would be horrified and enraged that most modern western Christians affirm the weaponization of secular political structures against those with whom they disagree. The American church is deeply divided because of political conflict, but, as we have already seen, very few Christians challenge the underlying presupposition that we *need* aggression against peaceful behavior to maintain social order. The difference between right and left is a matter

---

111. Bryan, *Render To Caesar*, p. 81

112. Oakes, *Empire*, p. 25

of emphasis, not structure. The anger and hostility which American Christians show towards one another because of the battle for political power compromises the witness of the church and undermines our values. If Paul was to write a letter *"To the Church of God in America"* addressing our current political climate, his tone would resemble Galatians and include a similar criticism to the one leveled at the Corinthians: *"Why not rather be wronged? Why not rather be defrauded?"*[113], questions for which conservative and progressive Christians would have no answer. Instead of living up to our identity as members of Abraham's family and seeking to edify one another through love, we would much rather be conformed to the detestable world of American politics by fighting over which party gets to dominate everyone else through the political system, all the while compromising the integrity and witness of Christ's church. With respect to politics, American Christians time and again wholeheartedly choose Caesar over Christ. Romans 13 simply provides cover for our preferred political policies.

It doesn't have to be this way. Our modern political context is undeniably different from the one in which the first believers were called to live. Like with any culturally embedded text, Romans 13 cannot be directly applied to the contemporary world without doing a considerable amount of damage to the text's original intention. Those of us who believe in the authority of Scripture must carefully derive principles from Paul's commentary while thoughtfully applying them in an age which is undeniably different from Paul's. The foundational principles upon which Paul's theologizing rests are messianic christology, inaugurated eschatology, incorporative ecclesiology, and cruciform ethics, all of which are intrinsically connected in Paul's thought. The Jewish tradition of Jeremiah 29:7, epitomized by Daniel, has been reinterpreted through the gospel without being fundamentally reworked. All of the tension inherent in the "seek the welfare of the city God will destroy" model must characterize Christian political engagement until the return of Christ. If this scrambles our political (and economic) categories, forcing us to oppose the prevailing cultural assumptions of our time, then so be it. Let's do our best to live at peace with all men.

So what do we do with a passage like Romans 13? In a post-Enlightment Western context, our political system is (nominally if not in practice) built upon the concepts of natural rights, representative government, democracy, and civic participation. What it means to 'be in subjection' to authorities who are supposed to represent us will necessarily look different than when living under the auspices of the Roman imperial order. Aren't we *supposed* to challenge our politicians, hold them to account, and seek to replace them when they fail to represent our

---

113. 1 Corinthians 6:7

interests? I would say we should. Criticism of the existing system is a part of what responsible citizens are supposed to do. Given the stated assumptions of Western government, our political leaders were never intended to exercise arbitrary authority over their population. Political leaders rule by consent of the governed, and we must hold them to account. Christians should be at the forefront of challenging unjust institutions and advocating for their replacement. This leaves us with a million questions, few of which I am able to answer. What exactly this looks like in practice is anyone's guess. Paul, however, has laid down a set of guiding principles which believers must not transgress.

Christians must never allow the political system to compromise their witness and values. Our loyalty is to God and God alone. We don't owe the political class anything except the debt of love which God has so graciously modeled for us in Christ. Every human being, including the most corrupt politician and bureaucrat, is created in God's image and deserves to encounter the gospel. We must attempt to be respectful, peaceful, considerate, and thoughtful when addressing political issues, especially with neighbors who do not share our political values. Believers should be the ones building bridges with people who hold a different set of political beliefs, especially if those people are other Christians. An excellent starting point for building peace in a participatory political system would be to follow Paul's advice in Colossians 4:5-6: "*Conduct yourselves with wisdom toward outsiders, making the most of the opportunity. Let your speech always be with grace, as though seasoned with salt, so that you will know how you should respond to each person*". What if Christians took this seriously?

The question of taxation, which may have been the factor prompting Paul to write Romans 13, is also a difficult one to answer. All taxes are collected involuntarily and under the threat of violence, therefore consistent Christians should never condone taxation as a mechanism for ordering society. Taxation is theft, full-stop. Nevermind that the U.S. federal government spends most of our tax dollars bombing innocent women and children in third-world countries, enabling degeneracy and ensuring that generations of Americans remain mired in poverty, and paying interest on the trillions of dollars of debt its accrued at the expense of productive American citizens. It's all bad. Any society which was truly based upon Christian values would abolish taxation and produce every good and service through voluntary, mutually-beneficial transactions. Philosophically this should be a central tenant of any Christian political philosophy, but practically we live in the real world. Taxation isn't going away any time soon and in order to follow the teachings of Jesus, Paul, and Jeremiah we should pay them. It doesn't mean we can't complain about how they are used and work to decrease both the crippling tax burden and the imperial policies it funds. The church should also do everything in its power to finance decentralized networks of charity which target help towards those in need, fulfilling our obligation to serve the (truly) poor while obviating the supposed justification for centralized entitlement programs. We must do better than our politicians. Thankfully, it's a low bar to clear.

It should go without saying that Christians must never resort to violence as a means of effecting political change. One of the major theses of this book is that the Bible doesn't justify modern authoritarian socialism of both the progressive or conservative variety because the entire political system is built on the assumption that arbitrary violence must be deployed against peaceful people for the sake of achieving subjective social ends. Followers of Jesus, the crucified Messiah, must never treat others like the Gentiles who crucified him. The greatest in Abraham's family is the humble slave. The last will one day be first. Fomenting violent rebellion against a political authority or physically threatening average people who do not share our beliefs are options which must not only be taken off the table but thrown in the garbage. I do believe that it is permissible for Christians to defend themselves and more importantly others when in imminent physical danger, but Christians must never initiate violence. Doing so is to deny our Messiah, the crucified king who was given authority over all creation because he was willing to empty himself in the incarnation and suffer a terrible death on our behalf. The cruciform witness of the one true family of God is always compromised when it advocates or participates in initiatory violence. If the context of Romans 13 tells us anything, it's that we should seek to live at peace with all men even if we are constantly wronged. No need to worry, though, because God will have the final say. Jesus will soon return, and until then the church must faithfully follow the example set by the son of David.

And thus concludes our study of Paul. We will now turn to Hebrews and the Catholic Epistles (James, 1-2 Peter, 1-3 John, and Jude) before ending our marathon through the New Testament with Revelation. As we read through Hebrews and the non-Pauline letters which follow it, we will find that they supplement the gospels, Acts, and Paul in many surprising ways while perfectly corresponding to their political and economic framework. The rest of the New Testament only further solidifies the incompatibility of authoritarian socialism with authentically biblical Christian values. We turn now to Hebrews.

CHAPTER 16 | Hebrews, James, 1-2 Peter, 1-3 John, and Jude

Dominion and Authority Forever

When He had made purification of sins, He sat down at the right hand of the Majesty on high.

Hebrews 1:3

Keep your behavior excellent among the Gentiles, so that in the thing in which they slander you as evildoers, they may because of your good deeds, as they observe them, glorify God on the day of visitation.

1 Peter 2:12

INTRODUCTION

The gospels and Paul dominate the New Testament. The towering figures of Jesus and his great apostle to the gentiles have cast a long shadow over other New Testament texts which are, in their own right, just as important for our understanding of early Christianity. Punctuated only by Acts, it is easy to view the canonical material between Matthew and Philemon as the New Testament's core while relegating the documents which follow to second-text status. Both the history of Christian theology and the emphasis of modern biblical scholarship engenders that impression. I think it's a mistake. Hebrews, James, 1-2 Peter, 1-3 John, and small yet not insignificant Jude make vital contributions to Christian theology without which our perspective would be incomplete. Furthermore, they each in their own way offer us a complimentary perspective on the political and economic concepts we have been studying in this book. While dedicating but a single chapter, even if lengthy, would seem to perpetuate the notion that Hebrews and the so-called "Catholic Epistles" are not quite as significant as the gospels and Paul, I find them to be in such harmonious agreement with the works which precede them canonically that a brief survey will supplement my thesis without unnecessary repetition.

The focal point is unavoidably 1 Peter 2:13-17, which could be aptly titled "The Romans 13 of the Catholic Epistles". While it will receive a protracted treatment, Peter comes to *the exact same conclusion* as Paul: the people of God must submit to authorities for the sake of peace and public witness while awaiting the return of Jesus to vindicate them from their enemies. Too late for a spoiler alert, I suppose. Hebrews presents the ascended Jesus as a cosmic priest in God's heavenly temple, and while atonement functions as the central theme in Hebrews it is predicated upon the messianic status of Jesus. James, steeped in the Jesus tradition, is overflowing with commentary on the rich and poor. The Johannine epistles display the crucified Jesus as the quintessential model for human relationships, and little Jude praises Jesus as the *only* Lord while viciously excoriating false teachers. Not a single sentence in any of these works can serve as an affirmation of authoritarian socialism as our all-too-short treatment of them will demonstrate. We begin our study with Hebrews.

HEBREWS

Background: Sitting at God's Right Hand

The author of Hebrews never identifies himself. He also never identifies his audience. Even though English translations often title this work "*The Letter to the Hebrews*", "*to the Hebrews*" appears nowhere in the text. From the earliest church to the modern era the authorship of Hebrews has been hotly contested. While many interpreters have associated Hebrews with Paul, arguing that it is his fourteenth canonical letter, this has never been a consensus view. The great church father Origen claimed that only God himself could know with certainty who penned Hebrews.[1] Modern scholarship has, correctly in my view, ruled out Pauline authorship altogether.[2] Ray Stedman acknowledges that Hebrews bears many striking theological similarities to Paul and was possibly penned by one of his associates, suggesting Apollos as the most likely candidate.[3] I remain agnostic. The prevalence of Jewish atonement theology suggests the work was written to a primarily Jewish audience,

---

1. Stedman, Ray. 1992. *Hebrews*. InterVarsity Press. p. 10

2. Bernier, *Rethinking the Dates*, p. 186

3. Stedman, *Hebrews*, pp. 10-11

but even this is debatable. Hebrews 12:4 implies the audience had not yet been persecuted physically (and therefore were not a part of the Judean community which suffers in the early chapters of Acts) while an ambiguous greeting by "*Those from Italy*" in 13:24 sheds little light on the intended audience (or author, for that matter) of Hebrews.[4] Bernier asserts that Hebrews 13:1-3 presupposes a functional temple in Jerusalem while the reference to Timothy in 13:23 assumes he is still alive; based on this limited information he argues Hebrews must have been written between 50-70 CE.[5] It is a frustratingly slim profile, and scholars have very little data to work with when reconstructing theoretical historical backgrounds for Hebrews. I suspect that these questions will remain unanswered until the age to come.

Not all hope is lost. While his attribution of authorship to Apollos pushes the evidence much too far, Stedman correctly observes that the writer of Hebrews and Paul have a whole lot in common. Hebrews 1:1-4, which introduces the letter, develops a Pauline-friendly exalted Christology: "*God, after He spoke long ago to the fathers in the prophets in many portions and in many ways, in these last days has spoken to us in His Son, whom He appointed heir of all things, through whom also He made the world. And He is the radiance of His glory and the exact representation of His nature, and upholds all things by the word of His power. When He had made purification of sins, He sat down at the right hand of the Majesty on high, having become as much better than the angels, as He has inherited a more excellent name than they*". Jesus, God's Son, died for sins and was subsequently exalted to the right hand of God through his ascension where he currently rules over all creation. Paul would approve. The author of Hebrews also operates within the framework of inaugurated eschatology, as "*these last days*" have been brought about by the work of Christ. The eschatological exaltation of Christ is *the* central theme of Hebrews and the foundation for the work's theology of Jesus as cosmic priest.[6] Hebrew's uniquely detailed emphasis on Jesus as priest is not at all in conflict with his status as Messiah; in fact, as Patrick Schreiner explains, Jesus's identity as universal Messiah is the context within which his role as priest is interpreted.[7] This is precisely the theme which I will highlight in our regrettably brisk stroll through Hebrews. As in the rest of the New Testament, Jesus is Lord of all creation.

---

4. Stedman, *Hebrews*, pp. 11-12

5. Bernier, *Rethinking the Dates*, pp. 185-195

6. Stedman, *Hebrews*, pp. 14-15

7. Schreiner, *The Ascension of Christ*, pp. 74-76

The Ascended Christ

The writer of Hebrews immediately follows his presentation of the exalted Christ with a series of Old Testament quotations which substantiate his claims. Included in catena of passages referenced in Hebrews 1:5-13 are Psalm 2, 2 Samuel 7, Psalm 45, and Psalm 110, all of which are either messianic or, in the case of Psalm 45, refer to the dominion of God over all creation. The messianic status of Jesus as exalted king is sealed by his ascension, the presupposition of Hebrew's exalted christology.[8] Even though the writer of Hebrews chooses to emphasise the priestly status of Jesus, it is intrinsically connected to his messianic identity as the string of citations demonstrates.[9] After reassuring the audience that his teaching is based on traditions which are derived from Jesus himself in Hebrews 2:1-4, the author describes the glory which Jesus received by virtue of his death and resurrection in 2:14. Combined with a combination of Psalm 8 in Hebrews 2:5-8, the writer portrays the church as ruling over creation with Christ, a fulfillment of God's original creational mandate for humanity.[10] Even as the writer of Hebrews begins transitioning to his discussion of Jesus's perpetual priesthood, he reminds the audience of the Christ's dominion over death and the help he gives *"to the descendants of Abraham"*, an ecclesiological reference point which could have been taken directly from one of Paul's epistles.

Much of Hebrews 3-10 is concerned with the priesthood of Jesus, but even within this long exposition his messianic status remains foundational for the logic of the text. In 8:1 the author reiterates his primary theme: *"Now the main point in what has been said is this: we have such a high priest, who has taken His seat at the right hand of the throne of the Majesty in the heavens"*, a point validated by the exegesis of Psalm 110 in Hebrews 7:11-22.[11] Psalm 110 envisions the restoration of Israel's monarchy and priesthood, both of which find their eschatological fulfillment in the ascended Messiah. In Hebrews 9:26-28, the eschatological age which was inaugurated by Christ, including Jesus's final offering for sin, will culminate in his victorious return to judge his opponents and rescue his people: *"now once at the consummation of the ages He has been manifested to put away sin by the sacrifice of Himself. And inasmuch as it is appointed for men to die once and after this comes judgment, so Christ also, having been offered once to bear the sins of many, will appear a second time for salvation without reference to sin, to those who eagerly await Him"*.

---

8. Hastings, Ross. 2025. *The Glory of the Ascension.* InterVarsity Press. pp. 55-56

9. Schreiner, *The Ascension of Christ*, pp. 82-88

10. Hastings, *Glory of the Ascension*, p. 223

11. Stedman, *Hebrews*, pp. 87-88

Hebrews 10:11-18 quotes Psalm 110 and Jeremiah 31, connecting the ascension of Jesus with the new covenant, made manifest through the Holy Spirit in the lives of believers.

Hebrews 11, famously cataloging the great faith of many Old Testament figures, strikingly appeals to the language of exile and restoration to describe the hope believers are to have through faith: *"All these died in faith, without receiving the promises, but having seen them and having welcomed them from a distance, and having confessed that they were strangers and exiles on the earth. For those who say such things make it clear that they are seeking a country of their own. And indeed if they had been thinking of that country from which they went out, they would have had opportunity to return. But as it is, they desire a better country, that is, a heavenly one. Therefore God is not ashamed to be called their God; for He has prepared a city for them"*[12]. Believers are to see themselves, like the great figures of faith who came before them, as exiles in a cosmic diaspora, faithfully awaiting the day of God's deliverance. The objective physical resurrection of Jesus precludes a reading of this passage which posits that our eternal destiny is non-physical. We will, like Jesus himself, inherit resurrection in the world to come. Just as Abraham looked forward to the fulfillment of God's promises (the point of Hebrews 11:8-12), the restoration of creation which will occur at the return of the (bodily) resurrected and ascended Christ enables the believer to continue in faithful hope despite living as exiles in a world which is hostile to Christian values.[13] This combination of eschatology, christology, and ecclesiology is, once again, entirely consistent with Paul and Jesus's proclamation of God's kingdom.

Hebrews 12-13, which brings the letter to its conclusion, also intersects with both the Jesus tradition and Pauline thought at several points. In 12:1-2, believers are to follow the cruciform example of Jesus, who endured the cross and yet *"has sat down at the right hand of the throne of God"*, another massive blow against Christians who accept yielding authoritarian political power as consistent with the witness of Jesus. Just a few verses later the writer of Hebrews channels Romans 12:18: *"Pursue peace with all men, and the sanctification without which no one will see the lord"*[14]. Hebrews makes no exception for those who do not share our political values. Another brilliant fusion of the exalted Christ, the status of his church, and the eschatological moment occurs in 12:22-24: *"But you have come to Mount Zion and to the city of the living God, the heavenly Jerusalem, and to myriads of angels, to the general assembly and church of the firstborn who are enrolled in heaven, and*

---

12. Hebrews 11:13-16

13. Stedman, *Hebrews*, pp. 125-126

14. Hebrews 12:14

to God, the Judge of all, and to the spirits of the righteous made perfect, and to Jesus, the mediator of a new covenant". Believers are, according to Hebrews, children of the firstborn, Jesus, who rules over all creation. Exiles belong to the city of God, not the empires of men. God's kingdom, according to Hebrews 12:28, *"cannot be shaken"*. To top it all off, the writer of Hebrews even warns against the love of money in 13:5: *"Make sure that your character is free from the love of money, being content with what you have"*. Once again this is not a critique of voluntary production and exchange. It is a warning against the dangers of idolizing money.

Hebrews is a brilliant literary work which deserves a much fuller treatment than the one given above, but even a cursory reading demonstrates with great clarity the cohesive relationship it shares with other New Testament texts. Politically speaking there can be no faithful reading of the christology, ecclesiology, or eschatology of Hebrews which justifies political authoritarianism, and Christians who either place their faith in secular political institutions or believe that they have a right to control and wield them against others will be sorely disappointed. The brief reference to the love of money in 13:5 does not justify centralized economic redistribution, either. Instead, the one family of Abraham, united under the resurrected and ascended Messiah, must conceptualize themselves as exiles and patiently await the final return of the king. Christ's atoning death and the work of God's Spirit will see them through to the end. While James has much to say about the rich and the poor, we will find that it too does not diverge an inch from the New Testament's conceptualization of political and economic structures.

JAMES

Background: The Earliest Christian Letter?

To my dear Catholic readers, I apologize in advance: I think James was written by the brother of Jesus. Please know that I love you and understand if you want to skip the next few paragraphs, but the eponymous attribution of the letter to Jesus's own brother is historically probable and solves a number of interesting exegetical puzzles, some of which dovetail pleasantly with my overall thesis. James 1:1-2 identifies the author, recipients, and occasion of the letter: *"James, a bond-servant of God and of the Lord Jesus Christ, To the twelve tribes who are dispersed abroad: Greetings. Consider it all joy, my brethren, when you encounter various trials"*. Both the Jesus tradition (in Mark 6:3, paralleled in Matthew 13:55) and Paul (in Galatians 1:19) identify James as a brother of Jesus using the Greek term *adelphos*. While this word is often employed by Paul to describe the church (including Galatians 1:2 and 1:11), its primary usage refers to genetic male siblings, which appears to be the natural meaning in Galatians 1:19 (which refers to him as *"James, the Lord's brother"* and not *"our brother"*) and the Synoptics, where the evangelists are plainly alluding to the family of Jesus. The church has historically attributed the authorship of James to this brother of Jesus, and I agree.[15]

The traditional authorship makes sense of the entire epistle in a way which cannot be matched by alternative theories. George Stulac's magnificent introduction to James not only convinced me that the brother of Jesus wrote the letter but also provides an entirely plausible historical background against which the text is entirely comprehensible. I quote from Stulac at length: *"the evidence supports the traditional view of authorship: that the epistle was written by James the brother of Jesus as the recognized leader of the church in Jerusalem. An earlier dating of this letter also makes clearest sense of the content of the letter . . . the epistle was authored by James between A.D. 40 and 50 . . . [in response to] the early diaspora of Acts 8, rather than the later dispersion after A.D. 70 . . . the letter was written by James the Just, the brother of Jesus, in a Palestinian (not Hellenistic) culture, either as a unified pastoral message or a compilation of brief messages, to the Jewish Christians scattered in the time recorded in Acts 8:1-3"*[16].

All of the pieces fall into place. The *"twelve tribes"* are Jewish Jesus-believers that were scattered after the persecution in Acts 8, which James first references in James 1:2 and serves as a recurring motif throughout the letter. James displays no knowledge of the Gentile mission or Paul's more developed theologizing and is easily read as a text composed by a Jew written entirely for other Jews.[17] Even the notorious passage in James 2:14-26 where the author contends that *"a man is justified by works and not by faith alone"*[18] is intelligible in a pre-Pauline context; Paul himself in texts such as Romans 3 and Galatians 2 is arguing not against general good works but rather Gentiles practicing *"the works of the Law"*, a problem arising during the Gentile mission of which James appears entirely ignorant. As we will see, James frequently alludes to the oral Jesus tradition, particularly as it relates to economic issues of riches and poverty. James excoriates the rich because they refuse to deal justly with their laborers, which is *exactly the same* economic arrangement Jesus condemned during his ministry! The work of Horsley, Crossley and others is relevant here; the exploitative economic arrangement in which the rich acquire wealth not through voluntary production and exchange but through expropriation legitimized by the political class offers a perfect explanation of the

---

15. Stulac, George. 1993. *James.* InterVarsity Press. p. 12

16. Stulac, *James*, p. 15

17. Stulac, *James*, pp. 15-16

18. James 2:24

frequent condemnations of the wealthy in James. The Jerusalem establishment, perceived to be in bed with the Roman occupiers, was persecuting the church and intensifying economic instability. They are the ones who are targeting Jewish Jesus-believers and oppressing the poor. The evidence is overwhelming. James wrote the letter to Jewish Christ-followers in response to the persecution initiated by the Jerusalem establishment against the church in Acts 8:1-3. Bernier, after extensively examining the evidence, concurs: the epistle of James was composed no later (and probably much earlier) than 62 CE, the year James was executed.[19] Within this context of persecution and injustice, James has much to say which is of interest to our economic analysis of the New Testament.

Miseries Will Befall the Rich

James 1:2-8 opens the letter with an encouragement to endure *"various trials"* through the wisdom and strength provided by God. Then in 1:9-11, James contrasts the glory of *"the brother of humble circumstances"* with the *"rich man . . .* [who will] *glory in his humiliation . . .* [who] *in the midst of his pursuits will fade away"*. The Greek word behind *"rich man"* is *plousios*, a term with which we became familiar in our study of the Synoptic tradition. In Judea as in much of the Roman Mediterranean, very few people accumulated wealth through voluntary market transactions; designating a person as *plousios* could easily connote immoral or unjust behavior, and the context of trials and persecution in James suggests this is the intended meaning. The eschatological reversal of riches is a major feature in the Jesus tradition, particularly accentuated in Luke. From the song of Mary in Luke 1:46-55 to the Lukan beatitudes in Luke 6:20-26, the *plousios* might have their fill now but will find themselves humiliated in the great eschatological conflagration while the poor will be vindicated by the righteous God of Israel. In James 1:27, those who truly honor God *"visit orphans and widows in their distress"*; the longstanding Jewish tradition of care for the vulnerable, exhibited in passages such as Jeremiah 49:11, must characterize the life of a believer in contrast with the self-serving *plousios*.

James 2:1-7 is a command to show no partiality between the rich and the poor. When believers assemble they are not to give preferential treatment to the well-dressed man while disregarding those who are poorly dressed, because *"God choose the poor of this world to be rich in faith and heirs of the kingdom which He promised to those who love Him"*[20], echoing the beatitudes in Matthew 5:2-12

---

19. Bernier, *Rethinking the Dates*, pp. 196-211

20. James 2:5

and Luke 6:20-26 in which the poor will inherit the kingdom of God, as well as Matthew 6:26-28 in which Jesus instructs his followers not to worry about clothing. Showing favoritism based on wealth and status has *"dishonored the poor man"*, and even worse, enabled the very oppression which James condemns (*"Is it not the rich who oppress you and personally drag you into court?"*) according to 2:6. This is another passage in which the authoritarian socialist reading falls flat. The wealthy who are being rightly criticized by James are oppressive and weaponize the legal system against the poor. James is not issuing a condemnation of peaceful, voluntary market transactions in which the production and consumption of goods and services are decentralized. Nowhere can this passage be used in opposition to capitalism; quite the opposite, in fact. Those who have acquired wealth through oppression and the manipulation of courts are the problem. The reliance upon (oftentimes legal) coercion under threats of violence to regulate, control, or appropriate the productive fruits of other people is a feature of socialism, and no quantity of egalitarian rhetoric can mask the fact that James is in reality denouncing economic arrangements based on violence. If we are to adopt an economic principle from this passage for the modern world, it must include a repudiation of the economically coercive system of authoritarian socialism.

James will follow his condemnation of favoritism by positing an alternative in 2:8-13; the behavior of believers must conform to Leviticus 19:18, *"you shall love your neighbor as yourself"*, quoted in James 2:8. Partiality, especially towards the poor, is a violation of the command to love your neighbor. Once again James appropriates a feature of the Jesus tradition. In his debate with a lawyer about the greatest commandment, Jesus quotes Leviticus 19:18 as the second greatest commandment.[21] Paul also cites Leviticus 19:18 multiple times in his epistles, including Romans 13:9. Favoritism towards the *plousios* is incompatible with the love of neighbor. Immediately after this instruction, James explains how *"faith, if it has no works, is dead"*[22], using charity towards those in need in 2:15-16 as a prime example of a working faith. This passage is conceptually identical to Matthew 25:34-46 in which those who inherit the kingdom at the eschatological judgment have helped the needy. Those who refuse to serve others won't make it. The call to radical charity issued by Jesus and followed by James is entirely compatible with capitalism and should not be confused with confiscatory entitlement programs in which rich (*plousios*, perhaps?) politicians take money from productive people under threat of violence and distribute it to politically-connected recipients. Believers must be concerned about those in need without ceding ground to the imperial

---

21. Mark 12:13, Matthew 22:39, and Luke 10:27

22. James 2:17

authorities. James doesn't even offer a hint that the rich should be given more control over the economy to 'fix' poverty, and in fact blames the rich for exacerbating poverty through oppression.

After warning his audience about the dangers of envy in 4:1-2, James 4:13-17 cautions against the arrogance of planning one's entire life around business and profit, presumptuously assuming we are in control of our destiny. Set within a larger rhetorical context where James compares the virtue of humility with the vice of arrogance, James will leverage this insight against the evil rich who have oppressed the poor in the following passage.[23] James is again in perfect alignment with the Jesus tradition; in Luke 12:13-21, Jesus teaches a parable in which a haughty rich man tears down his barns to build bigger ones, only to be struck down that very night by God. James has, throughout his letter, taken a hostile tone towards the rich, who will because of their arrogance and evil oppression fall to ruin.

This theme reaches its climax in James 5:1-6: "*Come now, you rich, weep and howl for your miseries which are coming upon you. Your riches have rotted and your garments have become moth-eaten. Your gold and your silver have rusted; and their rust will be a witness against you and will consume your flesh like fire. It is in the last days that you have stored up your treasure! Behold, the pay of the laborers who mowed your fields, and which has been withheld by you, cries out against you; and the outcry of those who did the harvesting has reached the ears of the Lord of Sabaoth. You have lived luxuriously on the earth and led a life of wanton pleasure; you have fattened your hearts in a day of slaughter. You have condemned and put to death the righteous man; he does not resist you*". The rich will be miserable because all of their wealth will be destroyed. The language James employs is reminiscent of Matthew 6:19-20, where Jesus instructs his audience not to "*store up for yourselves treasures on earth, where moth and rust destroy*". The rich will receive eschatological judgment because they have withheld the rightful earnings from those who labored in their fields. Since abject poverty was pervasive in first century Judea, day laborers who were not given their contractually-obligated wages were in danger of starvation.[24] This explains why James can describe the behavior of those rich landowners as "*condemn*[ing] *and put*[ting] *to death the righteous man*".

Far from being a critique of free-markets, James is railing against the wealthy people who act in an unjust manner to increase their own wealth. As we learned in our study of the gospels, rich landowners were enabled by the political and legal

---

23. Stulac, *James*, p. 158
24. Stulac, *James*, p. 166

institutions of their day. The socialists of the modern world, determined to grant a massive amount of economic power to a small handful of bureaucrats and politicians, are philosophically aligned with the rich oppressors James rightly condemns for their corruption and exploitation. Only through the most imprecise and inaccurate categorial definitions of 'capitalism' and 'socialism' could one possibly read this passage as an affirmation of the latter and a critique of the former. The Austrian definition of each term, predicated upon the objective difference between economic transactions based on consent against those based on coercion, allows us to draw the correct modern application: believers should condemn economic arrangements in which wealthy people are given arbitrary power over others. In other words, we must reject socialism root and branch.

In response to the oppressive rich and their impending eschatological judgment, James 5:7-11 encourages believers to remain faithful to God, enduring suffering until God acts to vindicate his people. Stulac explains the function of James 5:1-11: "[there are] *two purposes (encouragement and warning) James would have for Christians who are reading how he would address their rich, non-Christian oppressors. His encouragement is for them to leave judgment to God while they persevere in righteousness. His warning is for them to beware of God's judgment and flee from materialistic sin themselves*"[25]. This maps on perfectly with the general New Testament teaching on wealth and poverty. Wealth is morally neutral but must be acquired justly and used to build God's kingdom by serving others. It entails a massive responsibility which leads many into idolatry and ruin. Believers must commit to radical charity, voluntarily sharing their resources with those who truly need them while fleeing from the destructive love of money. God will judge the rich oppressors, but there can be no violent revolution against them until the final day without compromising the unique, cruciform identity of the church. So-called "Christian" socialists, in promoting an economic system which perpetuates violence and inequality, are just as much in danger of forging economic idols as those who are rich, and James empowers us to rebuke both parties. The solution, as always, are decentralized economic networks of voluntary production and exchange between peaceful people. Leveraging the monopolistic power of a secular state to remake the economy based on the subjective, short-sighted, and barbaric theory of socialism is antithetical to Christian values and will always result in greater wealth inequality and structural poverty. May the modern church one day learn this lesson.

---

25. Stulac, *James*, pp. 167-168

1 PETER[26]

Background: The 'Romans 13' of the Catholic Epistles

Contained in the first letter of the apostle Peter is a passage on the church and political authorities which rivals the infamous Romans 13. Since the Catholic Epistles are often neglected, pride-of-place is generally afforded to the much more famous passage in Paul. We have, I think, already solved the Romans 13 problem, and we will find, interestingly enough, that Peter's own commentary on the political authorities is functionally identical to Romans 13. By way of introduction, I quote 1 Peter 2:13-17: "*Submit yourselves for the Lord's sake to every human institution, whether to a king as the one in authority, or to governors as sent by him for the punishment of evildoers and the praise of those who do right. For such is the will of God that by doing right you may silence the ignorance of foolish men. Act as free men, and do not use your freedom as a covering for evil, but use it as bondslaves of God. Honor all people, love the brotherhood, fear God, honor the king.*" This passage looks and sounds familiar. Even a surface reading of 1 Peter 2, quoted entirely without reference to its rhetorical or historical context, should lead a perceptive reader to suspect Peter may not be offering a straightforward legitimation of any and all political powers.

When Peter writes his letter to a few churches in Asia minor, he has a particular set of goals in mind and begins establishing themes and concepts which will run throughout the duration of the letter, exactly like every other New Testament author. 1 Peter is not exceptional. Just as a modern reader understands that any given passage in a novel contributes to the plot development of the whole, New Testament authors also intended their works to be read (or heard) from start to finish. Reading a controversial passage like 1 Peter 2:13-17 without trying to understand its function within Peter's overarching rhetorical agenda and how it relates to every other part of the letter guarantees that the interpreter will misread the text. Romans 13:1-7 cannot be correctly interpreted in isolation, and neither can 1 Peter 2:13-17.

In order to establish the context, we must ask if Peter actually composed this letter, and, if so, what he intended to communicate. Twice in 1 Peter the author identifies himself; in 1:1 the author self-identifies as Peter, and in 5:1 he refers to himself as a "*fellow elder and witness of the sufferings of Christ*". Peter was no doubt

---

26. This section is based on an article which I published through the Libertarian Christian Institute; Bernardo, Alex. "Submit to the Authorities? What 1 Peter 2:13-17 Claims About Political Power." Libertarianchristians.Com. November 26, 2024. https://libertarianchristians.com/2024/11/26/submit-to-the-authorities/.

a generative force for the oral Jesus tradition, and an appeal to his eyewitness testimony would only strengthen the authoritative weight of 1 Peter. Why should the audience take this letter seriously? Because Peter, the purported author, was one of Jesus's most trusted disciples. He was with Jesus during his life, his ministry, his death (sort of), his resurrection, and his ascension. Peter can be trusted because he was a disciple of Jesus and heard his teachings firsthand. If the traditional attribution of 1 Peter to Peter the disciple can be substantiated then the perspective Peter takes in the letter is likely informed by his close proximity to Jesus and thus in harmony with the Jesus tradition. Furthermore, despite Peter's many shortcomings (which were on full display in the Gospels and, more painfully for Peter, Galatians), he is the center of Jesus's inner circle and the one to whom Jesus made the promise that *'on this rock I will build my Church'*[27]. Readers can trust what Peter says (if he actually wrote the letter) and are obligated to take him seriously.

Petrine authorship, however, cuts against a broad consensus in modern biblical scholarship. The assumption which has been made by the majority of New Testament scholars is that Peter couldn't have possibly composed this letter. Wasn't he just an illiterate fisherman from the ancient equivalent of Appalachia? Didn't plenty of writers in antiquity forge letters to legitimize their own arguments? Modern biblical scholarship was to a certain extent forged in the fires of Enlightenment skepticism, and as the discipline developed over the course of the nineteenth century the biases against 'religion' and in favor of 'science' as the only path to knowledge (which had political roots in the battle against establishment churches in Europe and the concurrent rise of nationalism) were embraced whole-heartedly by historians and theologians. Oftentimes this thoroughgoing skepticism has resulted in historical theories about the development of the New Testament which are, like the biblical legitimation of authoritarian socialism, almost entirely devoid of actual evidence, ironically the purported hallmark of Enlightenment rationalism. Besides the text's internal attestation, historian of the early church Eusebius, writing in the early fourth century, comments on the authorship of 1 Peter: *"As to the writings of Peter, one of his epistles called the first is acknowledged as genuine. This was anciently used by the ancient fathers in their writings as an undoubted work of the apostles."*[28] The ancients seemed to think 1 Peter is genuine, and I am inclined to agree.

There is another piece of internal evidence which sheds light on the author and occasion of the letter. Peter acknowledges that he himself did not physically write the letter in 1 Peter 5:12: *"Through Silvanus, our faithful brother (for so I*

---

27. Matthew 16:18

28. Eusebius, *Ecclesiastical Histories*, 3:3:1

regard him), I have written to you briefly". So yes, skeptics, Peter didn't technically *write* the letter. But he did have it written for him. How can an illiterate fisherman compose a work like 1 Peter? By employing a secretary. It's worth repeating Benjamin Laird's excellent description of this phenomenon: *"As the content and features of ancient writings are examined, it becomes increasingly apparent that writing in the Greco-Roman world often involved significant collaboration between an author and a number of individuals, each of whom served a specific role during the compositional process . . . for many individuals living during the first century, the composition of a personal letter, business or legal document, or virtually any time of literary work involved direct collaboration with a trained secretary . . . in addition to maintaining the necessary writing materials, secretaries were capable of composing documents in a variety of literary genres and in a style that was typically more efficient, rhetorically effective, and pleasing to the eye"[29]*. We have already established the compositional dynamic of collaboration in Paul, and it is historically plausible that Peter used Silvanus as a secretary to compose his letter. The assertion of Eusebius remains viable.

The identity of Silvanus also strengthens our case. According to R.E. Nixon (no relation, I'm sure, to Richard), 'Silvanus' is most likely the Latinized form of the Semitic 'Silas'[30], and we know from other New Testament documents that Silas was a leading member of the church in Jerusalem who possessed prophetic gifts[31]. This Silas not only receives a shout-out in 2 Corinthians 1:19 but is also responsible for crafting both of Paul's letters to Thessalonica[32]. Silas is likely responsible for the thematic similarities between those two letters[33], and we can rightly conclude that Peter and Paul, despite Peter's occasional lapses of judgment, were largely in agreement. According to Luke, Silas is an instrumental figure at the council of Jerusalem in Acts 15, where, addressing an issue at the heart of the New Testament and by extension 1 Peter, the church decides that Gentiles are a part of the family of Abraham by virtue of faith in Israel's Messiah and the gift of God's Spirit[34]. Not only does Silas participate in this foundational council, he is also responsible for delivering (and perhaps even composing) a letter to the confused

---

29. Laird, *Creating the Cannon*, pp. 15-16

30. Nixon, R.E.. 1996. *"Silas"*. In *New Bible Dictionary*, 3rd ed. ed. by I. Howard Marshall, A.R. Millard, J.I. Packer, and D.J. Wiseman, InterVarsity Press. p. 1101

31. Acts 15:22, 32

32. 1 Thessalonians 1:1 and 2 Thessalonians 1:1

33. Nixon, *"Silas"*, p. 1101

34. Acts 15:1-29

church in Antioch[35]. Silas will accompany Paul on his second missionary journey[36] and eventually wind up again in the presence of Peter, where he serves as Peter's secretary. After extensively reviewing the evidence, Bernier concludes that 1 Peter is authentically Petrine and was likely composed between 60 and 69 CE, the year of Peter's death.[37] We can now confidently presume Peter himself wrote the letter, but what was its occasion and how does it relate to 2 Peter 2:13-17?

In Acts 15 the leaders of the Jewish Jesus movement come to a radical conclusion: Gentiles who place their faith in Jesus and are given the Spirit now belong to Abraham's family without adopting the Law. This is also a key insight of Pauline ecclesiology and is on full display in Romans, Galatians, and Ephesians, where the Jew-plus-Gentile family of Abraham are holy, set apart from the rest of humanity by virtue of faith and the Spirit. Paul's Jewish anthropological dualism is reworked around the inaugurated eschatological reign of Israel's king. Peter struggles with Law-free Gentile inclusion in Galatians (in an event which possibly triggered the Jerusalem council in Acts 15) by compelling the Gentiles to live like Jews and requesting that they embrace particular aspects of the Jewish Law[38]. Paul, Jewish apostle to a Gentile world, composes an incensed response to Peter, arguing that because of Jesus all those who have faith are Abraham's descendants, not just those following the Jewish Law[39]. The identity of the church is rooted in Jesus, the Jewish Messiah who now by virtue of his ascension rules over all creation. Peter will come around to Paul's way of defining the church and argue passionately for it at the Jerusalem council[40]. The unique, set-apart identity of the church, rooted in Jesus the Messiah, is a central theme in 1 Peter and has a direct, often overlooked impact on the way in which Christians conceptualize political power. If this is starting to sound like our previous chapter on Romans, you are not suffering from a case of deja-vu; Peter comes around to Paul's Messianic, eschatological ecclesiology. As in Romans, it is the presupposition for Peter's instructions regarding political authorities.

So why, then, did Peter set out to write a letter to the churches scattered throughout Pontus, Galatia, Cappadocia, Asia, and Bithynia, all of which are in Asia Minor? *He is reminding them of their identity as members of the church and the need to be faithful witnesses to Christ in the midst of suffering.* A major recurring

---

35. Acts 15:22

36. Acts 15:36-41

37. Bernier, *Rethinking the Dates*, p. 223

38. Galatians 2:11-15

39. Galatians 3:1-4:11; see especially 3:1-9

40. Acts 15:7-11

motif in Paul, Peter is concerned about the faithfulness and public perception of believers experiencing intense social and political opposition. There are several places in the letter where Peter explicates his intentions[41], but 3:13-17 is by far the most significant: "*Who is there to harm you if you prove zealous for doing what is good? But even if you should suffer for the sake of righteousness, you are blessed. And do not fear their intimidation, and do not be troubled, but sanctify Christ as Lord in your hearts, always being ready to make a defense to everyone who asks you to give an account for the hope that is in you, yet with gentleness and reverence; and keep a good conscience so that in the thing in which you are slandered, those who revile your good behavior in Christ will be put to shame. For it is better, if God should will it so, that you suffer for doing what is right rather than for doing what is wrong.*"

Unlike in Romans, where Paul appears to be worried about the *potential* for persecution, Peter is writing to a church which is actively enduring opposition. This suffering is likely not systematic, as the work of Haddad and Burnett on Paul indicates; instead, it is probably due to the fact that believers engage in practices which their pagan neighbors find peculiar and culturally insensitive. Peter exhorts the churches to hold fast to their identity, being willing to defend their faith and maintaining a good reputation in the midst of it all, the lens through which 1 Peter 2:13-17 must be viewed. 1 Peter 3:13-17, revealing the purpose of 1 Peter, doesn't come out of nowhere. It is in fact the climax of a long section in the epistle which runs from 2:11-3:17. Notice what Peter says in 2:12, towards the beginning of this rhetorical unit, and compare it with the passage quoted above: "*Keep your behavior excellent among the Gentiles* [!], *so that in the thing in which they slander you as evildoers, they may because of your good deeds . . . glorify God on the day of visitation*". 1 Peter 2:11-12 and 3:13-17 are a classic example of *inclusio*, a set of passages which serve to bracket off a particular argument or rhetorical segment of a work. Notice that the themes in 2:11-12 and 3:13-17 are the same: keep your behavior excellent before outsiders and don't compromise your unique identity. Sounds like Paul. What does this mean for our reading of 1 Peter 2:13-17? All of the material in between these two passages *are functionally designed to reinforce that same basic point!* Just as Romans 13:1-7 cannot be read in isolation from Romans 12-13, particularly 12:1-2, Peter's commentary on submission to the governing authorities is contextualized by the material surrounding it. It is within the rhetorical *inclusio* of 1 Peter 2:11-12 and 3:13-17 that we find the politically controversial 1 Peter 2:13-17. Careful readers may have noticed that I have yet to comment on the rest of the material in this *inclusio*, 2:18-3:12. Two more extremely controversial issues, both of which require nuanced exegetical treatment before drawing modern principles,

---

41. 1 Peter 1:6, 3:13-17, 4:12-19, 5:9

are included in this passage; they too must shape how we interpret Peter's teaching on the identity of the church and political authorities. These two controversial sets of instructions address the relationship between slave and master and the relationship between wives and (presumably non-believing) husbands. An outline of 1 Peter 2:11-3:17 provides a useful visual aid:

A. 2:11-12 | Maintain Identity, Keep Behavior Excellent Before Outsiders
   a. 2:13-17 | Christians and Governing Authorities
   b. 2:18-25 | Slaves and Masters
   c. 3:1-7 | Wives and Husbands
   d. 3:8-12 | Summary of Previous Instruction
B. 3:13-17 | Maintain Identity, Keep Behavior Excellent Before Outsiders

In order to assess Peter's instructions about Christians and the governing authorities, we must set it within the rhetorical context of both the letter as a whole and the individual passage in which it is included, where Peter also provides instruction on the relationships between slaves and masters and wives and husbands. A faithful interpretation of Peter's statements will correspond to his overall agenda of reminding his audience of their identity and encouraging them to maintain that identity despite suffering. We are now in a position to analyze Peter's conception of political authorities.

The Set-Apart Family of God

Christianity does not replace Judaism. As we have seen, conceptualizing those two categories as separate entities in the first century is historically anachronistic. What would become known as 'Christianity' emerges from Second-Temple Judaism, and our 'New Testament' was written predominantly by Jews (with Luke-Acts a possible exception). Therefore the theological framework within which Jews like Peter were thinking was fundamentally Jewish. To this extent any analysis of 1 Peter, as with the Pauline epistles, cannot afford to ignore the Jewish intellectual milieu within which both men were raised. Like Paul, Peter would not have thought himself to be abandoning a category called 'Judaism' for a new one called 'Christianity'. Instead, the Jewish hope had been fulfilled in the eschatological reign of Israel's Messiah Jesus through whom the nations were, at the end of history, turning to the one true God of creation. Peter never abandons the exclusivistic Jewish notion of election; the idea that Abraham's family was distinct from the other nations based on God's gracious choice is the ecclesiological starting point in 1 Peter. As with Paul, the only real innovation in this Jewish theology of election among the early

Jesus-followers was that, because of the death, resurrection, and ascension of Jesus the Jewish messiah, Gentiles who place their faith in him are incorporated into the family of Abraham without having to follow the Jewish Law. This extended and redrew the boundary markers of Abraham's chosen family around faith. It was in no way a repudiation of ethnic Judaism; Abraham's family had been called to be a *'blessing to the nations'*[42] and the prophets had foretold that when God returns to rescue Abraham's family from their failure to be obedient that the nations would stream to the renewed Jerusalem[43] and that the *'earth will be full of the knowledge of the Lord as the waters cover the sea'*[44]. This is exactly what happens through the life, death, resurrection, and ascension of Jesus, and the Jewish leaders of the early church would (reluctantly, in Peter's case) acknowledge that Gentiles were fully welcome into Abraham's family *as Gentiles* by faith in the Messiah.

This is the historical and theological context in which 1 Peter must be grounded. In 1 Peter 1:1-2 Peter refers to his audience as 'aliens' and appeals to the language of election: *"Peter, an apostle of Jesus Christ, To those who reside as aliens, scattered throughout Pontus, Galatia, Cappadocia, Asia, and Bithynia, who are chosen according to the foreknowledge of God the Father, by the sanctifying work of the Spirit, to obey Jesus Christ and be sprinkled with His blood: May grace and peace be yours in the fullest measure"*. Paul himself could have composed this introduction. The one family of God may reside in different cities, but all belong to the one *"chosen"* community by the *"foreknowledge of God"*, the work of the Spirit, and Jesus the Messiah. Channelling Romans 1:5, 15:18, and 16:26, believers are to *"obey* [a form of *hypakoe*] *Jesus Christ"*. There is one family under one Lord. Peter hasn't forgotten what the word *christos* denotes. Jesus is truly, objectively the king of the world, and there are no other competitors. Jewish election theology is redefined around the Messiah; if Jesus is truly king, then his people are demarcated by obedience to him. The reason why Peter can refer to his mixed Jew-Gentile audience both as 'chosen' and as 'aliens', knowing that some of his recipients are, like Paul, Roman citizens, is because Jesus is the real king and therefore the power and prestige of the Roman empire is relativized in Christ. The echoes of Jeremiah 29:7 become increasingly audible. Peter hails Jesus as king, and the identity of God's family as His chosen people makes them 'aliens'. In accordance with the Jewish tradition inherited by Peter, resident aliens are called to seek the welfare of the city even though God plans on bringing the city to a violent, permanent end.

---

42. Genesis 12:3

43. Isaiah 2:2-4

44. Isaiah 11:9

To drive his ecclesiological point home, Peter directly quotes Leviticus 19:2 in 1:16: '*you shall be holy, for I* [God] *am holy*'. This statement functions as a refrain in Leviticus, reminding Israel that God has given them the Law so they may remain set apart and distinct from the other nations. Peter applies this election language of holiness to the church of those who believe in the Messiah, stating in 1:13-15 that the church must behave in a manner which is consistent with their identity. Peter employs the term "*obedient*" again in 1:14, clearly connecting the set-apartness of God's chosen people with the idea that they are obedient to Jesus, the world's real king. 1 Peter and Romans are in perfect alignment. Just as Paul introduces his gospel of king Jesus and the obedience of Gentiles in Romans 1, the first chapter of 1 Peter, functioning as an introduction to the rest of his letter, demarcates his christological and ecclesiological convictions. The church is called and set apart by God and are obedient to Jesus even, or perhaps especially, when they have to suffer for their faith. Peter will abandon none of these ideas as he continues to instruct his audience regarding how they should negotiate relationships given this complex set of realities. As in Romans 13, Peter doesn't magically suspend these principles when faced with the governing authorities.

Peter continues to build towards the chiastic instruction in 2:11-3:17. Peter refines his definition of the church and obedience in 1 Peter 2, preparing his audience for the difficult relational advice which includes his provocative statement about political submission. Peter continues the theme of Christian identity in 2:4-8 by articulating a claim also made by Paul in 1 Corinthians[45] and Ephesians[46] that the church is now the temple of God. I detect a slight hint of Genesis in 2:4, where the church is also the priestly class who ministers in the temple, and Peter will cite passages from Isaiah and Psalms[47] to substantiate this claim: the church is to "*offer up spiritual sacrifices acceptable to God through Jesus Christ*"[48]. Not only does this passage brilliantly express Peter's high view of the church, it also reveals that the boundaries between God's people and the rest of the world have been redefined around Christ. This short but dense section has massive ecclesiological implications, and Peter will continue to develop his theology of the church in the following section.

1 Peter 2:9-10 contains another brief chiasm, with Peter beginning and ending the section by applying Israel-language ('*chosen race*', '*holy nation*', '*people of God*', '*received mercy*') to his ethnically mixed audience and then stating boldly

---

45. 1 Corinthians 3:16-17

46. Ephesians 2:21-22

47. Isaiah 28:16, Psalm 118:22, and Isaiah 8:14

48. 1 Peter 2:4

in the middle that God has constituted the church *"so that you may proclaim the excellencies of Him who has called you out of darkness and into his marvelous light[49]"*. God promised Abraham in Genesis 12:3 that his family would be a blessing to the nations, a promise fulfilled through the family of Abraham, now defined by Christ and not the Law, sharing the Gospel with all nations. At the center of God's activity in the world is his set-apart, chosen family. Just as Paul encourages the church in Rome to refuse conformity and be transformed by the renewing of their minds in Romans 12:1-2, Peter expects his audience to live publicly remodeled lives.

This observation alone, as in Romans, should cause anyone reading Peter's letter to rethink their commitment to secular political authorities, and the next section of the letter, leading directly into the 'Romans 13 of the catholic epistles', blows every facile political reading of 1 Peter to pieces. It is frustrating, but sadly predictable, that many interpreters ignore it. 1 Peter 2:11-12 reads as follows: *"Beloved, I urge you as aliens and strangers to abstain from fleshly lusts which wage war against the soul. Keep your behavior excellent among the Gentiles, so that in the thing in which they slander you as evildoers, they may because of your good deeds, as they observe them, glorify God in the day of visitation."* The casual reader might skim over this passage, quickly moving on to the more controversial section which follows, much like Romans 13:1-7 is often read in isolation from its immediate rhetorical context. That would be a massive mistake. Peter makes several critical moves in this short section which must be recognized in order to interpret the following material. The first move addresses the identity of the church. Peter has already referred to his audience, some of which were Roman citizens, as 'aliens' in 1:1. He repeats this again in 2:11, identifying them as 'aliens and strangers'. His mixed Jew and Gentile community, comprising both Romans and non-Romans, are to perceive themselves as possessing a new identity which relativizes all others. This necessarily precludes any notion of a 'national identity' or automatic, uncritical obedience to the whims of the state. Those that aren't 'in Christ' are outside the family of God. For now. Peter reminds his audience that they must flee from lust and urges them to keep their behavior excellent among outsiders. The public perception of believers, a major concern in the Pauline epistles, reappears in full force. Peter is just as anxious as his apostolic counterpart for the witness of believers in a skeptical world. The family of God should *look* different from their Roman neighbors.

Peter utilizes yet another Pauline rhetorical maneuver, this time taken from Ephesians 4:17, of referring to those outside the church as *"Gentiles"*. Peter, the Jew of Jews who, even after a revelation from God that he should not call Gentiles

---

49. 1 Peter 2:9

unclean[50] still had a moment of crisis where he refused to eat with them[51] (and was excoriated by Paul in Galatians), now uses the term '*Gentile*' in reference to those outside the church regardless of their ethnic identity. By reapplying the term '*Gentile*' to unbelievers, Peter is drawing a bright red line between insiders and outsiders; Peter's audience are on the inside, while the rest of the world is out. The hope, of course, is that outsiders will be brought in, and by behaving excellently before "*the Gentiles*" unbelievers will comprehend the wisdom of Israel's God. Peter knows the church is facing intense pressure from the outside world and in 2:12 instructs his audience to behave well in front of the 'Gentiles' so that, even though they may slander the church, they will because of the good deeds of the church glorify God when Jesus finally returns to set the record straight. The purpose of Christian behavior is to convict outsiders and reveal the true king, Jesus. Before we even make it to 2:13-17, we can see what Peter is about to do: submitting to the authorities is an extension of Christians "*keeping their behavior excellent among the Gentiles*" so that they may one day "*glorify God*". Peter's advice about government, slaves, and wives is a pragmatic response to a world in desperate need of the gospel. It does not legitimize, condone, or create a timeless theological framework legitimizing ancient social institutions.

Peter, in the exact same manner as Paul, is essentially appropriating an eschatological reading of Jeremiah 29:7. Believers are distinct from but not in open conflict with the pagan authorities and must seek peace with all men. It's little wonder that Peter opens his letter by referring to the church as "*aliens*" or exiles and ends by calling Rome "*Babylon*" in 1 Peter 5:13. The tension we found inherent in the Jewish Jeremiah 29:7 tradition is on full display in 1 Peter, as Sprinkle helpfully summarizes: "*this passage* [1 Peter 2:13-17] *is situated in the middle of a letter where Peter called the church "exiles" (1:1), "foreigners" (1:17), and "foreigners and exiles" (2:11). He explicitly called Rome "Babylon" (5:13). The church's submissive posture toward Babylon is shaped by their identity as exiles and foreigners. Like the literal Jewish exiles in Jeremiah's day, Christians are to be good citizens, seek the good of the city they live in, and submit to governing authorities, because they are exiles who belong to a different kingdom*"[52]. This consistent attitude towards pagan rule throughout the New Testament is the presupposition for a properly historical reading of 1 Peter 2:13-17.

---

50. See Acts 10-11, as well as 15

51. Galatians 2:11-21

52. Sprinkle, *Exiles*, p. 168

"For the Lord's Sake": 1 Peter 2:13-17

The passage itself can only be comprehended in terms of the context in which Peter has placed it. Recall that this section is the first in a set of three dealing with the complexities of Christian involvement in ancient institutions. Peter has established his audience as the true people of God, exiles who find their identity only in Christ and are called to set an example for outsiders. It should not surprise us when Peter introduces this unit with a statement that is unfortunately easy to gloss over: *"Submit yourselves"*, says Peter, *"for the Lord's sake"*[53]. Why should his audience submit? Because the institutions which he is about to describe are eternally valid and reflect God's intention for creation? No. They submit *"for the Lord's sake"*. This is in keeping with what Peter commanded only words before, that believers ought to keep their behavior excellent among the Gentiles so that the Gentiles will see their good deeds and glorify God. When Peter says *"submit yourselves for the Lord's sake to every human institution, whether to a king as the one in authority or to governors"*, he is simply reiterating the church's missional responsibility as reflecting God's wisdom to outsiders. Peter is, like Paul, appropriating the Jewish tradition of Jeremiah 29:7, exemplified by Daniel. Believers must not compromise either their values or their witness but are also responsible for promoting peace in light of God's eschatological vindication.

Peter expects that submission to authorities will shame those critical of the church. In 2:15 Peter claims that by submitting to the authorities the church will *"silence the ignorance of foolish men"*, quite possibly the same *"foolish men"* who are *"distressing the church with various trials"* in 1:6 and *"slandering* [the church] *as evildoers"* in 2:12. The church is suffering, and by demonstrating a willingness to submit believers might silence any claims that the church is somehow engaged in illicit activities. For Peter (as for Paul, Daniel, and Jeremiah) the authorities exist and the church is obligated to build a pragmatic relationship with them. Is Peter saying the authorities are eternal and will exist forever? Does this mean that Christ shares his messianic, kingly, ascended, and exalted status with human leaders? Of course not. Even though the Messiah has inaugurated God's eschaton, believers still live in the real world. Peter knows Jesus is the true king *and* that the authorities still exercise actual power over human beings. The church must find a pragmatic way to live in the tension between an objectively enthroned Christ and the present reality of an old creation which is fading but has yet to fully fade away. Peter's approach to this historical and theological tension is a christological application of Jeremiah 29:7. Believers submit when they can *"for the Lord's sake"*,

---

53. 1 Peter 2:13

not for the sake of the authorities, so that in the end God will be glorified on the day Jesus returns.

Another important consideration has to do with the precise identity of the authorities. Peter lists them in 2:13-14: "*whether to a king as the one in authority, or to governors as sent by him for the punishment of evildoers and the praise of those who do right*". As we learned in Chapter 5, the Roman political system was necessarily decentralized. In a time before phones, email, cars, or airplanes, it would have been impossible for a small number of politicians in Rome to micromanage the entire Mediterranean basin. The general system of imperial management in the ancient and medieval world, perfected during the height of Roman imperialism, often relied on local leaders in conquered or annexed territory to perform the day-to-day operations of local governance. So long as the taxes got paid and the peace was kept imperial authorities were generally satisfied. This was, as I argued in my analysis of the gospels, why the Herods and Sanhedrin held real political power while having to present Jesus to Pilate as a threat to the *Pax Romana*. Peter (and Paul, for that matter) is not instructing his audience to submit to Caesar, a conspicuous omission in Peter's list of political authority figures which is readily explained by the decentralized nature of Roman power. The likelihood that anyone of his audience, located in Asia Minor far away from the imperial capital, would ever come into contact with a Roman emperor was pretty much nonexistent. Instead, they would be governed by local client-kings or governors who, as long as their territory remained at peace, usually ruled by the standards of the region's cultural customs. With the exception of the *imperium*, a not insignificant political trump card, the Romans governed with a light touch. Local 'kings and authorities' were delegated with the task of maintaining order. Submission to these local authorities contributed to the public peace and increased the likelihood that outsiders would view believers with respect.

1 Peter 2:14 (in perfect parallel with Romans 13:3-4) follows the prevailing ancient political theory that political authorities exist "*for the punishment of evildoers and the praise of those who do right*". At this point in the argument, it is worth quoting Haddad's great political insight on the language of evil and good in Romans 13 and 1 Peter 2: "*Peter relies upon a general theory of government whose purpose is to reward good conduct and promote public morality. This general theory was widely held and can be located among several authors. In Aristotle's Politica, for example, he provides a detailed description of this theory. He suggests that the polis exists for the good life and that justice is expressed by judicial procedure, in regulating what is right and wrong. In his Legatio ad Gaium, Philo of Alexandria not only affirms this theory of government but states that "no law can be complete unless it includes two provisions—honors for things good and punishments for things evil . . . for penalties are*

good for the morals of the multitude, who fear to suffer the like . . . When Paul [and by extension Peter] *says that "rulers are not a terror to good conduct, but to bad" (Rom 13:3a), he is only affirming a positive theory of civil authority that ancient society already subscribed to*[54]*."*

Peter, like Paul, asserts that political leaders have a very specific function: promote the good and punish the bad. If believers acknowledge this reality and willingly offer submission *"for the Lord's sake"*, they should have nothing to fear from anyone in power. The church maintains excellent behavior among the gentiles (we haven't forgotten 2:12!) and by doing so appear to the authorities as doers of good, worthy, perhaps, of praise. The public witness reveals to the authorities that Jesus is king and silences those who are causing trouble for the church. Peter, *"witness of the sufferings of Christ"*[55], is under no illusion that the Romans consistently (or even usually) embody the rhetoric of upholding the good in practice, but he does seem to think a reminder of their philosophically articulated political standards empowers believers to seek peace through submission.

Peter returns to ecclesiology in 2:15-16, using language reminiscent of Paul in Galatians[56]: *"act as free men, and do not use your freedom as a covering for evil, but use it as bondslaves of God. Honor all people, love the brotherhood, fear God, honor the king"*. While his audience is free, citizens of another kingdom, as a matter of political pragmatics they submit to political authorities which exist to punish bad and praise good. Just as Jeremiah evocatively describes the destruction of Babylon while simultaneously exhorting the Jewish exiles to seek the city's welfare, Peter, labelling Rome "Babylon" in 5:13, is acclimating his audience to the prophetic tradition of pagan imperialism with all its complex tension. Peter was intimately familiar with the fate of Babylon. His use of the term is an epithet, not an honorific. Submit in the present, wait for the future. Every human empire will one day fall like Babylon. As with Romans 13:1-7, so with 1 Peter 2:13-17; this passage is not a legitimation of any and every government, ruler, or political policy.

What makes 1 Peter 2:13-17 a more interesting test case than Romans 13 for Christians seeking to deduce applicable principles from the New Testament is the passage's rhetorical context. Peter's exhortation about authorities is part of a larger unit which runs from 2:11-3:17 and includes instructions regarding the institution of slavery and marriage. Authoritarians who would oppose my thesis on the basis of 1 Peter 2:13-17 face a difficult obstacle in 2:18-3:7: Peter doesn't challenge the institution of slavery or patriarchal marriage but instructs both slaves

---

54. Haddad, *New Creation*, p. 67

55. 1 Peter 5:1

56. Galatians 5:1, 13

and wives to submit. Left-wing Christians, for all their histrionics about slavery and "The Patriarchy", never feel compelled to uphold those two institutions on the basis of 1 Peter. Neither would I. Peter doesn't obligate us to reinstitute slavery or oppress women. What then, explains the firewall between 1 Peter 2:17 and 2:18? If slavery and patriarchal marriage are not universally valid institutions, and if modern Christians are morally obligated to oppose them, why shouldn't we apply the same logic to 1 Peter 2:13-17? I think we should. A brief historical and contextual examination of the surrounding material may help us think more clearly about carefully applying these ancient texts in the modern world.

Slavery and Patriarchy: 1 Peter 2:18-3:7

Should slaves always submit to their masters? Authoritarian socialists would tell you no. In fact, very few people in the modern Western world would support the institution of slavery. The abolition of slavery as a legally recognized institution is one of the few unequivocally positive social developments in human history. The ancients, however, knew nothing of universal emancipation. Right after Peter finishes encouraging his audience to 'submit to the authorities', he exhorts slaves in 2:18 to "*be submissive to your masters in all respect, not only to those who are good and gentile, but also to those who are unreasonable*". Does this mean Peter would have been opposed to the abolition movement? Of course not. Just as the modern Western mind can hardly fathom a world devoid of involuntary centralized authority, slavery was a ubiquitous institution in antiquity, rarely questioned by ancient thinkers. Slavery was so embedded in Roman society that, as Wright correctly observes, it was as essential to the ancient economy as electricity is to the modern one[57].

One conspicuous exception are the early followers of Jesus. Paul is uncomfortable with the social value attached to slavery and declared it relativised by the dawning of the eschatological age. Paul's infamous statement in Galatians 3:28 that "*there is neither Jew nor Greek, there is neither slave nor free, there is neither male nor female; for you are all one in Christ Jesus*" is, in a sense, the perfect summation of the New Testament witness to slavery. It is a part of the old creation which still exists but, like the rulers of this age, is fading away. Believers should live as if it was already dead and gone, which is the basis for Paul's subtly subversive letter to his dear friend (and slaveowner) Philemon. While the New Testament is *directionally* supportive of the abolition of slavery, there was no possibility of overthrowing the institution in antiquity. Instead, believers were instructed to recognize no

---

57. Wright, *Faithfulness of God*, p. 32

difference between slave or free. All have equal standing in Christ. The Christian slaveowner is to treat the Christian slave as a brother[58].

But what happens if a believing slave is owned by an unbelieving master? This is the question addressed in 1 Peter 2:18-25. His answer: treat an unbelieving slavemaster like the political authorities. Christian slaves submit to their masters for the Lord's sake, assured that their identity is found not in their status as a slave but as a child of the one true God. Peter acknowledges in 2:20 that slaves may suffer unjustly: "*if you do what is right and suffer for it you patiently endure it, this finds favor with God*". Peter then follows this statement with 2:21-25 (in a manner once again reminiscent of Paul[59]), telling the slaves in his audience (with an eye towards the rest of the congregation) that sometimes Christians are called to suffer unjustly because Christ did the same for us. Suffering can glorify God: "*Christ also suffered for you, leaving an example for you to follow in his steps*" (2:21)[60]. Slavery is a grave moral evil for which modernity is much better off having legally abolished it. Peter is dealing with a different reality where the church, tasked with revealing God to the world, must sometimes submit to unjust authorities.

The parallels between 1 Peter 2:13-17 and 2:18-25 are self-evident. It is completely appropriate for modern Christians to celebrate the death of institutional slavery while fighting to ensure it never returns. Anyone who attempts to enslave another person is a criminal. We should all be able to agree on that. The dangers of modernization, though, are ever present. Christians will correctly contextualize Peter's statements on slavery, recognizing that it does not obligate us to affirm the institution, while simultaneously decontextualizing his teaching regarding political authorities. If we accept that the realities of antiquity sometimes required the submission of slaves to masters then maybe we should also accept that the realities of antiquity sometimes required Christians to submit to political authorities. If we are absolutely certain about the moral legitimacy of abolition then it's high time we start dreaming about the abolition of arbitrary authoritarian government.

We find the same principle at work in Peter's directive to wives. The final institution which Peter addresses is marriage; particularly the vexing question of how wives should relate to their husbands. There were many women in the early church who came to faith in Christ without the support of their husbands, and Peter presupposes his audience includes at least a few such women. In 1 Peter 3:1 he offers advice: "*In the same way* [!], *you wives, be submissive to your own husbands so that even if any of them are disobedient to the word, they may be won without a*

---

58. Philemon 1:15-16

59. Philippians 2:5-11

60. 1 Peter 2:21

word by the behavior of their wives". Remember, Peter has *literally* just instructed slaves to remain obedient to their masters and how unjust suffering was in imitation of Christ. The framing for this exhortation is the *inclusio* which begins in 2:12, exhorting believers to keep their behavior excellent among outsiders for the glory of God. In a society which practiced patriarchal marriage this advice is not an affirmation of an imbalance in husband-wife relationships, as if Peter is telling women they must always and in every situation submit. Rather, given the realities and expectations of married women in the Greco-Roman world, submission to husbands was the most effective way of "*keep*[ing] *your behavior excellent among the Gentiles*". It is important to appreciate the dynamics and expectations of marriage in antiquity. New Testament scholar Holly Carey describes a series of laws passed by Augustus, briefly referenced in Chapter 4, part of which regulated marriage with the intention of strengthening the Roman empire. These laws included, quite naturally for a patriarchal society, women submitting to their husbands: "*such legal changes made marriage and child-bearing matters of civic responsibility, and they rewarded both male and female citizens who contributed in this way to the public good. It was believed that marriage and the creation of a family were not just personal affairs but contributed to the stability of the community*"[61].

Roman household legislation generated a troublesome legal twist: any Christian wife who was disobedient to her non-Christian husband would have been perceived as socially and politically subversive, an outcome which Peter was desperately trying to avoid. This sociological dynamic is only further reinforced by what Peter says in 3:2-6, where he encourages women to be chaste, respectful, and modestly dressed, all of which conform to the social expectations for Roman women. Carey explains: "*Another expectation of women was that they conduct themselves modestly. This was important because a woman's conduct was a direct reflection of her husband . . . in terms of dress, the virtue of modesty was less about avoiding revealing attire . . . and more about wearing simple clothing. Ultimately, modesty was about showing self-control rather than being self-indulgent*"[62]. Peter even appeals to Sarah and her obedience to Abraham as a model for believing women, an exegetical insight which comports well with Paul's general hermeneutic of Israel's Scripture being written "*as examples . . . for our instruction*"[63].

Peter, faced with a culturally embedded set of assumptions the transgression of which could spell disaster, finds submission the most pragmatic solution. Just as believers submit to political authorities and slaves to their masters for the Lord's

---

61. Carey, Holly. 2023. *Women Who Do*. Eerdmans. p. 29

62. Carey, *Women Who Do*, p. 35

63. 1 Corinthians 10:11

sake, so that outsiders will be ashamed that they ever slandered the church on judgment day, women must likewise yield to their husbands, becoming model examples of the virtuous wife. The hope, if their husbands are unbelievers, is that they will be *"won without a word by the behavior of their wives"*[64]. Husbands are likewise to *"show her* [their wives] *honor as fellow heir*[s] *of the grace of life"*[65]. Peter's advice for wives, as with slaves, is part of a pragmatic approach to several complicated social and political realities which is intended to maintain the identity of the church in the face of outside afflictions and reveal God's glory to the world. This is the *function of* this set of exhortations in 1 Peter, and any modern interpretation or application of Peter's words must take this purpose into account.

The rhetorical section ends with an extended summary which runs from 3:8-3:17, further revealing the intentions of Peter's advice about government, slavery, and marriage: *"To sum up, all of you be harmonious, sympathetic, brotherly, kind hearted, and humble in spirit; not returning evil for evil or insult for insult, but giving a blessing instead; for you were called for the very purpose that you might inherit a blessing*[66] *... who is there to harm you if you prove zealous for what is good? But even if you should suffer for the sake of righteousness, you are blessed ... sanctify Christ as Lord in your hearts, always being ready to make a defense to everyone who asks you to give an account for the hope that is in you ... and keep a good conscience so that in the thing in which you are slandered, those who revile your good behavior in Christ will be put to shame"*[67]. Verse 17 rounds out the section nicely: *"for it is better, if God should will it so, that you suffer for doing what is right rather than for doing what is wrong"*. We have come full circle.

Are we to say, then, that Peter would wish for us to reimpose the institution of slavery or expect women (and men, for that matter) to conform their modern marriages to the standards of ancient Roman patriarchalism? May it never be. Peter isn't affirming the universal validity of these social arrangements, baptizing them in the name of Jesus and telling his audience that they must never work for change, push boundaries, or live in light of the new creation. He is, like the entire Jewish tradition before him, navigating the complex socio-cultural tensions inherent in a fallen world marked by sin. While, as Peter will say in his second epistle,[68] we are awaiting God's promised new heavens and new earth, believers must wisely and pragmatically exist in the interim between the inauguration and consummation

---

64. 1 Peter 3:1

65. 1 Peter 3:7

66. 1 Peter 3:8-9

67. 1 Peter 3:13-16

68. 2 Peter 3:13

of God's eschatological kingdom. If we can peacefully work for change in a way which doesn't compromise the witness of Abraham's family, as many abolitionists of the nineteenth century did, then we should absolutely go for it. If conforming to an institution which is impossible to change at the moment will enhance our witness and doesn't compromise our values, then we should conform. Daniel is the quintessential example of this practical yet God-honoring practice. My point is simple: since modernism has correctly challenged slavery and arbitrary patriarchal marriages, then maybe, just maybe, we can challenge the hegemonic ideology of state omnipotence. In a society which is nominally committed to "democracy", perhaps Christians can help the rulers of this world which are passing away pass away a little faster. There will be no slavery, patriarchal marriages, or human government in the world to come. Eliminating two out of three in the interim is a good start, but I think we should go for the sweep.

Let's tie all of the threads together. The point of this long and complex argument has been to demonstrate that Peter doesn't justify the timeless and eternal power of human authorities. Peter instructs his audience to submit for the Lord's sake to political rulers, appeals to the conventional Greco-Roman concept of good governance, and tells his audience they should have nothing to fear if they do what is right. This is exactly what Paul is doing in Romans 13:1-7 and corresponds perfectly with the political tradition of Jeremiah 29:7 within which both Peter and Paul were raised. It is also entirely consistent with his advice to slaves and wives while contributing to the overall purpose of the letter, which is to maintain the identity of the church as God's chosen people in the midst of intense social pressures to conform. Peter is pragmatic while at the same time appealing to God's final victory. The political authorities are a part of the old creation that is passing away but still exercise very real power. Christians must find creative ways to live within this tension as did Jeremiah, Daniel, and others. The rest of 1 Peter gives us a few more powerful indicators that he does not, in fact, assert that earthly political authorities have eternal value.

Remember Peter twice uses exilic language when referring to his audience as 'strangers' or 'exiles' in 1:1 and 2:11, and all throughout the letter he is constantly reminding them of their identity as God's one true family. To every Roman citizen in his audience, the message was loud and clear: your true citizenship is in Christ, not the Roman empire. I think twenty-first century Christians should take the hint. Peter also operates within the high and royal christology of the early church. God's promises to David were fulfilled in Jesus, and believers are obligated to re-arrange their political allegiances accordingly. Peter specifically mentions Christ's glory and dominion twice: *"so that in all things God may be glorified through Jesus Christ, to whom belongs the glory and dominion forever and ever. Amen"* in 4:11, and *"to Him* [Christ] *be dominion forever and ever. Amen"* in 5:11. As if to place one final nail in the coffin of implied statism, he designates Rome as *"Babylon"* in 5:13. Baylon, the paradigm of pagan imperialism for which Jeremiah prophesied its cataclysmic downfall, has a new heir. According to the book of Revelation none of Babylon's offspring will survive[69]. Peter, like Paul, Daniel, and Jeremiah, has his eyes set to the past, present, and future of God's messianic agent: Jesus is the Christ, whether the pagans like it or not.

2 Peter

All These Things Will Be Destroyed

Peter makes it easy for us to identify the purpose of his second letter. He informs his audience in 2 Peter 3:1-2: *"This is now, beloved, the second letter I am writing to you in which I am stirring up your sincere mind by way of reminder, that you should remember the words spoken beforehand by the holy prophets and the commandment of the Lord and Savior spoken by your apostles"*. Peter wants the recipients to remember what the apostles taught them about the prophets and Jesus, whom he calls *"Lord and Savior"*. Peter should know; he was *"an eyewitness . . . of His Majesty"*, having heard God declare Jesus His *"beloved Son with whom I am well pleased"* during the transfiguration.[70] This is, of course, if 2 Peter was actually written by Peter, a position which all but a slim minority of scholars reject. Even Bernier, generally conceding the reliability of canonical authorial attribution, is skeptical, claiming that of all the works in the New Testament *"2 Peter is the strongest candidate for pseudonymous authorship in the New Testament corpus"*[71]. I think Peter wrote it as a matter of faith, which is hardly an intellectually rigorous argument, but fully confess the skeptics aren't without evidence. Nothing in what I am about to say hinges upon the Petrine authorship of the letter entitled '2 Peter', but I will refer to the author henceforth as "Peter".

Why does Peter remind the audience of his apostolic eyewitness credentials? You won't be surprised. False teachers have infiltrated the church, and Peter is counting them. That old chestnut. Peter denies the false teachers any hermeneutical legitimacy, boldly prefacing his withering condemnation of them by stating *"no prophecy of Scripture is a matter of one's own interpretation, for no prophecy was ever*

---

69. See especially Revelation 18-19.

70. 2 Peter 1:16-18. The Synoptic tradition of the transfiguration can be found in Mark 9:1-13, Matthew 17:1-13, Luke 9:28-36, analyzed in Chapter 9 above.

71. Bernier, *Rethinking the Dates*, p. 229; for his entire analysis see pp. 224-229.

made by an act of human will, but . . . by the Holy Spirit from God"[72]. The ruthless rhetoric of 2 Peter 2:1-22 is unmatched among the New Testament epistles (save Revelation) and makes Paul's feisty letter to Galatia appear downright tame. Peter will have none of their lies and tells the false prophets in no uncertain terms that they can go straight to hell (or, more accurately, *tartaroo*, but that's a conversation for another day)[73], where God will punish them justly for promoting false doctrine. Peter has little time for the nuanced political reflection on offer in 1 Peter because he is too busy combating proto-heretics. Yet he leaves the perceptive reader a small but not insignificant number of insights which helpfully contribute to our analysis of political categories in the New Testament.

The first is his unwavering commitment to the messianic status of Jesus. Peter consistently utilizes royal and messianic titles when speaking about Jesus[74] which should not be interpreted metaphorically. Just because 2 Peter, by virtue of its contextual function, offers no detailed analysis of messianic theology doesn't mean it deviates from the Davidic christology of every other New Testament work. Peter simply presupposes Jesus is king and expects his audience is in agreement. They have, as he states in 1:1-2, *"received a faith . . . by the righteousness of our God and Savior, Jesus Christ . . . Jesus our Lord"*. In 1:3-11, Peter encourages the recipients of his letter to continue to grow in the knowledge of Jesus, which will enable them to *"become partakers in the divine nature"* and *"escape the corruption that is in the world by lust"*. This knowledge results in *"moral excellence, and in your moral excellence, knowledge, and in your knowledge, self-control, and in your self-control, perseverance, and in your perseverance, godliness, and in your godliness, brotherly kindness, and in your brotherly kindness, love"*, making the believer *"neither useless nor unfruitful"*, compared with those reject the true knowledge of Jesus, an obvious shot at the false teachers. This path will lead to *"the entrance into the eternal kingdom of our Lord and Savior Jesus Christ"*.

Aside from the royal christology and kingdom theology which are foundational to this passage, modern Christians can deduce another important political principle from 2 Peter 1:3-11. Believers are to increase in the knowledge of Jesus, by which they will gain entrance into the eternal kingdom inaugurated through Jesus and awaiting its eschatological completion. The list of moral qualities which characterize believers shaped by Jesus include moral excellence, godliness, kindness, and love. Are any of these compatible with authoritarian socialism, a political and economic arrangement based upon the arbitrary monopolization of

---

72. 2 Peter 1:20-20

73. 2 Peter 2:4

74. 2 Peter 1:1, 2, 11, 16; 3:2, 15, 18

violence against peaceful people to achieve subjective social ends? Absolutely not. Is it befitting of a Christ-follower, with all the messianic resonances of "Christ", to support political systems which suppress speech, fine and imprison people for consensual behavior, tax labor, enable degeneracy, and wage never-ending wars? Most Americans, indoctrinated to accept the myth of the nineteenth-century nation-state model, would say "yes". They are wrong. Even post-nationalist models proposed by scholars like Moxnes result in the authoritarian violence of nationalism being concentrated in the hands of an even smaller number of (still very subjective) global elites. Their authoritarian project will result in the disasters of nationalism globally scaled. If Jesus is the king and we belong to his kingdom, we must abandon any and all attempts, progressive, conservative, or otherwise, to wield arbitrary state power against others to achieve our subjective social ends. Authoritarianism is not "*moral excellence*", it is little more than a rhetorical cover for the most debased, perverse, and sinful human inclinations. The western church stands condemned for ever believing a system predicated on violence could possibly be compatible with a faith rooted in the crucified Messiah.

Nationalism and globalism will on the final day be supplanted by the kingdom of God once and for all. Peter himself says as much in 2 Peter 3:1-13. Just as God "*destroyed*" the world through the flood while rescuing Noah, "*the present heavens and earth are being reserved for fire, kept for the day of judgment and destruction of ungodly men*". While this is directed at the false teachers whom Peter condemns, all ungodly men will not survive the coming eschatological judgment, including the Babylonian-like rulers of this world who are passing away. Peter's language of "destruction" is not a reference to the end of the world (he uses the term to describe the flood in Genesis, which served as a purification of the world and not its physical termination) but the ultimate cosmological restoration, including the permanent, eternal removal of wickedness. Because of this, the lives of believers are transformed by eschatological hope, as 2 Peter 3:11-13 attests: "*Since all these things are to be destroyed in this way, what sort of people ought you to be in holy conduct and godliness, looking for and hastening the coming of the day of God, because of which the heavens will be destroyed by burning, and the elements will melt with intense heat! But according to His promise we are looking for new heavens and a new earth, in which righteousness dwells*". The "*new heavens and a new earth*", imagery borrowed from Isaiah 65:17 and detailed in Revelation 21-22 empower believers to live faithfully in the dark present through the brilliant light of our future hope. Jesus the ascended king will one day return and restore all creation, definitively purging the world of sin and wickedness, including the domination of man over man. Because of this hope and the cruciform ethical standards it sustains, Christians must think twice before mindlessly condoning political and economic systems shamelessly rooted in the very wickedness God will eventually purge.

1 JOHN

We Love Because He First Loved Us

Like 2 Peter, the first epistle of John gives no direct instructions regarding political power or authority. The political implications of 1 John are, however, massive. The principles embedded in 1 John may actually have the most political relevance of any work in the New Testament which does not directly address political institutions. In 1 John 2:1 the author states his intentions: "*I am writing these things so that you do not sin*", which is a terse digest of the introduction in which he claims eyewitness testimony and a desire for his audience to "*have fellowship with us; and indeed our fellowship is with the Father, and with His Son Jesus Christ. These things we write, so that our joy may be made complete*"[75]. Even though "*First John is . . . permeated by a gentile pastoral tone*"[76], the author is not primarily interested in the pleasantries of epistolary correspondence. 1 John (and the sequel, 2 John) deals with a specific, recurring problem: the rise of false teachers. As Meye Thompson succinctly articulates, "*The main purpose of these two epistles is to combat a tangle of erroneous teaching and practice*"[77]. In contradistinction to these false teachers, the author reflects on the identity and practice of the church, encouraging them to remain faithful to the true, apostolic teaching.

While the Johannine epistles are generally considered pseudonymous, Bernier contends that the likely authors were either John son of Zebedee or John the Elder (from Revelation) who wrote sometime between 60-100 CE.[78] I'm fine with either; the dating and attribution of 1-3 John has little impact on their political consequences. I will call the author "John" going forward, placing these interesting but peripheral questions to the side. The false teachers in question, dubbed "antichrists", are named and shamed by John in 2:18-25 and 4:1-6. Modern speculation about a figure labeled "the antichrist" who heralds the end times entirely ignores John's transparent definition of the term. Here is what John actually says about the "antichrists": "*Children, it is the last hour; and just as you heard that antichrist is coming, even now many antichrists have appeared; from this we know that it is*

---

75. 1 John 1:1-4

76. Meye Thompson, *1-3 John*, p. 18

77. Meye Thompson, *1-3 John*, p. 18

78. Bernier, *Rethinking the Dates*, p. 118

the last hour. They went out from us, but they were not really of us; for if they had been of us, they would have remained with us; but they went out, so that it would be shown that they all are not of us"[79]. Far from signaling the "end times", John states it is "*the last hour*", a reference to inaugurated eschatology, and describes the "*antichrists*" (plural!) as those who were once in the church and have now left. Meye Thompson correctly identifies John's opponents: "*The warnings against antichrists in 2:18-27 are warnings against counterfeit teachers and the beliefs they are passing out among the unsuspecting . . . By labeling these false teachers as antichrists the Elder makes it plain how seriously he regards their offense*"[80].

But what was the content of their false teaching? According to 1 John 2:22, "*Who is the liar but the one who denies that Jesus is the Christ? This is the antichrist, the one who denies the Father and the Son*". Antichrists deny the gospel; they say Jesus is not the Messiah. They also deny that Jesus came in the flesh, as John asserts in 4:2-3: "*By this you know the Spirit of God: every spirit that confesses that Jesus Christ has come in the flesh is from God; and every spirit that does not confess Jesus is not from God; this is the spirit of the antichrist, of which you have heard that it is coming, and now it is already in the world*". The antichrists, once part of the people of God but now on the outside, reject two fundamental Christian beliefs: The Messianic identity of Jesus and his fleshly incarnation. This, for John, is what the antichrist false teachers are peddling. The term "*antichrist*" itself means "against Christ", and constitutes a denial of his Messianic identity and incarnation. As Meye Thompson summarizes, "*The antichrist usurps the rightful role of the Messiah, the Christ, and deceives his followers*"[81].

John must delineate the boundaries between believers and antichrists, and the question of who is in and who is out preoccupies the letter. On the outside are those who deny the messianic identity of Jesus and his coming in the flesh. Those on the inside affirm both, as 4:3 attests. In 3:1-3, the "*children of God*" are known not by the world but by God, and at the return of Christ "*will be like Him*"; everyone fixed on this hope purifies themselves, "*just as He is pure*". Christology, inaugurated eschatology, and ethics all characterize the believing identity. "*The world*" in 1 John does not denote God's material creation but rather "*the lust of the flesh and the lust of the eyes and the boastful pride of life . . . [which] is passing away*"[82]. Believers must abstain from the practices and beliefs which characterise the world and the antichrists because they have a different identity bestowed by God. John's

---

79. 1 John 2:18-19

80. Meye Thompson, *1-3 John*, pp. 71-72

81. Meye Thompson, *1-3 John*, p. 75

82. 1 John 2:15-17

demarcation of God's family reaches its denouement in 5:1-4: "*Whoever believes that Jesus is the Christ is born of God, and whoever loves the Father loves the child born of Him. By this we know that we love the children of God, when we love God and observe His commandments. For this is the love of God, that we keep His commandments; and His commandments are not burdensome. For whatever is born of God overcomes the world; and this is the victory that has overcome the world—our faith*". In a remarkably Pauline flourish, all who have faith ("*believes*" is a *pist-* root) in Jesus *the* Christ (its a messianic title, after all) loves God and observes (conceptually synonymous with 'obedience') His commandments. By doing so they overcome the corrupt world with all of its lusts. The antichrists are on the outside, but those who have faith in the Messiah are God's children. The familiar union of christology, ecclesiology, ethics, and (implied) eschatology are foundational for John's argument.

Ethics are also a major theme in 1 John; the antichrists have given into the world and are morally bankrupt, and true believers must not follow in their footsteps. Proper behavior is also intrinsic to a believer's identity as a child of God; those who place their faith in Messiah Jesus are transformed in ethical practice. For John, the centerpiece of Christ-centered ethics is love. In 1 John 2:1-11, those who know God, his children, keep his commandments and "*ought to walk himself in the same manner as He walked . . . because the darkness is passing away and the true Light is already shining*"[83]. What does it mean to be in the light and follow God's commandments, the identity-markers of God's family? Loving others: "*The one who says he is in the Light and yet hates his brother is in the darkness until now. The one who loves his brother abides in the Light and there is no cause for stumbling in him*"[84]. For John love is cruciform, as he explains in 3:13-16: "*Do not be surprised, brethren, if the world hates you. We know that we have passed out of death into life, because we love the brethren. He who does not love abides in death. Everyone who hates his brother is a murderer; and you know that no murderer has eternal life abiding in him. We know love by this, that He laid down His life for us; and we ought to lay down our lives for the brethren*". Just as Jesus died for us, so we must learn to sacrifice ourselves for others. Love, combined with faith in Jesus as the Messiah who came in the flesh, are the fulfillments of God's commandments and the sign, accompanied by the Spirit, that one is a part of God's family: "*This is His commandment, that we believe in the name of His Son Jesus Christ, and love one another, just as He commanded us. The one who keeps His commandments abides in Him, and He in him. We know by this that He abides in us, by the Spirit whom He has given us*"[85].

---

83. 1 John 2:6-8

84. 1 John 2:9-10

85. 1 John 3:23-24

1 John 4:7-21 includes one of the most moving descriptions of cruciform love in the entire New Testament. The centerpiece of this masterful passage is 4:8-14, where Peter combines the identity of God's family, the gift of the Spirit, Jesus's messianic status as king and savior over the entire world with the model of cruciform love: "*The one who does not love does not know God, for God is love. By this the love of God was manifested in us, that God has sent His only begotten Son into the world so that we might live through Him. In this is love, not that we loved God, but that He loved us and sent His Son to be the propitiation for our sins. Beloved, if God so loved us, we also ought to love one another. No one has seen God at any time; if we love one another, God abides in us, and His love is perfected in us. By this we know that we abide in Him and He in us, because He has given us of His Spirit. We have seen and testify that the Father has sent the Son to be the Savior of the world*". What more needs to be said? God takes the initiative, sending his son to die as a propitiation for our sins. In this is love; it takes the initiative and is willing to sacrifice on behalf of others. There is no validly Christian definition of love which isn't based on initiative and sacrifice. Christian love is cruciform love, plain and simple. Any attitude or behavior towards another person which doesn't conform to the cross cannot be properly categorized as love and is therefore an incomplete keeping of God's commands, unbecoming of His children and functionally synonymous with the antichrists' system of values. "*We love, because He first loved us*"[86].

"*The central thrust of libertarian thought*", according to Rothbard, "*is to oppose any and all aggression against the property rights of individuals in their own persons and in the material objects they have voluntarily acquired*"[87]. The non-aggression principle is universally valid and offers no carveouts for government officials: "*The distinctive feature of libertarians is that they coolly and uncompromisingly apply the general moral law to people acting in their roles as members of the State apparatus. Libertarians make no exception*"[88]. Indeed we do not. What has this to do with 1 John and the question of political principles? The church is defined against the world; it has a unique identity as God's children, through faith in the one true Messiah and the Spirit, and obeys the commandments of God through practicing cruciform love to all people. Just as the libertarian views the non-aggression principle as a universal moral imperative, the Christian ought to view cruciform love as a universal moral imperative. It is, after all, what distinguishes believers from the world.

---

86. 1 John 4:19

87. Rothbard, *For a New Liberty*, p. 55

88. Rothbard, *For a New Liberty*, p. 56

Nowhere in 1 John does John hint that the principle of cruciformity is suspended because of the democratic political process. The appropriation of state power, even under the rhetorical guise of justice and love, is an unequivocal violation of our God-given mandate to love others like Jesus. Using state power against another individual "for their own good" places the interests of the one wielding power above the interests of the one against whom power is brandished. We can dress it up however we like, fooling ourselves into believing we are morally superior for weaponizing the political process to achieve our subjective social goals, but we inevitably wind up looking much more like "*the world*" with all its selfish lusts against which John warned. Placing one's hope in the political process is, in the most contemptible way possible, a rejection of the universal messianic reign of Jesus and his unique, Spirit-empowered mandate for the church as a display of cruciform love for all humanity. Progressivism and conservatism alike are a rejection of everything God calls the church to be and do. It is impossible to support either of those political philosophies and extend cruciform love to other people. The church must do better. If we accept, as John says we ought, that believers are defined by cruciformity, then we must not make exceptions in the quest for political power. What point is there in gaining the world while forfeiting our souls? Shouldn't the church rather be wronged than side with the wrongdoers? 1 John is a wake-up call to every Western Christian. We can identify with the state and its arbitrary monopoly on violence, or we can reject violence altogether by emulating the crucified, resurrected, and ascended Messiah. We can only choose one.

2 John

Reject those Who Reject the Messiah

2 John as a short letter which is directed at the same problem addressed by the first Johannine epistle: false teachers. The antichrists are, according to 2 John 1:7, still denying Jesus came in the flesh, and true believers must follow the commandments of God by loving one another[89]. The clear thematic overlap between 1 and 2 John suggests a tight literary relationship, and Meye Thompson proposes 2 John was perhaps supposed to serve as either a cover letter of 1 John or written to another community in response to a common opponent.[90] Either way, the christological, ecclesiological, and eschatological principles found in 1 John characterize 2 John as well. John instructs his recipients to unequivocally reject false teachers, refusing

---

[89]. 2 John 1:4-6

[90]. Meye Thompson, *1-3 John*, pp. 149-150

to greet them or let them into a true believer's home: *"Anyone who goes too far and does not abide in the teaching of Christ, does not have God; the one who abides in the teaching, he has both the Father and the Son. If anyone comes to you and does not bring this teaching, do not receive him into your house, and do not give him a greeting"*[91]. Believers should take any denial of the messianic status of Jesus seriously, especially if it is accompanied by a docetic theology which denies his incarnational physicality. One of the many reasons the church has been unable to offer a compelling response to various global political crises is because we have abandoned the New Testament's high royal christology, and 2 John serves as a warning to all who would undermine the universal Lordship of Israel's ascended Messiah.

3 JOHN

Imitate What is Good

Third John is distinctive for two reasons. First, it is the shortest letter in the entire New Testament. Second, it never mentions the name Jesus. Written to an individual named Gaius[92], 3 John shames a man named Diotrephes for his pride and sowing division[93] while praising another leader named Demetrius for his *"good testimony from everyone"*[94]. Gaius must *"not imitate what is evil, but what is good. The one who does good is of God; the one who does evil has not seen God"*[95]. How does this contribute to our study of political and economic themes in the New Testament? Assuming 3 John shares the same ethical values as the other letters bearing John's name, imitating God includes cruciform love towards all people with no carve outs for participation in the political process. Diotrophes is accused in 3 John 1:9 for *"lov*[ing] *to be first among them"*, the arrogance which accompanies prestige, and believers must imitate not the ego of Diotrephes but the good testimony of Demetrius. Authoritarian socialism, the political and economic instantiation of human pride and power, will always be opposed to the gospel of a crucified Messiah. No imitation of the *"good"* could possibly include participation in any system based on the arbitrary initiation of violence.

---

91. 2 John 1:9-10

92. 3 John 1:1

93. 3 John 1:9-10

94. 3 John 1:12

95. 3 John 1:11

JUDE

The Eternal Dominion of Jesus Christ

Jude, the final Catholic Epistle, is an appropriate letter with which to conclude this chapter. The author identifies himself in Jude 1:1 as *"Jude, a bond-servant of Jesus Christ and brother of James"*. Bernier argues the author of Jude is most likely a brother of Jesus himself and suggests that his short letter was composed no later than 96 CE.[96] Like 2 Peter, Jude is a savage critique of false teachers whom his audience must reject[97]. There are several places where Jude hails Jesus as Messiah, particularly 1:4 (*"our only Master and Lord, Jesus Christ"*), 1:17, and 1:21 (both of which refer to Jesus as *"our Lord Jesus Christ"*). No truly Christian political theology can deny or explain away the exalted Christology of Jude, and believers are obligated to follow Jude 1:4 in proclaiming Jesus, and no one else, as *"our only Master and Lord"*. The ascended Christ is currently ruling over all creation, and his people are called to faithfully obey him until he returns to judge and save. By now the political consequences are conspicuous. Jude 1:24-25 ends his short letter with a sweeping pronouncement of the eternal dominion of Jesus: *"Now to Him who is able to keep you from stumbling, and to make you stand in the presence of His glory blameless with great joy, to the only God our Savior, through Jesus Christ our Lord, be glory, majesty, dominion and authority, before all time and now and forever. Amen"*. I agree.

---

96. Bernier, *Rethinking the Dates*, pp. 230-235

97. Jude 1:3-16; this occupies the bulk of his letter.

CHAPTER 17 | Revelation

The Fall of Babylon

Revelation is intended to reveal, not conceal.

Michael Gorman[1]

To Him who sits on the throne, and to the Lamb, be blessing and honor and glory and dominion forever and ever.

Revelation 5:13

INTRODUCTION

In the fall of 2024 I was tasked with preaching a sermon on the book of Revelation. After briefly explaining to my congregation how the genre of Revelation, apocalyptic literature, was intended to function, I addressed two of its main themes: the universal lordship of Jesus and our call to follow him. After the service I was approached by a woman who wanted to discuss the sermon with me. She explained how Revelation scared her and that she had considered leaving the sanctuary when I announced the topic of my sermon. Laughing, she confessed appreciating her stay; after hearing me speak, Revelation made a little more sense to her. Her perception of Revelation, as well as her anxiety, is not unusual.

In my experience there are two paths Christians take when confronted with Revelation. Some believers, observing the baffling and often disconcerting imagery, choose to ignore the work entirely. The vivid language, imagery, and symbolism is unnerving, too dark for fruitful comprehension or spiritual edification. For many who walk this path, the New Testament functionally ends with Jude. On the second path, however, are those who are obsessively fixated on Revelation,

---

1. Gorman, *Reading Revelation Responsibly*, p. 22

granting it a hermeneutical priority over the rest of Scripture. On this path, the language of Revelation must be decoded in order to penetrate the eschatological mysteries of God. The world is about to end, you know, and Revelation when properly untangled discloses every detail of the coming tribulation. With a newspaper in one hand and Revelation in the other, the New Testament is reduced to little more than supplemental data for deciphering Revelation. This second path has spawned thousands of theological conspiracy theories which invariably end in failure, yet it continues to be tread under heavy traffic.

Both paths are dead ends. Revelation is neither inapproachably frightening nor a blueprint for the end of history. As one of the New Testament's most theologically rich works, it demands to be read within its larger canonical and historical context. There is no way of productively interpreting Revelation or applying it in the modern world without coming to grips with its intended purpose. As with every other biblical work, the *function* of Revelation determines any theological conclusions or practical principles which can be drawn from it. Fortunately the author of Revelation states his intentions in the opening passages and identifies the genres he employs while communicating to his recipients. By carefully analyzing the opening passages of Revelation the work becomes more readily comprehensible. In fact, I think Paul's letter to the Romans is much more difficult to interpret than Revelation once one identifies how Revelation was designed by its author to work. The political and economic principles embedded in Revelation's text are entirely consistent with the New Testament witness and are, in truth, their most vivid thematic expressions.

This chapter is not intended to solve all of Revelation's mysteries, of course, and is for that reason limited in scope. By demonstrating how Revelation was intended to function and examining several key passages I will show, yet again, that this text offers no justification for the modern political and economic model of authoritarian socialism. Quite the opposite, actually. While commentators debate how the book of Revelation is structured, I will be dividing it into five sections. Within each I highlight individual passages relevant to our study. Chapter 1 introduces the author, genres, and recipients of Revelation while establishing its main themes. This section will serve as the contextual foundation for Revelation and the hermeneutical framework through which I will exegete the text. Chapters 2-3 are letters addressed to seven churches in Asia minor. Revelation was written *to them*, and the epistolary section of the text elucidates the historical context of its recipients and the impact John hoped his writings would have. Chapters 4-5 depict the ascended Christ seated in the heavenly throne-room, ruling over all creation, and is the central vision of Revelation. These chapters contextualize everything that follows and is thus foundational for Revelation as a whole. Chapters 6-20 are a long series of cyclical visions which culminate in the final defeat of evil through Jesus and the conclusive victory of his church over the world. Revelation 21-22 includes a breathtaking description of God's final plan for creation, the restoration of all creation in the new heavens and new earth. Those who have been faithful to the Messiah despite intense opposition will inherit the world to come, offering hope to a persecuted church and the final vision of a world renewed at long last.

THE BEGINNING OF THE END: REVELATION 1

Author, Recipient, Genre

In the opening verses of Revelation, the author identifies himself, his intended audience, and the genres employed throughout his lengthy correspondence. Too many readers of Revelation do not account for what the author plainly discloses about his work: "*The Revelation of Jesus Christ, which God gave Him to show to His bond-servants, the things which must soon take place; and He sent and communicated it by His angel to His bond-servant John, who testified to the word of God and to the testimony of Jesus Christ, even to all that he saw. Blessed is he who reads and those who hear the words of the prophecy, and heed the things which are written in it; for the time is near. John to the seven churches that are in Asia*"[2]. John, the author, provides his readers with an abundance of details which illuminate Revelation. Of primary importance is the author's self-identification; his own name, John, is stated in 1:2 and 1:4. This leads us to another important question: who, exactly, is John? The lack of autobiographical details suggests he was a well-known teacher with whom his audience would need no introduction. We also learn in Revelation 1:9 that John was exiled to the island of Patmos in the Aegean Sea "*because of the word of God and the testimony of Jesus*". John had been punished for his faith. While some interpreters hypothesize that John, son of Zebedee, is responsible for both the gospel of John and Revelation,[3] this theory lacks substantial historical evidence, meaning the "*precise identity of John is therefore elusive*"[4]. The traditional dating of Revelation which posits it was composed during the reign of emperor Domitian (between 81-96 CE) is almost certainly correct; after the fall of Rome it became customary for both Jews and Christians to refer to Rome as "*Babylon*", John of Patmos's preferred

---

2. Revelation 1:1-4

3. Gorman, *Reading Revelation Responsibly*, pp. 27-28

4. Gorman, *Reading Revelation Responsibly*, p. 28

title for the world empire (see Revelation 18:1-4; compare with 1 Peter 5:13), and Domitian was notorious for his vendetta against Jesus followers.[5]

Domitian's antagonistic reign was only one among a number of problems plaguing believers in the late first century. Revelation is addressed *"to the seven churches that are in Asia"*, each of which receive an individualized dispatch in Revelation 2-3. These churches are beset with the same obstacles identified in the Pauline, Petrine, and Johannine letters, including persecution, social ostracization, idolatry, complacency, and false teachers. Revelation is intended to help the seven churches in Asia navigate the complex and oftentimes painful realities of first-century life, enabling them to think theologically and remain faithful to Jesus in difficult circumstances. It is imperative that modern interpreters, especially those who believe the Bible is reliable and authoritative, take 1:4 seriously. Revelation was written *"to the seven churches that are in Asia"*, not to modern Americans. In 1:11 John identifies these churches by name: *"Ephesus . . . Smyrna . . . Pergamum . . . Thyatira . . . Sardis . . . Philadelphia . . . [and] Laodicea"*. Not only is Revelation designed to serve those communities, John is instructed by *Jesus himself* to write to the seven churches in Asia![6] This may be one of the most important (and neglected) insights in the first chapter of Revelation. It was not written to us, but to an ancient audience *with the expectation that they would understand it and respond in sincere faith*! Revelation cannot, based on its own witness, provide a detailed map of modern socio-political conflicts, nor is it written to directly confront the problems of our time. Any reading of Revelation which attempts to modernize it is a *misreading* of the text according to the text itself; exegesis which ignores the historical context of Revelation cannot be properly labeled "biblical" and should be immediately discarded. We cannot know what Revelation means for us today until we discern how it was designed to function for the seven churches in Asia for whom it was originally composed. Revelation would have made sense for its original audience even if it is difficult for us to understand today. Reflecting on the author and recipient has already oriented us to the occasion of Revelation. John of Patmos (whoever he may have been) was a teacher persecuted for his faith during the reign of Domitian and wrote an extended correspondence to seven congregations in Asia, encouraging them to remain faithful in the midst of social and political resistance.

What of Revelation's genre? It is improper to speak of Revelation conforming strictly to one type of literature, and in fact the author specifically names three: apocalypse (1:1), prophecy (1:2), and letter (1:4). Revelation is, as Gorman

---

5. Gorman, *Reading Revelation Responsibly*, p. 28

6. Revelation 9:11

puts it, "*a hybrid genre*"[7], a unique combination of all three styles. The first, and most significant, is the category of "apocalyptic", deeply misunderstood in certain Christian traditions. Reading along with an English Bible, one could be forgiven for observing that Revelation 1:1 appears to say nothing about "apocalyptic" at all. That would be a linguistic mistake. As Christopher Holmes observes, it's a matter of translation: "*We derive the English title of the book, "Revelation," from the first three words in Greek: apokalypsis Iesou Christou, "apocalypse of Jesus Christ." The Greek word apokalypsis has the literal sense of uncovering. In the New Testament and earlier Christian literature, the word refers to making something fully known*"[8]. The word *apokalypsis* can be translated as "*reveal*", from which the book of Revelation derives its name. I offered a brief explanation of apocalyptic literature in Chapter 6 which I will further refine here.

The standard definition of apocalyptic literature generally accepted among biblical scholars was developed by John Collins. It is worth repeating: "*'Apocalypse' is a genre of revelatory literature with a narrative framework, in which a revelation is mediated by an otherworldly being to a human recipient, disclosing a transcendent reality which is both temporal, insofar as it envisages eschatological salvation, and spatial, insofar as it involves another, supernatural world*"[9]. Apocalyptic literature was a popular style of writing in antiquity, especially in (although not limited to) Jewish circles, and there are several examples of extracanonical apocalyptic works which have enabled historians like Collins to discern the genre's literary conventions.[10] Within the Christian canon, apocalyptic is exemplified in the works of Daniel, Zechariah, and Revelation, while apocalyptic language is utilized by nearly every New Testament author. As Walton argues, apocalyptic literature is simply a subset of biblical prophecy,[11] and prophecy itself is not primarily futuristic. The classical prophets were intermediaries between God and His people, delivering (revealing) urgent divine messages which would result in dire consequences if left unheeded. Apocalyptic literature is a subset of prophetic literature and functions the same way; any futuristic elements in apocalyptic, as in general prophecy, are intended to produce either ethical change or engender hope in the present. Repeating one more quote from Chapter 6, Walton correctly observes that "*Apocalyptic does not*

---

7. Gorman, *Reading Revelation Responsibly*, p. 29

8. Holmes, Christopher. 2024. *Unspoiled Endings*. Fortress Press. p. 10

9. Collins, *Daniel*, p. 4

10. Holmes, *Unspoiled Endings*, pp. 22-36

11. Walton, *Prophets*, pp. 127-134

have the purpose of foretelling the future. Instead, it reveals how God's plans and purposes begun in the past will find future completion"[12].

Apocalyptic symbolism and imagery are not complex cosmic secrets which require decoding but rather an *encoding* of current events within the framework of a theological matrix to which the audience has already subscribed. Their experiences are vividly, theologically elucidated through the poetic rhetoric of apocalypticism, reminding them of how God is working through the chaos of the present age and will save His people at the end of history. All of Revelation's evocative imagery possessed historical referents which were discernible to the seven churches in Asia. Since apocalyptic was a popular literary convention, John assumes his audience understood how the symbolism and imagery worked. The seven churches would not have read Revelation as a cryptic but woodenly literalist schematic of end-time events but rather as a prophetic critique of evil which challenged and comforted the faithful in light of God's eventual victory over evil which, in the context of Revelation, has already begun with the death, resurrection, and ascension of Jesus. Aside from being one of the only examples of an apocalyptic work from antiquity which isn't pseudonymous[13], Revelation is unique because *"a crucial act of deliverance has already taken place with the death and resurrection of Jesus"*[14]. The seven churches of Asia are called to remain obedient to Jesus until the final consummation knowing that the battle has, in a very real sense, already been won.

Holmes identifies five aspects of apocalyptic literature which characterize the genre, all of which are applicable to Revelation. Apocalyptic emphasizes the sovereignty of God, provides access to the divine perspective of history, highlights God's ultimate victory, utilizes sensory language, and conveys hope.[15] We have already surveyed the other twenty-six documents included in the New Testament; nothing about the apocalypticism of Revelation differentiates it theologically from the works which canonically precede it, save for its literary convention which relies heavily upon symbolic imagery. Even so, the teachings of Jesus contain more than a few apocalyptic flourishes.[16] Once we look past the aesthetic differences, most of which are attributable to genre, the picture painted by Revelation appears comfortingly familiar. Jesus is king, believers are his people, and God will prevail. This corresponds with the goal of apocalyptic literature in general, as Gorman describes: "[apocalpyptic's] *basic function seems fairly clear: to sustain the people of*

---

12. Walton, *Prophets*, p. 134

13. Collins, John. 1998. *The Apocalyptic Imagination*. 2nd ed. Eerdmans. p. 270

14. Collins, *The Apocalyptic Imagination*, p. 271

15. Holmes, *Unspoiled Endings*, pp. 35-36

16. Mark 13 and parallels, for example.

God, especially in times of crisis, particularly evil and oppression. Apocalyptic literature both expresses and creates hope by offering scathing critique of the oppressors, passionate exhortations to defiance (and sometimes even preparation for confrontation), and unfailing confidence in God's ultimate defeat of the present evil. Usually articulated in symbolic, even cryptic language, this hope means that apocalyptic is also the language and literature of resistance"[17].

Gorman also offers a crucial explanation regarding the relationship between Revelation's apocalyptic imagery and its historical referents: *"Understanding the book of Revelation as apocalyptic literature will encourage us to try to understand the real-world situations, depicted in cosmic terms, that it reflects and addresses. It will also encourage us not to take the symbolism "literally," that is, to think of actual pale-green horses or multi-headed beasts or thousand-year periods. These are all symbolic, but that does not make the realities to which they point any less real . . . Like a good political cartoon or poem, an apocalypse appeals to the imagination to address the most profound realities that God's people can experience or hope for"*[18]. These realities are theologically indistinguishable from the other New Testament writings; Revelation, when properly understood as a manifestation of apocalyptic literature, offers its readers the *exact same* christology, ecclesiology, and eschatology we find in the gospels, Paul, Peter, and John. It does not provide us with a constellation of disparate concealed futuristic predictions but reveals the single plan of God for creation to which the seven churches in Asia would have already known and affirmed. What distinguishes Revelation within the Christian canon is its style, not its substance. Holmes perfectly distills the message of Revelation: *"For all of its strange visions and startling imagery, Revelation's single unveiling aligns with one of the most basic affirmations of early Christianity: God has been revealed as Lord in and through the life of Jesus Christ"*[19].

Within the framework of apocalyptic, Revelation is also a prophecy and a letter. biblical prophecy, as I have already elaborated in detail, is not primarily about the future but the present; any predictions of an eventual judgment or restoration is provided to impact current behavior. Prophecy is, strictly speaking, a mediated message from God directed at effecting change in the moment, not a mechanically precise description of some future event. To this end, Revelation functions exactly as the classical Jewish prophets whose works are included in the Old Testament: *"prophecy is speaking words of comfort and/or challenge, on behalf of God, to the*

---

17. Gorman, *Reading Revelation Responsibly*, p. 15

18. Gorman, *Reading Revelation Responsibly*, p. 21

19. Holmes, *Unspoiled Endings*, p. 11

people of God in their concrete historical situation"[20]. And, of course, "*their concrete historical situation*" refers to the concrete historical situation of the seven churches in Asia, not modern Christians in Europe and North America. Revelation is a letter, written to a particular group of people, a historical insight which has massive exegetical implications. The laws of hermeneutics are not suspended because Revelation is simultaneously apocalypse and prophecy; the function of Revelation is contingent upon what John intended to communicate with his audience, and it cannot mean anything for us until we control for its historical context. Epistles directed to the seven churches in Asia are found in Revelation 2-3 and are an example of the literary phenomenon of 'embedded letters', as Greg Carey articulates: "*Embedded letters, including those in Revelation, alter voices. Such letters enable the author to allow another voice, whether actual or fictional, to speak for a while. Revelation's letters present themselves as coming from the ultimate authority, the risen Jesus. From another perspective, the letters allow John the opportunity to present his point of view by appropriating the voice of Jesus*"[21]. Coincidently, this is precisely what John does in Revelation 1:12-20.

We are now in a position to understand how Revelation functions. The work was written by John, exiled on the island of Patmos for proclaiming the gospel, to seven churches in Asia who were experiencing concrete social and political pressure, probably under the reign of Domitian in the latter half of the first century. By appropriating the popular convention of apocalyptic literature, John is able to remind his audience of the victory which God has already won through Jesus and will see to completion on the final day, a message with which his recipients would have already agreed. As a prophetic work, John is comforting believers who are experiencing suffering because of their faith while challenging others who have become complacent. Revelation, through its use of apocalyptic imagery and symbolism, is investing real-world events with their full cosmic significance. For this reason I will, to a greater extent than in any chapter before, include a multitude of block quotes directly from Revelation. The imagery deserves to be *experienced*, not just blandly described, and despite its aesthetic idiosyncrasies Revelation will feel warmly familiar. John does not deviate one inch from the core teachings of the apostolic church. His message is fairly straightforward: Jesus is king, believers are God's people, demarcated from the rest of humanity by faith and the Spirit, and God will one day vindicate and rescue all who are in Christ. It's no accident that this is exactly what John says in the opening verses of Revelation, to which we will now turn.

---

20. Gorman, *Reading Revelation Responsibly*, p. 23

21. Carey, Greg. 2025. *Rereading Revelation*. Eerdmans. p. 12

Ruler of the Kings of the Earth: Revelation 1:4-7

The entire narrative of Revelation is summarized by John in 1:4-7: *"John to the seven churches that are in Asia: Grace to you and peace, from Him who is and who was and who is to come, and from the seven Spirits who are before His throne, and from Jesus Christ, the faithful witness, the firstborn of the dead, and the ruler of the kings of the earth. To Him who loves us and released us from our sins by His blood—and He has made us to be a kingdom, priests to His God and Father—to Him be the glory and the dominion forever and ever. Amen. Behold, He is coming with the clouds, and every eye will see Him, even those who pierced Him; and all the tribes of the earth will mourn over Him. So it is to be. Amen"*. If we grasp this message, Revelation becomes readily comprehensible. If John's prose sounds an awful lot like Acts or Paul, that's because it is. We see the three themes of christology, ecclesiology, and eschatology, ever-present throughout the New Testament, framing the introduction of John's apocalypse.

The resurrected Jesus has ascended to the father and now, *currently*, rules over all *"the kings of the earth"*. He rescued his people, transferring them to his kingdom and empowering them as priests to God, because of which Jesus has *"the glory and the dominion forever"*. Jesus is returning to judge and save, because of which the entire world, including those who oppose him, will be forced to reckon with his arrival. Revelation, as is characteristic of the apocalyptic genre, *"abounds with citations and allusions to what Christians call the Old Testament . . .* [particularly in its] *images and themes"*[22], as allusion to the royal Psalm 89, Daniel 7, and Zechariah 12 attest. As in Paul's formulation of the gospel, Revelation portrays the universal reign of Jesus happening in accordance with Scripture. Craig Koester explains John's unique application of Israel's Scriptures: *"John frequently paraphrases and alludes to Old Testament passages when recounting his visions, but he never gives exact quotations from the Old Testament according to any known text"*[23]. Yet another similarity with the Pauline *euangelion*; the life, death, resurrection, and ascension of Jesus didn't fulfill a small handful of random Old Testament prooftexts, they are the conclusion of the entire narrative arc of Scripture. Jesus has inaugurated the eschatological event by ruling over creation and has called a faithful people to be his kingdom on earth. For John this is an objective, historical reality, irreducible to a personal, spiritual interiority. The political consequences of radical eschatological messianism are in John identical to that found in the work of other New Testament authors.

---

22. Holmes, *Unspoiled Endings*, p. 18
23. Koester, Craig. 2001. *Revelation and the End of All Things*. Eerdmans. p. 51

The rest of John's work is, in a sense, an unpacking of Revelation 1:4-7. If one grasps this passage, reflecting on its significance, the narrative logic of Revelation becomes comprehensible. Jesus is king, believers are his people, and the end has already begun. This is, in short, the message of Revelation. Besides the aesthetic of apocalypticism, Revelation is canonically unique because it offers a blunt, direct critique of Roman imperialism and can, therefore, be properly categorized as "anti-imperial". In contradistinction to Paul, whose political theology is best described as *supra*political, directing his churches to conceptualize themselves as beyond the rulers of this age who are passing away, John graphically depicts the fall of Babylon (i.e. Rome) in Revelation 17-20. Jewish apocalyptic literature was inherently political, which partially explains the opaque symbolism, and by situating the announcement of Jesus's universal rule at the outset of his work within the matrix of apocalyptic John is unquestionably making a political point.[24] As Jipp notes, "*At the center of John's Apocalypse is the question of power and authority . . . the book centers upon a conflict between the rule of God and the Lamb versus the rule of Satan and his powers . . . Of all the writings in the New Testament, it is the book of Revelation that is the most dominated by political, martial, and royal imagery*"[25]. Gorman describes Revelation as "*a theopolitical text*" which directly challenges the pretensions of empire with the sovereign rule of Israel's Messiah.[26]. Revelation 1:4-7, far from being a mere rhetorical nicety at the introduction of a letter, is a denunciation of everything which opposes the Messiah and his church. There can be only one king, and he already sits on the throne.

John begins his apocalyptic vision in 1:9-11, being commanded to "*Write in a book what you see, and send it to the seven churches*". In Revelation 1:12-20, the ascended Christ appears to John, who describes his encounter with Jesus in language which is lifted straight out of Daniel.[27] Jesus reassures the frightened John, instructing him to "*not be afraid; I am the first and the last, and the living One; and I was dead, and behold, I am alive forevermore, and I have the keys of death and of Hades*"[28]. Because of this, Jesus orders John in 1:19-20 to "*write the things which you have seen, and the things which are, and the things which will take place after these things*" and share this writing with the seven churches in Asia. Jesus, the ruler of all creation, has a message which John is obligated to relay. We will discover the concrete historical situation in which these congregations find themselves, and,

---

24. Sprinkle, *Exiles*, p. 127

25. Jipp, *Messianic Theology*, pp. 284-285

26. Gorman, *Reading Revelation Responsibly*, p. 43

27. Koester, *Revelation*, pp. 52-53

28. Revelation 1:17-18

as is the aim of all biblical prophecy, Jesus will both challenge and comfort these communities while encouraging them to remain faithful until the end.

TO THE SEVEN CHURCHES: REVELATION 2-3

Revelation 2-3 contains a series of letters directed *"to the seven churches that are in Asia"*, including Ephesus, Smyrna, Pergamum, Thyatira, Sardis, Philadelphia, and Laodicea. If any section in Revelation serves as a reminder that John was not, in fact, writing to modern western Christians, this is it. Each of the seven churches receive a message from Jesus, mediated through John, directly addressing challenges with which they were faced. Each church was generally dealing with one of three problems; some were threatened by external hostility and persecution, others were internally divided and in danger of capitulating to pagan values, while the third category included churches which were comfortably complacent.[29] In all cases John seeks to confront the seven churches with the knowledge that Jesus was Lord over everything, engendering a change in perspective which would either strengthen the resolve of hope or challenge infighting and complacency.[30] Theologically, the letters revolve around the three main themes of christology, ecclesiology, and eschatology, all of which have political and economic implications for both the original audience of Revelation and modern Christians seeking to draw principles from the texts.

Ephesus, Pergamum, and Thyatira were *"dealing with internal conflicts over acceptable and unacceptable forms of Christian faith and practice"*, including leaders who promoted false teachings intended to accommodate faith in Christ with idolatrous pagan practices.[31] The letter to Ephesus, found in Revelation 2:2-7, accuses them of *"hav*[ing] *left your first love"*[32]. They are in danger of falling away and called to repent, with John reminding them of the glory which awaits those who remain faithful: *"To him who overcomes, I will grant to eat of the three of life which is in the Paradise of God"*[33]. Pergamum, addressed in 2:12-17, is accused of tolerating false teachers. They must rid themselves of the false teachers to receive their eternal reward. The church in Thyatria is prompted in 2:18-29 by the *"Son of God"* to continue in perseverance. While they have been mostly faithful, an evil prophetess named Jezebel has arisen in the church, and the Son of God intends to

---

29. Koester, *Revelation*, p. 56

30. Koester, *Revelation*, pp. 56-57

31. Koester, *Revelation*, p. 57

32. Revelation 2:4

33. Revelation 2:7

judge her and those who follow her abominable teaching. If they continue in faith and abandon the prophetess, they will be vindicated on the final day: *"He who overcomes, and he who keeps My deeds until the end, to him I will give authority over the nations; and he shall rule them with a rod of iron . . . as I have received authority from My Father"*[34]. Those who follow Jesus, ruler of the world, will co-reign with him in the age to come.

Smyrna and Philadelphia were experiencing hostility from their pagan neighbors, including physical persecution. While the Romans had no systematic, empire-wide policy of discrimination against Jesus-believers, local political authorities would, as Paul experienced in Acts, often make life difficult for those who followed Christ.[35] Smyrna's short letter is found in Revelation 2:8-11, dictated to John by *"The first and the last, who was dead, and has come to life"*[36]. Their opponents were presumably Jewish, and John warns that some believers in Smyrna will be thrown in prison or possibly even face death. They are comforted, however, with the knowledge that Jesus *"will give you the crown of life . . . He who overcomes will not be hurt by the second death"*[37]. Even in suffering the church must bear faithful witness, trusting in the decisive justice of God. Philadelphia is also portrayed as enduring persecution from Jewish opponents in 3:7-13. The one exhorting them "has the key of David"[38], and the Philadelphians who endure the painful suffering will inherit a glorious future, heralded in 3:11-12: *"I am coming quickly; hold fast what you have, so that no one will take your crown. He who overcomes, I will make him a pillar in the temple of My God, and he will not go out from it anymore; and I will write on him the name of My God, and the name of the city of My God, the new Jerusalem, which comes down out of heaven from My God, and My new name"*. It is more than worth it to endure until the end.

The churches in Sardis and Laodicea, rather conspicuously, appear to be safe from any immediate threats. There are no instructions about false teachers or persecution, but both churches receive an extremely negative evaluation of their behavior. What precipitated these two bellicose epistles? As Koester explains, *"The dangers to these congregations come not from overt hostility but from the kind of comfortable conditions that lead to complacency"*[39]. Sardis, a city which had the good geographical fortune of proximity to gold, fertile farmland, and major trade

---

34. Revelation 2:26-27

35. Koester, *Revelation*, p. 63

36. Revelation 2:8

37. Revelation 2:10-11

38. Revelation 3:7

39. Koester, *Revelation*, p. 66

routes, was relatively well-off.[40] Material comfort had lulled the church of Sardis into a spiritual sleep from which Jesus implored them to wake. Laodicea is the recipient of John's final letter in 3:14-22. The Laodiceans are famously described as *"lukewarm . . . neither hot nor cold"* in 3:15, *"Because you say, "I am rich, and have become wealthy, and have need of nothing," and you do not know that you are wretched and miserable and poor and blind and naked"*[41]. Laodicea, wealthy in part because of a booming textile industry[42], had turned their back on following Jesus, tempted, like the rich young ruler, by the allure of wealth. Jesus calls the church to repentance, trusting not in their own riches but in the wealth which can only be provided by Jesus himself. He stands at the door and knocks; the Laodiceans must answer.

All of these churches are, despite the differing historical setting of each community, confronted with the same set of theological truths. Christologically, Jesus is the Davidic king who currently sits on the cosmic throne and will one day judge all opponents. Ecclesiologically, the churches are commanded to consider their set-apart identity, refusing to collude with pagan values or the false teachers who perpetuate them, and must remain distinct from the surrounding culture until the coming day of the Lord. Eschatologically, Jesus has already won the decisive victory, inaugurating the end of history, and will soon return to consummate his kingdom by ushering in the new heavens and new Earth in which those who are faithful to him will live forever, wisely ruling over God's renewed creation. While each church is confronted with a different problem, the solution is always the same: Jesus is the only Lord, believers are his people, and the end has already begun.

Revelation 2-3 poses a significant dilemma for modern readers. Not once does John suggest that the seven churches in Asia should turn to authoritarian socialism as a mechanism for overcoming their problems. He advocates for no new law, no new tax, or no new government intervention. Even the decadent Sardisians and Laodiceans are not threatened with a comprehensive system of progressive taxation by which the Romans would confiscate their surplus and redistribute to those who have less, a political policy preferred by many modern progressive Christians. Couldn't the Romans easily readjust imperial policy and put an end to the greed which consumed these two churches? Would not more political representation allow the churches in Smyrna and Philadelphia to strike back against their oppressive neighbors? And wouldn't Ephesus, Pergamum, and Thyatira be better

---

40. Koester, *Revelation*, pp. 66-67

41. Revelation 3:17

42. Koester, *Revelation*, p. 69

off if restrictions were placed on speech, criminalizing the wicked words of false teachers? John would have none of it. His solution, inelegant by the sophisticated posturing of modern authoritarian socialism, is to double-down on the emerging orthodoxy of the church. There is no king but Jesus, no kingdom but the church, and no way out save for faithfulness until the end. While the political context of the modern church has changed and we must, of course, change with it, the underlying principles remain the same. Even though Revelation is more directly confrontational towards Rome than any other New Testament writing, John still retains a suprapolitical ecclesiology. While the ancient church must endure within an evil world, it has already begun to transcend it. The modern church should follow suit.

We now understand the author, recipients, and historical context of Revelation, its narratival and generic dynamics, and its main themes. Revelation 4-5, to which we will turn next, is the central vision in Revelation and must be incorporated into any serious Christian political theology. As John concludes the epistolary section of Revelation in 3:21-22, he prepares his audience for the vision they are about the experience with him: *"He who overcomes, I will grant to him to sit down with Me on My throne, as I also overcame and sat down with My Father on His throne. He who has an ear, let him hear what the Spirit says to the churches"*. The next two chapters of Revelation are set in the heavenly throne room, and the description of God and his Lamb reveal a stunning truth: no one will ever rise to greater heights of power than Jesus.

THE COSMIC THRONE ROOM: REVELATION 4-5

Gorman accurately refers to Revelation 4-5 as the work's *"Central and Centering Vision"*[43], underscoring the significance of John's epic description of God's cosmic throne-room, within which one man, having passed through death, now sits at the Father's right hand. In a work characterized by complexity, the exalted christology of Revelation is refreshingly straightforward and leaves the audience with no un-certainty about who rules the universe. In 4:1-11, John is taken into heaven *"in the Spirit"* and shown *"what must take place after these things"*. He sees a throne upon which *"One"* is sitting, emanating rainbows, lightning, thunder, and fire while flanked by twenty four crowned elders and *"four living creatures"*. The living crea-tures praise the enthroned being, *"day and night they do not cease to say, "Holy, holy, holy, is the Lord God, the Almighty, Who was and Who is and Who is to come."*. . .

---

43. Gorman, *Reading Revelation Responsibly*, p. 102

to Him who lives forever and ever"[44] while the elders, "*casting their crowns before the throne*", say "*Worthy are You, our Lord and our God, to receive glory and honor and power; for You created all things, and because of Your will they existed, and were created.*"[45].

The temple is "*depicted as a blend of temple and throne-room scenes from the Ancient Near East, as reflected in Isaiah 6 and Daniel 7* [from which much of the imagery is drawn], *and from the Roman Empire, where the emperor was honored and worshiped as sovereign of the universe*"[46], images which would have been familiar to an ancient audience. Cutting through the pastiche of Old Testament allusions, royal imagery, and apocalyptic symbolism, John makes one remarkably powerful point: God, the one who brought creation into existence, will always and forever sit on His throne. God, not man, possesses authentic power: "*in the proper order of things, all creation is oriented towards its Creator. Human beings are not at the center*". Given the social and political resistance John's audience was facing, Revelation's presentation of God's heavenly throne-room is a direct critique of all human authority. The twenty-four elders, placed in a position of power by God, do not fancy themselves as sovereign. Instead of projecting their own power, they throw their crowns at God's feet, directing attention to His throne instead of theirs.[47] John is intended to provide a sort of literary shock-and-awe; the persecuted believers in his audience would find solace in God's eternal reign while simultaneously scandalizing the complacent and culturally compromised. Revelation 4 is the prophetic function at its finest, comforting and challenging the people of God.

Despite sitting in the presence of God's glorious throne, John is unsettled. Revelation 5:1-5 depicts God holding a book secured with seven seals. An angel asks if anyone can open the book, yet no one in heaven or on earth is able to open the book and view its contents. John perceives this as a cosmic catastrophe and weeps. He is quickly comforted in 5:5 by "*one of the elders* [who] *said to me, "Stop weeping; behold, the Lion that is from the tribe of Judah, the Root of David, has overcome so as to open the book and its seven seals*"". In antiquity wax seals were placed on the edge of royal documents and usually stamped with the ring of the person who validated them; this was designed to ensure the contents had not been maliciously altered and that the text was a representation of the author's intended communication.[48] There is only one worthy to open the scroll, revealing what is

---

44. Revelation 4:8-9

45. Revelation 4:10-11

46. Gorman, *Reading Revelation Responsibly*, p. 103

47. Koester, *Revelation*, pp. 74-75

48. Koester, *Revelation*, pp. 76-77

about to take place: Jesus. The Lion, however, is also enigmatically described as *"a Lamb standing, as if slain"* starting in 5:6. John's mixed imagery makes perfect contextual sense; as the Lion of Judah, Jesus is the conquering Davidic son who rules over all creation as promised in Israel's Scriptures. As a slain Lamb, however, his kingly power was revealed through his paradoxical death on a cross.[49] These two images, appearing contradictory by human standards of power, perfectly encapsulate the Davidic dominion of Jesus, accomplished in part by his sacrificial death. Real power is, as the gospels, Paul, and other New Testament authors attest, inherently cruciform.

John plays on this contrast between the image of Jesus as a Lion and Lamb throughout the rest of his throne-room vision. Jesus takes the book out of God's hand in 5:7, causing the creatures and elders to praise him: *"they sang a new song, saying, "Worthy are You to take the book and to break its seals; for You were slain, and purchased for God with Your blood men from every tribe and tongue and people and nation. "You have made them to be a kingdom and priests to our God; and they will reign upon the earth. ""*[50]. Jesus, the crucified Lord, has purchased through his blood people from all over the world, incorporating the nations into God's family, and because of his accomplishment they will inherit the kingdom and rule over creation with him. John's christology, ecclesiology, and inaugurated eschatology are no different from any other New Testament author, only represented in apocalyptic language. The angels will join the creatures and elders in praise, *"saying with a loud voice, "Worthy is the Lamb that was slain to receive power and riches and wisdom and might and honor and glory and blessing. ""*[51]. In 5:13, everything and everyone acknowledges the power of Jesus: *"And every created thing which is in heaven and on the earth and under the earth and on the sea, and all things in them, I heard saying, "To Him who sits on the throne, and to the Lamb, be blessing and honor and glory and dominion forever and ever. ""*.

The constellation of christological language and the objective, politically consequential manner in which they are used hardly needs comment; John, along with his other canonical associates, believes the crucified, resurrected, and ascended Jesus *is currently* ruling over all creation, having ushered in the end of history which will be completed on the final day. The rest of Revelation is essentially a commentary, set within an apocalyptic framework, on Jesus's eventual defeat of all competitors and the need for his people to remain faithful until the very end. While the apocalyptic imagery employed in Revelation 6-20 is directed at the

---

49. Koester, *Revelation*, p. 78

50. Revelation 5:9-10

51. Revelation 5:12

specific historical situation of the seven churches in Asia, the cosmic kingship of Jesus, seated at the right hand of God and worthy to open the book, is both literal and timeless, challenging and comforting believers in all generations.

Revelation 4-5 provides the audience of John's apocalypse with a set of hermeneutical directions for reading the rest of the text, but the vision of God's throne-room in which the Lion-Lamb Jesus shares dominion is politically consequential. Revelation, as with most apocalyptic literature, is a 'political' text, and John envisions a war between the evil empires of man (Babylon, the current instantiation of which is Rome) and God, His people, and His Messiah. This war is fought and won by the sacrifice of Jesus, simultaneously the Lion of David and the Lamb of the cross, and a revelation that God rules through sacrifice, not violent military conquest.[52] Not only are God's family called to emulate the cruciform example of Christ, the cross is a repudiation of *all human systems of power* which rely on arbitrary authoritarian violence. As Jipp appropriately comments, "*Jesus is the conquering, triumphant Davidic Messiah, but this military battle and act of conquering has taken place through the highly paradoxical sacrificial death of Jesus the slaughtered Lamb . . . Thus, the popular ancient Mediterranean kingship ideology . . . which was the legitimation of the king's rule in his powerful and violent acts of military success, is subverted through Jesus's victory*"[53].

None of this is compatible with modern authoritarian socialism. All of the justifications for the arbitrary appropriation of political power made by Christian progressives and conservatives are shattered by John's image of a kingly yet crucified Lion-Lamb who possesses dominion over an eternal kingdom and through whom his people will rule over all creation. There can be no authentically Christian political theology which is not rooted in the cruciform witness of Israel's eschatological Davidic Messiah. Gorman elucidates the centrality of John's throne-room vision: "*As a narrative whole, Revelation first builds to this astonishing image, and then everything afterwards flows from it . . . only when chapters 4 and 5 are read as Revelation's hermeneutical key to reality, divinity, history, and ethics will we be able to place the visions of judgment in proper perspective*"[54].

Gorman's insight leads us to the rest of Revelation, primed by John's introduction in chapter 1, the epistolary section in chapters 2-3, and the throne-room vision of chapters 4-5. While biblical scholarship has yet to produce a consensus view of Revelation's general outline[55], all of the material included in Revelation

---

52. Sprinkle, *Exiles*, pp. 133-136

53. Jipp, *Messianic Theology*, p. 294

54. Gorman, *Reading Revelation Responsibly*, pp. 108, 111

55. Koester, *Revelation*, p. 38

6-22 is predicated upon chapters 1-5. John's visions begin in Revelation 4 and conclude with Revelation 22, but I have found it helpful if somewhat arbitrary to view Revelation 4-5 as a visionary introduction which concludes with the final eschatological restoration in Revelation 21-22. Therefore the next several sections in this chapter will briefly review the material included in Revelation 6-20, again somewhat arbitrarily subdivided for the sake of clarity. These chapters do not progress in a straightforward manner, and Koester's cyclical analysis of Revelation is on-point: "*Reading Revelation as a whole shows that the book moves in a non-linear way. This insight goes back to the third century . . . and many recent interpreters have found this approach helpful. An outline of the book looks like a spiral, with each loop consisting of a series of visions*"[56].

The cyclical, non-linear apocalyptic visions contribute to the effect John intends his apocalypse to have on its audience: "*Those who read Revelation as a whole encounter visions that alternatively threaten and assure them . . . Threatening visions and assuring visions function differently, but they serve the same end, which is that listeners might continue to trust in God and remain faithful to God*"[57]. In other words, the apocalyptic narrative, if we can properly refer to it as a 'narrative', does not progress in a straightforward manner. Revelation 6-20 is meant to feel chaotic, challenging the reader to reflect upon the depths of human evil, instantiated in imperial power, and the ultimate deliverance of God. The final two chapters resolve the tension created by the cycles of crisis and salvation which precede it. It is not my aim to provide a detailed commentary of the text, nor will I attempt to answer the convoluted historical and theological questions surrounding several famous passages in Revelation unless they directly relate to my analysis in this chapter. Despite the cyclical chaos of Revelation 6-20, the same three themes materialize time and time again; christology, ecclesiology, and eschatology, all of which are in direct opposition to the modern political and economic paradigm of modern authoritarian socialism, dominate the narrative. The goal of my short but inclusive sprint through the rest of Revelation will only further refine what has been repeatedly demonstrated in other New Testament texts. Our modern political and economic categories are hopelessly broken and in need of consistent, irreducible, and universally applicable definitions. Modern applications of the powerful theological principles embedded in Revelation will forever be handicapped until we come to terms with its analysis of divine and human power. We begin our short journey through a long text.

---

56. Koester, *Revelation*, p. 39

57. Koester, *Revelation*, p. 39

THE LONG CYCLE: REVELATION 6-20

Israel and the Nations: Revelation 6-7

A cycle of judgment begins in Revelation 6 with the release of four horsemen who bring wrath and judgment upon the earth.[58] The scene changes in 6:9-11, portraying those who have been martyred for the faith resting in heaven, awaiting the day when God will execute vengeance against their killers. They are assured of God's coming judgment. More believers will die for their faith before the final day, but rest assured it will happen. 6:12-17 is another depiction of judgment, this time against *"the kings of the earth and the great men and the commanders and the rich and the strong and every slave and free man . . .* [they seek to be hidden] *from the presence of Him who sits on the throne, and from the wrath of the Lamb; for the great day of their wrath has come"*. Everyone falls under the Lamb's wrath; no king, great man, commander, or wealthy person (John uses the adjectival plural of *plousious*) can escape the anger of God. Revelation consistently depicts judgment in universal terms; no one will avoid the coming conflagration save for those who are identified with the Lamb. Importantly, judgment is the exclusive prerogative of the Lamb; the dispensation of wrath belongs to Jesus alone. The church will not take up judgment against the world before the appointed time. Authoritarian socialism supplants the rightfully granted power of Jesus to judge and save at the end of history. The contrast between the martyrs and those judged by Jesus in Revelation 6 *"press readers to give up the idea that they can remain neutral, asking them whether they identify with the martyrs or with the rest of humanity"*[59]. Weaponizing state power against others (including those designated *plousious*, which likely refers to men who acquired wealth through unjust and immoral means)[60] is choosing to side *"with the rest of humanity"* against the patient anticipation of Christ's martyrs.

In Revelation 7:1-3, angels implementing God's wrath upon the earth are instructed to withhold harm until "we have sealed the bond-servants of our God". In 7:4-8, John describes the first group of people who are sealed: *"I heard the number of those who were sealed, one hundred and forty-four thousand sealed from every tribe of the sons of Israel"*. The second group, already seated before the throne of God, is described in 7:9-12 as "a great multitude which no one could count, from every nation and all tribes and peoples and tongues, standing before the throne and before the Lamb, clothed in white robes, and palm branches were in their hands".

---

58. Revelation 6:1-8

59. Koester, *Revelation*, p. 86

60. As its frequent Lukan usage would suggest.

In 7:13-17 their identity is revealed: *"These are the ones who come out of the great tribulation, and they have washed their robes and made them white in the blood of the Lamb. For this reason, they are before the throne of God; and they serve Him day and night in His temple; and He who sits on the throne will spread His tabernacle over them. They will hunger no longer, nor thirst anymore; nor will the sun beat down on them, nor any heat; for the Lamb in the center of the throne will be their shepherd, and will guide them to springs of the water of life; and God will wipe every tear from their eyes"*.

While these numbers have been subject to numerous theological conspiracy theories, many of which are based upon a flawed understanding of apocalyptic literature, John is actually making an important point about the nature of God's family, so much so that Gorman calls Revelation 7 *"one of the most important texts about the church in the entire New Testament"*[61]. By drawing upon the language of Israel and the nations, John's ecclesiological insight is fundamentally identical to Acts, Paul, and Peter, all of whom believe that the eschatological inauguration of God's kingdom results in the nations worshiping Israel's God through the appointed Messiah. John's point is twofold: the church is the united Jew and Gentile family of God, and this family is set apart and marked out for eschatological salvation, even if, as John depicts, many will die for their faith before the final day.[62] Revelation 7, then, should be read as an apocalyptic extension of passages such as Acts 15, Romans 4, Galatians 3, and Ephesians 2. John will appeal to the fullness of God's family repeatedly throughout Revelation, and many of his apocalyptic visions illustrate, in symbolic terms, the people of God in opposition to evil and destined for eternal salvation. The church is set apart from the world, and there is, as in other New Testament texts, a clear dividing line between insiders and outsiders. Gorman accurately identifies the underlying principle of Revelation 7 for the modern world; Christians today must embody John's vision by embracing our unique identity as Christ followers, rejecting temporal systems of power, and faithfully awaiting the day of Jesus's return.[63] Acquiescing to authoritarian socialism compromises the unique identity of the crucified Messiah's global family.

judgment and Vindication: Revelation 8-11

Revelation 8-11 continues the cyclical pattern of judgment and vindication characteristic of John's apocalypse. The chapters further develop what has come before.

---

61. Gorman, *Reading Revelation Responsibly*, p. 133

62. Gorman, *Reading Revelation Responsibly*, p. 133

63. Gorman, *Reading Revelation Responsibly*, pp. 133-135

Revelation 8-9 reveals that God is in complete control of the calamities befalling the earth; they are neither arbitrary nor erratic but executed with precision by the hand of God. According to Revelation 9:4 the judgment is directed against those who are not marked out by God, with the result that outsiders suffer a terrible fate through God's agent of wrath. John himself makes an important comment in Revelation 10:4-7 about the symbolic and general nature of his work: "*When the seven peals of thunder had spoken, I was about to write; and I heard a voice from heaven saying, "Seal up the things which the seven peals of thunder have spoken and do not write them." Then the angel whom I saw standing on the sea and on the land lifted up his right hand to heaven, and swore by Him who lives forever and ever, who created heaven and the things in it, and the earth and the things in it, and the sea and the things in it, that there will be delay no longer, but in the days of the voice of the seventh angel, when he is about to sound, then the mystery of God is finished, as He preached to His servants the prophets*". Based on the text itself, Revelation is not, as we have been arguing all along, a detailed depiction of the events which will accompany the final days but an apocalyptic prophecy designed to challenge and comfort believers in the present by appealing to a future hope in which they already believed.

The two witnesses of Revelation 11:1-13 are an extension of John's ecclesiology and "*represent the community of faithful Christians. The witnesses are depicted as lampstands, and in 1:20 the lampstands represented Christian congregations . . . the imagery fits the practice of providing two witnesses to sustain a truth claim in court (Deut. 19:15)*"[64]. Gorman also identities the faithful witnesses as a symbolic representation of the church[65], and they are described using imagery of faithfulness from the Old Testament, including a willingness to endure unto death in emulation of Jesus[66]. Following this in 11:15-18, John relays one of the most consequential statements about christology and eschatology in the entire New Testament: "*Then the seventh angel sounded; and there were loud voices in heaven, saying, "The kingdom of the world has become the kingdom of our Lord and of His Christ; and He will reign forever and ever." And the twenty-four elders . . . worshiped God, saying, "We give You thanks . . . because You have taken Your great power and have begun to reign. And the nations were enraged, and Your wrath came, and the time came for the dead to be judged, and the time to reward Your bond-servants the prophets and the saints and those who fear Your name, the small and the great, and to destroy those who destroy the earth.*"". The kingdoms of man *have already become* the kingdom of our Lord, God has *already begun to reign*. John is unambiguous: because Jesus, God's

---

64. Koester, *Revelation*, p. 108

65. Gorman, *Reading Revelation Responsibly*, p. 108

66. Koester, *Revelation*, pp. 108-109

Messiah, has ascended to the right hand of the Father, the kingdom is already here and Jesus already rules over creation. We find, yet again, the themes of ecclesiology, christology, and eschatology masterfully woven together in Revelation 11, with a clear political implication: Jesus is, *right now*, king over all creation.

A Dragon, a Woman, and Two Beasts: Revelation 12-16

In Revelation 12-16, John introduces his audience to three new characters: a dragon, a woman, and two beasts. Each of these figures have symbolic significance and possess real-world referents; the intention of Revelation as a form of prophecy is to challenge and comfort the seven churches in Asia, and biblical scholarship has worked tirelessly to reconstruct a plausible historical background for these texts. While these chapters are rife with imagery from the Old Testament, Jipp argues that the messianic Psalm 2 dominates chapters 12-14.[67] John prefaces these visions with an announcement that Jesus has already begun to rule over creation in Revelation 11, intentionally frontloading the rhetorical (and thus theological) context of the following visions. Psalm 2 is therefore an appropriate framework for reflecting upon the messianic significance of these passages. Revelation 12 narrates a conflict between a woman in labor and a great red dragon, described with imagery borrowed from Daniel and Zechariah which in context referred to earthly kings. 12:9 identifies the dragon with *"the devil and Satan, who deceives the whole world"*, and he wages war against the woman, who, according to 12:5, has given *"birth to a son . . . who is to rule all the nations with a rod of iron; and her child was caught up to God and to His throne"*. Jesus, obviously. Although the dragon is a great deceiver, *"the kingdom of our God and the authority of His Christ have come"*, enabling the church to *"over*[come] *him because of the blood of the Lamb"*[68].

The dragon is easily identified. John himself says the dragon represents *"the devil and Satan"*, the powerful force which is in constant conflict with God and his people.[69] The woman, who gives birth to the Messiah, most likely represents the people of God. Given the various symbolic ways in which John portrays his ecclesiology, the woman, adorned *"with the sun, and the moon under her feet, and on her head a crown of twelve stars"* according to 12:1, *"suggests that the woman is not primarily an individual (such as Mary, the mother of Jesus), but a symbol of the entire people of God, from whom come first the Messiah Jesus then other children"*[70]. One

---

67. Jipp, *Messianic Theology*, pp. 301-305

68. Revelation 12:10-11

69. Gorman, *Reading Revelation Responsibly*, p. 123

70. Gorman, *Reading Revelation Responsibly*, p. 131

of apocalyptic literature's functions is to invest real-world events with their full cosmic significance; casting the seven churches as in a battle with celestial forces of evil reveals their true enemy. Behind the persecutions, cultural accommodations, and comfortable complacency is a force which threatens to destroy the church if left unchecked. Those who remain faithful to Jesus will overcome the dragon. He isn't acting alone.

Two beasts are assisting the dragon, and they dominate John's vision in Revelation 13. The imagery of Revelation 13 draws heavily upon Daniel 7 and is congruent with Daniel's theology; the evil empires are at war with God and his people until *"One like a Son of Man . . . was given dominion, Glory, and a kingdom, That all peoples, nations and men of every language Might serve Him"*[71]. As we have already seen, the evangelists were convinced that Jesus was this messianic "Son of Man", a royal title congruent with New Testament christology. Before even analyzing the symbolism, the message of Revelation 13 is deducible: God, through the Messiah, will defeat the evil human empires. The first beast, presented in 13:1-10, emerges from the sea and is empowered by the dragon. The beast *"blasphemes against God"* and *"makes war with the saints"*, deceiving everyone except the faithful: *"All who dwell on the earth will worship him, everyone whose name has not been written . . . in the book of life"*[72]. The saints must overcome and refuse to worship the first beast. A second beast, this time from the earth, resumes in Revelation 13:11-18 the work of the dragan and the first beast, deceiving, waging war, and tricking the world into worshiping him. In 14:8, the beast is revealed as *"Babylon"*, the metaphor which John will employ for the remainder of his visionary cycles.

Gorman helpfully summarises the scholarly consensus on Revelation 13, and I largely agree with his analysis: *"Most interpreters of Revelation would identify the first beast, from the sea (that is, coming from the west by way of the Aegean Sea to reach the cities of western Asia Minor), as the Roman empire, the emperor, (perhaps one specifically, such as Domitian), or an imperial power. The second beast, from the earth (that is, of local origin), is then seen as those who promote the imperial cult, perhaps local government and/or religious officials in and around cities like Ephesus and Pergamum"*[73]. If, as Burnett argues, the imperial cult was not as pervasive as many New Testament scholars have previously thought, the second beast could simply refer to political opposition from the local authorities irrespective of any cultic ties. Either way, just as the imagery in Daniel 7 undoubtedly refers to real-world imperial powers, John of Patmos could only have one possible target in mind: Rome.

---

71. Daniel 7:13-14

72. Revelation 13:8

73. Gorman, *Reading Revelation Responsibly*, p. 124

Revelation is, in this sense at least, the most authentically 'anti-imperial' text in the entire New Testament. God's people must oppose the deceitful dragon and his beasts until their final defeat, even if it costs them everything.

With a nod to the English metal band Iron Maiden, we turn to perhaps the most notorious text in Revelation: 666, the number of the beast. Revelation 13:16-18 discusses this enigmatic mark: *"And he causes all, the small and the great, and the rich and the poor, and the free men and the slaves, to be given a mark on their right hand or on their forehead, and he provides that no one will be able to buy or to sell, except the one who has the mark, either the name of the beast or the number of his name. Here is wisdom. Let him who has understanding calculate the number of the beast, for the number is that of a man; and his number is six hundred and sixty-six"*. The second beast, a symbolic representation of imperial power, also has a real-world referent. The number *"six hundred and sixty-six"* is *"an example of gematria, the ancient practice of assigning significance to the mathematical sum of the letters in a word in systems where letters are used to represent numerals, whether Hebrew, Greek, or Latin"*[74]. Serendipitously, two of the most deranged Roman emperors of the first century, Nero and Domitian, bear titles that, when translated through the process of gematria, add up to the exact number found in Revelation 13: six hundred and sixty-six.[75] The symbolism borrowed from Daniel, the identification of the dragon-beast power with Babylon, and the use of gematria allow us to see beyond John's imagery. He is clearly envisioning an evil imperial power and possibly even a single emperor.[76] Many of the churches in Asia minor would have faced economic hardships as a result of their faith, and it's probable that believers in Sardis and Laodicea were tempted to engage in unjust or exploitative economic practices, explaining the reference to buying and selling with the mark[77]. Either way, John expects his audience to avoid associating with the dragon and his beasts.

He says as much in Revelation 14. The *"one hundred and forty-four thousand"* return in Revelation 14:1-5 as those who have overcome and are already with the Lamb. An angel, preaching an *"eternal gospel"*, issues a warning to all creation in 14:6-7 that the time of judgment is at hand and humanity must glorify God or face the consequences. The imminent judgment is revealed in 14:9-12: *"Then another angel, a third one, followed them, saying with a loud voice, "If anyone worships the beast and his image, and receives a mark on his forehead or on his hand, he also will drink of the wine of the wrath of God, which is mixed in full strength in the cup of*

---

74. Gorman, *Reading Revelation Responsibly*, p. 126

75. Gorman, *Reading Revelation Responsibly*, pp. 126-128

76. Gorman, *Reading Revelation Responsibly*, p. 128

77. Koester, *Revelation*, pp. 131-132

His anger; and he will be tormented with fire and brimstone in the presence of the holy angels and in the presence of the Lamb. And the smoke of their torment goes up forever and ever; they have no rest day and night, those who worship the beast and his image, and whoever receives the mark of his name." Here is the perseverance of the saints who keep the commandments of God and their faith in Jesus". Babylon will fall, and those who consort with her, bearing her mark, will not escape the wrath of God. The saints who retain their faith in Jesus and follow God despite all opposition, however, will be rewarded. Revelation 15-16 unveil a long series of judgments which will be soon turned against the evil empire: *"Babylon the great was remembered before God, to give her the cup of the wine of His fierce wrath"*[78]. Time is running out for the empires of men.

The Fall of Babylon: Revelation 17-20

"Come here, and I will show you the judgment of the great harlot who sits on many waters, with whom the kings of the earth committed acts of immorality"[79]. John introduces the great harlot in Revelation 17:1-7, a woman who sits atop a scarlet beast, commits adultery with the kings of the earth, and drinks the blood of the saints. She is identified by the title inscribed on her forehead: *"Babylon the Great, the Mother of Harlots and of the Abominations of the Earth"*[80]. Curiously, the beast upon whom the harlot is seated possesses many heads and multiple horns. John, appropriating imagery from Daniel and Roman imperial ideology, is assuredly not referring to an actual woman.[81] The target of his thinly veiled critique is obviously Rome, the new Babylon, who has contributed greatly to the sufferings (and temptations) of seven churches in Asia. John inquires about the nature of this powerful harlot, and an angel willingly clarifies her identity in 17:8-18. The woman, along with the kings and kingdoms represented by the multi-headed beast, *"will wage war against the Lamb"*, an effort which will fail in the long run: *"the Lamb will overcome them, because He is Lord of lords and King of Kings, and those who are with HIm are the called and chosen and faithful"*[82]. This is the essence of Revelation. The evil empire loses, Jesus and his people win. Remain faithful until the end. In case anyone in John's audience wasn't taking the hint, the chapter ends in 17:18 with

---

78. Revelation 16:19

79. Revelation 17:1-2

80. Revelation 17:5

81. Gorman, *Reading Revelation Responsibly*, pp. 128-130

82. Revelation 17:14

one final referent: "*The woman whom you saw is the great city, which reigns over the kings of the earth*". It's Rome, of course.

Revelation 18 is an indictment of the crimes committed by Babylon, beginning with an angelic announcement of her downfall: "*Fallen, fallen is Babylon the great . . . For all the nations have drunk of the wine of her immorality, and the kings of the earth have committed acts of immorality with her, and the merchants of the earth have become rich by the wealth of her sensuality*"[83]. After exhorting God's people to "*Come out of her . . . so that you will not participate in her sins*" in 18:4, 18:5-8 describes her great arrogance. The kings of the earth, according to 18:9-10, have committed acts of immorality with her and will weep as the city burns. John turns against the merchants who participated in her evil in 18:11-20, condemning them for conducting business with her: "*The merchants of these things, who became rich from her, will stand at a distance because of the fear of her torment, weeping and mourning*"[84]. What is particularly interesting about the visions of Revelation 18 is, as Sprinkle points out, their emphasis on (what moderns label) economics: "*John's oracle here draws from several passages in Isaiah and Jeremiah that condemn Babylon and from Ezekiel's oracle of judgment against the city of Tyre* [Ezekiel 26-28], *which also focuses on economic sins*"[85]. John describes the various goods traded through the city of Rome which will be forfeited after its judgment, a cause for celebration because God has acted on behalf of the saints. Revelation 18:21-24 concludes the chapter with an angel throwing a millstone into the sea as an example of what God will do with Babylon, because "*all the nations were deceived by your sorcery . . . And in her was found the blood of prophets and of saints and of all who have been slain on the earth*".

Gorman, along with a large number of New Testament scholars, read passages like Revelation 18 as a critique of 'capitalism', which he implicitly defines as "*economic networks that favored the elite and permitted human exploitation*"[86]. There is just one problem: Gorman is operating with a fundamentally flawed definition of capitalism. Capitalism is an economic arrangement based upon private, decentralized, and voluntary production and exchange between consenting parties. Any arbitrary economic intervention by a third party is, *by definition*, not capitalism, and transactions based on fraud and deceit cannot by any objective standard be considered either voluntary or consensual. Scholars like Gorman, brilliant as they may be, have completely failed on a definitional level to construct philosophically

---

83. Revelation 18:2-3

84. Revelation 18:15

85. Sprinkle, *Exiles*, p. 140

86. Gorman, *Reading Revelation Responsibly*, p. 44

coherent categories for political and economic terms which would lead them to logically consistent political and economic conclusions. John isn't obscure; the kings and merchants have committed adultery with the great whore of Babylon, becoming rich and powerful by their association with her. He says, quite literally, that the "*merchants . . . became rich from her*" in 18:15. Gorman is indeed correct in one respect. Much of the wealth and power in antiquity was derived from imperial policies which institutionalized arbitrary power and involuntary, coercive economic exploitation. We have an economic term to describe this sort of market system: socialism. In socialist economic systems, production and consumption are determined by a small oligarchy of politically-connected elites with the goal of imposing, under threat of violence, their subjective social preferences on all of society. In the modern world this takes the form of imperialism under the guise of democracy, and contemporary thinkers, including brilliant intellectuals like Gorman, have completely internalized the lies of nineteenth-century authoritarian socialism. If there is a modern application of Revelation 18, it should be an outright refusal of the faithful to participate in the coercive violence of socialism, which has always and everywhere enriched the elites at the expense of everyone else. We cannot allow Christianity to be held hostage by unclear political and economic reasoning and the interpretive mistakes which they generate.

Revelation 19-20 envisions the final, decisive defeat of all evil. It begins with "a great multitude in heaven, saying, "*Hallelujah! Salvation and glory and power belong to our God; because His judgments are true and righteous; for He has judged the great harlot who was corrupting the earth with her immorality, and He has avenged the blood of His bond-servants on her.*"" in 19:1-2. One warrior rises to fight against the great harlot and the evil forces which empower her: "*And I saw heaven opened, and behold, a white horse, and He who sat on it is called Faithful and True, and in righteousness He judges and wages war. His eyes are a flame of fire, and on His head are many diadems; and He has a name written on Him which no one knows except Himself. He is clothed with a robe dipped in blood, and His name is called The Word of God. And the armies which are in heaven, clothed in fine linen, white and clean, were following Him on white horses. From His mouth comes a sharp sword, so that with it He may strike down the nations, and He will rule them with a rod of iron; and He treads the wine press of the fierce wrath of God, the Almighty. And on His robe and on His thigh He has a name written, "KING OF KINGS, AND LORD OF LORDS.*""[87].

Jesus has returned, battling the enemies of God and His people, and will stand in victory. As Jipp notes, the description of Jesus is designed by John to portray him as the rightful king of the cosmos. The Elder, again borrowing imagery

---

87. Revelation 19:11-16

from Psalm 2 and Roman imperial propaganda, shows Christ waging the final fight against everything evil and prevailing, a triumph which was inaugurated through his death and completed by the last, permanent vanquishing of his enemies. Christ's followers do not wage physical war against the harlot and the beast; they remain faithful to the one true king, embodying his cruciform witness until the end when, as Paul says in 1 Corinthians 15:25, *"he has put all His enemies under his feet"*.[88] The harlot, the beast, and all who worship them are judged in 18:19-21, just before Jesus establishes his millennial reign in 20:1-6. A number of eschatological systems have been generated from this passage, but they are all, in their own way, missing the point. Revelation, an epistle of apocalyptic prophecy, employs symbolism, including numeric imagery (666, right?), throughout the entire work. As Gorman notes, this passage is yet another example of an apocalyptic trope which was designed to comfort and challenge Revelation's original audience (and by extension, modern Christians) with the knowledge that God will win in the end.[89] Revelation 20:7-15 bears this out. The devil and the beast are cast into an eternal lake of fire, after which God sits in judgment: *"Then I saw a great white throne and Him who sat upon it, from whose presence earth and heaven fled away, and no place was found for them. And I saw the dead, the great and the small, standing before the throne, and books were opened; and another book was opened, which is the book of life; and the dead were judged from the things which were written in the books, according to their deeds. And the sea gave up the dead which were in it, and death and Hades gave up the dead which were in them; and they were judged, every one of them according to their deeds. Then death and Hades were thrown into the lake of fire. This is the second death, the lake of fire. And if anyone's name was not found written in the book of life, he was thrown into the lake of fire"*[90]. The war is over. Jesus is victorious. The eschatological consummation commences.

NEW HEAVENS AND NEW EARTH: REVELATION 21-22

In Isaiah 65:17, the prophet envisioned the coming day of God's judgment and salvation as a restoration of all creation: "behold, I create new heavens and a new earth". After Jesus has defeated all his enemies, the great cosmic restoration commences. Revelation 21-22 envisions the coming cosmic reconstitution: *"Then I saw a new heaven and a new earth; for the first heaven and the first earth passed away, and there is no longer any sea. And I saw the holy city, new Jerusalem, coming down*

---

88. Jipp, *Messianic Theology*, pp. 305-307

89. Gorman, *Reading Revelation Responsibly*, pp. 144

90. Revelation 20:11-15

out of heaven from God, made ready as a bride adorned for her husband. And I heard a loud voice from the throne, saying, "Behold, the tabernacle of God is among men, and He will dwell among them, and they shall be His people, and God Himself will be among them, and He will wipe away every tear from their eyes; and there will no longer be any death; there will no longer be any mourning, or crying, or pain; the first things have passed away." And He who sits on the throne said, "Behold, I am making all things new." And He said, "Write, for these words are faithful and true." Then He said to me, "It is done. I am the Alpha and the Omega, the beginning and the end. I will give to the one who thirsts from the spring of the water of life without cost. He who overcomes will inherit these things, and I will be his God and he will be My son"[91].

There is little more to say. Revelation 1:4-7 has come full-circle. All of God's enemies have been defeated, including death, and the resurrected faithful will live eternally with God and the Lamb in a restored world. Gorman says it best: *"this vision . . . is the climax of the book of Revelation, the New Testament, the entire Bible, the whole story of God, and also the story of humanity"*[92]. It is, in other words, our destiny. If the seven churches in Asia heed John's warnings from Revelation 2-3, they too will inherit the world to come. The new creation is appropriately glorious, constructed (symbolically) with the finest metals and jewels imaginable.[93] There is no need for a temple because, according to 21:22-23, the glory of God and his Lamb will fill the new creation. The entire world will be suffused with the perfect knowledge of God, as one of John's final visions attests: *"Then he showed me a river of the water of life, clear as crystal, coming from the throne of God and of the Lamb, in the middle of its street. On either side of the river was the tree of life, bearing twelve kinds of fruit, yielding its fruit every month; and the leaves of the tree were for the healing of the nations. There will no longer be any curse; and the throne of God and of the Lamb will be in it, and His bond-servants will serve Him"*[94]. It is finished.

Revelation ends with a final note of caution. In 22:6-21, John reminds his audience that all of these visions will surely come to pass. The seven churches in Asia, and indeed all believers who live in the interim between Christ's eschatological inauguration and Revelation's eschatological consummation, must remain faithful, rejecting the power of all dragons, beasts, harlots, and devils by embodying the cruciform witness of the world's one true king, Jesus. Revelation, a fitting end to the Christian canon, is at its core a repudiation of authoritarian socialism, the imperial policy of political and economic exploitation which has unfortunately come

---

91. Revelation 21:1-7

92. Gorman, *Reading Revelation Responsibly*, p. 163

93. Revelation 21:9-21

94. Revelation 22:1-3

to characterize the modern world and its bestial social order. Believers have but two choices laid before us by Revelation. We can either surrender to the prevailing winds of our day, functionally rejecting the Messianic status of Jesus, our unique identity as his holy, set-apart family, and the time between the inauguration and consummation of the eschaton in which we find ourselves, or we can abandon the entire system and remain faithful to Jesus alone. The Western church finds itself both compromised and comfortable, in need of sharp rebuke. There is, in my view, no returning from the precipice of failure unless we entirely abandon authoritarian socialism and the violent, coercive, and evil structures of power which propagate it. It doesn't have to be this way. The world desperately needs the gospel, and it is up to us and us alone to proclaim it. If we do, we will win. The choice is ours to make, and the time is at hand. To quote John one last time, *"He who testifies to these things says, "Yes, I am coming quickly." Amen. Come, Lord Jesus"*[95].

---

95. Revelation 22:20

Rethinking Politics, Economics, and
New Testament Interpretation

DEFINITIONS STILL MATTER

It's been quite a journey. As we draw this study to a close, I would like to supply a brief reflection and synthesis of our analysis, provide a few examples of how biblical scholars could draw better interpretive conclusions by thinking clearly about political and economic categories, and offer a few words of encouragement for my long-suffering readers. I have repeated myself numerous times throughout this book, and I do not wish to do so again at length here. One of my central theses has been confirmed by the evidence. The New Testament is incompatible with modern authoritarian socialism. We began by defining 'capitalism' and 'socialism' demonstrating that *by its very definition* socialism requires the initiation, by either threat or action, of coercive violence against peaceful people. Progressivism and conservatism both accept, to varying degrees, the inevitability of arbitrary authority and are therefore structurally identical. The real political spectrum lies not between the so-called 'left' and 'right', both of which employ socialist economic policies to achieve their preferred social ends, but rather liberty and authority, with liberty being a morally consistent commitment to the non-aggression principle in all areas of life. For Christians, this entails a consistent ethic of cruciformity which doesn't exclude political and economic activity.

The New Testament canon begins with the claim that Jesus is the promised Davidic king in Matthew 1:1 and concludes by calling him *"Lord Jesus"* in Revelation 22:21. Everything between these two passages is essentially a proclamation of or commentary on the messianic identity and work of Jesus. The prophet from Nazareth announced the imminent kingdom of God and established it through his life, crucifixion, resurrection, and ascension, where he currently sits at the right hand of God, ruling over all creation. Because of this, the eschatological promises are already in the process of being fulfilled. The apostles, empowered by the Spirit, have affected the ingathering of all nations, who are now included in the family of Abraham on the basis of faith in Israel's Messiah and God's gracious gift of the Spirit. The church is God's holy, set-apart people, called to proclaim the gospel of Jesus Christ to the entire world. While the eschaton has been inaugurated, it will not be fully consummated until Christ's return. The rulers of this age are passing away but still possess power, and believers adopt the Jewish model of living peacefully among pagans articulated in texts such as Jeremiah 29:7 and Daniel. The church must emulate the cruciform example of Jesus, refusing violence and dominion while testifying to a king who conquered through sacrifice, not war. This means Abraham's family is responsible for providing radical charity, wisely supplying the needs of those who lack. The church is also suprapolitical, transcending the evils of human authority, but must submit so long as the gospel is not compromised. Political citizenship can be leveraged for the sake of witness but is not a value in and of itself. The world is divided into two groups of people, those who place their faith in Messiah Jesus and those who don't. God will return and vindicate his people in the end, and our task is to remain faithful to Jesus until the final day. The New Testament's christology, ecclesiology, and eschatology is incompatible with modern authoritarian socialism. If we are serious about the reliability and authority of Scripture, we are obligated to reject it.

In the opening chapter I outlined three goals I wished to accomplish in this book. First, I wanted to define modern economic and political concepts and compare them with the ancient world in which the New Testament was written. Check. Second, I hoped to demonstrate the complexities of applying biblical texts to modern social and political questions and explore the use of modern social and political categories in biblical interpretation. Done. Finally, I intended to analyze several prominent New Testament texts which are often assumed to address 'political' and 'economic' issues. The word 'several' was a massive understatement. Whether or not you, dear reader, are convinced by my conclusions, I hope we can agree that I certainly achieved my stated objectives. Some might even say I achieved them too much. Fair criticism. I do hope, however, that there will be some interpreters (any many lay readers) who are challenged to rethink how they apply political and economic concepts when reading the New Testament. I believe the work of several excellent scholars would be greatly enhanced with a more precise understanding of those categories, working with definitions which are consistent, irreducible, and universally applicable. Before we close I will provide four concrete examples.

SAY IT LIKE YOU MEAN IT: A RESPONSE TO NEW TESTAMENT SCHOLARSHIP

N.T. Wright

We will begin with the work of N.T. Wright, the most prolific biblical scholar of his generation and a man who had an incredible impact on my personal interpretive development. Although I now diverge from his scholarship at several critical points, he has been one of the most passionate and articulate defenders of messianic christology and high ecclesiology in the field and I largely agree with his general approach to both subjects. He is also a fantastic writer and communicator, an asset which his uncritically reflexive detractors fail to appreciate. We must give credit where credit is due. His work is far from perfect, though. In Chapter 2 we learned that Wright is wrong about free markets precisely because of his inconsistent economic reasoning, and I believe the same lack of conceptual clarity also hinders Wright's ability to think precisely about political concepts as well. Consider the following quotation, taken from his discussion of Romans 13 in *Paul and the Faithfulness of God*: "*It merely states that the One God wants human authorities to run his world, and that the people of the One God should respect such authorities . . . They were, however, prepared not only to obey those authorities under normal circumstances but also, when necessary, remind them of their proper vocation*"[1].

The second half of Wright's quotation isn't objectionable on its own. It is, in essence, the principle of Jeremiah 29:7. The problem is with his ambiguous claim that "*God wants human authorities to run his world*", a task which is clearly delegated to the Messiah and his people in the New Testament. Wright seems to assume the necessity, indeed the *inevitability*, of arbitrary human authority. His short critique of free-market economics in *History and Eschatology*[2], flawed both categorically and empirically, betrays a deep misunderstanding about the political power which necessarily accompanies centralized economic systems. Wright makes several demonstrably false claims about free markets and then proceeds to criticize economic arrangements which are the result of government policy. While he doesn't use the term 'capitalism', we know what Wright means. If, however, Wright were operating within the Austrian tradition where capitalism is simply a label which denotes decentralized, voluntary networks of production and consumption between peaceful people, he would never have arrived at such an incoherent conclusion. Or, at the very least, his critique of free markets would

---

1. Wright, *Faithfulness of God*, p. 1303
2. Wright, *History and Eschatology*, p. 19; see Chapter 2 for an extended discussion.

be far more reserved. Wright's political corollary requires supporting market interventions which he (subjectively, I might add) finds preferable by delegating increasing power to non-productive politicians and bureaucrats. They will use this power to arbitrarily regulate the behavior of others without their consent. I agree with Wright in one respect: the church should call authorities to account. In the modern Western world where government theoretically exists by consent of the governed, shouldn't the church leverage its citizenship to oppose centralized economic authority and the awful political and corporate incentives they perpetuate? If Jesus is king and the church is his family, shouldn't his people be advocating for economic arrangements which are based on peace and consent?

What accounts for this glaring lacunae in Wright's political theology? It is, in my view, his uncritical acceptance of modern authoritarian socialism. His comments about the Thatcher and Reagan governments are revealing; Wright objects to their administrations because he thinks they loosened the tight grip of government too much, endangering years of bureaucratic policymaking which was, according to the propaganda of authoritarian socialism, established to "help" people. Or something like that. Any libertarian analysis of Ronald Reagan's administration reveals a great gulf between his political rhetoric and actual policy record, and the evidence of history suggests Reagan wasn't the great champion of limited government his admirers and critics make him out to be. Politicians don't always tell the truth. The subtext of Wright's invective against free markets is an unstated commitment to arbitrary, centralized authority, a subjective cultural preference which is neither inevitable nor desirable. If Wright had been willing to rethink his political and economic presuppositions, especially in light of his christology and ecclesiology, he would not have made such erroneous claims. Wright, assuming himself to be on the side of justice, ironically (and tragically) winds up advocating for a world built on violence and justice, a contradiction easily resolved by greater intellectual precision.

Joshua Jipp

Joshua Jipp concludes his excellent book *The Messianic Theology of the New Testament* with a chapter entitled *"Politics, Power, and Eschatology"*[3]. Jipp summarizes the chapter with the following comments: "*The Scriptural promise for God to rule the world through a righteous, just, and peace-loving messianic king is ultimately fulfilled in the surprising manner of the King's death and resurrection. This results in an ethic whereby God's people entrust themselves and their cause to God and not to*

---

3. Jipp, *Messianic Theology*, pp. 388-404

the violent coercive methods of the human kings, kingdoms, and governments of the world[4]. Literally every word of this statement corresponds with the thesis of this book. Jesus is king of the world, and his followers are obligated to follow his non-violent example. Jipp states it even more bluntly earlier in the chapter: *"citizens of Christ's kingdom will reject the use of violence, brute force, and coercion in all areas of life"*[5]. He is absolutely correct. It is also, in short, the non-aggression principle. Libertarians do not believe the non-aggression principle is somehow suspended because a person is elected to office or works in government bureaucracy. If murder and theft are objective moral evils, government officials have no more of right than anyone else to murder and steal. Jipp is certainly correct that believers are obligated to reject the initiation of violence *"in all areas of life"*, including, I presume, the political process and economic transactions.

It logically follows, then, that Jipp should arrive at the correct political conclusion: believers must reject the paradigm of modern authoritarian socialism which is inherently built on violence and coercion in the name of an ill-defined 'justice'. Shouldn't Jipp just come out and say it? Unfortunately his analysis of Messiah-centered economic practices is much too vague. Jipp rightly affirms that *"Christ's kingship consistently relativizes and critiques the typical this-worldly assumptions about who are worthy subjects of Christ's rule based on their wealth and status . . .* [believers] *must not . . .* [follow] *the normal practices of kings, lords, and the powerful who use their wealth for power and exploitation . . . Those who are friends of God engage in countercultural economic practices"*[6]. I concur entirely! Believers are obligated to provide radical charity and use their wealth in service of others. Our economic practices should be countercultural, and "countercultural" would include opposing the inherent violence of authoritarian socialism, right?

There is nothing "free-market" about the United States; the federal government is nearing (at the time of writing in late 2025) forty *trillion* dollars in debt, it has fought a long series of unnecessary wars for the duration of my entire lifetime, it takes a large portion of the income of productive citizens and transfers the money to politically connected corporations, NGO's, and people who refuse to work, enabling degeneracy and decadence while continuing to devalue our currency and perpetuating a never-ending cycle of debt-dependency by manipulating the money supply through the Federal Reserve's artificial credit expansion. This is socialism on a scale unimaginable before the twenty-first century, all predicated on violence, coercion, and the idolatry of greed. The Messiah's family should oppose

---

4. Jipp, *Messianic Theology*, p. 404
5. Jipp, *Messianic Theology*, p. 398
6. Jipp, *Messianic Theology*, pp. 396-397

it. Socialism is evil, capitalism is just. It's that simple. Jipp, however, cannot bring himself to say it like that, which I believe is attributable to a lack of precision regarding basic political and economic concepts. If we are called to oppose violence in *"all areas of life"* then we should be against taxation, inflation, militarization, and entitlement programs, all of which are only possible due to the threat of coercive violence. I hope Jipp doesn't believe there is a mysterious carveout for government officials. Jesus shows us a better way, and scholars like Jipp, equipped with consistent, irreducible, and universally applicable definitions of basic political and economic concepts, would be in a position to show the world what it really means to follow Jesus.

Michael Gorman

The most obvious example is found in the otherwise brilliant and nearly flawless work of Michael Gorman. He is, much to my dismay, simply wrong about capitalism. Gorman's conception of capitalism from his book *Reading Revelation Responsibly* attributes to markets all of the problems inherent in socialism[7], a mistake easily remedied by a concrete categorization of economic concepts. It leaves a noticeable scar on an otherwise impeccable analysis of Revelation and generates the unstated but rather explicit policy prescription that John's apocalypse somehow condones the intervention of pagan government into peaceful and voluntary market transactions, a conclusion which is directly at odds with what John himself says about Rome and the merchants she enables in Revelation 18. Gorman can only sustain this illogical and contradictory line of thinking because of our chronic inability to conceptualize political behavior and economic exchange in a coherent manner. Scholars like Gorman, working in the progressive-leaning institution of American higher education and whose paychecks depend in part upon taxpayer-subsidized, federally-guaranteed student loans, have little incentive to ask difficult questions about the real nature of political power and economic central planning. It's an omission of inconsistency, I'm sure, but results in a nominally 'anti-imperial' scholar legitimizing the very economic mechanisms which enable the expansion of imperialism.

In the final chapter of *Cruciformity*, entitled *"Cruciformity Today"*[8], Gorman explores the consequences of his magisterial study for believers in the modern world. Following the example of Christ, Christians must conform to the cross: *"Cruciform faith does not allow—cannot even imagine—the separation of faith toward*

---

7. Gorman, *Reading Revelation Responsibly*, p. 44

8. Gorman, *Cruciformity*, pp. 368-401

God and love toward neighbor . . . Cruciform love resists the temptation to make myself the focus of everything, even of my spirituality"[9]. Cruciformity should also, according to Gorman, engender a radical skepticism: "*The cross examines not only the values of the status quo but also the motives of those who criticize the status quo. Pride and self-righteousness have no place in a spirituality of the cross . . . Every convention, every value, every virtue—they are all at risk. Scrutiny of everything becomes the order of the day*"[10]. Even better, Gorman's theory of power is identical to the one proposed in this book: "*True power is not "imperial" in nature; it is not the ability to influence or control people against their will with the possibility or threat of enforcing one's will should they not comply*"[11]. I, of course, agree, but Gorman's rejection of capitalism implies he doesn't believe his own words, or at least is unwilling to apply them consistently. Gorman openly renounces the only economic arrangement based on peaceful, voluntary consent and willingly endorses state power as a means of suppressing economic activity to which he (subjectively) objects. Taking Gorman at his word, that isn't the 'cruciform' position in any way.

It gets worse. In the first episode of Nijay Gupta's *Engaging Scripture* podcast, Gupta interviews Michael Gorman on the twentieth anniversary of his book *Cruciformity*. Gorman discusses the idolization of rights and turns the conversation to the COVID pandemic, demonizing American Christians who challenged the mask mandates and were skeptical of the mRNA injections produced by FDA-enabled pharmaceutical companies.[12] Gorman's response to the COVID pandemic is neither cruciform nor skeptical. Gorman, is, in fact, standing firmly beside the rich and powerful who violently weaponized government power against the rest of society during the pandemic. Tom Woods provides a staggering array of evidence in his book *Diary of a Psychosis*[13] that the so-called "non-pharmaceutical" interventions which the public health establishment promised were scientifically-based did absolutely nothing to prevent the spread of COVID while in practice destroying millions of lives. The most comprehensive study of masking demonstrated empirically that the mask mandates were ineffective and unnecessary[14], a position held by none other than Anthony Fauci, then head of the NIAID, just before the

---

9. Gorman, *Cruciformity*, pp. 388-389

10. Gorman, *Cruciformity*, p. 384

11. Gorman, *Cruciformity*, p. 395

12. Gupta, Nijay. "Cruciformity: Interview with Dr. Michael J. Gorman." *Engaging Scripture: Conversations in Biblical studies*, February 1, 2022. Podcast, 46:00. https://podcasts.apple.com/us/podcast/engaging-scripture-conversations-in-biblical-studies/id1608115229?i=1000549733640. The conversation begins around the 39-minute mark.

13. Woods, Thomas. 2023. *Diary of a Psychosis*. The Libertarian Institute.

14. Woods, *Diary of a Psychosis*, pp. 388-389

lockdowns were implemented in March 2020[15]. Fauci repeatedly lied to the public during the pandemic, misleading Americans into believing his solutions were based on hard, scientific evidence.[16] They weren't. Laurie Calhoun chronicles how the exact same propaganda used to artificially generate support for the US invasion of Iraq was turned against American citizens in the COVID era, deliberately misleading the public into accepting a massive increase in government power.[17] Gorman, honorably opposed to American militarism[18], was completely blinded by the COVID propaganda. The mRNA injections themselves were publicly funded and privately profited, with several Moderna executives becoming newly-minted billionaires at the expense of American taxpayers.[19] Between the CARES Act, eviction moratoriums, corporate bailouts, the Fed massively expanding the money supply, business being artificially shuttered, and hardworking Americans losing their jobs because unelected government bureaucrats deemed their work "unessential", the COVID era constituted the greatest upward transfer of wealth in American history.[20] The political and corporate class lied to the American public about the efficacy of mRNA injections, and as of late 2025 more evidence is beginning to surface about the faulty data presented by the corrupt pharmaceutical companies and the terrible, possibly fatal, side effects generated by their lucratively profitable products.

Gorman—the scholar who wrote the book *Cruciformity* and passionately exhorts believers to reject violence, embrace sacrificial love, and question everything—supported the entire COVID regime, enabling the politicians, bureaucrats, and corporate executives to accumulate wealth and power at the expense of everyone else. There was nothing cruciform about the COVID era, plain and simple, and Gorman shouldn't get to stand on a pedestal and condemn those who correctly saw through the lies and propaganda. Many of us who were skeptical about the COVID narrative cared deeply about our neighbors. Was it worth the

---

15. Deace, Steve , and Todd Erzen. 2021. *Faucian Bargain*. Post Hill Press. pp. 26-27

16. "*Delete This': New Smoking Gun Emails Reveal Fauci COVID Coverup.*" ZeroHedge, September 10, 2025. https://www.zerohedge.com/covid-19/delete-new-smoking-gun-emails-reveal-fauci-covid-coverup.

17. Calhoun, Laurie. 2023. *Questioning the COVID Company Line.* The Libertarian Institute.

18. Gorman, *Reading Revelation Responsibly*, pp. 50-5

19. Tognini, Giacomo. "*Surging Moderna Stock Mints the Vaccine Maker's Fifth Billionaire.*" Forbes, June 15, 2021. https://www.forbes.com/sites/giacomotognini/2021/06/15/surging-moderna-stock-mints-the-vaccine-makers-fifth-billionaire/.

20. Collins, Chuck, and Omar Ocampo. "*U.S. Billionaire Wealth Is Up 88% Since the Pandemic—Now Topping $5.5 Trillion.*" Institute for Policy Studies, March 25, 2024. https://ips-dc.org/u-s-billionaire-wealth-is-up-88-since-the-pandemic-now-topping-5-5-trillion/.

years of student learning loss, destroyed careers and businesses, broken families, fractured communities, the expansion of political and corporate power, and the potentially dangerous side-effects of a novel mRNA injections? Perhaps Gorman was more concerned about his own rights and his own sense of security than seeking to understand why many Americans opposed the mask and mRNA mandates. If cruciformity must engender a radical skepticism towards all claims to power and *always* avoid the use of arbitrary force against others, Gorman should start taking his own advice. None of this, by the way, detracts from his excellent work. I think Gorman's intentions are pure, but it is his unwillingness to grapple with fundamental political and economic concepts which have hindered his ability to think critically about *all* of the modern applications of his cruciform theology.

Richard Horsley

Is it appropriate, to close out this penultimate section of the book, that I revisit the work of Richard Horsley one final time. The fourth section of Horsley's book *You Shall Not Bow Down and Serve Them* is entitled "*The Bible and the New form of Empire*"[21]. In this lengthy section he repeatedly conflates 'capitalism' with 'empire', blaming all of the world's problems on a concept he never bothers to define. He illogically claims "*the state is not irrelevant but instrumental to global capitalism's expansion*" and then cites NAFTA, the IMF and World Bank, NATO, and the US military as examples of capitalism's great evils.[22] There is just one little problem: literally all his examples are the product of government policy. Had Horsley been familiar with traditions other than Marxism, maybe he would have realized that the notion of 'state capitalism' is a contradiction in terms. Horsley is in reality objecting to forms of socialism which he doesn't like, but he has no principle objection to the arbitrary use of power. His actual political solution is woefully predictable. He wants to give as much money and power as possible to people who think like him, and his critique of capitalism is intended to anathematize those who would challenge his pretensions to power. Any good libertarian hates all of the institutions to which Horsley rejects much more than he does, and in distinction to him we would like to see the mechanisms of power which enabled them in the first place be completely dismantled. Horsley, blinded by unsystematic political and economic thinking, has done little more than project the nineteenth-century power politics of nationalism onto the global stage. The supposedly anti-imperial

---

21. Horsley, *Bow Down*, pp. 155-219

22. Horsley, *Bow Down*, p. 212

Horsley, like many of his colleagues in theology and Biblical studies, can always be reliably counted upon to take the side of empire.

IT DOESN'T HAVE TO BE THIS WAY

There is a better way. I believe the New Testament. Jesus inaugurated the kingdom of God through his life, death, resurrection, and ascension. He now sits as king over all creation, dispensing the Spirit upon everyone, Jew and Gentile alike, who are faithful to him alone. Abraham's family is set apart to proclaim the gospel to all nations, heralding the end of history on the final day when Jesus returns, restoring creation and vindicating his people. The church must bear the cruciform witness of our king, sacrificially and nonviolently serving others, proclaiming the crucified Lord in both word and deed. This ethic of cruciformity must be applied in all areas of life, *especially* with respect to politics and economics. There is, as both Jipp and Gorman skillfully argued, no place for arbitrary coercion in the Messiah's family. This places us at odds with the world, of course, but so does the gospel of a crucified Messiah. We make no apologies for the truth, and we do not compromise our principles.

The church is obligated by the authority of Scripture to think through and apply biblical principles in every generation. The themes of christology, ecclesiology, and eschatology must shape our approach to the world today, a world which is simultaneously dissimilar and in some ways surprisingly familiar to antiquity. Being the set-apart, suprapolitical people of a universal king will manifest itself differently today than it did in the first century, and leveraging our citizenship for the gospel will likewise look distinct. Jesus didn't promise us it would be easy. Grounding political and economic concepts in consistent, irreducible, and universally applicable definitions allows us to see that the cruciform ethic of God's eschatological kingdom must be our starting point. It ends with eternity. The road is long and difficult, and there is only one way to reach our destination. We must keep moving forward. I hope that the words of this book have challenged you to think about what it means to practice our faith in a politically and economically complex world. The church can and will ultimately succeed through the power of God's Spirit and the reign of Israel's Messiah. Let's keep pushing ahead until his return.

BIBLIOGRAPHY

Abernethy, Andrew, and Gregory Goswell. 2020. *God's Messiah in the Old Testament.* Baker Academic.

Achtemeier, Paul. 1985. *Romans.* John Knox Press.

Allison Jr., Dale. 2009. *The Historical Christ and the Theological Jesus.* Eerdmans.

Allison Jr., Dale. 2025. *Interpreting Jesus.* Eerdmans.

Archer, Gleason. 2007. *A Survey of Old Testament Introduction.* Moody Publishers.

Bailey, Kenneth. 2008. *Jesus Through Middle Eastern Eyes.* InterVarsity Press Academic.

Baily, Kenneth. 2011. *Paul Through Mediterranean Eyes.* InterVarsity Press Academic.

Barker, James. 2025. *Writing and Rewriting the Gospels.* Eerdmans.

Barnett, Paul. 1993. "*Apostle*". In *Dictionary of Paul and His Letters*, edited by Hawthorne, Gerald; Martin, Ralph; Reid, Daniel. InterVarsity Press.

Bates, Matthew. 2017. *Salvation By Allegiance Alone.* Baker Academic.

Bauer, David. 2013. "*Genealogy*". In *Dictionary of Jesus and the Gospels*, 2nd ed. edited by Green, Joel. InterVarsity Press.

Baylis, Albert. 1996. *From Creation to the Cross.* Zondervan.

Beard, Mary. 2015. *SPQR: A History of Ancient Rome.* Liveright.

Beldman, David. 2017. *Deserting the King.* Lexham Press.

Bennema, Cornelis. 2025. *Imitation in Early Christianity.* Eerdmans.

Bernardo, Alex. "Submit to the Authorities? What 1 Peter 2:13-17 Claims About Political Power." Libertarianchristians.Com. November 26, 2024. https://libertarianchristians.com/2024/11/26/submit-to-the-authorities/.

Bernier, Jonathan. 2022. *Rethinking the Dates of the New Testament.* Baker Academic.

"Bible." Orthodox Church in America. https://www.oca.org/questions/scripture/bible.

Bird, Michael. 2008. *Introducing Paul.* InterVarsity Press.

Bird, Michael. 2013. "*Christ*". In *Dictionary of Jesus and the Gospels*, 2nd ed. ed. by Joel B. Green, InterVarsity Press.

Bird, Michael. 2023. *A Bird's-Eye View of Luke and Acts.* InterVarsity Press.

Blomberg, Craig. 2009. *Jesus and the Gospels*. 2nd ed. B&H Academic.

Blomberg, Craig. 2024. *Jesus the Purifier*. Baker Academic.

Bock, Darrell. 2002. *Jesus According to Scripture*. Baker Academic.

Bond, Helen. 2024. "*Biography*". In *The Next Quest for the Historical Jesus* edited by Crossley, James and Keith, Chris. Eerdmans.

Bronner, Stephen. 2017. *Critical Theory*. Oxford University Press.

Brown, Raymond. 1993. *The Birth of the Messiah*. 2nd ed. Doubleday.

Bruce, F.F.. 1996. "*Acts, Book of The*". In *New Bible Dictionary*, 3rd ed. ed. by I. Howard Marshall, A.R. Millard, J.I. Packer, and D.J. Wiseman, InterVarsity Press.

Bruce, F.F. 1997. *Israel and the Nations*. InterVarsity Press.

Bruno, Chris, John Lee, and Thomas Schreiner. 2024. *The Divine Christology of the Apostle Paul*. InterVarsity Press.

Bryan, Christopher. 2005. *Render Unto Caesar*. Oxford University Press.

Burnett, Clint. 2024. *Paul and Imperial Divine Honors*. Eerdmans.

Cadbury, Henry. 2006. *The Peril of Modernizing Jesus*. Wipf and Stock.

Cahill, Thomas. 2013. *Heretics and Heroes*. Anchor Books.

Calhoun, Laurie. 2023. *Questioning the COVID Company Line*. The Libertarian Institute.

Capes, David, Rodney Reeves, and Randolph Richards. 2007. *Rediscovering Paul*. InterVarsity Press.

Carey, Greg. 2025. *Rereading Revelation*. Eerdmans.

Carey, Holly. 2023. *Women Who Do*. Eerdmans.

Catechism of the Catholic Church, 2nd ed. (Vatican City: Libreria Editrice Vaticana, 1997), § 74-131.

Chen, Kevin. 2024. *Wonders From Your Law*. InterVarsity Press.

Cohen, Shaye. 2006. *From the Maccabees to the Mishnah*. 2nd ed. Westminster John Knox Press.

Collins, Adela, and John Collins. 2008. *King and Messiah as Son of God*. Eerdmans.

Collins, Chuck, and Omar Ocampo. "*U.S. Billionaire Wealth Is Up 88% Since the Pandemic—Now Topping $5.5 Trillion*." Institute for Policy Studies, March 25, 2024. https://ips-dc.org/u-s-billionaire-wealth-is-up-88-since-the-pandemic-now-topping-5-5-trillion/.

Collins, John. 1984. *Daniel with an Introduction to Apocalyptic Literature*. Eerdmans.

Collins, John. 1998. *The Apocalyptic Imagination*. 2nd ed. Eerdmans.

Comfort, Phillipl. 1993. "*Temple*". In *Dictionary of Paul and His Letters*, edited by Hawthorne, Gerald; Martin, Ralph; Reid, Daniel. InterVarsity Press.

Crossan, John, and Jonathan Reed. 2004. *In Search of Paul*. HarperSanFrancisco.

Crossley, James, and Robert Myles. 2023. *Jesus: A Life in Class Conflict*. Zer0 Books.

Crowe, Brandon. 2020. *The Hope of Israel*. Baker Academic.

Cruse, C.F. 1998. *Eusebius' Ecclesiastical History*. Hendrickson Publishers.

Cummins, S.A.. 2024. "*John the Baptist*". In *Dictionary of Jesus and the Gospels*, 2nd ed. edited by Green, Joel. InterVarsity Press.

Deace, Steve, and Todd Erzen. 2021. *Faucian Bargain*. Post Hill Press. pp. 26-27

DeCamp, Dave. "Support for Israel Has Cost US Taxpayers At Least \$22.76 Billion in One Year." Antiwar.com. October 7, 2024. https://news.antiwar.com/2024/10/07/support-for-israel-has-cost-the-us-taxpayer-at-least-22-8-billion-in-one-year/.

"*Delete This': New Smoking Gun Emails Reveal Fauci COVID Coverup*." ZeroHedge, September 10, 2025. https://www.zerohedge.com/covid-19/delete-new-smoking-gun-emails-reveal-fauci-covid-coverup.

Dempster, Stephen. 2024. *The Return of the Kingdom*. InterVarsity Press.

Dennis, John. 2024. "*Death of Jesus*". In *Dictionary of Jesus and the Gospels*, 2nd ed. edited by Green, Joel. InterVarsity Press.

Donfried, Karl. 2002. *Paul, Thessalonica, and Early Christianity*. Eerdmans.

Downs, David. 2013. "*Economics*". In *Dictionary of Jesus and the Gospels*, 2nd ed. ed. by Joel B. Green, InterVarsity Press.

Dunn, James. 1998. *The Theology of the Apostle Paul*. Eerdmans.

Dunn, James. 2003. *Jesus Remembered*. Eerdmans.

Dunn, James. 2006. *The New Perspective on Paul*. Eerdmans.

Dunn, James. 2009. *Beginning from Jerusalem*. Eerdmans.

Dunn, James. 2011. *Jesus, Paul, and the Gospels*. Eerdmans.

Elliott, Neil.. 2004. "*Romans 13:1-7 in the Context of Imperial Propaganda*". In *Paul and Empire*. ed. by Richard Horsley, Trinity Press International.

Fee, Gordon. 1999. *Philippians*. InterVarsity Press.

Fee, Gordon, and Douglas Stuart. 2003. *How to Read the Bible for All Its Worth*. 3rd ed. Zondervan.

Ferda, Tucker. 2024. *Jesus and His Promised Second Coming*. Eerdmans.

Ferguson, Everett. 2003. *Backgrounds of Early Christianity*. 3rd ed. Eerdmans.

Fichera, Angelo . "FACT FOCUS: Who's to Blame for the National Debt? It's More Complicated than One Culprit." *Associated Press*, May 18, 2023. https://apnews.com/article/fact-check-national-debt-donald-trump-barack-obama-ee3e613646fe500edf803e57959c776e.

Foucault, Michel. 1982. *The Foucault Reader*. Edited by Paul Rabinow. Pantheon Books.

Furnish, Victor. 2009. *The Moral Teaching of Paul*. 3rd ed. Abingdon Press.

Galbraith, Deane. 2024. *"Religion, Visions, and Alternative Histories"*. In *The Next Quest for the Historical Jesus* edited by Crossley, James and Keith, Chris. Eerdmans.

Green, Joel. 2013. *"Kingdom of God/Heaven"*. In *Dictionary of Jesus and the Gospels*, 2nd ed. ed. by Joel B. Green, InterVarsity Press.

Goodacre, Mark. 2004. *"A World Without Q"*. In *Questioning Q*, ed. by Mark Goodacre and Nicholas Perrin, InterVarsity Press.

Goodacre, Mark. 2025. *The Fourth Synoptic Gospel*. Eerdmans.

Gorman, Michael. 2001. *Elements of biblical Exegesis*. Hendrickson Publishers.

Gorman, Michael. 2001. *Cruciformity*. Eerdmans.

Gorman, Michael. 2004. *Apostle of the Crucified Lord*. Eerdmans.

Gorman, Michael. 2011. *Reading Revelation Responsibly*. Cascade Books.

Green, Joel. 2024. *"Passion Narrative"*. In *Dictionary of Jesus and the Gospels*, 2nd ed. edited by Green, Joel. InterVarsity Press.

Gupta, Nijay. 2020. *Paul and the Language of Faith*. Eerdmans.

Gupta, Nijay. "Cruciformity: Interview with Dr. Michael J. Gorman." *Engaging Scripture: Conversations in Biblical studies*, February 1, 2022. Podcast, 46:00. https://podcasts.apple.com/us/podcast/engaging-scripture-conversations-in-biblical-studies/id1608115229?i=1000549733640.

Gutierrez-Morfin, Noel . "Trump Says He's 'Fine' With Gay Marriage in '60 Minutes' Interview." *NBC News*, November 14, 2016. https://www.nbcnews.com/feature/nbc-out/trump-says-he-s-fine-gay-marriage-60-minutes-interview-n683606.

Haddad, Najeeb. 2021. *Paul, Politics, and New Creation*. Lexington Books/Fortress Academic.

Haddad, Najeeb. 2023. *Paul and Empire Criticism*. Cascade Books.

Hastings, Ross. 2025. *The Glory of the Ascension*. InterVarsity Press.

Hayes, Christopher. 2013. *"Rich and Poor"*. In *Dictionary of Jesus and the Gospels*, 2nd ed. ed. by Joel B. Green, InterVarsity Press.

Hayek, F. A.. 1954. *Capitalism and the Historians*. University of Chicago Press.

Hayek, F.A. 1954. *The Counter-Revolution of Science*. The Free Press; (Liberty Press, 1979).

Hayek, F.A. 2007. *The Road to Serfdom: The Definitive Edition*. Edited by Bruce Caldwell. The University
of Chicago Press.

Hayes, John, and Carl Holladay. 1987. *biblical Exegesis: A Beginner's Handbook*. John Knox Press.

Heilig, Christoph. 2022. *The Apostle and the Empire*. Eerdmans.

Herman, Arthur. 2017. *1917: Lenin, Wilson, and the Birth of the New World Disorder*. HarperCollins.

Holland, Drew. 2025. *The Place of the Past*. Cascade Books.

Holmes, Christopher. 2024. *Unspoiled Endings*. Fortress Press.

Hoppe, Hans-Hermann. 1989. *A Theory of Capitalism and Socialism*. 2nd ed. (2013). Mises Institute.

Hoppe, Hans-Hermann. "Marxist and Austrian Class Analysis." *Journal of Libertarian Studies 9 No. 2*, (1990): 79-93.

Horsley, Richard. 2003. *Jesus and Empire*. Fortress Press.

Horsley, Richard. 2004. *Paul and Empire*. Trinity Press International.

Horsley, Richard. 2004. "*1 Corinthians: Paul's Assembly as an Alternative Society*". In *Christianity at Corinth*, edited by Adams, Edward; Horrell, David. Westminster John Knox Press.

Horsley, Richard. 2021. *You Shall Not Bow Down and Serve Them: The Political Economic Projects of Jesus and Paul*. Cascade Books.

Horton, Scott. 2021. *Enough Already: Time to End the War on Terrorism*. The Libertarian Institute.

Horton, Scott. 2022. *Hotter Than the Sun: Time to Abolish Nuclear Weapons*. The Libertarian Institute.

Horwitz, Steven. 2020. *Austrian Economics: An Introduction*. Cato Institute.

Irvin, Tucker B. 2013. *Survey of Economics*. 8th ed. South-Western, Cengage Learning.

Jeffers, James. 1997. *The Greco-Roman Worlds of the New Testament Era*. InterVarsity Press.

Jipp, Joshua. 2020. *The Messianic Theology of the New Testament*. Eerdmans.

Johnson, Alan. 2004. *1 Corinthians*. InterVarsity Press.

Keith, Chris. 2024. "*Beyond What is Behind*". In *The Next Quest for the Historical Jesus* edited by Crossley, James and Keith, Chris. Eerdmans.

Kensky, Meira. 2025. "*Gospel of Luke*". In *Judeophobia and the New Testament*, edited by Rollens, Sarah, Eric Vanden Eykel, and Meredith Warren. Eerdmans.

Kidner, Derek. 1979. *Ezra and Nehemiah*. InterVarsity Press.

Kingsbury, Jack. 1988. *Matthew as Story*. 2nd ed. Fortress Press.

Kirk, Alan. 2023. *Jesus Tradition, Early Christian Memory, and Gospel Writing*. Eerdmans.

Koester, Craig. 2001. *Revelation and the End of All Things*. Eerdmans.

Kostenberger, Andreas. 2004. *John*. Baker Academic.

Kreitzer, Larry. 1993. "*Kingdom of God/Christ*". In *Dictionary of Paul and His Letters*, edited by Hawthorne, Gerald; Martin, Ralph; Reid, Daniel. InterVarsity Press.

Laird, Benjamin. 2023. *Creating the Canon*. InterVarsity Press.

Lawrence, Louise. 2013. "*Social-Scientific Criticisms*". In *Dictionary of Jesus and the Gospels*, 2nd ed. edited by Green, Joel. InterVarsity Press.

Licona, Mike. 2024. *Jesus, Contradicted*. Zondervan.

Malina, Bruce, and Richard Rohrbaugh. 1992. *Social-Science Commentary on the Synoptic Gospels*. Fortress Press.

Marx, Karl, and Frederick Engels. 1848. *The Communist Manifesto*. International Publishers (1948).

Matson, Mark. 2004. "*Luke's Rewriting of the Sermon on the Mount*". In *Questioning Q*, ed. by Mark Goodacre and Nicholas Perrin, InterVarsity Press.

McGrath, James. 2024. *Christmaker*. Eerdmans.

McGuinn, Patrick J. 2006. *No Child Left Behind and the Transformation of Federal Education Policy, 1965-2005*. University Press of Kansas.

McKnight, Scott. 1993. "*Collection for the Saints*". In *Dictionary of Paul and His Letters*, edited by Hawthorne, Gerald; Martin, Ralph; Reid, Daniel. InterVarsity Press.

McKnight, Scot. 2011. *The King Jesus Gospel*. Zondervan.

Mell, Ulrich. 2025. *Gospel as Letter*. Fortress Press.

Menger, Carl. 2007. *Principles of Economics*. Mises Institute. (1871)

Meyer, Ben. 1994. *Five Speeches that Changed the World*. Wipf & Stock.

Meye Thompson, Marianne. 1992. *1-3 John*. InterVarsity Press.

Miller, Zeke. "Axelrod: Obama Misled Nation When He Opposed Gay Marriage In 2008." *Time*, February 10, 2016. https://time.com/3702584/gay-marriage-axelrod-obama/.

Mises, Ludwig von. 1949. *Human Action*. Yale University Press; (Martino Publishing, 2012).

Moloney, Francis. 2002. *The Gospel of Mark*. Hendrickson.

Morgan, Teresa. 2015. *Roman Faith and Christian Faith*. Oxford University Press.

Moxnes, Halvor. 2018. *Jesus and the Rise of Nationalism: A New Quest for the Nineteenth-Century Historical Jesus*. I.B. Tauris.

Nixon, R.E.. 1996. "*Silas*". In *New Bible Dictionary*, 3rd ed. ed. by I. Howard Marshall, A.R. Millard, J.I. Packer, and D.J. Wiseman, InterVarsity Press.

Nongbri, Brent. 2013. *Before Religion: A History of the Modern Concept*. Yale University Press. p. 12

Novenson, Matthew. 2004. *Paul and Judaism at the End of History*. Cambridge University Press.

Novick, Tzvi. 2018. *An Introduction to The Scriptures of Israel*. Eerdmans.

Oakes, Peter. 2009. *Reading Romans in Pompeii*. Fortress Press.

Oakes, Peter. 2020. *Empire, Economics, and the New Testament*. Eerdmans

Oakman, Douglas. 2012. *The Political Aims of Jesus*. Fortress Press.

O'Keeffe, Conner. "Tariffs Will Not Make America Great Again." Mises.Org. January 29, 2025. https://mises.org/mises-wire/tariffs-will-not-make-america-great-again.

Pagden, Anthony. 2013. *The Enlightenment*. Random House.

Park, Wongi. 2024. "*Race, Ethnicity, and Whiteness*". In *The Next Quest for the Historical Jesus* edited by Crossley, James and Keith, Chris.

Powell, Jim. 2005. *Wilson's War: How Woodrow Wilson's Great Blunder Led to Hitler, Lenin, Stalin, & World War II*. Crown Forum.

Reid, Daniel. 1993. "*Principalities and Powers*". In *Dictionary of Paul and His Letters*, edited by Hawthorne, Gerald; Martin, Ralph; Reid, Daniel. InterVarsity Press.

Reinhartz, Adele. 2024. "*Beyond the Jewish Jesus Debate*". In *The Next Quest for the Historical Jesus* edited by Crossley, James and Keith, Chris. Eerdmans.

Rhoads, David, Joanna Dewey, and Donald Michie. 1999. *Mark as Story*. 2nd ed. Fortress Press.

Richman, Sheldon. 2001. *Tethered Citizens*. The Future of Freedom Foundation.

Richter, Sandra. 2008. *The Epic of Eden*. InterVarsity Press.

Rosner, Brian. 2007. *Greed As Idolatry*. Eerdmans.

Rothbard, Murray. 2000. *Egalitarianism as a Revolt Against Nature and Other Essays*. 2nd ed. Mises Institute.

Rothbard, Murray. 2010. *For a New Liberty: The Libertarian Manifesto*. 2nd ed. Mises Institute.

Russell, Bertrand. 1940. *The History of Western Philosophy*. Simon & Schuster, Inc.; (Touchstone, 1972).

Schellenberg, Ryan. 2013. "*Eschatology*". In *Dictionary of Jesus and the Gospels*, 2nd ed. ed. by Joel B. Green, InterVarsity Press.

Schenck, Kenneth. 2013. "*Gospel: Good News*". In *Dictionary of Jesus and the Gospels*, 2nd ed. ed. by Joel B. Green, InterVarsity Press.

Schiess, Kaitlyn. 2023. *The Ballot and the Bible*. Brazos Press.

Schreiner, Patrick. 2020. *The Ascension of Christ*. Lexham Press.

Schreiner, Thomas. 2019. *Handbook on Acts and Paul's Letters*. Baker Academic.

Schuler, Eric. "Obama's Most Important Legacy: Endless, Limitless War." Antiwar.com. May 6, 2016. https://www.antiwar.com/blog/2016/05/06/obamas-most-important-legacy-endless-limitless-war/.

Schweitzer, Albert. 1968. *The Quest of the Historical Jesus*. Macmillan.

Sloan, Paul. 2025. *Jesus and the Law of Moses*. Baker Academic.

Smith, James. 2005. *Marks of an Apostle*. Society of biblical Literature.

So, Paul. "Why Critical Race Theory Is Not Marxism." Midwestern Marx Institute. December 2, 2021. https://www.midwesternmarx.com/articles/why-critical-race-theory-is-not-marxism-by-paul-so.

Sowell, Thomas. 2011. *Economic Facts and Fallacies*. Basic Books.

Sprinkle, Preston. 2024. *Exiles*. David C Cook.

Stedman, Ray. 1992. *Hebrews*. InterVarsity Press.

Stein, Robert. 1992. *Luke*. Broadman & Holman.

Stein, Robert. 1994. *The Method and Message of Jesus' Teaching*. Westminster John Knox Press.

Stendahl, Krister. 1976. *Paul Among Jews and Gentiles*. Fortress Press.

Stockman, David. 2013. *The Great Deformation*. Public Affairs.

Stockman, David. 2024. *Trump's War on Capitalism*. Hot Books.

Stulac, George. 1993. *James*. InterVarsity Press.

Sumney, Jerry. 2017. *Steward of God's Mysteries*. Eerdmans.

Sunstein, Cass. 2011. *Going to Extremes: How Like Minds Unite and Divide*. Oxford University Press.

The American Vision. 2011. 1st ed. McGraw-Hill Glencoe.

"The Chicago Statement on Biblical Inerrancy." Defendinginerrancy.com. https://defendinginerrancy.com/chicago-statements/.

Thielman, Frank. 2022. *Paul, Apostle of Grace*. Eerdmans.

Thiessen, Matthew. 2023. *A Jewish Paul*. Baker Academic.

Thompson, James. 2011. *Moral Formation According to Paul*. Baker Academic.

Tognini, Giacomo. "*Surging Moderna Stock Mints the Vaccine Maker's Fifth Billionaire*." Forbes, June 15, 2021. https://www.forbes.com/sites/giacomotognini/2021/06/15/surging-moderna-stock-mints-the-vaccine-makers-fifth-billionaire/.

Towner, Philip. 1996. *1-2 Timothy & Titus*. InterVarsity Press.

Volle, Adam. "Historical Materialism." Britannica. December 2, 2021. https://www.britannica.com/topic/historical-materialism.

Wall, Robert. 1993. *Colossians and Philemon*. InterVarsity Press.

Walton, John. 2009. *The Lost World of Genesis One*. IVP Academic.

Walton, John. 2024. *The Lost World of the Prophets*. InterVarsity Press.

Walton, John, and Harvey Walton. 2019. *The Lost World of the Torah*. InterVarsity Press.

Ware, James. 2025. *The Final Triumph of God*. Eerdmans.

Wittgenstein, Ludwig. 1953. *Philosophical Investigations*. 3rd ed. (2001) Blackwell Publishing.

Winter, Bruce. 1994. *Seek the Welfare of the City*. Eerdmans.

Winter, Bruce. 2001. *After Paul Left Corinth: The Influence of Secular Ethics and Social Change*. Eerdmans. p. 280

Woods, Thomas. 2014. *Real Dissent: A Libertarian Sets Fire to the Index Card of Allowable Opinion*. Self-published.

Woods, Thomas. 2023. *Diary of a Psychosis*. The Libertarian Institute.

Woolf, Greg. 2012. *Rome: An Empire's Story*. Oxford University Press.

Wright, N.T. 1992. *The New Testament and the People of God*. Fortress Press.

Wright, N.T. 1996. *Jesus and the Victory of God*. Fortress Press.

Wright, N.T.. 2000. *"Paul's Gospel and Caesar's Empire"*. In *Paul and Politics*. ed. by Richard Horsley, Trinity Press International.

Wright, N.T. 2003. *The Resurrection of the Son of God*. Fortress Press.

Wright, N.T. 2011. *Justification*. InterVarsity Press.

Wright, N.T. 2013. *Paul and the Faithfulness of God*. Fortress Press.

Wright, N.T. 2019. *History and Eschatology*. Baylor University Press.

Yang, Seung. 2013. *"Sermon on the Mount/Plain"*. In *Dictionary of Jesus and the Gospels*, 2nd ed. ed. by Joel B. Green, InterVarsity Press.

Zetterholm, Magnus. 2009. *Approaches to Paul*. Fortress Press.

Zlotow, Walt. "Why So Many Progressives Promoting Endless Ukraine Bloodbath?" Antiwar.Com. June 7, 2023. https://www.antiwar.com/blog/2023/06/07/why-so-many-progressives-promoting-endless-ukraine-bloodbath/.

SUBJECT INDEX

SCRIPTURE INDEX

Alex Bernardo holds a bachelor's degree in Biblical Studies from Cincinnati Christian University and a Master of Arts in Teaching from Northern Kentucky University. He teaches seventh-grade social studies in Independence, Kentucky, where he lives with his wife and daughter. Alex is the host of *The Protestant Libertarian Podcast* and previously served in ministry for nearly a decade, bringing a passion for faith, education, and thoughtful dialogue to his work.